Los Angeles
THE ROUGH GUIDE

KU-470-491

There are more than one hundred Rough Guide titles
covering destinations from Amsterdam to Zimbabwe

Forthcoming titles include
Central America • Chile • Indonesia • Japan • New Orleans

Rough Guide Reference Series
Classical Music • European Football • The Internet • Jazz
Opera • Reggae • Rock Music • World Music

Rough Guide Phrasebooks
Czech • Egyptian Arabic • French • German • Greek • Hindi & Urdu
Indonesian • Hungarian • Indonesian • Italian • Japanese • Mandarin Chinese
Mexican Spanish • Polish • Portuguese • Russian • Spanish • Swahili
Thai • Turkish • Vietnamese

Rough Guides on the Internet
www.roughguides.com

Rough Guide Credits

Text Editor:	Andrew Rosenberg
Series Editor:	Mark Ellingham
Editorial:	Martin Dunford, Jonathan Buckley, Samantha Cook, Jo Mead, Kate Berens, Amanda Tomlin, Ann-Marie Shaw, Paul Gray, Chris Schüler, Helena Smith, Judith Bamber, Kieran Falconer, Orla Duane, Olivia Eccleshall, Ruth Blackmore, Sophie Martin, Jennifer Dempsey, Sue Jackson, Geoff Howard (UK); Andrew Taber (US)
Online Editors:	Alan Spicer, Kate Hands (UK); Geronimo Madrid (US)
Production:	Susanne Hillen, Andy Hilliard, Link Hall, Helen Ostick, James Morris, Julia Bovis, Michelle Draycott
Cartography:	Melissa Flack, Maxine Burke, Nichola Goodliffe
Picture research:	Eleanor Hill
Finance:	John Fisher, Celia Crowley, Neeta Mistry
Marketing & Publicity:	Richard Trillo, Simon Carloss, Niki Smith, Katherine Allen (UK); Jean-Marie Kelly, SoRelle Braun (US)
Administration:	Tania Hummel, Alexander Mark Rogers

Acknowledgements

Special **thanks** go to my wife and family, as well as Dick Wright. In LA, Susan Bejeckian, Marjorie Bettenhausen-Schmaehl, Michelle Bolton, Burks Hamner, George Lysak, Janet Marangi, Dino Nanni, Jane Quine, Sris (in Venice), Elana Tuizer, and Earnie Yasuhara provided invaluable assistance. Thanks to everyone else at Rough Guides, too, namely Helen Ostick and Melissa Flack, and Susanne Oosta for help with the index and page references also Narrell Leffman for Oz basics, and Russell Walton for proofreading. And of course, this book could not have been written without the cheerful, sage guidance of Andrew Rosenberg and Martin Dunford.

This edition published November 1998 by Rough Guides Ltd, 62–70 Shorts Gardens, London WC2H 9AB.
Distributed by the Penguin Group:
Penguin Books Ltd, 27 Wrights Lane, London W8 5TZ.
Penguin Books USA Inc, 375 Hudson Street, New York 10014, USA.
Penguin Books Australia Ltd, 487 Maroondah Highway, PO Box 257, Ringwood, Victoria 3134, Australia.
Penguin Books Canada Ltd, 10 Alcorn Avenue, Toronto, Ontario, Canada M4V 1E4.
Penguin Books (NZ) Ltd, 182–190 Wairau Road, Auckland 10, New Zealand.

Printed in England by Clays Ltd, St Ives PLC
Typography and **original design** by Jonathan Dear and The Crowd Roars.
Illustrations throughout by Edward Briant.

A catalogue record for this book is available from the British Library.

ISBN 1-85828-344-2

Los Angeles

THE ROUGH GUIDE

Written and researched by
Jeff Dickey

Additional material by Jamie Jensen

THE ROUGH GUIDES

Help us update

We've gone to a lot of trouble to ensure that this second edition of the *Rough Guide to Los Angeles* is accurate and up-to-date. However, things inevitably change, and if you feel we've got it wrong or left something out, we'd like to know: any suggestions, comments or corrections would be much appreciated. We'll credit all contributions and send a copy of the next edition – or any other *Rough Guide* if you prefer – for the best correspondence.

Please mark letters "Rough Guide to Los Angeles" and send to:
Rough Guides, 62–70 Shorts Gardens, London WC2H 9AB
or
Rough Guides, 375 Hudson St, New York, NY 10014.

E-mail should be sent to:
mail@roughguides.co.uk

Online updates about Rough Guide titles can be found on our Web site at www.roughguides.com

The Author

Jeff Dickey is a film and video writer and director who spent five years in LA, getting a taste of the movie biz at USC's film school and in the byzantine world of Hollywood. Although he has since moved to the Pacific Northwest, he still yearns for LA's pulsing dark heart. He has contributed to Rough Guides to California and the USA.

Rough Guides

Travel Guides • Phrasebooks • Music and Reference Guides

We set out to do something different when the first *Rough Guide* was published in 1982. Mark Ellingham, just out of university, was travelling in Greece. He brought along the popular guides of the day, but found they were all lacking in some way. They were either strong on ruins and museums but went on for pages without mentioning a beach or taverna. Or they were so conscious of the need to save money that they lost sight of Greece's cultural and historical significance. Also, none of the books told him anything about Greece's contemporary life – its politics, its culture, its people, and how they lived.

So with no job in prospect, Mark decided to write his own guidebook, one which aimed to provide practical information that was second to none, detailing the best beaches and the hottest clubs and restaurants, while also giving hard hitting accounts of every sight, both famous and obscure, and providing up-to-the-minute information on contemporary culture. It was a guide that encouraged independent travelers to find the best of Greece, and was a great success, getting shortlisted for the Thomas Cook travel guide award, and encouraging Mark, along with three friends, to expand the series.

The Rough Guide list grew rapidly and the letters flooded in, indicating a much broader readership than had been anticipated, but one which uniformly appreciated the Rough Guides' mix of practical detail and humor, irreverence and enthusiasm. Things haven't changed. The same four friends who began the series are still the caretakers of the Rough Guide mission today: to provide the most reliable, up-to-date and entertaining information to independent-minded travelers of all ages, on all budgets.

We now publish 100 titles and have offices in London and New York. The travel guides are written and researched by a dedicated team of more than 100 authors, based in Britain, Europe, the USA and Australia. We have also created a unique series of phrasebooks to accompany the travel series, along with the acclaimed series of music guides, and a best-selling pocket guide to the Internet and World Wide Web. We also publish comprehensive travel information on our Web site: www.roughguides.com

Contents

List of Maps

MAP SYMBOLS

Interstate	◉	Hotel
U.S. Highway	■	Restaurant
Highway	🕯	Lighthouse
Road under construction	⌂	Mountain range
Pedestrianized road		Marshland
Walkway	(i)	Information centre
Railway		Building
Ferry route	⊞	Church
International border		Cemetery
State border		National/State Park
Chapter division boundary		Park
River		Beach
Airport		

Introduction

A maddening collection of freeways and beaches, fast-food joints and palm trees, seedy suburbs and high-gloss neighborhoods and extreme lifestyles, **Los Angeles** is California's biggest and most stimulating city – and an unconventional one by any standard. Indeed, LA's character is so shifting and elusive – understandable "only dimly, and in flashes," according to F Scott Fitzgerald – that the city might be freely dismissed by many outsiders if it weren't so central to the world's mass culture. Its multiple personalities and lack of any unifying design make it seem at first neither approachable, nor perhaps even enjoyable; but once the free-spirited chaos of the place takes hold, you'll be hard-pressed to resist.

Made up of scores of distinct municipalities, LA is a model for modern city development, having traded urban centralization for suburban sprawl and high-rise corporate towers for strip malls. It gets more than ample opportunity to show off its wares because of its stature as international entertainment center, which paints a picture of a sunny and glamorous place like no other. It is certainly unique, an unpredictable and addictive assault on the senses where mud-wrestling venues and porn cinemas stand next door to chic boutiques and trendy restaurants, the whole of it under constant threat of the next earthquake, flood, or natural disaster.

Despite this uniqueness, LA has much in common with other major US cities. With the largest combined port in the country (and biggest in the world outside of China), LA is a center for transpacific trade and a dominant **financial hub** in its own right. Predictably, real estate is a chief concern of the local economy, as is the media industry; defense-related businesses, on the other hand, have met their demise in recent years and will probably never regain the promi-

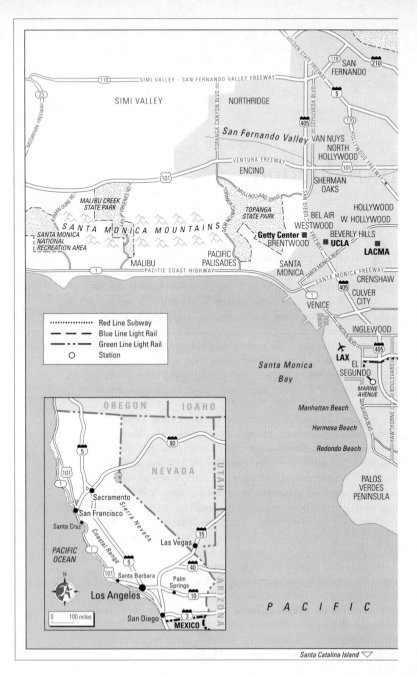

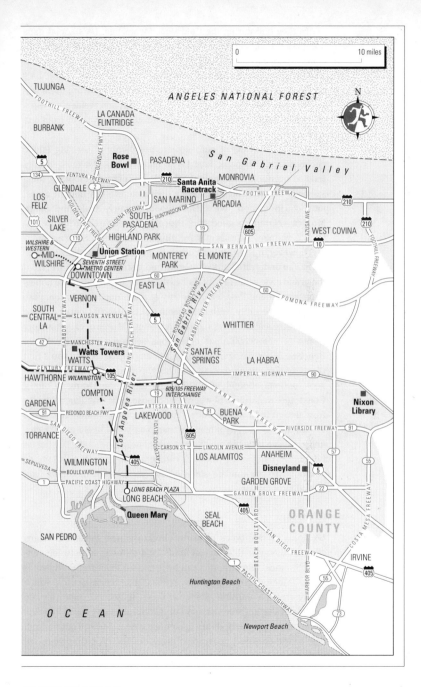

nence they had during the Cold War. Meanwhile, LA's **social gaps** are quite broad, and there's no end in sight for the nasty racial divisions broadcast to the world in the 1992 riots and the OJ Simpson trial three years later. Not a simple matter of black versus white, LA's unparalleled diversity sometimes gets in its way: there are more languages spoken here than in any other US city, and residents – especially white suburbanites – tend to cordon themselves off from one another.

This also means of course there are plenty of thriving ethnic enclaves, from Hispanic East LA to Little Tokyo. But most visitors tend to overlook these **neighborhoods**, except when looking for a specialty cuisine, and concentrate their time in a few notable areas, namely **Hollywood**, **West Hollywood**, **Beverly Hills** and **Santa Monica** – certainly a good start, especially if you've come for the typically Los Angeles thrills of stargazing and shopping. Such an itinerary, however, misses out on a number of the city's less glitzy charms. LA has an underrated mix of modern and historic **architecture**, from the grand civic scale of City Hall to the rustic Craftsman-style homes peppered around Pasadena. The city's **museums** have gotten quite an upgrade recently, with the opening of the **Getty Center** art museum; there's also the top-notch **LA County Museum of Art** among plenty of uniquely LA art collections scattered about the basin. **Beaches**, of course, should be a part of any trip to LA, and you'll find plenty of them around, most popularly, perhaps, in **Venice**, though good options abound in **Malibu** and along the **Orange County Coast**, too. Regardless of where you choose to be, you'll never be far from decent food and nightlife – fitting for an entertainment capital.

To access the city's many attractions, you'll likely need a **car**, unless you've targeted relatively compact neighborhoods. Driving on LA's much-ballyhooed freeways can be a challenge, but as long as you don't try to emulate some of the crazier local motorists, you should have few problems.

Climate

LA holds several types of warm **climate zones**, including desert, semi-arid, and Mediterranean areas, and differences between constituent cities' temperatures can be great: for example, Pasadena is ten to fifteen degrees hotter on average than Santa Monica, which can resemble a maritime climate at times. In general, toasty air and sunny skies reign: summer and fall months are fairly warm and dry; winter and spring periods are cooler and wetter, but still quite warm. Due to the enclosed geographic design of the LA basin, there are high levels of smog, worst during a few summer months in the east-

Average daytime temperatures in LA

	Jan	Feb	Mar	Apr	May	June	July	Aug	Sept	Oct	Nov	Dec
Max °F	65	66	68	71	73	77	83	82	81	77	73	68
Max °C	18	19	20	22	23	25	28	28	27	25	23	20
Min °F	47	48	49	53	55	60	63	63	60	57	53	49
Min °C	8	9	9	12	13	16	17	17	16	14	12	9

ern parts of the region. Torrential rainstorms do occur during the winter months, and disastrous storms and mudslides affect hillside neighborhoods across the city with uneasy frequency.

Basics

Getting there from Britain and Europe

Though flying to Los Angeles from Europe is pretty straightforward, finding the best deal can be more complicated than you might think, with prices fluctuating wildly according to how and when you go. The majority of budget options involve non-stop services from Britain, although many others turn out to be so-called "direct" flights, which can land several times, waiting an hour or so at each stop – a flight is called direct as long as it keeps the same flight number throughout its journey. The first place the plane lands is your point of entry into the US, which means you'll have to collect your bags and go through customs and immigration formalities there, even if you're continuing on to Los Angeles on the same plane. This can be a real pain after a ten-hour journey, so it's worth finding out before you book a ticket.

Fares, routes and agents

Although you can fly to the US from any of the regional airports, the only **non-stop flights** from Britain to Los Angeles are from London. The non-stop **flight time** is around eleven hours; add an hour at least for each intervening stop on direct flights, twice that if you have to change planes. Following winds ensure that return flights are always an hour or two shorter than outward journeys. Because of the time difference between Britain and the West Coast (eight hours almost all year), flights usually leave Britain mid-morning, while flights back from the US tend to arrive in Britain early in the morning.

Britain remains one of the best places in Europe to obtain flight bargains, though **fares** vary widely according to season, availability and the current level of inter-airline competition. The comments that follow can only act as a general guide, so be sure to shop around carefully for the best offers by checking the **travel ads** in the weekend papers, on the **holiday pages** of ITV's *Teletext* and, in London, scouring *Time Out* and the *Evening Standard*. Giveaway magazines aimed at young travelers, like *TNT*, are also useful resources.

Stand-by deals (open-dated tickets which you pay for and then decide later when you want to

---

Sample air fares from Britain

The prices given below (in £ sterling) are a general indication of the (minimum) transatlantic air fares currently obtainable from specialist companies; remember to add £40–50 airport tax to these figures. Each airline decides the exact dates of its seasons. Prices are for departures from London and Manchester.

LOW		SHOULDER		HIGH	
April 11–30, Nov 1–Dec 14, Dec 25–March 28		March 29–Apr 10, May 1–Jun 30, Sept 1–Oct 31		July 1–Aug 31, Dec 15–24	
one-way	return	one-way	return	one-way	return
215	310	215	350	255	490

One word of **warning**: it's not a good idea to buy a **one-way** ticket to the States. Not only are they rarely good value compared to a round-trip ticket, but US immigration officials usually take them as a sign that you aren't planning to go home, and may refuse you entry.

fly – if there's room on the plane) are few and far between, and don't give great savings: in general you're better off with an **Apex** ticket. The conditions on these are pretty standard whoever you fly with – seats must be purchased seven days or more in advance, and you must stay for at least one Saturday night; tickets are normally valid for up to six months. Some airlines also do less expensive **Super-Apex** tickets, which fall into two categories: the first are approximately £150 cheaper than an ordinary Apex but must be bought 21 days in advance and require a minimum stay of seven days and a maximum stay of one month, the second are around £100 less than an Apex, must be purchased fourteen days in advance and entail a minimum stay of a week and a maximum stay of two months – such tickets are usually non-refundable or changeable. **"Open-jaw"** tickets can be a good idea, allowing you to fly into LA, for example, and back from San Francisco for little or no extra charge; fares are calculated by halving the return fares to each destination and adding the two figures together. This makes a convenient option for those who want a fly-drive holiday (see opposite).

Generally, the most expensive time to fly is **high season**, roughly between June and August and around Christmas. May and September are slightly less pricey, and the rest of the year is considered low season and is cheaper still. Keep an eye out for slack season bargains, and, additionally, make sure to check the exact dates of the seasons with your operator or airline; you might be able to make major savings by shifting your departure date by a week – or even a day. **Weekend rates** for all return flights tend to be around £20 more expensive than those in the week.

For an overview of the various offers, and unofficially discounted tickets, go straight to an **agent** specializing in low-cost flights (we've listed some below). Especially if you're under 26 or a student, they may be able to knock up to thirty percent off the regular Apex fares when there are no special

airline deals. Agents will usually offer non-stop flights, or "direct" flights via another airport in the USA, although you may be offered other, stranger combinations (London–Los Angeles via Amsterdam, Manchester–Los Angeles via Paris for example) – all worth considering if the price is right.

The same agents also offer cut-price seats on **charter flights**. These are particularly good value if you're traveling from a British city other than London, although they tend to be limited to the summer season, be restricted to so-called "holiday destinations" and have fixed departure and return dates. Brochures are available in most high street travel agents, or contact the specialists direct.

Finally, if you've got a bit more time, or want to see a bit more of the USA, it's often possible to stop over in another city – **New York** especially – and fly on from there for little more than the cost of a direct flight to Los Angeles. Also, with increased competition on the London–Los Angeles route, thanks to Virgin Atlantic among others and price wars between US carriers, the cost of a connecting flight from LA to San Francisco has been brought down to as low as £40 – so if you want to see California's other star city, you're in luck. Many airlines also offer **air passes**, which allow foreign travelers to fly between a given number of US cities for one discounted price.

Courier flights

It's still possible, if not as common as it used to be, for those on a very tight budget to travel as **couriers**. Courier firms offer opportunities to travel at discounted rates (as low as £200 return to the West Coast) in return for delivering a package. There'll be someone to check you in and to meet you at your destination, which minimizes any red-tape hassle. However, you'll have to travel light, with only a cabin-bag, and accept tight restrictions on travel dates. For phone numbers, check the *Yellow Pages*, as these businesses come and go.

Packages

Packages – fly-drive, flight/accommodation deals and guided tours (or a combination of all three) – can work out cheaper than arranging the same trip yourself, especially for a short-term stay. The obvious drawbacks are the loss of flexibility and

Flights from Britain

The following carriers operate **non-stop flights** from London to Los Angeles (all from Heathrow unless otherwise stated):

Air New Zealand, five times a week.
American Airlines, daily.
British Airways, daily from Heathrow and Gatwick.

United Airlines, daily.
Virgin Atlantic, daily.

The following carriers operate **one-stop direct flights** from London to Los Angeles (all from Gatwick unless otherwise stated):

Continental, daily via Denver, Miami, Houston or Newark to Los Angeles.
Delta, daily via Cincinnati or Atlanta to Los Angeles.

Northwest, four times a week via Detroit or Minneapolis to Los Angeles.
TWA, daily via St Louis to Los Angeles.

The following carriers operate direct flights from **regional airports** to the US:
American Airlines, from Manchester to Chicago and New York, and from Glasgow to Chicago.

British Airways, from Manchester and Glasgow to New York.

Delta, from Manchester to Atlanta.
Northwest, from Glasgow to Boston.

Air New Zealand ☎0181/741 2299
American Airlines ☎0345/789789
British Airways ☎0345/222111
Continental ☎01293/776464
Delta ☎0800/414767

Northwest ☎01424/224400
TWA ☎0345/333333
United ☎0181/313 0999
Virgin Atlantic ☎01293/747747

the fact that most operators use hotels in the mid-range bracket, but there is a wide variety of options available. High-street travel agents have plenty of brochures and information about the various combinations.

Fly-drive

Fly-drive deals, which give cut-rate (sometimes free) car rental when buying a transatlantic ticket, always work out cheaper than renting on the spot and give especially great value if you intend to do a lot of driving. On the other hand, you'll probably have to pay more for the flight than if you booked it through a discount agent. Competition between airlines (especially Northwest and TWA) and tour operators means that it's well worth phoning to check on current special promotions.

Northwest Flydrive offers excellent deals for not much more than an ordinary Apex fare; for example, a return flight to LA and a week's car rental costs around £350 per person in low season. Several of the other companies listed in the box overleaf offer similar, and sometimes cheaper, packages.

Watch out for hidden extras, such as local taxes, and "drop-off" charges, which can be as much as a week's rental, and Collision Damage Waiver insurance. Remember, too, that while you can drive in the States with a British license, there can be problems renting vehicles if you're under 25. For more car-rental and driveaway details, see p.14.

Flight and accommodation deals

There's really no end of combined **flight and accommodation deals** to Los Angeles, and although you can often do things cheaper independently, you won't be able to do the *same* things cheaper – in fact, the equivalent room booked separately will normally be a lot more expensive – and you can leave the organizational hassles to someone else. Drawbacks include the loss of flexibility and the fact that you'll probably have to stay in hotels in the mid-range to expensive bracket, even though less expensive accommodation is almost always available.

A handful of tour operators (see overleaf) offer quite deluxe packages: a week in LA plus return flight should run you anywhere from £650–1000. Discount agents can set up more basic packages for just over £500 each.

Discount flight agents in Britain

Bridge The World 1–3 Ferdinand St, London NW1 ☎0171/916 0990.

Campus Travel 52 Grosvenor Gardens, London SW1 ☎0171/730 2101; branches nationwide.

Council Travel 28a Poland St, London W1V ☎0171/437 7767.

Destination Group 41–45 Goswell Rd, London EC1 ☎0171/253 9000.

STA Travel 86 Old Brompton Rd, London SW7 ☎0171/361 6262; branches nationwide.

Trailfinders 42–50 Earls Court Rd, London W8 ☎0171/937 5400; branches nationwide.

Travel Bug 597 Cheetham Hill Rd, Manchester M8 5EJ ☎0161/721 4000.

Travel Cuts 295a Regent St, London W1 ☎0171/255 2082.

Touring and adventure packages

There are plenty of specialist **touring and adventure packages** which include transportation, accommodation, food and a guide. These work best if you're planning on seeing more of California than just Los Angeles. Some of the more adventurous carry small groups around on minibuses and use a combination of budget hotels and camping (equipment, except a sleeping bag, is provided). Most also have a food kitty

Specialist holiday operators

Airtours Wavell House, Helmshore, Rossendale, Lancs BB4 4NB ☎01706/240033. *Multi-center holidays including combinations of Los Angeles, San Francisco and Las Vegas.*

American Airlines Holidays PO Box 5, 12 Coningsby Rd, Peterborough PE3 8XP ☎0870/605 0506. *Flight plus accommodation and fly-drive deals.*

American Connections 10 York Way, Lancaster Rd, High Wycombe, Bucks HP12 3PY ☎01494/473173. *City breaks.*

Bon Voyage 18 Bellevue Rd, Southampton, Hants SO15 2AY ☎01703/330332. *Flight-plus-accommodation deals.*

Bridge Travel Service Bridge House, Broxbourne, Herts EN10 7DT ☎01992/456101. *Packages to Disneyland.*

British Airways Holidays Astral Towers, Bettsway, London Rd, Crawley, West Sussex RH10 2XA ☎01293/723121. *City breaks and fly-drive deals.*

Contiki Travel Wells House, 15 Elmfield Rd, Bromley, Kent BR1 1LS ☎0181/290 6777. *West Coast coach tours.*

Cosmos Tourama House, 17 Homesdale Rd, Bromley, Kent BR2 9LX ☎0181/464 3444. *Packages to Los Angeles/Anaheim.*

Destination USA 41–45 Goswell Rd, London EC1 ☎0171/253 2000. *Tailor-made accommodation and fly-drive deals.*

Funway 1 Elmfield Park, Bromley, Kent BR1 1LU ☎0181/466 0222. *Package holidays.*

Kuoni Kuoni House, Dorking, Surrey RH5 4AZ ☎01306/742888. *Multi-center flight-plus-accommodation-plus-car deals.*

North America Travel Service 7 Albion St, Leeds LS1 5ER ☎0113/246 1466. *Also branches in Nottingham, Manchester and Barnsley.*

Northwest Flydrive PO Box 45, Bexhill-on-Sea, East Sussex TN40 1PY ☎01424/224400. *Flight-plus-accommodation and fly-drive specials.*

Premier Holidays Westbrook, Milton Rd, Cambridge CB4 1YQ ☎01223/516516. *Flight-plus-accommodation deals.*

Road Runner 64 Mount Pleasant Ave, Tunbridge Wells, Kent TN1 1QY ☎01892/512700. *Hosteling-based touring and adventure packages.*

Travelpack 523 High Rd, Wembley HA0 2DH ☎0990/747101. *Escorted tours and tailor-made holidays throughout California.*

United Vacations PO Box 377, Bromley, Kent, BR1 1LY ☎0181/313 0999. *City breaks, tailor-mades and fly-drives.*

Up & Away 19 The Mall, Bromley, Kent BR1 1LY ☎0181/289 5050. *Tailor-mades and fly-drives to Los Angeles and Californian National Parks.*

Virgin Holidays The Galleria, Station Rd, Crawley, West Sussex RH10 1WW ☎01293/617181. *Packages to a wide range of California destinations.*

of around £25 per week, with many meals cooked and eaten communally, although there's plenty of time to leave the group and do your own thing. In any case, we've listed a few in the tour operators box opposite if you're interested.

Flights from Ireland

Both Delta and Aer Lingus fly to Los Angeles **direct** from Ireland. The **cheapest flights** from Ireland – if you're under 26 or a student – are available from USIT. Student-only return fares range from IR£389 to IR£569. Ordinary Apex fares are only marginally higher.

USIT can be contacted at Aston Quay, O'Connell Bridge, Dublin 2 (☎01/677 8117), while Aer Lingus is at 40 O'Connell St, Dublin 1 (☎01/844 4777), and Delta Airlines is at 24 Merrion Square, Dublin 2 (☎01/676 8080 or 1-800/768080).

Flights from Europe

It is generally far cheaper to fly non-stop to Los Angeles from London than any other European city. However, for the best deals to New York from Brussels and Paris, contact **Nouvelles Frontières**, 87 Boulevard de Grenelle, 75015 Paris (☎41.41.58.58) and 2 Boulevard M. Lemonnier, 1000 Brussels (☎02/547 4444). Its London branch is at 2–3 Woodstock St (☎0171/629 7772), although you'll have to go through the Paris or Brussels branch in order to actually book tickets.

Other options are the cut-price charter flights occasionally offered from major European cities; ask at your nearest travel agent for details. In Germany, look for discount **youth fare** deals which United offers (to those under 26 booking 72 hours or less in advance) from Frankfurt, its continental hub (☎069/605020).

Insurance

Most travel agents and tour operators will offer you **travel insurance** when you book your flight or holiday, and some will insist you take it. These policies are usually reasonable value, though as ever, you should check the small print. If you feel the cover is inadequate, or you want to compare prices, any **travel agent**, **insurance broker** or **bank** should be able to help. If you have a good "all risks" home insurance policy it may well cover your possessions against loss or theft even when overseas, and many private medical schemes also cover you when abroad – make sure you know the procedure and the helpline number. On all policies, the cover should include a sensible amount for medical expenses – at least £1,000,000, which will cover the cost of an air ambulance to fly you home in the event of serious injury or hospitalization. Typical insurance policies can be had from Endsleigh Insurance, 97–107 Southampton Row, London WC1B 4AG (☎0171/436 4451), at £43 for three weeks to cover life, limb and luggage (with a 25 percent reduction if you choose to forgo luggage insurance); and Columbus Travel Insurance, 17 Devonshire Square, London EC2M 4SQ (☎0171/375 0011), which does an annual multi-trip policy offering twelve months' cover for £185.

Getting there from Australia and New Zealand

Los Angeles is the main point of entry in the US if traveling from Australia or New Zealand, thus there are plenty of flights that arrive in LA direct from those places – though there is very little price difference between airlines. If you travel via Asia, you may well have to stop over for the night, but there is a non-stop service too, via the Pacific. Air passes and round-the-world tickets can be good value if you're planning on covering more ground than just Los Angeles.

Flights and fares

Tickets purchased direct from the airlines are usually at published rates, which are often more expensive than a RTW fare. **Travel agents** offer the best deals on fares and have the latest information on limited special offers, such as, free stopovers and fly-drive-accommodation packages. Flight Centres and STA (which offer fare reductions for ISIC card holders and under 26s) generally offer the lowest fares. Seat availability on most international flights out of Australia and New Zealand is often limited, so it's best to book several weeks ahead.

Air fares are seasonal, and the differences can add up to as much as A/NZ$300. Generally speaking, **low season** is from mid-January to the

end of February and October to the end of November; **high season** mid-May to the end of August and December to mid-January; **shoulder seasons** cover the rest of the year. Travel time between Auckland/Sydney and LA is around 12–14 hours on a non-stop flight – though some flights do allow for stopovers in Honolulu and a number of the South Pacific Islands.

Traveling **from Australia**, fares to Los Angeles from eastern capitals cost much the same; from Perth they're about A$400 more. There are **daily non-stop** flights from Sydney to LA on United Airlines and Qantas for around A$1899 in low season. However, the best deals are on Air New Zealand via Auckland either direct or with stopovers in Honolulu, Fiji, Tonga or Papeete, starting at A$1850. Air Pacific can also take you via a stopover in Fiji for around the same price. The best deal for flying via Asia is on JAL A$1550 (A$1880 in high season), which includes a night's stopover accommodation in Tokyo in the fare, while fares on Philippine Airlines, via Manila, start at around A$1750. If you don't want to spend the night Cathay Pacific and Singapore Airlines can get you there for around A$1880, via a transfer in either Hong Kong or Singapore.

From New Zealand, the best deals are out of **Auckland** (add about NZ$150–300 for Christchurch and Wellington departures), on either Air New Zealand or United Airlines. Both companies fly non-stop to LA or via Honolulu for around NZ$2099/2499. Meanwhile, Air Pacific, via Fiji, and Qantas, via Sydney, both start around NZ$2150. JAL offers the best fares via Asia, starting at NZ$1850/2250, with a transfer or stopover in Tokyo.

Round-the-world and air passes

If you intend to take in Los Angeles as part of a world trip, a round-the-world (**RTW**) ticket offers the best value for money. There are any number of airline combinations to choose from, however, the most US oriented are Cathay Pacific-UA's

Airlines

Air New Zealand Australia ☎ 13/2476; New Zealand ☎ 09/357 3000. *Daily flights to LA from major Australasian cities, via transfers in Auckland, or several times a week via either Auckland and Honolulu/Papeete, or Auckland, Fiji/Tonga and Honolulu.*

Air Pacific Australia ☎ 02/9957 0150 & 1800/230 150; New Zealand ☎ 09/379 2404. *Once a week to LA from Sydney, Melbourne, Brisbane and major New Zealand cities via a stopover in Nadi (Fiji).*

Cathay Pacific Australia ☎ 13/1747; New Zealand ☎ 09/379 0861. *Daily to LA from major Australasian cities via a transfer or stopover in Hong Kong.*

Delta Air Lines Australia ☎ 02/9262 1777 & 1800/251 878; New Zealand ☎ 09/379 3370. *Coupons for extended travel in the US.*

JAL Japan Airlines Australia ☎ 02/9272 1111; New Zealand ☎ 09/379 9906. *Several flights a week to LA from Sydney, Brisbane, Cairns and Auckland via an overnight's stopover in either Tokyo or Osaka included in the fare (codeshare with Air New Zealand).*

Northwest Airlines Australia ☎ 02/9231 6333. *Coupons for extended travel in the US.*

Philippine Airlines Australia ☎ 02/9262 3333. *Several flights a week to LA from Sydney and Brisbane via either a transfer or overnight stopover in Manila.*

Qantas Australia ☎ 13/1211; New Zealand ☎ 09/357 8900 & 0800/808 767. *Daily to LA from major Australian cities either non-stop or via Honolulu and daily from Auckland via Sydney.*

Singapore Airlines Australia ☎ 13/1011; New Zealand ☎ 09/379 3209. *Twice a week to LA from major Australian cities and once a week from Auckland via Singapore.*

United Airlines Australia ☎ 13/1777; New Zealand ☎ 09/379 3800. *Daily to LA from Sydney, Melbourne and Auckland either direct or via Honolulu.*

Discount travel agents

Anywhere Travel, 345 Anzac Parade, Kingsford, Sydney ☎ 02/9663 0411.

Brisbane Discount Travel, 260 Queen St, Brisbane ☎ 07/3229 9211.

Budget Travel, 16 Fort St, Auckland, plus branches around the city ☎ 09/366 0061 & 0800/808 040.

Destinations Unlimited, 3 Milford Rd, Auckland ☎ 09/373 4033.

Flight Centres Australia: 82 Elizabeth St, Sydney, plus branches nationwide ☎ 13/1600. New Zealand: 205 Queen St, Auckland ☎ 09/309 6171, plus branches nationwide. *Good flight discounts plus a comprehensive range of tours and packages.*

Northern Gateway, 22 Cavenagh St, Darwin ☎ 08/8941 1394.

STA Travel Australia: 702 Harris St, Ultimo, Sydney; 256 Flinders St, Melbourne; *www. statravelaus.com.au*, email *traveller@ statravelaus.com.au*; other offices in state capitals and major universities (nearest branch ☎ 13/1776, fastfare telesales ☎ 1300/360 960). New Zealand: 10 High St, Auckland (☎ 09/309 0458, fastfare telesales ☎ 09/366 6673), plus branches in Wellington, Christchurch, Dunedin, Palmerston North, Hamilton and at major universities. *Discounts for students and under 26.*

Thomas Cook Australia: 175 Pitt St, Sydney; 257 Collins St, Melbourne; plus branches in other state capitals (local branch ☎ 13/1771, Thomas Cook Direct telesales ☎ 1800/063 913). New Zealand: 96 Anzac Ave, Auckland ☎ 09/379 3920. *Rail and bus passes, travelers checks.*

Tymtro Travel, Level 8, 130 Pitt St, Sydney ☎ 02/9223 2211 or 1300/652 969.

"Globetrotter", Air New Zealand-KLM-Northwest's "World Navigator" and Qantas-BA's "Global Explorer," all of which offer six free stopovers worldwide with a maximum of three in the US, limited backtracking, and additional stopovers (around A/NZ$120 each), from low season fares of A$2599/NZ$3189 (high season $3299/$3699). More US-oriented, but only available in Australia, is Singapore-TWA's "Easyworld" fare, allowing unlimited stopovers worldwide, with a maximum of eight within the US, and limited backtracking within the US (flat rate A$3150).

Specialist agents and operators

Adventure World, 73 Walker St, Sydney ☎ 02/956 7766; 8 Victoria Ave, Perth ☎ 09/9221 2300; 101 Great South Rd, Auckland ☎ 09/524 5118. *Agents for a vast array of international adventure travel companies that operate trips out of San Francisco and LA, such as Trek America's "off the beaten track" 18-35 adventures, as well as city-stays and Disney passes.*

American Travel Centre, 2nd Floor, 262 Adelaide St, Brisbane ☎ 07/3221 4788. *All US travel arrangements.*

Creative Tours, booking through travel agents only. *Escorted coach tours, air passes, Anaheim-Disneyland packages.*

Insight, bookings through travel agents only. *Offers, Disneyland packages, car rental and bus tours.*

Peregrine Adventures, 258 Lonsdale St, Melbourne ☎ 03/9663 8611, plus offices in Brisbane, Sydney, Adelaide and Perth. *Agents for AmeriCan's 7–21 day small group active camping trips.*

Sydney International Travel Centre, 75 King St, Sydney ☎ 02/9299 8000. *Can arrange individually tailored holidays, fly-drive packages, Disneyland passes, city-stays, bus and rail tours.*

Wiltrans/Maupintour, 10/189 Kent St, Sydney ☎ 02/9255 0899. *Five-star all inclusive escorted Californian sightseeing holidays out of Los Angeles.*

Gay and lesbian

Pride Travel, 254 Bay St, Brighton, Melbourne ☎ 03/9596 3566 or 1800/061 427; Sydney ☎ 1800/808 696.

Silke's Travel, 263 Oxford St, Darlinghurst, Sydney ☎ 02/9380 5835; *www.magna.com. au./~silba.*

If you intend to venture from Los Angeles to other destinations in the US, there are a number of good value air, train and bus passes that can be booked before you leave. For instance there are various **coupon deals** available with your international ticket for discounted flights within the US. A minimum purchase of three coupons usually applies, for example: American Airlines' Coupon Pass costs US$330 for the first three, and between US$60 and US$100 for subsequent tickets (maximum of ten total). If you prefer to travel overland, Amtrak and Greyhound Ameripass offer myriad routings and destinations throughout the US; Amtrak fares start around US$270, Greyhound fares around US$90.

Package holidays

There are a variety of **package holidays** to Los Angeles available to travelers from Australia and New Zealand, but few that include international flights. Occasionally Qantas, Air New Zealand or United Airlines, in conjunction with wholesalers, offer flight-accommodation packages to LA, but most packages are for land travel only. Adventure World, Creative Tours, and Insight all offer four to eight night city-stays, which include hotel accommodation in Downtown LA, Beverly Hills, Hollywood or Anaheim, tours of LA's famous haunts and homes, and passes to Hollywood's

Universal Studio and Disneyland. Booking can be made from most travel agents, but before you book ask about any special conditions or hidden costs that may apply, as full refunds on package holidays are uncommon.

In addition there are a number of operators that specialize in overland adventure trips and sightseeing tours from LA, such as AmeriCan's ten-day round-trip "Californian Cooler," that includes sightseeing tours of LA, San Francisco, Las Vegas and Santa Barbara, plus Disneyland passes, entry to the Grand Canyon and Yosemite National Parks, and wine tasting to boot; it goes for about A$720, and includes a mix of hotel room shares and camping. Trek America offers a fourteen-day LA-to-Seattle "Pacific Crest," starting with Disneyland and Hollywood Studios, then heading to Big Sur, east to Yosemite, back to San Francisco, then following the coastal range up to Mount Rainier and Olympic National Parks; this starts at A$1100, with a similar mix of hotel room shares and camping.

Insurance

Some form of **travel insurance** is highly recommended, and it's available from most travel agents, some banks or direct from insurance companies, for periods ranging from a few days to a year or even longer. All are fairly similar in premium and coverage which includes medical expenses, loss of personal property and travelers checks, cancellations and delays, as well as most adventure sports. If you plan to indulge in high-risk activities such as mountaineering, bungee jumping or scuba diving check the policy carefully to make sure you'll be covered as it may be necessary to tailor a policy to suit your requirements. Cover More, 9/32 Walker St, North Sydney (☎02/9202 8000 or 1800/251 881), and Ready Plan, 141 Walker St, Dandenong, Melbourne (☎03/9791 5077 or 1800/337 462), also 10/63 Albert St, Auckland (☎09/379 3208), give the best value coverage. A normal policy for Los Angeles – or the US in general – costs around A$130/NZ$145 for two weeks, A$190/NZ$210 for one month, A$280/NZ$310 for two months.

Getting there from North America

As a major center for national and international travel, LA is well served by air, rail, and road networks. The best means of getting to LA from North America is undoubtedly airline travel, with many transcontinental flights offering daily service to LA from across the US and Canada. Rail travel is a distant second choice, with few options save for Amtrak, the nation's underfunded train system. The cheapest and most cost-effective travel choice is to go by bus, although it's also the least comfortable and the most time-consuming.

By air

Los Angeles International Airport, or "LAX," is the obvious choice if you're **flying** into LA, one of the country's busiest air hubs and a common stopover point on trips between North America and East Asia. While LAX is undoubtedly the most familiar, other airports also offer flight alternatives in the region, notably **John Wayne International** in Orange County, but also smaller airports in Burbank, Van Nuys, and Ontario (in the San Gabriel Valley).

As airlines tend to match each other's prices, there's generally little difference in their quoted fares. Barring a **fare war**, round-trip prices from New York start at around $300, slightly more from Toronto and Montreal. Flights from major US air hubs, such as Denver, Atlanta, and Chicago, will often cost you less than shorter trips from smaller, closer airports, unless you're flying on a **regional carrier** like Reno Air, in which case you can expect to pay much less – in many cases, less than $100 from western US cities. What makes more difference than your choice of carrier are the conditions governing the ticket: whether it is fully refundable, the time and day, and, most importantly, the **time of year** you travel. Least expensive is a non-summer-season midweek flight, booked and purchased at least three weeks in advance. Some **no-frills carriers** can often provide very good value as well. Southwest Airlines is one of the most notable of these, but New York-based operator Tower Air also offers some of the most competitive fares in the country, including a $241 rate between New York and LA ($162 one-way).

Airlines serving LA

Aer Lingus ☎1-800/223-6537 or 212/557-1110; *www.aerlingus.ie*

Aero California ☎1-800/237-6225

Aeromexico ☎1-800/237-6639 or 713/939-7535; *www.wotw.com/aeromexico*

Air Canada ☎1-800/776-3000; *www.aircanada.ca*

Air France ☎1-800/237-2747; in Canada, ☎1-800/667-2747; *www.airfrance.fr*

Air New Zealand ☎1-800/262-1234; in Canada, ☎1-800/563-5494; *www.airnz.com.*

Alaska Airlines ☎1-800/426-0333; *www.alaska-air.com*

American Airlines ☎1-800/433-7300; *www.americanair.com*

America West Airlines ☎1-800/235-9292; *www.americawest.com.*

British Airways ☎1-800/247-9297; in Canada ☎1-800/668-1059; *www.british-airways.com*

Canadian Airlines in Canada ☎1-800/665-1177; in US ☎1-800/426-7000; *www.cdnair.ca*

Continental Airlines ☎1-800/525-0280; *www.flycontinental.com.*

Delta Airlines ☎1-800/221-1212; *www.delta-air.com.*

Hawaiian Airlines ☎1-800/367-5320; *www.hawaiianair.com.*

Iberia ☎1-800/772-4642; in Canada, ☎1-800/423-7421; *www.iberia.com/ingles/home.html*

KLM ☎1-800/374-7747; in Canada, ☎1-800/361-5073; *www.klm.nl*

Korean Airlines ☎1-800/438-5000

Lufthansa ☎1-800/645-3880; in Canada, ☎1-800/563-5954; *www.lufthansa-usa.com*

Mexicana ☎1-800/531-7921; *www.mexicana.com*

Northwest Airlines ☎1-800/225-2525; *www.nwa.com*

Reno Air ☎1-800/736-6247; *www.renoair.com*

Southwest Airlines ☎1-800/435-9792; *www.iflyswa.com*

Tower Air ☎1-800/221-2500; *www.towerair.com*

TWA ☎1-800/221-2000; *www.twa.com*

United Airlines ☎1-800/241-6522; *www.ual.com*

US Airways ☎1-800/428-4322; *www.usairways.com*

Virgin Atlantic Airways ☎1-800/862-8621; *www.fly.virgin.com/atlantic*

Western Pacific ☎1-800/930-3030; *www.syspac.com/~inno/index.html*

Travelers intending to fly **from Canada** may find that, with less competition on these routes, fares are somewhat higher than they are for flights wholly within the US. You will often find that it's worth the effort to get to a US city first and fly on to LA from there.

Shopping for tickets

While it's good to call the airlines directly to inquire about their official fares, you can cut costs by going through a **specialist flight agent** – either a **consolidator**, who buys up blocks of tickets from the airlines and sells them at a discount, or a **discount agent**, who in addition to dealing with discounted flights may also offer special student and youth fares and a range of other travel-related services such as travel insurance, rail passes, car rentals, tours, and the like. Bear in mind, though, that penalties for

changing your plans can be stiff. Remember too that these companies make their money by dealing in bulk – don't expect them to answer lots of questions. Some agents specialize in **charter flights**, which may be cheaper than anything available on a scheduled flight, but again departure dates are fixed and withdrawal penalties are high check the refund policy. If you travel a lot, **discount travel clubs** are another option – the annual membership fee may be worth it for benefits such as cut-price air tickets and car rental.

Don't automatically assume that tickets purchased through a travel specialist will be cheapest – once you get a quote, check with the airlines and you may turn up an even better deal. Always exercise caution and *never* deal with a company that demands cash up front or refuses to accept payment by credit card.

Discount travel agents in the USA and Canada

Council Travel ☎1-800/226-8624; *www.ciee.org. Student/budget travel agency with branches in many US cities.*
Educational Travel Center ☎1-800/747-5551 or 608/256-5551; *www.edtrav.com. Student/youth and consolidator fares.*
Now Voyager ☎212/431-1616; *www. nowvoyagertravel.com. Courier flight broker and consolidator.*
Skylink ☎1-800/AIR-ONLY or ☎212/573-8980. *Consolidator with branches in Chicago, Los Angeles, Montreal, Toronto, and Washington DC.*
STA Travel ☎1-800/781-4040 or 213/934-8722; *www.sta-travel.com*; offices in New

York, Chicago, Seattle, Philadelphia, and Boston. *Worldwide discount travel firm specializing in student/youth fares; also student IDs, travel insurance, car rental, rail passes, etc.*
TFI Tours International☎1-800/745-8000 or 212/736-1140. *Consolidator with offices in New York, Las Vegas and Miami.*
Travel Avenue ☎1-800/333-3335 or 312/876-6866; *www.travelavenue.com. Full-service travel agent offering discounts in the form of rebates.*
Travelocity *www.travelocity.com. Online consolidator.*

By train

If you have additional money to spend and want a bit more luxury and space on your trip through the use of private cabins and dining cars, or simply have the time and inclination to tour the greater US, an **Amtrak train** may be just the ticket for you.

To arrive by way of the Midwest and Southwest, ride on the **Southwest Chief**, which begins in Chicago and travels through Kansas City, Albuquerque, and Flagstaff before arriving in LA. The **Sunset Limited** is another option, a route that takes you from central Florida through New Orleans, Houston, and Tucson and reaches LA via

Palm Springs and Pomona. A shorter but even more memorable route is the **Coast Starlight**, which runs between Seattle and San Diego and features some of the most appealing scenery anywhere, from coastal whale-watching between San Luis Obispo and Santa Barbara to an evening trip around Mt Shasta to a journey through the wooded terrain of the Pacific Northwest.

One-way cross-country fares are around $250 or so, though Americans traveling round-trip can take advantage of "**All-Aboard America**" fares, which are zone-based and allow three stopovers in between your origin and eventual return. This enables you to visit one or more

Amtrak rail passes

Foreign travelers have a choice of four **rail passes** that include the LA area; the **Coastal Pass** permits unlimited rail travel on the East and West coasts, but not in between the two.

	15 day (June-Aug)	15 day (Sept-May)	30 day (June-Aug)	30 day (Sept-May)
Far West	$240	$185	$310	$240
West	$315	$195	$395	$260
Coastal	—	—	$275	$225
National	$425	$285	$535	$375

On production of a passport issued outside the US or Canada, the passes can be purchased at Amtrak stations in the US. In the **UK**, buy them from Destination Marketing, 2 Cinnamon Row, York Place, London SW11 3TW (☎0171/253 9009); in **Ireland**, contact USIT (☎01/602 1620); in **Australia**, Walshes World (☎02/9232 7499); and in **New Zealand**, Atlantic & Pacific (☎09/302 9720).

For all information on **Amtrak fares and schedules**, and to make reservations, use the toll-free number ☎1-800/USA-RAIL. Do not call individual stations.

cities without paying anything extra. Travel within the West from Denver to the Pacific costs $198 between September and May, or $228 June to August; within the West and Midwest (west of Chicago) costs $258/318; and for the entire US the cost is $318/378. **Foreign travelers** can take advantage of the rail passes as well (see box overleaf). While Amtrak's basic fares are pretty good value, if you want to travel more comfortably, the cost rises quickly. **Sleeping compartments**, which include small toilets and showers, start at around $100 for one or two people, but can climb as high as $400 depending on the class of compartment, number of nights, season, etc, but all include three meals per day.

By bus

Bus travel is a slow, often frustrating way to get to LA, and in the end you won't really save that much money. **Greyhound** (☎1-800/231-2222) is the sole long-distance operator, and its fares average 10¢ per mile – costing you around $300 for a coast-to-coast trip. The main reason to go Greyhound is if you're planning to visit a number of other places en route; the company's **Ameripass** is good for unlimited travel within a certain time; 7 days of travel costs $199; 15 days, $299; 30 days, $409; and 60 days, $599. Because the pass is valid from the date of purchase, it's a bad idea to buy it

---

Green Tortoise

A counterculture alternative to long-distance bus travel is the colorful **Green Tortoise** line, whose buses, furnished with bunks, foam cushions, coolers, and sound systems, run between the major cities of the West Coast, from LA to Seattle. In the summer, they also cross the country from New York to Boston; transcontinental trips that amount to mini-tours of the nation, taking around a dozen days at a cost of $319–389, not including contributions to the food fund, and allowing plenty of stops for hiking, river-rafting, and hot springs. Other Green Tortoise trips include excursions to major national parks (in 16 days for $499), and north to Alaska, and winter trips to Central America and Mexico, as well as year-round excursions to Yosemite. For information call ☎1-800/227-4766.

---

in advance. **Foreign visitors** can buy Ameripasses before leaving home, in which case they will be validated once you start your travels. In the **UK**, a 4-day pass costs £70; 5-day, £90; 7-day, £110; 15-day, £160; 30-day, £215; and 60-day, £330. Greyhound's London office is at Sussex House, London Rd, East Grinstead, West Sussex RH19 1LD (☎01342/317317).

Alternatively, the **US Bus Pass** (☎617/984-1556) allows unlimited travel on special buses that ply fixed routes through certain parts of the US. Passes are valid for a certain number of consecutive days: 5 days, $99; 10 days, $179; 15 days, $229; 20 days, $270; 30 days, $349; 45 days, $459. Prices are somewhat higher if you want to keep your start date/place open.

By car

Obviously, for a city built on concrete and asphalt, LA is the perfect place to access **by car**, and although there are numerous freeways within the region to expedite your travel, see "Introducing the City," pp.39–52, there are really only three main routes outside Southern California that can quickly get you to the metropolis: **Interstate 5**, a north–south corridor that connects LA to Mexico and Canada through the West Coast; **Interstate 10**, a transcontinental east–west route that begins in Jacksonville and ends in Santa Monica, where it becomes the Pacific Coast Highway; and **Interstate 15**, running along a mostly deserted stretch of the Far West before it reaches Las Vegas and drops down into LA in the eastern San Gabriel Valley. Another option is **Highway 101**, the famed coastal route that takes you along the cliffs and crannies of the Pacific Ocean and terminates in Downtown LA, after traveling through the San Fernando Valley and Hollywood where it is known as the "Hollywood Freeway".

Driving your own car gives the greatest freedom and flexibility, but if you don't have one or don't trust the one you have, one option worth considering is a **driveaway**. Certain companies, operating in most major cities, are paid to find drivers to take a customer's car from one place to another. The company will normally pay for your insurance and one tank of gas; after that, you'll be expected to drive along the most direct

Car rental agencies in North America

Alamo
☎ 1-800/354-2322; *www.goalamo.com*.

Avis
☎ 1-800/331-1212; *www.avis.com*.

Budget
☎ 1-800/527-0700; *www.budgetrentacar.com*.

Dollar
☎ 1-800/421-6868.

Enterprise Rent-a-Car
☎ 1-800/325-8007; *www.pickenterprise.com*

Hertz
☎ 1-800/654-3131; in Canada ☎ 1-800/263-0600; *www.hertz.com*.

National
☎ 1-800/CAR-RENT; *www.nationalcar.com*.

Rent-A-Wreck
☎ 1-800/535-1391.

Thrifty
☎ 1-800/367-2277; *www.thrifty.com*.

US Rent-a-Car
☎ 1-800/777-9377.

Value
☎ 1-800/468-2583.

route and to average 400 miles a day. Companies are keen to use foreign travelers with German visitors being the most desired, but if you are at least 21 and can convince them that you're a safe choice, they'll take something like a $350 deposit, which you can get back once you've returned the car in good condition. Look under "Automobile Transporters and Driveaways" in the *Yellow Pages* for more information.

Absolutely necessary unless you're planning to spend all your time in relatively compact Downtown, Beverly Hills, or Santa Monica, **renting a car** is the usual story of phoning one of the major companies – Avis, Hertz, Budget, etc – listed in the box above, of which Thrifty tends to be the cheapest. Most companies – have offices at destination airports, and addresses and phone numbers are comprehensively documented in the *Yellow Pages*.

Also worth examining are **fly-drive deals**, which offer bargain-rate and sometimes free car rental when buying an airline ticket. They usually work out better than renting on the spot and are especially good value if you intend to do a lot of driving.

Packages

Many operators run all-inclusive **packages** that combine plane tickets and hotel accommodation with for example sightseeing, wining and dining, and excursions to major tourist sites. Even if the "package" aspect doesn't excite you, these deals can still be more convenient and sometimes even work out to be more econom-ical than arranging the whole thing yourself, provided you don't mind losing a little flexibility. With such a great range of packages available, a general overview is difficult – travel agents will have copious brochures detailing what's available.

Insurance

Before purchasing a **travel insurance policy**, North American visitors should check to make sure they're not already covered by their regular health insurance. After making a claim, always save **forms** and **documentation** so you can be reimbursed after your journey, and make sure to be prompt in processing your claim – many providers have time limits on making a claim. Holders of official **student/teacher/youth cards** are entitled to accident coverage and hospital inpatient benefits, and students may find that their **student health coverage** extends during vacation or one term past enrollment.

While **homeowners'** and **renters' insurance** often covers up to $500 in stolen goods during a vacation, few if any providers cover against theft during traveling. For more options, **specialist travel insurance companies** offer certain types of coverage with varying premiums, depending on your situation and needs (see box overleaf). Policies are comprehensive for accidents, illnesses, lost luggage, or canceled flights, but maximum payments tend to be low. **Student/youth travel agencies** sometimes provide the best deals, with policies costing $48–69 for fifteen days of travel depending on level of coverage,

$80–105 for a month, $149–207 for two months, and $510–700 for a year. However, if you're planning on engaging in high-risk sports like skiing, you can expect to pay a **surcharge** of twenty to fifty percent.

Most North American travel policies apply only to items lost, stolen, or damaged while in the custody of officially recognized third-parties like airlines, hotel porters, and so on. Even in these cases, you'll still have to contact the police within a reasonable time limit.

Entry requirements for foreign visitors

Under the Visa Waiver Scheme, designed to speed up lengthy immigration procedures, citizens of Andorra, Argentina, Australia, Austria, Belgium, Brunei, Denmark, Finland, France, Germany, Iceland, Ireland, Italy, Japan, Liechtenstein, Luxembourg, Monaco, the Netherlands, New Zealand, Norway, San Marino, Slovenia, Spain, Sweden, Switzerland, and the United Kingdom visiting the United States for a period of less than ninety days only need a full passport and a visa waiver form. The latter will be provided either by your travel agency, or by the airline during check-in or on the plane, and must be presented to immigration on arrival. The same form covers entry across the land borders with Canada and Mexico as well as by air. However, those eligible for the scheme must apply for a visa if they intend to work, study, or stay in the country for more than ninety days.

Prospective visitors from parts of the world not mentioned above require a valid passport and a **non-immigrant visitor's visa**. How you'll obtain a visa depends on what country you're in and your status when you apply, so telephone the nearest embassy or consulate (see box opposite).

In **Britain**, only British or EU citizens, and those from other countries eligible for the visa waiver scheme, can apply by post – fill in the application form available at most travel agents and send it with a full passport and a SAE to the nearest US embassy or consulate. Expect a wait of one to three weeks before your passport is returned. All others must apply in person, making an appointment in advance. Visa application fees in Britain are currently US$20.

Canadian citizens are in a particularly privileged position when it comes to crossing the border into the US. Though it is possible to enter the States without your passport, you should really have it with you on any trip that brings you as far as California. Only if you plan to stay for more than ninety days do you need a visa. Bear in mind that if you cross into the States in your car, trunks and passenger compartments are subject to spot searches by US Customs personnel, though this sort of surveillance is likely to decrease as remaining tariff barriers fall over the next few years. Remember too, that without the proper paperwork, Canadians are legally barred from seeking gainful employment in the US.

Australian and New Zealand passport holders staying less than ninety days do not require a visa, providing they arrive on a commercial flight with an onward or return ticket. For longer stays, US multiple entry visas cost A$26. You'll need an application form, available from the US visa information service (☎1902/262 682), one signed passport photo and your passport, and either post it or personally lodge it at one of the American embassy or consulate addresses below. For postal applications in Australia, payment can be made at any post office (US visa application payment form no.828); you'll also need to include the receipt of payment and a SAE. Processing takes about ten working days for postal applications; personal lodgements take two days – but check details with the consulate first.

Whatever your nationality, visas are not issued to convicted felons and anybody who owns up to being a communist, fascist or drug dealer.

US embassies and consulates

Australia
Moonbah Place, Canberra, ACT ☎02/6270 5000

39 Castlereagh St, Sydney ☎1800/805 924

Britain
24/31 Upper Grosvenor Square, London W1A 1AE ☎0171/499 9000; visa hotline ☎0891/200290

3 Regent Terrace, Edinburgh EH7 5BW ☎0131/556 8315

Queens House, 14 Queen St, Belfast BT1 6EQ ☎01232/241279

Canada
100 Wellington St, Ottawa, ON K1P 5T1 ☎613/238-5335

Suite 1050, 615 Macleod Trail, Calgary, AB T2G 4T8 ☎403/266-8962

Suite 910, Cogswell Tower, Scotia Square, Halifax, NS B3J 3K1 ☎902/429-2480

Complex Desjardins, South Tower, Montréal, PQ H5B 1G1 ☎514/398-9695

2 Place Terrasse Dufferin, Québec City, PQ G1R 4T9 ☎418/692-2095

360 University Ave, Toronto, ON M5G 1S4 ☎416/595-1700

1095 W Pender St, Vancouver, BC V6E 2M6 ☎604/685-4311

New Zealand
29 Fitzherbert Terrace, Thorndon, Wellington ☎04/472 2068

Cnr. Shortland and O'Connell sts, Auckland ☎09/303 2724 or Non-Immigrant Visas, Private Bag 92022, Auckland.

Health matters

Foreign visitors don't require any inoculations to enter the States. What you will require is insurance (see pp.7, 10, 15 & 16), as medical bills for the most minor accident can be astronomical – and there's no way they can be escaped.

If you have a serious **emergency** while in the US, medical services will get to you quickly and charge you later. For emergencies or ambulances, call ☎**911**, the national emergency line. Lists of **doctors** can be found in the telephone directory under "Physicians and Surgeons" and "Clinics," and a **consultation** will run you from $50–100. Prescribed medicines aren't cheap, either, and you should keep your receipts for later reimbursement from your insurance carrier.

Drugstores provide a wide array of over-the-counter lotions, creams, and ointments, but because of tight federal regulation, some easily attainable products in Europe, like codeine-based painkillers, need a prescription in the US. Brand names also vary, so ask the pharmacist for assistance.

24hr pharmacies

Kaiser Permanente, in the LA Medical Center, 4867 Sunset Blvd, Hollywood ☎213/667-8301

Horton & Converse Pharmacy, 11600 Wilshire Blvd, West LA ☎310/478-0801

West LA Medical Center Pharmacy, 6041 Cadillac Ave, West LA ☎323/857-2151

Information and maps

The best way to get free information and maps about LA is to write or call any of its constituent cities' visitors bureaux. These promotional offices will send you copious material on their respective areas, and occasionally a simple map or two. However, in a region like LA, there are numerous ways to get lost, so you're better off investing a few extra dollars in a detailed map, just so you stay on the right boulevards and freeways.

USA/California tourist offices abroad

California Tourism Information Office, Suite 433, High Holborn House, 52-54 High Holborn, London WC1V 6RB ☎0171/242 3131, fax 242 2838.

US Travel and Tourism, Martin Place, Sydney ☎02/9234 9155.

USA Tourist Service, 75 King St, Sydney ☎02/9299 1222.

Map and travel book outlets

AUSTRALIA AND NEW ZEALAND

Travel Bookshop, Shop 3, 175 Liverpool St, Sydney ☎02/9261 8200.

Bowyangs, 372 Little Bourke St, Melbourne ☎03/9670 4383.

The Map Shop, 16a Peel St, Adelaide ☎08/8231 2033.

Perth Map Centre, 891 Hay St, Perth ☎08/9322 5733.

Specialty Maps, 58 Albert St, Auckland ☎09/307 2217.

Worldwide Maps and Guides 187 George St, Brisbane ☎07/3221 4330.

CANADA

Open Air Books and Maps, 25 Toronto St, Toronto, ON M5C 2R1 ☎416/363-0719.

Ulysses Travel Bookshop, 4176 St-Denis, Montréal ☎514/843-9447.

World Wide Books and Maps, 736a Granville St, Vancouver, BC V6Z 1G3 ☎604/687-3320.

UK

Blackwell's Map and Travel Shop, 53 Broad St, Oxford OX1 3BQ ☎01865/792792; *bookshop.blackwell.co.uk.*

Daunt Books, 83 Marylebone High St, London W1M 3DE ☎0171/224 2295; 193 Haverstock Hill, NW3 4QL ☎0171/794 4006.

Heffers Map Shop, 3rd Floor, in Heffers Stationery Department, 19 Sidney St, Cambridge CB2 3HL ☎01223/568467; *www.heffers.co.uk.*

James Thin Melven's Bookshop, 29 Union St, Inverness IV1 1QA ☎01463/233500; *www.jthin.co.uk.*

John Smith and Sons, 57–61 St Vincent St, Glasgow G2 5TB ☎0141/221 7472; *www.johnsmith.co.uk.*

The Map Shop, 30a Belvoir St, Leicester LE1 6QH ☎0116/247 1400.

National Map Centre, 22–24 Caxton St, London SW1H 0QU ☎0171/222 2466; *www.mapsworld.com.*

Newcastle Map Centre, 55 Grey St, Newcastle upon Tyne NE1 6EF ☎0191/261 5622.

Stanfords, 12–14 Long Acre, London WC2E 9LP ☎0171/836 1321; 29 Corn Street, Bristol BS1 1HT ☎0117/929 9966.

The Travel Bookshop, 13–15 Blenheim Crescent, London W11 2EE ☎0171/229 5260; *www.thetravelbookshop.co.uk.*

Waterstone's, 91 Deansgate, Manchester M3 2BW ☎0161/832 1992; *www.waterstones.co.uk.*

US

Adventurous Traveler Bookstore, PO Box 1468, Williston, VT 05495 ☎1-800/282-3963; *www.AdventurousTraveler.com.*

Book Passage, 51 Tamal Vista Blvd, Corte Madera, CA 94925 ☎415/927-0960.

The Complete Traveler Bookstore, 199 Madison Ave, New York, NY 10016 ☎212/685-9007.

Map Link, 30 S La Petera Lane, Unit #5, Santa Barbara, CA 93117 ☎805/692-6777.

The Map Store Inc., 1636 First St, Washington, DC 20006 ☎202/628-2608.

Phileas Fogg's Books & Maps, #87 Stanford Shopping Center, Palo Alto, CA 94304 ☎1-800/533-FOGG.

Sierra Club Bookstore, 6014 College Ave, Oakland, CA 94618 ☎510/658-7470.

Travel Books & Language Center, 4931 Cordell Ave, Bethesda, MD 20814 ☎1-800/220-2665.

Traveler's Bookstore, 22 W 52nd St, New York, NY 10019 ☎212/664-0995.

Information

The **California Visitors Bureau** (CVB) is the main source of **information** about the city, with offices Downtown and in Hollywood see box overleaf. Independent offices in smaller LA cities also offer valuable material, which relate more to their own specific attractions and less to the area in general. For a much broader perspective

of Southern California, as well as the entire state, call or write to the **California Office of Tourism**, 801 K St, Suite 1600, Sacramento, CA 95814-3520 (☎916/322-2881 or 1-800/862-2543).

If all else fails, you can find racks of free **promotional material** like simple maps, hotel and restaurant pamphlets, and magazine-sized city guides at small kiosks across the city, or at stands in most hotels.

Maps

Generally speaking, the **maps** in this book will be sufficient in helping you find your way around the main parts of town and their key attractions. For a pocket-sized, laminated map, you may wish to check out *Streetwise Los Angeles* ($4.95), available in many bookstores.

For a much more **detailed view** of the city, Thomas Brothers Publishing sells its *Thomas Guide to Los Angeles County* at many area bookstores. Published yearly for counties across Southern California, the Thomas guides are the best maps available for regional travel, especially for venturing beyond the well-known parts of the city into more unfamiliar territory. If you're staying for several weeks, consider spending $25 to purchase one. If you're interested in highly specific views of **rural terrain**, as well as the urban layout, DeLorme's large-format *Atlas and Gazetteer* of *Southern and Central California* ($16.95) is an extensively detailed map that is best for showing national forests, parkland, hiking trails, and minor dirt and gravel roads.

Rand McNally operates a chain of comprehensive **travel stores** across the region, and nation. For locations, call ☎1-800/333-0136 or simply visit one of the company's better stores, its excellent branch in the Westside's Century City Mall. If you happen to be one of its members, the Automobile Club of Southern California, 2601 S Figueroa St, south of Downtown (☎213/741-3686), provides maps, guides, and other **motoring information**, while the national office of the AAA also provides maps and assistance to its members, as well as to British members of the AA and RAC (☎1-800/222-4357).

The Internet

You can obtain plenty of information about LA, whether you're planning your trip or you're already here and checking to see what's on in the clubs, from the **Internet**. Given LA's role as a center for commercial entertainment, it should come as no surprise that the city is the subject of a number of interesting, off-the-wall **Web sites** that relate to Hollywood and the surrounding movie culture. Along with these, other sites also offer information on city hotels, restaurants, and clubs, along with quirkier pages devoted to bizarre architecture or celebrity murders. Some of these sites are listed in the accompanying box, and you can find even more by using a search engine like Yahoo, Hotbot, or Altavista. Don't forget to visit our own site *www.roughguides.com/travel* for other Internet suggestions for LA and beyond.

LA Web sites

ArtScene *artscenecal.com/index.html*
Copious listing of the galleries and museums of Southern California, broken down by neighborhood and geography.

California Surf Report
www.surfscene.net/surf/index.html
Hot surfing news for the Southern California

counties of Los Angeles and Ventura. There are daily surf reports by a correspondent who's been shootin' tubes for thirty years.

Club LA *www.clubLA.com*
Searchable lists and reviews of trendy bars, dance clubs, and comedy spots, plus fashion advice and gossip tidbits.

LA Web sites (cont.)

E! Online *www.eonline.com*
Breathless, gossipy and visually gorgeous, this site has features such as "Celebs Under the Knife," a diary of a genuine striving starlet, and pages of star profiles and movie reviews.

I Love LA *www-leland.stanford.edu/~jenkg/angeles/la.html*
Despite the corny title, the best link page about LA, featuring sites on the area's art, architecture, history, landmarks, media, books, and transportation.

LA Grim Society *desperado.scvnet.com/~grim/index.html*
Surprisingly cheerful look at the books, movies, and events relating to death in LA, past and present.

LA Movie Theaters *www.primenet.com/~otto/movieville/movieville.html*
Coverage of all the first-run, art, and revival houses of the city.

LA Nocturne *www.nocturne.com*
Covering both the dark side of LA, and LA after dark: reviews of pool halls, diners, and clubs, plus books and movies that explore the sordid allure of the city.

Los Angeles County Museum of Art *www.lacma.org*
Reviews of current and future shows, such as the 1999 Vincent Van Gogh exhibition – based entirely on the holdings of Amsterdam's Van Gogh Museum.

Murals of LA *www.usc.edu/Library/Ref/LA/PubArt/LA_murals/*
Excellent listing by neighborhood of the many murals across the city, from resplendent Madonnas in East LA to beachside curiosities in Venice, with accompanying pictures.

The Rock and Roll Road Map *www.net101.com/rocknroll/*
Visit the sites that made local, and national, music history, in the LA area.

Southern California Earthquake Map *www.crustal.ucsb.edu/scec/webquakes/*
A disturbing diagram showing the sites of the last 500 temblors picked up by local seismographs, plus informative earthquake links.

Union Station: Los Angeles Rail Transit *www.westworld.com/~elson/larail/*
Good information about the subways, trains, and light rail options available in the metropolis, along with history and trivia about the Angel's Flight funicular railway.

Virtual Hollywood Walking Tour *www.historicla.com/hollywood/index.html*
Wander through movie history along Hollywood Boulevard, taking in the famous sights and surroundings of this faded, but still colorful stretch.

Telephones and mail

As one of the main US nodes for commercial and business activity, LA has an excellent communications infrastructure, with all manner of modern, high-tech links to the rest of the country and world. Although various degrees of investment have made some areas better hooked up than others – the Westside, for example – generally, most communication services are more than adequate throughout the region, with the singular exception of the US mail, which is quite slow and prone to misplacing letters and packages.

Telephones

Regional **telephone service** in the LA area is generally divided between US West and Pacific Bell, two former chunks of the Bell system monopoly. **Public phones** are common and most tend to function, at least those in well-trafficked areas,

and a local call within a given area code will likely cost you 25¢, though potentially as much as 35¢. Outside the immediate calling zone, you'll have to dial a 1, plus the area code and telephone number. City calls outside your area code are technically long distance calls, and cost a bit more depending on where you're calling from and dialing to.

Beyond the local area, regular **long distance calls** to other parts of the US and world are most expensive during daylight hours typically (8am–6pm) with evening charges somewhat reduced (6–11pm) and early morning hours cheapest of all (11pm–8am). Detailed rates are listed at the front of **telephone directories**, which are commonly available in hotel rooms and less frequently at public phone booths, which tend to offer more tattered copies. Most LA hotels have gotten into the practice of charging a **fee** often around a dollar for each local phone call, in addition to their extremely costly long distance rates. You can get around these charges by using a calling card with a free ☎1-800 access number for long distance calls, and by using a lobby pay phone for local calls.

A great number of companies provide long distance services, either through a **calling card** issued from phone companies or purchased at airports, hostels, and some retailers or major **credit card**. You're better off sticking with the big names – Sprint, AT&T, MCI, and the like – and avoiding smaller companies with unfamiliar names, as some of these are fly-by-night operations that will take your credit information and tack on exorbitant fees. Amazingly, this is a legal

---

Public service numbers

Emergencies ☎911 for fire, police, or ambulance

Other lines:
Ambulance ☎213/483-6721
Fire ☎213/384-3131 or 262-2111
Paramedics ☎213/262-2111
Police ☎213/625-3311
Poison control center ☎1-800/777-6476
Earthquake tips ☎818/787-3737

Information:
Operator ☎0
Local directory information ☎411
Long distance information ☎1 +area code/555-1212
Information for toll-free numbers ☎1-800/555-1212

International telephone calls

International calls can be dialed direct from private or (more expensively) public phones. You can get assistance from the **international operator** ☎00, who may also interrupt every three minutes asking for more money, and call you back for any money still owed immediately after you hang up.

In **Britain**, it's possible to obtain a free **BT Chargecard** (☎0800/800838), from which all calls from overseas can be charged to your quarterly domestic account. To use these cards in the US, or to make a **collect call** (to "reverse the charges") using a BT operator, contact the carrier: AT&T ☎1-800/445-5667; MCI ☎1-800/444-2162; or Sprint ☎1-800/800-0008. To avoid the international operator fee, BT credit card calls can be made directly using an automated system: AT&T ☎1-800/445-5688;

MCI ☎1-800/854-4826; or Sprint ☎1-800/825-4904.

British visitors who are going to be making a number of calls to the US, and who want to be able to call ☎1-800 numbers, otherwise inaccessible from outside the country, should take advantage of the **Swiftcall** telephone club, for which you need a touch-tone phone. Call your nearest office (see below; daily 8am–midnight), and once you've paid by credit card for however many units you want, you are given a PIN. Any time you want to get an international line, simply dial ☎0171/488 0800, punch in your PIN, and then dial as you would were you in the US, putting a 1 before the area code, followed by the number. Calls to the USA – including ☎1-800 calls – cost about 14p per minute, a **saving** of over fifty percent:

Swiftcall numbers

UK ☎0800/769 5555   Ireland ☎0800/409278   USA ☎1-800/513-7325

Telephone cards such as Australia's Telstra Telecard or Optus Calling Card and New Zealand Telecom's Calling Card can be used to make calls abroad, which are charged

back to a domestic account or credit card. Apply to Telstra ☎1800/626 008, Optus ☎1300/300 300, or NZ Telecom ☎04/382 5818.

The telephone code to dial **TO the US** from the outside world excluding Canada is 1.
To make international calls **FROM the US**, dial 011 followed by the country code:

Australia 61	Denmark 45	Germany 49	Ireland 353
Netherlands 31	New Zealand 64	Sweden 46	United Kingdom 44

practice, thanks to loopholes in US telecommunications law.

Many major hotels, government agencies, and car rental firms have **toll-free numbers** that are recognizable by their ☎1-800 prefix. Some of these numbers are meant to be accessed nationally, others only within the state of California – dialing is the only way to find out. Numbers with a ☎1-900 prefix are **toll calls**, typically sports information lines, psychic hotlines, and phone sex centers, and will cost you a variable, though consistently high, fee for just a few minutes of use. Alphabetic **letters** attached to a phone number, such as ☎555-JOKE, simply correspond to numbers displayed on the telephone itself.

Finally, LA is a patchwork of long-distance telephone numbers with separate **area code** zones that are constantly being split up into smaller sections. For years, almost all of Central LA from

Downtown to Santa Monica had one area code, 213. Since 1991, though, new area codes have popped up frequently, and some of the current

Area codes for LA

213 Downtown, Mid-Wilshire, Hollywood, South Central LA, East LA
310 West Hollywood, Beverly Hills, West LA, Westwood, Santa Monica, Venice, Malibu, South Bay, San Pedro
562 Long Beach, Whittier, Southeast LA
626 Pasadena, Arcadia, San Gabriel Valley
714 Orange County
805 Santa Clarita, Lancaster, northern deserts
818 Burbank, Glendale, San Fernando Valley
909 Pomona, Inland Empire

ones listed in the box overleaf will no doubt be updated in a few years.

Mail

Regular hours for US **post offices** are from 9am to 5pm Monday through Friday, and from 9am to noon or 1pm on Saturday. Moreover, blue **mail boxes** are found throughout the area, and you can send mail weighing under an ounce to anywhere in the US with a single 32¢ stamp, soon to rise to 33¢. You must, however, list a **return address** and include the **zip code** of the recipient. These codes can be found at post offices and at the front of telephone directories. If sending mail to Europe, postcards, aerograms, and letters weighing less than one-half ounce cost 60¢, with the time of arrival usually taking about a week.

If you're **receiving mail**, senders should address material to General Delivery what's known overseas as **poste restante** and include your name and the address of the main post office at 900 N Alameda St, Downtown LA, making sure to include the 90086 zip code (☎213/617-4543). You can pick up letters from this post office located next to Union Station Monday to Friday, 8am to 3pm. Mail will be held for thirty days before it's returned to the sender. If you're receiving material at a **local address**, senders should also write "c/o" before the regular occupant's name, though non-discriminating mail carriers are likely to deliver it anyway.

Letters and postcards are the easiest items to send from LA to countries overseas, but if larger **parcels** must be sent, you can find packaging requirements listed at the front of telephone directories, understanding that green **customs declaration forms** available from post offices are a necessity. International parcel **rates** for items weighing less than a pound run from $10 to $12, depending on the package's destination.

Telegrams, faxes and email

To send a **telegram**, otherwise known as a wire, go to the nearest Western Union office, which you will find listed in the telephone directory. For added ease, credit card users can dictate messages over the telephone. **International telegrams** are similar in cost to the cheapest international phone calls, if even slightly less, and messages sent in the morning will arrive at their destinations on the following day. For **domestic telegrams**, ask for a **mailgram**, which will be delivered to any address in the country the next morning.

Public **fax** machines can be found at photocopy centers and, occasionally, bookstores; many hotels have faxes, but will charge you a higher rate for using their machines either sending or receiving. To fax a document at a public machine, simply "swipe" a major credit card through a scanner and wait; otherwise, the staff at a photocopy center will fax it for you.

Public access to **email** and the Internet is fairly well available in Los Angeles. So-called "cybercafés," with terminals at each table, charge roughly $7/hour for full access to the Web; try *The World Café*, 2820 Main St, Santa Monica (☎310/392-1661; *www.worldcafe.la.com*). Additionally, many public libraries have computers available with internet access. If you don't already have one, you can set up a free email account at *www.rocketmail.com*, *www.hotmail.com*, *www.yahoo.com* or *www.juno.com* before you depart

Costs, money and banks

Costs

The local economy has picked up, thus LA is not quite as affordable as it was a few years ago – though there are, as always, bargains to be had. For museums and similar attractions in the Guide, we generally quote prices for adults; you can assume that children get in half-price – and some establishments allow kids under 8 in for free. There are a few free attractions in the city as well, mostly historical and cultural monuments like adobes and old railroad stations.

Unless you're staying in a hostel, where dorm rooms cost from $12–15, **accommodation** will be your greatest expense on a visit to LA. Adequate lodging is rarely available for under $30, and a minimally decent room will run anywhere from $40–80, with fancier hotels costing much, much more – up to $400 in some cases. Surprisingly, **camping** in LA is an alternative, but only if you're staying in more rural areas, where you can get into a campground for around $15–20 per night.

Unlike lodging, there is a wide range of price choices for **food**, from hot dog stands to the chic restaurants (see "Restaurants and Cafés," p.232). You could get by on as little as $15 a day, but realistically you should target around $30 – and remember, too, that LA has plenty of spots great for a splurge. Beyond eating, the city has many alternatives for **bars**, **nightlife**, **music**, and **shop-**ping, and the associated costs depend largely on neighborhood and reputation: you can find a perfectly good watering hole or club with a good location and fair prices, as long as there's no trendy social cachet attached to it. At the more faddish spots, you can expect to pay more for the atmosphere and receive less in service and treatment.

For **transportation**, US gas prices are relatively cheap, and LA's mass transit network leaves much to be desired, so your best bet may be to **rent a car** from any of the vendors around the airport, especially if you're traveling in a group. Regional distances are huge, and if you're headed anywhere beyond Central LA, or more specifically beyond the Westside, you'll undoubtedly find many of the **public transit** choices to be time-consuming hassles – necessary only if you can't afford a car or are frightened by the sight of the city's chaotic boulevards and freeways.

Finally, an 8.25 percent **sales tax** will be added to the cost of most items you purchase, and is implicit in some fees, such as amusement park charges. Exceptions are made for food and medicine. Additionally, many municipalities tack on a **hotel tax** of around 14 percent, which can drive up lodging costs quite dramatically.

Getting and changing money

ATM cards, or "debit cards," are the best and most convenient means of **getting money** for domestic visitors, see box above, provided you use automatic tellers in popular, well-lit locations and avoid getting money at night, particularly in unfamiliar urban environments. Foreign cash-dispensing cards linked to international networks, such as Plus or Cirrus, can be used throughout LA, call the issuing bank or credit company to get a list of area locations, but all ATM users should

Stolen travelers checks and credit cards

Keep a record of the numbers of your **travelers checks** separate from regular bank checks. If you lose them, you can call the issuing companies at the numbers listed below. Similarly, stolen **credit cards** can be reported to these toll-free numbers, and in both cases, you'll need to provide information on where and when you made your last transactions, and the specific numbers of the checks and cards. If you're lucky, the issuing companies may be charitable enough to give you an emergency advance – though you certainly shouldn't count on it.

American Express cards ☎ 1-800/528-4800
American Express checks ☎ 1-800/221-7282
Citicorp ☎ 1-800/645-6556
Diners Club ☎ 1-800/234-6377

Mastercard/Access ☎ 1-800/826-2181
Thomas Cook/Mastercard ☎ 1-800/223-9920
Visa cards ☎ 1-800/227-6811
Visa checks ☎ 1-800/336-8472

remember that most banks now charge "double fees" for cash withdrawals not made at their own machines, resulting in added costs of up to $3 per transaction.

US **travelers checks** are the safest way to carry money for foreign visitors, and the better-known travelers checks, such as those issued through American Express and Visa, are treated as cash in most shops. The usual fee for travelers check sales is one or two percent, though this fee may be waived if you buy the checks through a bank where you have an account. It pays to get a selection of denominations. Make sure to keep the purchase agreement and a record of check serial numbers safe and separate from the checks themselves. In the event that checks are lost or stolen, the issuing company will expect you to report the loss immediately; see box above for access numbers. Most companies claim to replace lost or stolen checks within 24 hours.

While you can pay for items with ATM cards and travelers checks at some establishments, many lower-end businesses may still demand actual **cash** for transactions. Be sure to have plenty of $10 and $20 bills, as higher denominations may not be accepted by many merchants or service providers.

Credit cards are the most widely accepted form of payment for major hotels, restaurants, and retailers, even though some smaller merchants still do not accept them. However, a card may actually be requested of you if you're renting a bike, windsurfer, or other such item, or so you can establish a "tab" at hotels for incidental charges; in any case, you can always pay the bill in cash when you return the item or check out of your room.

Credit cards can also come in very handy as a backup source of funds, and they can even save on exchange-rate commissions; just be sure someone back home is taking care of the bills if you're away for more than a month. Make sure you have a **personal identification number** PIN that's designed to work overseas. Remember that all cash advances are treated as loans, with interest accruing daily from the date of withdrawal; there may be a transaction fee on top of this.

Visa and Mastercard are honored at all credit-friendly businesses, while Diners Club, Discover, and American Express are not quite as widespread in acceptance, though Diners Club cards can be used to cash personal checks at Citibank offices. American Express cards will only assist you in getting cash or travelers checks from company offices, or in using travelers-check dispensers at airports.

Bank hours are generally from 10am to 4pm or 5pm on Monday to Thursday, and from 10am to 6pm on Friday. Although few US banks keep **foreign currency** on hand, you should be able to order most major currencies from your bank's foreign desk if you give them a few days' notice, or you can use the major **exchange bureaux** located at LAX, where at least one outlet will be open daily until 11.30pm; call ☎ 310/417-0366 for details.

Emergencies

If your checks or cards are stolen, **emergency access numbers** are listed in the box above, but if you know someone magnanimous enough to send you money during a crisis, he or she can take money to the nearest **American Express Moneygram** office (☎ 1-800/543-4080) and have it instantaneously wired to you, minus a ten-per-

Money: a note for foreign travelers

Even when the exchange rate is at its least advantageous, most western European visitors find virtually everything – accommodation, food, gas, cameras, clothes and so on – to be better value in the US than it is at home. However, if you're used to traveling in the less expensive countries of Europe, let alone the rest of the world, you shouldn't expect to scrape by on the same minuscule budget once you're in the US.

Usually, one **pound sterling** will get you between $1.45 and $1.70 in American currency, a **Canadian** or **Australian dollar** between 70¢ and 90¢, and a **New Zealand dollar** between 60¢ and 75¢.

BILLS AND COINS

US **bills** typically come in denominations of $1, $5, $10, $20, $50, and $100, with ones and twenties being the most common. All of the common US bills are printed in the **same size and color**, making it necessary to carefully examine each before handing one over, just to make sure you don't mistakenly offer a $50 for

a $1 cup of coffee. Currently, the US Treasury Department has been printing what look to be irregular $100, $50, and $20 bills with enlarged portraits. These are simply the **new versions** of old bills, made more difficult to counterfeit through additional security features like watermarks and special inks.

A dollar is made up of a range of **coins**, including the 1¢ **penny**, 5¢ **nickel**, smaller and thinner 10¢ **dime**, larger 25¢ **quarter**, and the more uncommon 50¢ **half-dollar**. Change is usually necessary for laundromats, vending machines, and public telephones, even though some automatic devices like vending machines are increasingly fitted with slots for dollar bills.

Finally, you should figure in costs for **tipping** into your travel budget. Expect to pay about 15 percent to servers in restaurants, down to 8–10 percent for truly wretched service, and 20 percent for upscale establishments. Taxi drivers expect the same sort of tip, and hotel porters receive one dollar per bag, maids one dollar per evening of lodging, and valet attendants a flat dollar, beyond the valet fee itself.

cent commission that varies inversely according to the amount sent. The entire process should take no longer than ten minutes. For similar, if slightly pricier, services, **Western Union** has offices throughout LA (information at ☎1-800/325-6000 in the US; ☎0800/833 8333 in the UK; and ☎1800/649 565 in Australia), with credit card payments subject to an additional $10 fee.

It's also possible to have money **wired** directly from a bank in your own country to a bank in the US, even though this is somewhat unreliable as it involves two separate institutions. If you choose this option, the person making the transfer will need to know the **telex number** of the bank to which the funds are being sent. This should be considered an expensive last resort in getting money.

If you have a few days' leeway, sending a postal **money order**, exchangeable at any post

office through the mail, is a cheaper option. The equivalent for foreign travelers is the **international money order**, for which you need to allow up to seven days in international air mail before arrival. An ordinary **check** sent from overseas takes two or three weeks to clear.

Foreign travelers in trouble have the final option of throwing themselves on the mercy of their nearest national **consulate** see "Directory" for a list of locations. You may get repatriated, but never expect to get money loaned to you.

International Money Transfers can be made from any bank in Australia and New Zealand to a nominated bank abroad and cost around A$25/NZ$30, but be warned – the whole process can take anywhere between a couple of days and several months. If you desperately need money, wire services are faster, but about twice as expensive.

Crime and personal safety

Crime throughout LA has decreased markedly in the last few years, corresponding to the improvement in the local economy and to less belligerent, and more effective, policing. Much of LA's reputation for violence, lawlessness, and chaos is largely a media phenomenon, promoted by Hollywood as a way to cast the city as a dark, dangerous metropolis. The movie stereotypes of LA – rampant muggings, frequent drive-by shootings, and chaos always ready to erupt – were intensified with the outbreak of the 1992 riots, and have still not appreciably diminished. The great challenge regarding crime in the city is separating the reality of theft and violence from the media-fueled fantasy. Members of the notorious LA gangs, for instance, are a rare sight outside their own territories, and they tend to kill each other rather than tourists.

Most places in Central LA, from Downtown to the coast, are fairly non-threatening during the daytime, though the number of safe spots diminishes **at night**. Much of Downtown, west of Skid Row at least, is walkable during the morning and afternoon hours. At night, you should stay in your Downtown hotel room – the area closes up after dark anyway. Mid-Wilshire should be treated like Downtown, with special care given to the dicey Westlake neighborhood, which is a major spot for drug-dealing. The tourist center of Hollywood is best explored on foot, and, if you don't mind a few prostitutes and petty thugs, is a prime spot for after-hours dancing and drinking. West Hollywood is a busy, dynamic, and generally safe place throughout the day and night, as are most Westside areas from Beverly Hills to Santa Monica. Most of South Central LA should only be visited during the day, with some areas like Compton off-limits at all times to unaccustomed visitors.

Further out, you should have few problems in the major tourist areas – Burbank, Pasadena, coastal Long Beach, Malibu, Orange County – though there are some scattered places where the street gangs are particularly visible – sections of Southeast and East LA, North Long Beach, Pacoima in the San Fernando Valley, and the attractions therein should be approached with caution.

Mugging and theft

If you're unlucky enough to get **mugged**, most of the time you should hand over your cash without argument. Some criminals tend to be quite well-armed, and unless you create a disturbance in a public setting – and are willing to chance a gun-shot – the criminal may not just run away if you struggle. Moreover, since **drugs** are an increasing motivation in many personal robberies, and many criminals are stoned or high when committing their actions, trying to predict what the mugger will do is pointless.

Of course, **prevention** is always the best solution, and you can avoid many problems by simply steering clear of neighborhoods that look dangerous, especially at night. Deserted areas should be avoided in the evening, as should places where the residents watch visitors suspiciously or with hostility. When walking, carry the bulk of your cash, and all of your credit cards, in a **hidden place** separate from a token sum of cash you can use to "buy off" the mugger. Fifty or so dollars, easily accessible on your person, should be an adequate sum to send the criminal looking for his next victim; almost all violent lawbreakers are male. After the crime occurs, immediately report it to the police so you can later attempt to recover your loss from an insurance provider – unlikely, but worth a try. Also, keep **emergency numbers** for credit cards and travelers checks handy, so they can be canceled after the crime occurs.

One prime spot to be mugged is at an **ATM** in an untouristed location. Despite your vigilance, a criminal may manage to sneak up on you and demand you make the maximum withdrawal – $200 – and hand it over. On rare instances, some muggers also operate as **kidnappers** and force you to ferry them from one ATM to another throughout an evening, just so they can slowly pile up your money. Needless to say, you should treat ATM use with the strictest caution and not worry about looking paranoid – LA residents have gotten used to viewing the machines as nocturnal invitations for street crime. Your best choice is to use the automatic tellers available at major hotels and entertainment areas, where it's more difficult for muggers to get away with robbing customers.

Finally, a few **simple rules** are worth remembering: don't flash money around, leave your wallet open, or count money in public; don't excessively peer at maps or guide books on the street; don't look terrified or drunk, even if you are; and at night, make sure you walk on the edge of the sidewalk toward the street, so you can dash toward the road if a confrontation occurs.

Hotel room theft

To avoid being the victim of a **hotel room theft** – a more frequent problem for lower-end establishments, though even the elite hotels are not immune from it – lock your valuables in the room **safe** when you leave, and always keep doors locked with chains as well as bolts. Don't open the door to suspicious individuals, and if a visitor

claims to be a hotel representative, phone the front desk to make sure of it.

If you manage to **lose your passport**, call your country's consulate listed in the "Directory" and pick up or have sent to you an application form, to which you must attach a notarized photocopy of your ID and a $30 reissuing fee. Because the process of issuing you a new passport can take up to six weeks, you should also spend another $10 to have the consulate telex record departments back home.

Car crime

Crimes committed against tourists driving **rental cars**, particularly in Florida, made international headlines a few years ago. In major urbanized areas like LA, any car you rent should have nothing on it, such as a special license plate, to distinguish it as a rental car.

When driving, under no circumstances should you stop in unlit or deserted urban areas, and especially not if someone is waving at you and claiming there's something wrong with your vehicle. Similarly, if you are "accidentally" rammed by the driver behind you, do not stop immediately but instead drive on to the nearest well-lit and trafficked spot, preferably near a police station. Keep doors locked and windows rolled up, or never more than slightly open, and view suspiciously those who approach your car to ask for directions or money. Hide valuables in the glove compartment or leave them in the hotel safe. Should a "**carjacking**" occur, in which you're asked to hand over your car at gunpoint, flee the vehicle as quickly as possible and get away from the scene, then call the police. There is absolutely no reason why you should die for the sake of an automobile.

Breaking the law

Whether intentionally or not, foreign visitors may find themselves breaking various American laws on occasion. Aside from **speeding** or **parking violations**, one of the most common ways visitors bring trouble on themselves is through **jaywalking**, or crossing the road against red lights or away from intersections. Fines can be stiff – over $50 in most cases – and the police will most assuredly not take sympathy on you if you mumble that you "didn't know it was illegal."

Drinking laws provide another source of irritation to visitors, particularly as the law prohibits swilling liquor, wine, or beer in most public spaces like parks, beaches, and such. Other infringements can include **walking on certain beaches** after dark, **insulting a police officer** which is often interpreted as vociferous argument, and **riding a bicycle at night** without proper lights and reflectors.

Travelers with disabilities

Travelers with mobility challenges or physical disabilities will find LA, along with the US in general, more amenable to their needs than most places in the world. Because of the passage of the 1990 Americans with Disabilities Act, all public buildings must be wheelchair-accessible and have suitable toilets. Accordingly, the city has sloped curbs at most street corners, subways have elevator access, and city buses have adjustable entry platforms, along with space and handgrips for wheelchair users. Most hotels and restaurants, especially those built within the last decade, also have adequate accommodations for wheelchairs.

Getting to and from LA

Most **airlines**, transatlantic or domestic, accommodate those with disabilities, some of them even allowing attendants of those with serious conditions to accompany them on the trip. Similarly, almost every **Amtrak train** includes one or more cars with accommodation for disabled passengers, along with wheelchair assistance at train platforms, adapted on-board seating, free travel for guide dogs, and fifteen percent discounts on fares, with 24 hours' advance notice. Passengers with hearing impairment can get information by calling ☎1-800/523-6590.

Information for disabled travelers

Australia and New Zealand

ACROD Australian Council for Rehabilitation of the Disabled, PO Box 60, Curtin, ACT 2605 ☎02/6282 4333.

Disabled Persons Assembly, 173–175 Victoria St, Wellington ☎04/811 9100.

UK

Access Travel, 16 Haweswater Ave, Astley, Lancashire M29 7BL ☎01942/888844, fax 891811.

Holiday Care Service, 2nd floor, Imperial Building, Victoria Rd, Horley, Surrey RH6 7PZ ☎01293/774535, fax 784647; Minicom ☎01293/776943.

RADAR Royal Association for Disability and Rehabilitation, 12 City Forum, 250 City Rd, London EC1V 8AF ☎0171/250 3222; Minicom ☎0171/250 4119.

Tripscope, The Courtyard, Evelyn Rd, London W4 5JL ☎0181/994 9294, fax 994 3618.

US and Canada

California Office of Tourism, 801 K St, Suite 1600, Sacramento, CA 95814-3520 ☎916/322-2881 or 1-800/862-2543. *Publishes a free, two-hundred-page* Travel Planning Guide *that lists "handicap facilities" for accommodations and attractions.*

Directions Unlimited, 720 N Bedford Rd, Bedford Hills, NY 10507 ☎914/241-1700. *Tour operator with customized tours for people with disabilities.*

Mobility International USA, PO Box 10767, Eugene, OR 97440 ☎541/343-1284. *Answers travel questions and operates an exchange program for the disabled.*

Society for the Advancement of Travel for the Handicapped SATH, 347 Fifth Ave, #610, New York, NY 10016 ☎212/447-7284. *Non-profit travel-industry group that answers travel-related queries.*

Travel Information Service ☎215/456-9600. *Telephone information and referral service, with a support line for the hearing impaired* (☎215/456-9602).

Travelin' Talk, PO Box 3534, Clarksville, TN 37043 ☎615/552-6670. *Network that assists travelers with disabilities by enabling contact with other people with similar conditions. Also publishes a quarterly newsletter.*

Twin Peaks Press, Box 129, Vancouver, WA 98666 ☎360/694-2462 or 1-800/637-2256. *Publishes the* Directory of Travel Agencies for the Disabled, *listing more than 370 agencies worldwide, as well as* Travel for the Disabled.

On the other hand, traveling by **Greyhound** and **Amtrak Thruway** service is not recommended. Buses are not equipped with platforms for wheelchairs, though intercity carriers are required by law to provide assistance with boarding. Passengers unable to travel alone, and in possession of a doctor's certificate, may receive two-for-one fares to bring a companion along with them.

The city's major **car rental** firms provide vehicles with hand controls, even though these are typically available on pricier models. The American Automobile Association (☎213/741-3686) produces the *Handicapped Driver's Mobility Guide*, and **parking regulations** for disabled motorists are now uniform: licenses for the disabled must carry a three-inch-square international access symbol, and placards bearing this symbol must be hung from the car's rearview mirror (blue colors signify permanent disability, while red signifies a temporary condition of up to six months). Additionally, self-service gas stations are required to provide **full service** to disabled motorists at self-service prices.

Disabled access

The major hotel and motel chains are the best bet for accessible **accommodation**, even though there are any number of good local alternatives. At the higher end of the scale, *Embassy Suites* (☎1-800/362-2779 voice; 1-800/458-4708 TDD) has been working to meet new standards of access that meet or, in some cases, exceed ADA requirements, involving building new facilities, retrofitting older hotels, and providing special training to all employees. The same is true, to a somewhat lesser degree, with *Hyatt Hotels* (☎1-800/233-1234).

Citizens or permanent residents of the US who have been "medically determined to be blind or permanently disabled" can obtain the **Golden Access Passport**, a free lifetime pass to federally operated parks, monuments, historic sites, and recreation areas that charge admission fees. The pass must be picked up in person, from the areas described, and it also provides a fifty percent discount on fees charged at facilities for camping, boat launching, and parking. The **Golden Bear Pass**, also free to the disabled, offers similar benefits for state-run parks, beaches, and historic sites that charge admission fees.

Many US **tour companies** cater to disabled travelers or specialize in organizing **group tours**. The California Office of Tourism (☎1-800/862-2543) can provide you with a list of such companies, or you can ask the National Tour Association, 546 E Main St, PO Box 3071, Lexington, KY 40596 (☎606/226-4444 or 1-800/755-8687), a group that can put you in touch with operators whose tours match your needs.

Women's LA

Although a woman traveling alone is not as much of a conspicuous target in LA as she might be in other parts of the world, or the US, sexual harassment is not uncommon, either. Beyond offensive comments, forms of violence against women, notably rape and assault, are high in this country, even though crime rates have nationally and locally decreased in recent years. However, despite the threats, LA overall is a good place for women to visit and offers numerous resources for their assistance.

As a rule, women should **never hitchhike** anywhere in the city alone. This mode of travel is an open invitation to every thug and would-be rapist motoring down the highway; if you're driving, you should avoid hitchhikers just as steadfastly – many of them have been known to have a bent for kidnapping, rape, robbery, and even murder on occasion. If you can, try not to travel at night by **public transportation**, especially in the city's riskier parts of town; if this is your only means of transit, sit as close to the bus driver as possible. Better yet, find another person to team up with for added security.

Also on the danger list is **walking** through desolate, unlit streets at night; you're better off taking cabs to your destination, if even for just a few blocks. Perception is key for most criminals, and if you don't appear to be confused, scared, or drunk, and project a serious countenance

instead, your chances of attack will be lessened.

One option for women travelers to the US that's unavailable, and unnecessary, in most European countries is **pepper spray**, which comes in a small, ergonomic canister that you can carry in a purse or jacket. Upon contact with an attacker's eyes, the spray causes terrible, temporary pain – giving you the opportunity to flee the scene and alert the police. While you should never enter an airport with the spray, and always get rid of it before you return home, you can purchase this over-the-counter weapon after taking a short test or training class on its proper use. The local police will have more details on the best way to buy and use the spray, and to avoid danger so you don't have to use it.

If you listen to the advice of locals, and stick to safer parts of town, going into **bars** and **clubs** should pose no problems, as women's privacy is often respected, especially in dance and rock clubs. If in doubt, gay and lesbian bars are generally trouble-free alternatives.

Should your **vehicle break down** on the road, don't stand by it waiting for assistance. Instead, flag down a police car – the worse the neighborhood, the fewer of them you'll see – or go to the nearest store, hotel, or restaurant and call for the police or a tow truck. If disaster strikes, **rape counseling services** are available throughout the city, and can be accessed through the local sheriff's office, which can make arrangements for personal help and counseling, along with tracking down the criminal that attacked you.

It's hardly surprising that a city as big as LA should have a well-organized **women's network**, with many resource centers, bookstores, publications, and clubs. Women travelers are unlikely to encounter any problems that aren't applicable to all the West Coast, but the resources here are much more developed. The **National Organization for Women (NOW)** is the most prominent women's group, whose lobbying has done much to effect positive legislation. NOW branches, listed in phone books across the region, can provide referrals for specific concerns, such as rape crisis centers, counseling services, feminist bookstores, and lesbian bars. National information can also be found in *Places of Interest to Women*, Ferrari Publications, PO Box 37887, Phoenix, AZ (☎602/863-2408), an annual guide for women traveling to the US, Canada, Mexico, and the Caribbean.

On a more local level, there's plenty of detailed information, too, though there's an inevitable crossover with the city's sizable lesbian community. *LA Woman*, Los Angeles' largest women's magazine, profiling local personalities and providing a calendar of events, is available from most newsstands and bookstores – notably the Sisterhood Bookstore, 1351 Westwood Blvd, south of Westwood Village (☎310/477-7300) that sells books, music, cards, jewelry, and literature pertaining to the women's movement. The annual *Women's Yellow Pages* (☎310/398-5761), another good resource, lists more than 1400 women-owned businesses and services. Call for a copy of the latest edition.

The media

Although LA's local press has a deserved reputation for sensationalism, with helicopter pursuits of police chases and constant celebrity gossip, you can nevertheless find good outlets for regional and national information, fewer for foreign news. With the growth of cable TV, there are more television viewing choices than before, without a concomitant rise in quality, but area radio stations can often fill needs for information and entertainment that you can't get from other sources.

Newspapers

For such a large city, LA supports surprisingly few daily **newspapers**. At the top of the list is the *Los Angeles Times*, the most widely circulated and read newspaper in Southern California, and probably the top paper in the Western US. Having recently reduced its daily rate to 25¢, the paper is also impressively cheap and available at news boxes and dealers throughout town. Friday's *Calendar* section is an essential source for **entertainment** and **cultural listings**. Upscale hotels often distribute the newspaper to your door for free, along with, less frequently, a copy of the *New York Times*. However, most **other major newspapers** domestic and foreign tend to be found mainly at city and university libraries and a few large magazine stands.

As far as other dailies go, the *Los Angeles Daily News* is more conservative, with a strong San Fernando Valley slant, while *La Opinion* is one of the country's major Spanish-language newspapers, and is read by many in the local community. The *Orange County Register*, a right-of-center paper, is mainly found in that suburb and offers little for LA readers.

There are a few good **alternative weeklies**, most notably the free *LA Weekly* found at libraries and retailers everywhere, which provides engaging investigative journalism and copious entertainment listings. The *OC Weekly*, the liberal Orange County counterpart of the *LA Weekly*, is a fine alternative source that manages to create quite a stir in suburbia.

Every community of any size has at least a few **free newspapers** that cater to the local scene, with some also providing specialist coverage of interests ranging from cycling to business investment. Like the *LA Weekly*, many such papers are also good sources for **listings** for bars, restaurants, and nightlife in their immediate areas.

Both the USC and UCLA campuses have libraries with recent **overseas newspapers**. Day-old English and European papers are on sale in Hollywood at Universal News Agency, 1655 N Las Palmas Ave (daily 7am–midnight), and World Book and News, 1652 N Cahuenga Blvd (24hr).

Television

LA network **television** is generally a steady diet of talk shows, sitcoms, soap operas, and game shows. There are some **Spanish-language stations** on the UHF portion of the dial that offer an

Broadcast television stations

2 KCBS (CBS)
4 KNBC (NBC)
5 KTLA (WB)
7 KABC (ABC)
9 KCAL (no affiliate)
11 KTTV (Fox)
13 KCOP (UPN)
28 KCET (PBS)

ethnic alternative, along with a few **Asian-oriented stations**. Perhaps the best choice for broadcast television is KCET, on UHF channel 28, one of the nation's top producers of informational and educational television and an intelligent break from the normal vacuous shows.

Most motel and hotel rooms are hooked up to some form of **cable TV**, though the number of channels available to guests varies from place to place. Also varying are the locations of broadcast stations transmitted over cable, which may jump around to assorted spots on the dial, depending on the cable provider.

Most cable stations are actually no better than the big broadcast networks, though some of the specialized channels are interesting. The **Arts and Entertainment** (A&E) channel offers mildly appealing documentaries on art, culture, and history, while The Learning Channel (TLC) provides a lower-budgeted alternative. **Cable News Network** (CNN) and **Headline News** both have round-the-clock news. **Home Box Office** (HBO) and **Showtime** present big-budget Hollywood

flicks, while **American Movie Classics** (AMC) and **Turner Classic Movies** show entries from the Golden Age of Cinema. On a lighter note, **ESPN** is your best bet for all kinds of sports, **MTV** for youth-oriented music videos and animated programming, and **VH-1** for Baby Boomer sounds.

Many major **sporting events** are transmitted on a pay-per-view basis, and watching an event like a heavyweight boxing match will set you back around $50, billable directly to your motel room. Most hotels and motels also offer a choice of **recent movies** that have just finished their theatrical runs, at around $7 per film, and some places also provide **X-rated titillation** for a similar cost.

Radio

Radio stations are even more abundant than TV stations, and the majority stick to predictable commercial formats. **AM stations** are best for news and traffic information and talk radio, while **FM stations**, particularly the federally and subscriber-funded **public** and **college stations** found between 88 and 92 FM, broadcast diverse and intriguing programming, from bizarre underground rock to obscure local theater. Of these stations, **KCRW** is one of the most interesting, particularly at night when its music varies between trance, dub, trip hop, and ambient.

LA also features a range of decent **specialist music stations** – classical, jazz, and so on – as well as **Spanish-language stations** that offer an alternative cultural take on the city, provided you can understand the Mexican-dialect language.

FM radio stations

85.9 KCSN Latino classics and salsa
88.9 KXLU Underground hip-hop and Saturday night performer interviews
89.3 KPCC Jazz and blues concerts, plus talk radio
89.9 KCRW New, eclectic music, and one of the few good sources of world news
90.7 KPFK Left-leaning opinions, politics, and news, with some music too
91.5 KUSC Classical, jazz, world music

92.3 KKBT R&B, soul, reggae
93.1 KCBS Classic rock
95.5 KLOS Album rock
97.1 KLSX Rock music and New York shock-jock Howard Stern in the morning
101.1 KRTH Pop oldies
105.1 KKGO Classical music
105.9 KPWR Hip-hop
106.7 KROQ Modern rock

AM radio stations

640 KFI Talk radio, weather and traffic
980 KFWB Timely local news, plus various talk shows

1070 KNX News with half-hourly sports reports
1150 KXTA Sports radio

Staying on

If you're planning on staying on in Los Angeles, as many aspiring actors, rock'n'rollers, and other dreamers have before you, you've got your work cut out. While there is work to be had, many people toil for years before getting anything resembling a chance at the big time, and most don't get that chance at all.

Foreign visitors and students

Foreign visitors should apply for a special **working visa** at any American Embassy *before* setting off. Different types of visas are issued, depending on your skills and length of stay, but unless you've got relatives, parents, or children over 21, or a prospective employer to sponsor you, your chances are slim at best.

Illegal work is not as easy to find as it used to be, now that the government has introduced fines as high as $10,000 for companies caught employing anyone without a **social security number** which effectively proves you're part of the legal workforce. Even in the traditionally more casual establishments like restaurants and bars, things have really tightened up, and if you do find work it's likely to be of the less visible, poorly paid kind – dishwasher rather than waiter. Making up a social security number, or borrowing one from somebody else, is of course completely illegal, as are **marriages of convenience**; usually inconvenient for all concerned and with a lower success rate than is claimed.

Foreign students have a slightly better chance of a prolonged stay in Los Angeles, especially those who can arrange a "year abroad" through their university at home. Otherwise you can apply directly to a university; if they admit you and you can afford the painfully expensive fees charged to overseas students, it can be a great way to get to know the country, and maybe even learn something useful. The US grants more or less unlimited visas to those enrolled in full-time further education. Another possibility for students is to get onto an **Exchange Visitor Program**, for which participants are given a J-1 visa that entitles them to accept paid summer employment and apply for a social security number. However, most of these visas are issued for jobs in American **summer camps**, which aren't everybody's idea of a good time; they fly you over, and after a summer's work you end up with around $500 and a month to six weeks to blow it in. If you live in Britain and are interested, contact **BUNAC**, 16 Bowling Green Lane, London EC1 (☎0171/251 3472), or Camp America, 37 Queens' Gate, London SW7 (☎0171/581 7373). In Australia, contact **ASSE International**, PO Box 1323, Rozelle, Sydney (☎02/9819 4777 or 1800/077 509, *www.asse.com*).

Apartment hunting

If you do manage to secure a job and are intent on making your mark in Southern California, there is a small bit of good news: **apartment-hunting** in LA is not the nightmare it is in, say, New York or San Francisco – although accommodation still doesn't come cheap. Apartments are almost always rented unfurnished so you'll have to buy furniture; expect to pay at least $700 a month for a studio or one-bedroom apartment and upwards of $1500 per month for two to three bedrooms. Most landlords will expect one month's rent as a deposit, plus one month in advance.

The best way to find somewhere is to ask around – particularly near universities or college campuses, where apartment turnover is unusually frequent. Otherwise rooms for rent are often advertised in the windows of houses and the local papers have "Apartments For Rent" sections. The best source is the *LA Weekly*, although you should also scan the *LA Times* classifieds.

The Guide

Introducing the City

F ittingly for a city synonymous with urban sprawl, much of **Los Angeles** lies in a fairly flat basin, contained within and around the Santa Monica, San Gabriel, Santa Ana and Verdugo mountains, and hemmed in by the Pacific Ocean to the west – a geography best appreciated from the crest of the Hollywood Hills, where on any given night, you're likely to see the city lights spread out before you in a seemingly perfect – and endless – illuminated grid. These confines, however, are not as perfect as they look, home not only to a surprisingly varied terrain of undulating hills, precipitous coastal bluffs, high mountain ranges, and rocky canyons, but also to every social extreme imaginable, from mind-boggling beachside luxury to some of the most severe inner-city poverty anywhere in the US.

Los Angeles is, of course, known for its movie stars, shopping arcades, freeways, theme parks, beaches, and fancy homes, all of which you'll immediately become acquainted with in any short stay, but it's worth your time to seek out its series of impressive museums, rugged parks, and expansive gardens, too. This may mean venturing outside of the obvious stops of Beverly Hills, Santa Monica, Downtown, and Hollywood, but to get a true sense of the city – not a traditional city by any means, but a series of interconnected districts and separate municipalities, many of which have little in common with one another – such travels are an absolute necessity.

Starting in the center of the region, **Downtown** (Chapter 2) has always been the hub of LA's political and financial life, a district that in recent decades has tried to match some of the cultural attractions found throughout the "Westside" (ie, everything west of La Brea Avenue) and Hollywood. Downtown was originally the focus of a Spanish settlement known as the Plaza, then jumped around geographically and culturally, changing from a Mexican social center to a middle-class commercial zone to a high-rise business district – all in a matter of decades. Although Westsiders see Downtown as inhospitable and isolated, nowhere else in the city is there as much variation of class, culture, and design as there is here, all within a fairly compact, centralized area.

Just west of Downtown, beyond the 110 freeway, **Mid-Wilshire** (Chapter 3) is the so-called "linear city" built around part of the commercial strip of Wilshire Boulevard. Containing a recently arrived population of Hispanic immigrants to the east and upper-middle-class Anglos to the west, Mid-Wilshire is home to some of LA's best Art Deco architecture and finest residential designs, and is also a good place to take in some culture along "Museum Row," the moniker for a stretch of Wilshire designed to give it some highbrow cachet. There are visible ethnic neighborhoods in Koreatown and the predominantly Jewish Fairfax District; and don't forget the chic grunginess of Melrose Avenue, a unique zone that actually has little in common with the rest of Mid-Wilshire, or practically any other place in LA.

The short version of the city's early Spanish name, "El Pueblo de la Reina de los Angeles," means "The Village of the Queen of the Angels."

North of Mid-Wilshire is LA's most famous area, **Hollywood** (Chapter 4), the birthplace of the modern American movie business and still an essential stop for most visitors, though it's seen far better days. The site of grand old cinema palaces, the renowned "Walk of Fame," and countless movie legends, Hollywood lost most of its big studios long ago, but the faded allure remains. Hollywood, Sunset, and Santa Monica boulevards are the district's main drags, all of which lead into the trendy West Hollywood, a center for gays, seniors, and Russian immigrants. In the hills above Hollywood, you can search for your favorite cliff-hanging mansion or take a break in sizable Griffith Park, location of LA's famed observatory.

West of Mid-Wilshire and Hollywood, in the heart of the city's Westside, **Beverly Hills** and **West LA** (Chapter 5) are where today's nouveau riche prefer to eat, drink, and dwell, breathing in the rarefied air of Brentwood, Bel Air, and northern Beverly Hills, places which offer you much to gaze upon enviously (Rodeo Drive's high-fashion attire, Bel Air's wooded estates), but only at a comfortable distance. Suspicious security guards are less of a concern in Westwood, where you can wander along UCLA's fine, expansive campus, and in the Sepulveda corridor, which holds the new Getty Center. Less hyped is Culver City, on the southern end of West LA, with a few small-scale museums, much experimental modern architecture, and several major historical sites of the movie business, on a par even with Hollywood.

Santa Monica and **Venice** (Chapter 6) lie at the ocean's edge, sixteen miles from Downtown on the western boundary of LA. Known for their piers, amusement parks, and surfers, these towns give LA its popular beach image, if somewhat mistakenly – temperatures are far cooler here than in much of the sweltering metropolis. South of these cities, Marina del Rey is a bleak zone of oceanside high-rises and Playa del Rey a decaying resort town, though in between is a refreshing surprise, the Ballona Wetlands – a several hundred acre refuge for all manner of birds, mammals, worms, and crustaceans.

Despite having some of the worst reputations in town, if not the entire country, **South** and **East LA** (Chapter 7) are nonetheless

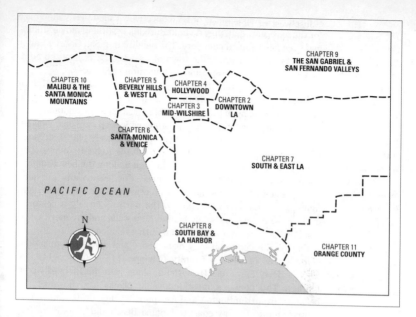

important parts of the city. Well off the path of most tourists, not least for its worrisome crime rate, South Central LA has an impressive array of historic architecture, cultural institutions, and social activity. The less appealing of the two, South LA's highlights are fairly isolated, with most of its interesting spots found in the distant city of Whittier. East of Downtown, East LA is the heart of the city's Mexican-American community, with a fairly vibrant street life.

Due south of South Central LA, the **South Bay** and **LA Harbor** (Chapter 8) comprise largely residential and industrial districts that feature some compelling oceanside scenery and charming architecture. Just south of the airport, Manhattan and Hermosa beaches are small, middle-class beachfront communities with a walkable scale and a lack of pretension, things missing in Redondo Beach, further south. At the southwestern corner of LA, the Palos Verdes Peninsula is a stately mound that is home to some of the city's priciest real estate and most dramatic ocean vistas. San Pedro, on the other hand, is a working-class city that's suffered some tough times, but still appeals for its authentically nautical character. Nearby, Long Beach is the metropolis' second-largest city, highlighted by the tourist attraction of the Queen Mary ocean liner.

East and north of the Hollywood Hills, the **San Gabriel** and **San Fernando valleys** (Chapter 9) were the focus of LA's postwar suburban expansion, when housing tracts replaced orange groves and real estate speculators made money by the bushel. Today, although

The San Fernando Valley also contains North Hollywood, named so in 1923, when it was annexed to LA – though it shares little in common with its more famous neighbor to the south.

the San Fernando suburbs of LA, collectively called the "Valley," are for the most part dull, they do hold Burbank's working movie studios and Glendale's famed cemetery. The neighboring San Gabriel Valley has an even better draw: the town of Pasadena, a centralized community with a rich cultural and architectural heritage.

The best natural turf in the LA region is probably around **Malibu** and **the Santa Monica Mountains** (Chapter 10), northwest of Santa Monica. With many of their acres protected as state or regional parklands, the mountains are quite pristine, with deep canyons, isolated waterfalls, numerous hiking trails, and deceptively placid streams, offering visitors a chance to trek through the rugged, undeveloped part of the metropolis, or to drive through it along the beautiful, circuitous stretch of Mulholland Highway. For less natural pursuits, there is Pacific Palisades, home to a few architectural spiritual highlights, while the city of Malibu to the north is largely a celebrity enclave, with the stars safely behind high walls and greenery thickets. Further west are excellent, and fairly secluded, beaches.

Finally, the geographically dispersed – and densely populated – communities of **Orange County** (Chapter 11) include sights like Knott's Berry Farm and Disneyland, along with the Richard Nixon Library. The county's most enjoyable places are, however, its beaches, from Huntington and Newport beaches on the north and central Orange County coast to Laguna Beach and Dana Point further south. The most distant places of interest will take you almost halfway to San Diego, where you can chase the swallows of Mission San Juan Capistrano or visit Nixon's old haunt of San Clemente.

Arriving in LA

Most people arrive in Los Angeles **by air**. European and many domestic **flights** use Los Angeles International Airport – always known as **LAX** – sixteen miles southwest of Downtown (☎310/646-5252). If you're on a budget, and not planning to rent a car (in which case see "Driving and car rental," p.45), the cheapest way of getting to your final destination is to take the free **"C" shuttle bus** (not "A" or "B," which serve the parking lots), running 24 hours a day from each terminal, to the LAX Transit Center at Vicksburg Avenue and 96th Street. From here, local **buses** leave for different parts of LA – see "City transport" on p.45 for more details.

More convenient, but also more expensive, you can ride a minibus service such as **Airport Shuttle** (☎1-800/545-7745) or **SuperShuttle** (☎1-800/554-3146 or 310/782-6600), which run to Downtown, Hollywood, West LA, and Santa Monica (the SuperShuttle also goes to Long Beach and Disneyland) and deliver you to your door; most have flashing signs on their fronts, advertising their general destination. If you're heading for the Santa Monica area, or the South Bay, another possibility is the **Coast Shuttle**

(☎310/417-3988). Fares vary depending on your destination, but are generally around $20. The shuttles run around the clock from outside the baggage claim areas, and you should never have to wait more than fifteen or twenty minutes. Pay the fare when you board.

Taxis from the airport are always expensive: expect to pay at least $25 to Downtown, $30 to Hollywood, and $90 to Disneyland. Unlicensed taxi operators may approach you and offer flat fares to your destination; generally, such offers are best avoided. Don't even consider using the **Metro** system to get to your destination from LAX. The first train stops miles from the airport, and the overall journey involves three time-consuming transfers (very difficult with luggage) before you even arrive Downtown. Other destinations are completely inaccessible by rail.

The vast majority of flights into LA use LAX, but if you're arriving from elsewhere in the US, or Mexico, you may land at one of the **other airports** in the LA area – at Burbank, Long Beach, Ontario, or Orange County's John Wayne International Airport. These are similarly well served by car rental firms. If you want to use public transportation, phone the MTA Regional Information Network (Mon–Fri 6am–7pm, Sat 8am–6pm; ☎213/626-4455 or 1-800/COMMUTE, outside LA ☎1-800/2LA-RIDE) on arrival and tell them where you are and where you want to go.

By bus

LA's main **Greyhound** bus terminal, at 1716 E Seventh St, is in a seedy section of Downtown – though access is restricted to ticket holders and it's safe enough inside. There are other Greyhound terminals elsewhere in the city, which handle fewer services: in Hollywood at 1409 Vine St; Pasadena at 645 E Walnut St; North

---

Arriving in LA

Rather surprisingly, the busiest airfield in LA, or anywhere in the nation, is Van Nuys Airport – not LAX – due to its smaller planes and quicker take-offs and landings.

> **Amtrak Departures:**
>
> Los Angeles to: Anaheim (7 daily; 45min), Fullerton (for Disneyland; 9 daily; 35min), Glendale (7 daily; 33min), Palm Springs (1 daily; 2 hr 22min), Sacramento (1 daily; 14hr 12min), San Bernardino (1 daily; 1hr 40min), San Clemente (1 daily; 1hr 30min), San Diego (8 daily; 2hr 45min), San Francisco (1 daily; 12hr 40min), San Juan Capistrano (8 daily; 1hr 13min), Santa Barbara (5 daily; 2hr 45min), Tucson (1 daily; 8hr 50min), Van Nuys (5 daily; 35min), Ventura (4 daily; 1hr 50min).
>
> **Greyhound Departures:**
>
> Los Angeles to: Las Vegas (10 daily; 5hr 30min), Palm Springs (6 daily; 3hr), Phoenix (5 daily; 8hr 50min), Portland (5 daily; 23hr), Salt Lake City (2 daily; 17hr 15min), San Diego (18 daily; 2hr 45min), San Francisco (12 daily; 8hr), Seattle (4 daily; 27hr), Tijuana, Mexico (15 daily; 3hr 30min), Tucson (5 daily; 11hr 20min). (Number of daily buses dependent on varying schedules for each weekday.)

Hollywood at 11239 Magnolia Blvd; Santa Monica at 1433 Fifth St; and Anaheim at 1711 S Manchester Blvd. Only the Downtown terminal is open around the clock; all have toilets and left-luggage lockers.

　Green Tortoise offers $30 one-way fares to LA from San Francisco and stops in Hollywood at *McDonald's* on Vine Street, a block south of Sunset Blvd, and in Santa Monica at the *HI-LA/Santa Monica*, 1434 Second St at Santa Monica Blvd. However, schedules can be infrequent and trips typically take longer than the average bus ride. Call ☎ 1-800/227-4766 for more information.

By train

For some detailed background on Union Station, see p.58.

Arriving in LA by **train**, you'll be greeted by the expansive architecture of Union Station, on the north side of Downtown at 800 N Alameda St – from which you can also access the recently constructed Gateway Transit Center, where you can connect to bus lines. Union Station is the hub for three main commuter rail lines: **Metrorail**, the subway and light-rail system used (sparingly) by locals and visitors, **Metrolink**, another train system, which chiefly connects distant suburbs, and **Amtrak** trains, which also stop at outlying stations in the LA area. For information call Amtrak at ☎ 1-800/USA-RAIL.

By car

The main routes by **car** into Los Angeles are the interstate highways, all of which pass through Downtown. From the east, I-10, the **San Bernardino freeway**, has replaced the more sonorous Route 66, which is now called the **Foothill** freeway, or I-210. (A slower alternative from the east is Highway 60.) The **Golden State** freeway, or I-5, is the chief north–south access corridor, with the **San Diego** freeway, I-405, used commonly as an alternative. Of the non-interstate routes into the city, US-101, the scenic route from San Francisco known as the **Ventura** freeway, cuts across the San Fernando Valley and Hollywood into Downtown. Hwy-1 follows the entire coast of California and links up with US-101 in Ventura County, and is also known as **Pacific Coast Highway** (PCH), using surface streets through Santa Monica, the South Bay, and Orange County.

Information

For free maps, accommodation suggestions, and general information, the **California Visitors Bureau** operates two **visitor centers**: Downtown at 685 S Figueroa St (Mon–Fri 8am–5pm, Sat 8.30am–5pm; ☎ 213/689-8822), and in Hollywood at the Janes House, 6541 Hollywood Blvd (Mon–Fri 9am–5pm; ☎ 213/236-2331). You can also call toll-free for information at ☎ 1-800/228-2452.

　Other LA suburbs have their own **visitor centers**: in Santa Monica at 1400 Ocean Ave (daily 10am–4pm; ☎ 310/393-7593); Anaheim near Disneyland at 800 W Katella Ave (daily 9am–5pm; ☎714/999-8999); Beverly Hills, 239 S Beverly Drive (☎310/271-8174 or 1-800/345-2210); and Long Beach, 1 World Trade Center, Suite 300 (☎310/436-3645).

All these centers offer free **maps** of their area, but you'd do better to purchase Gousha Publications' fully indexed *Los Angeles and Hollywood Street Map* ($2.95), available from vending machines in visitor centers and most hotel lobbies. Of course, the maps in this book should suffice for most of your needs, but if you're in LA for a considerable period of time, the fully indexed *LA County Thomas Guide* ($17) is the definitive **road atlas**, a meticulous, up-to-date guide of hard-to-find streets, which every driver in this city should have – and many do.

A color map insert, including detailed plans of Downtown, Hollywood, the Westside, and Santa Monica and Venice, can be found at the back of this book.

City transport

The only certainty when it comes to **getting around** LA is that wherever and however you're going, you should allow plenty of time to get there. Obviously, this is partly due to the sheer size of the city, but the confusing entanglements of freeways and the gridlock common during rush hour can make car trips lengthy undertakings – and with most local buses stopping on every corner, bus travel is hardly a speedy alternative.

Driving and car rental

The best way to get around LA – though by no means the only way – is to **drive**. Despite traffic being bumper-to-bumper much of the day, the **freeways** are the only way to cover long distances quickly. The system, however, can be confusing, especially since each stretch can have two or three names (often derived from their eventual destinations, however far away) as well as a number. Four major freeways fan out from Downtown: the Hollywood freeway (a section of US-101) heads northwest through Hollywood into the San Fernando Valley; the Santa Monica freeway (I-10) runs south of Mid-Wilshire and West LA to Santa Monica; the Harbor freeway (I-110) goes south to San Pedro – heading northeast it's called the Pasadena freeway; and the Santa Ana freeway (I-5) passes Disneyland and continues south through Orange County – north of Downtown it's called the Golden State freeway. **Other freeways** include the San Diego freeway (I-405), which roughly follows the coast through West LA and the South Bay; the Ventura freeway (Hwy 134), which links Burbank, Glendale, and Pasadena to US-101 in the San Fernando Valley; and the Long Beach freeway (I-710), which connects East LA and Long Beach. For **shorter journeys**, especially between Hollywood and West LA, the wide avenues and boulevards are a better option (sometimes the only one), not least because you get to see more of the city.

The first major highway in LA, the Pasadena Freeway, opened on December 31, 1939, and was then known as the Arroyo Seco Parkway.

City transport

An LA freeway primer

Visitors exploring most places between Hollywood and the coast will have few difficulties with freeway driving – almost all the traveling can be done on surface streets. However, for those headed to more far-flung parts of LA, freeway travel is essential. Understanding the particular character and quirks of the system, and of individual highways, is thus important to prevent you from spending most of your time in nerve-wracking gridlock.

The basic rules for driving in LA are no different than in other major cities: don't tailgate, stay with the flow of traffic, and avoid "road rage" at all costs (certain of your fellow travelers are known to carry weapons). Beyond this, LA freeway travel presents its own unique challenges. For one, city drivers are not good at handling inclement weather, and you can expect to double your expected travel time during an episode of rain, even if only a drizzle. Second, the huge asphalt network of highways creates its own unpredictable logic – often, traffic will slow down randomly for no apparent reason, with the cause sometimes miles away on a different route, and the result being a sudden shift from 60mph+ to less than 10mph. Furthermore, alternate route planning is critical, especially if traveling to Orange County, because gridlock can occur at any time of the day (especially from 6am to midnight). However, getting off a congested freeway in an unfamiliar location can be a bad idea, especially if you're lacking a detailed city map, in which case you may find yourself in a high-crime zone and, because of rush-hour traffic lights on entry ramps, unable to quickly escape from it. To assist your planning, AM news radio stations offer frequent traffic updates that announce "SigAlerts," which list where the nasty tie-ups are. To avoid traffic tickets, stick around the speed limit (55mph in town), stay out of the left lane – it attracts the most attention from the highway patrol – and never tear through the winding concourse of Pacific Coast Highway, a favorite strip for the traffic police.

The busiest roads are Highway 101 and the 405 freeway, with particularly hellish confluences at the Downtown "stack," where four highways overlap each other near the Civic Center, and the section of the 405 at the 10 freeway, the busiest junction in LA, if not the entire US. Some individual roads present their own sorts of difficulties. On a few freeways, such as the 101 south through the Universal City district, you only have a few yards to accelerate from a dead stop to 55mph, while on others, notoriously the antiquated 110 freeway in Highland Park, exit-ramp speeds can suddenly drop to 5mph. At the LA River, transferring from the south 5 to the south 110 is a hair-raising merge around the base of a cliff, while following the 10 freeway through East LA plunges you briefly, and chaotically, into the confusion of Interstate 5. Finally, shipping trucks, or "big rigs," are a constant sight throughout LA County, but are almost ubiquitous on the Terminal Island Expressway, a short road near the harbor; and the Long Beach freeway, or 710, which offers the added pitfalls of frighteningly narrow lanes and uneven, rutted asphalt.

All the major **car rental** firms have branches all over the city, and most have their main offices close to LAX, linked to each terminal by free shuttle buses. A number of smaller rental companies specialize in everything from Gremlins to Bentleys. Rent-a-Wreck, 12333 W

Pico Blvd (☎310/478-0676), has mid-Sixties Mustang convertibles and other, less appealing vehicles, and Dream Boats, 2929 Pico Blvd, Santa Monica (☎310/828-3014), also deals in Mustangs, as well as pink Cadillacs. Expect to pay around $50 per day.

Parking is a particular problem Downtown, along Melrose Avenue's trendy Westside shopping zone, and in Beverly Hills and Westwood. Anywhere else is less troublesome, but watch out for restrictions – some lampposts boast as many as four placards listing do's and don'ts. Sometimes it's better to shell out $5 for valet parking than get stuck with a $30 ticket for parking in a residential zone.

Public transport

The bulk of LA's public transport is operated by the LA County Metropolitan Transit Authority (**MTA** or "**Metro**"), which is still sometimes abbreviated to its old name, the RTD. Its brand-new, massive **Gateway Transit Center**, to the east of Union Station on Vignes Street, may eventually serve 100,000 commuters a day traveling by Metrorail, light rail, commuter rail, Amtrak, and the regional bus systems. The Center comprises **Patsaouras Transit Plaza**, from which you can hop on a bus, the glass-domed **East Portal**, through which you can connect to a train, and the 26-story **Gateway Tower**, at which you can find an MTA customer service office on the ground floor.

See p.58 for more on the Gateway Transit Center.

Metrorail

Hampered by a series of construction scandals and budget difficulties, LA's **Metrorail** system is beginning to come into at least partial use. The light rail network may one day cover the whole of LA County, but as of now it consists of three lines. The underground **Red Line** reaches from the Transit Center west to the intersection of Wilshire and Western avenues, but will soon cut through Hollywood and Universal City, eventually reaching the San Fernando Valley and, its planners hope, become the city's central transport line in the next century. Of more use to residents than visitors, the **Green Line** runs between industrial El Segundo and colorless Norwalk along the middle of the Century freeway. Tantalizingly close to LAX, but in practical terms absolutely useless if you are in a hurry, the placing of the line has attracted much criticism. Currently the most complete route, the **Blue Line** leaves Downtown and heads above-ground through South Central LA to Long Beach. It's a safe journey through some of the most economically depressed areas of the city, and shows the normality of everyday commuters' lives rather than the violence of media repute. A trolley line from Downtown to Pasadena is also under construction, though MTA has yet to announce an estimated due date. **Fares** on all journeys are $1.35 one way. Peak-hour trains run at five- to six-minute intervals, at other times every ten to fifteen minutes. Don't bring your own refreshments on the trains – the fine is $250.

City transport

Other forms of rail transit primarily serve more distant areas of the metropolis. **Amtrak** connects to points in Ventura, Riverside, and Orange counties, and beyond (see box on p.43), while **Metrolink**, operated by the Southern California Regional Rail Authority (the "SCRRA"), will take you to far-off "exurbs" like Lancaster, Moorpark, Fontana, and Oceanside, along with some of LA's closer, more familiar suburbs (call the SCRRA at ☎ 1-800/371-LINK for more details).

Buses

Carless Angelenos are still most at ease with **buses**. Although initially bewildering, the gist of the MTA bus network is quite simple: the main routes run east–west (ie between Downtown and the coast) and north–south (between Downtown and the South Bay). Establishing the best transfer point if you need to change buses can be difficult, but with a bit of planning you should have few real problems – though you should always allow plenty of time.

A detailed bus map appears in the color map section at the back of this book.

Area brochures are available free from MTA offices, and you can pick up diagrams and timetables for individual bus routes, as well as regional bus maps showing larger sections of the metropolis (complete system maps are unavailable). Buses on the major arteries between Downtown and the coast run roughly every fifteen minutes between 5am and 2am, while other routes, and the **all-night services** along the major thoroughfares, are less frequent, usually every thirty minutes or hourly. At night be careful not to get stranded Downtown waiting for connecting buses.

The standard **single fare** is $1.35; **transfers**, which can be used in one direction within the time marked on the ticket (usually three hours), cost 25¢ more; **express buses** (a limited commuter service), and any others using a freeway, are usually $1.85, but can be as much as $3.85. Put the correct money (coins or bills) into the slot when getting on. If you're staying in LA a while, you can save some money with a **monthly pass**, which costs $42 (slightly more to include express buses) or a **semi-monthly pass** (good for two weeks), which is sold for $21.

There are also the mini **DASH** buses, also called "LADOT" lines, with a flat fare of 25¢. Several lines travel a circuit around Hollywood, and five routes go through the center of Downtown

MTA BUS ROUTES

MTA's buses fall into six categories, as outlined below, with some of the routes being characterized by their passengers. The early morning east–west route along Wilshire Boulevard is full of Latin American service workers traveling to the homes of their Westside employers, whereas tourists dominate the route west along Santa Monica Boulevard to the beach and pier. The drivers add to the atmosphere too: some deliver a chirpy running commentary, while others are sour and abrupt. Whatever bus you're on, if traveling alone, especially at night, sit up front near the driver. Try and sit near a ventilation hatch, too, as the air conditioning can emit a rather sickly odor.

#1–99 – local routes to and from Downtown.

#100–299 – local routes to other areas.

#300–399 – limited-stop routes (usually rush hour only).

#400–499 – express routes to and from Downtown.

#500–599 – express routes for other areas.

#600–699 – special service routes (for sports events and the like).

MAJOR LA BUS SERVICES

From LAX to:
Downtown #42, #439.
Long Beach #232.
San Fernando Valley/Getty Center #561.
San Pedro #225.
Watts Towers #117.
West Hollywood #220 (for Hollywood change to #4 along Santa Monica Boulevard).

To and from Downtown:
Along Hollywood Blvd #1.
Along Sunset Blvd #2, #3, #302.
Along Santa Monica Blvd #4, #304.
Along Melrose Ave #10, #11.
Along Wilshire Blvd #20, #21, #22, #320.

From Downtown to:
Santa Monica #20, #22, #320, #322, #434.
Venice #33, #333, #436.
Forest Lawn Cemetery, Glendale #90, #91.
Exposition Park #38, #81.
East LA #68.
Pasadena #401, #402.
Huntington Library #79, #379.
Burbank Studios #96.
San Fernando Valley #424, #425, #522.
San Pedro #445, #446, #447 (transfer to LADOT #142 for Santa Catalina ferry).
Manhattan Beach, Hermosa Beach, Redondo Beach #439.
Palos Verdes #444.
Long Beach #60.
Orange County, Knott's Berry Farm, Disneyland #460.

roughly every ten minutes between 6.30am and 6pm on weekdays, every fifteen minutes between 10am and 5pm on Saturday, and not at all on Sunday. Other DASH routes travel through Mid-Wilshire, Pacific Palisades, Venice, and several sections of South Central LA.

Other **local bus services** include Orange County's "OCTD" lines (☎714/636-7433), Long Beach's "LBTD" (☎310/591-2301), Culver City's bus network (☎310/253-6500), and Santa Monica's Big Blue Buses (☎310/451-5444).

Taxis

You can find **taxis** at most airline, train, and bus terminals and major hotels – otherwise call ahead. Among the more reliable companies are Independent Cab Co (☎1-800/521-8294), LA Taxi (☎310/859-0111), and United Independent Taxi (☎213/653-5050 or 1-800/822-TAXI). The basic fare is $1.90, plus $1.60 for each mile. The driver won't know every street in LA but will know the major ones, so ask for the nearest junction and give directions from there.

Cycling

Cycling in LA may sound perverse, but in some areas it can be one of the better ways of getting around. There are beachside bike paths between Santa Monica and Redondo Beach, and from Long Beach to Newport Beach, and many equally enjoyable inland routes, notably around Griffith Park and the grand mansions of Pasadena. Contact the AAA (☎213/741-3686) or the LA Department of Transportation (☎213/485-3051) for maps and information.

More information on cycling and rollerblading can be found in "Sports and Outdoor Activities," p.287.

The best place to **rent a bike** for the beaches is on Washington Street around Venice Pier, where numerous outlets include Spokes 'n' Stuff (☎310/306-3332); in summer bike rental stands line the beach. For Griffith Park, use Woody's Bicycle World, 3157 Los Feliz Blvd (☎213/661-6665). Prices range from $8 a day for a junker to $15 a day or more for a ten-speed. For similar prices, many beachside stores also rent **roller skates** and **rollerblades**.

Walking and hiking

Although some people are surprised to find sidewalks in LA, let alone pedestrians, **walking** is in fact the best way to see much of Downtown and a few other districts. You can structure your stroll by taking **guided walking tours**, the best of which are organized by the Los Angeles Conservancy (☎213/623-CITY), whose treks around Downtown's battered but still beating heart are full of Art Deco movie palaces, once-opulent financial monuments, and architectural gems like the Bradbury Building (see p.66). Among many alternatives, the Conservancy runs Downtown tours every Saturday, leaving from the rear entrance of the *Biltmore Hotel*, 506 Grand St at 10am (reservations required; $5). You can also take guided **hikes** through the wilds of the Santa Monica Mountains and Hollywood Hills, free of charge every weekend, with a variety of organizations, including the Sierra Club (☎213/387-4287), the State Parks Department (☎818/880-0350), and the Santa Monica Mountains National Recreation Area (☎818/597-1036).

City tours

One quick and easy way to see something of LA is from the window of a **guided bus tour**. These vary greatly in cost and quality, with the **mainstream tours** carrying large busloads around the major sights and only worth considering if you're very pushed for time – none covers anything that you couldn't see for yourself at less cost. **Specialist tours** tailored to suit particular interests, which usually carry smaller groups of people, are often a better value. **Studio tours** of film and TV production areas are covered on day-trips by most of the mainstream operators, though again you'll save money by show-ing up independently.

Mainstream tours

By far the most popular of the mainstream tours is the half-day jaunt to the **homes of the stars** – the tours' starting point, near the Chinese Theatre, is thick with tourists lining up for their tickets. Usually taking in the Farmer's Market, Sunset Strip, Rodeo Drive, and Hollywood Bowl, this tour is much less tempting than it sounds – frequently no more than a view of the gate at the end of the drive-way of the house of some TV or celluloid celebrity. Other programs include tours around the Westside at night, beach areas, shopping strips, the *Queen Mary*, and day-long excursions to Disneyland and the Mexican border city of Tijuana.

Costs are \$30 minimum per person, with informational leaflets found strewn over hotel lobbies and visitor centers. You can make reservations at, and be picked up from, most hotels. Otherwise con-tact one of the following booking offices:

Casablanca Tours, in the *Hollywood Roosevelt* hotel, 7000 Hollywood Blvd (☎213/461-0156).

Hollywood Fantasy Tours, 6715 Hollywood Blvd (☎213/469-8184).

Hollywood Tours, 6328 Hollywood Blvd (☎213/957-2480 or 1-800/523-8864).

Starline Tours, at the Janes House building, 6541 Hollywood Blvd (☎213/463-3333).

Specialist tours

Unless otherwise noted, typical specialist tours are around \$30+ per person. For more suggestions, pick up the free *LA Visitors Guide* from hotels and visitor centers.

City transport

Black LA Tours, 3420 W 43rd St, STE 108 (☎213/750-9267). Black historical and entertainment tours.

The California Native, 6701 W 87th Place (☎310/642-1140). Sea kayaking and adventure hikes. Tour uninhabited islands off the coast of California for $99 and up.

Grave Line Tours, PO Box 931694, Hollywood (☎213/469-4149). Two-and-a-half hours in the back of a 1969 Cadillac hearse pausing at the scenes of many, though by no means all, of the eventful deaths, scandals, bizarre sex acts, and drugs orgies that have tainted Hollywood and the surrounding area. Leaves Tuesday through Sunday at 9.30am from the corner of Hollywood Boulevard and Orchid Avenue, with overflow cortege running at 12.30pm and 3.30pm.

Googie Tours (☎213/980-3480). Pilgrimages to Southern California's remaining space-age glass and formica diners – emblems of the so-called "Googie" style. Choose between the six-hour "San Gabriel Valley" and "Behind the Orange Curtain" tours, the three-hour "Coffee Shop Moderne & More" journey, or the four-hour night-time "Cocktails 'n' Coffee Shops" trip.

SPARCtours, "the Murals of LA", 685 Venice Blvd, Venice (☎310/822-9560). Public art in LA is alive and well, and this is an enlightening tour of the "mural capital of the world."

Studio tours

For a small insight into how a film or TV show is made, or just to admire the special effects, there are guided tours costing $7–36 at Warner Brothers Studios, NBC Television Studios, and Universal Studios, all in or near Burbank; see p.190 for details. If you want to be part of the audience of a network or cable TV show, the street just outside the Chinese Theatre is the major solicitation spot, with TV-company lackeys regularly handing out free tickets and offering to bus you to their studios and back. All you have to do, once there, is laugh and clap on cue.

Chapter 2

Downtown LA

Relatively small and often overlooked, **DOWNTOWN LA** still puts on a fairly representative mix of much of what LA has on display: old adobes, decaying theaters, modern museums, and sleek corporate towers, with the last giving mostly flat LA its little-known skyline. In fact, it's only recently that Downtown has become vertical at all. In the 1980s, Canadian and Japanese money built the shimmering glass spires now visible from a great distance, but before that there were few such buildings; indeed, until 1960, **City Hall** was, at 28 stories, the town's tallest structure. LA's building boom has fizzled out in recent years, but it's only a matter of time before overseas money turns on the real estate tap once more and gives the city a few more big steel boxes to put on its postcards.

Although the gleaming modernity is tempting, your wanderings through Downtown should begin at the **Plaza**, the original nineteenth-century town site and now the remodeled center of a cleaned-up district known as "**El Pueblo de Los Angeles**," which also holds the similarly historic **Olvera Street**. To the south, LA's **Civic Center** is a rather bland seat of local government enlivened by the classic form of City Hall and a few other choice buildings.

Further south stand the dilapidated facades along **Spring Street** and **Broadway**. Since their heyday in the 1920s as the respective financial and cultural centers of the city, the two streets have dramatically changed. Broadway is still a thriving commercial area, but now has an Hispanic character, with T-shirt stands and fast food vendors lining its corridor, and many of its once-grand movie palaces surviving in one form or another. Spring Street, however, presents a bleaker picture: the decline of banking and financial services spelled death for the strip, and the only shouts you're now likely to hear amid the deserted neoclassical buildings come from the many homeless people in the area.

Similarly deserted, at least on weekends and at night, **Bunker Hill** is Downtown's new center, essentially a financial district whose charms are limited to museums and architecture. Somewhat more interesting are **Chinatown** and **Little Tokyo** in the north and east of Downtown, mostly for their predictable wealth of ethnic restaurants,

A full color map of Downtown and around is included in the insert at the back of the guide.

△ Chinatown

CESAR CHAVEZ AVENUE

Union
Station

El Pueblo de
Los Angeles

HOLLYWOOD FREEWAY 101

SANTA ANA FREEWAY

LA River

Ahmanson
Theatre

TEMPLE STREET

Children's
Museum

Mark Taper
Forum

City
Hall

Geffen
Contemporary

Dorothy
Chandler
Pavilion

1ST STREET

BEAUDRY AVENUE

HILL ST

BROADWAY

SPRING ST

MAIN STREET

2ND STREET

N

●1

MOCA

●2

LITTLE
TOKYO

CENTRAL AVENUE

Angels Flight
Railway

3RD STREET

●3

BUNKER
HILL

●4

OLIVE STREET

Bradbury
Building

●5

Grand
Central
Market

4TH STREET

SKID ROW

Central
Library

5TH STREET

SAN PEDRO STREET

HOPE STREET

●6

PERSHING
SQUARE

●7

6TH STREET

ACCOMMODATION

WILSHIRE

BOULEVARD

Biltmore 6
Figueroa 12
Holiday Inn 9
Hotel Inter-Continental 4
Kawada 2
Mayfair 11
New Otani 1
Omni Los Angeles 8
Orchid 10
Sheraton Grande 3
Westin Bonaventure 5
Wyndham Checkers 7

ℹ ●8

Red Line Metrorail

7TH STREET

110

GARMENT
DISTRICT

Flower
Markets

●9

MAIN STREET

8TH STREET

●10

BROADWAY

Cooper
Building

9TH STREET

● Metrorail Stations

– – Dash Mini-Bus Routes

HARBOR FREEWAY

Museum of
Neon Art

Blue Line Metrorail

OLYMPIC BOULEVARD

GRAND AVENUE

●12

FIGUEROA STREET

HOPE STREET

0   500 yds

LOS ANGELES STREET

SAN PEDRO STREET

12TH STREET

DOWNTOWN LA
ACCOMMODATION

LA
Convention
Center

PICO BOULEVARD

though neither is really a vital cultural center – the city's newly
arrived Asian residents migrate more toward suburban areas like
Monterey Park and Gardena. Central American immigrants prefer
Westlake, west of Downtown, comprising the bulk of the population
in the busy **MacArthur Park** and **Echo Park** communities. To the
northeast, the **Southwest Museum**, **Lummis House**, and **Heritage
Square** offer more sedate trips through local culture and history.

If all this fails to excite you, there's always the **LA River** on
Downtown's eastern border: a bleak concrete channel designed for
flood control and, not surprisingly, the forbidding setting for a number of Hollywood action flicks.

Some history

For well over two hundred years, the center of Downtown LA has been in motion. Spaniards constructed the original townsite, the Plaza district, in 1781, but the tract was soon destroyed by fire and rebuilt further southeast in 1818, where it stayed for some seventy years. Encompassing the historic Pico House and Plaza Church, this was the focus of commercial activity during the Mexican years of rule and the early American period.

By the end of the nineteenth century, however, the city's commercial focus had relocated to Broadway, full of department stores and vaudeville theaters, while the financial center had become Spring Street. The Plaza was left to decay until the 1920s, when renovation projects slowly brought the area back, this time as a tourist center. Meanwhile, Broadway and Spring were still in their heyday in the 1920s, and, along with City Hall, completed in 1928, were the most visible emblems of LA's emerging metropolis – by then numbering over a million people in its city limits and over two million in the surrounding county. These symbols wouldn't last for long.

Although the Civic Center is still LA's seat of government, it has since lost its financial and cultural counterparts to the south. Cold War-era urban renewal projects shoved the city center five blocks to the west and accordingly doomed the great boulevards. Bunker Hill, previously a residential area full of elegant Victorian dwellings, replaced Spring Street in the 1960s as Downtown's financial nucleus, thanks to a drastic facelift engineered by LA's mega-bureaucracy, the **Community Redevelopment Agency**. However, while Spring Street found its counterpart on the western side of Downtown, nothing replaced Broadway. The Museum of Contemporary Art, plunked down at the top of the hill in the 1980s, was one attempt to draw back the crowds, as was the placement of nearby facilities for theater and music such as the Mark Taper Forum, Dorothy Chandler Pavilion, and Ahmanson Theater. Despite these institutions' prestigious track records, they have failed miserably at resurrecting the kind of social vitality that once existed along Broadway. For most visitors, the new center of Downtown may be brimming with high culture and modern architecture, but it is absolutely bereft of anything else.

The Plaza district

Because so much of LA's architectural heritage has been destroyed, it is perhaps surprising that **the Plaza** still exists. In the early 1920s, some city planners wanted to demolish it to make way for a larger Civic Center, and in the 1950s the Hollywood Freeway narrowly missed plowing through it. Luckily, the area was saved by its 1953 designation as the **El Pueblo de Los Angeles State Historic Park**. Comprising twenty-seven buildings, including eleven open to the public and four museums, the park is an essential stop on any historic journey through LA and also acts as the site for community celebrations during yearly events such as Cinco de Mayo.

In the immediate vicinity of the Plaza, **Union Station** and the adjacent **Gateway Transit Center** provide hubs for the train and bus activity throughout the region, while just north sits the latest version of LA's uninspiring **Chinatown**.

The Plaza and Olvera Street

Within the El Pueblo de Los Angeles historic monument, you can find the original center of LA: the square known as **the Plaza**, which in 1870 was reconstructed into a circular design now visible just off North Los Angeles Street. However, the true focus of the early settlement was the *zanja madre*, or "mother ditch," which ran from the then-wild Los Angeles River through what is now **Olvera Street**. The canal was used for domestic and agricultural purposes as early as 1781; even into the 1870s, water pioneer **William Mulholland** had an early job overseeing the many ditches that supplied the town's water. Then, just as now, *aqua* was serious business, and it is no accident that a historic route like Olvera Street follows the path of an antique irrigation ditch.

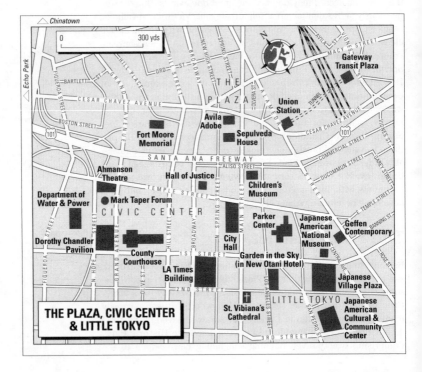

THE PLAZA, CIVIC CENTER & LITTLE TOKYO

Although open to pedestrian traffic (daily 10am–8pm), Olvera has been closed since 1930 to automobiles. Thanks to preservationist **Christine Sterling**, the area was reimagined as a Mexican marketplace, filled with food and merchandise vendors, where you can trace the original path of the *zanja madre* watercourse by a series of marked bricks. Along the street, the **Avila Adobe** (daily 10am–5pm) claims to date from 1818, but was actually rebuilt in concrete after the 1971 Sylmar earthquake. Mainly interesting for its period antiques, the Adobe also offers two vaguely diverting programs: one on Ms Sterling and the other giving a dubious "History of Water in Los Angeles." Nearby, the **Sepulveda House** (Mon–Sat 10am–3pm) is an 1887 Eastlake structure that has rooms highlighting different periods in Mexican-American history, with various displays of antiques, furniture, and so on.

The Sepulveda House also serves as a visitor center, offering free guided walking tours (Tues–Sat 10am–1pm; hourly).

Just west of the Plaza, the Catholic **Plaza Church**, a small adobe structure with a gabled roof, has long served as a sanctuary for illegal Central American refugees. From 1861 to 1923, the building was remodeled or reconstructed four different times, and still evokes a sense of the city's Mexican heritage, even though very little remains from the original church. Its Sunday Mariachi Masses are also something of a cultural institution (11.30am & 4.30pm).

To the south, the red-brick **Old Plaza Firehouse** (Mon–Sat 10am–3pm) was only operational for thirteen years, beginning in 1884, subsequently becoming a saloon, lodging house, and pool hall before attaining museum status in 1960. If you like old firefighting equipment, this is definitely the place for you.

Nearby **Old Masonic Hall** (Tues–Fri 10am–3pm) was the first Masonic Hall in the city when built in 1858 and still holds the occasional freemason meeting, as well as a cache of club memorabilia such as swords, compasses, jewels, and the like. The adjacent **Pico House** is a three-story Italianate building that was the former home of the last Mexican governor of California, Pio Pico, while the **Merced Theater** next door represented the last gasp of the Plaza's commercial vitality, as LA's first indoor theater. Close by, LA's original settlement of Chinese immigrants was centered on the **Garnier Building**, an 1850 brick-and-stone structure that has slowly been restored, but does not yet allow visitors.

The Pico House, Merced Theater, and Garnier Building are all currently closed to visitors, though plans are in the works to soon open them to the public.

Before you leave the area, it's worth walking three blocks west to the junction of Sunset Boulevard and Hill Street, the site of the **Fort Moore Pioneer Memorial**, a series of bas reliefs serving as sculptural hagiography to early LA figures who provided "for its citizens water and power for life and energy," an inscription written on the interior wall of what has been described as "the most spectacular man-made waterfall in the United States": an 80ft wide, 50ft high wall of water serving as a colossal monument to the city's aqueous needs. Not surprisingly, it was shut off twenty years ago.

The Plaza
district

Union Station

The Mission-style **Union Station**, across Alameda Street from the Plaza, is an impressive, if underused, architectural landmark that was once the focus of much hostility from the railroad companies, who originally saw the idea for a centralized rail terminus as a threat to their oligarchy, and members of the local Chinese community, many of whom were forcibly evicted from the site of the station when it was constructed in the 1930s. Today, it's a pretty quiet place – rail travel simply isn't that important to LA anymore – that is also one of the city's best-preserved monuments to the lost age of mass transportation. The station's design encompasses grand arches, a high clock-tower, and a Spanish-tiled roof, while its Art Deco motifs include geometric designs and Streamline Moderne lettering. Even though it's no longer the heart of the region's transit system, the station continues to serve as the confluence for Amtrak, Metrolink, and Metroline commuter trains.

For information on train transportation into and around Los Angeles, see p.47–48.

Less glamorous is the recently completed **Gateway Transit Center**, connected to Union Station via a tunnel below the train tracks. Serving as a regional hub for bus lines, the center comprises three distinct parts: the **Gateway Tower**, a 26-story building that dominates the flat space around it and contains a customer service center on its ground floor; the **Patsaouras Transit Plaza**, which is the bus mall itself, decorated with insipid public art and worth avoiding at night; and, under a glass ceiling, the **East Portal**, a light and airy space marred only by an Orwellian-looking mural supposedly dedicated to LA's ethnic diversity.

There's nothing much to see beyond here, just the largest municipal **jail** in the US and the similarly forbidding **Metropolitan Detention Center**, with razor wire-style decor that was used for the cover photograph of author Mike Davis' dark tome about LA, *City of Quartz* (see p.336).

Chinatown

The city's current incarnation of **CHINATOWN**, between North Broadway and North Hill streets, is not the bustling affair you might expect from Chinatowns in other big US cities. It's only been sited here since 1938, when the previous version was obliterated to make way for Union Station. Because many of the newly arrived Chinese in the late nineteenth century were impoverished laborers, as well as racial targets, they endured wretched social conditions and periodic lynch mobs for many decades. Many cities, such as Burbank and Pasadena, evicted them or at least kept them from buying land. Chinatown was developed as a source of refuge as well as ethnic identity, although the Chinese residents weren't necessarily safe even in their own homogenous community.

For recommendations of restaurants in Chinatown, see p.243.

Currently home to 14,000 people, today's Chinatown is meant as much for tourists as for residents. With its quasi-Chinese architecture and narrow, pedestrian alleys with names like Bamboo Lane, it's not particularly authentic, and for a truer and more modern experience of Chinese-American culture, you're better off visiting Alhambra and Monterey Park several miles east of Downtown. Indeed, if you're not here to sample some of its main attractions – the restaurants – there's not much point coming at all.

Civic Center

Marked by City Hall's great white pillar, the **Civic Center** is the focus of government for the city and county of LA, with various state and federal entities also occupying space in the district. Bounded on the east and west by San Pedro and Figueroa streets and on the north and south by the Hollywood freeway and First Street, the area is an unexciting hive of bureaucracy that offers but a few interesting cultural and architectural sights. Even in the face of this, LA's political power-brokers have spent significant time and treasure vainly trying to pump some life into the area.

City Hall and around

One exception to the dreariness is **City Hall**, 200 N Spring St, known popularly as *Dragnet*'s imposing symbol of civic fortitude and as the Daily Planet office in the original *Superman* series. The building is a hodgepodge of styles: from its classical temple base rises a sleek modern tower crowned with a miniature version of the Mausoleum at Halicarnassus – one of the Seven Wonders of the World. Although its 28th-story observation deck is not open to the public, you can get a look at the building's grand marble arches and columns during a **free tour** (daily 10am & 11am; ☎213/485-4423 for reservations).

North of City Hall, the **Children's Museum**, 310 N Main St (summer Tues–Fri 9.15am–1pm, Sat–Sun 10am–5pm; rest of year weekends only; $5, children $3) holds mediocre science exhibits, "high-tech" toys, and disused municipal equipment – such as an old city bus. At the corner of Main and Temple, the **Triforium** is a 1975 public art monstrosity decorated with shafts of colored glass and loudspeakers strategically placed between massive concrete legs that all but ruins the surrounding **Fletcher Bowron Square**, dedicated to LA's pioneering reform mayor who cleaned up City Hall after his predecessor, Frank Shaw, was booted from office in a 1938 corruption scandal. More compelling is the public artwork **Molecule Man**, 255 E Temple St, Jonathan Borofsky's piece showing two perforated figures about to embrace and illustrating the watery composition of the human body. Some even suggest it's a comment on adjacent **Parker Center**, headquarters of the Los Angeles Police Department – rather than perforated by water molecules, the figures are said to be riddled with bullet holes.

The LA Times family dynasty

The *Los Angeles Times* began life in 1881 as the mouthpiece for **Harrison Gray Otis**, the arch-conservative publisher whose virulently anti-labor opinions and actions led him to be called the most "unfair enemy of trades unionism on the North American continent." Tensions he fostered with unions and leftists turned violent in 1910, when the original Times building was bombed. After the explosion, Otis not only rebuilt the structure, but he emerged even stronger and more powerful than ever, with control over numerous elected officials. Having already kept the Southern Pacific railroad from monopolizing development of the LA Harbor, Otis also engineered public support for the giant construction projects that deviously brought Northern California's Owens Valley water to LA, or more precisely, to the San Fernando Valley, where he and other investors made a fortune in suspicious real-estate purchases. Roman Polanski's film *Chinatown* chronicles the chicanery of these powerful figures.

The *LA Times* directly reflected his strong opinions and, when he died in 1917, his legacy was passed to his son-in-law, Harry Chandler, who maintained the paper's fight against unions and political reform until his death in 1941. With a personal fortune of up to a billion dollars, Chandler was a plutocrat and a kingmaker who usually got his way with city politicians, controlling many of them much like his father-in-law had. His one great defeat was the 1937 election of reformist mayor Fletcher Bowron.

In 1960, the paper changed course dramatically with the ascension of Harry's son Otis to the publishing throne. Through his progressive efforts, the *LA Times* finally rejected its small-town conservatism and became nationally recognized for its journalistic quality. Yet not surprisingly, the *Times* has recently taken another turn, slashing its payroll and cutting its cover price in half. True to LA's spirit, the publisher who introduced these drastic changes is a breakfast cereal tycoon.

Just to the south, near Spring and First streets, the concrete and glass **Times-Mirror Complex** contains the production facilities for the *Los Angeles Times*, the West Coast's biggest newspaper. Built in the colossal PWA Moderne style in the mid-1930s, and given a 1973 expansion, the building supplanted an earlier version, closer to Broadway, that was bombed, rebuilt, then torn down. Take one of its **public tours** (Mon–Fri 11.15am; ☎213/237-5757) if you're interested in seeing how the paper operates.

Civic Center West

The municipal buildings in the **Civic Center West** are largely functional and drab, though not all without interest. The **County Courthouse**, at Hill and First streets, is worth a glance as the venue of 1995's OJ Simpson trial, if not for its faceless late-1950s architecture. Better is the **Department of Water and Power Building**, at the corner of Hope and First streets, a modern structure that casts an appealing glow at night with its narrow horizontal bands of light. To celebrate itself, it also features an array of fountains, ironically turned off to conserve water. Nearby is the **Hall of Justice**, Broadway and Temple streets, famous for its own turbulent trial – that of the Manson Family. The 1925 structure is a compelling counterpart to City Hall, its high granite columns typifying the Beaux Arts style of the time. See it while you can: the building is closed to the public and under threat of the wrecking ball.

Further west, LA has grouped together its three leading music and theater establishments in the **Music Center**, north of First Street at 135 Grand Ave, an ugly slab of concrete plaza with a notable lack of visitors (outside of performances). The site for **Disney Hall**, across First Street, planned as the city's next concert hall, has had problems of its own. Despite its groundbreaking design – seemingly one of colossal broken eggshells – by maverick architect Frank Gehry, four years of construction have resulted only in a parking garage. Multimillionaire mayor Richard Riordan even had to dip into his own pocket to right the project, but it remains years behind schedule with no completion date in sight.

Venues for classical music and theater performances are listed beginning on p.271.

Little Tokyo

Southeast of the Civic Center, **LITTLE TOKYO** is a more vital ethnic center than nearby Chinatown, if not quite a flourishing residential neighborhood, full of smart shops and restaurants, well-heeled visitors, and some business and cultural institutions rather important to LA's Japanese population. The area, principally the small section bound by First and Third streets north and south and Central Avenue and San Pedro Street east and west, was originally named in 1908, eventually home to 30,000 Japanese immigrants before they were forcibly removed to internment camps in 1942. Decades later, LA's powerful Community Redevelopment Agency funneled new money to the district, and it returned to prominence, even if most Japanese-Americans now live well outside the area.

Little Tokyo is best explored on foot, starting at the **Japanese American Cultural and Community Center**, 244 S San Pedro St, reached via the gentle contours and heavy basalt rocks of **Noguchi Plaza**, designed by sculptor Isamu Noguchi, who grew up in nearby Boyle Heights. Inside the center, the **Doizaki Gallery** (Tues–Fri noon–5pm, Sat–Sun 11am–4pm; free) features a wide range of Japanese art and calligraphy. Also on the premises is the **Japan America Theater**, which hosts cultural events such as Kabuki theater, as well as more contemporary plays. The best part of the center, however, is the **James Irvine Garden** (Mon–Fri 8am–5pm, Sat–Sun from 9am; free), also known as *Seiryu-en*, or Garden of the Clear Stream, for its 170-foot stream symbolizing the struggles and successes of the Japanese-American community. It may not technically be a Japanese garden (it uses local materials not native to the islands), but it's still an excellent spot for a respite from LA's Downtown turmoil. More authentic is the **Garden in the Sky**, located on the *New Otani Hotel*'s third-floor terrace, 120 S Los Angeles St, a half-acre strolling garden, or *shuyu*, that uses the technique of "borrowed scenery," in which existing distant panoramas are worked into the visual setting, a neat trick that allows you to contemplate the grandeur of City Hall during your walk.

The New Otani Hotel *also holds a delight-ful Japanese restaurant,* A Thousand Cranes, *a listing of which is on p.244.*

The most active part of Little Tokyo is **Japanese Village Plaza**, an outdoor mall near First Street and Central Avenue that is lined with sushi bars, numerous upscale retailers, and Zen rock gardens. Adjacent to the plaza is the area's most familiar symbol: the **Fire Tower**, a small canopy sitting atop slender wooden beams. Across First Street, the **Japanese American National Museum** (daily 10am–5pm, Fri closes at 8pm; $4), housed in a former Buddhist temple constructed in 1925, focuses on local *Issei* pioneers and the period of Japanese internments during World War II. Amid the genealogies and assorted curios are some proud old portraits of community leaders.

A ticket to the Geffen gets you same-day admission into the Museum of Contemporary Art; see p.67.

Just beyond the borders of Little Tokyo is the **Geffen Contemporary**, Central Avenue at First Street (Tues–Sun 11am–5pm, Thurs closes at 8pm; $6), a branch of the Museum of Contemporary Art. Occupying an old city warehouse, the museum was first opened in 1983 as overflow space for the main facility on Bunker Hill but soon gained its own popularity, and in 1986 it became a fixture on the art scene, betraying its former (and better-known) name, the "Temporary Contemporary." Even today, MOCA's permanent holdings are usually shown at its main facility, leaving the Geffen as the spot for the risk-taking work of artists that many museums don't usually touch.

West of Little Tokyo, **St. Vibiana's Cathedral**, 114 E Second St, is a modest replica of Barcelona's church of San Miguel del Mar, with a simple white Italianate design. For years the regional seat of the Catholic Church, as well as a sanctuary for recently arrived Latin American immigrants, the 1871 cathedral has fallen on tough times, the Church having abandoned the structure to build a $50 million replacement further west. Now walled off with a high security fence, the cathedral sits empty, the cross-hatched stress fractures on its bell tower vivid reminders of the 1994 Northridge earthquake.

Old Downtown

Spring Street and Broadway form the linear axes of **Old Downtown**, a once-thriving district that has lost some of its charm over the years. On Spring Street, dilapidation has turned the strip into a ghost town, with looming neoclassical facades announcing their grand presences to a few lone street people. To the east, the **Garment District** and **Flower Market** more than make up for Spring Street's lost mercantile energy, but lack the atmosphere the old strip used to have. Paralleling Spring to the west, Broadway is much more vibrant, but its character has changed as well: whereas movie palaces and fine restaurants once drew white middle-class crowds, its current swap meets (or flea markets) and bargain discounters now draw working-class Hispanics.

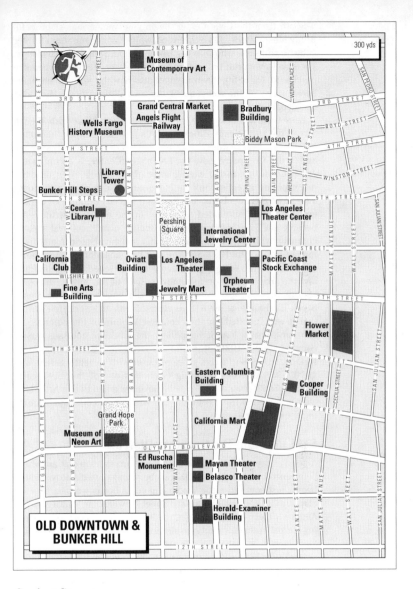

Map labels:
- 2ND STREET
- Museum of Contemporary Art
- HOPE STREET
- SAN PEDRO STREET
- 3RD STREET
- FIGUEROA STREET
- Grand Central Market
- Angels Flight Railway
- Wells Fargo History Museum
- Bradbury Building
- BOYD STREET
- WERDIN PLACE
- LOS ANGELES STREET
- Biddy Mason Park
- 4TH STREET
- FLOWER STREET
- OLIVE STREET
- GRAND AVENUE
- HILL STREET
- BROADWAY
- SPRING STREET
- MAIN STREET
- WINSTON STREET
- Library Tower
- Bunker Hill Steps
- 5TH STREET
- Central Library
- Pershing Square
- Los Angeles Theater Center
- SAN JULIAN STREET
- International Jewelry Center
- 6TH STREET
- California Club
- WILSHIRE BLVD
- Oviatt Building
- Los Angeles Theater
- Pacific Coast Stock Exchange
- MAPLE AVENUE
- WALL STREET
- Fine Arts Building
- Jewelry Mart
- Orpheum Theater
- 7TH STREET
- Flower Market
- 8TH STREET
- Eastern Columbia Building
- CECILIA STREET
- Cooper Building
- 9TH STREET
- Grand Hope Park
- Museum of Neon Art
- California Mart
- OLYMPIC BOULEVARD
- MIDWAY PLACE
- Ed Ruscha Monument
- Mayan Theater
- Belasco Theater
- SANTEE STREET
- 11TH STREET
- Herald-Examiner Building
- 12TH STREET
- 0   300 yds

OLD DOWNTOWN & BUNKER HILL

Spring Street

Formerly known as the "Wall Street of the West," **Spring Street** feels a bit like a post-apocalyptic movie set, its imperious banking and commercial buildings all closed. As such, you'll have a tour of the place mostly to yourself.

South from the Civic Center, begin your wanderings at peaceful **Biddy Mason Park**, 333 S Spring St, which commemorates a former midwife and slave who won her freedom in an 1855 legal challenge. The small memorial provides a timeline of her life, from when she purchased, for $250, the property that is now the park, to when she became one of the founders of the local First African Methodist Episcopal Church.

Less than a block away, at Spring's intersection with Fourth Street, the 1904 **Brady Block** was LA's first "skyscraper," though it only boasts twelve stories. Nearby, at no. 433, the **Title Insurance and Trust Company**, now the LA Design Center, is an appealing Art Deco design in the Zigzag style of the late 1920s. Although many of the street's bank buildings are in disuse, the **Security Trust and Savings Bank**, no. 514, is a (failed) example of a modern use for an outmoded structure. In the mid-1980s, the bank became the Los Angeles Theater Center, a multicultural theater company with a $4 million annual city subsidy. Unfortunately, the money ran out in 1991 and the site was abandoned once more, even though the company's name remains etched on the building and the space is still occasionally rented out for performances by various arts groups. Further south, the one-time **Pacific Coast Stock Exchange**, at no. 618, is chiseled with an inscription stating that it was "created for the economic welfare of the community, state and nation." As it happened, the moderne colossus wasn't completed until 1930 – the first full year of the Great Depression. Nearby, at Spring Street's intersection with Seventh Street, the 1910 **I N Van Nuys Building** celebrates one of the city's early titans, a San Fernando Valley land baron, in grand Beaux Arts style, with ornamental Ionic columns and white terra cotta walls adorning the old office space.

Skid Row and the Garment District

A good portion of LA's homeless population, estimated at anywhere between 60,000 and 180,000, can be found on **Skid Row**, which begins just south of Little Tokyo and continues down past Seventh Street, at its seediest along Fifth Street between San Pedro and Los Angeles streets – a stretch known as "the Nickel." Unless you're looking for exceptionally gritty inspiration – as arty folk like the Doors (who posed in these parts for the cover of their Morrison Hotel album) and Charles Bukowski have before – you're best off skipping Skid Row entirely.

Further south is the bustling **Garment District**, twenty square blocks of clothing manufacturers and discounters. The biggest retailer here, the **California Mart**, at Ninth and Los Angeles streets, fills three million square feet and seemingly has just as many visitors. The **Cooper Building**, just across Los Angeles Street, offers designer merchandise at bargain prices; indeed, most shrewd

Angelenos avoid the high-priced Westside boutiques and head to this district to do their clothes shopping. Good discounts can also be had at the **Flower Market**, 754 S Wall St (daily 6–11am, Mon, Wed & Fri opens at 8am; free), home to more than ninety wholesale florists.

Broadway

Long ago the commercial nucleus of Los Angeles, **Broadway** is now a worthwhile mix of historic architecture and frenetic activity. Its blocks from Second to Ninth streets make up the busiest commercial strip in the western US, and, despite rapid cultural and demographic changes, the street still retains a measure of its old exciting character and allure.

An instructive place to begin exploring the strip's former color is at its southern end, with the **Herald-Examiner Building**, 1111 S Broadway, a grand Mission-style edifice occupying a city block and featuring blue-and-yellow domes and ground-level arcades. The building was first home to William Randolph Hearst's *Los Angeles Examiner*, the progressive counterpart of the *Los Angeles Times*, which grew to have the widest afternoon circulation of any daily in the country. After it merged with Hearst's *Herald-Express*, though, trouble soon began. Declining circulation followed a devastating six-year labor strike beginning in 1967, and the paper went out of business in 1989. Although the building is closed to the public, its landmark design is frequently host to movie crews eager for an opulent setting – fitting, considering that Orson Welles had the news magnate and the building in mind when he directed his thinly-veiled critique of Hearst, *Citizen Kane*.

One block to the west, at 1040 S Hill St, the wild **Mayan Theater** is a stunning work of the pre-Columbian revival, its ornamental design, including sculpted reliefs of Aztec gods and bright paintings of dragons and birds, every bit as outlandish as its Chinese Theatre counterpart in Hollywood. Like that, this one is still in use – though as a dance club called, aptly, *The Mayan* (see p.266). The neighboring **Belasco Theater**, 1050 S Hill St, has similar brash appeal, with a Spanish Baroque design and a bright green color.

Nearby, the **Theater District** begins with the **United Artists Theater**, 929 S Broadway, a 1927 Spanish Gothic movie palace with a lobby designed after a church nave. Appropriately, the theater is now the site of the Gene Scott Ministry. A block away, stuck amidst the theaters, is the Art Deco **Eastern Columbia Building**, 849 S Broadway, with terra cotta walls of gold and aquamarine, a giant clock face (non-functional), and sleek dark piers on its roof, all essential viewing for anyone remotely interested in 1920s architecture. Further along, at no. 744, the **Globe Theater** is a Beaux Arts design that has been clumsily converted into a flea market. The street continues with a rash of old moviehouses, some of which, such as the

*The Los
Angeles
Conservancy
helps run the
Last
Remaining
Seats program
and also offers
architectural
tours of the
Broadway the-
aters and
Spring Street
banks. For
more informa-
tion, call
☎213/623-
CITY.*

*While in the
area, consider
a meal at
Clifton's
Cafeteria, 648
S Broadway,
cheesily deco-
rated with
mooseheads,
massive logs,
and waterfalls;
see p.239 for
listing.*

State, no. 703, the **Orpheum**, no. 630, and the **Palace**, no. 615, still show movies today. The exquisite lobby of the **Los Angeles**, no. 640, garishly dressed up in French Second Empire style, can only be seen on tours or during the Last Remaining Seats festival in June.

Finally, the **Million Dollar Theater**, no. 307, has appeared in numerous Hollywood movies and is renowned for its glorious Baroque auditorium, which is put to full use by the church that now occupies it. Across the street, the **Bradbury Building**, no. 304, has perhaps the finest atrium of any structure in the city. Built in 1893, the building's wrought-iron railings and elevators contrast sharply with its glazed brick walls under an overhead skylight of iron and glass. The lobby, which is as far as the public can go, should be rec-ognizable to most from films such as *Citizen Kane* and *Blade Runner*.

As you leave on the Third Street side, passing by the Victor Clothing Company mural of a **dancing Anthony Quinn**, stop at the broadly ethnic **Grand Central Market**, between Third and Fourth streets, which provides a good taste of modern Broadway – as do the pickled pigs feet and sheeps brains it sells, if you can stomach them.

Pershing Square and around

Sitting at the foot of Bunker Hill, uninspiring **Pershing Square**, the city's oldest park, acts as a buffer between the new and old parts of Downtown. Constructed in 1866 and known throughout the years variously as Public Square, City Park, La Plaza Abaja, and St Vincent's Park, it was renamed for the last time in 1918, in honor of World War I general **John Pershing**. By the 1960s, the place had deteriorated into little more than grounds for assorted layabouts and homeless folk, though since then, there have been efforts to revital-ize it. One recent renovation, a homage to the work of Mexican archi-tect Luis Barragan, features brightly painted concrete elements, including a massive purple campanile that chimes on the hour, and an almost inhuman lack of grass and trees.

The buildings around the square hold much greater visual appeal than the square itself, such as the **Biltmore Hotel**, on the west side of the park, its three brick towers rising from a Renaissance Revival arcade along Olive Street. To the east, the **International Jewelry Center** holds more than six hundred jewelers, the majority of them offering competitive prices on gold, diamonds, and other precious stones and metals, most of which come from the Middle East. If this doesn't satisfy your passion for pricey shopping, try the other **Jewelry Center**, 629 S Hill St, a green Art Deco gem, or the **Diamond Mart**, at the corner of Seventh and Hill streets, which occupies the former Pantages Theater, maintaining its Hollywood look with its own wraparound marquee.

At 617 S Olive St, the Art Deco **Oviatt Building** is another sump-tuous survivor that recalls the vibrant nature of Old Downtown in vivid modern color. The ground floor housed LA's most elegant haberdashery, catering to dapper types such as Clark Gable and John Barrymore, since converted into the *Cicada* restaurant (see p.244). The building's elevators, which open onto the street-level exterior lobby, feature hand-carved oak paneling designed and fashioned by Parisian craftsman René Lalique. Also, the intricate 1928 design of the structure's exterior – especially the building's grand sign and its ornamental clock – testify to an era when modernity and elegance weren't mortal enemies.

Bunker Hill and around

First developed as middle-class residential property in the 1870s, **BUNKER HILL** was an upscale neighborhood for just a few decades; by the 1940s it was little more than a collection of fleabag dives and crumbling old Victorian mansions, its middle-class having migrated to the suburbs. In the 1960s, the whole thing was plowed asunder, and Bunker Hill became the latest nucleus for the Downtown area.

The best way to approach Bunker Hill's **Financial District** is on the **Angels Flight Railway**, a funicular train originally banished from the hillside along with the residents it once served. In the last few years, the two orange-and-black train cars have come out of storage to be resurrected as an old-fashioned transit line – this time for tourists. You can board the train just north of the intersection of Hill and Fourth streets for a quarter, though an **escalator** at the corner of Olive and Fourth streets will give you the same views of the city for free.

The Museum of Contemporary Art

From the top of Bunker Hill, you must walk through the billion-dollar **California Plaza**, a large complex of offices and condominiums, to reach the **Museum of Contemporary Art**, 250 S Grand Ave (Tues–Sun 11am–5pm, Thurs until 8pm; $6, students $4), a collection of reddish sandstone pyramids, blocks, and slabs that effectively hide the museum itself, which is recessed underneath a ground-level courtyard and bookstore. Built in 1986 and designed by noted architect Arata Isozaki, MOCA – as the museum is better known – is Downtown's latest attempt to wrest the city's art cachet from the swankier Westside, a move not entirely successful, though it has enlivened the corporate surroundings and contributed to Bunker Hill's emergence as a spot to visit, rather than simply a place to work.

A ticket to MOCA also gains you admission to its companion museum, the Geffen Contemporary, over in Little Tokyo; see p.62.

While some critics fault the museum for not showing more of its permanent collection more regularly – indeed, the constant rotation of exhibitions insure that you never know exactly what will be on display – there's little doubt this is one of the best modern art museums west of the Mississippi, featuring notable works such as Andy Warhol's *Telephone*, Jackson Pollock's *Number One*, and several of Claes Oldenburg's oversized papier-mâché hamburgers and fast foods. **Abstract Expressionism** is represented by Franz Kline and Mark Rothko and includes a second important Pollock work, his imposing, hypnotic *Number Three*, plus ten of Sam Francis' vivid splashes of color. The museum has a growing collection of **Pop Art**, by the likes of Robert Rauschenberg and James Rosenquist, the centerpiece of which is Rauschenberg's *Coca-Cola Plan*, a battered old cabinet containing three soda bottles and angelic wings tacked onto the sides. Jasper Johns' well-known *Map* is also here, a blotchy diagram of the US states.

Noted **minimalists** shown at the museum include Robert Irwin and Donald Judd, whose metal boxes should keep you entranced if you like his mechanized style; **postmodernist** works are well represented too, by names like Eric Fischl, David Salle, and Barbara Kruger, whose giant declamatory mural once occupied the south wall of the Geffen Contemporary. The museum is also strong on **photography**, with prints from Diane Arbus, Robert Frank, and Larry Clark, along with several of Cindy Sherman's goofy, ghastly self-portraits. Local artists such as Manuel Ocampo, Robert Williams, and Lari Pittman make occasional appearances as well.

Around MOCA

if you've overdosed on modern art, a welcome tonic is the **Wells Fargo History Museum**, just down the street at 333 S Grand Ave (Mon–Fri 9am–5pm; free). Located at the base of the Wells Fargo Center, the museum displays an old stagecoach, mining equipment, antiques, photographs, a two-pound chunk of gold, and a re-created assay office from the nineteenth century, and is not quite as self-serving as you might expect.

Among the generally faceless Bunker Hill skyscrapers are a few standouts, such as the **Gas Company Tower**, 555 W Fifth St, a stunning modern high-rise whose crown symbolizes a blue natural-gas flame; the **Westin Bonaventure**, at Figueroa and Fifth streets, a collection of bright metallic cocktail shakers that passes for a hotel; and the **1000 Wilshire Building**, one of LA's few postmodern creations: a bizarre trompe l'oeil with ridiculously oversized windows. The biggest of the bunch, though, is the **Library Tower**, at Grand Avenue and Fifth Street, designed by I M Pei's firm and, at 73 stories, LA's tallest building. Formerly the First Interstate World Center, its new moniker comes from its relationship with its neighbor, LA's **Central Library** (Mon & Thurs–Sat 10am–5.30pm, Sun 1–5pm), which burned in a series of 1980s fires and needed $125 million for repair and renovation. Developers Maguire Thomas Partners offered the money on the condition that the library sell its air rights so a super-tower could be built across the street, and thus the historic library, designed in 1926 by Bertram Goodhue, now sits dwarfed by the tower that shares its name. Despite the difference in scale, the library remains a marvel, featuring a newly-designed atrium – oversized to the rest of the building, critics say – and a more pedestrian-friendly exterior with gardens, fountains, and engaging animal sculptures. Likewise, the nearby **Bunker Hill Steps**, across Fifth Street, are a well-designed stairway with floral landscaping, a thin, winding water-fall, and small sculpted figures, with several restaurants along the way, if you want to eat and rest.

On the downslope, a reminder of old LA sits at Sixth and Flower streets, **The California Club**, an exclusive men's social club that was, according to its founders, designed to "provide an atmosphere of the finest type of American Club life." It was also a favorite spot for the Committee of 25, an informal grouping of local politicians and busi-nessmen who decided important city issues behind the club's closed doors. Just over a block away, the **Fine Arts Building**, 811 W Seventh St, presents a more welcoming environment, with bold arches, Romanesque styling, and an eye-catching lobby, with splendid medieval carvings and weird art exhibits under gloomy lighting.

If you've tired of all the art and architecture and just wish to indulge in LA's true pastime – shopping – visit the **Seventh Street Marketplace**, at Seventh and Figueroa streets, an outdoor, subter-ranean shopping mall that's cool and leafy, quite a switch from most LA malls. Also, be sure to see Kent Twitchell's **Harbor Freeway Overtone** mural, two blocks east near the 110 freeway, a depiction of the members of the LA Chamber Orchestra. It's a strange juxta-position with **Dome City** to the south, just west of the freeway. A unique attempt to address the homelessness problem, the "city" is actually a series of eighteen white geodesic-like domes (looking like displaced igloos) that provide housing for those without it.

South of Bunker Hill

A bit removed from the rest of Downtown, serene **Grand Hope Park**, a grassy public space between Grand and Olympic avenues and Hope and Ninth streets, was created by Bunker Hill Steps designer Lawrence Halprin, and features a red-and-yellow clock tower, wood-en canopies, and concave fountains with gilt mosaics. Less impres-sive are the lines of doggerel on the canopies, to wit: "Dawn is a tale of intrigue carved in citrus and jasmine." The park is popular with visitors to the neighboring **Museum of Neon Art**, 501 W Olympic Blvd (Tues–Sun 11am–6pm; $5), which displays the adulterated vis-age of Mona Lisa smiling through blue-and-yellow tubing. The muse-um has recently relocated from its former site on Universal's CityWalk and offers a small exhibition space featuring contemporary neon designs and a range of bizarre kinetic art, plus some great old neon theater signs, such as that from the Melrose Theater, with its sweeping, streamlined lettering .

Around Downtown

Just west beyond the Harbor Freeway, the **Temple-Beaudry** and **Pico-Union** barrios are home to thousands of newly arrived immigrants from Central America, areas more depressed in some ways than the noted ghettos of South Central LA. They should generally be avoided at night, and **MacArthur Park** and the **Westlake** neighborhood along Wilshire Boulevard, despite the appeal of their faded Victorian architecture, should only be viewed by car – petty theft and drug dealing are rampant. North of Westlake, **Echo Park** is another immigrant center, but, like **Angelino Heights** to its east, is safer, with a surprising picturesque appeal. Further east is **Elysian Park**, a green space that surrounds **Dodger Stadium**. Finally, **Highland Park**, northeast of Downtown, has some decent museums, none very far from the stark concrete channel of the **LA River**.

Westlake and MacArthur Park

With Wilshire Boulevard as its linear axis, **Westlake** is the tumultuous focus of much immigration to the city, thronged with Panamanians, Hondurans, Mexicans, and other recent arrivals waiting for American citizenship or, in some cases, hiding from the law. The activity centers on the intersection of **Wilshire and Alvarado**, where street vendors hawk their wares in front of busy swap meets. The most prominent image in the area is the classy sign for the departed **Westlake Theater**, 638 Alvarado St, now sitting atop a grubby flea market.

Across Alvarado Street, **MacArthur Park** was originally developed in the 1890s when its surrounding area was a suburb of Los Angeles; it has since gone from being a middle-class leisure spot to a center of criminal activity. To the south, **Bonnie Brae Street** and **Alvarado Terrace** still feature a number of quaint Victorian dwellings, such as an odd creation at 1036 S Bonnie Brae St that is a striking mix of Queen Anne and French chateau styles.

Echo Park and Angelino Heights

About a mile north of Westlake along Glendale Boulevard, **Echo Park**, a tranquil arrangement of lotuses and palm trees set around an idyllic lake, features several familiar images used in Roman Polanski's film *Chinatown*, notably a palm tree-laden island reachable by a red footbridge and an assortment of row- and paddleboats. In the large, white **Angelus Temple** on the northern side of the lake, the evangelist **Aimee Semple McPherson** used to preach fire and brimstone sermons to five thousand people, with thousands more listening in on the radio. The first in a long line of media evangelists, "Sister Aimee" died in 1944, but the building is still used for services by her Four Square Gospel ministry, which dunks converts in its huge water tank during mass baptisms.

Just east of Echo Park on a hill overlooking the city, **ANGELINO HEIGHTS** was LA's first suburb, laid out in the flush of a property boom at the end of the 1880s and connected by streetcar to Downtown. Though the boom soon went bust, the elaborate houses that were built here, especially along **Carroll Avenue**, have survived and were recently restored as reminders of the optimism and energy of the city's early years. You may recognize some of the houses from television commercials or from Michael Jackson's *Thriller* video, which used the neighborhood to spooky effect. The best of the lot is the **Sessions House**, no. 1330, a Queen Anne masterpiece with Moorish detail and decorative glass. All the homes are private and not generally open to visitors, though the Angelino Heights Community Organization (☎213/413-8756) sometimes offers tours.

Elysian and Highland parks

Two miles north of the Civic Center, quiet **Elysian Park** was laid out in 1886 and has been shrinking ever since. The LA Police Academy first took a chunk of the park for its training facility; later, the Pasadena Freeway sliced off another section. Finally, after city bureaucrats booted a good number of tenants from the land, **Dodger Stadium** was constructed in the early 1960s to host the games of the transplanted Brooklyn baseball team, the LA Dodgers, and the park became a fraction of its former self. However, it's still worth a look, especially for its awe-inspiring views of the metropolis – when the smog doesn't intercede. **Angels Point**, on the upper western rim of the park, is your best vantage point, marked by an abstract sculpture with a palm tree growing out of its center.

Dodger Stadium is one of the most strikingly sited anywhere, overlooking Chavez Ravine.

Along the Pasadena Freeway to the east, **HIGHLAND PARK** was the very first district annexed to LA, in 1895. Twelve years later, it became home to the **Southwest Museum** (Tues–Sun 11am–5pm; $5), the oldest museum in LA. Its name is a bit deceptive: there are in fact displays of Native American artifacts from all over North America, with exhibits of pre-Columbian pottery, coastal Chumash rock art, and a full-size Cheyenne tepee. The museum also hosts traveling exhibitions, and has a worthwhile educational program of lectures, films, and theatrical events. Meanwhile, its Braun Research Library has an unmatched collection of recordings and photographs of Native Americans from the Bering Straits to Mexico, and the gift shop's not bad either, with Navajo rugs, kachina dolls, and turquoise jewelry, as well as an extensive selection of books and specialist publications. Nearby, the **Casa de Adobe**, 4603 N Figueroa St, administered by the museum, is a 1917 re-creation of a Mexican hacienda, containing a small museum of its own detailing LA history into the nineteenth century. Call ☎213/221-2163 to visit.

Just down the road, at 200 E Ave 43, the **Lummis House** (Fri–Sun noon–4pm) is the well-preserved home of the museum's founder, Charles F. Lummis, also the city librarian and an early champion of civil rights for Native Americans, who worked to save many of the region's missions. Lummis built this house for himself in an ad hoc mixture of Mission and medieval styles, naming it El Alisal after the many large sycamore trees (*alisal* in Spanish) that shade the gardens. He constructed the thick walls out of rounded granite boulders taken from the nearby riverbed, and living room beams from old telephone poles; the solid wooden front doors are similarly built to last, reinforced with iron and weighing tons, while the plaster-and-tile interior is rustically outfitted with hand-cut timber ceilings and homemade furniture, all a fitting reflection of its rugged owner, one of the few individuals to reach LA by walking – from Cincinnati.

Across the Pasadena Freeway, **Heritage Square**, 3800 Homer St (Sat–Sun noon–4pm; $5), is an outdoor museum featuring a jumble of Victorian structures collected from different places in the city, most coming from Bunker Hill and expendable after the 1960s urban renewal campaign there. The strip sites a railway station next to an octagonal house next to a Methodist church, all the more incongruous by its positioning next to the freeway.

The LA River

"A beautiful, limpid little stream with willows on its banks" is how water czar William Mulholland once described the **LA River**, the long gutter that runs along Downtown proper's eastern border. While the river may have often been tranquil, it was also quite volatile, periodically flooding neighboring communities until, in 1938, a typically drastic solution was imposed: its muddy bottom was turned into cement and its earthy contours became a hard, flat basin. The river mutated into a flood channel, which it remains, snaking through the city for 58 miles. You're not allowed to poke around it, but you can view the channel by driving across several Downtown bridges, or by renting movies. The river has been used in numerous films, notably *Grease*, in which the channel hosts a wild drag race, and the *Terminator* series, in which cyborgs run amok in its bleak setting.

Chapter 3

Mid-Wilshire

T he ethnically and visually diverse neighborhood of **MID-WILSHIRE** – for want of a better name – takes in the general area around **Wilshire Boulevard** between Downtown and Beverly Hills, running roughly parallel to Hollywood, and is often bypassed by visitors for those more starry regions. It was the site of LA's first major suburban expansion, when the 1920s middle class began migrating west along the expanding strip of Wilshire Boulevard and shopping at places like the **Bullocks Wilshire** department store, the first one built with the automobile in mind.

Today, communities of middle-income Asians, old-money whites, working-class African-Americans, and various groups of Hispanics are all located within a few miles of each other along this approximately five-mile corridor; not surprisingly, the area was one of the hardest hit during the 1992 riots, when diversity became outright racial hatred. **Koreatown**, on the eastern end of Mid-Wilshire, was the site of some of the bleakest images of the conflict, with Korean shop-owners brandishing rifles on the roofs of their businesses and rioters looting and setting flame to any convenient nearby buildings. Luckily, LA has, in the last six years, settled into a quiet ethnic tolerance. This has meant renewed growth for Koreatown, if not necessarily for the impoverished Hispanic neighborhoods to the east, once the province of the suburban middle class in the early twentieth century, who have since continued their white-flight trajectory and left for good. To the west, just north of Wilshire Boulevard, much of the old Anglo-Saxon money in places like **Hancock Park** has also fled, but the area still visually resembles its 1920s heyday, and is now populated by a mix of Asians, Jews, and African-Americans.

Further along Wilshire, the **Miracle Mile** shopping strip has been in steady decline for several decades, but still boasts enough interesting Art Deco architecture to make a visit worthwhile. The western side of the strip, however, has recently been rejuvenated by the creation of **Museum Row**, a collection of institutions celebrating everything from the city's tar-soaked fossils to its worldly art to, inevitably, its car-worship. **Fairfax Avenue**, west of Museum Row, takes you through the human hive of the **Farmers Market** to the heart of the city's Jewish population. Further west, the **Third Street** shopping district, along with **La Brea Avenue**, is where the hip and trendy buy the latest designer clothes, eat in the smartest cafés, and hobnob with other would-be bohemians. These same activities occur more conspicuously on the celebrated **Melrose Avenue**, which borders the southern fringe of Hollywood. Fittingly perhaps, the western edge of Mid-Wilshire is marked by an imposing symbol of mass consumerism, the concrete monstrosity of the **Beverly Center**, looming over everything in sight.

Wilshire Boulevard

Named for oil magnate and socialist H Gaylord Wilshire, a unique individual even for LA (see box, p.76), **Wilshire Boulevard** runs from Downtown to Beverly Hills and Santa Monica, but is at its most visually appealing in Mid-Wilshire, from Vermont to Fairfax avenues. This stretch of road was for many decades LA's prime shopping strip, until the same middle class that created this "linear city" in the 1920s and 1930s disappeared for good in the 1970s and 1980s. These days, the facades along the boulevard have lost their consumer relevance, but continue to serve as beacons of a faded era, when Zigzag and Streamline Moderne architecture were the rage and designers built apartment blocks to resemble Egyptian temples and French castles.

East of Vermont, surrounding grim **Lafayette Park**, are a few excellent examples of these early styles. The Romanesque **Park Plaza Hotel**, 607 S Park View St, is adorned by intricately crafted sculptures on the front and sides of the building; the **First Congregational Church**, at Commonwealth Avenue and W Sixth Street, is a 1930 English Gothic cathedral; and the **Town House**, 2959 Wilshire Blvd, is a neoclassical hotel sporting an old-fashioned neon sign on its roof. The best example of the period-revival styles may be the **Granada Building**, 627 S Lafayette Park Place, a shopping and residential complex posing as an exquisite Spanish Colonial village.

Better still is the **Bullocks Wilshire** department store, 3050 Wilshire Blvd, an early Art Deco piece and the most complete and unaltered example of late-1920s architecture in the city, with its terra cotta base and striking oxidized copper tower. Built in 1928, in what was then a suburban beanfield, it was the first department store in LA outside Downtown, and the first to construct its main entrance, a porte-co-chère entry for cars, at the back of the structure adjacent to the parking lot – pandering to the automobile in a way that was to become the norm. The inside also echoed the time's obsession with modernization and transportation, decked out with murals and mosaics featuring planes and ocean liners glowing with activity. Badly vandalized during the 1992 riots, the store subsequently closed, but the building has since reopened as the law library of adjacent **Southwestern University**, and is off-limits to the general public, unless you can talk a student into giving you an impromptu tour.

The **Ambassador Hotel**, just west of Vermont Avenue at 3400 Wilshire Blvd, is another landmark of the boulevard's golden age. From the early 1920s to the late 1940s, when the hotel was the winter home of transient Hollywood celebrities, its *Cocoanut Grove* club was a favorite LA nightspot. The large ballroom hosted some of the early Academy Award ceremonies, and was featured in the first two versions of *A Star is Born* – though the hotel's most notorious event occurred on June 5, 1968, when **Bobby Kennedy** was fatally shot in the hotel kitchen while trying to avoid the press after winning the California presidential primary. Converted into a film location and closed to public view, the establishment has recently been the object of a bizarre struggle between the local school district and Donald Trump, both of whom would like to demolish the historic hotel.

A few blocks west, past the impressively modern **St Basil's Roman Catholic Church**, 3611 Wilshire Blvd, and the lustrous mosaics, marble, and gold of the Byzantine **Wilshire Boulevard Temple**, Wilshire at Hobart Boulevard, another of LA's great Art Deco monuments rises at the corner of Wilshire and Western Avenue: the **Wiltern Theater**, once one of the city's prime movie palaces, featuring a bluish Zigzag Moderne facade and narrow windows that made the building seem larger than it actually was. The Warner Brothers Western Theater, as it was known upon its 1930 completion, was nearly

Henry Gaylord Wilshire

Aline Barnsdall, the 1920s heiress who commissioned Frank Lloyd Wright
to build her Hollyhock House in Hollywood (see p.91), was not the only
socialist who became rich thanks to overflowing oil profits. Decades
before, Henry Gaylord Wilshire gained his notoriety from the petroleum
industry, and like Barnsdall was a scion to a family dynasty, as well as an
entrepreneur. By the time he was 30, in the 1880s, he had already come to
California and founded the Orange County town of Fullerton. Shortly
thereafter, he became heavily involved in social causes and took up the
Socialist banner in two unsuccessful runs for Congress, losing both in New
York and California. These defeats did not deter his frenetic activity, however, and before long he was in London hanging out with members of the
Fabian Society, as well as a then-unknown George Bernard Shaw. The turn
of the century found him back in LA, this time buying up chunks of land
from Pasadena to Santa Monica, including some of the Westlake neighborhood a few miles west of Downtown. Although Wilshire is often cred-
ited with creating the eponymous boulevard, the strip had actually been a
wagon trail well before the Spanish had begun to populate the area and
had by Wilshire's time become known as the "Old Road," though it was little more than an uneven dirt path. The oil baron soon developed the street
and the property around it, eventually helping the boulevard to connect
Downtown with the ocean and creating one of the city's biggest thoroughfares in the process. Wilshire, though, had worse luck than the street he
named. After another failed congressional attempt, he lost much of his
money in foolhardy investments, managing to drop a cool $3 million. Still,
he survived well enough to see his beloved horse path become one of the
city's most significant boulevards, a status it still holds to this day.

destroyed in the 1980s until local conservationists stepped in; it has
since been converted into a concert hall (see p.271).

Koreatown

*If you want to
eat Korean food
there's simply
no better place
than
Koreatown; see
p.246 for the
top restaurants
in the area.*

To get a good look at LA's cultural diversity, head south to Olympic
Boulevard, between Vermont and Western avenues, to find the center of **KOREATOWN**, the largest concentration of Koreans outside
Korea (up to 100,000 people) and five times bigger than Chinatown
and Little Tokyo combined. In reality, the comparison is unfair, for
Koreatown is an active residential and commercial district, not just a
tourist sight. Moreover, the low-scaled buildings and mom-and-pop
stores that define the stereotype of ethnic enclaves elsewhere are
absent: the district is loaded with big, glossy modern buildings and
more multi-story minimalls than you'll see anywhere else in LA. In
fact, were it not for the Korean letters on the signs and the top-notch
Korean restaurants inside those malls, you may mistake this for just
another faceless LA district.

While Koreatown has some history of being tension-filled, your
chance of running into trouble is slim, and in any case it's unlikely

you'll have any reason to linger: there simply aren't enough interesting destinations to make a lengthy trip here worthwhile. One exception is the **Korean-American Museum**, 3333 Wilshire Blvd (Tues–Sat 11am–4pm; free), which displays photographs, antiques, and craftwork of Korean immigrants and citizens, from their 1910 arrival in LA to the current era, with particular attention given to the simple, elegant furniture of various dynastic periods.

Hancock Park

Further west, Wilshire passes through the sloping, tree-lined neighborhood of **Hancock Park**, named after yet another oil magnate, G Allan Hancock, who developed this expansive parcel of real estate in the 1920s as an elite suburb. Nowadays, LA has engulfed the surrounding land, but the area manages to retain its charm thanks to its well-preserved Historic Revival architecture along the curving streets. Be sure to check out the **Getty House**, 605 S Irving at Sixth St, the mayor's official residence – although current head Richard Riordan only uses it for city functions – and somewhat of an architectural oddity, its green-and-cream color scheme and Tudor design bucking the stereotype of a mayoral mansion. In any case, the house is open for tours only on the first Tuesday of each month (10am, 12.30pm, and 3pm), but can be readily appreciated from the street at any time. As for the name, the oil company simply owned it for a time before donating it to the city.

There are plenty of other lovely houses, mock-Tudor and otherwise, in the neighborhood, though none, unfortunately, are open to the public. Still, you can check out some grand exteriors, such as Paul R Williams' magnificent **Rothman House**, 541 Rossmore Ave, a half-timbered jewel that fits in quite nicely with the historic character of the surrounding neighborhood. Further west is a bizarre example of Medieval Norman, the **Sisson House**, on Hudson Avenue at Sixth Street, featuring a gloomy facade and three-story tower.

Bordering Hancock Park to the west and cutting across Wilshire Boulevard, the Mid-Wilshire blocks of **La Brea Avenue** have emerged as one of the city's trendier shopping districts in recent years, attracting increasingly large amounts of weekend visitors, who come to sample the edgy galleries, hip boutiques, chic restaurants, and antique furniture dealers. Indeed, this shopping strip makes a good prelude for a vigorous walk up to the more serious consumer precinct of Melrose Avenue (see p.56).

The Miracle Mile

Like so many of LA's iconic districts, the **Miracle Mile**, along Wilshire Boulevard between La Brea and Fairfax avenues, was creat-

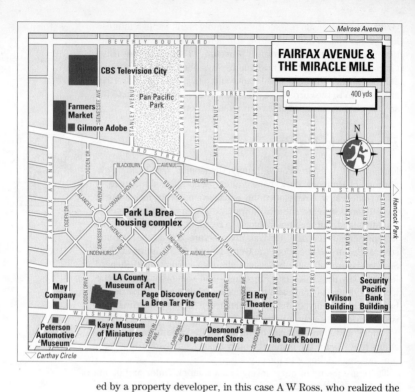

**FAIRFAX AVENUE &
THE MIRACLE MILE**

0   400 yds

N

BEVERLY BOULEVARD

CBS Television City

Pan Pacific Park

Farmers Market

Gilmore Adobe

1ST STREET

2ND STREET

3RD STREET

BLACKBURN AVENUE

HAUSER BLVD

BURNSIDE

3RD STREET

Park La Brea housing complex

4TH STREET

LINDENHURST AVE

6TH STREET

LA County Museum of Art

May Company

Page Discovery Center/
La Brea Tar Pits

El Rey Theater

Wilson Building

Security Pacific Bank Building

WILSHIRE BOULEVARD (THE MIRACLE MILE)

Peterson Automotive Museum

Kaye Museum of Miniatures

Desmond's Department Store

The Dark Room

Carthay Circle

Hancock Park

ed by a property developer, in this case A W Ross, who realized the growing importance of the city's auto culture and summarily began developing this stretch of road in 1921. Though it never became LA's version of Fifth Avenue, as Ross thought it would be, the Miracle Mile was quite a successful enterprise in its time, luring big-name department stores like Coulter's, Desmond's, and May Company to the then-fringes of the city. (These retail operations, like the Bullocks Wilshire store to the east, had their main entrances in rear parking lots to please their car-driving customers.) With the inevitable suburban shift of middle-class dollars, Miracle Mile was left to decay, its vivid Art Deco designs to fade and crumble. Though there have been some attempts at recent renovation, you'll have to look pretty closely at the one-time Moderne marvels – and try to ignore the encroaching office supply and supermarket chains – to envision this shopping strip in its glory days.

Architectural terms like Art Deco and Zigzag Moderne are explained in greater detail in the "Glossary," pp.341–345.

The strip begins in earnest with the **Security Pacific Bank Building**, just east of La Brea Avenue at 5209 Wilshire Blvd, a miniature black-and-gold version of the luminous Richfield Building, a Downtown monument that was destroyed in 1968; both were designed by the firm of Morgan, Walls and Clements, perhaps LA's greatest purveyor of Art Deco and Historic Revival styles (see box). Just past this is the **Wilson Building**, 5217 Wilshire Blvd, a grand Zigzag tower unfortunately marred by a colossal neon beer ad on its crown. The former **Dark Room**, no. 5370, a Streamline Moderne retail shop shaped like a camera, has been clumsily transformed into a low-end restaurant, its "lens" now used to advertise the daily special. Other Art Deco classics, like the Zigzag **office buildings** at nos. 5410 and 5464, have fared even worse, their facades allowed to crack and wither while their ground-level offices sit vacant and dusty. **Desmond's Department Store**, no. 5514, now seems like a relic, even though

---

The great unknown architects

Frank Lloyd Wright's exploits in pre-Columbian styles in 1920s Los Angeles are well known, as are Rudolf Schindler's and Richard Neutra's early modernist efforts. However, the firm of **Morgan, Walls and Clements**, had equal, if not greater, success in the age of Art Deco, even though its name is now largely forgotten.

The most conspicuous works of Octavius Morgan, J A Walls, and Stiles O Clements were the beloved Art Deco movie palaces that have survived the years and re-emerged as shrines to the Golden Age of Hollywood. The old Warner Brothers Western Theater, now called the Wiltern (see p.75), was a triumph of the Zigzag Moderne that was saved from the wrecking ball by community activism in the 1980s. Others of the firm's theaters, such as the El Capitan (p.99), have survived through massive renovation efforts, or by becoming churches, like the Moderne spire-topped Leimert Theater, and even nightclubs, as in the pre-Columbian fantasy of the Mayan Theater (p.266). While much of these architects' work has been preserved, some of their designs have been left to rot or to be remodeled beyond recognition, as in Downtown's former Pantages Theater, 534 S Broadway, and Globe Theater, 744 S Broadway, both Beaux Arts designs. However, the firm's best work was not confined to moviehouses, but included a variety of commercial buildings throughout the Mid-Wilshire and Hollywood areas and a range of styles, from the Spanish Churrigueresque of the McKinley Building, Wilshire Blvd at Oxford Ave, and the Hollywood Chamber of Commerce, Sunset Blvd at Hudson Ave, to the monumental Assyrian design of the Samson Tyre and Rubber Company, now The Citadel (p.156), an ancient temple stranded alongside a busy freeway. Along with being adept at period-revival architecture, Morgan, Walls and Clements were also skilled at early Beaux Arts designs, as in the I N Van Nuys building Downtown (p.64), and the Streamline Moderne, shown best in the radiant pylons of the KFL Building, 133 N Vermont Ave, and the Owl Drug Company, 6380 Hollywood Blvd. Perhaps their best remaining structure is the Spanish Colonial Chapman Building and Market, at Sixth Street and Alexandria Avenue, which occupies a full city block and hides a secluded interior courtyard full of clubs and restaurants.

Although many of their extant structures are closed to the public, their Andalusian Adamson House in Malibu, Pacific Coast Hwy at Serra Rd (p.200), is not, offering the best chance to see what made their romantic escapist designs of the period so appealing to the architecture world.

---

its bold Moderne tower and wraparound corners remain stylish. One building, however, has not only withstood the years, but flourished: the **El Rey Theater**, no. 5519, a thriving concert venue that has been renovated in a yellow-and-red design, with a sleek king's head and flashy neon marquee, unmistakable amid its new concrete-box neighbors. Just to the north, a series of **apartment blocks**, between Burnside and La Brea avenues around Sixth Street, manages to impress with its wild 1920s and 1930s period-revival styling, everything from French chateaux to Hansel-and-Gretel cottages to Spanish Colonial villas to pop-Baroque confections, many of them preserved with their original outlandish designs.

Museum Row

As you continue west, the fading Art Deco monuments of the Miracle Mile give way to the cultural institutions of **Museum Row**, a one-time dilapidated shopping zone that became, with the help of LA's political leaders in the early 1990s, a city arts center.

The museums begin at the **La Brea Tar Pits**, on Wilshire at Curson Avenue, where a large pool of smelly tar ("*la brea*" in Spanish) surrounds full-size models of mastodons struggling to free themselves from the grimy muck, a re-creation of prehistoric times, when such creatures tried to drink from the thin layer of water covering the tar in the pits, only to become entrapped. Millions of bones belonging to the animals (and one set of human bones) have been found here and reconstructed in the adjacent **George C Page Discovery Center**, 5801 Wilshire Blvd (Tues–Sat 10am–5pm; $6, students $3.50), a Westside branch of the Natural History Museum in Exposition Park (see p.150). Along with watching researchers clean and categorize the bones of recent finds behind glass, you can also examine the mounted remains of many early or extinct creatures, including bison, saber-toothed tigers, wolves, and giant ground sloths, their skeletons stained brown from the goo. Unlucky animals were not the only ones attracted to the tar, as oil drillers for years pumped the liquid black gold from the ground and created an industry as endemic to Southern California as the movie business. In fact, it was an oil geologist, William Orcutt, who found the modern world's first saber-toothed tiger skull here in 1916, and an oil magnate, G Allan Hancock, who the same year donated this property to the county. Outside, tar still seeps through the grass, but most of the black stuff is kept out of range behind chain-link fences.

The next stop is the intriguing **Carol and Barry Kaye Museum of Miniatures**, 5900 Wilshire Blvd (Tues–Sat 10am–5pm, Sun 11am–5pm; $7.50), housing the world's most comprehensive collection of miniatures – originally a hobby for founder Carole

Kaye, but soon becoming a museum-sized storehouse of both genuine art pieces and colorful kitsch. Exhibits include a Victorian mansion, Japanese garden, Hollywood Bowl (complete with pint-sized Ella, Satchmo, and Dizzy), and a re-creation of Fontainebleau Palace, not to mention myriad tiny kings, politicians, and celebrities, from Marie Antoinette to Abe Lincoln to Nancy Reagan. Particularly interesting is a pygmy version of emperor Domitian's Domus Augustana, which renders the dining room of the Roman palace with detailed classical architecture and opulent period furnishings.

The nearby **Peterson Automotive Museum**, 6060 Wilshire Blvd (daily 10am–6pm, Fri until 9pm; $7), is the baby of media mogul Robert Peterson, its three floors paying sumptuous if superficial homage to the automobile, with special exhibits of movie stars' cars, customized lowriders, and vintage footage of land-speed record attempts in the desert. It fails to explain the reasons behind the collapse of LA's early public transport system and is not critical by any means, but it has enough mint-condition classic models on its upper floors to gratify anyone's automotive desires.

The ground floor features an asphalt path that takes you on a journey through the city's vehicular past, from crude early-twentieth-century flivvers and seminal hot rods that raced on dangerous wooden tracks, to a 1930s Streamline Moderne gas station, post-World War II gas guzzlers, and so on, running right up to a display of a modern wreckage, illustrating the need for air bag use. However, the museum's best exhibit is its re-creation of the *Dog Café*, a departed LA landmark of pop roadside architecture that was literally a giant bulldog smoking a pipe, under which patrons entered to sample the restaurant's famed tamales and ice cream.

The Los Angeles County Museum of Art

The **LA County Museum of Art**, or LACMA, 5905 Wilshire Blvd (Mon–Tues & Thurs noon–8pm, Fri noon–9pm, Sat–Sun 11am–8pm), is an unimpressive series of buildings along Museum Row that was plopped down in 1965 in a fit of municipal-mindedness that has never really taken root. The buildings aside, though, some of the collections of applied art here are among the best in the world, and despite the loss of Armand Hammer's stock of paintings to his own museum in Westwood (see p.118), it justifies a lengthy visit. If you arrive on a Wednesday before 1pm, check out the schedule of films playing in the **Leo S Bing Theater**, where you can see anything from a Hitchcock classic to a screwball comedy for only $2.

LACMA is enormous, and there's no way you could see the lot in one go; you're best off either focusing on the contemporary art and traveling exhibitions in the **Anderson Building** or diving into the fine selection of world art in the **Ahmanson Building**.

The Ahmanson Building, Robert Gore Center and Japanese Pavilion

Alongside many excellent collections of Southeast Asian sculpture and Middle Eastern decorative arts in the Ahmanson Building, the Fearing Collection consists of funeral masks and sculpted guardian figures from the early civilizations of pre-Columbian Mexico. Another highlight is the array of ancient Egyptian sculpture and icons, including finely crafted designs of deities, on the second floor of the building. These are across from the European art rooms, which begin with a good overview of Greek and Roman art and continue into the medieval era with religious sculptures and ecclesiastical ornamentation, notably several stone carvings of the Passion cycle. The Renaissance and Mannerist eras are represented by compelling works such as Fra Bartolommeo's *Holy Family*, painted in a balanced High Renaissance manner, Paolo Veronese's *Two Allegories of Navigation*, great Mannerist figures filling the frame from an imposing low angle, El Greco's uncommonly reserved portrait *The Apostle Saint Andrew*, and Titian's *Portrait of Giacomo Dolfin*, a carefully tinted study by the great colorist. Northern European painters are well represented in subsequent rooms, including Hans Holbein's small, resplendent *Portrait of a Young Woman with White Coif*, a number of Frans Hals' pictures of cheerful burghers, and Rembrandt's probing *Portrait of Marten Looten*.

In adjacent galleries are Georges de la Tour's *Magdalen with Smoking Flame*, a chiaroscuro work of a girl ruminating by candlelight while holding an ominous skull on her lap, Jean-Jacques Feuchère's wickedly grotesque bronze sculpture of *Satan*, and an excellent grouping of Auguste Rodin's smaller works, which compare favorably to the larger pieces in the museum forecourt's **B Gerald Cantor Sculpture Garden**, where casts of characters from the *Gates of Hell*, as well as a towering Balzac, stare out at the passing traffic. Elsewhere inside are some lesser works by Degas, Gauguin, Renoir, and the like – necessary viewing only for devotees of Impressionism. Similarly, the collection of American art, on the entry level, is somewhat spotty, with a few interesting pieces by John Singleton Copley (the regal *Portrait of a Lady*) and Winslow Homer (the dusty realism of the *Cotton Pickers*), but far too many unremarkable pieces.

Where the museum excels is in its specializations, notably the prints and drawings in the **Robert Gore Rifkind Center for German Expressionist Studies**, which includes a library of magazines and tracts from Weimar Germany, and the **Pavilion for Japanese Art**. This is a recent addition to the museum, built to resemble the effects of traditional *shoji* screens, filtering varying levels and qualities of light through to the interior – the most effective building in the LACMA. Displays include painted screens and scrolls, ceramics, and lacquerware, rivaling the collection of the late Emperor Hirohito as the most extensive in the world, all of which are viewed on a gradually sloping ramp that meanders down through the building until it reaches a small waterfall at the bottom.

The Anderson Building

Contemporary art is showcased in the Anderson Building, which was greeted in 1986 with a hail of critical brickbats for the way it abutted Wilshire Boulevard with a huge, impenetrable wall and for being little more than a giant concrete cube. Even the adjoining modern **sculpture garden** is similarly bleak, with an uninspired Alexander Calder mobile typifying the charmless works in its cramped space. Luckily, the Anderson Building's other exhibits have a better reputation than its architecture. Rotating exhibitions are presented on the structure's ground floor, while on the second and third floors, American and international modernist art are the focus, the twentieth century art on display including selections from Picasso, Magritte, and abstract expressionists like Mark Rothko and Franz Kline among the more prominent pieces. Less celebrated, but

---

The people vs ED Kienholz

Long before Robert Mapplethorpe and Andres Serrano stirred up controversy in the art world, **Ed Kienholz** was making waves with his *Back Seat Dodge '38*, offending politicos and the public alike. Now sitting near a stairway on the second floor of the LA County Museum of Art, Kienholz's work consists of a broken-down old Dodge with fading blue paint and dimming headlights sitting on an artificial grass mat surrounded by empty beer bottles. An open door reveals two wire-mesh bodies, their grubby clothes ripped and torn, intertwined in an act of sexual frenzy and looking thoroughly decomposed. Ominous, crackly music adds to the sordid effect. Now recognized as a triumph of early social protest art, Kienholz's piece was called many other things upon its debut in the mid-1960s – indecent, morally depraved, pornographic.

LA County Supervisor Kenneth Hahn was one of the loudest voices to vilify both Kienholz and the museum for exhibiting the work, calling for the museum to be shut down unless it was removed. The battle that ensued was resolved with an appropriately ridiculous solution: the piece would be left in the gallery, but its car door would have to be closed most of the time, and opened only infrequently by a museum guard stationed near the controversial sculpture. Both Kienholz and Hahn moved on from the fight relatively unscathed: Hahn became a local legend for securing support for rapid transit, building the Martin Luther King Jr. General Hospital, creating the freeway emergency "call box" system, and funding sports complexes (he had earlier successfully lured the Dodgers away from Brooklyn); while Kienholz went on to establish an international reputation for daring assemblage art. He carried his fixation with cars to the grave. When he was buried in 1994, in a strangely modern version of an Egyptian funeral rite, his wife drove him and his possessions down into the ground, burying him along with his favorite car – a Packard.

Museum Row

just as appealing, is Nam June Paik's *Video Flag*, an arrangement of 84 television screens flashing violent or bizarre images to create the hypnotic effect of a pulsating stars-and-stripes. Also fascinating is *Hammering Man*, one of Jonathan Borofsky's gargantuan, kinetic sculptures that resembles a huge silhouette of a nineteenth-century proletariat. Not far away, Ed Kienholz's *Back Seat Dodge '38* looks just as perverse as it did when it caused a public outrage in the 1960s (see box above). On a similar note, Michael McMillen's multimedia assemblage *Central Meridian* is a creepy walk-in garage that includes an old beater propped up on blocks and lit with red neon, containing a small, malformed figure in the front seat and a glowing fire in the back.

South of Wilshire

The Academy Awards have also been hosted at the Dorothy Chandler Pavilion and Shrine Auditorium; for more background on the Oscars, see p.112.

A few blocks southwest of Wilshire, the period-revival architecture of **Carthay Circle**, a 1920s property development, is one of LA's best spots to see classic Spanish Colonial designs. A few more blocks to the south, **South Carthay** also holds plenty of 1920s and 1930s Historic Revival styles, with the added benefit of being one of the region's few totally protected architectural areas, known officially and clumsily as a Historic Preservation Overlay Zone. On the western edge of the neighborhood, the attractive **Center for Motion Picture Study**, 333 S La Cienega Blvd, contains the Margaret Herrick Library, a voluminous institution containing books on actors, filmmaking, and festivals, screenplays from a variety of eras, film production photographs, and etchings. Formerly the home of the Beverly Hills Water Department, it was given a once-over in 1988 under the auspices of the Academy of Motion Picture Arts and Sciences, though its original spirit was kept intact – a municipal shrine to water designed to look like a Spanish Colonial church.

More of LA's festivals are detailed beginning on p.293.

Two miles to the southeast, and a mile south of Wilshire, **St Elmo's Village**, 4836 St Elmo Dr (☎213/931-3409), is a two-decade-old art project of colorful murals and sculptures intended to foster a creative environment for local youth. It's now also the site of the **Festival of the Art of Survival**, an annual celebration of hippie-flavored folk and popular art and music held each Memorial Day.

Fairfax Avenue and around

Just beyond Museum Row, **Fairfax Avenue**, between Santa Monica and Wilshire boulevards, is the backbone of the city's Jewish culture, full of countless temples, yeshivas, kosher butcher shops, and delicatessens. There's little in the way of sights, but it's a refreshingly vibrant neighborhood, easily explored on foot.

At Fairfax's junction with Third Street are the ramshackle buildings and white clapboard tower of the **Farmers Market** (June–Sept Mon–Sat 9am–8pm; Oct–May Mon–Sat 9am–6.30pm, Sun 10am–5pm; free), created in the 1930s by an advertising writer and a local entrepreneur as an act of civic boosterism, intended to highlight the region's agrarian delights. Inside the market is a dynamic rabbit warren of food stalls and produce stands, attracting both locals and out-of-towners. Also on the Farmers Market property, just to the east, the **Gilmore Adobe** is a structure from 1852 that sits among the other buildings owned by the Gilmore Company, a family business that also owns the market itself. The L-shaped house was the birthplace of one Earl Gilmore, grandson of Arthur Gilmore, a one-time farmer who owned the huge Rancho La Brea tract – once encompassing much of Hollywood, West Hollywood, and the Wilshire area. The younger Gilmore had his moment too, backing the car that set the 1939 land speed record at Bonneville Flats.

Just north, **CBS Television City** is a thoroughly contemporary, sprawling black cube – and something of an architectural eyesore – but also a worthwhile destination if you're in town to sit in a TV-show audience for a sitcom or game show. East of here is tranquil **Pan Pacific Park**, which once featured the wondrous Pan Pacific Auditorium, a renowned creation belonging to the Gilmore clan that burned in a 1989 fire.

West of the Farmers Market, the **Third Street** shopping district, running from La Jolla Avenue to La Cienega Boulevard, is another of LA's trendy consumer zones, though with a bit less flash and pretension than most. Although there are numerous good antique stores, restaurants, and coffee shops, most visitors are actually drawn by the forbidding concrete goliath nearby: the **Beverly Center**, Third Street at La Cienega Boulevard, a huge shopping mall that is the nexus of much weekend activity for area teenagers, though its stores are nothing special and its look far from attractive, recently repainted in a hideous purple, brown, and green color scheme and bedecked with giant fashion ads. The Center is perhaps more notable for its concessions to car culture, locating its three shopping floors far up on top of its five-story parking garage and forcing customers up a series of Pompidou-Center-style escalators to reach the chain stores.

More appealing is the small enclave of Streamline Moderne designs west of the mall at **Kings Road and First Street**, apartment blocks and small houses designed by Milton Black, among other big names of the genre. The best examples are the unnamed apartment building at **8360 First Street**, with sloping contours and a typically aerodynamic design, and the private residence at **127 S Kings Road** by Black that provides a visual parallel across the street, dwellings that give you a fairly uncluttered view of what many buildings in prewar LA resembled: beached ocean liners.

If you're interested in seeing one of CBS's daily offerings live, call ☎213/852-2624 for detailed information.

Melrose Avenue

The unofficial border between Mid-Wilshire and Hollywood, **Melrose Avenue** has become LA's central shopping strip for both locals and tourists. An eccentric world of its own, Melrose manages to live up to its considerable hype by maintaining its edgy veneer and irreverent attitude – despite the onslaught of corporate chain stores that have diluted some of its appeal – with enough trashy salons and funky boutiques to make it an essential stop on any trip through Southern California.

For a full run-down of the Melrose retail scene, see "Shopping," p.301.

Although it runs south of Hollywood starting at Hoover Street in Silver Lake, Melrose only becomes intriguing west of La Brea Avenue, where it shifts from being a grimy, down-at-the-heels traffic corridor to a colorful shopping zone with a wide range of independent businesses selling everything from Goth-clubwear to Day-glo beanbags to retro-1950s fast food. Clothing is definitely the top attraction around these parts, and stores like Retropolis, no. 7270, selling outré clothing from past decades, Red Balls, no. 7365, full of brash colors and clashing designs, and Aardvark's, no. 7579, shouldn't disappoint. There are also plenty of record shops, galleries and suchlike to check out beneath the flashing neon.

As Melrose continues west, things get a bit more corporate, with chain stores like the Gap competing for customers, and beyond Fairfax Avenue, the street turns increasingly chic and pricey until it reaches West Hollywood, where its color and vitality dissolve into a bleak array of elite boutiques and most of the window-shoppers also vanish.

Chapter 4

Hollywood

HOLLYWOOD is the birthplace of the modern movie business and one of LA's prime tourist attractions, an enduring – if often misleading – symbol of glamour, money, and overnight success. Its seediness, however, is also well known. Even in the 1930s, novelist Nathanael West described its dark side in vivid detail, and Raymond Chandler made a career out of telling bleak stories of its violence and corruption. Nonetheless, these pejorative aspects have only served to enhance its romantic appeal and to keep the visitors coming.

Ironically, Hollywood began its existence as a temperance colony, as well as a home to a great number of Protestant religious institutions, including what was alleged to be the world's biggest Presbyterian church. However, the need for water left the town with little choice but to merge with LA in 1910, after which Hollywood became the focus of the film industry, due mostly to its eclectic shooting locations, cheap labor, low taxes (unlike the East Coast), and, most importantly, the influence of **Thomas Ince**, a producer who set up shop here and established a production studio that was to become a template for later filmmaking companies. Hollywood vaulted to domestic economic success, though its international dominance took a bit more luck: two world wars that crippled Europe's vibrant film industry.

Thomas Ince was also active in Culver City's early days in the film industry; see p.128 for details.

This dominion lasted until the 1950s, when anti-trust actions, television, and revitalized European competition damaged the movie industry, and by the 1960s large-scale financial flight further weakened Hollywood's film business. In recent years, Hollywood has continued to sustain companies involved in motion pictures, but these are typically smaller production businesses and support facilities for editing, lighting, and props – the industrial side of the biz. Except for Paramount, all the major studios have since moved out to new digs in Burbank, Culver City, and the like.

Although the district has been gravely wounded by the departure of the big studios, tourism revenues have helped to make up some of the economic loss, and city redevelopment schemes are always in the works – though not always successful. The MTA's expansion of its **Red Line** subway, intended to provide slick new mass transit, has managed only to damage the roadbed along Hollywood Boulevard and financially cripple the businesses that lie along it. Despite this, Hollywood is an aged survivor of economic and cultural turmoil, and while its renovation is hard to picture, so too is its demise.

A trip through Hollywood from east to west conveniently follows the westward drift of the movie business itself. The far eastern boundary of Hollywood begins just beyond Echo Park at **Silver Lake**, initial home of the movie studios and now a center for Latin American immigrants and a well-established gay community. To the north, **Los Feliz**, was home in the 1920s to many of the residences of Hollywood bigwigs. Nowadays, it's a charming mixed-income community with a few examples of classic architecture on its northern side, where the neighborhood's wealthy reside. Even further north lies **Griffith Park**, the site of LA's famed **observatory**, among other less well-known vaguely cultural institutions.

A detailed color map of the Hollywood area appears in the insert at the back of the book.

The district's main drag is, of course, **Hollywood Boulevard**, and, despite its grunginess, essential viewing – the basis for much of the myth and lore surrounding the entire district. This street and its neighbor to the south, **Sunset Boulevard**, were the central streets of the Golden Age of Hollywood, from the 1920s through the early 1950s, during which time the stars lived in exclusive homes in the **Hollywood Hills**, rising above the boulevards.

In recent years, the economic core of the area has migrated west once more and now resides in **West Hollywood**, actually a separate city unto itself, attracting a mix of gay activists, youthful poseurs, self-appointed trendsetters, and neo-bohemians. All these assorted folks congregate on the legendary **Sunset Strip**, a traffic corridor loaded with nightclubs, bars, and huge billboards.

Silver Lake and Los Feliz

As the original home to the region's film studios and their elite circles, **Silver Lake** and **Los Feliz** are fitting places to begin a tour of Hollywood. Unfortunately, Silver Lake has not seen fit to preserve very much of its heritage, and it only resembles its former self in a few dusty pockets; on the whole, more noteworthy now for its striking views of the city and fine modern architecture. Los Feliz has preserved a marginally greater proportion of its history and maintains a number of landmark buildings, thanks in no small measure to the financial wherewithal and aesthetic sensibilities of its residents, and remains a pleasantly low-key area that lacks some of the pretension found in the Hollywood Hills to the west.

Silver Lake

Strictly as a body of water, **SILVER LAKE** is not a pretty sight – little more than a utilitarian reservoir, built in 1907, just before the area around it briefly became LA's movie capital. The neighborhood which bears the same name, however, features a number of fine homes and soaring views of the LA basin. With its wealthy white denizens occupying the hills, Silver Lake's poorer Hispanic residents tend to congregate near Sunset Boulevard not far from the old studios. Rich or poor, though, both communities include a sizable gay population, and the overall mix gives the area a certain contemporary vitality.

Silver Lake and Los Feliz

Silver Lake's hills rise just to the west around the reservoir. From the aptly-named **Apex Street**, wealthy residents are afforded great views of the city, which you can get too, if you don't mind driving up the precipitously steep incline to reach the top. Closer to the lake, a cluster of austere houses by one of LA's preeminent modernists, Richard Neutra, can be found at **Neutra Place**, a small spur just south of the intersection of Glendale and Silver Lake boulevards; further south, the area around the intersection of **Sunset and Silver Lake boulevards** is the dynamic, if seedy, heart of the neighborhood, with grubby-chic dance clubs, dingy bars, and a range of cheap restaurants.

Silver Lake is bordered to the east by an area once known as **EDENDALE**, another early home to movie studios. Although most of the district's history has been paved over, a symbol of its fleeting glory is at 1712 Glendale Boulevard, now a storage facility but once the studio where movie pioneer Mack Sennett's former **Keystone Film Company** employed such legends as Fatty Arbuckle, Charlie Chaplin, Gloria Swanson, and the Keystone Kops, using much of the surrounding terrain for shooting locations. If you're a devotee of Laurel and Hardy, you may wish to wander south to one such location on Vendome Street, where near no. 930 a **long stairway** saw the duo trying to move a grand piano up its incline, in the 1932 film *The Music Box*.

The early history of the movie business is discussed at length on pp.328–330.

Los Feliz

Named after nineteenth-century soldier and landowner José Feliz, **LOS FELIZ** is a residential neighborhood of fairly mixed ethnicity, including large contingents of Hispanics and gays, though it was once all home to the glittering mansions of movie stars and studio bosses, a legacy that has left it with no small amount of eye-opening architecture.

Just northwest of Silver Lake and occupying a prime perch below Griffith Park, the district numbered among its 1920s denizens Cecil B DeMille, W C Fields, and Walt Disney, who also had his first studio at 4649 Kingswell Ave, just off the bend in Hollywood Boulevard. Other early movie companies had facilities in the area, including the current **KCET Studios**, 4401 Sunset Blvd, which was constructed in 1912 and is Hollywood's oldest film studio in continuous use, and the old **Vitagraph Studios**, which has been reincarnated as the **ABC**

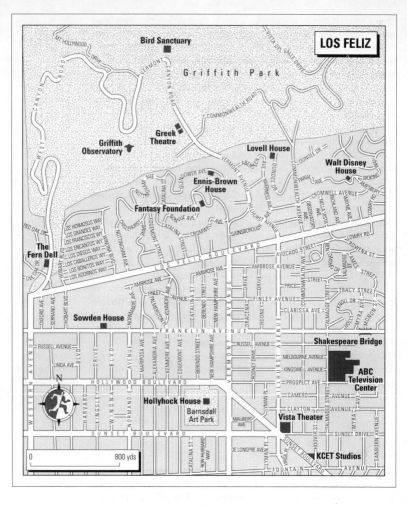

Television Center, 4151 Prospect Ave (call ☎ 310/557-777 for free tickets to see a television show, the only way to visit). More evocative is the **Vista Theater**, at the convergence of Sunset and Hollywood boulevards, a recently renovated, quasi-Egyptian neighborhood moviehouse near where film pioneer **D W Griffith** constructed his Babylonian set for the 1916 film *Intolerance*, which cost $2 million and employed fifteen thousand extras. The movie was a parable about social bigotry and a response to critics of his earlier hit, *The Birth of a Nation*, which glorified the Ku Klux Klan; however, audiences were largely intolerant of *Intolerance*, and as a reminder of the movie's failure, the colossal film set (featuring elephant statues, hanging gardens, and massive pillars) sat for three years at the intersection, becoming a perverse tourist attraction.

Just after the movie set's destruction, **Frank Lloyd Wright** began constructing a house up the road, on a picturesque hillside overlooking the city, the **Hollyhock House**, 4800 Hollywood Blvd (hourly tours Tues–Sun noon–3pm; $2). Completed in 1921, covered with Mayan motifs and imbued with Art Deco fervor, it's an intriguingly obsessive dwelling, whose original furniture (now replaced by detailed reconstructions) continued the conceptual flow. The bizarre quality of the building was obviously too much for its oil heiress owner, Aline Barnsdall, who lived here only for a short time before donating both the house and the surrounding land to the city authorities for use as a cultural center. In keeping with this wish, the grounds of the house became known as **Barnsdall Art Park**, in which the **Municipal Art Gallery** (Wed–Sun 12.30–5pm, Friday until–8.30pm; $1.50) was erected to give exposure to new Southern Californian artists. Other cultural attractions at the site include the **Barnsdall Arts Center** (Mon–Thurs 9.30am–9.30pm, Fri–Sat 9.30am–4pm; free), featuring arts and crafts in assorted media from photography to jewelry; and the **Junior Arts Center** (Mon–Fri 10am–5pm, Sat 10.30am–2pm; free), showing off local children's art of, not surprisingly, wildly varying quality. If you've no interest in art or architecture, the park is still worth a visit as one of the few quiet spots around here to enjoy a view: the Hollywood Hills in one direction, all of Downtown LA and beyond in the other.

Further into the residential heart of Los Feliz, the **Shakespeare Bridge** on Franklin Avenue near St George Street, a 1925 charmer with small Gothic arches and turrets, leads toward the **Walt Disney House**, 4053 Woking Way, an oversized cartoon cottage that calls to mind its former owner's films as well as his secretive nature, inaccessible as it is perched on its high slope. Further into the hills, Richard Neutra's **Lovell House**, 4616 Dundee Drive, is a set of sleek, white rectangles and broad window bands that looks quite contemporary for a 1929 building. Much more garish and bizarre are the **Sowden House**, 5121 Franklin Ave, a pink box with concrete jaws designed by Frank Lloyd Wright's son Lloyd, and the **Ennis-Brown House**, 2655 Glendower Ave, the elder Wright's own pre-Columbian monster looming over the Los Feliz hillside, a fascinating experiment in so-called "knit-block" design, comprising hundreds of bulky concrete blocks, that looks like a monumental Mayan temple. Unlike most of the area's houses, which are well-guarded fortresses, the Ennis-Brown House is open to the public bimonthly throughout the year (tours are $10, or $5 for students and kids, and are available only by reservation; ☎213/668-0234).

Not far away, at 2495 Glendower Ave, the **Fantasy Foundation** (daily 10am–4pm; free) boasts a truly amazing hoard of more than 300,000 items of horror, fantasy, and sci-fi memorabilia. Forrest J

Ackerman, former editor of *Famous Monsters of Filmland* magazine and winner of science fiction's first Hugo award, has filled eighteen rooms of his "Ackermansion" with such delights as the robot from *Metropolis*, the facial molds of Boris Karloff, Bela Lugosi, and Lon Chaney, the Creature from the Black Lagoon, and the fake breasts worn by Jane Fonda in *Barbarella*. Sixty-nine years in the making, this is a unique collection enhanced by the draw of the man himself: numerous personal anecdotes and bits of gossip make his one-on-one tour a must.

Griffith Park

Griffith Park, north of Los Feliz, is the nation's largest municipal park, a sprawling combination of gentle greenery and rugged mountain slopes acquired by mining millionaire **Griffith J Griffith** in 1884. Almost immediately, Griffith wanted to be rid of it, but could find no buyers and, in 1896, deeded the space to the city for public recreation, since which it has become a standard field trip for grade-school kids and a requisite stop for anyone taking a trip through Hollywood.

In its five square miles, the park contains 53 miles of **trails** and many facilities for natural explorations and excursions. Near the entrance to the park off of Los Feliz Boulevard, Fern Dell Drive leads into the **Fern Dell**, a bucolic glade of ferns that acts as a border between the park to the east and an exclusive neighborhood to the west. Along Canyon Drive to the northwest, a hiking trail leads past a rock quarry to the lush **azalea gardens**, tucked away in an often untraveled section of the park. Further north, the **Sunset Ranch**, 3400 N Beachwood Dr, provides evening horse rides through the area for $35 by reservation (☎213/469-5450), and the **LA Equestrian Center**, just across the LA River, offers horse rentals for $15 or evening rides for $33, with a barbecue to boot (☎818/840-8401).

If you'd rather just view the park's animals, instead of ride them, you can do so at the **bird sanctuary**, on Vermont Canyon Road (daily during daylight hours; free). Caged animals, meanwhile, are plentiful in the **LA Zoo**, 5333 Zoo Drive (daily 10am–5pm; $8.25, kids $3.25), one of the biggest zoos in the country and home to more than 1600 creatures, dividing its animals by continent first, with pens representing various parts of the world. Although some renovation has recently improved the zoo, it's still not terribly impressive, especially in comparison to its San Diego counterpart, two hours south. The park also has a **recreation center**, Los Feliz Boulevard at Riverside Drive (☎213/665-4372), offering a swimming pool and various indoor and outdoor sports, and a **ranger station**, 4730 Crystal Springs Rd (daily during daylight hours), with information and maps on hiking paths. To bike around the park, rentals are available at **Woody's Bicycle World**, 3157 Los Feliz Blvd (☎213/661-6665).

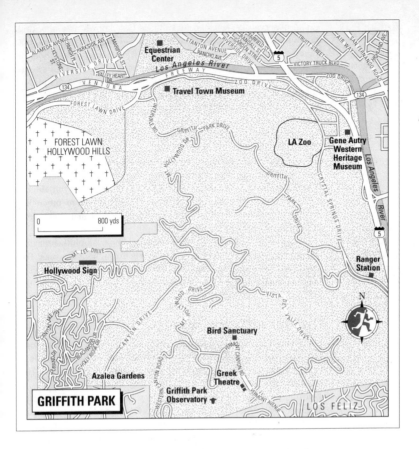

The Griffith Observatory and Greek Theatre

The **Griffith Observatory** is unquestionably one of LA's icons, a domed Art Deco monument to science and a perennial favorite of Hollywood filmmakers, who have made its PWA Moderne silhouette known to most everyone. Just after the turn of the century, Griffith J Griffith offered $700,000 to the city to build the observatory and theater on the parkland he had previously donated. The city declined, principally because "the Colonel," as he was known, had just been released from California's San Quentin Prison for trying to murder his wife – a 1903 incident in which Griffith, drunk and deluded with the wild idea that his wife was orchestrating a papal conspiracy, shot Mary Griffith through the eye. Although convicted of attempted murder, Griffith only spent a year in prison, and it wasn't until 1919, after his death, that LA finally took his money and later built the observatory and theater.

A review of
Rebel Without a
Cause *appears
in "LA on
Film," p.330.*

The observatory, finished in 1935, is best known as a shooting location for Nicholas Ray's classic film *Rebel Without a Cause*, but it has appeared in many other movies as well, ranging from modern action films like *The Terminator* to numerous B-grade 1950s sci-fi flicks. There are moderately interesting science shows in its **planetarium** (Tues–Fri 3–7.30pm, Sat–Sun 1.30–7.30pm, shows every 90min; $4); the **Hall of Science** (daily 12.30–10pm, in winter opens Tues–Fri at 2pm and closed Mon; free), displays curiosities like a cloud chamber, Foucault's pendulum, and Tesla coil; the **Laserium** (Sun–Thurs 6pm & 8.45pm, Fri–Sat & various holidays 6pm, 8.45pm & 9.45pm; $7), shows the type of laser-beam rock concerts that typically attract druggy teens; and a powerful **telescope** sits mounted on the roof (daily 7–10pm; free). One Saturday a month at 1pm, the LA Astronomical Society gathers on the front lawn, and its members set up their telescopes to see the sun through filters and chat about planets and stars with passersby.

*Ticket infor-
mation for the
Greek Theatre
can be found
on p.271.*

Not far away is the **Greek Theatre**, an open-air amphitheater that offers rock, country, and classical concerts throughout the year. The unimpressive design for the theater is said to be Griffith's, though it was not until 1930, eleven years after the Colonel's death, that the structure was completed.

Griffith Park's museums

On the north side of the park, several **museums** compete for visitors' attention, with varying degrees of success. The most worthwhile is undoubtedly the **Gene Autry Western Heritage Museum**, 4700 Western Heritage Way (Tues–Sun 10am–5pm; $7, students $5), bearing the name of the "singing cowboy" who cut over six-hundred records from 1929, starred in numerous Hollywood Westerns during the height of the studio era, and had his own television show in the 1950s. Displaying a large and comprehensive collection of artifacts relating to the American West, the museum includes engaging sections on native peoples, European exploration, nineteenth-century pioneers, the Wild West, Asian immigrants, and, of course, Hollywood's versions of all of the above. Catholic missionaries, gun-slinging criminals, tribal medicine men, Romantic painters, and Tinseltown directors are but a few of the colorful figures the museum honors, and sometimes criticizes.

*The more-
famous Forest
Lawn Glendale
cemetery is
profiled on
p.189.*

Somewhat less intriguing is the nostalgic **Travel Town Museum**, 5200 Zoo Drive (daily 10am–5pm; free), touted as a transportation museum but more a dumping ground for old trains and fire trucks, most of them presented without context or full explanation. Bounding Griffith Park's northwest rim, **Forest Lawn Hollywood Hills**, 6300 Forest Lawn Drive, is a cemetery of the stars that, while not quite as awe-inspiringly vulgar as its Glendale counterpart, is no less pretentious, with showy grave-markers and fancy memorials indicating the importance of each celebrity in the Hollywood firmament. Luminaries like **Buster Keaton, Stan Laurel, Ernie Kovacs, George Raft**, and **Liberace** can be found here, along with the likes of **Andy Gibb** and **Jack Webb**.

Hollywood Boulevard

From the 101 freeway to the edge of West Hollywood, **Hollywood Boulevard** is movie history incarnate, with renovated movie palaces sitting near noted hangouts for the stars of old, and crowds of tourists poring over the famous and infamous locales where legendary Tinseltown wonder boys and girls used to carouse, and occasionally overdose.

Although the hills to its north and the flatland to its south hold much interest, the boulevard itself contains the great majority of Hollywood's most popular and best-known attractions. With the densest concentration of faded glamour and film mythology in the world, a pervasive sense of nostalgia makes the area deeply appealing in a way no measure of commercialism can diminish.

West from Barnsdall Park in Los Feliz, few engaging sights greet travelers on this side of the 101 freeway, other than the fascinating

debacle of LA's ongoing **Metrorail** construction (see box below), but once you cross the freeway and reach Gower Street, you enter the glamour stretch of Hollywood Boulevard – the section up to La Brea Avenue. An unofficial dividing line between the east and west sides of this historic district is **Highland Avenue**, which also runs through the heart of the area.

East of Highland Avenue

Perhaps the nucleus of Hollywood nostalgia, the intersection of **Hollywood and Vine** was said to be the place for unknowns to be "discovered" by movie bosses and self-described big shots. Naturally, this was based more on rumor than fact, but the legend spread because real movie stars, such as Tom Mix and Rudolph Valentino, were often spotted in the area, feeding the frenzy that this "crossroads of the stars" was a good place to get a career boost from a Hollywood luminary. Nowadays, relatively few loiter at the spot waiting to be discovered, but many visitors do come to trace the **Walk of Fame**, which officially begins at the junction, a series of metallic stars inlaid into the sidewalk and honoring various celebrities of the past and present. The laying of the stars began in 1960, instigated by

---

LA's mass transit troubles

In recent years, LA has been plagued by colossal transportation problems, its freeways carrying the nation's heaviest volume of traffic. Even when gridlock doesn't occur, average highway speeds continue to drop to the 11mph average that analysts have predicted for the early part of the next century. Although the city once had a mass transit system – the **Red Cars** that old-timers remember fondly – it's been a metropolis built around freeways since the 1950s. In 1988, the Metropolitan Transit Authority (MTA), began work on the **Red Line**, a subway project that was planned to carry riders from Downtown to the San Fernando Valley. Sharing a colorful name is thus far the only thing the old and new mass transit systems have had in common. Not only has Red Line construction been plagued by political problems (US Representative Henry Waxman has reportedly forbidden the train to travel down the Wilshire corridor beyond Western Avenue, where it is most needed), it has also led to traffic nightmares, exorbitant cost overruns, and occasional chaos. In 1994, thanks to dubious construction work and subsiding earth, a section of Hollywood Boulevard collapsed into a giant **sinkhole**. This humiliating episode made national news but was by no means the end of the problems; indeed, the concrete lining of the subway tunnels was later found to be about half the width required for proper earthquake protection. Along with this, large chunks of the boulevard were found to be sinking as much as half a foot. Despite all this, the MTA continued to funnel huge sums of money into the system, reportedly as much as $6 billion, and the Red Line has pressed on, gobbling sections of the street while moving on to new terrain under the Cahuenga Pass and Universal City. Transit stations on the line are scheduled to open during 1999 and 2000.

---

the local Chamber of Commerce, which thought that by enshrining the big names in radio, television, movies, music, and theater, it could somehow restore the boulevard's faded glamour and boost tourism, but in fact the sidewalk honors are more a matter of money than talent, and many celebrities have to part with several thousand dollars for the privilege of being included, among them Marlon Brando (1717 Vine St), Marlene Dietrich (6400 Hollywood Blvd), Elvis Presley (6777 Hollywood Blvd) and Ronald Reagan (6374 Hollywood Blvd).

Just north of the intersection, on Vine Street, are a small cache of historic pop culture buildings. The most familiar, the **Capitol Records Tower**, 1750 Vine St, resembles a stack of now-defunct 45-rpm records and continues to serve as the music company's headquarters (although the building will soon undergo a facelift and expansion). Allegedly, its 1950s design derives from an offhand suggestion by composer Johnny Mercer, although this story is probably more Tinseltown legend than fact. Nearby, at 6233 Hollywood Blvd, the 1929 **Pantages Theater** has a rather colorless facade but a stunning Baroque interior, though you'll have to buy a show ticket to see for yourself.

Around the corner, a bit of literary history can be found at 1817 Ivar Ave, the site of the fleabag rooming house where author and screenwriter **Nathanael West** lived during the 1930s after coming west to revive his flagging financial situation. (The author vividly described Ivar Street as "Lysol Alley.") Gazing over the street's assortment of extras, hustlers, and make-believe cowboys, he penned the classic satirical portrait of Hollywood, *The Day of the Locust*, the apocalyptic finale of which was inspired by West's viewing of Hollywood Hills wildfires in the summer of 1935. Across the street, the former **Knickerbocker Hotel**, 1714 Ivar Ave, is now an old people's retirement center, but was once where the widow of legendary magician Harry Houdini conducted a rooftop seance in an attempt to help him make the greatest escape of all. During the 1930s and 1940s, the hotel had a reputation for rooming some of Hollywood's more unstable characters and hosting a number of aerial suicides.

Further down Ivar Avenue, at no. 1623, the **Francis Howard Library**, a branch of LA's library system, designed by Frank Gehry, is a depressingly successful attempt at fortress architecture, with blank walls, faceless facades, and maximum security above all else. More inviting is the **Janes House**, 6541 Hollywood Blvd, a 1903 Queen Anne dwelling that has not only managed to survive the century, but has also become the home of the Hollywood **visitors center** (daily 9am–5pm).

On a more risqué note, the purple-and-pink **Frederick's of Hollywood**, no. 6608, sells racy lingerie and offers visitors a glimpse of famous undergarments from the 1940s to the present in its lingerie museum (Mon–Sat 10am–6pm, Sun noon–5pm; free), where the centerpiece of the collection is the Celebrity Lingerie Hall of Fame, featuring the underclothing of many different movie, TV, and pop music stars: Zsa Zsa Gabor's girdle, Cyd Charisse's leotard, Ava Gardner's skirt, and Madonna's bustier, among many others. Frederick's was one of the stranger targets in the city's 1992 riots, in which bandits made off with a clutch of celebrity skivvies. Untouched in the violence were the dining booths of the Musso and Frank Grill across the street, no. 6667, a 1919 restaurant that has been a fixture since the days of silent cinema. Here, famous writers, actors, and studio bosses would meet to slap backs, cut deals, and drink potent lunches. It's no accident that this was the place where, in Tim Burton's *Ed Wood*, the title character – notorious B-movie director of *Plan 9 from Outer Space* – goes to drown his sorrows, only to encounter a loaded Orson Welles doing the same thing.

Restaurants in Hollywood are listed beginning on p.247.

Likewise, theater king Sid Grauman's Egyptian Theater, no. 6712, embodies the spirit of a distant age. Built in 1922, the theater is a classically garish example of the heroic age of movie palace architecture, when vulgarity could be triumphant and fun, with a pseudo-ancient forecourt, "hieroglyphic" murals, and grand auditorium decorated with sunbursts and an iconic winged scarab. Neglected for decades, and damaged by earthquakes and vandalism, the building was closed in 1992 but has been renovated and is now the headquarters of the American Cinematheque organization, showing a range of documentaries, foreign films, and classic Hollywood productions.

Unless you've nothing else to do with the kids, avoid the neon-lit buildings to the theater's west, all flash and no substance: The Guinness Book of World Records, no. 6764 (daily 10am–midnight, Fri–Sat closes at 2am; $9), Ripley's Believe It or Not, no. 6780 (daily 10am–11pm; $9), and the Hollywood Wax Museum, no. 6767 (daily 10am–midnight, Fri–Sat closes at 2am; $8.25), of which only the Wax Museum provides a shred of interest, mostly for the kitsch value of seeing Elvis or Bogie as a pallid mannequin.

A few blocks north, the Hollywood Studio Museum, 2100 N Highland Ave (Sat–Sun 10am–4pm; $4), occupies a historic horse barn, which originally stood at the corner of Selma and Vine streets.

The trio of DeMille, Lasky, and Goldwyn gave rise to Paramount Studios; for the lowdown, see pp.328–329.

In 1913, Cecil B DeMille, Jesse Lasky, and Sam Goldfish (later Goldwyn) rented one half of the structure while the barn's owner continued to stable horses in the other. From this base, the three collaborated to make *The Squaw Man*, Hollywood's first true feature film; although copies of the film are long gone, the movie's success propelled them to move their operation – including the barn itself – to the current Paramount lot at Marathon Street and Van Ness Avenue. Later, the barn was moved to its current location to become a public monument to Hollywood history, and it now displays clothing and props from old studio films, original Bell & Howell cameras of the silent era, and other knickknacks from early filmmaking days.

West of Highland Avenue

Mann's **Chinese Theatre**, 6925 Hollywood Blvd, is the focal point of
tourist activity in Hollywood, and it looks the part, with its outlandish
dragon reliefs, ancient-looking wallpaper (with pictures of stags,
herons, and wise men), spiky Oriental motifs, imposing columns, and
a plush, dark-red design throughout. Originally the property of **Sid
Grauman**, a local P T Barnum of movie exhibitors who, with the
Egyptian Theater down the block and other such properties, established a reputation for creating garish movie palaces with gloriously
vulgar designs based on exotic themes. Because the theater hasn't
been extensively remodeled, you can still appreciate its 1927 chinoiserie splendor (with several thousand other visitors on any given
day) by buying a ticket or freely wandering around the forecourt,
where legend tells that actress Norma Talmadge once "blindly"
strode into its wet cement. With this intentional action, movie history
was made, and from the end of the silent era to the present, stars
from Mary Pickford to Al Pacino have plunged their palms into the
soft cement, and have consequently made this theater an obligatory
stop on the tourist circuit.

*To catch a
current film in
an old movie
palace, see the
listings on
p.283.*

Similarly, the **El Capitan Theater**, no. 6834, is a colorful 1926
movie palace, with a Baroque and Moorish design and wild South
Seas interior of sculpted angels and garlands. In recent years, a
restoration has brought back the facility's full glory, and has once
again illuminated one of LA's great marquees, a multicolored profusion of flashing bulbs and neon tubes. The theater mostly shows
Disney cartoons and comedies, which even if you're not up for, are
worth the price of a ticket to glimpse the grand old Hollywood architecture.

The nearby **Hollywood Roosevelt** hotel, no. 7000, provides even
more movie nostalgia, its History of Hollywood exhibit, on the second floor, displaying photographs, props, and filmmaking equipment from eight decades of Tinseltown history. Just as enticing is the
hotel itself, home to the *Cinegrill* restaurant, a watering-hole once
frequented by legendary drinkers such as W C Fields and William
Faulkner and now also serving as a cabaret. In 1929, the first
Academy Awards were presented here, and the building is said to be
haunted by the ghost of Montgomery Clift, who has been known to
whisper in the ears of hotel guests.

The Cinegrill *is
also a major
cabaret venue;
see p.280 in
"Performing
Arts and Film"
for details.*

Across the street, the **Hollywood Entertainment Museum**, no.
7021, in the lower level of the Hollywood Galaxy Building (Tues–Sun
10am–6pm; $7.50), presents less spectral amusements, such as the
full set of the TV show *Cheers* and the bridge of the Enterprise from
Star Trek, along with rotating exhibitions and various curiosities
from Hollywood history. The museum's real jewel is the **Max Factor
Collection**, a display of beauty artifacts from Hollywood's Golden
Age that was formerly housed in its own building on Highland
Avenue. From the early glop used for actors under the nasty klieg

lights of the time to up-to-the-minute scientifically designed formulas, the collection presents makeup from different historical eras and also features the famed "beauty calibrator," which was supposed to engineer the perfect facial design for actors but actually resembles something out of a horror flick, a ghoulish-looking head cage containing rows of measuring pins that poke in at the wearer's skin.

To catch a peek at a current Hollywood production, visit the nearby **Motion Picture Production Office**, no. 6922 at Room 602 (Mon–Fri 8am–5pm), which issues a free "shoot sheet" every weekday from 10.30am, detailing exactly what's being filmed around town that day. Most film shoots hire a couple of off-duty LAPD officers for "security," but not all sets are impenetrable.

Hollywood Boulevard's historic stretch largely ends where it hits La Brea Avenue, at which corner stands a metallic sculpture of movie goddesses Dorothy Dandridge, Dolores del Rio, Anna May Wong, and Mae West. For a respite from the Hollywood scene, the **Wattles House and Park**, 1824 N Curson Ave (house by appointment only; ☎213/874-4005), is a relaxing spot at the edge of the Hollywood Hills. This 1907 estate contains an expansive manor house and a small city park with picturesque grounds and palm trees. The park is usually accessible; the house is somewhat more difficult to visit, though no less interesting, with its Mission Revival design, impressive front arcade, and Craftsman detailing.

Back on Hollywood Boulevard, the strip becomes more residential until it finally disappears into the hills past Laurel Canyon Boulevard, which forms the western boundary of the district itself. There's not much to see other than Frank Lloyd Wright's Mayan-inspired **Storer House**, 8161 Hollywood Blvd, stylized pre-Columbian blocks set on an imposing hillside perch that, unfortunately, can only be viewed from the street: high-rolling movie producer and owner Joel Silver doesn't let inquisitive folks get past the driveway.

Sunset and Santa Monica boulevards

Although Hollywood Boulevard is the undisputed center of Hollywood history and tourism, the area around **Sunset** and **Santa Monica boulevards** was the actual focus of the film industry. At the start of this century, these streets hosted five of the seven major film studios (minus MGM and Universal), but by the 1930s, four of the studios had left due to limited studio space in the area. Cities like Burbank, for example, offered huge parcels of land to these studios, with lower taxes than LA, and only **Paramount** stayed in its Hollywood location.

Today, both these streets are less touristy than Hollywood Boulevard, with more modest and intermittent attractions; however, they remain a crucial part of a completist's trip through Hollywood nostalgia. For most visitors to the area, the interesting spots are grouped in pockets and should be explored by car, not on foot.

Sunset Boulevard

Famous as the title of the classic 1950 movie that featured Gloria Swanson as an aging, predatory movie star, **Sunset Boulevard** runs through Hollywood into West Hollywood, where it becomes the colorful Sunset Strip. Along with **RKO Studios** to the south, three film-making giants left sizable holes in the street's cultural landscape when they departed over six decades ago. Within a twelve-block distance from Western Avenue to Gower Street, **Warner Brothers** (1918-29), **Columbia** (1920-1934), and **William Fox Studios** (1924-35) marked the American film industry's early ascent, though all their studio buildings have been changed, destroyed, or rendered unrecognizable by their current owners – although the Warner Brothers facility, 5858 Sunset Blvd, is now locally familiar as the home of a TV station. Other, smaller studios also occupied space along Sunset, and many actors would frequently try to get the attention of movie producers or casting directors by loitering around the corner of Sunset and Gower Street, the so-called **Gower Gulch**. Here, film extras in need of a few days' work would make appearances in the hope of being hired for the latest B-grade Western. The gulch's air of desperation earned it the moniker "Poverty Row," which also collectively described the town's smaller studios, such as nearby Columbia.

Adjacent to the old Warner Brothers studios, the **Hollywood Palladium**, 6215 Sunset Blvd, was best known for hosting the big names in swing, jazz, and big band music, notably Glenn Miller, and the place still puts on concerts today. Down a few blocks, at no. 6360, the white concrete **Cinerama Dome** is an unmistakable sight, its hemispheric auditorium containing a monumental movie screen. The dome was originally built to accommodate the three-projector Cinerama films sweeping Hollywood at the end of the 1950s, but the movie fad faded even before the theater was completed, and today it still projects films on, alternately, curved and flat screens. Around the time the dome was completed, the Spanish Revival **Hollywood Athletic Club**, no. 6525, was closing its doors. From 1923, the club was a favorite of the likes of Charlie Chaplin, Clark Gable, John Barrymore, and Johnny "Tarzan" Weismuller and featured an Olympic-sized pool and equally Olympic drinking parties. Perhaps the most colorful antics of the club's Hollywood guests belonged to John Wayne: often either pitching pool balls at passing cars or pummeling wooden doors. After 1958, the club became a Jewish seminary and university before it was closed twenty years later. In the 1990s, it has been reopened as a recreational club for young celebrities, with some of its current clientele engaging in behavior that might have made "the Duke" himself proud.

On a less sordid note, **Crossroads of the World**, no. 6672, Robert Derrah's 1930s hybrid of Tudor, Italian, French, Spanish Colonial, and Streamline Moderne styles, with most buildings in the complex designed in different styles, is a small, early version of an outdoor shopping mall – one of the rare appealing designs of that ilk. A not-so-welcome mall stands at 7101 Sunset Blvd, better known as the former site of **Tiny Naylor's**, a memorable diner (with car hops) in the "Googie" style – neon lights, boomerang angles, and bright colors. Less than a block away, the **Charlie Chaplin Studio**, 1416 N La Brea Ave, was a 1918 creation, built a year before he teamed with other celebrities to create the United Artists studio. Now owned by Polygram Records, the complex preserves Chaplin's foot imprints near Stage 3. A few blocks to the west, the **Guitar Center**, a musical instrument store, does the same thing for rock stars, with handprints of your favorite guitar wizards – Eddie Van Halen, Slash, and so on. Finally, just before Sunset Boulevard dips into West Hollywood and becomes the famous "Strip," the **Directors Guild of America**, no. 7920, is a modern building that is typical of 1980s design, with shiny geometry and an oversized scale, which provides a number of excellent screening rooms and theaters, some of which are open to the public for special events.

Santa Monica Boulevard

For a street with such a familiar name, **Santa Monica Boulevard** has relatively few noteworthy attractions, at least in Hollywood. A grungy strip with the occasional prostitute and low-end drug dealer, the boulevard is home to sizable communities of Russian immigrants and working-class gays, and does have the distinction of bordering Hollywood's last remaining studio. Still, for modern excitement, you're better off heading to West Hollywood, where the street becomes a bit more lively.

A standard stop on many celebrity-death tours, the **Hollywood Memorial Cemetery**, 6000 Santa Monica Blvd, is actually quite fascinating. In the southeastern corner of the cemetery, the cathedral mausoleum sets a solemn tone for the place and displays a collection of tombs that includes the resting place of **Rudolph Valentino**. In 1926, ten thousand people packed the cemetery when the celebrated screen lover died at 31, and to this day on each anniversary of his passing (August 23), at least one "Lady in Black" will likely be found mourning – a tradition that started as a publicity stunt in 1931 (the first weeping damsel claimed to be a former paramour of Valentino's but was exposed as a hired actress). Fittingly, outside the mausoleum, the most ostentatious grave in the cemetery belongs to **Douglas Fairbanks Sr**, who, with his wife Mary Pickford, did much to introduce social snobbery to Hollywood. Even in death Fairbanks keeps his distance from the pack, his memorial, complete with sculptured pond, only reachable by a shrubbery-lined path from the mausoleum. More lighthearted is the headstone of **Mel Blanc**, "the man of a thousand voices" – among them Bugs Bunny, Porky Pig, and Tweety Pie – whose epitaph simply reads "That's All, Folks."

Sunset and Santa Monica boulevards

South of the cemetery, **Paramount Studios** is the last of the old studio giants, its lot a heterogeneous collection of different chunks of film history. While its facilities are largely closed to the public, the studio's famed **gate**, comprising two great arches with metallic detailing, can be viewed at 5555 Melrose Ave, even though the original studio entrance – which Gloria Swanson rode through in *Sunset Boulevard* – is now inaccessible. The company came into being when Cecil B DeMille, Sam Goldwyn, and Jesse Lasky merged their operation with **Adolph Zukor's Famous Players**, which owned property across Melrose Avenue at 650 N Bronson, and adopted the Paramount name in late 1910s, becoming second in stature only to Culver City's MGM. It soon subsumed the facilities of **RKO Studios** when that company went under, and in its heyday, Paramount churned out more than a hundred films a year and had biggies like the Marx Brothers, Cary Grant, D W Griffith, Marlon Brando, and countless others under contract. In 1967, the conglomerate Gulf & Western devoured the studio but later adopted its name to fully cash in on its snow-capped image and reputation. Today, Paramount has a hand in film, TV, and multimedia and isn't likely to leave its familiar confines any time soon.

There are only two other interesting sights along this stretch of Santa Monica Boulevard, the first of which is the **Formosa Café**, no. 7156, a notorious bar where celebrities, including Humphrey Bogart and Marilyn Monroe, came to drown their sorrows. It's still open, and its colorful ambience, though faded, was put to good use in the recent film *LA Confidential*, in which a city cop mistakenly calls Lana Turner a "two-bit hooker" and for his error receives a splash of booze in the face.

Hollwood's bars are detailed beginning on p.262.

Nearby, at 1041 Formosa Ave, is **Warner Hollywood Studios**, owned by Warner Brothers but until 1975 the home of **United Artists Studios**, built in 1919 as a home to the production company of **Charlie Chaplin** (his second), **Douglas Fairbanks Sr**, **Mary Pickford**, and **D W Griffith**. With their studio as the symbol of the **star system** in the silent era, these four artists controlled their careers through the company, at least for a while, and helped craft the Hollywood marketing machine that sold movies by celebrity appeal, a system that endures to this day.

The Hollywood Hills

Once the exclusive home to Hollywood's glitterati, and still a lofty location for the city's up-and-comers, the **HOLLYWOOD HILLS** are perhaps the best-known urban mountains in the US. Roughly paralleling Hollywood itself, and forming the eastern end of the Santa Monica Mountains chain, these canyons and slopes are filled with prime views of the basin and with your everyday million-dollar mansions, though all are fairly inaccessible. Most of the appealing sights in this area are located just north of Hollywood Boulevard, on narrow, snaking roads that are easy to get lost on. If you want to do serious exploring in these hills, bring a detailed map along to keep from getting yourself hopelessly lost.

The eastern Hollywood Hills

On the eastern side of the area, **Beachwood Drive** heads into the hills north of Franklin Avenue and was the axis of the **Hollywoodland** residential development, a 1920s product of *Los Angeles Times* news baron **Harry Chandler**, who found ample time for real-estate speculation when he wasn't strong-arming city politicians (see p.341). The self-important **stone gates** of the development sit at Beachwood's intersection with Westshire and Belden drives; although the neighborhood is quite relaxing, the chief reason most people come to the area is for the view of the **Hollywood sign** at the top of Mt Lee above. The sign began life as little more than a billboard for the development and originally contained its full name; however, the "land" part was removed in 1945, and the rest has become the familiar symbol of the entertainment industry. The current incarnation has also literally lost its radiance: at one time, the sign featured 4000 light bulbs that beamed the district's name as far away as LA harbor.

Such illumination is a distant memory now, as is the public's easy access to the sign, for it has gained a reputation as a suicide spot, ever since would-be movie star Peg Entwhistle terminated her career and life here in 1932, aged 24. It was no mean feat – the sign being as difficult to reach then as it is now: from the end of Beachwood Drive she picked a path slowly upward through the thick brush and climbed the fifty-foot-high "H," eventually leaping from it to her death. However, stories that this act led a line of failed starlets to make their final exit from Tinseltown's best known marker are untrue – though many troubled souls may have died of exhaustion while trying to get to it. Less fatal mischief has been practiced by students of nearby Cal Tech, who on one occasion took to renaming the sign for their school.

Because of this history, there's no public road to the sign (Beachwood Drive comes nearest, but ends at a closed gate) and you'll incur minor cuts and bruises while scrambling to get anywhere near. In any case, infrared cameras and radar-activated zoom lenses have been installed to catch graffiti writers, and innocent tourists who can't resist a close look are also liable for the $107 fine. It's simply not worth the bother.

If you've seen the disaster epic *Earthquake*, you may remember the **Hollywood Reservoir's** dam bursting and flooding the LA basin; however, this manmade lake is anything but dramatic – just a calm, quiet spot hemmed in among the hills between Griffith Park and the

Hollywood Freeway, good for an afternoon stroll along one of its perimeter's footpaths. If you take such a walk, perhaps to admire the stone bear-heads staring out from the dam walls, you'll encounter surprisingly few tourists, despite the reservoir's appearance in a number of Hollywood films. Although opening and closing times vary widely throughout the year, the **lake access road** is generally open from 7am until noon and 2pm until 7pm on weekdays, and 7am till 7.30pm on weekends: to get to it, go north on Cahuenga Boulevard past Franklin Avenue and turn right onto Dix Street and left to Holly Drive and climb up to Deep Dell Place; from there it's a sharp left on Weidlake Drive. Follow the winding little street to the main gate.

The Hollywood Hills Earthquake, *along with numerous other Los Angeles-oriented films, is reviewed in "LA on Film," pp.331–335.*

Offering a different sort of tranquility, the **Vedanta Temple** (also known as "Little Taj"), 1946 Vedanta Terrace, off Dix Street near the Hollywood Freeway, is a miniature white-domed, golden-spired structure reminiscent of Agra, India. The temple sits in the midst of a residential neighborhood, home to the **Vedanta Society**, a group derived from India's Ramakrishna Order. The land's initial owner, William Mead, was a property developer and patron of the society who gave the site to its members upon his death in 1929; his original 1901 house still sits near the complex, but unless you're a member of the society, you'll probably not be allowed access to the house or the temple.

West across Cahuenga Boulevard, pristine **Whitley Heights** is a small pocket of Spanish Colonial architecture, worth a pass both for its well-maintained houses and great city views. The neighborhood, accessible from Milner Road off Highland Avenue, was laid out by business tycoon **H J Whitley**, an Owens Valley water conspirator who engineered, and profited from, the sale of San Fernando Valley real estate (under his aptly named corporation, "Suburban Homes"). He was also known as the "Father of Hollywood," as his Whitley Heights soon became a movie-star subdivision for such silent-screen greats as Marie Dressler, Gloria Swanson, Rudolph Valentino, and one-time "Ben Hur" Francis X. Bushman – a legacy that has recently earned the area "official" status as a historic zone.

The Hollywood Bowl and around

Just north of Whitley Heights, and west of the Hollywood Freeway, sits the renowned **Hollywood Bowl**, 2301 N Highland Ave (☎213/850-2000), an outdoor auditorium opened in 1921 that principally functions as the summer home of the Los Angeles Philharmonic, which gives evening concerts from July to September. These are far less highbrow than you might imagine, and it's the long-standing practice to eat a picnic on the grounds before making the climb to your seat, but increasingly the food consumption tends to continue throughout the show, often rendering the music barely audible above the crunching of popcorn and the clink of empty wine bottles rolling down the steps. Tickets start at just $1, but if you're really broke, come to the Bowl Tuesday through Friday between 9.30am and noon to listen to rehearsals for free. Near the entrance is the **Hollywood Bowl Museum** (Tues–Sat 10am–4pm, closes in summer at 8.30pm; free), which shows a decent video on the Bowl's history and contains a collection of musical instruments from around the world, along with architectural drawings by the Bowl's designer, Lloyd Wright (Frank's son).

*More informa-
tion on sum-
mer concerts
at the Bowl is
detailed on
p.276.*

One of the elder Wright's memorable 1920s houses, the **Freeman House**, just south of the Bowl at 1962 Glencoe Way (tours Sat 2pm & 4pm; $10, students $5; ☎213/851-0671), doesn't actually seem like much from the outside, done in concrete "knit-blocks." Inside, though, you get an outstanding panoramic view of Hollywood, while Wright's familiar geometric decorations and pre-Columbian motifs are pleasing enough. Another early-1920s design, the **High Tower**, is notable for a different reason. Inaccessible to the public, though viewable at the end of High Tower Drive, the Italian-styled campanile is the literary home of Raymond Chandler's **Philip Marlowe** – and Elliott Gould, playing Marlowe, lived in a dumpy apartment at the tower's apex in Robert Altman's 1973 film *The Long Goodbye*.

*Arnold
Schwarze-
negger and
David
Carridine both
appear in
cameos in* The
Long Goodbye*.*

The western Hollywood Hills

When he was directing *Chinatown*, Roman Polanski spent many hours in Jack Nicholson's house on **Mulholland Drive**, and later remarked of LA, "[t]here's no more beautiful city in the world...provided it's seen at night and from a distance." With its striking panorama of the illuminated city-grid, stretching on seemingly without end, Mulholland easily justifies the director's wry comment.

From its starting point near the 101 freeway to its terminus at LA County's beachside boundary, the road travels 21 miles through winding mountain passes and steep canyons and offers a stunning overview of the region's size and character. The stretch between the 101 and 405 freeways is the best, especially at night, when views of brightly lit LA keep drivers dangerously distracted. Although nighttime parking is forbidden, as well as hazardous, daytime views of the same scenes are best experienced at a **roadside park**, off of

*Mulholland
follows a cir-
cuitous path
deep into the
Santa Monica
mountains; for
a description,
see p.202–203.*

Mulholland Drive just west of Hillside Drive. Here, telescopes allow you to peek at Hollywood, Downtown, and the many palatial homes of the wealthy, including a bizarre red-and-yellow striped house – one of Madonna's former residences (difficult to find in person, near Canyon Lake Drive off of Beachwood Drive).

Further west lies the northern edge of **Runyon Canyon Park**, which actually improves on the views from Mulholland's crest. Park your car in the dirt near its chained gate and wander inside to a rocky outcropping that overlooks the city. Below, a path winds down to closer views of Hollywood until it eventually reaches the base of the hills themselves. Here, the foundation of a **ruined estate** offers a certain decrepit charm amid the high canyon walls and low foliage. If you have the stamina, take the long hike back up the hill to Mulholland; otherwise, exit the park at Vista or Fuller streets and call a cab to take you back up to the top. Follow Mulholland west past the Woodrow Wilson Drive entrance to the elite subdivision of **Mount Olympus**, a residential exercise in 1950s vulgarity that is to neoclassical architecture what a toga party is to ancient drama, with Doric columns and "heroic" sculptures added pell-mell to charmless stucco boxes. Much more appealing in its late-1950s style is the **Chemosphere**, at 776 Torreyson Drive, a giant UFO-like house you can stare at from below, sitting on a huge Space-Age pedestal and overlooking the San Fernando Valley to the north.

Mulholland Drive continues toward a series of enjoyable parks, including **Fryman Canyon Overlook**, a good place for a hike in the adjacent Santa Monica Mountains; and **Coldwater Canyon Park**, which merges with **Wilacre Park** and also provides a solid workout.

West Hollywood

Between La Brea Avenue and Beverly Hills, **WEST HOLLYWOOD** is the newest of LA's constituent cities. For many years the vice capital of LA, with prostitution, gambling, and drugs all occupying prominent places on the debauched **Sunset Strip** and a whole criminal subculture flourishing in the absence of effective law-enforcement and with the tacit approval of lethargic locals, the area was incorporated in 1984, a move meant to serve several functions: to provide a refuge for the area's gay community, protect the interests of pensioners through rent control, and crack down on crime along Sunset.

In the years since, it has done reasonably well in achieving these goals, becoming one of the most dynamic and colorful parts of the region. However, this success has not entirely eliminated strife, and the new waves of Russian and Armenian immigrants making their homes near Santa Monica Boulevard have made for an uneasy mix with the city's traditional constituents. Not surprisingly, West Hollywood is in many ways more akin to less-prosperous Hollywood, in its freewheeling character and attitudes, than it is to the prosaic wealth of Beverly Hills.

Except for the Sunset Strip – the well-known asphalt artery that holds LA's best clubs, bars, and billboards – West Hollywood's principal attractions lie west of **La Cienega Boulevard** around the colossal **Pacific Design Center**. The area to the east generally blends with the less inviting parts of lower Hollywood and has little appeal beyond a few clubs and restaurants.

Details of West Hollywood's bars begin on p.262; clubs on p.267.

The Sunset Strip

Sunset Boulevard from Crescent Heights Boulevard to Doheny Drive, long known as the **Sunset Strip**, is a roughly two-mile long

ACCOMMODATION

Bel Age	5
Chateau Marmont	1
Le Mondrian	2
Le Montrose	8
Le Parc	10
Le Reve	9
Park Sunset	3
Ramada	7
Summerfield Suites	6
Sunset Marquis	4

WEST HOLLYWOOD

conglomeration of chic restaurants, plush hotels, and popular night-clubs. These establishments first began to appear during the early 1920s, along what was then a dusty dirt road serving as the main route between the Hollywood movie studios and the West LA "homes of the stars." F Scott Fitzgerald and friends spent many leisurely afternoons over drinks here, around the swimming pool of the long-demolished *Garden of Allah* hotel, and the nearby *Ciro's* nightclub was *the* place to be seen in the swinging 1940s, surviving today as the original *Comedy Store*. With the rise of TV, the Strip declined, only reviving in the 1960s when a scene developed around the land-mark *Whisky-a-Go-Go* club, which featured seminal psychedelic rock bands such as Love and Buffalo Springfield during the heyday of West Coast flower power. Since the incorporation of West Hollywood, the striptease clubs and "head shops" have been phased out, along with the attendant crime and vice, and this fashionable area now rivals Beverly Hills for entertainment-industry executives per square foot.

Some tourists come to the strip just to see the enormous **bill-boards**, which take advantage of a very permissive long-standing municipal policy. The ruddy-faced and reassuring Marlboro Man is now a fixture, but there are many more along the strip that consistently re-invent the medium: fantastic commercial murals animated with eye-catching gimmicks, movie ads with stars' names in gargantuan letters, and self-promotions for mysterious actresses – note the amply-bosomed "Angelyne" looming in Day-Glo splendor.

The Strip starts in earnest at the **Chateau Marmont Hotel**, 8221 Sunset Blvd, famous for its bungalows and chic clientele – among them numerous Hollywood celebrities from the 1920s to the present – and infamous as the spot where John Belushi died of a heroin overdose, its grim Norman exterior adding to the Strip's dark atmosphere. Across the street, the **House of Blues**, no. 8430, is a corrugated tin shack that is one of the area's chief tourist attractions, although it pales in comparison with the more authentic scene found around the **Whisky-a-Go-Go**, no. 8901, and the **Roxy**, no. 9009, both famed for 1960s performers like Janis Joplin and bands like The Doors. Although these clubs have survived recent decades, others have long since disappeared, like **Gazzarri's**, no. 9039, famous for hosting acts such as Van Halen, the Byrds, and Guns N' Roses early on in their careers; it's now *Billboard Live* dance club. Newer venues like the **Viper Room**, no. 8852, and the **Sunset Hyatt**, no. 8401, have already established their own sordid histories – Johnny Depp's trendy lair for rockers is the spot where River Phoenix OD'd, and the upscale hotel was the staging ground for the lurid antics of Led Zeppelin and The Who. Moreover, some famous spots have been sharply renovated to evoke the past. The former **Sunset Tower**, no. 8358, a 1929 Art Deco monument with radiator-grill decorations over its garage and sixteen stories of refurbished splendor, has become the *Argyle* hotel, with no real loss of its original design or character.

See "Live Music," p.270, for some background on the LA music scene.

La Cienega Boulevard

La Cienega Boulevard is the cultural dividing line between Hollywood's funky seediness to the east and West LA's snooty affluence to the west, featuring excellent hotels, clubs, and restaurants and hosting an array of lively record and book stores along Melrose Avenue and Santa Monica Boulevard. Still, the real focus is Cesar Pelli's **Pacific Design Center**, 8687 Melrose Ave, a hulking complex known as the "Blue Whale," loaded with interior design boutiques and furniture dealers. The entire center is now open to the public for viewing, but purchasing anything inside requires the assistance of a professional designer, which few visitors are likely to have in tow. Still, you're likely to be satisfied with just a snoop around, not so much in the octagonal, green-paneled **Center Green**, but in **Center Blue**, a blue-paneled barn offering a mix of vast showrooms and intimate boutiques that can be explored in near-solitude. Outside the center, a small **amphitheater** inset with **stars** honors architects and designers like Frank Gehry, Lawrence Halprin, and Pelli himself.

A full listing of LA's galleries can be found starting on p.313.

Other architectural novelties exist on the surrounding streets, not least of which is the **Margo Leavin Gallery**, 817 N Hilldale Ave; an art center with a facade featuring a Claes Oldenburg-designed knife blade of giant proportions cutting through the stucco. To the west, at 858 N Doheny Drive, the 1928 **Wright House** was created by Frank's son Lloyd and features a bulky concrete-block design and pre-Columbian decoration – a small counterpart to Frank's monumental Ennis-Brown House in the Hollywood Hills (see p.106).

Back east of La Cienega Boulevard, the **Schindler House**, 835 N Kings Rd (Wed–Sun 11am–6pm, tours by appointment ☎213/651-1510; $5 donation), was for years the blueprint of California modernist architecture, with sliding canvas panels designed to be removed in summer, exposed roof rafters, and open-plan rooms facing onto outdoor terraces. Coming from his native Austria via Frank Lloyd Wright's studio to work on the Hollyhock House (see p.91), R M Schindler was so pleased with the California climate that he built this house without any bedrooms, romantically planning to sleep outdoors year-round in covered sleeping baskets on the roof. However, like other newcomers unfamiliar with the region's erratic climate, he misjudged the weather and soon moved inside.

Chapter 5

Beverly Hills and West LA

Although Downtown has the skyscrapers and Hollywood the history, it's **BEVERLY HILLS** and **WEST LA** where tourists tend to spend most of their time. Not only do these areas, along with West Hollywood, boast the best hotels and restaurants, they relentlessly – and successfully – market themselves as the height of LA chic, in this case little more than a stylized European flair that, under the facade, lacks any of the "real" flavor of, say, Melrose Avenue. Of course, with its interesting architecture and plentiful gardens, there's more to **Beverly Hills** than just the elite boutiques of Rodeo Drive, but for most visitors, the entire focus of the area lies within the three sides of the shopping zone known as the **Golden Triangle**. Above Beverly Hills, the canyon roads lead into the well-guarded enclaves of rich celebrities, while to the west, the bleak modern towers of **Century City** loom in the distance – the ultimate anti-pedestrian urban design.

West LA has a somewhat amorphous definition, anything from a small neighborhood by the 405 freeway to everything west of Hollywood and Mid-Wilshire. Locals, however, recognize it as the area between Beverly Hills and Santa Monica, stretching south to the 10 freeway. One of West LA's main districts, **Westwood**, somewhat resembles Century City along Wilshire Boulevard, in this part of town a sunless chasm running between towering office blocks. However, closer to UCLA, the so-called "Village" suddenly becomes pedestrian-friendly and the university itself is full of nice buildings and somewhat provocative public art, a welcome respite from its surrounding areas. To the west, along the **Sepulveda Pass**, the wooded wealth of **Bel Air** and **Brentwood** are split by the 405 freeway, which leads to the hilltop site of the new **Getty Center**, a travertine icon of monumental proportions that promises to be LA's greatest artistic center. A southern neighbor, **Culver City**, is far less conspicuous than its West LA counterparts, even though it contains several movie studios and a trove of wild, deconstructivist architecture.

A color map of Beverly Hills and West LA can be found in the insert at the back of this book.

Beverly Hills

BEVERLY HILLS is inextricably linked with images of suntanned Ferrari drivers, fur-clad poodle-walkers, and outrageously priced consumer goods, illustrating how successful this city has been in marketing itself to the rest of the world – and in drawing visitors by the millions. Inevitably, this self-promotion doesn't quite match reality, but if you've come to town for the experience of fawning over celebrities and pressing your nose against the display windows, you probably won't leave disappointed.

Beverly Hills has more police per capita than any city in the world.

The small city's heart is **Rodeo Drive**, which slices through a nominal downtown with much pomp and circumstance, containing the Beverly Hills of the popular imagination. More picturesque sights are tucked away in the slopes and canyons north of downtown, but even there, you'll find the gated-off mansions you might have come to expect after visiting area stores that require an invitation to enter.

Any proper trip into Beverly Hills begins on Wilshire Boulevard, where you encounter the **Academy of Motion Picture Arts and**

The Academy and the Oscar

The Academy of Motion Picture Arts and Sciences was formed in 1927 by titans of the film industry such as Louis B Mayer, Cecil B DeMille, Mary Pickford, and Douglas Fairbanks. Officially created to advance the cause of filmmaking, this organization was actually intended to combat trade union expansion in Hollywood, which it tried to do, unsuccessfully, for ten years, after which it concentrated instead on standardizing the technical specifications of filmmaking – everything from streamlining script design to approving industry standards for sound and lighting. To expand its membership and appeal, the Academy began to include notable artists and craftworkers from most segments of the business and to promote its award show as an event of national significance.

This show was, of course, the **Academy Awards**, which began two years after the organization's creation and was designed to give the industry's stamp of approval to its own film product. Called the **Oscar**, an award with many dubious explanations for its name – everything from its being a forgotten acronym to the name of Academy librarian Margaret Herrick's uncle – the Academy's official blessing was a much sought-after honor even in its early years. From their infancy, however, the Academy Awards have generally recognized the best work produced by the **studio system**, not necessarily the best films overall, so as not to bite the hand that feeds. This is why landmark works such as *Citizen Kane*, *Vertigo*, and *Taxi Driver* have typically been ignored and event films like *The Greatest Show on Earth* and *Out of Africa* grab the accolades. Even in recent years, despite the renowned strength of independent studios (actually subsidiaries of the majors), the top awards have gone to old-fashioned flicks like *Forrest Gump* and *Braveheart*, letting the lower-budgeted films clean up in "secondary" categories like screenwriting and cinematography.

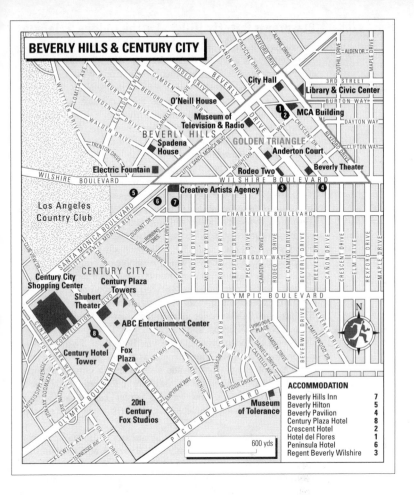

BEVERLY HILLS & CENTURY CITY

Sciences (AMPAS), 8949 Wilshire Blvd, an unremarkable building that houses the headquarters of the organization that puts on the Oscars every year. This film association also offers occasional public screenings of industry work in its excellent main theater, along with maintaining the nearby Margaret Herrick Library for film research (see p.84). This stretch of Wilshire features other classic venues for watching movies, including the Zigzag Moderne **Wilshire Theater**, no. 8440, nowadays a home to traveling stage productions; the exuberant neon of the **Fine Arts Theater**, no. 8556; and the once grand, now subdivided, **Music Hall Theater**, no. 9036. There's also the intriguingly Moorish, onion-domed former **Beverly Theatre**, 206 N Beverly Drive, now converted into the Israel Discount Bank.

Beverly Hills' restaurants are listed beginning on p.251.

Downtown Beverly Hills, aka the Golden Triangle

Downtown Beverly Hills, successfully labeled the "**Golden Triangle**" by the city's PR department, is a shopping district like no other, the ritzy wedge between Rexford Drive and Wilshire and Santa Monica boulevards, dotted with the city's top retailers, hotels, and restaurants. The apotheosis of this haute couture is, of course, Rodeo Drive, which cuts right through the triangle in a three-block concentrated showcase of the most exclusive names in international fashion. One worth looking into is Fred Hayman, 273 N Rodeo Drive, housing the autographed photos of a number of Hollywood celebs alongside its mostly Italian designer-menswear. Also meriting a peek is Ralph Lauren, 444 N Rodeo Drive, which caters to well-heeled WASPs who fancy themselves as canine-coddling English gentry. Besides the thousand-dollar suits and monogrammed Wellingtons, there are exquisitely carved walking sticks, mounted game heads, and an assortment of wooden and bronze dogs. In the midst of these snooty shops is Frank Lloyd Wright's decidedly unstodgy **Anderton Court**, 328 N Rodeo Drive, which resembles a boxy, miniaturized version of the Guggenheim museum crowned by a jagged horn, and is home to a few cramped retailers who must contend with Wright's awkward experiment in space and light. At the foot of Rodeo along Wilshire are LA's premier department stores: Barney's, Giorgio Armani, Neiman-Marcus, and the like.

Listings of some of the best shops on Rodeo Drive can be found beginning on p.303.

Adjacent to Rodeo Drive and Wilshire Boulevard, **Two Rodeo**, the area's mock-European tourist route, is a less appealing consumer zone. A cobblestone street leads visitors into a curving shopping alley designed to resemble an Old World footpath, or at least a Disney version of one. However, this "street" cannot escape its LA identity: the entire concourse is built on top of a multi-story parking garage.

Despite being the home of Hollywood, Los Angeles does not yet have a proper film museum.

A few more interesting sights lie in and around Rodeo's elite commercial zone, most prominently the **Museum of Television and Radio**, 465 N Beverly Drive (Wed–Sun noon–5pm, Thurs closes at 9pm; $6, students $4), which holds more than 75,000 TV and radio programs, any of which you can watch or listen to; LA's first real attempt at providing a media museum of scholarly value. The institution also has a well-designed theater for public screenings of old and recent shows. The building itself is immaculate white geometry from the leading practitioner of that sort of architecture, Richard Meier – more famous for his Getty Center (see p.123).

A few blocks away on Crescent Drive is the period-revival former **MCA Building**, 360 Crescent Drive, a surprisingly successful neo-Georgian mansion with a central Florentine fountain and surrounding gardens you can wander through – one of the few buildings in Beverly Hills that manages to convince you of its eighteenth-century heritage, despite being constructed in 1940. Another triumph is the adjacent **Beverly Hills City Hall**, a 1932 concoction of Spanish

Revival and Art Deco architecture that resembles a squat version of LA's City Hall for its Moderne tower, but which is topped off with an ornate dome dripping with Baroque details and vivid colors. Across Rexford Drive, the **Civic Center and Library** are built in a postmodern design with Art Deco elements, meant to complement the style of City Hall.

The Civic Center's designer, Charles Moore, also created the Piazza d'Italia in New Orleans.

Outside the triangle

Just west of the triangle is the **Electric Fountain**, created in 1930 by the Beverly Hills Women's Club. Depicting the history of the West on a circular frieze along its base, the fountain spews water from the hands of a nameless Indian sitting atop its central column, deep in a rain prayer. You may find it difficult to concentrate like he is, though, as the nearby intersection of Wilshire and Santa Monica boulevards is one of the loudest in the city.

Across the intersection sits the conspicuous headquarters of **Creative Artists Agency**, where powerbrokers, led by Mike Ovitz, made their company into one of the most feared and respected institutions in town. With its white-marble curtain wall and curved glass, the I M Pei-designed structure befits the imperious mood of the company in the late 1980s, when it virtually ruled Hollywood and eventually drove actors' salaries up into the $20 million range, where they have remained ever since. Although Ovitz is long gone and "CAA" has lost some of its clout, it remains a key agency to the stars.

Mike Ovitz went on to become president of Disney, where his style didn't play out quite as well – though when he left, he did receive a contract settlement reportedly worth around $100 million.

Meanwhile, the area above Santa Monica Boulevard is less familiar to most visitors but still worth checking out. On the north side of the boulevard, between Camden and Bedford drives, a **cactus garden** holds one of the largest municipal collections of cacti in the world, managing to offer a tranquil setting despite its menacing array of sharp, spiny plants. Further north, away from the massive thoroughfares and buildings, the residential side of Beverly Hills features palm-lined streets and Mercedes-lined driveways. There are a number of lesser-known stars who live along these streets, but the real interest is the architecture that some residents have chosen for their dwellings. Without a doubt the most peculiar is the **Spadena House**, Carmelita Drive at Walden Avenue, commonly known as the "Witch's House," its sagging roof, gnarled windows, and jagged wooden fence straight out of a fairy tale. It was actually built as the headquarters for a Culver City movie company in the early 1920s, later moving to its present location. Another outlandish design, the **O'Neill House**, 507 N Rodeo Drive, looks like a melting birthday cake, with its undulating white curves and asymmetrical design – a style sometimes referred to as California Art Nouveau or Gaudi-esque.

The curving blocks heading into the hills become increasingly upmarket, converging on the pink plaster **Beverly Hills Hotel**, on Sunset and Rodeo, constructed in 1912 to attract wealthy settlers to what was then a town of just five hundred people. Much has changed in the intervening years, and the hotel's Mission style has been updated by a slew of renovators, who have managed to keep the core design of the building and its attendant gardens intact. Currently owned by the Sultan of Brunei, the hotel's social cachet makes its *Polo Lounge* a prime spot for movie execs to power-lunch.

The northern hills and canyons

Above the *Beverly Hills Hotel*, in the **northern hills and canyons**, a number of gardens and parks offer much-needed solace and are fairly well concealed. One such place, the wooded **Virginia Robinson Gardens**, 1008 Elden Way (tours Tues–Thurs 10am & 1pm, Fri 10am; $5, students $3; by appointment only at ☎310/276-5367), holds six acres of flora and a thousand-plus varieties of plants, including some towering Australian king palm trees. Ms Robinson was the heiress to the Robinson's department store chain who, upon her death, donated her land and Mediterranean-style estate (not open to the public) to LA County. To the east, you can roam the thirteen-acre **Greystone Park**, 905 Loma Vista Drive (daily 10am–6pm; free), though its centerpiece, a Tudor mansion – the biggest house in Beverly Hills – once owned by oil scion Edward Doheny, Jr, is closed to the public. Still, its limestone facade and intricately designed chimneys are worth a look, as are the grounds, which feature a stunning view of the LA basin, a widely sloping front lawn, several koi-filled fishponds, and a concrete-filled swimming pool.

For a look inside the Greystone Mansion, it helps to be a member of a film crew; the house is busy year-round hosting Hollywood movie and music video productions.

Two miles northwest, **Franklin Canyon**, an isolated niche of the Santa Monica Mountains National Recreation Area, features two fairly remote reservoirs and a ranch, and it routinely welcomes a cast of picnickers, joggers, even wedding parties to its grounds. To reach the area, follow Franklin Canyon Drive north into the parkland until you hit a fork in the road. The lake route, to the left, takes you to the upper reservoir; the ranch route, to the right, leads to a series of hiking trails and a central lawn.

Further west, in the verdant canyons and foothills above Sunset Boulevard, a number of palatial estates lie hidden away behind landscaped security gates. **Benedict Canyon Drive** climbs from the *Beverly Hills Hotel* past many of them. The most famous was the lavish **PickFair** mansion, 1143 Summit Drive, originally a 1910 hunting lodge that was remodeled for Mary Pickford and Douglas Fairbanks in 1919, soon becoming home to LA's very first private swimming pool. The mansion lasted for seven decades, until its 1987 demolition by would-be movie star Pia Zadora. Further up Benedict Canyon, Harold Lloyd's 1928 **Greenacres**, 1040 Angelo Drive, where he lived for forty years, has secret passageways and a large private screening room that are still intact (and off-limits to the public), though the grounds, which contained a waterfall and a nine-hole golf course, have since been broken up into smaller lots.

Century City

With its towering office blocks and giant boulevards, **Century City** is perhaps LA's most egregious example of building for the automobile and leaving human traffic in the dust. Originally part of the 20th Century-Fox studio lot, Century City began taking shape in the early 1960s during the height of glass-and-steel corporate modernism and is tainted with the excesses of that era, most noticeably at the east end of Constellation Boulevard with the **Century Plaza Towers**: huge, triangular buildings looming over a bleak concrete plaza and the low, charmless box of the **ABC Entertainment Center**, a plodding mall designed like a bomb shelter, whose one appeal is the Shubert Theater, a popular spot for traveling musicals. Somewhat better are the **Century Plaza Hotel**, 2025 Avenue of the Stars, an elliptical 1966 structure (with an accompanying contemporary tower for elite guests), and the postmodern **Fox Plaza**, 2121 Avenue of the Stars, memorable as the staging ground for Bruce Willis' manic heroism in the film *Die Hard*, and often referred to as the "Fox Tower."

Other buildings on the site are flash-frozen from around 1970, such as the **Century City Shopping Center**, 10250 Santa Monica Blvd, where locals snap up the familiar goods offered by stores like Macy's and Bloomingdale's. Its single-level, open-air design makes the mall one of the more pleasant in the region, and even features a prominent celebrity-owned restaurant: Steven Spielberg's *Dive!*, a cartoon submarine that sells all manner of sandwiches and burgers.

Near the mall's food court is the AMC Theater (see p.281), one of the best spots in LA to catch a first-run movie.

The current home of **20th Century-Fox**, just south at 10201 Pico Blvd, occupies much smaller digs than it used to, much of its former 225 acres having been sold to make way for Century City. Nowadays, you have to crane to see the New York street scene intact from the production of *Hello Dolly!*, hidden behind high walls and scaffolding. In any case, the studio keeps the public out – apparently not learning any lessons from the hugely successful tour services offered by Warner Brothers and Universal Studios.

Around Century City

East of Century City, below Beverly Hills, an inauspicious white building houses the **Simon Wiesenthal Center for Holocaust Studies**, 9786 Pico Blvd. The US headquarters of the organization devoted to tracking down ex-Nazis, the center has an extensive library of Holocaust-related documents, photographs and accounts – but the main draw for visitors is the affecting **Beit HaShoa Museum of Tolerance** (Mon–Thurs 10am–4pm, Fri 10am–3pm, Sun 11am–4pm; $8), an extraordinary interactive resource center aimed at exposing the lies of revisionist historians. The most technologically advanced institution of its kind, it uses videotaped interviews to provide LA's frankest examination of the 1992 riots, and leads the visitor through re-enactments outlining the rise of Nazism to a harrowing conclusion in a replica gas chamber. The corresponding **Martyrs Memorial and Museum of the Holocaust**, 6505 Wilshire Blvd (Mon–Thurs 9am–5pm, Fri 9am–3pm, Sun 1–5pm; free), several miles to the east, traces anti-Semitism through the years and serves as a memorial to those who died in the Holocaust, as well as an affecting presentation of survivors' thoughts and memories. Look for the model of Sobibor, one of the death camps, created by one of its survivors.

On a less sober note, the **Westside Pavilion**, west at Pico and Westwood boulevards, is another of LA's great shopping mall complexes, with a bright, postmodern design, high pedestrian bridge, and a long, interior skylight. Some blocks to the north, visible throughout the mostly flat Westside, the **Mormon Temple**, 10777 Santa Monica Blvd, is a marble hilltop colossus with a 257ft tower crowned by the angel Moroni. Although the main part of the building isn't open to non-Mormons, outsiders are allowed access to the **visitors center** (daily 9am–9pm; free), where you can get a look at a 12ft marble sculpture of Jesus.

Westwood and the UCLA Campus

Just west of Beverly Hills and Century City along Wilshire Boulevard, **WESTWOOD** is, for the most part, pleasantly low-scaled and crowded with students, shoppers, and theater-goers, though it sits alongside some of the tallest buildings this side of Downtown. In the 1970s and 1980s, this section of Wilshire exploded with oil-rich high-rise developments, where penthouse apartments with private heliports in twenty-story condos sell for upwards of $12 million – a dramatic contrast to the modest bungalows found just a block away – and the intersection of Wilshire and Westwood boulevards is now choked with overflowing traffic, with some of LA's longest waits for a green light.

The Hammer Museum is now under the auspices of UCLA, a move that has resulted in a greater emphasis on contemporary art shows at the museum.

At this intersection, inside one of the great towers, the **Armand Hammer Museum of Art and Culture Center** (Tues–Sat 11am–7pm, Thurs until 9pm, Sun 11am–5pm; $4.50, students $3, Thurs 6–9pm free) is one of the city's most debated art stashes, amassed over seven decades by the flamboyant and ultra-wealthy boss of the Occidental Petroleum Corporation. Art critic Robert Hughes called the paintings here "a mishmash of second or third-rate works by famous names," but while the Rembrandts and Rubenses may be less than stunning, the nineteenth-century pieces like Van Gogh's intense and radiant *Hospital at Saint Remy* more than make amends, as do some American works, such as a Gilbert Stuart portrait of George Washington, who stares with a regal glow; Thomas Eakins' painting of *Sebastiano Cardinal Martinelli*, depicted with the artist's blunt, penetrating realism; and John Singer Sargent's *Dr Pozzi at Home*, another of the artist's skilled character studies.

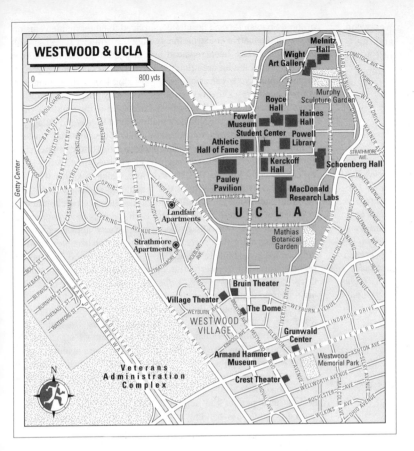

Across Wilshire from the museum, at the end of the driveway behind the tiny Avco cinema, you'll find Hammer's speckled marble tomb, sharing the tiny cemetery of **Westwood Memorial Park** with the likes of movie stars Peter Lorre and Natalie Wood, wildman jazz drummer Buddy Rich, and, to the left of the entrance in the far northeast corner, the lipstick-covered plaque that marks the resting place of **Marilyn Monroe**. You can see some of these stars on the radiant mural inside the **Crest Theater**, 1262 Westwood Blvd, also notable for its brash marquee.

Westwood Village

North of Wilshire Boulevard, **Westwood Village** is one of LA's more user-friendly neighborhoods, a grouping of low-slung brick buildings that went up in the late 1920s, along with the adjacent campus of the nascent University of California at Los Angeles (UCLA). Much of the original Spanish Revival design has survived the intervening years of more unimaginative construction, though the ordinary businesses of the old days have been replaced by fancy boutiques and designer novelty shops. It's an area that's easily explored on foot – if you're driving, dump your car at one of the parking lots before beginning your wanderings – and one very much shaped by the proximity of the university campus, which is really the lifeblood of the area.

Broxton Avenue, the Village's main strip of Westwood Village, is filled with record stores, moviehouses, and diners, though it doesn't attract as many visitors as it did before a late-1980s gang-related shooting. Its focus, the tower near the end of the street, is the 1931 **Fox Westwood Village**, 961 Broxton Ave, which, together with the neon-signed **Bruin** across the street, is sometimes used by movie studios for "sneak previews" of films to gauge audience reaction and is now part of the Mann theater chain. Both theaters have impressive Moderne designs, the Village being particularly appealing for its great Zigzag spire that resembles a neon church steeple. Another familiar Westwood image is **The Dome**, 1099 Westwood Blvd, now a record store but formerly the offices of the Janss Investment Corporation, which from 1929 operated under this Moderne building's Islamic dome, creating the surrounding Westwood real estate development and many other districts out of a 3300-acre parcel that was formerly the Rancho San José de Buenos Ayres. The firm supervised the building of many period-revival Spanish structures in Westwood, and nowhere is its design signature more evident than at the one-time **Ralph's Grocery Store**, 1150 Westwood Blvd, a Spanish Romanesque creation with a red-tile roof and cylindrical corner tower that is now a Mexican restaurant. Some Richard Neutra designs also pepper the neighborhood, notably the blocky white geometry and glass banding of the **Landfair Apartments**, 10940 Ophir Drive, now used for student housing, and the nearby **Strathmore Apartments**, 11005 Strathmore Drive, a faded, grungy heap of cubes and angles.

Moviehouses like the Fox Westwood Village and Bruin are listed in "Performing Arts and Film," beginning on p.275.

UCLA

The University of California at Los Angeles, or **UCLA**, is one of the country's most prominent academic and athletic institutions, and is also an enjoyable spot to explore for its Italian-style architecture, art exhibition spaces, and laid-back vibe. Anchoring Westwood Village at its northern end, the campus' focus of interest lies toward the northeast, where the original quadrangle from the late 1920s still acts as a nexus for social activity.

The campus originally occupied the site of the Downtown Library, later moving to the location of the current Los Angeles City College, but by 1925 had outgrown its East Hollywood environs. After new land was purchased in Westwood, UCLA became a model of Northern Italian Romanesque design: intended by architect George

Kelham to resemble the red brick structures of Milan and Genoa, the buildings around the central quadrangle, such as the library and science halls, seem to be plucked straight from a "Lombard" Romanesque blueprint. This pristine quality was diminished by the rash of concrete bunkers and steel boxes added from the 1950s to the 1970s, but recent years have seen creative experimentation by the likes of Frank Gehry and Robert Venturi, along with more regard for visual continuity.

Before embarking on your journey around UCLA, be sure to pick up a **map** at any of the various information kiosks scattered around the campus. A good place to start your wanderings is at the **Mathias Botanical Garden**, 405 Hilgard Ave (daily 8am–4pm; free), a rustic glade on the east side of the university that offers sloping paths, small waterfalls, and greenery from dawn redwoods to fern groves to extensive lily beds. Just north, modern **Schoenberg Hall** houses the music school and pays homage to the twelve-tone composer, Arnold Schoenberg, who taught at the campus for fifteen years. Immediately around the corner lies the central **quadrangle**, a grassy space bordered by UCLA's most graceful buildings. To the east, **Haines Hall** and the **Physics-Biology Building** introduce you to the Lombard Romanesque style of the early campus, but it is with **Royce Hall** and **Powell Library**, west of the courtyard, that this style is most fully realized. The former, recently restored, is modeled on Milan's Church of St Ambrosio, with high bell towers, rib vaulting, and grand archways; while the Library, designed by Kelham, has a spellbinding interior with lovely Romanesque arches, dome, and stairwell, and an array of medieval ornament to complement its ecclesiastical feel.

The quadrangle ends with a great stairway that parallels the Romanesque **Moore Hall of Education**, as well as **Kerckoff Hall**, the sole example of Gothic architecture on campus and home to the student union. Further south, one of the best contemporary structures, Robert Venturi's **MacDonald Research Labs**, is well worth seeking out for its postmodern style, featuring off-color, brick upper stories with irregular windows, a concrete base, and quasi-Egyptian colonnade.

The **Fowler Museum of Cultural History**, Bruin Walk at Westwood Plaza (Wed–Sun noon–5pm, Thurs open until 8pm; free) offers an immense range of multicultural art with some political works thrown in for good measure. Among the museum's highlights are its extensive collections of African and Polynesian art and various folk designs, including a particularly interesting display of pre-Columbian headdresses that show the color and variety of the art of the Americas before Cortés and Pizarro arrived. Not far away, in the center of campus, sculptor Robert Graham's work is displayed in a **courtyard collection** near Rolfe Hall, a series of miniature humans, many of them female nudes, with austere gazes and explicit anatomies posed on top of cylindrical pedestals – a good example of UCLA's risk-taking approach to public art.

*Franklin
Murphy was
chancellor of
UCLA during
most of the
1960s; he also
helped develop
the Los Angeles
County
Museum of
Art.*

To the northeast, the **Franklin Murphy Sculpture Garden** (always open; free) is LA's best outdoor display of modern sculpture, containing numerous modern works in its collection, notably Rodin's *Walking Man*, a typically stark nude; Gaston Lachaise's Amazonian *Standing Woman*, a proud, if grotesque, 1932 sculpture; David Smith's abstract geometry, the stainless-steel *Cubi XX*; and George Tsutakawa's *OBOS-69*, a superior example of fountain art. One of the most appealing works is Joan Miro's birdlike abstraction *Mere Ubu*, north of the main lawn of the garden in its own space. Just north of the Murphy Garden, the **Wight Art Gallery** (Mon–Fri 9am–5pm; free) has a less intriguing collection of contemporary works on display, though its holdings are significant and include the **Grunwald Center for the Graphic Arts**, located off campus at 10899 Wilshire Blvd (by appointment only at ☎310/443-7076), which has around 35,000 drawings, photographs, and prints covering the entire post-medieval era, from Dürer to Picasso, with some exceptional Expressionist works by Emil Nolde and Käthe Kollwitz. Back on campus, east of the Wight Gallery, UCLA's **film school** has produced offbeat film-makers like Francis Ford Coppola, Alison Anders, and Alex Cox; it also has one of the most extensive collections of old films and TV programs in the world, examples of which are shown daily, often for free, in the large auditorium in **Melnitz Hall**. Check the bulletin board in the lobby or phone ☎310/206-FILM for the current schedule.

*UCLA has won
more college
basketball
championships
– eleven –
than any other
team in history, their most
recent coming
in 1995.*

UCLA is also well known for its athletic prowess, on display at the **Athletic Hall of Fame** (Mon–Fri 8am–5pm; free) near the center of campus, where you can check out the myriad awards in basketball, football, volleyball, and other sports that the school has received, along with viewing its glossy tribute to coach John Wooden's clutch of ten basketball championships. That team plays just west of here, at **Pauley Pavilion**.

For a more contemplative experience, travel north of the UCLA campus to the **UCLA Hanna Carter Japanese Garden**, 10619 Bellagio Rd (Tues 10am–1pm, Wed noon–3pm; free; by appointment only at ☎310/206-6632), constructed in Japan and featuring plants native to that country, including magnolias and Japanese maples. Adding to the atmosphere are a pagoda, teahouse, some quaint bridges, and assorted ancient Buddha sculptures in gold and stone.

Bel Air, Brentwood, and the Getty Center

The gap through the Santa Monica Mountains known as the **Sepulveda Pass** runs alongside some of LA's most exclusive residential neighborhoods, as well as LA's newest art jewel, the **Getty Center**. The pass was, like the eponymous boulevard and nearby community, named for Mexican soldier Francisco Sepúlveda, who gained ownership in 1839 of the Rancho San Vicente y Santa Monica, which once encompassed the surrounding area. It holds both the 405 freeway and part of Sepulveda Boulevard, the longest road in the city or county of Los Angeles, which leads from Long Beach into the San Fernando Valley.

Just northwest of UCLA and east of the 405 freeway, **BEL AIR** is an insular community that defines an elite subdivision, with opulent black gates fronting Sunset Boulevard and security guards driving about to catch loiterers and interlopers. Surprisingly, despite its famous name and reputation, not a lot goes on in Bel Air, as there are hardly any businesses (but for a very fine hotel with an exquisite garden, see p.224) and the residential architecture can only be called, at best, tasteful – and in any case is near-impossible to see, often hidden behind thick foliage.

Indeed, if you want to have a more enjoyable experience among the well-heeled, **BRENTWOOD** to the west is a much better bet. Best known for being the former home of O J Simpson (curiosity-seekers will find the Tudor mansion at the southeast corner of Rockingham and Ashford), the neighborhood also contains a few other residences of note, such as Frank Gehry's **Schnabel House**, 526 N Carmelina Ave, one of his 1980s experiments in form that features a chunky group of metal cubes connected to an incongruous Moorish dome. Further along, Frank Lloyd Wright's **Sturges House**, 449 Skyeway Rd, a giant wooden shingle cantilevered off a hillside and hovering over the street below it. The neighborhood also has an upscale shopping strip along San Vicente Boulevard, with all the standard boutiques and restaurants (*Mezzaluna*, 11750 San Vicente Blvd, the eatery where Nicole Simpson supped her last, has now shut its doors).

North along Sepulveda Boulevard near the crest of the Santa Monica Mountains is the **Skirball Cultural Center**, 2701 N Sepulveda Blvd (Tues–Fri 10am–4pm, Sat noon–5pm, Sun 10am–5pm; $7, students $5), a home to Judaic studies, art, and religious interpretation, recently relocated from South Central LA. Devoting its attention to describing some of the history, beliefs and rituals of Judaism, the Center concentrates on the more mystical elements of the faith, but is most interesting for describing the American Diaspora, embodied in stark photographs of turn-of-the-century immigrants and written mementos of their arduous travel and assimilation. It also offers a wide collection of artifacts, everything from archeological discoveries around the Mediterranean to folk art to religious items, including Hanukkah lamps and a replica of a Holy Ark (a cabinet for Torah scrolls) from a German synagogue.

The Getty Center

Off Sepulveda and west of the 405 freeway, Getty Center Drive leads up to the monumental **Getty Center** (Tues–Wed 11am–7pm,

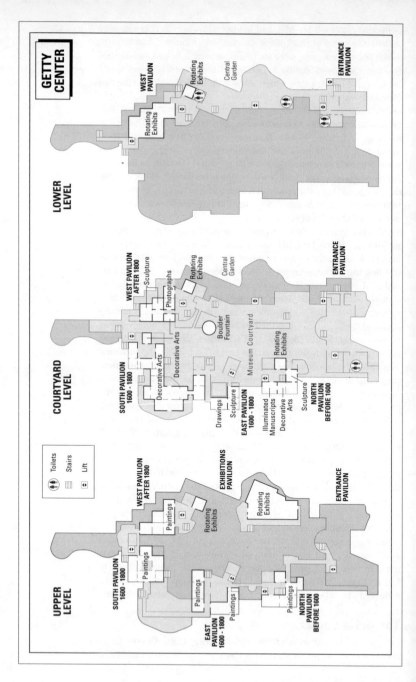

GETTY CENTER

LOWER LEVEL

WEST PAVILION
Rotating Exhibits
Rotating Exhibits
Central Garden
ENTRANCE PAVILION

COURTYARD LEVEL

WEST PAVILION AFTER 1800
Sculpture
Photographs
Rotating Exhibits
Central Garden
Decorative Arts
SOUTH PAVILION 1600 - 1800
Decorative Arts
Boulder Fountain
Museum Courtyard
Rotating Exhibits
ENTRANCE PAVILION
Drawings
Sculpture
EAST PAVILION 1600 - 1800
Illuminated Manuscripts
Decorative Arts
Sculpture
NORTH PAVILION BEFORE 1600

UPPER LEVEL

Toilets
Stairs
Lift

WEST PAVILION AFTER 1800
Paintings
Paintings
Rotating Exhibits
EXHIBITIONS PAVILION
SOUTH PAVILION 1600 - 1800
Paintings
Paintings
Rotating Exhibits
ENTRANCE PAVILION
Paintings
EAST PAVILION 1600 - 1800
Paintings
Paintings
NORTH PAVILION BEFORE 1600

Thurs–Fri 11am–9pm, Sat–Sun 10am–6pm; free), a gleaming museum palace and research complex that towers over the city. The Center, designed by modernist Richard Meier and built over fifteen years at a cost of around $1 billion, contains the vast art holdings of oil mogul J Paul Getty and has been constructed with no small amount of fanfare and controversy. Originally Meier planned for the whole museum complex to be constructed from white metallic panels – his signature style – but protests from the Brentwood neighbors below (regarding sun glare) forced him to re-design part of it in travertine, which has given the center a classical look, leading some to dub it the "American Acropolis." It's a bit of an exaggeration, but there's no overestimating the amount of money the center will be spending to outbid its competitors on trophies of world art: by law, it must disburse hundreds of millions each year from its endowment of more than $3 billion. This has resulted in outcries from competitors that the Center has inflated art prices to an astronomical level, at which only the Center can compete. J Paul himself would have been proud.

Getty started building his massive collection in the 1930s, storing much of it in his house until the **Getty Museum** opened in 1974 on an ocean bluff near the end of Sunset Boulevard. That site is now closed, but will reopen in 2001 as a showcase for the foundation's antiquities (see below), temporarily held here. Properly speaking, the museum itself has moved to the grounds of the Center, which also includes six other buildings for art research, conservation, acquisition, and such, none of which are open to the public. However, the museum alone provides more than enough interest to fill a day.

As the collection is determined by the enthusiasms of Getty himself, there's a formidable array of ornate **furniture** and **decorative arts**, with clocks, chandeliers, tapestries, and gilt-edged commodes, designed for the French nobility from the reign of Louis XIV, filling several overwhelmingly opulent rooms. However, it's the museum's paintings, sculpture, and photographs that will overwhelm you. As long as the **antiquities** collection is still around, be sure to check out its selection of ancient **Greek art**; highlights include the *Getty Kouros*, a rigidly posed figure of a boy that conservators openly state could be a later forgery, a *Cult Statue of Aphrodite* from the Golden Age of Greece (fifth century BC), with flowing robe and voluptuous limestone figure, and a Hellenistic *Statue of a Victorious Youth*, wearing only an olive wreath, that was carefully restored after having been recovered from the sea floor, where it had been dumped centuries earlier. Athenian vases are also well represented, as are ancient kylikes, or drinking vessels. The museum also has an excellent collection of medieval **illuminated manuscripts**, featuring vellum leaves depicting scenes from the Bible such as the Passion cycle, as well as notable saints and even lectionaries, in which exquisitely

You cannot stop at the Getty Center on a whim. Reservations for parking, which cost $5, are always made in advance and are difficult to get on weekends or holidays. However, if you arrive by cab or bus (the #561 line, which you can pick up at LAX), you are assured entry.

drawn and gilded letters introduce chapters from Scripture and maintain their radiance to this day. One of the most interesting volumes is the *Apocalypse with Commentary by Berengaudus*, an English Gothic creation that shows the Book of Revelation in all its fiery detail, including an image of the Four Horsemen of the Apocalypse looking suspiciously like feudal knights.

In **painting**, European art is principally represented from the post-Renaissance era, but there are a few notable exceptions, among them Andrea Mantegna's stoic *Adoration of the Magi*, Correggio's *Head of Christ*, an affecting portrait that rivals Rembrandt for the sheer quality of the subject's emotional expression, and Titian's well-known *Venus and Adonis*, depicting in muted colors the last moments between the lovers before Adonis is gored by a wild pig. **Mannerist** works include Pontormo's haunted *Portrait of a Halberdier* and Veronese's *Portrait of a Man*, perhaps the painter himself – a sword-wearing nobleman gazing proudly at the viewer – with rich, ornamental details and a low angle to emphasize the fellow's grandeur.

The finest works from the seventeenth century are Flemish and Dutch. Among the highlights are Rubens' *Entombment*, a pictorial essay on transubstantiation, Hendrik ter Brugghen's *Bacchante with an Ape*, showing a drunken libertine clutching a handful of grapes, an action mirrored by his pet monkey, and a trio of Rembrandts that emphasize the artist's interest in character and composition: *Daniel and Cyrus before the Idol Bel*, in which the Persian king tries foolishly to feed the bronze statue he worships; *An Old Man in Military Costume*, the exhausted, uncertain face of an old soldier; and the great portrait of *Saint Bartholomew*, wherein the martyred saint is shown to be a quiet, thoughtful Dutchman – the knife that will soon kill him barely visible in the corner of the frame.

While some lesser French neoclassical works are present in the collection, the best work from the general period is Gericault's later *Portrait Study*, a sensitive portrait of an African man that is one of many the artist created. The Getty Center is also known for bidding on **Impressionist works**; as such, these acquisitions read like a laundry list of late-nineteenth-century French art: a portrait of *Albert Cahen d'Anvers* by Renoir, the inevitable Monet haystacks, and one of Degas' ballet dancers. Van Gogh's *Irises* was the subject of a bruising 1980s bidding war, in which an Australian financier beat out other competitors (at a price of more than $50 million), but later defaulted on his payments, after which the painting went into legal limbo before the Getty Trust snatched it up for an unknown price.

Other significant works from the nineteenth century include *Bullfight* by Goya, in which the bull stares triumphantly at a group of unsuccessful matadors; J M W Turner's frenzied *Ships at Sea, Getting a Good Wetting*, all hazy colors and soft lines; and Caspar Friedrich's elegant and understated *A Walk at Dusk*, a Romantic painting of a lone man bowing before a stone cairn during twilight.

The institution also boasts a wide collection of **drawings**, among them Albrecht Dürer's meticulous *Study of the Good Thief*, a portrait of the crucified criminal who was converted on the cross; his *Stag Beetle*, precise enough to look as if the bug were crawling on the page itself; and William Blake's bizarre watercolor of *Satan Exalting over Eve*, an expressionless devil hovering over his prone captive.

As far as **sculpture** goes, best are Benvenuto Cellini's *Hercules Pendant*, a small, finely rendered piece of jewelry that shows the ancient hero in shock, mouth agape, and Gianlorenzo Bernini's slightly larger *Boy with a Dragon*, done when he was only sixteen, depicting a plump toddler bending back the jaw of a dragon with surprising ease.

Finally, the Getty's **photographs** are quite renowned, with the requisite displays of Stieglitz, Strand, Weston, Adams, Arbus, and other such notables, but again, it's the museum's less familiar works that are its most intriguing: an 1849 *Portrait of Edgar Allan Poe*, by an unknown photographer, has the writer staring at the camera with manic intensity; Thomas Eakins' photo study *Students at the Site for 'The Swimming Hole'*, which the painter used as a dry-run for his famous painting, showing his pupils jumping naked from a flat rock into a muddy pond; and August Sander's feral *Frau Peter Abelen*, an androgynous woman with slicked-back hair, white culottes, business shirt and tie, holding an unlit cigarette between gritted teeth.

Culver City

Several miles south of Beverly Hills and Westwood, triangular **CULVER CITY** is one of the Westside's more undiscovered charms, its history rich with movie lore and its current face shaped by groundbreaking architectural experiments. Wedged between Venice Boulevard and the 405 freeway, it's also one of LA's most ethnically diverse cities, with a well functioning mix of whites and blacks amid a growing population of Hispanics and Asians.

The most impressive Culver City building is probably the **Ivy Substation**, at Culver and Venice boulevards, a 1907 Mission Revival power station for the old Red Car public transit line. Given an austere, modern renovation in a palm-tree filled park, the substation has been reborn as a performing arts theater and exhibition space for public events, though one that's irregularly open. Two other major structures can be found nearby, including the **Helms Bakery**, 8800 Venice Blvd, a PWA Moderne landmark with a heavy, Art Deco volume that now features an array of local furniture dealers and craft shops inside, as well as the *Jazz Bakery* (a club listed on p.273) – though bread hasn't been made on the premises in many years. To the west, the **Culver Theater**, Washington Boulevard at Duquesne Avenue, is a striking late-Moderne moviehouse that's a sometimes filming location, mostly for its streamlined marquee.

While its old-fashioned architecture is certainly compelling, Culver City's greatest historic structures are its movie studios, many of which still function, albeit in different guises. The man responsible for creating the two greatest studio complexes was **Thomas Ince**, who helped found modern Hollywood and whose 1915 **Ince Studios**, 9336 Washington Blvd, was the first such operation in Culver City, today instantly recognizable as the plantation in *Gone with the Wind*. The structure's grand Colonial Revival design now houses unimpressive office space and is known as the Culver Studios. Ince's later, bigger creation was **Triangle Pictures**, 10202 Washington Blvd, which he helped build with the financial aid of Harry Culver, a journalist and realtor who founded the city specifically for the movie business. Though the Triangle's original classical colonnade still sits along the boulevard, the studio itself went through many incarnations, to be purchased by Samuel Goldwyn, then Metro-Goldwyn-Mayer, and later turned over to Sony Pictures, which now occupies the grounds. (Unfortunately, Sony has seen fit to create its own version of monumental architecture nearby – a huge out-of-place office complex with a diagonally slanting glass wall.)

Restaurants in West LA are listed begining on p.232.

A few blocks east, on a triangle of land formed by Duquesne Avenue and Culver and Washington boulevards, the early-twentieth-century **Culver Hotel** has emerged from its decades-long decay to return to its original splendor. Duck inside to check out its checkered-marble flooring, red-and-black interior design, and intricate iron railings. This structure, like quite a few others in town, has received assistance from Culver City's redevelopment fund – a recent attempt to bring back the look of the old town, including additions such as historic lampposts and jacaranda trees. Nowhere is this reinvigorating spirit more evident than at **City Hall**, 9770 Culver Blvd, a postmodern municipal building entered through a detached facade near the street, which is a re-creation of an enormous entry wall from the former City Hall. In between the freestanding archway and the building proper you'll find a pleasant park with a peek-through movie camera detailing the city's film history. To see more revitalization, ride the adjacent **Culver Trolley** (Mon–Fri 11.30am–3pm; free) to the **Hayden Tract**, a stretch of Hayden Avenue that, apart from being the city's latest business district, is also one of LA's most fertile spots for wild modern architecture (see box opposite).

On the northern edge of Culver City, The **Museum of Jurassic Technology**, 9341 Venice Blvd (Thurs 2–8pm, Fri–Sun noon–6pm; $3), is without question the region's most unusual museum – if it can even be called that. This "institution" offers a range of oddities from the pseudo-scientific to the paranormal, including several regularly rotating exhibits such as a trailer-park art display, showing various junk collections next to tiny models of RVs and mobile homes about to be swallowed up by the earth; depictions of folk superstitions, with a memorable image of dead mice on toast used as a cure for bedwetting; written and oral narratives of crank scientists and researchers, many of whom have reputedly disappeared under strange circumstances or gone mad; and a series of unearthly insects, like an Amazonian bug that kills its prey through the use of a giant head spike. The effect is entirely unnerving, these vivid exhibits shown in a dark environment without windows or sunlight.

The gray boxes of Eric Moss

Most small towns, even in LA, are known for their conservatism in design and attitude. Culver City is a major exception. With architect/artist **Eric Owen Moss**, this city has not only welcomed his bizarre buildings, it has also helped subsidize the business sites for many of his clients and prominently advertised his groundbreaking work. The Hayden Tract provides excellent examples of this. Here, you can find a whole series of Moss' designs, including one of his latest creations, the **Pittard Sullivan** building, 3535 Hayden Ave, a giant gray box with massive wooden ribs poking out of its sides, almost like contemporary flying buttresses. This work is not dissimilar to nearby **8522 National**, another of his gray boxes that is shattered by a deconstructive glass-and-metal entryway and a white stairway attached to the outside of the building and leading nowhere. Adjacent to this is **The Box**, one of the works that first gained acclaim for Moss. This time, the familiar gray box, with a cubic window riveted to one of its corners, looks ready to come off its hinges and tumble down onto the street below.

Another pocket of his earlier works sits near Ince Boulevard and Lindblade Street, where the **Gary Group** building offers a fragmented white-and-red sign with – again – a ladder to nowhere, while the side of the structure is a concrete wall ornamented with jutting brick cubes and an array of metal chains. Somewhat less discordant, the adjoining **Paramount Laundry** is no more conventional: a series of fat red columns that support a metal awning, even as one of them sits several feet out of place. Other notable Mossworks in LA include the **Petal House**, 2828 Midvale Ave, a renovation of an earlier house, featuring a blossoming, unfolding roof, and the **708 House**, 708 El Medio Ave, another strange reworking of an old house, this time into a brightly colored box with the house's numbers plastered in giant form across its face.

Chapter 6

Santa Monica and Venice

Synonymous in people's minds with the sun-and-surf culture of LA, the beach cities of **SANTA MONICA** and **VENICE** actually defy visitors' expectations: not only can surfing here be hazardous to your health (thanks to several sewage drains that periodically dump into the ocean), but both places are colder than the rest of the basin. Indeed, Santa Monica's average midsummer temperatures sit comfortably around 66° F. Perhaps for this reason, these areas have become home to at least one-quarter of LA's population of British and Irish expatriates, many of whom have opened bars, nightclubs, and restaurants in the area.

A color map of Santa Monica and Venice can be found in the insert at the back of this book.

Located on the western edge of LA, and next to the great crescent of Santa Monica Bay, both cities are some of the region's most enjoyable spots, with little of the standard pretension found elsewhere and much in the way of laid-back attitudes, art studios and galleries, and pleasant low-scale development, not to mention bustling beachside strips that never fail to abound with colorful characters. Santa Monica still has somewhat of a reputation as a white enclave, but ethnic diversity is increasing, even though the overall population is stagnant, due to the city's iron-clad rent control policy. Multiculturalism, however, has been a long-established reality in Venice, which was one of the few coastal cities not to use restrictive covenants to keep blacks from living there. Today, the district is home to a much wider range of classes, races, and cultures than is Santa Monica, juxtaposing run-down burger shacks by upscale boutiques, with the latest modern architecture often sitting next to ramshackle wooden heaps. Nowhere are these visual contrasts more apparent than near **Abbot Kinney Boulevard**, where chic salons lie only a few short blocks from one of LA's bleakest ghettos, Oakwood.

Further south, the colorless real estate development of **MARINA DEL REY** offers few spots of interest, but **PLAYA DEL REY** maintains a certain faded charm, which turns eerie near the airport, where you can find LA's only urban ghost town.

Santa Monica

Breezy **Santa Monica** is one of the most sought-after places to live in LA, as well as one of the most difficult to get into. Rent control keeps the number of affordable rentals limited, sometimes non-existent, and higher-end offerings are often exorbitant. It's easy to understand the desire of locals to move here: the city has relatively low crime rates, plenty of cool ocean air, decent attractions, and a generally unpretentious character. While its main sights are limited in number, Santa Monica most rewards casual wandering through its tree-lined neighborhoods or along its oceanside sands.

That Santa Monica became the fashionable resort that it is today is somewhat a fluke. As little as a century ago, most of the land between Santa Monica and what was then Los Angeles was covered by ranch lands and citrus groves, interrupted by the occasional outposts of Hollywood and Beverly Hills. Like so much of the state, the land was owned by the Southern Pacific Railroad, which tried – and failed – to make Santa Monica into the port of Los Angeles, losing out to other interests who dredged the harbor at San Pedro, near Long Beach, which was really a blessing in disguise for Santa Monica.

The linking of the beachfront with the rest of Los Angeles by the suburban streetcar system meant the town instead grew into one of LA's premier getaways – a giant funfair city that was the inspiration for Raymond Chandler's anything-goes "Bay City," described in *Farewell My Lovely*. While working- and middle-class residents frequented the Santa Monica pier for its thrill-rides and junk food, the town's elite sailed out to the gambling boats anchored offshore, where they could indulge in a bit of illicit excitement beyond the reach of the local authorities. Today Chandler wouldn't recognize the place: changes in the gaming laws and the advent of the private swimming pool have led to the removal of the offshore gambling ships and many of the popular bathing clubs, and Santa Monica is among LA's more elegant seaside towns – and also well known for its rent control and stringent planning and development regulations.

For more on the development of the harbor in San Pedro, see p.166.

The city lies across Bundy Drive from West LA, and splits into three general areas: **oceanside Santa Monica**, holding a fair bit of Santa Monica's history and tourist attractions, sits on the coastal bluffs and includes the pier and beach; **Main Street**, running south from the pier towards Venice, is a style-conscious quarter with designer restaurants and quirky shops; and Santa Monica's interior, or as we've termed it, **the rest of the city**, is home to the city's exclusive neighborhoods and its best museums.

Oceanside Santa Monica

Although Santa Monica reaches fairly well inland, most visitors are content to limit themselves to the city's **oceanside** amusements, with

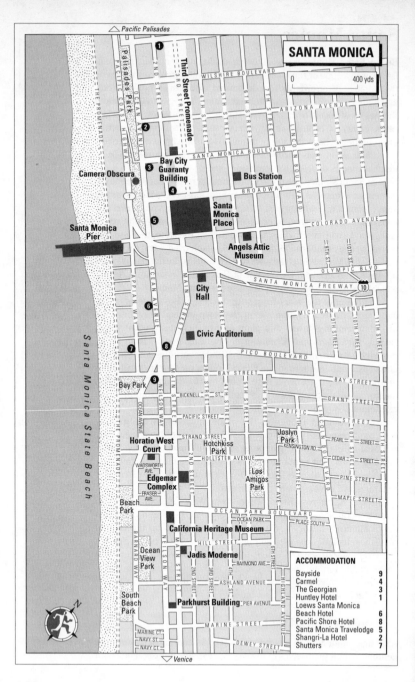

❶

Third Street Promenade

SANTA MONICA

0   400 yds

WILSHIRE BOULEVARD

2ND STREET

3RD STREET

4TH STREET

5TH STREET

6TH STREET

7TH STREET

ARIZONA AVENUE

9TH STREET

10TH STREET

12TH ST.

LINCOLN BOULEVARD

❷

OCEAN AVENUE

PACIFIC COAST HIGHWAY

Palisades Park

SANTA MONICA BOULEVARD

❸ Bay City
Guaranty
Building

Camera Obscura

■ Bus Station

❹

BROADWAY

Santa
Monica
Place

**Santa Monica
Pier**

❺

COLORADO AVENUE

**Angels Attic
Museum**

OLYMPIC BLVD

9TH ST.

10TH ST.

11TH ST.

SANTA MONICA FREEWAY

10

**City
Hall**

OCEAN AVENUE

MAIN STREET

4TH STREET

❻

APPIAN WAY

SANTA MONICA

MICHIGAN AVENUE

9TH STREET

10TH STREET

11TH STREET

Civic Auditorium

❼   ❽

PICO BOULEVARD

BAY STREET

GRANT STREET

BAY STREET

THE PROMENADE

OCEAN AVENUE

NELSON WAY

❾
Bay Park

3RD STREET

4TH ST.

5TH STREET

6TH STREET

PACIFIC

STREET

BICKNELL

PACIFIC STREET

LINCOLN BOULEVARD

PEARL   STREET

10TH STREET

11TH STREET

STRAND STREET

**Horatio West
Court**

Hotchkiss
Park

Joslyn
Park

KENSINGTON RD

CEDAR   STREET

WADSWORTH
AVE.

2ND STREET

HOLLISTER AVENUE

**Edgemar
Complex**

FRASER
AVE.

Los
Amigos
Park

BEVERLY AVE.

PINE STREET

MAPLE STREET

Santa Monica State Beach

**Beach
Park**

BARNARD WAY

OCEAN PARK BOULEVARD

OCEAN PARK

PLACE SOUTH

California Heritage Museum

**Ocean
View
Park**

NELSON WAY

MAIN STREET

HILL STREET

Jadis Moderne

RAYMOND AVE.

6TH STREET

HIGHLAND AVENUE

ACCOMMODATION	
Bayside	9
Carmel	4
The Georgian	3
Huntley Hotel	1
Loews Santa Monica	
Beach Hotel	6
Pacific Shore Hotel	8
Santa Monica Travelodge	5
Shangri-La Hotel	2
Shutters	7

**South
Beach
Park**

2ND STREET

3RD STREET

Parkhurst Building

PIER AVENUE

MARINE STREET

MARINE CT.

NAVY ST.

NAVY CT.

DEWEY STREET

N

the main attraction being the **Santa Monica Pier**, extending from Colorado Avenue over the Pacific Coast Highway, a busy tourist zone that has weathered many different storms.

The pier, constructed in 1874, was once one of LA's prime entertainments, offering the standard nerve-jangling rides, junk food vendors, and carnival atmosphere. Rebuilt and reconstructed several times, it was often threatened with demolition by developers and bureaucrats, narrowly averting this fate on several occasions in the 1970s (thanks largely to citizen advocacy groups). Other factors conspired against the pier, too, such as merciless storms in 1982 that nearly pounded the old pier into the sea and a growing reputation as a hangout for gangs and petty thugs from outside the area, with violent episodes as all-too-frequent events. Many visitors stayed away, especially at night when skirmishes between gangs and the police often took place, and business suffered accordingly.

In recent years, the establishment of a substation of the Santa Monica Police Department has eliminated most of the violent crime, as has an uptick in the local economy, and nightly tourist traffic is once again visible, attracting everyone from local business workers to puberty-stricken adolescents.

Although featuring an assortment of fast food stands, video game parlors, and watering holes, the pier's main appeal is its restored 1922 wooden **carousel** (50¢ per ride). To the south, a **children's park** comprises a number of stone sculptures that can be climbed on or crawled under, while further out on the pier, **Pacific Park** provides only a dim memory of the freewheeling amusement park of old, with its roller coaster and other such rides off limits to those who don't pay an entry fee. Near the end of the pier, anglers cast their lines into the murky depths of Santa Monica Bay, while below the pier, **Santa Monica State Beach** is a crowded strip of sand with little privacy for those who wish to sunbathe or relax. Swimming is a gamble due to pollution from nearby storm drains, but the threat of water-borne infections doesn't keep some locals, or unknowing tourists, from venturing out into the waters.

The grand beach houses just north of the pier were known as the "Gold Coast," because of the Hollywood personalities who lived in them. The largest, now the **Sand and Sea** beach club, was built as the servants' quarters of a massive 120-room house, now demolished, that belonged to William Randolph Hearst. MGM boss Louis B Mayer owned the adjacent Mediterranean-style villa; it was later rumored to be the place where the Kennedy brothers had their liaisons with Marilyn Monroe. If you're not intending to stretch out on the sands, you can follow the **bike path**, which begins at the pier and heads twenty miles south to Palos Verdes, a stretch that is one of the area's top choices for cycling.

East of the beach, across Pacific Coast Highway, **Palisades Park** overlooks the bay with stunning clear-day views from Malibu to Palos

For more on cycling in LA, see "Sports and Outdoor Activities," p.289.

Verdes – even as it sits precariously atop high bluffs that are constantly being eroded, and which occasionally tumble down to block the highway. Like the pier, the park has in recent years been the focus of renewed police activity, which has swept many of the homeless out, and is generally safe – although one clear danger you should avoid is venturing too close to the bluffs themselves, the rims of which are frequently fenced off with pylons to keep you from tumbling down with the shifting earth.

*The camera
obscura tool
was used by
artists such as
Jan Vermeer
as a visual aid
for painting.*

Within the park, the **Camera Obscura**, 1450 Ocean Ave (Mon 9am–2pm, Tues–Fri 9am–4pm, Sat–Sun 11am–4pm; free), provides a unique appeal with an old-fashioned visual device that prefigures modern photography. Through a reflective, rotational mirror on its roof, this "dark room" projects images of the outside world onto a circular screen.

Two blocks east of Ocean Avenue, between Wilshire Boulevard and Broadway, the **Third Street Promenade** is the closest the Westside comes to having an energetic street life. A pedestrianized stretch popular with street vendors and itinerant evangelists, and lined by a variety of fashionable clothing outlets and restaurants, the promenade underwent a successful refurbishment several years ago and now attracts a lively crowd of characters who come to hang out in the cafés, pubs, and nightclubs, play a game of pool, or browse through the many secondhand and fine-art book shops. It's especially busy on weekends, when huge numbers of tourists and locals vie for space amid the bohemian street poets, sidewalk jazz bands, and occasional bellowing lunatics.

The mall is anchored at its southern end by the trendy **Santa Monica Place**, a white stucco shopping precinct that is surely one of architect Frank Gehry's less-inspired works, with the usual assortment of upmarket chain stores and a mandatory food court. Just to the north, the entire commercial area is marked by one of the city's great visual icons, the 1929 **Bay City Guaranty Building**, Third Street at Santa Monica Boulevard, a Zigzag Moderne marvel that was for years Santa Monica's tallest building and which still features a colorful, non-functional, clock that towers over the shopping strip

*Accommod-
ation listings
in Santa
Monica,
including the
Shangri-La,
begin on
p.225.*

below. A little further north, the 1939 **Shangri-La Apartment Building**, now a hotel at Ocean and Arizona avenues, is perhaps the city's finest example of the later Streamline Moderne style that used nautical motifs to great effect, making this structure look like a giant, landlocked ocean liner.

Main Street

The completion of the Santa Monica Freeway in 1965 brought the city's beachfront homes within a fifteen-minute drive of Downtown and isolated the bulk of the town from **Main Street**, five minutes' walk from the pier – a collection of novelty shops, kite stores, and classy restaurants that is now one of the chief shopping districts on the Westside. The commercial operations are occasionally quirky, as shown by Jadis Moderne, Main and Hill streets, a prop rental operation not open to the public but featuring LA's best display window: a collection of 1930s horror-film mannequins posed in various demented dioramas, such as a mad scientist's lab, and surrounded by all sorts of antiquated technical junk and contraptions.

There's not much in the way of cultural entertainment along here, except perhaps the **California Heritage Museum**, Main Street at Ocean Park Boulevard (Wed–Sat 11am–4pm, Sun noon–4pm; $3), the city's effort to preserve some of its architectural past in the face of ever-encroaching development. Two houses were moved here to escape demolition: one hosts temporary displays on California cultural topics like the reign of the Dodgers and has several restored rooms that variously evoke the years from 1890 to 1930, while the other houses the *Victorian Restaurant*, which also serves tea on its patio at weekends (reserve on ☎310/392-8537). Additionally, there are several appealing architectural feats along the street, from the angular gray volumes and curious cube-frame of Frank Gehry's **Edgemar** shopping development, at no. 2415, to the great Spanish Colonial Revival design of the **Parkhurst Building**, Main Street at Pier Avenue, now occupied by a Giorgio Armani outlet. However, none matches the austere modernism of Irving Gill's nearby **Horatio West Court**, 140 Hollister Ave, a stripped-down Mission Revival from 1919, with cool white arches and simple geometric shapes.

Not all of Santa Monica has been so lucky as to escape the wrecking ball, however. Ocean Park Boulevard was one of the main routes to the coast via the old streetcars of the Pacific Electric, and the entire beachfront between here and the Venice border, now overshadowed by massive gray condominiums, used to be the site of a resort community developed by Abbot Kinney, the man behind the design of Venice itself. Along with vacation bungalows, a wharf, and a colorful boardwalk, the neighborhood also featured the largest and wildest of the old amusement piers: the fantastic **Pacific Ocean Park**, or "P-O-P" as it was known, which had a huge roller coaster, a giant funhouse, and a boisterous midway arcade, described by architectural historian Reyner Banham as a "fantasy in stucco and every known style of architecture and human ecology." Sadly, not a trace remains.

Santa Monica

The bars of Main Street, along with those in the rest of Santa Monica, are listed on p.263.

To see more modern buildings by Irving Gill, check out the Raymond House, p.172, and the Miltimore House, p.183.

The rest of the city

The interior of Santa Monica is marked mostly by quiet upscale neighborhoods, featuring copious foliage and modest architecture, alongside some entertainment-industry office parks and a few interesting museums and galleries.

Wilshire Boulevard, as elsewhere in LA, is the main commercial axis of this area, but further north, near the city border, **San Vicente Boulevard** is an interesting diversion, a grassy tree-lined strip and a

Santa Monica's restaurants are listed beginning on p.255.

Santa Monica

joggers' freeway that leads east to the wealthier confines of Brentwood. You can find LA's true health-mania just two blocks north of San Vicente, along Adelaide Drive between First and Seventh streets, where an entire stair-climbing culture has evolved along the giant **stairways** that connect Santa Monica with Pacific Palisades. On any given morning, crowds of locals trot up and down the street, just waiting for a chance to descend down the bluffs and charge back up again, red-faced and gasping for air, a spectacle that attracts many onlookers.

Two blocks south of San Vicente, the flashy novelty and clothing shops of **Montana Avenue** reflect the upward mobility of the area, as do its chic restaurants and upscale chain stores. This general area is home to the moneyed set of Santa Monica, but is fairly bland, save for the area's only example of world-class architecture, the wild **Gehry House**, 22nd Street at Washington Avenue, a fitting reflection of its architect Frank Gehry's taste for the unusual and experimental. Now partially hidden by foliage, the 1978 house features a chain-link facade, asphalt floors, a jagged, broken structure, and a complete shattering of conventional notions of architecture: not a unified design, but what appears to be a series of random ideas thrown together and bundled up with concrete walls and metal fencing.

Gehry's most recent bizarre creation is the new Guggenheim Museum in Bilbao, Spain.

Back towards the 10 freeway is **Angels Attic**, 516 Colorado Ave (Thurs–Sun 12.30–4.30pm; $6.50), an elegant 1895 Queen Anne structure that is home to a large collection of Victoriana, such as oversized dolls, turn-of-the-century arts and crafts, assorted wooden and tin toys, and a number of finely detailed miniatures. These tiny items are exquisitely rendered and surprisingly detailed, particularly the dwarf palace of Versailles, a more contemporary work. After reviewing the junior palaces and mini-houses, you can take a seat on the veranda for the museum's afternoon tea service, amid nineteenth-century furnishings.

The Highways performance space, in the 18th Street Arts Complex, is listed on p.279.

Further east is another of the town's ambitious young art spaces, the **Side Street Projects**, 1629 18th St (hours vary; information at ☎310/829-0779), which forms a part of the **18th Street Arts Complex**, Santa Monica's attempt at a trendy arts center.

Most of Bergamot Station's galleries are open Tues–Fri 11am–5.30pm.

The city also has a number of highly visible, and interesting, galleries selling works by emerging local and international artists, with many of them located at **Bergamot Station**, 2525 Michigan Ave, a collection of former railway sheds. The most intriguing dealers are Track 16, offering a wide display of cutting-edge material, much of it representational, with particular emphasis on social criticism and identity politics, and The Gallery of Functional Art, one of the town's most engaging art spaces, with a wide array of mechanical gizmos and eccentric furniture like cubist lamps, neon-lit chairs, wooden couches, and modified televisions. By the end of 1998, the **Santa Monica Museum of Art** will be moving into Bergamot Station as a staging ground for traveling exhibitions, having abandoned its previous digs at the Edgemar complex on Main Street.

Finally, at the corner of Ocean Park Boulevard, 28th Street leads south to a museum you'd be unlikely ever to stumble upon by chance, the **Museum of Flying** (Wed–Sun 10am–5pm; $7), at the Santa Monica Municipal Airport (now used only by private planes). The major employer in the early years of Santa Monica, the Donald Douglas Aircraft Company, had its main factory here – birthplace of the DC-3 and other planes which pioneered commercial aviation – and the old premises now display a number of vintage aircraft and related curiosities, which will appeal primarily to aeronautics buffs.

Venice

Immediately south of Santa Monica, **Venice** was laid out in the marshlands of Ballona Creek in 1905 by developer Abbot Kinney as a romantic replica of the northern Italian city (see box, p.139), though most of the architecture and canals of this new American Venice have long since disappeared. The lingering pseudo-European atmosphere has since proved just right for pulling in the artistic community he was aiming at, making Venice one of the coast's trendier spots. Not only are artists' studios and galleries a vital part of town, even the mainstream commercial enterprises get into the spirit. Main Street, for instance, is home to the offices of advertising firm **Chiat/Day/Mojo**, just south of Rose Street. Marked by Claes Oldenburg's huge pair of binoculars at the entrance, the Frank Gehry-designed offices have no assigned desks, leaving employees to roam free with laptops and mobile phones through spartan rooms lined with original modern art. A block north is the disturbing *Ballerina Clown*, a gargantuan sculpture by Jonathan Borofsky that looms over the intersection of Rose Avenue and Main Street. Elsewhere, a strong alternative arts scene centers around the **Beyond Baroque** literary arts center and bookshop in the old City Hall, 681 Venice Blvd (Tues–Fri 10am–5pm, Sat noon–5pm; ☎310/822-3006), which holds regular readings and workshops of poetry, prose, and drama.

Venice Beach and Venice Boardwalk

It's **Venice Beach** that draws most people down to the district, and nowhere else does LA parade itself quite so conspicuously as it does along the **Venice Boardwalk**, a wide pathway tracking alongside the sands that is packed weekends and all summer long with people-watchers, jugglers, fire-eaters, Hare Krishnas, and roller-skating guitar players. City authorities, in their zeal for order, have tried to force the many street vendors to get licenses to sell their goods (incense, love beads, tie-dyed shirts, and the like), but so far have failed to quell the anarchic spirit of the place. In any case, you'll have no difficulty picking up your choice of cheap sunglasses, T-shirts,

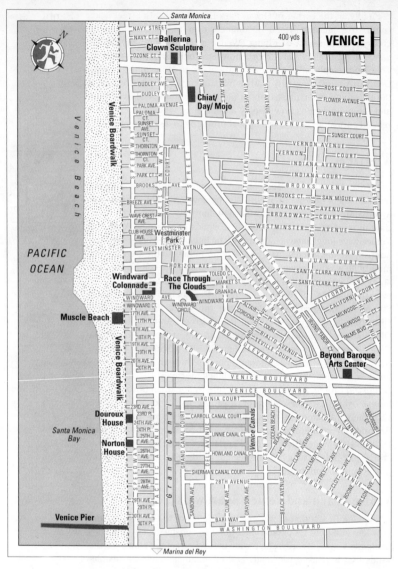

VENICE

0   400 yds

NAVY STREET
NAVY CT
Ballerina Clown Sculpture
OZONE CT
ROSE CT
DUDLEY AVE
DUDLEY CT
PALOMA AVENUE
PALOMA CT
SUNSET AVE
SUNSET CT
THORNTON CT
THORNTON AVE
PARK AVE
PARK CT
BROOKS AVE
BREEZE AVE
WAVE CREST AVE
CLUB HOUSE AVE
Westminster Park
WESTMINSTER AVENUE
HORIZON AVE

Chiat/ Day/ Mojo

ROSE   AVENUE
ROSE COURT
FLOWER AVENUE
FLOWER COURT
SUNSET   AVENUE
SUNSET COURT
VERNON AVENUE
VERNON COURT
INDIANA AVENUE
INDIANA COURT
BROOKS AVENUE
BROOKS CT   SAN MIGUEL AVE
BROADWAY AVENUE
BROADWAY COURT
WESTMINSTER AVENUE
SAN JUAN AVENUE
SAN JUAN COURT
SANTA CLARA AVENUE
SANTA CLARA COURT

HAMPTON   DRIVE

3RD   AVENUE
4TH   AVENUE
5TH   AVENUE
6TH   AVENUE
7TH   AVENUE

4TH   AVENUE
7TH   AVENUE

ELECTRIC   AVENUE
ABBOT KINNEY   BOULEVARD
CABRILLO AVE
ALHAMBRA COURT

PACIFIC OCEAN

Venice Beach

Venice Boardwalk

Windward Colonnade
WINDWARD
WINDWARD CT
17TH AVE
17TH PL
18TH AVE
18TH PL
19TH AVE
19TH PL
20TH AVE
20TH PL

Muscle Beach

Race Through The Clouds
TOLEDO CT
MARKET ST
GRANADA CT
WINDWARD AVE
ALTAIR PL
WINDWARD CIRCLE
CORDOVA PL
MINDANAO WAY
RIALTO AVENUE
SEVILLE COURT

CALIFORNIA AVENUE
CALIFORNIA COURT
CALIFORNIA AVE
MILWOOD CT
MILWOOD AVE
PALMS BLVD

IRVING TABOR CT

VENICE   WAY
MILDRED AVENUE
GRAND   BOULEVARD

Beyond Baroque Arts Center

VENICE   BOULEVARD
VENICE   BOULEVARD

Venice Boardwalk

23RD AVE
23RD PL
24TH AVE
24TH PL
25TH AVE
25TH PL
26TH AVE

Douroux House

Santa Monica Bay

Norton House

27TH AVE
28TH AVE
29TH AVE
29TH PL
30TH AVE
30TH PL

VIRGINIA COURT
CARROLL CANAL COURT
LINNIE CANAL CT
HOWLAND CANAL CT
SHERMAN CANAL COURT
28TH AVENUE

Grand Canal

GRAND CANAL COURT
DEL AVENUE
SANBORN AVE
CLUNE AVE
GRAYSON AVE
BARI WAY

Venice Canals

CARROLL CANAL
LINNIE CANAL
OCEAN AVENUE
BEACH AVENUE
BOONE AVE

OCEAN AVENUE
CLARK AVENUE
CLEMENT AVE
OLIVE AVENUE
BEACH AVE
WILSON AVE

WASHINGTON   WAY
MILDRED   AVENUE
ABBOT KINNEY BLVD
HARBOR   STREET

Venice Pier

WASHINGTON   BOULEVARD

personal stereos, tennis shoes, whatever you need for a day at the beach. South of Windward Avenue along the Boardwalk is **Muscle Beach**, a now-legendary outdoor weightlifting center where stern-looking, would-be Schwarzeneggers and other hardbodies pump serious iron, and high-flying gymnasts swing on the adjacent rings and bars. Incidentally, be warned that Venice Beach at night can be

American Venice

As with various other parts of LA, most notably Beverly Hills and San Marino, the development of Venice owed much to the desire to emulate European models; however, if it weren't for a lucky coin flip, this Old World simulation would never have existed. When **Abbot Kinney**, winner of the fabled toss with his former real estate partners, gained control of the area in 1904, he set about on a quixotic quest to build a paragon of learning, art, and culture from scratch. After deciding to base his ideal burg on the great Renaissance city-state, and after this area was linked up to the rest of LA by the Red Car mass transit line, Kinney began construction of the town by draining the land's marshes and quickly developing an extensive network of canals and roads, following this up with the creation of various theaters, performance venues, and sites for restaurants and cafés, as well as a think tank for the liberal arts. He even put his own money into the effort, investing about $1.5 million, and the initial payoff seemed great. Visitors were smitten with the new arts center, featuring bungalows and hotel rooms available for short stopovers, gondoliers (some from Italy) to navigate the waterways, and a pier for seaside relaxation.

Culture, however, only gets you so far; soon the crowds were demanding more amusement and less edification. In response, Venice shifted its focus to providing thrills and excitement to its seasonal vacationers and daily visitors, and Kinney oversaw the formation of what would be LA's greatest boardwalk. Minaret-topped palaces, rollercoasters, a ferris wheel, giant balloons, freak shows, and all other types of carnival recreations were soon found along Venice's once-austere oceanfront, and by 1911, under competition from his Ocean Park neighbors to the north, Kinney engineered the town's incorporation, even though it scarcely resembled his original notion for the community (aside from certain visual motifs like the canals). The city was successful for about a decade, until the oil industry moved in next door: when the derricks started their crude production, water pollution became a major threat to the beloved canals and before long, the central lagoon and outlying channels became fetid sites for waste disposal and general filth. Although the boardwalk was still attracting tourists, the decaying canals sullied the town's image, leading to a significant fall-off in short-term vacationers. Without any solution in sight, Venice's city leaders (which at that point did not include Kinney, who died in 1920) allowed the growing metropolis of LA to take over. Before long, the larger city paved over most of the canals and the main lagoon around the Windward Circle. Later decades would bring Depression-era economic convulsions, the demise of the carnivalesque boardwalk, and the severing of the Red Car line, all of which made Venice into a bleak shadow of its former self. The town's nadir may have come in 1958, when Orson Welles used it as a location in his film *Touch of Evil*, plausibly remaking it into a shabby, depressing Mexican border town rife with corruption and murder.

Later times would bring a new arts scene (with painters and poets finding cheap accommodations in Venice's oceanside apartment blocks), a redesigned boardwalk offering a contemporary sort of human entertainment, and rents steadily rising to keep pace with the newly popular boho-chic image. In recent years, gentrification has driven out many of the old residents from the quaint buildings, and little remains from Kinney's original plan, although a few vestiges, such as the fading colonnade and five renovated canals, are still visible here and there.

a dangerous place, taken over by street gangs, drug dealers, and various weirdos. Walking on the beach after dark is illegal, but you should have no problem supping at a beachside café or browsing at a record store.

Windward Avenue and around

Running from the beach into what was the Grand Circle of the canal system, **Windward Avenue** is Venice's main historical artery, once a canal but now paved over and ringed by a number of galleries and the Venice **post office**, inside of which a mural depicts the early city layout. On the west side of the circle, **Race Through the Clouds** is a 1987 office building with design elements paying homage to the old Venice rollercoaster (once the nation's biggest), including a sweeping neon track and complementary metal gridwork. Closer to the beach, the original Renaissance **arcade**, around Windward's intersection with Pacific Avenue, is alive with health-food shops, used-record stores, and rollerblade rental stands, though sadly, less and less of it remains with each passing year. Of the preserved columns, several are painted in Day-Glo colors that Kinney would no doubt have gasped at, while others retain their black-and-white dignity. Look closely at some of them and you'll see an odd touch: on their Ionic capitals are molded the faces of local businessmen – a pointed reminder of Venice's entrepreneurial roots, and its early hubris.

To drive over the canals, there's only one route: Dell Avenue, a one-way street that heads north from Washington Boulevard.

The five remaining **canals** are just a few blocks south, where the original 1904 bridges survive, and you can sit and watch the ducks paddle around in the still waters. The pleasant and secluded setting belies a much more disturbing reality, though, as the spread of a bird-borne disease in recent years led local health officials to capture, and kill, a large number of the waterfowl. While the birds have since made a comeback, some community members still hold a grudge against city officials for their heavy-handed approach. Also along the canals is some pricey real estate, though the houses don't necessarily look so expensive, with modernist cubes and Tudor piles sitting next to Colonial bungalows and postmodern sheds.

To the north, diagonally between Venice Boulevard and Main Street, the shopping strip of **Abbot Kinney Boulevard** features hair salons, antique stores, mid-range restaurants, and scattered old houses in between, a fairly worthwhile place to kill an hour or two, although strolling about in the dark is strongly discouraged: this street is also the southern border of Venice's notorious Oakwood district – the only coastal area hit with substantial violence during the 1992 riots.

Ocean Front Walk

Between the Grand Canal and the ocean is the thin line of Pacific Avenue, home to some of LA's finest contemporary architecture. Park either at the channel-side lot on the south, near Via Marina street, or curbside on the north, and follow **Ocean Front Walk**, actually the same route as the Venice boardwalk, by the colorful beachside houses. From the north, you'll first hit Antoine Predock's groundbreaking **Douroux House**, 2315 Ocean Front Walk, a great concrete frame with rooftop bleachers and a big red window that fully pivots toward the sea, allowing the ocean breezes to easily sweep through the geometric structure. Not far away is Frank Gehry's **Norton House**, 2509 Ocean Front Walk, a big yellow box with jagged wooden windowframes and a tiny metal staircase on the facade; further along is the contemporary Art Deco design of the **Yacht House**, 3900 Pacific Ave, just a block east of Ocean Front Walk, a great blue-and-white boat that maintains a streamlined appearance even as its bow remains firmly stuck in the concrete sidewalk. Finally, the **Doumani House**, Ocean Front Walk at Yawl Court, is an angular white cube with stepped windows and metallic tracery. All these structures are far more successful than their counterparts sitting across the stagnant Grand Canal – ostentatious houses that are little more than sham-palazzos and hokey neoclassical monstrosities.

Marina del Rey, the Ballona Wetlands and Playa del Rey

When Venice was at the height of its decay in the 1950s and 1960s, it had to deal with a new and unwelcome neighbor to the south: **Marina del Rey**, a county-controlled real estate development of huge proportions that blotted out the old city's southward views with coastal high-rise construction. As with the colossal towers plunked down along Wilshire Boulevard in Westwood, investment capital proved irresistible, even if it meant damaging the charm of nearby neighborhoods. Marina del Rey continues to be an eyesore, and you're unlikely to see any water whatsoever, unless you drive around the sizable marina; the whole area is ringed by giant business complexes and apartment superstructures, the latter of which more suggest the high-rise tenements of the East Coast than they do any notion of luxury living. Along the south end of the area, at the end of Fiji Way, **Fisherman's Village** is Marina del Rey's sole visitor's attraction, though it's difficult to see why, consisting as it does of uninspired pseudo-maritime architecture, low-end seafood joints, and endless trinket and T-shirt shops.

Ballona Wetlands

Further south, down Lincoln Boulevard, Marina del Rey gives way to a shocking surprise: the wide, undeveloped expanse of the **Ballona** (pronounced *by-oh-na*) **Wetlands**, what may be LA's last major wetlands area and a site of much recent controversy (see box overleaf).

Marina del
Rey, the
Ballona
Wetlands
and Playa
del Rey

Trouble in the wetlands

Before Abbot Kinney won his 1904 coin flip to create what is now Venice, the wetlands of LA's mid-coastal area stretched all the way to the border of the community of Ocean Park and had several other counterparts in the region. Since then, almost all the old bogs have been filled in by development, and only the Ballona Wetlands remain, a rich and diverse environment, with two hundred major bird species and a range of other creatures all subsisting on the land. Unfortunately, the Wetlands are also prime real estate, and for twenty years developers and environmentalists have battled for permanent control of them.

Essentially, real estate developers Maguire Thomas Partners planned the huge community of Playa Vista to sit on the disused property of Hughes Aircraft Corporation alongside the Wetlands, which would effectively disrupt, if not usurp, the natural surroundings. Activists have countered by citing the immediate danger to the ecosystem as well as the daunting size of the new community: 1000 acres that would include 28,000 residents, 5 million square feet of office space, and countless amounts of pollution, noise, and traffic. Unlike the current environs that have protected the Wetlands – a flood channel to the north and high bluffs to the south – Playa Vista would, they argue, effectively ruin the surrounding environment by its proximity, size, and character.

With $7 billion at stake, the developers fought a lengthy court battle that culminated in a draw: in exchange for a modified development, the real estate company agreed to set aside an avian preserve and create an interpretive center. With all the lingering hostility, though, the settlement still has not assuaged everyone's fears, and unless the project changes even further, the Ballona Wetlands will likely be a continuing topic of argument and legal action. Waiting to move in, one of Playa Vista's first tenants will be Steven Spielberg and friends, who plan to construct their new Dreamworks SKG studio here.

These three hundred fertile acres of ecological preservation, containing species such as herons, egrets, crabs, and shrimp in a mixed environment of fresh and salt water, have had their ecosystem disrupted in recent years by the erroneous introduction of foxes, which freely roam the land. Although off-limits to humans, this natural preserve can be toured at a distance by heading west on Jefferson Boulevard (off Lincoln) and taking a left onto Culver Boulevard. While you might not see any major animals, you will get a sense of the unique character of this terrain in the heavily urbanized LA basin.

Playa del Rey

To the west, Culver Boulevard leads to the declining resort community of **Playa del Rey**, once an essential link in the Red Car transit line and the site of a grand hotel, but since reduced to a faded, weather-beaten collection of commercial shacks and downscale houses. Although new investment has caused some property values along its marina channel to increase, this LA district has been decaying for decades – which gives it a surprising charm. Untrampled by the crowds of tourists and locals that can make Santa Monica and Venice unpleasant at times, this little neighborhood offers similar ocean views without the congestion. The **lagoon**, nestled near the beach along Pacific Street, is a quiet, peaceful location that is a popular spot for children's activities and dog-walking, and the **jetty**, stretching out to the marina breakwater, provides a good walk as well as an intimate view of sail- and motorboats cruising slowly through the channel on their way back to the marina. The adjacent northern edge of **Dockweiler Beach** also provides a certain amount of solace, as long as you avoid the speeding cyclists and rollerbladers along the bike path.

On the high bluff above the main part of Playa del Rey, the neighborhood of **Palisades del Rey** is a good spot for a hike, with the additional bonus of a few scattered bits of architectural interest, particularly a 1939 **ship house**, 5740 Whitlock Ave, with a pipe railing and array of glass brick to complement the seaworthy design of this late-Art Deco gem.

There used to be more to this neighborhood, and to Playa del Rey overall, but the need for a sound barrier between LAX and the ocean did much to ruin its residential setting. When the airport bought out the property here, it resulted in one of LA's strangest attractions: a modern **ghost town** stretching for several miles from Waterview Street to Imperial Highway along Vista del Mar. Guarding a disturbingly surreal atmosphere, chain-link fences keep intruders away from this network of empty streets, crumbling housing foundations, and defunct street lights. Head to Sandpiper Street to survey the scene close up – at least until the next blaring takeoff of a jumbo jet makes you jump back in your car.

Chapter 7

South and East LA

S outh and **East LA** are far removed from the tourist circuit, with
abysmal reputations for crime and are avoided generally by visitors and almost always by local Westsiders, many of them
believing any venture south of the I-10 freeway to be an open invitation to murder, mugging, or some other unpleasantry.

In truth, while these places can be dangerous and should be
largely avoided at night, the ghetto stereotypes are blown out of proportion, especially given the size and diversity of the area. Contained
mostly within the boundaries of the 405, 605, and 10 freeways,
South and East LA make up a huge section of the metropolitan basin
that encompasses a great range of cultures and races, with neighboring communities often separated by major differences in language, ethnicity, and religion. Hispanic population growth is a constant throughout these areas, and crude racial categorization is simply not possible in most of these parts: South Central LA is no more
uniformly African-American than the Westside is uniformly WASP.
Visitors are best off if they keep an open mind and explore some of
the more worthwhile destinations around here.

South Central LA

Lacking the scenic splendor of the coast, the glamour of West LA,
and the movie history of Hollywood, **SOUTH CENTRAL LA** hardly
ranks on the city's list of prime attractions – especially since it burst
onto the world's TV screens as the focal point of the April 1992 **riots**.
However, it's an integral part of the city, particularly in terms of size:
a big oval chunk bordered by Alameda Street and the 10 and 405
freeways. The population was once mostly black, but is increasingly
Hispanic and Asian, interspersed here and there with working-class
whites. Mostly made up of detached bungalows enjoying their own
patch of palm-shaded lawn, South Central has something of a com-
munitarian spirit that long ago disappeared elsewhere in LA. Yet, this
picture doesn't for long conceal the relative poverty of the area,

The gangs of LA

South Central LA is the heartland of the city's infamous **gangs**, said to number over one hundred thousand members between them. The gangs have existed for more than forty years and often encompass several generations of a family. The black gangs known as Crips and Bloods are the most famous, but there are also many expanding Hispanic gangs as well. The characteristic violence associated with these groups often stems from territorial fights over drug-dealing, with many gangs staking claim to certain neighborhoods through their names. For example, the "Shoreline Gangster Crips" denotes a local gang active in the central ghetto of Venice.

Each new wave of immigration adds to the roster of gangs, which usually, though not always, organize themselves by ethnicity, but it's only recently, with the massive influx of drug money, that violence has escalated and automatic weaponry (not least Uzi machine guns) has become commonplace. Although most fatalities (there are about 350 a year) are a direct result of drug-trade rivalry, in recent years there's been an increase in "drive-by shootings," the vast majority of which take place in established gangland areas and occasionally involve the death of bystanders. It was indicative of LA's entrenched racial and social divisions that the death of a white professional woman during a freak shootout in West LA in 1987 was one of the few gang-related deaths to excite widespread publicity and lead to major anti-gang initiatives on the part of the police. The resulting clampdowns have seen a thousand arrests made on a single night, but on the whole have made little real headway in tackling the real problem – and seem unlikely to do so until the outlook for people in LA's poorer sections improves.

Despite the violence, an outsider is unlikely to see much evidence of the gangs beyond the occasional blue or red scarf (the colors of the Crips and Bloods) tied around a street sign to denote territory and, in some areas, the presence of widespread graffiti consisting of various letters and symbols that are almost always indecipherable. Don't expect to witness any inter-gang warfare, unless you do something foolish like cruising down Vermont Avenue on a Saturday night. As for personal danger, driving through South Central LA by day is generally safe, but be wary of delays at traffic lights, and avoid the area after dusk unless you're with people who know their way around.

which gives most residents little chance of climbing the social ladder and which has engendered the creation of large, pervasive youth gangs. Nonetheless, there are compelling – and undervisited – sights to be found, best seen in daylight.

Inglewood

Bordered by the San Diego Freeway and the airport, on the western edge of South Central, **INGLEWOOD** was once the world capital for chinchilla farming, but is now known mostly for its major sporting venues, including the **Hollywood Park Racetrack**, 1050 S Prairie Ave, a landscaped track with lagoons and tropical vegetation, and the adjacent white pillars of **The Forum**, a 17,000-seat stadium that is the headquarters of both the LA Lakers (basketball) and the LA Kings (hockey) and is also a major concert hall.

Tickets for Lakers' and Kings' games are expensive and can be hard to get; for details on how to go about obtaining them, see "Sports and Outdoor Activities," p.287.

However, Inglewood is best seen for its pop architecture, starting with the grand **Academy Theater**, 3100 Manchester Blvd, now a church, with a giant Moderne spire and spiky neon globe that beckon to worshippers. Further west, the **Loyola Theater**, at Sepulveda and Manchester boulevards, is late Streamline Moderne – with a sweeping red goose-neck curve on its facade – that now serves as office space. The titans of popular design, though, are unquestionably **Randy's Donuts**, 805 Manchester Blvd, a 1954 fast-food shack topped by a colossal brown donut; and **Pann's**, a mile north at La Tijera Boulevard and Centinela, one of the last great coffee shops, with a big neon sign, boomerang design, surrounding exotic plants, gravel roof, and a wealth of primary colors.

The Centinela Adobe was once home to Ignacio Machado, an heir to one of the Mexican founders of Los Angeles.

Just south of *Pann's*, the historic **Centinela Adobe**, 7636 Midfield Ave (Wed & Sun 2–4pm; free), an 1834 structure that's the oldest building in the area, is currently furnished with period antiques and replicas, including a good array of Victorian clothing and furniture. On the site is a center for historic preservation, which contains a storehouse of information, curios, and memorabilia of Inglewood city history and culture.

Crenshaw

Just to the north, **CRENSHAW** and adjacent **Leimert Park** form the contemporary center of African-American social activity in LA. Where once the nucleus of black culture was along Central Avenue,

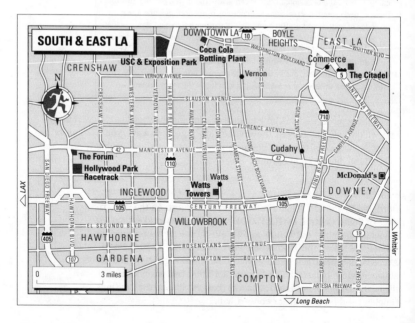

south of Downtown, it is now along **Crenshaw Boulevard**, which features many restaurants and book and record stores, as well as the Baldwin Hills Crenshaw Plaza, a multimillion-dollar shopping mall created with community redevelopment money. The first of Magic Johnson's inner-city theater complexes was constructed in the vicinity, too, although the best (former) moviehouse in the district is the **Leimert Theater**, 3300 43rd Place, an Art Deco marvel by architects Morgan, Walls and Clements (see p.79) that features a towering oil-derrick sign with concrete ornamentation and neon accents. The building, since converted into a Jehovah's Witness Hall, lies in the heart of **Leimert Park Village**, an array of shops and restaurants mostly frequented by African-Americans and African immigrants. The chief cultural institution in the Village is the **Museum in Black**, 4331 Degnan Blvd (Tues–Sat noon–6pm; free), a wide survey of African and African-American art and history, from knives, cooking utensils, and totemic statuary of the Old World to racist advertising and political propaganda of the New.

Above Crenshaw and Leimert Park, the black upper-middle class resides in pleasant **Baldwin Hills**, named after Wall Street gambler and Santa Anita racetrack-builder E J "Lucky" Baldwin, who acquired the old Rancho La Cienega, of which this is a part, just before he died in 1909. Later, the area would host the Olympic Village for LA's 1932 summer games and become the site of a catastrophic 1963 dam-burst and flood, due in no small part to environmental damage from oil-drilling, which continues to this day.

*Olympic
Boulevard,
just a few
miles north of
the former
Olympic
Village in
Baldwin Hills,
was named in
honor of the
1932 games.*

West Adams

The faded **West Adams** neighborhood, along Adams Boulevard from Crenshaw Boulevard to Hoover Street, was one of the more unlikely spots where movie stars once lived, full of striking late-nineteenth-century architecture and notable celebrities such as musical director Busby Berkeley, silent comic Fatty Arbuckle, silent vamp Theda Bara, and sound-era actresses Butterfly McQueen and Hattie McDaniel. Berkeley's estate, the 1910 **Gusti Villa**, 3500 W Adams Blvd, a French Beaux Arts creation, markedly contrasts with neighbors like the **Lindsay House**, no. 3424, a bulky stone curiosity, now a Catholic church, with a half-Craftsman, half-Mission Revival design of surprising pedigree: Irving Gill, who usually designed austere works of pre-Moderne severity, co-built this in 1905 with Charles Whittlesey before he developed his mature style. Similar in many respects, the **Walker House**, no. 3300, is a Whittlesey structure that is a Craftsman-Mission hybrid which has also been turned into a church. Further east, the **Britt House**, no. 2141, is a great classical revival structure with towering Ionic columns that is home to an ath-letic foundation. The finest building in the area – and at last, one open to the public – is the French Renaissance **William Clark Memorial Library**, 2520 Cimarron St (Mon–Fri 9am–5pm; free),

South
Central LA

*Along with
creating the
library,
William Clark
founded the LA
Philharmonic
Orchestra and
was a US
Senator –
representing
Montana.*

with tight, symmetrical composition, yellow brick walls, elegant formal gardens, and a grand entrance hall. Its collection, amassed by millionaire Clark, heir to a copper fortune, comprises 90,000 books, with rare volumes by Pope, Fielding, Dryden, Swift, and Milton, as well as a huge set of letters and manuscripts by Oscar Wilde. Four Shakespeare folios and a group of works by Chaucer are also highlights, as are critical documents in American history like those regarding the Louisiana Purchase.

The USC Campus

Further east, the USC (University of Southern California) **CAMPUS** is an enclave of wealth in one of the city's poorest neighborhoods. For many years a breeding ground for political and economic fat cats, from hatching LA's shadow rulers for the secretive "Committee of 25" to supplying Richard Nixon with advisers like H R Haldeman. USC, or the "University of Spoiled Children" as some call it, is one of the most expensive universities in the country, its undergraduates thought of as more likely to have rich parents than fertile brains. Indeed, the stereotype is often borne out, both by their easygoing, suntanned, beach-bumming nature, and by USC's being more famous for its sporting prowess than its academic strength. Alumni include O J Simpson, who collected college football's highest honor, the Heisman Trophy, when he played for USC. There have been attempts to integrate the campus population more closely with the local community, but for the moment at least USC is something of an elitist island, right down to its own fast-food outlets.

The **campus** often resembles an armed camp, literally fenced off from the world around it (you can only enter by car through carefully monitored guard stations) and constructed with a rigid and austere design – and hardly any green space. Based around a similar Italian Romanesque style as UCLA, USC's 1920s buildings exhibit nice detail and ornamentation, but its later modern versions of the Romanesque are much uglier, with the **Social Science Building** and **Philips Hall of Education** being two singularly unappealing structures from 1968 that are so massive and inhuman as to recall the rest of Mussolini's Fascist architecture.

Though sizable, the campus is reasonably easy to get around. If you do want to visit, you might find it easiest to take the free hour-long **walking tour** (Mon–Fri 10am–2pm by appointment; ☎213/743-2183). Without a guide, a good place to start is the **Doheny Library** (during academic year Mon–Thurs 8.30am–10pm, Fri 8.30am–5pm, Sat 9am–5pm, Sun 1–10pm; free), an inviting Romanesque structure, where you can pick up a campus map and pass an hour or so investigating the large stock of overseas newspapers and magazines on the second floor – although they tend to be at least three weeks behind the times. Another place for general information is the **Student Union** building, just across from the library and straight out of *Beverly Hills 90210*. Food is priced to make the college money, and the **bar** is an underused and claustrophobic room with mirrored walls and watery beer. A **café** under the Wolfgang Puck banner provides some good news, however, with tasty, if still pricey, pizzas and salads.

USC's art collection is housed in the **Fisher Gallery** on Exposition Boulevard (during academic year Tues–Fri noon–5pm, Sat 11am–3pm; free), which stages several major international exhibitions each year and has a broad permanent stock, best for its nineteenth-century American works, including Thomas Cole's *The Woodchopper*, a Hudson River School painting, and Albert Bierstadt's landscape of *A Stream in the Rocky Mountains*, a grand Romantic vista. Elsewhere, you can see smaller shows of students' creative efforts in the **Helen Lindhurst Fine Arts Gallery** (Mon–Fri 9am–5pm; free) and the **Helen Lindhurst Architecture Gallery and Library** (Mon–Fri noon–6pm, Sat noon–5pm; free), a structure which itself is quite creative, with concrete-porch-level glass boxes doubling as skylights for the underground library. Much less appealing is the public art nearby, the *Pascal Fountain*, an unintentionally frightening pair of quasi-human figures with elongated metallic bodies – Giacometti meets *Battlestar Galactica*.

The campus is also home to the **George Lucas Film School**, named after the producer who studied here, which is a decidedly mainstream counterpart to the UCLA film school in Westwood. Ironically, **Steven Spielberg**, one of the biggest box-office directors in the history of film, couldn't get in to USC when he applied as an aspiring director. Now, his name is hallowed here, and writ large on the wall of the imposing and expensive cinema-and-TV-school sound-mixing center he later funded. A short walk away, the **Arnold Schoenberg Institute** (Mon–Fri 9am–5pm; free) is a study center devoted to a composer whose wide influence on modern musical thought – largely through his experiments with atonal sounds and twelve-tone structures – is even more remarkable when you consider that he had no formal training. Schoenberg, born in Austria in 1871, came to the US to escape the Nazis, and spent the fourteen years before his death in 1951 in LA. The reception area holds a mock-up of his studio, while the small auditorium displays his personal mementos. During the academic year, students often give free lunchtime concerts of his music, which can sound rather prickly to the uninitiated.

Between USC and Exposition Park, sports fans may want to stop at the **Coliseum** on Hoover Boulevard. The site of the 1932 and 1984 Olympic Games has fallen on hard times lately, with football's LA Raiders having relocated to Oakland and no new tenant in sight. However, USC's home games are still played here, and the great arch on the facade and the muscular, headless commemorative statues create enough visual appeal to make for a worthwhile stop-off.

Exposition Park

Once known as Agricultural Park because of its produce vendors and farming exhibits, **Exposition Park** is, given the bleak nature of the surrounding area, one of the most appreciated spots in LA, incorporating lush landscaped gardens and a number of decent museums. Although this area just south of USC – along with the residential quarters north of the school – was once home to LA's elite, "white flight" and economic downturns have left it behind. Nevertheless, compelling reasons remain to explore beyond USC's fenced-in compound.

Large by any standards, the park itself retains a sense of community – a feeling bolstered by its function as a favorite lunchtime picnic place for schoolkids. After eating, their field trips usually involve the **California Museum of Science and Industry**, one of several museums in the park (unless otherwise stated all daily 10am–5pm; free). Although largely uncritical, the institution has scores of working scientific models, thousands of pressable buttons, and a full array of the incubating chickens, recycling displays, and techno-gizmos common to most museums of this ilk. Just outside, the **Hall of Health** includes a replica "classic" American diner offering displays on what not to eat if you want to stay healthy, along with cutaways of human anatomy and bodily systems. At the neighboring **Technology Hall**, you can, with the aid of a few machines, wreck the American economy, experience a tepid version of an earthquake, and play around with electrical charges – however, all the simulations are lightweight and geared more to children than adults. Closer to Exposition Boulevard, the **Aerospace Building**, marked by the DC10 parked outside, is rather bland, offering a few models and displays pertaining to space and weather prediction and a slew of old jets and rocket paraphernalia. The building itself – a white cubic mass with a jet stuck on the side – is something of a landmark, designed by Frank Gehry and prefiguring some of his later, better work.

In the vicinity, an **IMAX Theater** plays a range of short, eye-popping documentaries on a gigantic curved screen, and the nearby **California African-American Museum** has diverse, temporary exhibitions on the history, art, and culture of black people in the Americas, with special focus given to the contribution of African-Americans in painting and sculpture throughout the centuries.

The **Natural History Museum of Los Angeles County** (Tues–Sun 10am–5pm; $6, students $3.50), in the northwest corner of the park, also has much appeal. Apart from housing the biggest collection of material, it's the nicest building around here – an explosion of Spanish Revival styles with echoing domes, travertine columns, and a marble floor. Foremost among the exhibits is a tremendous stock of dinosaur bones and fossils, and some individually imposing skeletons (usually casts), including the crested "duck-billed" dinosaur, the skull of a Tyrannosaurus Rex, and the astonishing frame of a

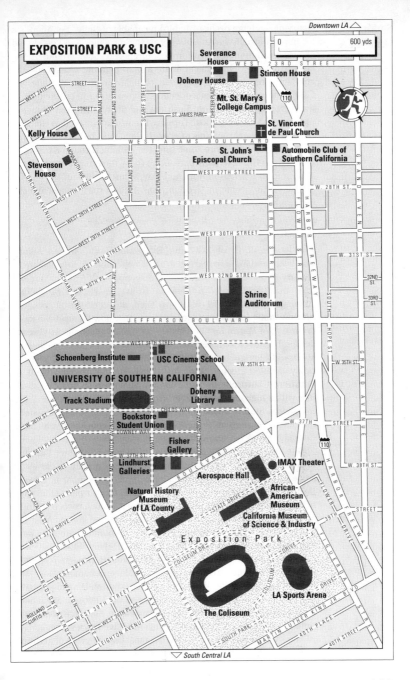

EXPOSITION PARK & USC

0   600 yds

Severance House
WEST 23RD STREET
Stimson House
Doheny House
110
Mt. St. Mary's College Campus
St. James Park
ST. JAMES PARK

St. Vincent de Paul Church

Kelly House

WEST ADAMS BOULEVARD

St. John's Episcopal Church
Automobile Club of Southern California

Stevenson House

WEST 27TH STREET

WEST 28TH STREET

WEST 30TH STREET

WEST 32ND STREET

Shrine Auditorium

JEFFERSON BOULEVARD

Schoenberg Institute
USC Cinema School

UNIVERSITY OF SOUTHERN CALIFORNIA

Track Stadium
Doheny Library

Bookstore
Student Union
Fisher Gallery

Lindhurst Galleries
IMAX Theater
Aerospace Hall
African-American Museum
Natural History Museum of LA County
California Museum of Science & Industry

Exposition Park

The Coliseum
LA Sports Arena

Diatryma – a huge prehistoric bird incapable of flight. Yet, there's a lot beyond strictly natural history in the museum, and you should allow several hours at least for a comprehensive look around. In the fascinating pre-Columbian Hall are Mayan pyramid murals and the complete, reconstructed contents of a Mexican tomb, while the Californian history sections document the early (white) settlement of the region during the Gold Rush era and after, with some stunning photos of LA in the 1920s. Topping the whole place off is the gem collection: several roomfuls of crystals, enhanced by special lighting.

On a sunny day, spare some time for walking through Exposition Park's **Rose Garden** (daily 9am–5pm; free), the flowers of which are at their most fragrant in April and May, when the bulk of the 45,000 annual visitors come by to admire the 16,000 rose bushes and the downright prettiness of their setting.

North of USC

Just to the north of USC and Exposition Park, around Adams Boulevard and Figueroa Street, is a fine collection of early twentieth-century architecture. Indeed, the intersection itself features three of LA's best period-revival designs from the 1920s: **St John's Episcopal Church**, 514 W Adams Blvd, an architectural competition's winning Italian Romanesque entry that now features the modern image of Martin Luther King, Jr, in stained glass; the **St Vincent de Paul Church**, catercorner to St John's, a wildly ornamental Mexican Churrigueresque creation with a sparkling, tiled dome and richly detailed steeple; and the church-like **Automobile Club of Southern California**, 2601 S Figueroa St, a Spanish Baroque structure with a high octagonal tower. Nearby, the **Stimson House**, 2421 S Figueroa St, is a Romanesque castle-home made of red sandstone that features a great crenelated tower and appears ready for a Crusader battle.

One long block to the west, **Chester Place** and **St James Park** are pedestrian-friendly zones that were once the private enclaves of some of LA's most prominent citizens, including oil baron Edward Doheny, whose **Doheny House**, 8 Chester Place, is a palatial triumph of Spanish Gothic, with a palm conservatory, French rococo interior, and immense dining hall built to seat one hundred guests. After the 1958 death of Doheny's wife, this and the surrounding property were given to Mount St Mary's College, and the Doheny House is now a campus building. Right by here is the **Wilson House**, 7 Chester Place, an Islamic creation with appealing ornamentation; the **Severance House**, 650 W 23rd St, a 1904 Mission Revival structure with some Victorian detailing in back; and the Victorian **Stevenson House**, 2639 Monmouth Ave, notable mainly as the place where two-time presidential candidate Adlai Stevenson lived as a youth.

Across the street from USC lies the most bizarre piece of architecture in the area, the **Shrine Auditorium**, 665 W Jefferson Blvd, a

1920s Islamic fantasy with onion domes and streetside colonnade that seems like a vestige of D W Griffith's *Intolerance* set in Hollywood and which is actually, and appropriately, a frequent venue for award shows like the Oscars.

Central Avenue

The focus of black commercial and cultural activity in the interwar years, **Central Avenue** had a vigor and popularity that has never really been recaptured. Because pre-1960s segregation and restrictive housing covenants prevented African-Americans from living in large sections of LA, especially to the west, this avenue from Eighth Street to Vernon Avenue became the hub for numerous restaurants, nightclubs, and jazz halls – including such notable establishments as the *Down Beat Club* and the *Last Word*, among many other hot spots – where a broad mixture of blacks, from blue-collar workers to celebrities, created a real cultural cachet for the strip, one that occasionally attracted white liberals from the Westside.

With the demise of official segregation, Central Avenue met an inevitable decline, but here and there, there are still appealing sights to visit. The greatest piece of Streamline Moderne architecture in the area, or perhaps anywhere in the city, lies at the north end of the street: the **Coca-Cola Bottling Plant**, 1334 S Central Ave, a huge, landlocked Art Deco ocean liner with rounded corners, porthole windows, racing stripes, metal railings, and nautical doors that is not only in excellent condition, but is also still in use by the soft drink giant. Eleven blocks south, pioneering black architect Paul R Williams' **Second Baptist Church**, 2412 Griffith Ave, is a striking north Italian Romanesque church that is now home to what has long been one of the most prominent religious institutions in LA, the First AME Church, notable for its social activism and role in city politics. Further south, the **Dunbar Hotel**, 4225 S Central Ave, marks the first US hotel built specifically for blacks (by a dentist) and patronized by almost every prominent African-American, including such luminaries as W E B DuBois and Duke Ellington, during the 1930s through the 1950s. However, you can only see the hotel's restored lobby and facade, as it is now a home for the elderly.

Watts, Compton, and Gardena

Beyond the empty shell of the old Art Deco campus of **Pepperdine University**, Vermont Avenue and 79th Street, South Central becomes grittier and much more dicey. If areas like West Adams and Exposition Park are unfairly described as dangerous, places like **WATTS** and adjacent Willowbrook often justify the description (see box overleaf). Now more Hispanic than black, Watts provides only one valid reason to visit (and only during the day), the Gaudiesque **Watts Towers**, sometimes called the Rodia

Pepperdine's current digs are in Malibu, on an ocean-side hilltop; see p.201.

LA's riots

The district of Watts achieved notoriety as the scene of the six-day **Watts Riot** of August 1965. The arrest of a 21-year-old unemployed black man, Marquette Frye, on suspicion of drunken driving, gave rise to charges of police brutality and led to bricks, bottles, and slabs of concrete being hurled at police and passing motorists during the night of the 11th. The situation had calmed by the next morning, but the following evening both young and old black people were on the streets, venting an anger generated by years of what they felt to be less than even-handed treatment by the police and other white-dominated institutions. Weapons were looted from stores and many buildings set afire (though few residential buildings, black-owned businesses, or community services, such as libraries and schools, were touched); street barricades were erected, and the events then took a more serious turn. By the fifth day the insurgents were approaching Downtown, which, along with the fear spreading through white LA, led to the call-out of the National Guard: 13,000 troops arrived, set up machine-gun placements and road blocks, and imposed an 8pm-to-dawn curfew, which caused the chaos to subside. In the aftermath of the uprising, which left 36 dead, one German reporter said of Watts, "It looks like Germany during the last months of World War II."

Ten years later, Watts hit the headlines for a second time when members of the Symbionese Liberation Army (SLA), who had kidnapped publishing heiress Patti Hearst, fought a lengthy – and televised – gun battle with police until the house they were trapped in burned to the ground. The site of the battle, at 1466 E 54th St, is now a vacant lot, though the surrounding houses are still riddled with bullet holes.

LA experienced another round of urban turmoil in 1992 with the unexpected acquittal of five white Los Angeles police officers (charged

Towers, at 1765 E 107th St. Constructed from iron, stainless steel, old bedframes, and cement, and decorated with fragments of bottles and around 70,000 crushed seashells, these striking pieces of folk art are surrounded by more than a little mystery. Their maker Simon Rodia had no artistic background or training at all, but labored over the towers' construction from 1921 to 1954, refusing offers of help and unable to explain either their meaning or why on earth he was building them. Once finished, Rodia left the area, refused to talk about the towers, and faded into complete obscurity. The towers managed to stave off condemnation for many decades and were eventually declared a landmark. However, 1994's earthquake left the towers shrouded in scaffolding, and they have not yet been fully repaired; call the adjacent Watts Tower Arts Center, 1727 E 107th St (☎213/847-4646) to check on their condition and accessibility.

Between Watts and the Harbor Area, only a few districts are of passing interest. Despite its fame as the home of many of LA's rappers – NWA, for example, sang venomously of its ills on their "Straight Outta Compton" – **COMPTON** is not a place where strangers should attempt to sniff out the local music scene. History

with using excessive force after they were videotaped kicking and beating black motorist Rodney King), which could almost have been calculated to provoke a violent backlash in LA's poverty-stricken ghetto. What few predicted, however, was the sheer scale of the response to the verdict, surpassing the violence of the Watts Riots. It again all began in South Central LA, with motorists being pulled from their cars and attacked, and quickly escalated into a tumult of arson, shooting, and looting that spread from Long Beach to Hollywood. Downtown police headquarters were surrounded by a mixed crowd of blacks, Hispanics, and whites, chanting "No Justice, No Peace," and it took the imposition of a four-day dusk-to-dawn curfew, and the presence on LA's streets of several thousand well-armed US National Guard troops, to restore calm – whereupon the full extent of the rioting became known. The worst urban violence seen in the US this century had left 58 dead, nearly 2000 injured, and caused an estimated $1 billion worth of damage. With much of the devastation in the city's poorest areas, a relief operation of Third World dimensions was mounted to feed and clothe those most severely affected by the carnage. A second trial, on charges that the officers violated Mr King's civil rights, resulted in prison sentences for two of the officers – too little too late.

Though ignited by a single incident, the riots were a very real indication of the tensions in a city whose controllers (and its affluent inhabitants) have traditionally been all too ready to turn a blind eye to social problems. Prompted by the King case, the Christopher Commission was set up to investigate racial prejudice within the LAPD. Sadly, its recommendations had all too blatantly not been implemented by the time of the O J Simpson trial in 1995, when the world was once again reminded that race is always an issue in Los Angeles.

buffs secure in their cars, however, might chance a stop at the **Dominguez Ranch Adobe**, 18127 S Alameda St (Tues & Wed 1–4pm, second & third Sun of each month 1–4pm; free conducted tour ☎213/636-3030), now restored and chronicling the social ascent of its founder, Juan Jose Dominguez – one of the soldiers who left Mexico with Padre Junipero Serra's expedition to found the California missions and whose long military service was acknowledged in 1782 by the granting of these 75,000 acres of land. As the importance of the area grew, so did the influence of Dominguez's descendants, who became powerful in local politics.

One of the safer segments of South Central LA, **GARDENA**, a few miles south, is best known for its large Japanese population and, more importantly, a city ordinance which permits gambling – rare in California. Along Vermont and Western avenues, half a dozen or so clubs devoted to poker are combined with restaurants and cocktail lounges, which charge a half-hourly rental on seats ($1–25). Food and drink are served around the clock, though the bars are kept separate from the tables. The whole effect is somewhat tacky, which shouldn't be a concern to gamblers desperate to part with their money.

Southeast LA

Following the path of Interstate 5, the terrain of **SOUTHEAST LA** is generally made up of low-grade industrial sites – incinerators, salvage operations, auto wrecking yards – and their dingy bedroom communities, along with large expanses of de-industrialized urban desert overflowing with weeds and economic depression. In the years after World War II, Southeast LA was a center for auto manufacture and tire-making, but the subsequent loss of blue-collar jobs has meant the disappearance of much of the white and black population, replaced by Mexican and Central American immigrant laborers, many of whom work at or below the minimum wage in dreadful sweatshop conditions. Because this is one of the prime centers for new arrivals, population density in some places has become overwhelming – the tiny town of **Cudahy** packs nearly 25,000 people on one square mile of land, and not surprisingly has one of the country's highest poverty rates – while in other industrial towns, residential zones are practically forbidden, and filthy sweatshops manage to evade labor laws through a lack of local oversight.

If, for some reason, you should wind up in this bleak terrain, there are several things worth checking out, starting in **Vernon**, an inhospitable burg whose highlight is the **Farmer John's Mural**, 3049 E Vernon Ave, a bucolic trompe l'oeil on a meat-packing operation, featuring a team of little pigs scampering about a farm and even managing to scale the building walls – an amusing scene that almost makes you forget the business inside. Further east, in Commerce, is **The Citadel**, 5675 Telegraph Rd, built like a huge Assyrian temple, with great carvings of priests and warriors on the exterior walls and a design modeled after the ancient architecture of Khorsabad, in the Middle East. Designed by Morgan, Walls and Clements, this structure started life as the Samson Tyre and Rubber Company, was later abandoned, and has recently been resurrected as a fashion store outlet, with a convenient location just off the 5 freeway.

To the south, the community of **Downey** is uneventful in itself, but does feature a true pop architecture icon – the country's very first **McDonald's** fast-food restaurant, 10207 Lakewood Blvd, created in 1953, a year before the chain officially started, and boasting a much more exuberant, colorful design than the mansard-roofed clones of today. With big yellow-neon arches that stretch over, and into, the building itself and a deviously winking chef, "Speedee," on its 60-foot-high sign, this "Googie" design is more than just an old burger joint.

Whittier and around

To the east, across the convergence of the 5 and 605 freeways, the small town of **WHITTIER**, originally founded by Quakers, has played at least a marginal role in American history. It was here that **Richard**

Nixon – a Quaker himself – was raised, went to law school, and started his first law office, a story which, if you don't already know it, many of the locals will be happy to recount for you in detail. You can find out more at the **Whittier Museum**, 6755 Newlin Ave (Sat–Sun 1–4pm; $2), which, along with telling of the lore and history of the city, gives further details of Nixon's activities here and prominently displays the personal desk he used in his first law practice. For a look at another local politician who wound up disgraced, there's the arcing **Pico Adobe**, 6003 Pioneer Blvd (Wed–Sun 10am–5pm; free), full of Victorian furnishings and various documents and memorabilia tracing the life of **Pio Pico**, one-time Mexican territorial governor who lived here for a period. Constructed in 1842, when California was still in Mexican hands, the house saw Pico lose his governorship, re-emerge on the LA City Council, make a fortune in real estate, and finally go bankrupt, eventually dying penniless. Several miles south, at 10211 S Pioneer Blvd, the **Clarke House** (Tues & Fri 11am–2pm; free) is another of Irving Gill's Mission Revival and pre-Moderne melds, with Italian-styled balconies and Tuscan columns used to offset a number of pre-Columbian effects – such as Mayan icons and early North American hieroglyphs – and the tight modern geometry of the setting. Neighboring **Heritage Park**, 12100 Mora Drive (daily 7am–10pm; free), is also worth a look, a collection of re-created, local historic buildings, such as a windmill, aviary, and carriage barn, and an accompanying English garden. Less refined is the **LA County Sheriffs Museum**, 11515 S Colima Rd (Mon–Fri 9am–4pm; free), which features a replica of an early jail and a sizable set of law-enforcement antiques and old-fashioned deadly weapons – from classic tommy guns to razor-sharp ice picks. Look, too, for the menacing meat hooks and crude knives that were popular tools in LA's mid-nineteenth century "Hell Town" days.

Southeast LA

If you just can't get enough of Nixon, make sure to check out his library and birthplace in Orange County, p.209.

East LA

You can't visit LA without being made aware of the Hispanic influence on the city's demography and culture, whether through the thousands of Mexican restaurants, the innumerable Spanish street names, or, most obviously, the sheer volume of Spanish spoken by people on the streets. None of this is surprising given LA's proximity to Mexico, but equally apparent are the clear distinctions between the Latino community and white LA. As a rule, it's the former who do the menial jobs for the latter, and, although a great number of Hispanics live in the US lawfully, they're also the people who suffer most from the repeated drives against illegal immigration. During the 1992 riots, there were charges of brutality and racism against Immigration and Naturalization Service agents, who may have used the chaos as an opportunity to hunt down undocumented foreign workers.

East LA

Of the many Hispanic neighborhoods all over LA, the most prominent is **EAST LA**, a Spanish-speaking enclave that begins two miles east of Downtown, across the concrete-clad dribble of the Los Angeles river. There was a Mexican population here long before the white settlers arrived, and from the late nineteenth century onward millions more arrived, coming here chiefly to work on the land. As the white inhabitants gradually moved west towards the coast, the Mexicans stayed, creating a vast community that's more like a Hispanic island than an integrated part of an American city.

Activity in East LA (commonly abbreviated to "ELA" or "East Los") tends to be outdoors, in cluttered markets and busy shops. Non-Hispanic visitors are comparatively thin on the ground, but you are unlikely to meet any hostility on the streets during the day – though you should steer clear of the rough and very male-dominated bars, and avoid the whole area after dark.

Guadalupe, the Mexican image of the mother of God, appears in mural art all over East LA, nowhere better than at the junction of Mednik and Cesar Chavez avenues. When a housing project across the street was demolished in the early 1970s, one wall, bearing a particularly remarkable image of Mother Mary surrounded by a rich band of rainbow colors, was saved from the wrecking ball and reinstated across the street. Lined with blue tile, it now forms an unofficial shrine where worshippers place fresh flowers and candles.

Other than the street life and murals, there are few specific "sights" in East LA. The best plan is just to turn up on a Saturday afternoon (the liveliest part of the week) and stroll along **Cesar Chavez Avenue**, formerly Brooklyn Avenue, going eastward from Indiana Street and look at the wild pet shops, with free-roaming parrots and cases of boa constrictors, and at the **botanicas**, which cater to practitioners of Santeria – a religion that is equal parts voodoo and Catholicism. Browse amid the shark's teeth, dried devil fish, and plastic statuettes of Catholic saints and buy magical herbs, ointments, or candles after consulting the shopkeeper and explaining (in Spanish) what ails you. Only slightly less exotic fare can be found in **El Mercado de Los Angeles**, 3425 E First St, an indoor market not unlike Olvera Street but much more authentic.

Afterwards, drive through the LA district of **Boyle Heights**, which through the 1940s was a center for Jewish culture but has since become a solid Hispanic neighborhood. Go to the junction of **Soto and Cesar Chavez**, where at 5pm each afternoon, *Norteños* combos (upright bass, accordion, guitar, and banjo sexto) freely showcase their talents, hoping to be booked for weddings; failing that, listen to the mariachi bands that strike up at 6.30pm outside the *Olympic Donut Shop*, at First and Boyle, four blocks south of Cesar Chavez Avenue.

Of the other nearby areas east of Downtown LA, the only one of conceivable interest is **MONTEREY PARK**, northeast of East LA, which contains the highest percentage of Asian residents of any city in the nation (40 percent) and is one of the central gateways for Taiwanese and mainland Chinese immigrants arriving in the US. It's also home to a number of authentic Chinese restaurants, as well as many nightclubs, ethnic grocers, and theaters, on its main drag, **Atlantic Boulevard**.

Chapter 8

The South Bay and LA Harbor

S tretching below Los Angeles Airport down to the edge of Orange County, the beach towns of the **SOUTH BAY** and **LA HARBOR** share little in common except their proximity to the sea. While much of oceanside South Bay is the province of wealthy white Angelenos, poorer blacks and Hispanics reside many miles inland, in places like Carson and Hawthorne, and in bleak districts like North Long Beach. However, the public beaches in the area offer more ethnic diversity, and the climate and scenery combine to make this into one of the city's most visually appealing regions.

While not much of a draw for visitors, the LA harbor is the busiest cargo port in the world, a massive complex divided between San Pedro and Long Beach, consisting of so many ship passages, trucking routes, and artificial islands that the huge Vincent Thomas Bridge had to be built to carry travelers over the entire works. The emphasis on industrial development has had its consequences, though, and only now are the natural environment and many forms of wildlife making a comeback – the entire area was long one of LA's dirtiest. Not only was the harbor a significant source of pollution, DDT was pumped directly into the sea near Palos Verdes and even now sits in a giant deadly "bubble" offshore, still playing havoc with the ecosystem.

The South Bay begins south of the airport with three **south beach cities** that aren't terribly captivating, though Manhattan Beach, the nicest of them, is reasonably attractive. Further south, and visible all along this stretch of the coast, the large, vegetated **Palos Verdes Peninsula** occupies a wild, craggy stretch of coastline, with some rustic parks and pricey real estate, while comparatively rough-hewn **San Pedro** is a working-class community that forms part of the site for the LA harbor. Its counterpart, **Long Beach**, is best known as the resting place of the *Queen Mary*, even though it is also the region's second-largest city, with nearly half a million people.

Perhaps the most enticing, and certainly the strangest, place in the area is **Santa Catalina Island**, twenty miles offshore and easily

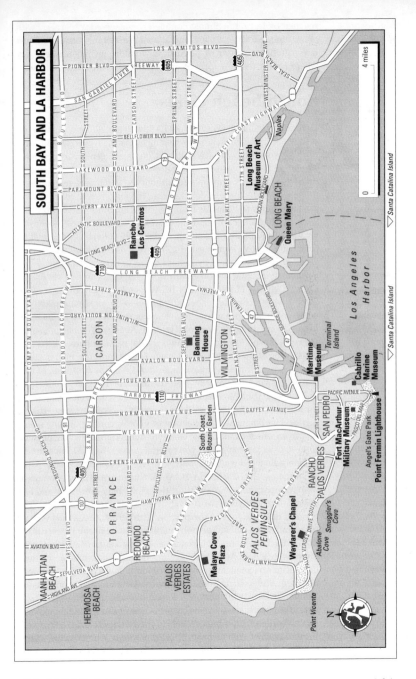

SOUTH BAY AND LA HARBOR

LOS ALAMITOS BLVD
PIONEER BLVD
SAN GABRIEL RIVER FREEWAY
605
405
SEAL BEACH BLVD
WESTMINSTER AVE

CARSON STREET
SPRING STREET
WILLOW STREET
BELLFLOWER BLVD
SAN DIEGO FREEWAY
PACIFIC COAST HIGHWAY
1

ARTESIA BOULEVARD
SOUTH STREET
DEL AMO BOULEVARD
LAKEWOOD BOULEVARD
19
PARAMOUNT BLVD
CHERRY AVENUE
ATLANTIC BOULEVARD
LONG BEACH BLVD
WILLOW STREET
405
710
LONG BEACH FREEWAY

7TH STREET
ANAHEIM STREET
OCEAN BOULEVARD
Long Beach
Museum of Art
LONG BEACH
Queen Mary
Naples

Rancho
Los Cerritos

COMPTON BOULEVARD
REDONDO BEACH FREEWAY
SOUTH STREET
WILMINGTON BOULEVARD
ALAMEDA STREET
SAN DIEGO FREEWAY
DEL AMO BLVD
SEPULVEDA BLVD
SEASIDE BOULEVARD
TERMINAL IS. FREEWAY
47
Los Angeles Harbor

CARSON
Banning
House
WILMINGTON
AVALON BOULEVARD
ANAHEIM STREET
B STREET
Terminal
Island
42

91
REDONDO BEACH BLVD
FIGUEROA STREET
HARBOR FREEWAY
110
Maritime
Museum
Cabrillo
Marine
Museum

TORRANCE
190TH STREET
SEPULVEDA BLVD
TORRANCE BOULEVARD
HAWTHORNE BLVD
PACIFIC COAST HIGHWAY
NORMANDIE AVENUE
WESTERN AVENUE
CRENSHAW BOULEVARD
GAFFEY AVENUE
9TH STREET
5TH STREET
PACIFIC AVENUE
SAN PEDRO
PASEO DEL MAR
Fort MacArthur
Military Museum
Angel's Gate Park
Point Fermin Lighthouse

South Coast
Botanic Garden
107
405

MANHATTAN
BEACH
HERMOSA
BEACH
REDONDO BEACH
PALOS VERDES
ESTATES
AVIATION BLVD
ARTESIA BLVD
SEPULVEDA BLVD
HIGHLAND AVE
HAWTHORNE BOULEVARD

Malaya Cove
Plaza
PALOS VERDES DRIVE SOUTH
PALOS VERDES DRIVE NORTH
CREST ROAD
PALOS VERDES
PENINSULA
PALOS VERDES
RANCHO
PALOS VERDES
Wayfarer's Chapel
Abalone
Cove
Smuggler's
Cove
Point Vicente

N

Santa Catalina Island
Santa Catalina Island

0   4 miles

reached by ferry. It's almost completely conserved wilderness, with many unique forms of plant and animal life, notably bison, and just one significant center of population, **Avalon**, an independent city where almost the only form of motorized transport is the golf cart.

South beach cities

Beyond the industrial zone below LAX, which includes a Chevron oil refinery and LA's main sewage treatment plant, is an eight-mile strip of three **south beach cities** that sit on small, gently steeped hills, where pleasantly low-scaled development and modest amusements provide a laid-back atmosphere without too much pretension. Along the cities' shared beachside bike path, the joggers and roller skaters are more likely to be locals than poseurs from other parts of LA, and each city has a beckoning strip of white sand, with most oceanside locations equipped for surfing and beach volleyball. These little towns are also well connected to the rest of the city – within easy reach of LAX and linked by regular buses to Downtown LA.

Those 1960s purveyors of beach culture, the Beach Boys, formed in nearby – and unlovely – Hawthorne.

Accessible along the bike path from Venice, or by car via Pacific Coast Highway, **MANHATTAN BEACH** is the most northern of the three towns, a likable place with a well-to-do air, home mainly to white-collar workers whose middle-class stucco homes sit near the beach, along the main drag of **Highland Avenue**. The beach itself is the main reason to come; surfing is a local pastime here, with a two-week international surf festival each August, and the city is also a major center for beach volleyball, evidenced by the profusion of nets across the sands. If you can, visit the **historical center**, a mile from the beach at 1601 Manhattan Beach Blvd (Sat–Sun noon–3pm; free), for its locally crafted pottery from the early part of the twentieth century and its illuminating collection of photos, tracing the city's history, from when it was known as Shore Acres right up to the present. If these whet your appetite, you can purchase a map ($1) that details a history-flavored **walking tour**.

To the south, **HERMOSA BEACH**, across Longfellow Avenue, is more downscale than Manhattan Beach, its houses smaller and less showy, but it does have a lively beachside strip, known as **The Strand**, near the foot of the pier on 12th Street, that's packed with restaurants and clubs. The only building of note in the vicinity is the **Either/Or** bookstore, 124 Pier Ave, once a haunt of elusive writer Thomas Pynchon. Apart from ocean-oriented amusements, the town does offer an excellent **green belt** (a long, grassy median), running between Valley Drive and Ardmore Avenue, that connects to Manhattan Beach and provides a good place for a workout.

A listing for the Either/Or bookstore appears on p.310.

Further south, despite some good strips of sand, and fine views of Palos Verdes' stunning greenery, **REDONDO BEACH**, across Herondo Street, is less inviting, with hardly any noteworthy sights. Condos and large hotels line the beachfront, "The Pier" is an unremarkable tourist trap, and the exclusive eateries around the yacht-lined **King Harbor** are off-limits to the hoi polloi.

The Palos Verdes Peninsula

South of the beach cities, the **PALOS VERDES PENINSULA**, a great green mound marking LA's southwest corner, features rugged beaches and secluded coves, sweeping views of the coastline from Malibu to Orange County, and some of the most expensive real estate in LA County. Originally intended as a "millionaires' colony" by 1920s developers, Palos Verdes has more or less worked out according to plan, with several gated communities like **Rolling Hills**, numerous multimillion-dollar estates, and an armada of private security guards. Despite this, the peninsula is one of the best spots for experiencing nature in the area, with sea cliffs and tide pools, and its oceanside scenery is nothing less than awe-inspiring.

North Palos Verdes

The north section of the peninsula is generally ungated and accessible, with most attractions near the coast of **PALOS VERDES ESTATES**, the first city founded on the peninsula, in 1939, and the only one with significant architecture and public green space. First laid out by brothers John Olmsted and Frederick Law Olmsted Jr, sons of the developer of New York's Central Park, the town has nearly one-third of its space preserved as parkland (on which you may come across a roaming herd of peacocks), many circuitous streets that overlook the ocean, and a pseudo-European air that is a bit more subtle than that of Beverly Hills.

The Olmsted brothers laid out a similar series of green spaces in Seattle and Portland in the early twentieth century.

The best place to take in this Old World atmosphere is at **Malaga Cove Plaza**, Palos Verdes Drive at Via Corta, a Spanish Colonial Revival commercial center that the Olmsteds planned as a prototype for four other such centers in the city, none of which were ever built. Although the central plaza and arcaded buildings are attractive enough, the focus of the development is unquestionably the **Neptune Fountain**, a smaller-scale replica of a 1563 structure in Bologna, Italy of the same name. With its central bronze sculpture and late-Renaissance design, the fountain is another reminder of the European predilection of LA's nouveau riche, which is also evident in the city's seaside architecture, much of it with a strong Mediterranean flair. For starters, see the **Olmsted House**, Paseo del Mar at Via Arroyo, a Spanish Colonial estate with a walled garden that was built for Frederick Law Olmsted Jr, and the **Haggerty House**, 415 Paseo del Mar, an Italian-styled villa (now a church) that was built by the Olmsteds themselves.

Inland on the north peninsula, there are few compelling sights save the **South Coast Botanic Garden**, 26300 Crenshaw Blvd (daily

9am–5pm; $5), a relaxing spot that was once home to a giant land-fill. In the 1950s and 1960s, LA dumped 3.5 million tons of its trash here, creating one of the bigger eyesores in the region, but more recently, the turf has been covered by layers of soil and successfully reclaimed as a garden, filled with exotic bromeliads, an expansive cactus garden, different kinds of palm trees, numerous ferns and flowering plants, and even a small French-style garden. The only sign of its former life is the terrain itself, which, thanks to the subsiding of the garbage below, has a weirdly undulating landscape.

South Palos Verdes

South of Palos Verdes Estates along Palos Verdes Drive, the beaches are more easily visited, even as the neighborhoods turn increasingly stuffy and gated. The main city, **RANCHO PALOS VERDES**, is worthwhile for its significant natural attractions, one of which is the promontory of **Point Vicente**, Palos Verdes Drive south of Hawthorne Boulevard, sitting on high cliff walls above the Pacific Ocean. Here a **park** overlooks the sea and an **interpretive center** (daily 10am–5pm; $2) describes the geology and history of the area, along with showing artifacts of native cultures and whaling equip-

The whales tend to do their heaviest migrations from December to January and March to April.

ment from earlier in the century. Better exhibits are the **whales** themselves, often visible from the center during their seasonal migrations. Nearby, a **lighthouse** adds to the picturesque quality, as does the abandoned **Marineland** theme park, a bit further south, at Long Point – though it can only be glimpsed from the parking lot.

Continuing south on Palos Verdes Drive, **Abalone Cove**, reached from a parking lot on Barkentine Road or by a steep roadside stair-way, boasts rock and tide pools and offshore kelp beds alive with rock scallops, sea urchins, and, of course, abalone. While you're in the area, don't miss **Wayfarer's Chapel**, across the street at 5755 Palos Verdes Drive, a masterpiece of pitched glass and wood that was designed by Frank Lloyd Wright's son, Lloyd. A tribute to the eighteenth-century Swedish scientist and mystic Emanuel Swedenborg, and funded by the Swedenborgian Church, the ultimate aim is for the redwood grove around the chapel to grow and entan-gle itself in the glass-framed structure – a fusing of human handiwork with the forces of nature. A half-mile south, the coast at **Portuguese Bend** provides another dramatic ocean vista, and was once a key site where Portuguese whalers hunted gray whales for their blubber, to be turned into oil. Strangely enough, their trade came to an end thanks to a simple lack of firewood to run their operation, and the only trace of their activity is the name they inspired. Much more con-spicuous is **Smugglers Cove**, at the end of a path off Peppertree Drive, which is a renowned nudist beach just around Portuguese Bend.

San Pedro

Forming part of the site of the LA harbor, scruffy **SAN PEDRO**, in complete contrast to Palos Verdes, is a diverse blue-collar community peopled by immigrants from the Mediterranean and Scandinavia, with a rich, often violent, history. As one of several places along the West Coast where labor strife erupted during the Depression, the city has a long tradition of populism and a nagging antipathy toward the city of Los Angeles, which annexed it in 1909, despite local opposition. Its low-rise scale and maritime atmosphere have little in common with the metropolis itself, nor does its location – San Pedro is 20 miles south of Downtown, connected only by a thin strip along the 110 freeway. Indeed, San Pedro residents often talk about a return to the city's independent days, but the idea of LA ever giving up its share of America's busiest port is rather far-fetched, to say the least.

Some History

First called the "Bay of Smokes" for the many fires set by Tongva natives along its shoreline, this formerly Spanish-controlled city was named after St Peter and consolidated into the territory owned by Juan Domínguez, whose ranch house is still standing in Compton (see p.155). Later, around the time it was usurped by the US in the Mexican-American War, San Pedro became a major center for the nautical trade of animal skins and beef tallow and became, thanks to entrepreneur **Phineas Banning** (see p.341), linked to cities throughout the region by railway lines in the 1870s.

A decade later, the city was incorporated and began maturing as a port, with the action centered on **Timms Landing**, where animal hides were exported and seabound travelers embarked. Although little visual evidence remains, you can get a sense of the place by reading Richard Henry Dana's classic book *Two Years Before the Mast*.

Around this time, Henry Huntington of the Southern Pacific Railroad was threatening to thwart the region's progress. With an eye toward making Santa Monica the chief harbor of the region, Huntington came into conflict with many LA bigwigs, especially Harrison Gray Otis of the *Los Angeles Times*, whose newspaper did much to excite passions for a "free" harbor. The battle was successful, and San Pedro was the beneficiary: by the end of the century, construction on a massive 2-mile breakwater had begun, thanks to a generous federal subsidy, and was completed a decade later. Shortly thereafter, Los Angeles mounted its aggressive annexation drive and the military base Fort MacArthur was built next to the harbor.

The world wars and a booming maritime economy further helped San Pedro to attract shipbuilding industries and commercial canneries, and by the 1950s, despite occasional labor conflicts, the district had hit its peak. However, succeeding decades and industrial retrenchment saw the city begin to decline, and by the 1980s San

San Pedro

Pedro was decayed and weather-beaten, full of boarded-up businesses. Although redevelopment money and the opening of new museums has helped the city in recent years, most locals realize that if it weren't for the port, which is still busy, San Pedro would basically be dead.

Around the harbor

The LA harbor, aside from being the country's busiest, is the third biggest in the world, behind only those in Hong Kong and Shanghai.

San Pedro's **harbor** abuts the city's downtown and forms part of the massive complex of the LA harbor, though the actual focus of shipping activities is an industrial zone known as **Terminal Island**, a manmade island across the harbor's main channel. While you'll have to keep your distance from the oceanside docks and machinery, there are some points along the channel worth investigating.

To get a better sense of the harbor's history, start at the **Maritime Museum**, in the former Municipal Ferry Building, Sampson Way at Sixth Street (Tues–Sun 10am–5pm; free), which features art and artifacts from the glory days of fishing and whaling. There are also plenty of nautical models, from Spanish galleons to British steamships, which are complemented by full-sized versions behind the museum, a floating collection that includes several tugs and fishing boats, an old-fashioned schooner, and a racing yacht. Just west, more history is recalled at the **Bloody Thursday Monument**, Sixth Street at Beacon Street, a plaza that commemorates the two workers who were killed when police and private guards opened fire during a 1934 strike by local waterfront workers, many of them recently arrived immigrants.

A few blocks to the south, along Nagoya Way, don't bother with the banal, overrated **Ports o' Call Village** – a dismal batch of wooden and corrugated iron huts supposedly capturing the flavor of exotic seaports around the world. Somewhat more appealing is the **SS Lane Victory**, to the north in Berth 94, off Swinford Street (daily 9am–4pm; $2), a huge World War II cargo ship that also operated in Korea and Vietnam. A tour will take you through its many cramped spaces, including the engine and radio rooms, crew quarters, galley, and bridge. After it was decommissioned and declared a historic landmark, the ship wound up back near its birthplace: it was built just across the channel at the Terminal Island shipyard in 1945. Overhead is the towering **Vincent Thomas Bridge**, California's third-longest suspension bridge, created in 1963, for $21 million, to help speed vehicular access between San Pedro and Long Beach. While successful in this goal, it has also made the municipal ferry system, which had run for 22 years around the harbor, permanently obsolete.

The only other real spot of interest in this part of town is the opulent **Warner Grand Theater**, 478 W Sixth St, five blocks from Harbor Boulevard, a terrific 1931 Zigzag Moderne moviehouse, with dark geometric details, great columns and sunburst motifs, a style that almost looks pre-Columbian. Disused for years, the theater has been renovated as a repertory cinema and performing arts hall and is also the centerpiece of an effort to revive San Pedro's city center.

Point Fermin

At the southern tip of San Pedro, down Pacific Avenue, is **Point Fermin**, a cape named for an early Franciscan missionary, Padre Fermín Lasuén. In **Angel's Gate Park**, Gaffey Street at 36th Street, a recreational green on a hill overlooking the Pacific, a central pagoda contains the **Korean Bell of Friendship**, a 17-ton copper-and-tin colossus that was a 1976 gift from South Korea. Decorated with Korean characters, the bell has no clapper; instead, a hefty log strikes the instrument only on three key days of the year: Korean and American independence days and New Year's Eve. Nearby, the **Fort MacArthur Military Museum** (Sat–Sun noon–5pm; free) is the old site of Battery Osgood, a gun emplacement that maintained artillery that could fire seventeen miles out to sea. Principally used between world wars, and later retrofitted for surface-to-air missiles, the fort displays a clutch of military outfits and old photographs, as well as an array of bombs, mines, and missiles, all disarmed or deactivated.

On the park's south end, across Paseo del Mar, **Point Fermin Park** is a verdant strip of land sitting atop ocean bluffs. In the middle of the park, **Point Fermin Lighthouse** is an 1874 Eastlake structure with a cupola that once contained a 6600-candlepower light which beamed 22 miles out to sea. Ending its service during World War II, the lighthouse fell into disrepair until it was renovated in the 1970s. While not open to the public, it does feature a whale-watching station where you can read up on the winter migrations. Bottle-nosed dolphins can often be seen during their fall departure and spring return as well, and there's also the less seasonally dependent thrill of spotting hang-gliders swooping down off the sea cliffs. Just to the east of the lighthouse, fenced off by shoddy chain link, sits what's left of an early-twentieth-century resort known as "**Sunken City**": little more than crumbling pavement and foundation that is officially, though not practically, off-limits to the public.

Below the bluffs, a beachside path winds around the cape and reaches the excellent **Cabrillo Marine Museum**, 3720 Stephen White Drive (Tues–Fri noon–5pm, Sat–Sun 10am–5pm; free; parking $6.50), where a diverse collection of marine life has been imaginatively and instructively assembled: everything from predator snails and sea urchins to larger displays on otters, seals, and whales, as well as the rare "sarcastic fringehead" (a peculiar fish whose name makes sense once you see it). Fully visible from the aquarium, a short jetty extends to a 1913 **breakwater** that is over 9000 feet long and marks the harbor entrance. At the end of the breakwater sits the **Angel's Gate Lighthouse**, a steel monolith with Romanesque detailing that blasts its foghorn twice per minute, using a rotating green light to

The Cabrillo Marine Museum was designed by Frank Gehry, and his visual trademark of chain-link fencing is abundantly present at the museum.

direct ships into the protected harbor and helping them avoid the breakwater's three-million-ton rock seawall. If you use your binoculars from the aquarium, you can get a better look at this historic structure; however, don't expect to see a lone sailor manning the station – the lighthouse has been automated for twenty-five years.

Wilmington

Due north of San Pedro, **WILMINGTON** provides the starkest images of LA's petroleum economy, its oil wells and refineries dotting the industrial landscape and resembling something out of *The Terminator*, with massive towers spurting jets of flame and cargo trucks barreling down the bleak Terminal Island Expressway (which connects Downtown with the harbor via the 710 freeway).

It's also the surprising setting for the grand **Banning House**, 401 E Main St (guided tours hourly Tues–Thurs & Sat–Sun 12.30–2.30pm and 3.30pm on weekends; $2), an 1864 Greek Revival estate surrounded by a park that once held expansive gardens, largely gone today. The home was the residence of mid-nineteenth-century entrepreneur Phineas Banning, who made his fortune when the value of his land increased astronomically as the harbor was developed. Through his promotion of the rail link between Wilmington and Downtown LA, he also became known as "the father of Los Angeles transportation. " However, in his final years, he could only watch as LA's politicians extended the rail line to San Pedro, causing his own beloved city to begin its gradual decline. He died long before the town began its industrial re-emergence in the 1930s with the discovery of oil, but his house remains an engaging spot to visit, full of opulent Victorian touches (chandeliers, dinner settings) on the inside and with restored carriages and stagecoaches in an outside barn.

Banning originally wanted to call Wilmington "New San Pedro," but eventually named it after the Delaware town in which he grew up.

Several blocks south is the **Drum Barracks Civil War Museum**, 1052 Banning Blvd (hourly tours Tues & Thurs 10am–noon Sat 12.30–2.30pm; $2.50), originally part of a military base called Camp Drum that was built on sixty acres purchased from Banning. Throughout the 1860s, this base served as the Southwest headquarters for the US Army, through which California volunteers for Civil War duty would be processed to fight in the battles in the East. It was also a staging point for attacks on nearby Confederate troops, which in the early years of the war had made territorial gains in neighboring Arizona and New Mexico, and in later decades became a base for federal soldiers fighting in the Indian Wars of the Southwest. Today, the only structure remaining is the barracks that was used for "unaccompanied officers." The rickety building houses a collection of military antiques and memorabilia, such as a 34-star US flag, and assorted guns and muskets, including an early machine gun that could fire several hundred rounds per minute.

Long Beach

Like San Pedro, **LONG BEACH** is the home of the LA harbor, and is also a sizable Southern California city with many acres of tract homes and flat, sprawling development. Not surprisingly, most of its interesting sights – including the *Queen Mary* ship – are grouped near the water, away from the port, including the tourist-oriented amusements around **Shoreline Drive** and the historic architecture of **downtown**.

Once the stomping ground of off-duty naval personnel, Long Beach's porn shops and sleazy bars made the place just the wrong side of seedy. The last decade or so, however, saw a billion-dollar cash injection into the town that has led – around downtown at least – to a spate of glossy office buildings, a convention center, new hotels, a swanky shopping mall, and restoration of some of the best turn-of-the-century buildings on the coast. Inland from downtown, however, it's a different story – grim, uninviting housing projects on the perimeter of impoverished South Central LA.

Indeed, away from the water, the only real interest comes from **Rancho Los Cerritos**, 4600 Virginia Rd, northeast of the junction of the 405 and 710 freeways (Wed–Sun 10am–5pm; free), a U-shaped 1844 adobe in the Monterey style with a terrific garden, containing roses, herbs, exotic plants, and even an antiquated water tower. Rather fortunately, it's easily accessible, via the 710, to Long Beach's more prominent attractions near the harbor.

Shoreline Drive and around

From the turn of the century, Long Beach has sold itself as a resort community, and while it's difficult to imagine any romantic getaway nestled behind an industrial port basin, the city keeps trying. Its major seaside amusements now sit close to the curving strip of **Shoreline Drive**, even though the area was much more of a true entertainment center ninety years ago than it is today.

Around 1910, Long Beach developed its municipal pier, known as "The Pike" or the "Walk of a Thousand Lights," featuring street vendors, a band shell, bathhouse, rollercoaster, and throngs of tourists, as well as the legendary **Looff Carousel**, designed in 1911 by merry-go-round-builder Charles Looff, who used his carving skills to create the finely decorated and ornamented horses of the ride. After the carousel burned in 1943, the pier began its decline, accelerated by the later arrival of Orange County theme parks in the 1950s. Today, the pier is long gone and the modern focus of attention is the much less appealing **Shoreline Village**, just south of Shoreline Drive, a ragtag collection of shops and restaurants that offers little to see but the **Tallship California**, a sleek cutter which is a simulation of an 1848 vessel.

North of Shoreline Village is the **Breakers Hotel**, 200 E Ocean Blvd, a 1925 structure with twelve pink Spanish Revival stories

If you'd like to spend half a day playing sailor aboard the Tallship California, *call ☎1-800/432-2201 for more details.*

topped by a green copper roof, now used for senior citizens' housing. Two blocks south, Seaside Way connects with Shoreline Drive to create the circuit for the **Long Beach Grand Prix**, an Indy car race that typically attracts several hundred thousand spectators in mid-April, a good time to avoid the city if you don't like auto racing.

Around a lagoon south of Shoreline Drive, the just-opened **Aquarium of the Pacific** (daily 10am–6pm; $13, kids $6.50), divides its marine life into regions: Southern California, the Micronesian island chain of Palau, and the icy Bering Sea. There's the requisite range of familiar sea lions and otters, along with more exotic fare like leopard sharks and giant Japanese spider crabs.

If you want a closer view of local sealife, several tour operators have bases in the area. Between December and April, more than fifteen thousand whales cruise the "**Whale Freeway**" past Long Beach on their annual migration to and return from winter breeding and berthing grounds in Baja California. Both Shoreline Village Cruises (☎310/495-5884) and Star Party Cruises (☎562/799-7000) offer good whale-watching trips for around $10–15.

As you travel along Ocean Boulevard, you may notice the presence of several angular, pastel **islands** sitting offshore. These are not resort colonies, but rather Long Beach's idea to beautify its harbor by clothing its oil drilling platforms in colorful garb – in truth, petroleum still provides one of the town's major industries, with over four hundred oil and gas wells operating at any one time.

The Queen Mary

Long Beach's most famous attraction is not indigenous at all. The mighty ocean liner, the **Queen Mary**, moored on Pier H at the end of Queens Hwy S (daily 10am–6pm; free self-tours or $11 guided tours), was acquired by local authorities in 1964 with the specific aim of bolstering tourism, and has generally succeeded in doing so. The ship lies across the bay, opposite Shoreline Village, and is easily accessible either by a lengthy walk or free Long Beach Transit shuttle from downtown. Now retrofitted as a luxury hotel with 400 rooms, the ship doesn't tell the full truth of its history. The suggestion is that all who sailed on the vessel – the flagship of the Cunard Line from the 1930s until the 1960s – enjoyed the extravagantly furnished lounges and the luxurious cabins, all carefully restored and kept sparkling. However, a glance at the spartan third-class cabins reveals something of the real story, along with the tough conditions experienced by the desperate migrants who left Europe on the ship hoping to start a new life in the US. The red British telephone kiosks around the decks and the hammy theatrical displays in the engine room and wheelhouse (closer to *Star Trek* than anything nautical) don't help the authenticity, but it's nonetheless a marvelous ship, with a wealth of Moderne decor – Deco glasswork, geometric ornament, and streamlined edges and railings – as well as stores and restaurants and even a wedding chapel.

Downtown Long Beach

Even with the *Queen Mary* and the shoreline strip, **downtown Long Beach** is clearly the place to spend most of your time, with the best of the city's restored architecture and numerous thrift shops, antique emporiums, and bookstores. Running from Magnolia Avenue to Alamitos Boulevard, and Ocean Boulevard to Tenth Street, downtown Long Beach has a number of vivid sights, one of which is a famous **mural**, *Activities in Long Beach*, Third Street west of Long Beach Boulevard, that depicts the Long Beach population in a contemporary, multicultural fashion – surprisingly, a 1930s WPA creation. Once gracing the side wall of the Long Beach Municipal Auditorium before the building was destroyed, the mural has been preserved on a parking garage, at the end of a three-block strip known as **The Promenade**, a series of touristy restaurants and stores.

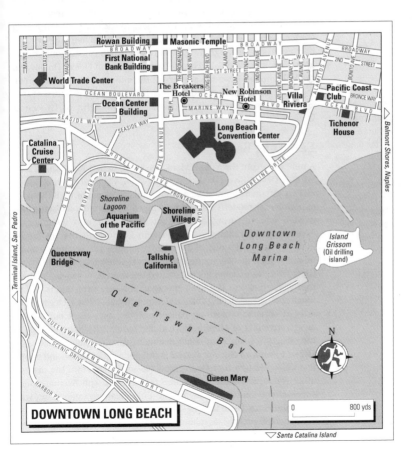

Also compelling is **Pine Avenue**, running a mile inland from Ocean Boulevard, where some of the city's best-preserved architecture sits in a moderately busy commercial zone. Highlights include the **Ocean Center Building**, 110 W Ocean Blvd, a 1929 Mediterranean-styled series of towers that once connected to the Walk of a Thousand Lights along the old pier; the **First National Bank Building**, 115 Pine Ave, a Beaux Arts structure from 1900 that has recently been refurbished, along with its resplendent clock tower; the 1903 **Masonic Temple**, no. 230, a triple-gabled building with a brilliant sun mural inside on its second story; and, best of all, the **Rowan Building**, no. 201, a vividly colored Art Deco creation from 1931 with detailed terra cotta ornamentation.

Further east, near Ocean Boulevard and Alamitos Avenue, is the **New Robinson Hotel**, 334 E Ocean Blvd, another Art Deco design, with imposing geometry and sharp vertical lines rising from a pleasant entry garden. Undeniably impressive is the **Villa Riviera**, 800 E Ocean Blvd, a fourteen-story apartment block that has a stunning Gothic Revival form, with high dormers on its pitched copper roof, narrow ground-level archways, and even a pointy octagonal turret above it all. Curved to accommodate the bend in Ocean Boulevard, the Villa monopolizes the scenery in the immediate area. Just down the block, the **Tichenor House**, 852 E Ocean Blvd, is a turn-of-the-century Craftsman structure designed by the firm of Greene & Greene.

The Greene brothers are better known for the Gamble House in Pasadena, which, unlike the Tichenor House, you can tour; see p.181 for more.

East Long Beach

A mile east from the Villa Riviera, the **Long Beach Museum of Art**, 2300 E Ocean Blvd (Wed–Sun 10am–5pm, Fri until 8pm; $2), is a 1912 Craftsman home that is now the site of some of LA's more experimental modern artworks. Fringed by an abstract **sculpture garden** and featuring an adequate collection of contemporary Southern Californian art, the museum is most interesting for its horde of video art – one of the country's biggest collections – much of which is on display in the **video annex**, where you can see everything from Nam June Paik's modified televisions, broadcasting only thin white lines, to Bill Viola's enigmatic video projections. A few blocks to the east, Irving Gill's **Raymond House**, 2724 E Ocean Blvd, is a 1918 classic with simple concrete arches and a rigid, cubic form, an effective mix of Mission Revival and modern styles, even though the structure itself is in some disrepair. Another mile further, the affluent **Belmont Shores** district is full of designer shops and yuppified cafés, though there's not much to see, aside from the historic 1929 **Belmont Theater**, Second Street at St Joseph Avenue, which successfully combines colorful, pre-Columbian ornamentation with streamlined Art Deco towers.

Second Street crosses manmade Alamitos Bay to reach the "island" community of **Naples**, supposedly modeled after the eponymous

Italian city, though closer in spirit to LA's Venice and Marina del Rey, with rows of T-shirt shops and trinket vendors and a busy yacht club. While the thin, circular **canal** may give you a romantic thrill (call Gondola Getaway for details, ☎310/433-9595), and pedestrian-friendly "Toledo," Naples' main road, holds some pseudo-Continental appeal, the place is little more than a tacky aquatic suburb.

Two miles north, **Rancho Los Alamitos**, 6400 Bixby Hill Rd (Wed–Sun 1–5pm; free), is a grand version of the typical nineteenth-century adobe you may have seen elsewhere in the region. First constructed in 1806, and later improved and renovated, the ranch house contains twenty rooms of furniture, antiques, glassware, and farm implements, as well as an on-site quarters for a blacksmith. However, the gardens are the main draw, with plots containing herbs, roses, cacti, jacaranda, and oleander set among terraces and landscaped walks. Nearby, the **Miller Japanese Garden**, 1250 Bellflower Blvd (Tues–Fri 8am–3.30pm Sun noon–4pm; free), provides more quietude amidst weeping willows and bamboo. The standard accoutrements are all here – teahouse, bridge, lanterns, pagoda, and meditation garden – and it's easy to spend an hour just wandering aimlessly around the grounds.

Santa Catalina Island

Overlooked by many visitors, **SANTA CATALINA ISLAND**, a mix of uncluttered beaches and wild hills 22 miles off the coast, is favored by Californians in the know. Initially claimed by the Portuguese in 1542 as San Salvador, and renamed by the Spanish in 1602, the island has actually been privately owned since 1811, most notably by businessman William Wrigley Jr (part of the Chicago-based chewing gum dynasty), who financed the construction of the Avalon Casino, still the island's major landmark, in the 1920s. Wrigley also used the island as a site for his baseball team, the Chicago Cubs, to hold spring training in a remote location.

The island has become a popular destination for boaters and nature lovers, and its small marina overflows with luxury yachts and cruise ships in summer. Even so, tourism has been held largely at bay: the hotels are unobtrusive among the whimsical architecture and cars are a rarity, as there's a ten-year waiting list to bring one over from the mainland. Consequently, most of the 3000 islanders walk, ride bikes, or drive electrically powered golf carts.

No longer a private playground for the Wrigley family, Catalina Island has since 1975 been almost entirely owned by the Catalina Island Conservancy.

Avalon and Two Harbors

The main city on the island, **AVALON**, can be fully explored on foot in two hours, with maps issued by the **Chamber of Commerce** at the foot of the ferry pier (☎310/510-1520). The town itself is a series of

T-shirt shops, restaurants, and boat operators, many of whom offer fishing trips or tours on glass-bottom boats. The best place to begin your journey is the **Avalon Casino**, at 1 Casino Way on a promontory north of downtown, a 1920s structure with mermaid murals, gold-leaf motifs, rippling arches, a large ballroom, and an overall design that some have dubbed "Aquarium Deco." Not designed as a gambling hall, despite its name, this moviehouse features an interior auditorium that is creatively outlandish: wild horses and unicorns roam through a painted forest on the side wall, sunbursts explode above the proscenium arch, the image of an Art Deco superman rides a wave on the front screen, and above it all, a waif-like Venus of Botticelli stands atop a seashell over the heads of two vigorous, thunderbolt-clutching gods. Not surprisingly, the muralist for the theater, John Beckman, also helped design the equally fanciful Chinese Theatre in Hollywood (see p.99).

Much more subdued, a small **museum** (daily 10.30am–4pm; $1.50) on the premises of the Casino displays Native American artifacts from Catalina's past, as well as tiles from local potters, and old photographs and biology exhibits on the surrounding area. To the south, R M Schindler's modern **Wolfe House**, a private residence at 124 Chimes Tower Rd, is a wood-and-stucco design that seems to hover above the road below, its stepped roof terraces out of proportion to the environment around it. Nearby, the **Zane Grey Pueblo Hotel**, 199 Chimes Tower Rd, is the former home of the Western author, who visited Catalina with a film crew to shoot *The Vanishing American* and liked the place so much he never left, building for himself this "hopi pueblo"-style house, complete with a beamed ceiling, stark white walls, and thick, wooden front door. The hotel's rooms are themed after his books and its pool is shaped like an arrowhead, with the complex also offering excellent views of Avalon and the bay below. Similarly, the **Inn on Mt Ada**, at Wrigley Terrace Road on the south hillside of Avalon, was the 1921 Colonial Revival home of William Wrigley and is now a palatial hotel, with sweeping ocean views and a fine garden with numerous cacti and succulents native to the region.

Several miles southwest of Avalon, the **Wrigley Botanical Garden**, 1400 Avalon Canyon Rd (daily 8am–5pm; $1), contains 37 acres of native foliage and trees, though more fascinating is the **Wrigley Monument**, just beyond the garden. This cenotaph honors the chewing-gum baron with a great tile staircase leading to an imposing Art Deco mausoleum, where Wrigley was to have been interred – which, for unclear reasons, never happened.

Northwest of Avalon, isolated **TWO HARBORS**, a small resort community, sits on a small strip of land that connects Cherry Cove and Catalina Harbor. With a large marina and several campground facilities, the town is suitable enough for outdoor activities like kayaking, snorkeling, and scuba diving, but there's little to really see.

The Santa Catalina interior

If possible, venture into the **interior** of Santa Catalina, which comprises 42,000 acres of largely untouched wilderness. You can take a bus tour if time is short; if it isn't, get a map and a free **wilderness permit**, which allows you to hike and camp, from the Chamber of Commerce or the **Parks and Recreation office** (☎310/510-0688), both in Avalon. Mountain biking requires a $50 permit from the **Catalina Island Conservancy**, 125 Calressa Ave (☎310/510-1421), which controls and manages 86 percent of the island terrain.

There are some unique animals roaming about the wildlands: keep an eye out for the Catalina Shrew, so rare it's only been sighted twice, and the Catalina Mouse, bigger and healthier than its mainland counterpart thanks to abundant food and lack of natural enemies. There are also foxes, ground squirrels, pigs, bald eagles, and quail, along with buffalo, which were descended from a smattering of fourteen left behind by a Hollywood film crew and have now become a sizable herd that wanders freely about the island.

Chapter 9

The San Gabriel and San Fernando Valleys

Along the eastern and northern limits of LA, the **SAN GABRIEL** and **SAN FERNANDO VALLEYS**, home to the bulk of LA's suburbs, are not as bland and homogenous as most people think – though San Fernando sometimes comes close. A broad range of classes, cultures, and terrains dot the areas, from the old-money hauteur of San Marino to the slapdash vigor of media-fueled Burbank

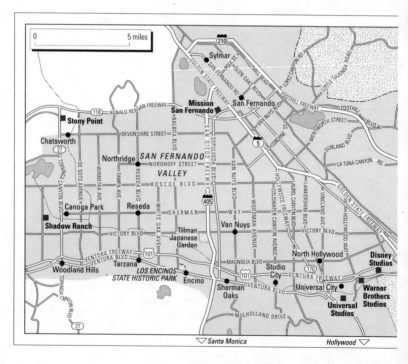

to the endless expanses of bleak asphalt in suburbs from North Hollywood to West Hills.

In the San Gabriel Valley, on the east side of the Verdugo Mountains, **Pasadena** is not only a geographical junction between the relatively flat San Fernando Valley and the sloped foothills of the San Gabriel Valley, it's also the region's only true cultural counterweight to the city of LA – a small, patrician town full of great architecture and diligent historic preservation. **South Pasadena** and **San Marino** also have their charms, particularly the latter's Huntington Gardens. The rest of the San Gabriel Valley holds more dispersed pleasures, worth a look only if you're staying in the LA region for at least a week.

West of Pasadena, in the San Fernando Valley, the upper-middle class suburb of **Glendale** is home to a fascinating cemetery, while **Burbank**, further west, is studio central, with the likes of Disney, Warner Brothers, and, in its own municipal enclave, Universal. In the **western San Fernando Valley**, LA's secessionist-minded suburbs, known collectively as "the Valley," offer historic attractions here and there, but are mostly known for their furnace-like temperatures and copious minimalls. At the apex of the triangular Valley, communities like **San Fernando** have a rich Spanish heritage, while further north,

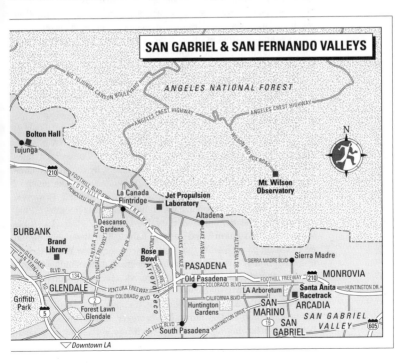

exciting **Magic Mountain** outdoes Disneyland for death-defying rides.

The San Gabriel Valley

Running along the Verdugo and San Gabriel mountains, the **San Gabriel Valley** largely escapes the derision many Angelenos have for the San Fernando Valley. Home to a good number of exclusive communities, it has an authentic cultural cachet in many places, especially along its foothills, even though it actually contains just as many grubby, inhospitable spaces as anywhere in the region.

After its early settlement by native Tongva tribes and the later arrival of Spanish landowners and missionaries, the San Gabriel Valley became by the turn of this century a choice spot for American agriculture, predominantly grapes, wine, and citrus crops. Railroads brought new migrants, and by the postwar era, the foothills of the San Gabriel mountains developed into another populous arm of suburban LA, with swimming pools and barbeques taking the place of ranch houses and orange groves. One thing that didn't change was the torrential flooding. Thanks to its specific climate and geography, the Valley has always been a prime spot for **winter deluges**, in which great cascades of water sweep down the hillsides; by the time they reach the foothills, they become mudslides, charging through the canyons and destroying all in their wake – including encroaching suburban homes. This problem has been an occasional impediment to hillside growth, but with the creation of huge "catch basins" to contain the watery mudslides, real estate developers have continued to push the envelope of growth further up into the mountains.

Pasadena

At the western edge of the San Gabriel Valley, **PASADENA** is a mix of old tradition and contemporary popular appeal. Located ten miles northeast of Downtown LA, and connected to it by the rickety, dangerous Pasadena Freeway (110 north), Pasadena was, like much of LA, settled by midwesterners, in this case from Indiana. However, unlike much of the metropolis, which has lost its nineteenth-century flavor to the onslaught of modernity, Pasadena has retained a visible sense of its old culture and genteel habits. The **Rose Parade**, an event dating back to 1890 that takes place every New Year's Day, is one reflection of this heritage, as are the grand estates of the **Arroyo Seco** neighborhood and the Spanish Revival character of **downtown Pasadena**, the civic and commercial heart of the city. Until fairly recently Pasadena had been slumping, its business core resembling the meaner parts of Downtown LA; however, urban renewal dollars have begun flowing and made the town into something of a year-round tourist magnet, not only for its **Old Pasadena** shopping strip,

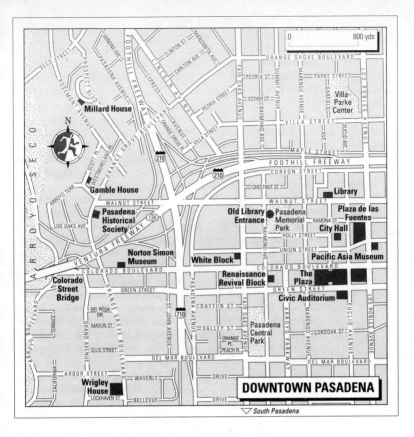

Map labels (from image):
- SECO STREET
- WINONA AVE
- PROSPECT BLVD
- CLINTON ST
- MANZANITA AVE
- CARLTON AVE
- FOOTHILL FREEWAY
- PASADENA AVENUE
- ROSEMONT AVENUE
- LINCOLN AVE
- CYPRESS
- FAIR OAKS AVENUE
- PEORIA STREET
- SUMMIT AVENUE
- ORANGE GROVE BOULEVARD
- PARKE STREET
- MARENGO AVENUE
- GARFIELD
- Villa Parke Center
- LOS ROBLES AVENUE
- PEORIA ST
- ESTHER ST
- RAYMOND AVE
- Millard House
- ORANGE GROVE BOULEVARD
- PEORIA STREET
- VILLA STREET
- EUCLID AVE
- SCOTT PL
- WESTMORELAND PL
- ORANGE GROVE BLVD
- VILLA STREET
- MAPLE STREET
- 210
- FOOTHILL FREEWAY
- CORSON STREET
- CHESTNUT ST
- Library
- Gamble House
- ARROYO TERR
- LIVE OAKS AVE
- WALNUT STREET
- WALNUT STREET
- Plaza de las Fuentes
- Pasadena Historical Society
- 134
- Old Library Entrance
- Pasadena Memorial Park
- RAMONA ST
- City Hall
- HOLLY STREET
- VENTURA FREEWAY
- Norton Simon Museum
- White Block
- UNION STREET
- Pacific Asia Museum
- COLORADO BOULEVARD
- COLORADO BOULEVARD
- Colorado Street Bridge
- ORANGE GROVE BOULEVARD
- PASADENA AVENUE
- Renaissance Revival Block
- The Plaza
- GREEN STREET
- GREEN STREET
- Civic Auditorium
- DEL ROSA DR
- MAYLIN ST
- ST JOHN AVENUE
- DAYTON ST
- FAIR OAKS AVENUE
- ARROYO PARKWAY
- MARENGO AVENUE
- EUCLID AVENUE
- LOS ROBLES AVENUE
- CORDOVA ST
- 710
- VALLEY ST
- Pasadena Central Park
- ORANGE PL
- PEACH PL
- GRAND AVENUE
- ELLIS STREET
- DEL MAR BOULEVARD
- DEL MAR BOULEVARD
- CALIFORNIA
- ARBOR STREET
- WAVERLY
- DRIVE
- Wrigley House
- LOCKHAVEN ST
- BELLEVUE
- DRIVE
- **DOWNTOWN PASADENA**
- ▽ South Pasadena
- 0   800 yds
- N

primarily a boutique and architecture zone, but also for its ever-popular architectural treasures like the **Gamble House**.

Downtown Pasadena

Downtown Pasadena, bordered by Lake Avenue, California Boulevard, the 210 freeway, and a sliver of the 710 freeway, is one of LA County's few traditional downtowns, with fine municipal architecture, restaurants, and shops; best of all, it's easily navigable on foot, with most places of interest located near **Colorado Boulevard**, the city's commercial axis.

On and around this boulevard, between Fair Oaks and Euclid avenues, is "**Old Pasadena**," a mix of antique sellers, used book and record stores, cafés, clothing shops, and theaters that gets quite crowded on weekends. Scattered among these businesses are some elegant buildings, such as the faded Italian-style **White Block**, Fair Oaks Avenue at Union Street, formerly the 1887 City Hall building,

Call the local
preservation
society,
Pasadena
Heritage, for
information
about taking a
tour of Hotel
Green and
other area
landmarks, at
☎ 818/793-
0617.

and the **Venetian Revival Building**, 17 S Raymond Ave, an 1894 Victorian design just recently renovated.

The streets to the north and south of Colorado Boulevard can be accessed through several pedestrian alleys that maintain their turn-of-the-century style. Standing out to the south is the marvelous **Hotel Green apartment block**, 50 E Green St, formerly a resort, finished in 1903, that centered around a now-demolished hotel across the street. Later additions included the apartments that remain today, plus a **bridge** that crossed Raymond Avenue to unite the structures. Although the walkway, once called the "Bridge of Sighs" after the Venetian version, has been sliced in half and now stops at the sidewalk, its design still fascinates, with everything from tiled domes and turrets to curvaceous arches that support the whole.

Pasadena's Old World trappings are most evident in its early municipal buildings, such as the city's centerpiece, **Pasadena City Hall**, 100 N Garfield Ave, one of several city buildings in Mediterranean Revival styles, in this case Spanish Baroque. Set on a wide city plaza, the structure has a large, tiled dome and an imperious facade with grand arches and columns, along with an elegant garden, patio, and fountain. Across Euclid Avenue from City Hall, **Plaza de las Fuentes** is a postmodern public square, with colorful tile work and a blocky pastel design. Significantly more interesting is the **Pacific Asia Museum**, diagonally across at 46 N Los Robles Ave (Wed–Sun 10am–5pm; free), designed to look like an imperial Chinese palace – with sloping tiled roof, inset balconies, and fortress-like appearance – and displaying thousands of treasures and more mundane objects from Korean, Chinese, and Japanese history, including jade and porcelain artworks, silk robes, intricately carved woodblocks, various swords and spears, and a large cache of paintings and drawings from across the Pacific Rim. One particular highlight is the **courtyard garden**, with koi fish, marble statues, and a variety of trees native to the Far East.

Also intriguing are the nearby remains of the neo-Romanesque city library in what is now **Pasadena Memorial Park**. The old library steps and entrance, which can be seen – though not accessed – from the corner of Walnut Street and Raymond Avenue, are encased by stone walls and lead nowhere. On a more functional level, the current **Public Library**, 285 E Walnut St, is a Spanish Renaissance gem, and the **Civic Auditorium**, 300 E Green St, a subdued cinquecento Italian creation that was built during the Depression.

Further east, **Lake Avenue** is a commercial strip that competes with Old Pasadena for visitors' attention, though in less quaint – and less successful – fashion, and is easily missed. Better is the **California Institute of Technology** ("Cal Tech") campus, a few blocks east of Lake Avenue, with its assortment of Spanish-style buildings, some designed by Bertram Goodhue, architect of Downtown LA's library (see p.68).

The Norton Simon Museum

Just across the 710 freeway from downtown Pasadena, the **Norton
Simon Museum**, 411 W Colorado Blvd (Thurs–Sun noon–6pm; $4),
does not have the famous reputation of the LA County or Getty museums, but its collections compare favorably in many respects. Established
and overseen by the industrialist Simon until his death in 1993, and since
administered by his movie-star wife Jennifer Jones, the museum, perhaps because of its distant location, sidesteps the hype of the LA art
world to concentrate on the quality of its presentation. You could easily
spend a whole day wandering through the spacious galleries.

The core of the collection is Western European painting from the
Renaissance to the early modern period. It's a massive one, much of
it rotated, but most of the major pieces are consistently on view.
Highlights include Dutch paintings of the seventeenth century –
notably Rembrandt's vivacious *Titus, Portrait of a Boy* and Frans
Hals' quietly aggressive *Portrait of a Man* – and Italian Renaissance
work from Pietro Longhi and Guido Reni. Among more modern
works, there's a good sprinkling of French Impressionists and post-
Impressionists: Monet's atmospheric, light-dappled *Mouth of the
Seine at Honfleur*, Manet's plaintive *Ragpicker*, and a Degas capturing the extended yawn of a washerwoman in *The Ironers*, plus
works by Cézanne, Gauguin, Van Gogh, and Picasso.

As a counterpoint to the Western art, the museum has a fine collection of **Asian sculpture**, including many highly polished Buddhist
and Hindu figures, some inlaid with precious stones.

The Arroyo Seco

Spanish for "dry riverbed," the **Arroyo Seco** is another of Pasadena's
districts with significant turn-of-the-century heritage, augmented by
abundant greenery and a pleasantly isolated setting, just northwest
of the 134 and 210 freeways. Orange Grove Boulevard leads you into
this neighborhood of fine houses, one of them occupied by the
Pasadena Historical Society, 470 W Walnut St (Thurs–Sun 1–4pm;
$4), decoratd with its original 1905 funishings and paintings, and
with fine displays on Pasadena's history. The building was once the
Finnish Consulate, and much of the folk art on display comes from
Pasadena's "twin town" of Jarvenpää in Finland.

Down the street, the **Gamble House**, 4 Westmoreland Place (hour-
long tours Thurs–Sun noon–3pm; $4), is the one attraction that real-
ly brings people out here. Built in 1908, and one of the masterpieces
of Southern Californian Craftsman architecture, it's a style you can
see replicated all over the state, freely combining elements from Swiss
chalets and Japanese temples in a sprawling, shingled house. Broad
eaves shelter outdoor sleeping porches, which in turn shade terraces
on the ground floor, leading out to the spacious lawn. The interior was
crafted with the same attention to detail, and all the carpets, cabi-
netry, and lighting fixtures, designed specifically for the house,

Arroyo culture

The neighborhood around the **Arroyo Seco** has shifted somewhat through the years, first by geography, later by culture. Orange Grove Boulevard, which now runs immediately to the west of the 710 freeway spur, was the original focus of the Arroyo and lined with a series of grand estates, tagged "Millionaire's Row." The local gentry, however, chose not to live in the Arroyo itself, and instead used it mainly as a source of wood and a place to picnic, and the palaces went into decline in the early part of this century, to be replaced eventually by the apartment blocks visible today. Meanwhile, just to the west, the Arroya Seco proper was being built up by numerous Arts and Crafts-movement intellectuals inspired by the designs of William Morris and Gustav Stickley. The resulting Swiss chalets, Tudor mansions, and Craftsman monuments were manifestations of a new **Arroyo Culture**; its artisan practitioners prized working with wood, clay, and stone. Not surprisingly, one of their heroes was Charles Lummis, famed for his boulder house in Highland Park (see p.71) and an equally prominent intellectual of the time. Architects Charles and Henry Greene and Frank Lloyd Wright were all attracted by the Arroyo too, if not full believers in its attendant culture. The culture faded, however, as much of the area was bought up by wealthy Angelenos, though fortunately, the architecture has been largely preserved.

remain in excellent condition. The area around the Gamble House is filled with at least eight other (private) houses by the two brothers (the firm of Greene & Greene) who designed it, including Charles Greene's own house, **368 Arroyo Terrace**. A quarter of a mile north of the Gamble House is a small, concrete block house by Frank Lloyd Wright, La Miniatura, also known as the **Millard House**, which you can glimpse through the gate opposite 585 Rosemont Ave. Almost incongruously, the 104,000-seat **Rose Bowl** is just to the north, out of use most of the year but home to a very popular **flea market** on the second Sunday of each month and, in the autumn, the place where the UCLA football team plays its home games. The other football was also played here in 1994, when the site hosted the World Cup Final.

To the south on Arroyo Boulevard, pass under the monumental spans of the **Colorado Street Bridge**, one of the area's structural wonders – a 1467ft monolith of curving concrete spans – to arrive at the **Wrigley House**, 391 S Orange Grove Blvd (tours Thurs 2–4pm; free), a 1914 Mediterranean mansion, formerly owned by gum king William Wrigley. The house is the administrative headquarters of the annual **Rose Parade**, which it appropriately celebrates by maintaining up to 1500 types of roses in its gardens.

Details on the Rose Parade appear in "Festivals," p.293.

South Pasadena

For all its historic architecture and small-town appeal, the separate city of **SOUTH PASADENA**, due south of downtown Pasadena, finds itself in a precarious spot – in the path of the 710 freeway, which highway engineers have been trying to finish for decades. Thanks to lawsuits and delaying tactics, however, the wrecking ball has not yet arrived for the grand old structures of the city (even though much of the property north of it has already been condemned), but it's hard to say how much longer the city can hold out against LA's insatiable desire for new freeway links.

The best place to start exploring South Pasadena is on **Fair Oaks Avenue**, the city's main strip, though its charm has been somewhat eroded by new minimalls and fast-food joints. Along here you'll find the **Rialto Theater**, 1023 Fair Oaks Ave, a 1925 movie palace that is not much from the outside, but has a faded splendor inside, with Moorish organ screens, Egyptian columns, winged harpies and a central Medusa head. It's worth the price of a movie ticket just to poke around inside. Almost as interesting, off nearby Monterey Road, Irving Gill's **Miltimore House**, 1301 Chelten Way, is a modular white structure with green trim that combines elements of Mission Revival and modern styles. Even so, it almost pales in comparison to the bizarre street design of the surrounding neighborhood, in which ancient live oaks jut out at random spots in the roadbed – the trees used to be part of a long-forgotten park.

Meridian Avenue, which parallels Fair Oaks Avenue several blocks to its west, takes you through the smaller-scaled Victorian-era homes south of the 110 freeway and into the larger residences north of it – many of them doomed. On the southern end, the **Meridian Iron Works**, 913 Meridian Ave (Sat 1–4pm; free), is an 1886 Pioneer-style building that was a hotel, blacksmith, ironworks, and bicycle dealer at different times in its history. Now officially the South Pasadena Preservation Society Museum, it features exhibits and photographs from its own history and on the heritage of the city itself, including unexpected curios from an ostrich farm.

To the north, Meridian Avenue runs into posh **Buena Vista Street**, which features a number of grand dwellings, including two by Charles and Henry Greene: the **Garfield House**, no. 1001, former home of murdered US President James Garfield's widow and a fairly well-preserved 1904 Swiss chalet with numerous Craftsman elements; and the adjacent **Longley House**, no. 1005, an impressively eclectic 1897 mix of revival styles from Romanesque to Moorish to Georgian.

A few blocks east, another Greene creation extends across the railway gully of the abandoned Southern Pacific and Santa Fe line, the 1906 **Oaklawn Bridge**, at the end of Oaklawn Avenue, a concrete ruin that spans the railway gap with a romantically weather-beaten and vine-covered look, and leads to the boulder pillars of an old waiting station, at Fair Oaks Avenue.

San Marino

East of South Pasadena, uneventful **SAN MARINO** is marked by some of LA's most privileged residents and widest neighborhood

San Marino is a "dry" town – no commercial alcohol sales allowed.

Additional information on staying at the Ritz Carlton, along with details on other San Gabriel Valley accommodation, can be found on p.227.

streets, not necessarily attractions in themselves by any means; indeed, the main reason to come out here is to see the legacy of railway man and real estate mogul **Henry Huntington**, preserved in his museum and gardens.

Before hitting the museum, though, you may want to check out the **El Molino Viejo**, 1120 Old Mill Rd (daily 1–4pm; free), a weathered adobe that was built as a water-driven flour mill in 1816 by Spanish missionaries from Mission San Gabriel. Its functional use ended only decades later, and it was allowed to rot until the 1920s, when restoration began. Since then, it's gone from being an industrial site to Henry Huntington's golf-course clubhouse to its current incarnation as the home of the California Historical Society. Inside, you can see mildly interesting historical exhibits and technical explanations of how water generated the power to make flour.

Just to the west, the towering **Ritz-Carlton Huntington Hotel**, atop a hill at 1401 S Oak Knoll Ave, began life as the *Wentworth Hotel* in 1906, to be taken over by Huntington in 1913, at which point the hotel expanded considerably. It consists of a Mediterranean-style main building, with attractive gardens out back, and, further away, small bungalow-styled residences for its swankiest guests – not surprisingly, the only part of the hotel off-limits to the public.

The Huntington Library

San Marino's most redeeming feature is the **Huntington Library, Art Collections and Botanical Gardens**, just off Huntington Drive at 1151 Oxford Rd (Tues–Fri 1–4.30pm, Sat–Sun 10am–4.30pm; $7.50; students $4). Part of this is made up of the collections of Henry Huntington, who was the nephew of childless multimillionaire Collis P Huntington. Henry, groomed to take over the company from his uncle, was dethroned by the board of directors and took his sizable inheritance to LA, where he bought up the existing streetcar routes and combined them as the Pacific Electric Railway Company, which in turn controlled the Red Car line that soon became the largest transit network in the world, and Huntington the largest landowner in the state. He retired in 1910, moving to the manor house he had built in San Marino, devoting himself full time to buying rare books and manuscripts, and marrying his uncle's widow Arabella and acquiring her collection of English portraits.

You can pick up a self-guided walking tour of each of the three main sections from the bookstore and information desk in the entry pavilion. The **Library**, right off the main entrance, is a good first stop, its two-story exhibition hall containing numerous manuscripts and rare books, among them a Gutenberg Bible, a folio edition of Shakespeare's plays, and the **Ellesmere Chaucer**, a circa-1410 illuminated manuscript of *The Canterbury Tales*. Displays around the walls trace the history of printing and of the English language from

medieval manuscripts to a King James Bible, through Milton's
Paradise Lost and Blake's *Songs of Innocence and Experience*, to
first editions of Swift, Coleridge, Dickens, Woolf, and Joyce.

To decorate the **main house**, a grand mansion done out in Louis
XIV carpets and later French tapestries, the Huntingtons traveled to
England and returned laden with the finest art money could buy.
Most of it still hangs on the walls. Unless you're a real fan of eighteenth-century English portraiture, head through to the back extension, added when the gallery opened in 1934, which displays, as well
as important works by Turner, Van Dyck, and Constable, the stars of
the whole collection: Gainsborough's *Blue Boy* and Reynolds' *Mrs
Siddons as the Tragic Muse*. Close by, you'll find paintings by
Edward Hopper and Mary Cassatt, and a range of Wild West drawings and sculpture, in the **Scott Gallery for American Art**.

For all the art and literature, though, it's the grounds that make
the Huntington truly appealing, and the acres of beautiful themed
gardens surrounding the buildings include a Zen Rock Garden, complete with authentically constructed Buddhist Temple and Tea
House, as well as a Desert Garden, with the world's largest collection
of desert plants, including twelve acres of cacti. While strolling
through these botanical splendors, you might also visit the
Huntingtons themselves, buried in a neo-Palladian **mausoleum** at
the northwest corner of the estate, beyond the rows of an orange
grove.

North of Pasadena

The tiny neighborhoods north of Pasadena, **ALTADENA** and **LA
CANADA FLINTRIDGE**, sit on hillsides that lead into the Angeles
National Forest, a fifty-mile wilderness in the San Gabriel Mountains.
Threatened by flood during heavy rains, these are some of the diciest
places to live in LA, and you can see part of their elaborate flood control system just off Oak Grove Drive, where the Hanamongna
Watershed Park and Devils Gate Reservoir are dramatic testaments
to the power of water: a huge green slope and massive catch basin
designed specifically to contain water, mud, rocks, housing debris,
and assorted other elements in the event of catastrophic flooding.

Immediately north of the park and reservoir is one of the corner-
stones of America's military-industrial complex: the **Jet Propulsion
Laboratory**, 4800 Oak Grove Drive, La Cañada Flintridge (for tours
call ☎818/354-9314; free), devoted to the research and development
of all manner of high-tech, space-related machinery, including orbiting
satellites, long-range missiles and rockets, and unmanned explorer
crafts. For obvious public-relations reasons, the lab chooses instead to
display a replica of the solar-system-exploring *Voyager* craft, and the
Magellan and *Galileo* vehicles that mapped Venus and Mars.

On a very different note, west off Foothill Boulevard, **Descanso
Gardens**, 1418 Descanso Drive, La Cañada Flintridge (daily

9am–4.30pm; $5, students $3), concentrates all the plants you might see in the mountains into 155 acres of landscaped park. There's also a Japanese tea house and garden, with an accompanying narrow red footbridge, and a tranquil bird sanctuary for migrating waterfowl. The gardens are especially brilliant during the spring, when all the wildflowers are in bloom.

North from the 210 freeway, the **Angeles Crest Highway** (Hwy-2) heads up into the mountains above Pasadena. This area was once dotted with resort hotels and wilderness camps, and today you can hike up any number of nearby canyons and come across the ruins of old lodges that either burned down or washed away towards the end of the hiking era in the 1930s, when automobiles became popular. One of the most interesting of these trails, a five-mile round trip, follows the route of the Mount Lowe Railway, once one of LA's biggest tourist attractions, up to the old funicular and the foundations of "**White City**" – formerly a mountaintop resort of two hotels, a zoo, and an observatory. Today, a brass plaque embedded in concrete is the only reminder of the resort, and even this is slowly becoming overgrown with pine trees and incense cedars. Further north, the Crest Highway passes through the **Angeles National Forest**, where you can hike and camp most of the year and ski in winter, to **Mount Wilson**, high enough to be a major site for TV broadcast antennae. At the peak, the Mount Wilson Observatory features a small **museum** (daily 10am–3pm; $1) that displays both 60- and 100-inch telescopes and various astronomical exhibits, some of them detailing the work of Edwin Hubble, who developed the now-dominant theory of cosmological expansion, along with being named for the famous orbiting telescope.

Like many other transit lines in the region, the Mount Lowe funicular was owned by Henry Huntington's Pacific Electric Railway company.

East of Pasadena

East of Pasadena, the San Gabriel Valley becomes a patchwork quilt of small, blocky municipalities, with few sights scattered across large distances. The one commonality these foothill communities have is Foothill Boulevard, which, before it was displaced by the Foothill Freeway (Hwy 210), was famously known as **Route 66**. Formerly the main route across the US, "from Chicago to LA, more than three thousand miles all the way," the strip has declined in recent decades and begun looking a bit decrepit. However, the romance of the open road remains, and along its path, you'll find numerous establishments advertising the route's nostalgia in bright, neon letters.

Route 66 has been the inspiration of everything from an early 1960s TV show to a famous song – (Get Your Kicks on) Route 66 – performed by the Rolling Stones, Depeche Mode, and many others.

If you follow Foothill Boulevard out of Pasadena nowadays, you'll come to the town of **ARCADIA**, a colorless suburb whose **LA County Arboretum**, 310 N Baldwin Ave (daily 9am–4.30pm; $5; students $3), contains plenty of impressive gardens and waterfalls, and, above all, a great assortment of trees. The arboretum was the 127-acre ranch home of "Lucky" Baldwin, who made his millions in the silver mines of the Comstock in the 1870s. He settled here in 1875, and built a fanciful white palace along a palm-tree-lined lagoon, later used in the TV show *Fantasy Island*, on the site of the 1839 Rancho Santa Anita. He also bred horses and raced them on a neighboring track that has since grown into the **Santa Anita Racetrack** (racing Oct to early Nov & late Dec to late April, Wed–Sun post time 12.30pm or 1pm; $3–$8), still the most glamorous racetrack in California, with a Depression-era steel frieze along the grandstand.

The foothill district of **SIERRA MADRE**, on the northern edge of town, lies directly beneath Mount Wilson and is worth a visit if you're a hiker. A seven-mile round-trip trail up to the summit has recently been restored and makes for an excellent, if tiring, trek. The trailhead is 150 yards up the private Mount Wilson Road.

South of Sierra Madre stands the valley's original settlement, the church and grounds of **Mission San Gabriel Archangel** (daily 9am–4.30pm; $3). Still standing at the corner of Mission and Serra in the heart of the small town of **San Gabriel**, the mission was established here in 1771 by Junipero Serra. Although partially covered in scaffolding following decades of damage by earthquakes and the elements, the church and grounds have recently been reopened, with the grapevine-filled gardens giving some sense of mission life.

The lone draw out in **MONROVIA**, east of Sierra Madre, is the zany **Aztec Hotel**, 311 W Foothill Blvd, a 1925 pre-Columbian creation from Mayan revivalist Robert Stacy-Judd that is still maintained as a boarding house. Its faux-ancient carvings and designs, monumental appearance, and stunning facade encase a lobby that features old bikes, vacuum cleaners, and other antiques, as well as the original gas pumps found along Route 66, which runs just outside the front door.

The San Fernando Valley

Home to acres of asphalt, countless minimalls, and non-stop tract housing, the **San Fernando Valley** is often considered to be the apotheosis of dull, vacuous suburbia, fit only for the likes of mall-hopping "Valley girls" and the cloistered lower middle class. Though of course an exaggeration, there's some truth to it, at least in terms of finding things to do; what few attractions there are center on the movie studios that left Hollywood long ago.

Its 1769 Spanish discovery predating the settlement of Los Angeles, the San Fernando Valley was first named after St Catherine, only later acquiring its present moniker with the development of Mission San Fernando at its northern tip. After the US took possession of the California territory and the railroad cut through it, the Valley rapidly transformed, going from a late-nineteenth-century tract of wheat fields to an interwar expanse of citrus groves to a post-World War II dynamo of industry, media, and, above all, suburban housing. The spark that enabled all this development to occur was

The San Fernando Valley

the 1913 construction of the LA Aqueduct, which irrigated the land with water diverted from California's northern Owens Valley.

The film Chinatown provides all the ugly details on the water troubles of the Valley.

While the Owens Valley farmers may have suffered, some of them even resorting to hydro-terrorism, the San Fernando Valley landowners – including many Downtown LA businessmen – got rich, and they in turn sold their land to make way for even more residential development. The agricultural ghosts are apparent only in street names such as Orange Grove Boulevard and Walnut Street.

Glendale

West of Pasadena, beyond the Verdugo Mountains, **GLENDALE** is a typical upper-middle-class suburb, unusual mostly for its size, extending from the Griffith Park area all the way past the northern reaches of foothill communities like La Cañada Flintridge. At least its downtown is compact, south of the 134 freeway along Brand Boulevard, though it has little to compel any visitor. However, if you're in the neighborhood, make sure to see the **Alex Theater**, 268 N Brand Blvd, a striking Art Deco piece from 1925 with a green-and-yellow, neon-trimmed design and a great pylon erupting from the facade; it's now used mainly as a performing arts center. North of the 134, the **Verdugo Adobe**, 2211 Bonita Drive (daily 8am–4pm; free), displays antiques and artifacts from the early nineteenth-century, including a colorful selection of dolls and puppets; while the **Casa Adobe de San Rafael**, 1330 Dorothy Drive (8am–5pm; free), is an old adobe set among birds of paradise, magnolias, and eucalyptus trees. To the northwest, the **Brand Library**, or "El Miradero," 1601 W Mountain St (Tues–Thurs 1–6pm, Fri–Sat 1–5pm; free), is a white oddity from 1902 said to be modeled on the East India Pavilion at Chicago's 1893 Columbian Exposition. In any case, it's a striking

Islamic design of domes and arches containing art materials from the main Glendale Library.

Seven miles north, **Tujunga** has a terrific collection of boulder houses and bungalows built in the 1910s and 1920s, the inspiration of a small community of Socialists who, like the dwellers in Pasadena's Arroyo Seco, believed earthy materials like wood and stone made for the best, and most moral, forms of construction. Their restored 1913 clubhouse, **Bolton Hall**, 10116 Commerce Ave (Tues & Sun 1–4pm; free), hints at their aims, with a rocky central tower and interior with exposed wooden beams; it now displays antiques from city history.

Forest Lawn Glendale

For most visitors, the main reason to come to the city is to visit the Glendale branch of **Forest Lawn Cemetery**, 1712 S Glendale Ave (daily 9am–5pm; free) – immortalized with biting satire by Evelyn Waugh in *The Loved One*, and at the vanguard of the American way of death for decades. Founded in 1917 by one Dr Hubert Eaton, this soon became *the* place to be buried, its pompous landscaping and pious artworks attracting celebrities by the dozen to buy their own little piece of heaven.

It's best to climb the hill and see the cemetery in reverse from the **Forest Lawn Museum** (open during park hours; free), whose hodge-podge of worldly artifacts includes coins from ancient Rome, Viking relics, medieval armor, and a mysterious, sculpted Easter Island fig-ure, discovered being used as ballast in a fishing boat in the days when the statues could still be removed from the island. How it ended up here is another mystery, but it is the only one on view in the US. Next door to the museum, the grandiose **Resurrection and Crucifixion Hall** houses the biggest piece of religious art in the world, *The Crucifixion* by Jan Styka – though you're only allowed to see it during the ceremonial unveiling every hour on the hour (and you'll be charged $1 to boot). Besides this, Eaton owned a stained glass "re-creation" of Leonardo da Vinci's *Last Supper* and, realizing that he only needed one piece to complete his trio of "the three great-est moments in the life of Christ," he commissioned American artist Robert Clark to produce *The Resurrection* – with its own unveiling ceremony every half-hour. If you can't stick around for the showings (with both, in any case, the size is the only aspect that's impressive), you can check out the scaled-down replicas just inside the entrance.

The Hollywood Hills branch of Forest Lawn is discussed on p.94.

From the museum, walk down through the terrace gardens – loaded with sculptures modeled on the greats of classical European art – to the **Freedom Mausoleum**, where you'll find a handful of the cemetery's better-known graves. Just outside the mausoleum's doors, Errol Flynn lies in an unspectacular plot (unmarked until 1979), rumored to have been buried with six bottles of whiskey at his side, while a few strides away is the grave of Walt Disney, who is not cryogenically preserved as urban legend would have it. Inside the mausoleum itself you'll find Clara Bow, Nat King Cole, Jeanette MacDonald, and Alan Ladd placed close to each other on the first floor. Downstairs are Chico Marx and his brother Gummo, the Marx Brothers' agent and business manager. Back down the hill, the **Great Mausoleum** is chiefly noted for the tombs of Clark Gable (next to Carole Lombard, who died in a plane crash just three years after marrying him), and Jean Harlow, in a marble-lined room which cost over $25,000, paid for by fiancé William Powell.

Burbank

Although Hollywood is the name that's synonymous with the movie industry, in reality many of the big studios moved out of Tinseltown long ago, and much of the nitty-gritty business of actually making films goes on over the hills in otherwise boring **BURBANK**, Johnny Carson's former job site (at NBC), and the frequent butt of his jokes.

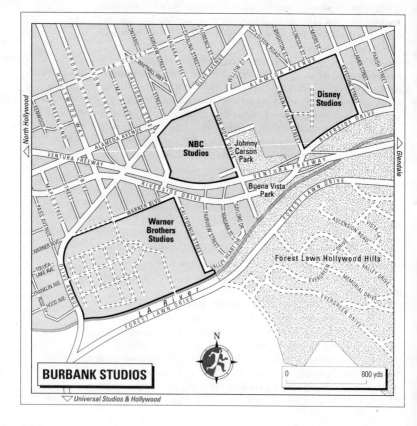

Hot, smoggy, and often downright ugly, Burbank nonetheless has a media district bustling with production activity, thanks to the explosion in demand from overseas markets, cable TV, and broadcast networks.

The San Fernando Valley

Disney is probably the most prominent of the studios, having recently constructed a postmodern building in the shape of a wizard's hat, visible from the 101 freeway, to house over seven hundred animators. This creation is slightly better than Disney's other public face, its **Studio Office Building**, 500 S Buena Vista St, a clumsy effort from Michael Graves that features five of the Seven Dwarves propping up the building's roof. Built in 1992, it already seems dated, and as for touring the studio, forget it – the company would rather have you plunk down your cash in Disneyland.

Nearby, **NBC**, or the National Broadcasting Company, 3000 W Alameda St (Mon–Fri 9am–3pm; $7; ☎818/840-3537), offers a frank and interesting ninety-minute tour of the largest production facility in the US. The studio also gives you the chance to be in the audience for the taping of a program (phone ahead for free tickets), and it's worth the price of admission just to see *Tonight Show* host Jay Leno in action.

Just across Ventura Boulevard, the **Warner Brothers Studio**, 4000 Warner Blvd at Hollywood Way, does offer tours of its facilities (Mon–Fri 9am–4pm; $29; reservations only, at ☎818/972-TOUR). These "insider" trips through the lot take you past the big soundstages, around the production offices, and through the outdoor sets for movies and TV shows, including the urban set used in the canceled *Lois and Clark* program, which features a replica of Gotham and a facade for the fictional *Daily Globe* newspaper. Ultimately, you won't get to see any actual filming, but if you want to see a major studio's actual working environment, the tour is worth the money.

As long as you're in the area, drop by the oldest **Bob's Big Boy** in existence, 4211 Riverside Drive, a "Googie" coffee shop from 1949 that's been used for a host of Hollywood flicks.

For guided tours of Googie-style architecture in the LA area, see p.52.

Universal Studios

Just to the south along the 101 freeway, the largest of the old studio backlots belongs to **Universal Studios**, whose tours (summer daily 8am–10pm, rest of year daily 9am–7pm; $36; ☎818/508-9600) are firmly tourist-oriented, four hours long, and, with several high-tech interactive rides, more like a trip around an amusement park than a film studio. The first half features a tram ride through a make-believe set where you can experience the fading magic of the Red Sea parting, a visit with the *Jaws* shark, and a "collapsing" bridge; the second takes place inside the corny Entertainment Center, where unemployed actors engage in Wild West shoot-outs and stunt shows based on the latest movies. The theme rides are based on the studio's more popular films, including *Back to the Future* (a jerky trip on a motion simulator) and

Jurassic Park (close encounters with prehistoric plastic). You never actually get to see any filming.

The **Universal Amphitheater**, which hosts pop concerts in summer, is also part of the complex – known as Universal City – as is a twenty-screen movie-theater multiplex, with a lobby reminiscent of 1920s movie palaces. **Universal CityWalk**, also on the same lot, is an outdoor mall – free to all who pay the $5 parking (redeemable at the cinemas) – with neon-lit themed restaurants, chain stores, and cutesy architecture. Here, rock bands churn out MOR covers, street performers warble syrupy ballads, and giant TV screens run ads for the latest Universal release, all a sanitized simulation of LA city life that's hard to get too excited about.

The western San Fernando Valley

Beyond Burbank, the **western San Fernando Valley** suburbs – some of the more well-known of which are **NORTH HOLLYWOOD**, **SHERMAN OAKS**, **VAN NUYS**, and **RESEDA** – are often collectively called "the Valley," immediately bringing to mind minimalls, fast-food joints, and a certain biting Frank Zappa song. There are a few isolated attractions – most of the adobe variety – but not much of a real reason to head out this way.

However, the lack of any real sense of culture or community has not kept these suburbs from making regular secessionist threats against the city of LA, or from complaining of high city taxes, crummy schools, and distant bureaucracy. Strengthened by a recent law that allows them secession by plebiscite, subject to state approval, the districts no longer have to get a green light from Downtown LA to go their own way. However, their course is far from certain, with residents split on a need for total Balkanization of the area versus a San Fernando megacity that would be the nation's seventh-largest.

Across from Universal Studios is **Campo de Cahuenga**, 3919 Lankershim Blvd, North Hollywood (Mon–Fri 8am–2pm; free), of major importance to American history as the spot where generals John Fremont and Andres Pico signed an 1847 treaty between the US and Mexico, thus ending the Mexican-American War and allowing the US to officially acquire California and the rest of the Southwest, all of which is recounted here in fairly interesting detail.

Further west, near the 405 freeway, the **Tillman Japanese Garden**, 6100 Woodley Ave, Van Nuys (Mon–Fri 9am–1pm; free; by reservation at ☎818/756-8166), is a pleasant little spot with features standard to many Japanese gardens: stone lanterns, a teahouse, bonsai trees, bamboo sprouts, low bridges, and artful streams and pools. Using recycled water to animate its setting, the garden is a placid and enjoyable locale, despite sitting in the middle of the Sepulveda Dam Recreation Area – a giant flood plain.

Due southwest, off Ventura Boulevard, the increasingly expensive hillside homes of **Encino** sit near **Los Encinos State Historic Park**,

16756 Moorpark St (Wed–Sun 10am–5pm, tours 1–4pm; grounds free, tours $2), which includes all that remains of an original Native American settlement and later Mexican hacienda that were once here. Along with a blacksmith's shop and central lake, the main attraction is an 1849 adobe house, featuring high-ceilinged rooms that open out onto porches, shaded by oak trees (in Spanish, "encinos") and kept cool by the two-foot-thick walls.

The San Fernando Valley

Encino hit the news in 1998 as the murder site of actor-comic Phil Hartman, shot while sleeping in his San Fernando estate.

At the western end of the Valley, in **West Hills**, are more (minor) historic points of interest, notably the **Shadow Ranch**, 22633 Vanowen St (Mon–Fri 10am–5pm, Sat 9am–5pm, Sun noon–5pm), the center of a nineteenth-century ranch of 23,000 acres that was controlled by land moguls I N Van Nuys and Isaac Lankershim, and now mainly notable for its great stand of eucalyptus trees imported from Australia over 120 years ago. To the northwest is the **Orcutt Ranch**, 23600 Roscoe Blvd (daily 8am–5pm; free), once belonging to the oil geologist who first found fossils in the La Brea Tar Pits, and featuring a traditional Spanish Colonial ranch house, romantic grotto, large garden sundial, and a plot of ancient oaks and bamboo.

The La Brea Tar Pits are described on p.80.

A few miles east, Topanga Canyon Boulevard heads into the far northwest reaches of the Valley to **Stony Point**, a bizarre outcrop of sandstone that has been used for countless low-budget Western shootouts, and in recent years as a popular venue for LA's contingent of lycra-clad rock climbers. The area, though crossed by both Amtrak and Metrorail trains, has a desolate spookiness about it, and it comes as little surprise to learn that during the late 1960s the Charles Manson "family" lived for a time at **Spahn Ranch**, just west at 22000 Santa Susana Pass Road.

At the northern tip of the Valley, the San Diego, Golden State, and Foothill freeways join together at I-5, the quickest route north to San Francisco. Standing near the junction, at 15151 San Fernando Mission Blvd, the church and many of the historic buildings of **Mission San Fernando Rey de Espana** (daily 9am–5pm; $4) had to be completely rebuilt following the 1971 earthquake. It's hard to imagine now, walking through the nicely landscaped courtyards and gardens, but eighty-odd years ago, director D W Griffith used the then-dilapidated mission as a film site for movies such as *Our Silent Paths*, his tale of the Gold Rush. There's a good collection of the pottery, furniture, and saddles of the time, along with a blacksmith's shop loaded with an array of old-fashioned metalworking instruments.

Beyond the Valley

West of Stony Point, at the end of Santa Susana Pass Road, the little town of **SIMI VALLEY** has acquired something of an infamous reputation, the site where four LAPD cops were acquitted in the beating of Rodney King. It also offers the **Ronald Reagan Presidential**

Library, off Olsen Rd at 40 Presidential Drive (Mon–Sat 10am–5pm, Sun noon–5pm; $4), where it helps to be a fan of the Gipper to enjoy your visit; otherwise, you're likely to find the dewy-eyed exhibits and affectionate portrait of the Reagan Administration execrable. Far more captivating is **Grandma Prisbrey's Bottle Village**, 4595 Cochran St, assorted famous and generic buildings – from the Leaning Tower of Pisa to simple shacks – constructed from bits of junk. Auto parts, defunct lightbulbs, pencil shards, glass bottles, and various other detritus all show up in the design of this miniature village, the highlight of which is undoubtedly the "Doll Head Shrine," an assortment of antique plastic doll heads stuck on poles to vividly resemble a childhood nightmare.

To the far north of San Fernando, the historic ruins of **Mentryville**, three miles west of I-5 at 27201 W Pico Canyon Rd (guided tours noon–4pm first & third Sun of month; $2), are where California's very first oil well was dug, in 1876. The boom only lasted for a few decades and, despite the original well remaining in operation until 1990, the site was mainly a ghost town for many years. A preserved red-and-white barn, a one-room 1880s schoolhouse, and the Victorian house of the town's founder, Alexander Mentry, evoke some of the old character.

To the east, in the town of **Santa Clarita**, the **William S Hart Museum**, 24151 San Fernando Rd (Wed–Fri 10am–1pm, Sat–Sun 11am–4pm; free) is an excellent assemblage of Western history, featuring native artworks, Remington sculptures, displays of spurs, guns, and lariats, Tinseltown costumes, and authentic cowhand clothing, housed in a Spanish Colonial mansion. The building was constructed by Hart, the star of numerous silent westerns in the 1910s and 1920s, and considered by aficionados to be one of the all-time cowboy greats, and donated, along with his estate, to LA county.

Magic Mountain is best visited on weekdays, when the lines for the rides are not quite as long.

Conveniently, a trip to the Hart Museum may be combined with a day at nearby **Magic Mountain**, Magic Mountain Parkway at I-5 (summer daily 10am–10pm; rest of year Sat–Sun only 10am–8pm; $33, parking $5), a three-hundred-acre complex that has some of the wildest rollercoasters and rides in the world – a hundred times more thrilling than anything at Disneyland. Highlights include the Viper, a huge orange monster with seven frightening loops, and the Psyclone, a modern coaster modeled on the rickety wooden Cyclone in Coney Island. The recent addition of an adjacent water park, **Hurricane Harbor**, has only boosted the fun.

The I-14 freeway, also called the Antelope Valley Freeway, branches off from I-5 into an extension of the bleak Mojave Desert and takes you to **Vasquez Rocks Park**, off Agua Dulce Canyon Road, where jagged, rocky outcroppings and an undulating terrain make for one of Hollywood's favorite film locations – everything from *The Flintstones* to *Bonanza* to *Star Trek* has been shot on these 745 acres. Even more mythically, the illicit treasure of legendary bandit

Tiburcio Vásquez, is supposedly buried around here. Further up I-14, in the town of **Lancaster**, the awe-inspiring **Antelope Valley Poppy Reserve**, on Lancaster Drive, spreads over 1800 acres – in spring, an endless, bright-orange sea of wild blossoms. Despite its isolation, it gets fairly crowded during the spring. If you prefer the sound of screaming fighter jets, continue north on I-14 to **Edwards Air Force Base** (☎805/258-3520 for tours and information), where you might be lucky enough to see experimental planes darting overhead – or even the space shuttle landing.

Chapter 10

Malibu and the Santa Monica Mountains

Reached by way of a popular beachside motorway, the Pacific Coast Highway (otherwise known as "PCH"), **MALIBU** and the **SANTA MONICA MOUNTAINS** hold some of LA's most expensive real estate and, ironically, some of its highest levels of danger. Built on eroding cliffs forever sliding into the ocean, the area's homes and businesses also face trouble inland, where summer hillside fires blacken the landscape and leave a slick residue of burnt chaparral – a perfect surface for the catastrophic floods and mudslides that come just a few months later. In recent years, the arrival of El Niño-driven wet weather has only made the situation more dire, with watery calamities a constant, inescapable threat.

That said, Malibu and its inland mountains feature some of LA's most picturesque scenery, its canyons, valleys, and forests making up a surprisingly large, pristine wilderness amid the surrounding urban development. From **Pacific Palisades**, a chic district just

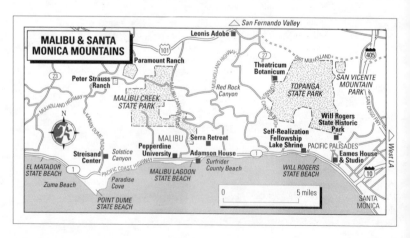

northwest of Santa Monica, to rustic **Topanga Canyon**, a wooded neighborhood with an artistic flavor, to beautiful **Point Dume**, a whale-watching promontory, these seaside and mountainous areas are best navigated by car, unless you prefer to hike on their rigorous parkland trails, of which there are many. North of PCH, **Mulholland Highway** provides an alternative trip through the area, winding through the Santa Monica Mountains and skipping Malibu entirely, instead reaching the ocean less than a mile from LA County's distant northwest boundary.

Pacific Palisades

Driving north on PCH beyond the bluffs of Santa Monica, you reach the sandy crescent of **Will Rogers State Beach** and, on the other side of the road, **PACIFIC PALISADES**, once an upper-crust community of artists and writers, but now just another pleasant seaside neighborhood. Indeed, that legacy is not all that's been erased: the district's hillsides are slowly but surely falling into the ocean, most noticeably at the point above Chautauqua Boulevard and PCH. With each winter's storms, more of the place gets washed down to the street below by simple erosion or catastrophic mudslides, blocking traffic on PCH, and shrinking the backyards of the clifftop homes.

There are a few remaining spots of interest among the suburban ranch houses, starting with the **Eames Studio Compound**, just off PCH at 203 Chautauqua Blvd, perhaps the most influential LA building of the late 1940s. Fashioned out of prefabricated industrial parts in 1947, the complex boasts a main residential unit and an adjacent studio building, both of which resemble large, colored metal-and-glass boxes – at the time of construction perceived as a great step toward complete architectural modernity. However, the compound's current appeal derives as much from the encroaching eucalyptus trees as from anything else. The metal frame of the neighboring **Entenza House**, 205 Chautauqua Blvd, is also something of a landmark, built by the same architect, Charles Eames, with help from Eero Saarinen. Significantly more captivating, the collection of **log cabins**, along Haldeman Road east of Rustic Canyon Recreation Center, is an unexpected sight in the woodsy hills that rise from Chautauqua Boulevard, self-consciously quaint houses that were the product of the "Uplifters Club," a branch of the LA Athletic Club that found residence in Pacific Palisades. Led by Wizard of Oz author L Frank Baum, the group's goals were to "uplift art, promote good fellowship, and build a closer acquaintance," but in practice consisted mainly of having booze-soaked fun during Prohibition. The bucolic charms of the houses, too, are somewhat deceptive – like Hollywood sets, many of the "cabins" have log facades that are merely pasted on.

To the north, Sunset Boulevard heads away from the ocean to **Will Rogers State Historic Park**, 14243 Sunset Blvd (summer daily 8am–7pm; rest of year daily 8am–6pm; free, parking $5), the home and ranch of the Depression-era cowboy philosopher and journalist Will Rogers, one of America's most popular figures of the time – after his death in a plane crash in 1935, there was a nationwide 35-minute silence. While he was renowned for his downhome, commonsense thinking, famously remarking that he "never met a man he didn't like," Rogers was also a Socialist with a pointed wit who once served as mayor of Beverly Hills. Now an informal **museum** (daily 10am–5pm; free), his ranch-style house is filled to overflowing with cowboy gear and Native American art, including a collection of ropes and lariats, sculptures by Frederic Remington, and the mounted head of a Texas longhorn. The 200-acre park has miles of foot and bridle paths, one of which leads up to the top of Topanga Canyon; on spring and summer weekends, professional polo matches take place on the park's main lawn and attract a fair crowd of local spectators.

Rogers was also something of a movie star, appearing in films such as State Fair and Connecticut Yankee.

Castellammare

The western section of Pacific Palisades, **Castellammare**, was named after a Latin port known as the "castle by the sea," with a 1920s design that mimicked Italian villas and Spanish Colonial estates. Although it's now essentially just another rich suburb, it does hold some period appeal in structures whose settings are just as dramatic as their architecture.

Located west of Sunset Boulevard, just before the street reaches PCH, Castellammare's exclusive neighborhoods look down at an incongruous sight on Sunset itself: the massive copper-lotus archway of the **Self-Realization Fellowship Lake Shrine**, 17190 Sunset Blvd (Tues–Sat 9am–4.30pm, Sun 12.30–4.30pm; free), a religious monument like no other. Sitting below a giant, golden-domed, hilltop temple of 58 stories, the lake shrine is an ecumenical ode to world faiths, with a heavy Eastern bent. Visitors are invited to circle the lake on a literal path of spiritual enlightenment, pausing to view such sights as the **Windmill Chapel** (Tues–Sun 1–4.30pm; free), a church built as a replica of a sixteenth-century Dutch windmill, along with an archway topped with metal lotus flowers, a houseboat that the shrine's Indian founder once used, a bird refuge, gardens with religious icons, and numerous plaques and signs quoting the Bible, Koran, and such. The temple, unfortunately, is strictly for monks.

The Getty Museum has been relocated to the Getty Center, in West LA. For a full rundown on that building's history and holdings, see p.123.

Up the bluffs from Sunset, the **Times Demonstration House**, 520 Paseo Miramar, is an idyllic 1927 Spanish Colonial structure that was, like other houses of the time, a type of public-relations project to show the glories of the Mediterranean style, both for its architectural elements – Spanish tile, dramatic hillside siting, expansive windows and balconies – and its alluring gardens. Closer to PCH, the area's most prominent house is the towering **Villa de Leon**, 17948 Porto Marina Way, a 1927 Italian Renaissance villa, visually unavoidable as you drive north on PCH, and perched precariously near a cliff.

Just around the corner, north of Sunset Boulevard's intersection with PCH, the **Getty Villa** sits on a hilltop overlooking the ocean. Once the site of the Getty Museum, this imitation Roman villa is closed to the public but due to reopen as an antiquities center in 2001.

Topanga Canyon

Around Topanga Canyon Boulevard north of PCH, **Topanga Canyon** is a stunning natural preserve, with hillsides covered in golden poppies and wildflowers, which forms part of the 150,000 acres of mountains and seashore northwest of LA protected as the **Santa Monica Mountains National Recreation Area**. Very few people take advantage of the fine views and fresh air here, thus missing out on the sight of the deer, coyotes, and the odd mountain lion that still live in the area. As elsewhere in these parts, the place is not without its element of danger, especially in winter and early spring, when mudslides threaten houses and waterfalls cascade down the cliffs. Most of the time, though, these hazards are of little concern to visitors, and park rangers offer free guided hikes throughout the mountains most weekends (for information and reservations phone ☎818/597-9192). There are also self-guided trails through the canyon's **Topanga State Park**, east of Topanga Canyon Boulevard, which features 9000 isolated acres of forest and wildlife, along with spectacular views over the Pacific.

The nearby community of **Topanga**, further up Topanga Canyon Boulevard, was a fermenting ground for West Coast rock music in the 1960s, when Neil Young, the Byrds, and other artists moved here and held all-night jam sessions in the sycamore groves along Topanga Creek, and the neighborhood retains an air of this history, although few real bohemians are left. If you'd like to revisit a bit of the old musical spirit, the **Topanga Community House**, 1440 Topanga Canyon Blvd, hosts gigs by graying rock bands, as well as occasional classical concerts. More enjoyable is the **Theatricum Botanicum**, close by at no. 1419, a wooded outdoor amphitheater known for its classical and modern plays, including well-regarded summer performances of Shakespeare (call ☎310/455-3723 for information and tickets). Originally created by old-time thespian Will Geer, known best as TV's Grandpa Walton, the theater is still very much a family affair, with daughter Ellen directing the plays.

To the south, Old Topanga Canyon Road leads, via Red Rock Road, to **Red Rock Canyon**, a stunning red-sandstone gorge that was formerly a Boy Scout retreat. Now a California state park, the colorful rock formations, surrounding gardens, and riparian wildlife give you a good reason to leave your car behind and go exploring on foot.

Malibu

Further up PCH, past a long stretch of gated beachfront properties, lies **MALIBU**, the very name of which conjures up images of beautiful people sunbathing on palm-fringed beaches and lazily consuming cocktails. And the image is not so far from the truth – even though you might not think so on arrival. As you enter the small town, the succession of ramshackle surf shops and fast-food stands, scattered along both sides of the highway around the popular **Malibu Pier** (primarily a fishing pier, at 23000 PCH), don't exactly reek of money, but the secluded estates just inland are as valuable as any in the entire US, despite their constant susceptibility to wildfires.

Malibu's name allegedly derives from a Chumash Indian word meaning "place where the surf is loud."

Adjacent to the pier, **Surfrider Beach** was the surfing capital of the world in the 1950s and early 1960s, popularized by the many *Beach Blanket Bingo* movies filmed here, and starring the likes of Annette Funicello and Frankie Avalon. It's still a big surfing spot: the waves are best in late summer, when storms off Mexico cause them to reach upwards of eight feet. Just to the west are **Malibu Lagoon State Beach** (parking $6), a nature reserve and bird refuge that provides bird-watching walks around the lagoon on occasional weekends, and a small **museum** (Wed–Sat 11am–3pm; $2) that details the history of the area from the early Chumash tribes to the later arrivals of Hollywood movie stars.

Most Malibu residents live in the houses and small ranches that hide away in the narrow canyons on the edges of the town, together forming a well-off, insular community with a long-established dread of outsiders. Up until the 1920s all of Malibu was owned by one **May K Rindge**, widow of the entrepreneur Frederick Rindge who died in 1905. Employing armed guards and dynamiting roads to keep travelers from crossing her land on their way to and from Santa Monica, Rindge also fought for years to prevent the Southern Pacific Railroad from laying down track through her property, as well as the state of California from building the Pacific Coast Highway across her land. Despite going as far as building a personal network of roads and her own private railroad, she ultimately lost her legal battle in the state's supreme court and the highway was eventually finished.

Before Rindge lost her money in the Depression, Rindge's daughter, Rhoda, and her husband Merritt Adamson hired architect Stiles O Clements to design the magnificent **Adamson House**, 23200 PCH (hourly tours Wed–Sat 11am–2pm; $2), one of LA's finest pieces of Spanish Colonial architecture, with an eye-catching interior design as well. Applying Mission Revival and Moorish elements, Clements' work features molded wooden ceilings, intricate glazed tiles, detailed ironwork, and Spanish and Middle Eastern furnishings, as well as expansive gardens and a central pool and fountain.

After May Rindge's mischief finally ceased, thanks in no small part to her financial difficulties, her son took over the ranch and quickly sold much of the land, establishing the **Malibu Colony**, along Malibu Colony Drive off of Malibu Road, as a haven for movie stars. There's very little to see here except the garage doors of the rich and famous; for a cinematic view inside, check out Robert Altman's *The Long Goodbye*, in which the colony plays home to washed-up artists and blasé murder suspects. Otherwise, head to the **Malibu Colony Plaza**, near the area's gated entrance – good for star-spotting and stocking up on food and drink before a day lounging on the sands. To the north, off of Cross Creek Road, relaxation of a different sort can be had at the **Serra Retreat**, 3401 Serra Rd (☎310/456-6631), a non-denominational religious haven named after Franciscan friar and missionary Junipero Serra, one of several such retreats operated by the friars throughout the West.

Downtown Malibu, further north on PCH, doesn't have much to grab your attention other than the **Malibu Castle**, a bizarre thirteenth-century Scottish castle – with arched windows, stone tower, and countless battlements – that sits on a hilltop and is a frequent film and TV location. Unfortunately, it's off-limits to the general public, and your best bet is seeing it from Civic Center Way, well below it. North of downtown, **Pepperdine University**, 24255 PCH, is even more eye-catching, its sloping green lawns and gigantic white cross visible throughout the area, though there's little to attract attention on the gated campus itself.

Pepperdine's original campus was in South Central LA (see p.153); it moved to Malibu in 1972.

Outside downtown Malibu, PCH takes you past the attractive, if uneventful, **Puerco Beach** and **Dan Blocker County Beach** – the latter dedicated to the actor who played Hoss in TV's *Bonanza* – until you come to Corral Canyon Road, which leads you into **Solstice Canyon Park**, one of LA's best hidden treasures. The park, which you can access through rugged mountaintop hiking trails or tranquil forested walks, is most interesting for its splendid garden ruins. A mile down placid Solstice Canyon Creek is a bucolic old cabin from 1865 sitting in a state of arrested dilapidation; past that are the remains of a modern estate known as **Tropical Terrace**. Burned down in a fire decades ago, the basic structure and foundation of this house are still standing, as are its surrounding brick steps and garden terraces, all overtaken by its natural setting, with trees sprouting through the concrete and vines covering the brickwork.

Point Dume and beyond

Four miles north of Malibu Pier, **Point Dume** is a great seaward promontory built on lava extruded from an ancient volcano, with stunning vistas of the ocean and, indeed, the entire Santa Monica Bay. Along with being a popular whale-watching spot during the migrating season, it's also the home of some of the local residents' favorite strips of sand, including **Zuma Beach**, just north at 30000 PCH (parking $6 for most area beaches), the largest of the LA

Point Dume
and beyond

*Rocker Neil
Young, who
hung out quite
a bit in nearby
Topanga,
released a
1975 album
entitled Zuma.*

County beaches and popular with San Fernando Valley high-school kids. Adjacent **Point Dume State Beach**, below the bluffs, is a lot more relaxed, especially up and over the rocks at its southern tip, where **Pirate's Cove** is used by nudists. The rocks here are also a good place to look out for seals and migrating gray whales in winter, as the point juts out into the Pacific at the northern lip of the bay. Just to the east, **Paradise Cove** is a secluded strip of land from which you can well see the fancy houses slowly tumbling into the surf from their cliffside perches.

Given Malibu's walled-off security and privacy, the **Barbara Streisand Center for Conservancy Studies**, north of Point Dume and PCH at 5750 Ramirez Canyon Rd (individual tours Wed 1–4pm, groups Tues & Thurs 1–4pm; free; by reservation only at ☎310/589-2850), comes as a bit of a shock, a 22-acre complex of houses and gardens that the entertainer donated to the Santa Monica Mountains Conservancy in 1993. Amid extensive flower, herb, and fruit gardens, you can get a glimpse into Streisand's former residences and properties on the grounds. The stained-glass windows and river-rock fireplace of the quaint "Barn" house, the Mediterranean and Art Nouveau stylings of the "Peach" house, and the Craftsman splendor of the singer's one-time production company building, the "Barwood," are a prelude to the finest building on the site, the "Deco" house, with its red-and-black color scheme, geometric decor, and stainless-steel panels taken from Downtown's Richfield Building, before that Art Deco monument was destroyed in 1968.

Several miles north of Point Dume, at 32100 PCH, **El Matador State Beach** is about as close as ordinary folk can get to the private-beach seclusion enjoyed by the stars, thanks mostly to its entrance at an easily missable turn off PCH. Another five miles north, where Mulholland Drive reaches the ocean, **Leo Carrillo State Beach Park**, 35000 PCH, marks the northwestern border of LA County. The mile-long sandy beach is divided by Sequit Point, a small bluff that has underwater caves and a tunnel you can pass through at low tide.

Mulholland Highway

Most familiar as the road running along the crest of Hollywood Hills, Mulholland Drive continues west of the 405 freeway and takes drivers through the heart of the Santa Monica Mountains, where it becomes **Mulholland Highway**, a lengthy, winding route that can easily take several hours to traverse, but is an excellent introduction to LA's largely unheralded natural environment.

The initial leg of this trip is not for the timid: for most of its first seven miles westward, from Encino Hills Drive to Topanga Canyon Boulevard, Mulholland is a bumpy dirt road loaded with broken rocks, fallen trees, and sizable mudholes, truly earning its nickname, **"Dirt Mulholland"** – though the awe-inspiring vistas and abundant greenery are reward enough. Also on the stretch is the towering hill-top of **San Vicente Mountain Park**, about a mile and a half past Encino Hills Drive, a decommissioned nuclear missile command center, operable between 1956 and 1968 as a radar site and launching pad for Nike thermonuclear missiles, turned into an unusual state park.

Mulholland Highway can be picked up from either Mulholland Drive, after the dirt road ends in the suburb of Woodland Hills, or from the Mulholland Drive exit off the 101 freeway. Just below the 101, west of Mulholland Drive, the **Leonis Adobe**, 23537 Calabasas Rd (Wed–Sun 1–4pm; free), is a pleasant re-creation of adobe life, an 1844 ranch that features a windmill, barn, and Spanish estate, along with a blacksmith, shop and restored carriage.

To the south, the highway itself takes you through the forest, brush, and sparse dwellings of the Santa Monica Mountains, sometimes via dizzying switchbacks and narrow cliffside passages. Interesting diversions along the way begin at **Malibu Creek State Park**, just south of Mulholland Highway on Las Virgenes Road, a scenic 4000-acre park that once belonged to 20th Century-Fox studios, which filmed many Tarzan pictures here and used the chaparral-covered hillsides to simulate South Korea for the TV show *M*A*S*H*. Pick up a map at the main entry station to avoid getting lost on its nearly fifteen miles of hiking trails. Further west on Mulholland, **Paramount Ranch**, 2813 Cornell Rd, is another old studio backlot, with an intact Western movie set used in, among other things, the canceled TV program *Dr. Quinn Medicine Woman*. The phony rail tracks and station behind the set and the dummy cemetery to the south are often thought by more than a few visitors to be real.

A few miles west of Cornell Road, accessed through a parking lot under an archway, the charming **Peter Strauss Ranch** was once the site of **Lake Enchanto Resort**, one of LA's favorite places for amusement in the 1930s and 1940s, with fishing, picnicking, and carnival rides, along with a great swimming pool, main island, cottages, cabanas, and a swinging dance floor. Years later, Lake Enchanto literally disappeared when a nearby dam burst and washed it away; however, it would later be resurrected variously as a resort, nudist colony, and, finally, a planned theme park with replicas of Egyptian pyramids and Mt Fuji, none of which succeeded. In the 1970s, the property passed into the hands of actor Peter Strauss, who, after yet another dam-burst, turned it over to its current caretakers, the Santa Monica Mountains Conservancy.

The last point of interest on Mullholland is one of Frank Lloyd Wright's less celebrated homes, the **Arch Oboler House**, 32436 Mulholland Hwy, a 1940s complex of wood and stone that the architect built for the now-forgotten film director Oboler, the creator of such works as *Bewitched* and *Bwana Devil*.

If you'd like to view Mulholland's scenery on horseback, the K C Malibu Stables, 400 N Kanan Rd (☎ 818/879-0444), provides guided equine tours of the area, during the daylight or twilight hours, and, occasionally, under moonlight, with prices generally around $20 per hour.

Chapter 11

Orange County

C onservative **ORANGE COUNTY** is one of the country's most well-known suburbs, not only as the home of **Disneyland**, the original modern theme park and one which has spawned legions of imitators, but also as a longtime bastion of right-wing politics. Fundamentally, however, Orange County is no different from the rest of suburban LA, a one-time agricultural zone thick with citrus crops that became, after the end of World War II, a choice living space for LA's white middle class. As such, there is plenty of room for bright green lawns and two-car garages, but no real sense of culture.

Inland Orange County, the initial heart of the suburbs, gets most of the press, with all the familiar theme parks, but is perhaps more notable for the rapid cultural changes taking place therein. Once Anglo bastions, towns like **Anaheim** and **Santa Ana** have rapidly become home to growing numbers of Hispanics and Asians, making many whites pack their bags one more time and relocate even further away, to Palm Springs, Phoenix, or Utah.

Still, unless you really have affection for said amusement centers, your trip to the county is probably best spent on the **Orange County Coast**, a collection of relaxing seaside towns populated by some of the wealthier, more libertarian county residents. Keep in mind, though, that the coast never really ends, but just blends into even more housing colonies even further south, between LA and San Diego.

Inland Orange County

The area throughout **INLAND ORANGE COUNTY** remains pure Eisenhower era: staunchly conservative suburbs made up of mile after mile of unvarying residential plots. It's still one of the US's fastest growing areas, if not expanding exactly the way the area's original residents would prefer. **Westminster**, for example, is now the home of Little Saigon, a center for Vietnamese expatriates, and neighboring cities are as likely to have large populations fluent only in Spanish as they are in English.

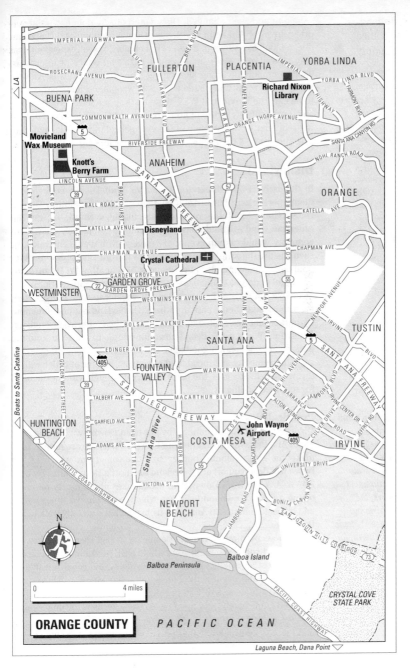

*Baseball's
Anaheim
Angels play at
Anaheim
Stadium and
hockey's
Mighty Ducks
play at
Arrowhead
Pond. For
ticket informa-
tion, see
"Sports and
Outdoor
Activities,"
p.287.*

One thing hasn't changed: **Disneyland** utterly dominates the colorless town of **Anaheim** and Inland Orange County, and the boom doesn't look like slowing. If you're not coming to see Disneyland, you may as well give Anaheim a miss; it hasn't an ounce of interest in itself. As mildly diverting alternatives, the creakier rides at **Knott's Berry Farm** recall antiquated notions of what amusement parks used to be like, the **Movieland Wax Museum** is sporadically entertaining, and, on an entirely different note, the **Crystal Cathedral** is an imposing reminder of the potency of the evangelical movement. And if all else fails, there's the **Richard Nixon Library and Birthplace**.

Disneyland

In the early 1950s, illustrator/filmmaker **Walt Disney** conceived a theme park where his cartoon characters – Mickey Mouse, Donald Duck, Goofy, and the rest, already indelibly imprinted on the American mind – would come to life, and his fabulously successful company would rake in even more money from them. The result of such wishful thinking, **Disneyland**, 1313 Harbor Blvd at Katella Ave, Anaheim, (summer daily 8am–1am; rest of year Mon–Fri 10am–6pm, Sat 9am–midnight, Sun 9am–10pm; $36, kids $30, parking $6; ☎714/781-4565) is the most famous, most carefully constructed, most influential theme park anywhere. Disneyland is a phenomenon, corporate America's ultimate fantasy, with the emphasis strongly on family fun. While it has been known for people to cruise around the park on acid, it is not a good idea; the authorities take a dim view of anything remotely antisocial, and anyone acting out of order will be thrown out. In any case the place is surreal enough without the need for mind-expanding drugs.

Practicalities

*Bear in mind
that
Disneyland is
not LA's only
large-scale
amusement
park; the
whirlwind
rides at Magic
Mountain, for
example, are
consistently
better (see
p.194).*

Disneyland is about 45 minutes by **car** from Downtown LA using the Santa Ana Freeway. By **train** from Downtown (there are nine a day), make the thirty-minute journey to Fullerton, from where OCTD buses will drop you off at Disneyland or Knott's Berry Farm. By **bus**, use MTA #460 from Downtown, which takes about ninety minutes, or the quicker Greyhound service, which runs thirteen times a day, and takes 45 minutes to Anaheim, from which it's an easy walk to the theme park.

As for **accommodation**, most people try to visit Disneyland just for the day and spend the night somewhere else, or at home. It's simply not the most appealing area, with seedy dives and run-down motels everywhere, and most of the hotels and motels close to Disneyland costing well in excess of $70 per night. However, the park is least-crowded immediately after opening, so one – perhaps the only – rationale for staying nearby is to get a jump on the morning crowds.

A massive central kitchen produces all the **food** that's eaten in the park (you're not permitted to bring your own), unloading popcorn, hot dogs, hamburgers, and other junk food by the ton. For anything healthier or more substantial, you'll need to leave the park and travel a good distance.

Inland
Orange
County

See p.260 for restaurant listings in Orange County.

The park

If you only have a one-day pass to Disneyland, you will not see everything you want to in one day. To try to fit in as much as you can, it may be best to choose just a few of the most popular rides – during peak periods lines on these can take up to hours – alongside a larger range of middling ones. The admission price does include them, and again, lines are shortest when the park first opens, so arrive early.

From the front gates, **Main Street** leads through a scaled-down, camped-up replica of a turn-of-the-century Midwestern town, filled with small souvenir shops, food stands, and penny arcades, directly to Sleeping Beauty's Castle, a pseudo-Rhineland palace at the heart of the park. **New Orleans Square**, to the west, contains two of the best rides in the park: the Pirates of the Caribbean, a boat trip through underground caverns, singing along with drunken pirates, and the Haunted Mansion, a riotous "doom buggy" tour in the company of the house spooks.

In nearby **Adventureland**, the antiquated Jungle Cruise offers little more than "tour guides" making crude puns about the fake animatronic beasts lurking in the trees. The Enchanted Tiki Room is a little better, with animatronic birds warbling assorted tunes.

Over four hundred "imagineers" worked to create the **Indiana Jones Adventure**, Disney's biggest opening in years. Two hours of waiting in line are built into the ride, with an interactive archeological dig and 1930s-style newsreel show leading up to the main feature – a speedy journey along 2500ft of skull-encrusted corridors in which you face fireballs, burning rubble, venomous snakes, and, inevitably, a rolling-boulder finale.

The Indiana Jones ride is based on, as you probably well know, the Raiders of the Lost Ark trilogy, one of the biggest moneymaking franchises in movie history.

Less fun is **Frontierland**, the smallest of the various themelands, taking its cues from the Wild West and the tales of Mark Twain, with any unsavory and complex elements carefully deleted. *Thunder Mountain Railroad* is a rather slow-moving rollercoaster, which takes you through a rocky setting resembling a cartoony version of Hollywood Westerns. Nearby, the focus of **Critter Country**, aside from a musical show with mechanized bears, is Splash Mountain, a log ride in which you can expect to get drenched.

Fantasyland, across the drawbridge from Main Street, shows off the cleverest but also the most sentimental aspects of the Disney imagination: Mr Toad's Wild Ride through Victorian England, Peter Pan flying over London, and It's a Small World, a tour of the world's continents in which animated dolls sing the same cloying song over and over again. The sole Fantasyland rollercoaster, the Matterhorn, is somewhat entertaining for its phony cement mountain and goofy abominable snowman appearing when you round a corner.

*Walt Disney's
original name
for Mickey
Mouse was the
somewhat less
mellifluous
"Mortimer
Mouse."*

On the park's northern end, **Toontown** is a cartoon village with noisy sound effects and Day-Glo colors – fun for the under-ten set, slow torture for adults.

On the eastern side of the park, **Tomorrowland** is Disney's vision of the future, where the Space Mountain rollercoaster zips through the pitch-blackness of outer space, bumbling scientists dabble with 3-D trickery in Honey, I Shrunk the Audience, and R2D2 pilots a runaway space cruiser through George Lucas' Star Tours galaxy of Luke Skywalker and Darth Vader. This idea of the future occasionally looks like a hangover from the past – note rides such as Autopia, where you drive a miniature car at a glacial pace, and the Submarine Voyage, a slow underwater look at crude sea monsters and plastic mermaids – but Tomorrowland has been given quite an overhaul recently, with many of its more outdated rides replaced.

In addition to these fixed attractions, **fireworks displays** explode every summer night at 9pm, and all manner of parades and special events celebrate important occasions – such as Mickey Mouse's birthday. Unfortunately, Disneyland's rulers have abolished the park's trademark Electric Light Parade in favor of a program called Fantasmic, involving familiar characters from Disney cartoons performing amid lasers, explosions, and screaming sound effects.

Around Disneyland

It's hard to escape the clutches of Disneyland even when you leave: everything in the surrounding area seems to have been designed to service the needs of its visitors. If you're a bit fazed by its excesses, you might prefer the more traditional **Knott's Berry Farm**, four miles northwest, off the Santa Ana Freeway at 8039 Beach Blvd (summer Sun–Thurs 9am–11pm, Fri–Sat 9am–midnight; rest of year Mon–Fri 10am–6pm, Sat 10am–10pm, Sun 10am–7pm; $30, kids $20), a relaxed, rough-around-the-edges park born during the Depression when people began lining up for the fried chicken dinners prepared by Mrs Knott, a local farmer's wife. To amuse the children while they waited for their food, Mr Knott reconstructed a Wild West ghost town and added amusements until the park had grown into the sprawling sideshow of rollercoasters and carnival rides that stands today. Unlike Disneyland, this park can easily be seen in one day, as it only has a few thrilling highlights – Montezooma's Revenge, a looping coaster, Bigfoot Rapids, a watercourse with giant innertubes, and a log ride and parachute jump – and a lot of space filled with concession stands and fast-food joints.

Across the street at 7711 Beach Blvd, the **Movieland Wax Museum** (summer daily 9am–7pm; $13, kids $7), is a Madame Tussaud's for Hollywood, displaying a collection of wax dummies posed in various scenes from movies and TV shows. The Marx Brothers, Captain Kirk, the crew from the *Starship Enterprise*, and Arnold Schwarzenegger may be far from essential viewing, but they're good for a laugh.

On the other side of Disneyland just off the Santa Ana Freeway, in the town of **Garden Grove**, the giant **Crystal Cathedral**, 12141 Lewis St (daily 9am–4pm; free), is a hugely garish Philip Johnson design of tubular space frames and plate-glass walls that forms part of the vision of televangelist Robert Schuller, who, not content with owning the world's first drive-in church (next door to the cathedral), commissioned this dramatic prop to boost the ratings of his nationally televised Sunday sermons. These shows reach their climax with the special Christmas production, using live animals in biblical roles and people disguised as angels suspended on ropes. Schuller raised $1.5 million for the construction of this colossus, which is visible throughout the local area, during one Sunday service alone – a statistic worth pondering as you wander the cavernous interior.

The Richard Nixon Library and Birthplace

Mickey Mouse may be its most famous resident, but conservative Orange County's favorite son was former US president Richard Milhouse Nixon, born in 1913 in what is now the freeway-caged **YORBA LINDA**, about eight miles northeast of Disneyland. Here, the **Richard Nixon Library and Birthplace**, 18001 Yorba Linda Blvd (Mon–Sat 10am–5pm, Sun 11am–5pm; $5), is an unrelentingly hagiographical library/museum that features oversized gifts from world leaders, amusing campaign memorabilia, and a collection of obsequious letters written by and to Nixon (including one he sent to the boss of *McDonald's* proclaiming the fast-food chain's hamburgers to be "one of the finest food buys in America"). However, it's in the constantly running archive of radio and TV recordings that the distinctive Nixon persona really shines through.

Although famously embarrassed in live 1960s TV debates with John F Kennedy, Nixon had earlier used the medium to save his political life. In 1952, the discovery of undeclared income precipitated the "funds crisis," which cast doubts on Nixon's honesty. Incredibly, his **"Checkers speech"** convinced 58 million viewers of his integrity with a broadcast to rival the worst soap opera. Exuding mock sincerity, he cast himself as an ordinary American struggling to raise a family and provide for his wife a "respectable Republican cloth coat," and climaxed his performance with the statement that, regardless of the damage it may do to his career, he would not be returning the cocker spaniel dog – Checkers – given to him as a gift and now a family pet.

Director Oliver Stone's film Nixon *is reviewed in "LA on Film," p.335.*

After viewing a few of these TV recordings, take a walk through the **World Leaders Gallery** of the autocrats and democrats of note during Nixon's golden years, with Mao, Brezhnev, and de Gaulle among the political bigwigs in the hall, all of them austerely cast in metal and arranged in rigid, pompous poses.

Throughout the museum, Nixon's face leers down in Orwellian fashion from almost every wall, but only inside the **Presidential**

Inland
Orange
County

Richard Nixon: A life in politics

Qualified as a lawyer and fresh from wartime (non-combat) service in the US Navy, Richard Milhouse Nixon entered politics as a Republican congressman in 1946, without so much as a civilian suit to his name. A journalist of the time observed that Nixon employed "the half-truth, the misleading quotation, the loose-joined logic" to cast doubts on his rival Jerry Voorhees – traits he would perfect in the years to come.

Shortly after arriving in Washington, the fresh-faced Nixon joined the **House Un-American Activities Committee** (HUAC), a group of reds-under-the-bed scaremongers led by the fanatical Joseph McCarthy. Through the now notorious anti-Communist "witch trials," McCarthy and Nixon wrecked the lives and careers of many Americans. Although these hearings eventually backfired on McCarthy (he was later censured by Congress), they helped launch Nixon to national prominence, culminating in his becoming Eisenhower's vice president in 1953, aged just 39. Seven years later, Nixon was defeated in his own bid for the nation's top job by the even younger John F Kennedy, a loss which led him into his "wilderness years." Staying out of the public spotlight, except to raise money for fellow Republicans, he took several highly lucrative corporate posts and wrote *Six Crises*, a book whose deep introspection came as a surprise – and convinced many of the author's paranoia. Seeking a power base for the next presidential campaign, Nixon contested the governorship of California in 1962. His humiliating defeat prompted a short-lived "retirement" and did nothing to suggest that six years later he would beat Ronald Reagan to the Republican nomination and be **elected president** in 1968.

Nixon had attained his dream, but the country he inherited was more divided than at any time since the Civil War. The **Vietnam War** was at its height, and his large-scale illegal bombing of Cambodia earned him world-

---

Auditorium (at the end of the corridor packed with notes attesting to the president's innocence in Watergate) do you get the chance to ask him a question. Many possibilities spring to mind, but the choice is limited to those already programmed into a computer. Ten or so minutes after making your selection, Nixon's gaunt features will fill the overly large screen and provide the stock reply, as endearingly and believably as ever.

On your way out, stop by the gift shop to admire (and perhaps purchase) its most popular item, a picture of Nixon meeting a dazed Elvis in the Oval Office.

The Orange County Coast

As Disneyland grew, so too did the rest of Orange County. Besides providing tourist services, the region also became a major center for light industry and home to many of the millions who poured into Southern California during the 1960s and 1970s – its population density is now even greater than that of neighboring LA County. Yet

wide opprobrium. Nixon was not, however, a conservative by modern standards. By breaking with his own party's right wing, he was able to re-establish diplomatic relations with China, begin arms reduction talks with the Soviet Union, create the Environmental Protection Agency, impose wage and price controls over an unruly economy, and quietly oversee the implementation of court-ordering busing to alleviate racial segregation. Nixon's actions surprised many and contributed, at least in part, to his decisive re-election in 1972.

Despite his huge victory, Nixon's second term ended prematurely over the cataclysmic **Watergate Affair**. In January 1973, seven men were tried for breaking into and bugging the headquarters of the Democratic Party in the Watergate building in Washington, an act that was discovered to have been financed with money allocated to the Campaign to Re-elect the President (CREEP). Nixon may not have sanctioned the actual bugging operation, but there was ample evidence to suggest that he participated in the cover-up. Ironically, his insistence on taping all White House conversations in order to ease the writing of his future memoirs was to be the major stumbling block to his surviving the crisis. Under threat of impeachment, Nixon **resigned** in 1974.

The full **pardon** granted to Nixon by his successor, Gerald Ford (appointed to the vice-presidency during Watergate to take the place of Spiro Agnew, who resigned in a separate scandal) did little to arrest a widespread public disillusionment with the country's political machine. The rose-tinted faith, long held by many Americans, in the unflinching goodness of the President *per se* seemed irredeemably shattered. Remarkably, however, the years since Richard Nixon's ignoble demise saw him quietly seek to establish elder-statesman credentials, opining on world and national affairs through books and newspaper columns. He died in 1994 and was buried at Yorba Linda.

---

it was expansion without style, and those who could afford to do so soon left the anonymous inland sprawl for the more colorful coast. As a result, the **ORANGE COUNTY COAST**, a string of towns stretching from the edge of the LA Harbor to the borders of San Diego County 35 miles south, is chic suburbia with a shoreline: swanky beachside houses line the sands, and the general ambience is easygoing, affluent, and conservative.

As the names of the main towns suggest – **Huntington Beach**, **Newport Beach**, and **Laguna Beach** – there's no real reason beyond sea and sand to come here. However, they do provide something of a counterpart to LA's more cosmopolitan side, and, despite recent destructive brushfires and washouts, they do form appealing stopovers on a leisurely journey south. You might even see a bit of countryside: unlike most of the county's other districts, the communities here aren't crammed together but are a few miles apart, in many instances divided by an ugly power station, but sometimes by a piece of undeveloped coastline. The one place genuinely meriting a stop is just inland at **San Juan Capistrano**, site of the best kept of all the Californian missions. Further on, there's little to see before you

reach adjoining San Diego County, except perhaps for **San
Clemente**, one-time stomping ground for Richard Nixon.

If you're in a rush to get from LA to San Diego, you can skip the
coast by passing through Orange County on the inland San Diego
Freeway. The coastal cities, though, are linked by the more adventurous Pacific Coast Highway (PCH), which you can pick up in Long
Beach.

Huntington Beach

*The town of
Westminster,
just north of
Huntington
Beach, has
plenty of
authentic
Vietnamese
restaurants in
its "Little
Saigon"; see
p.260 for rec-
ommendations.*

HUNTINGTON BEACH is the first place of any interest on the
Orange County coast, wildest of the beach communities and one that
you don't need a fortune to enjoy. It's a compact little place com-
posed of engagingly ramshackle single-story cafés and beach stores
grouped around the foot of a long **pier**, off PCH at Main Street. Here,
you can find the **Surfers Walk of Fame**, honoring the greats of the
sport and reminding visitors that this is the town where California
surfing began – imported from Hawaii in 1907 to encourage curious
day-trippers to visit on the Pacific Electric Railway. Top surfers still
flock to Huntington Beach for the annual **Pro Surfing
Championship**, an internationally televised event held each June.
Even more of this culture can be sniffed out at the **International
Surfing Museum**, 411 Olive Ave (Wed–Sun noon–5pm, summer
open daily; $2), which, along with marginally interesting memor-
abilia from surfing history, displays a great selection of boards, from
the fat models of yesteryear to the sleek, colorful ones of today.

In October, the largely blond and suntanned locals celebrate a
plausible **Oktoberfest**, with German food and music. Otherwise,
once you've exhausted the beach and the local shops, there's not
much else to see, though Huntington Beach is a good place to be
based for a while, with Orange County's cheapest beds in the **youth
hostel** at 421 Eighth St, three blocks from the pier (see p.229).

Newport Beach and Corona Del Mar

Ten miles south from Huntington, **NEWPORT BEACH** could hardly
provide a greater contrast. With ten yacht clubs and ten thousand
yachts, this is upmarket even by Orange County standards, an elite,
image-conscious town that people visit to acquire a tan they can
show off on the long stretches of sand or in the bars nearby. You'll
need a pocketful of credit cards and a presentable physique to join
them, but the sheer exclusivity of the place may be an attraction in
itself.

Newport Beach is spread around a natural bay that cuts several
miles inland, but *the* place to hang out is on the thin **Balboa
Peninsula**, located along Balboa Boulevard, which parallels the
three-mile-long beach. The most youthful and boisterous section is
about halfway along, around **Newport Pier** at the end of 20th Street.

To the north, beachfront homes restrict access; to the south, around
the touristy **Balboa Pier**, there's a marina from which you can
escape to Catalina Island (see p.173) or take a boat ride on the
Pavilion Queen (summer daily, hourly cruises 11am–7pm; rest of
year daily 11am–3pm; $6–8) around Newport's own, much smaller,
islands.

On the peninsula itself, there's little in the way of conventional
sights, but you might cast an eye over the exterior (there's no public
access) of the modernist **Lovell Beach House**, near the end of 13th
Street, designed by Rudolph Schindler and finished in 1926. Raised
on five concrete legs, its living quarters jutting out toward the sidewalk, the house formed the basis of the architect's international reputation. Away from the peninsula, Newport Beach is also home to the
Newport Harbor Art Museum, 850 San Clemente Drive (Tues–Sun
11am–5pm; $5, free Tues), another of Southern California's regional
art museums, which stages occasionally engaging exhibitions of contemporary work.

Just a few miles along PCH from Newport Beach, **CORONA DEL
MAR** is a much less ostentatious place, worth a short stop for its
good beach and the **Sherman Foundation Center**, 2647 E Pacific
Coast Highway, devoted to the horticulture of the American
Southwest and raising many vivid blooms in its botanical gardens.
Between here and Laguna Beach lies an invitingly unspoiled three-
mile chunk of coastline, protected as **Crystal Coves State Park**, per-
fect to explore on foot, and far from the tourist crowds.

Laguna Beach

Nestled among the crags around a small sandy beach, **LAGUNA
BEACH** grew up late in the nineteenth century as a community of
artists drawn by the beauty of the location. You need a few million
dollars to live here nowadays, but there's a relaxed and tolerant feel
among the inhabitants, who span everything from rich industrialists
to leftovers from the 1960s when Laguna became a hippie haven –
even Timothy Leary was known to hang out at the *Taco Bell* on PCH.
The scenery is still the great attraction, and despite the massive
growth in population Laguna remains enjoyable, with a still-flourish-
ing minor arts scene manifest in the many galleries jammed into the
narrow streets.

*A bit inland
from Laguna
Beach is the
convergence of
I-5 and I-405,
known in local
parlance as the
"El Toro Y."*

PCH passes directly through the center of Laguna, a few steps
from the small main **beach**. From the beach's north side, an elevated
wooden walkway twists around the coastline above a conserved **ecological area**, enabling you to peer down on the ocean and, when the
tide's out, scamper over the rocks to observe the tide pool activity.
From the end of the walkway, make your way through the legions of
posh beachside homes and head down the hill back to the center.
You'll pass the **Laguna Beach Museum of Art**, 307 Cliff Drive
(Tues–Sun 11am–5pm; $5), which has changing exhibitions from its

Laguna's festivals

Laguna hosts a number of large summer **art festivals** over a six-week period during July and August. The best-known, and most bizarre, is the **Pageant of the Masters**, a kind of great-paintings charade in which the participants pose in front of a painted backdrop to portray a famous work of art. It might sound ridiculous, but it's actually somewhat impressive, and takes a great deal of preparation – something reflected in the prices: $15 for the cheapest tickets for shows that sell out months in advance, though you may be able to pick up cancellations on the show night. The idea for the pageant was hatched during the Depression as a way to raise money for local artists, and the action takes place at the Irving Bowl, close to where Broadway meets Laguna Canyon Road, a walkable distance from the Laguna Beach bus station. The pageant is combined with the **Festival of the Arts** held at the same venue during daylight hours. The excitement of both festivals waned in the Sixties, when a group of hippies created the alternative **Sawdust Festival**, in which local artists and craftspeople set up makeshift studios to demonstrate their skills – now just as established but a lot cheaper and easier to get into than the other two. It takes place at 935 Laguna Canyon Rd and admission is $5.

stock of Southern California art from the 1900s to the present day. A few miles south is less-touristy **South Laguna**, where the wonderfully secluded **Victoria** and **Aliso beaches** are among several below the bluffs.

Dana Point

From South Laguna, it's possible to see **DANA POINT**, a town and promontory jutting into the ocean about four miles south. It was named after sailor and author Richard Henry Dana Jr, whose *Two Years Before the Mast* described how cattle hides were flung over these cliffs to trading ships waiting below. He ended his voyaging career here in 1830, and there's a statue of him and a replica of his vessel, *The Pilgrim*, at the edge of the harbor – though it's fairly unremarkable, as is the rest of the town. Its most recent claim to fame was as the place where a postal worker went berserk a few years ago and killed several people.

San Juan Capistrano and San Clemente

Three miles inland from Dana Point along the I-5 freeway, most of the small town of **SAN JUAN CAPISTRANO** is built in a Spanish Colonial style derived from the **Mission San Juan Capistrano**, Ortega Highway at Camino Capistrano (daily 8.30am–5pm; $4), right in the center of town. The seventh in California's chain of missions, this was founded by Junipero Serra in 1776, and within three years was so well populated that it outgrew the original chapel. Soon after, its **Stone Church** was erected, the ruins of which are the first thing you see as you walk in. The enormous structure had seven domes and a bell tower but was destroyed by an earthquake soon after its completion in 1812. For an idea of how it might have looked, visit the full-sized reconstruction – now a working church – just northwest of the mission.

The rest of the site is in an above-average state of repair, due to an ongoing restoration program, and the **chapel** is small and narrow, decorated with Indian drawings and Spanish artifacts from its earliest days, and set off by a sixteenth-century altar from Barcelona. In a side room is the chapel of St Pereguin, a tiny room kept warm by the heat from the dozens of candles lit by hopeful pilgrims who arrive here from all over the US and Mexico.

The other restored buildings reflect the mission's practical role during the Indian period: the kitchen, the smelter, and the workshops were used for dyeing, weaving, and candle-making. There's also a rather predictable **museum** (open during mission hours; free with admission), which gives a broad historical outline of the Spanish progress through California and displays odds and ends from the mission's past. The complex is also noted for its **swallows**, popularly thought to return here from their winter migration on March 19. They sometimes do arrive on this day – along with large numbers of tourists – but the birds are much more likely to show up as soon as the weather is warm enough, and when there are enough insects on the ground to provide a decent homecoming banquet.

Five miles south of San Juan Capistrano down I-5, the town of **SAN CLEMENTE** is a pretty little place, its streets contoured around the hills, effecting an almost Mediterranean air. Because of its proximity to one of the largest military bases in the state, **Camp Pendleton**, it's a popular weekend retreat for military personnel. It's also predominantly a retirement town which had a brief moment of fame during the 1970s, when President Nixon convened his "Western White House" here, meeting with old cronies and political allies. The 25-acre estate and house are visible from the beach, which is clean and virtually deserted.

Listings

Chapter 12

Accommodation

Since LA has more than one hundred thousand hotel rooms, finding **accommodation** is easy. Whether you're looking for a budget place to rest your head, or a world-class hotel where you can hobnob with Hollywood stars and entertainment industry tycoons, LA has something for everyone – though prices have been rising with the city's recent economic recovery.

Finding somewhere that's moderately-priced and well-located is somewhat more difficult, though not impossible. If you're driving, of course, you needn't worry about staying in a less than ideal location – a freeway is never far away. Otherwise, you'll need to be quite choosy about the district you stay in, as getting across town can be a time-consuming experience.

Motels and low-end hotels start at around $40 for a double, but many are situated in seedy or out-of-the-way areas. **Bed and breakfasts** are rare in LA; the few that exist tend to be quite expensive and frequently fully booked. We've listed the worthwhile ones together with hotels and motels. If you're traveling from Britain, try calling Colby International (☎0151/220 5848)), who can book B&B rooms, as well as private apartments, in advance. For those on a tight budget, **hostels** are dotted all over the city, many in good locations, though at some stays are limited to a few nights. **Camping**, perhaps surprisingly, is also an option: there are a number of campgrounds on the edge of the metro-

politan area – along the beach north of Malibu, and in the San Gabriel mountains, for example – but you'll need a car to get to them. **College rooms** are also sometimes available for rent during student vacation time: contact **UCLA**'s Interfraternity Council (☎310/825-7878) or **USC**'s off-campus housing office (☎1-800/USC-4632) for information.

LA is so big that it can make sense to divide your stay between several districts, just to make sightseeing more convenient. Prices – and options – vary by area. **Downtown** has expensive and mid-range hotels, with cheaper accommodations west of Downtown, across the 110 freeway, in somewhat dicier neighborhoods. **Hollywood** provides a good range of choices along Hollywood and Sunset boulevards, and **West Hollywood** has some of the most chic and trendy hotels anywhere in town, nearly all of them priced at a premium. **West LA** and **Beverly Hills** are predominantly mid-to-upper-range territory, with expensive establishments in Century City and the relatively few bargains around the Westwood campus of UCLA. Staying in **Santa Monica** can be costly or inexpensive, depending mainly on proximity to the ocean and trendy areas in town; just south, **Venice** offers a cheaper alternative.

Among options further out, the **South Bay** and **LA Harbor** have a good selection of low- to mid-range hotels strung mostly along the Pacific Coast Highway. The best choices in the **San Gabriel** and

Accommodation

San Fernando valleys are around Universal City and Pasadena, although scattered alternatives exist in North Hollywood and Burbank. The limited selections in **Malibu** are almost all upper-end resorts or inns, but if you really want to stay cheaply in the area, several roadside motels along Pacific Coast Highway may suffice. Finally, it's only worth staying in **Orange County**, thirty miles southeast of Downtown, if you're aiming for Disneyland or are traveling along the coast; also, hotels under $70 a night are a rarity and you must book at least a week in advance, especially if a convention is in town. Even so, many of the plentiful rooms along Katella Avenue and Harbor Boulevard in Anaheim are decrepit and depressing, despite costing up to $100 a night.

A map of the Downtown hotels can be found on p.54.

Since there are hardly any **booking agencies**, and visitor centers don't make accommodation reservations (though they will offer information and advice), you can only book a room through a travel agent or by phoning the hotel directly. Ask if there are special weekend or midweek rates; remember, too, that hotels are generally less expensive if booked by the week than the night.

Hotels and motels

Hotels and **motels** are listed below by neighborhood, with specific accommodation options for gay and lesbian travelers listed in a special section under "Gay and Lesbian LA," p.284. In case you're arriving on a late flight, or leaving on an early one, we've also listed a few places to stay near the airport: hotels near LAX are blandly similar and generally cost

around $60, but most have complimentary shuttle service to and from the terminals.

Prices increase at many tourist-oriented establishments during peak travel periods, typically over the summer and on weekends, especially those near major attractions like Disneyland and Universal Studios. However, weekday rates at business-oriented hotels, especially during conventions, can be just as expensive, or even more so, than weekend prices.

Downtown

Biltmore, 506 S Grand Ave at Fifth St ☎213/624-1011 or 1-800/245-8673. Italian Renaissance architecture combined with modern luxury to make your head swim: a health club modeled on a Roman bathhouse, cherub and angel decor, and a view overlooking restored Pershing Square. The well-appointed rooms match the stateliness of the overall design as well. ⑧–⑨.

Figueroa, 939 S Figueroa St at Olympic Blvd ☎213/627-8971 or 1-800/421-9092. Mid-range hotel on the southern side of Downtown, with a Southwestern flavor, cheery and sizable pastel rooms, a jacuzzi-equipped pool, 24-hour coffee shop, and even a few scattered statues of saints. ④–⑤.

Hotel Inter-Continental, 251 S Olive St at Fourth St ☎213/617-3300 or 1-800/442-5251. Fancy Bunker Hill hotel, home to financial kingpins and Academy Award attendees. Very plush, with elegant rooms, swimming pool, and weight room. Adjacent to MOCA. ⑧.

Kawada, 200 S Hill St at Second St ☎213/621-4455 or 1-800/752-9232. Comfortable and clean rooms in renovated, medium-sized hotel near the Civic Center and popular with value-oriented business travelers. ④.

New Otani Hotel and Garden, 120 S Los Angeles St ☎213/629-1200 or 1-800/421-8795. One of the city's better business hotels, featuring spacious suites, a good restaurant with Asian cuisine (see p.244), and a small Japanese garden using "borrowed scenery" technique, in which existing views are incorporated into design. Also with excellent views of Bunker Hill and Little Tokyo. ⑦.

Omni Los Angeles, 930 Wilshire Blvd ☎213/688-7777 or 1-800/843-6664. Large hotel on Bunker Hill with good access to numerous sights, nice if unimaginative rooms, and extra luxury in pricey "Towers" suites, along with health club and pool. ⑦.

Orchid, 819 S Flower St at Eighth ☎213/624-5855 or 1-800/874-5855. The best deal in the heart of Downtown, near the Seventh and Flower Metrorail station. Comfortable and safe, even if the rooms are a bit plain. Weekly rates. ②.

Park Plaza, 607 S Park View St, between Sixth St and Wilshire Blvd ☎213/384-5281. Facing MacArthur Park, this 1920s hotel has a marble floor, grand ballroom, tasteful mix of neoclassical and modern design, and sumptuous lobby popular with filmmakers – but ordinary rooms with limited charm. ④.

Sheraton Grande, 333 S Figueroa St ☎213/617-1133 or 1-800/325-3535. Palm-tree laden pool area, spacious rooms, and Old Masters reproductions add some charm to this chain hotel, unfortunately sited near the 110 and 101 freeways. ⑧.

Westin Bonaventure, 404 S Figueroa St, between Fourth and Fifth sts ☎213/624-1000 or 1-800/228-3000. Modern luxury hotel, with five glass towers, a six-story lobby with a "lake," and only so-so rooms. Breathtaking exterior elevator ride to a rotating cocktail lounge

that averages seven proposals of marriage a week. ⑥–⑨.

Wyndham Checkers, 535 S Grand ☎213/624-0000 or 1-800/WYNDHAM. One of the great LA hotels, with sleek modern design yet classical furnishings, nicely appointed rooms, rooftop pool and spa, and terrific Downtown views. ⑨.

West of Downtown

Churchill Suites, 444 S Occidental Blvd ☎213/487-1100. Westlake accommodations with daily or monthly rental, offering airy rooms with plants and paintings in a somewhat chancy neighborhood. Larger one- and two-bedroom suites also available. ⑤.

City Center Motel, 1135 W Seventh St at Lucas ☎213/628-7141. Bare but clean bargain accommodation with Sixties-style decor and free continental breakfast and airport shuttle bus. ②.

Holiday Inn Downtown, 750 Garland Ave at Eighth ☎213/628-5242 or 1-800/628-5240. On the western fringe of Downtown beside the Harbor Freeway, this *Holiday Inn* features a pool, cozy rooms, coffee-makers, and cable TV. Good access to Downtown's major sights, including LA Convention Center. ⑥.

Mayfair, 1256 W Seventh St ☎213/484-9789 or 1-800/821-8682. Grand 1920s building with classical arches and pillars in the lobby and fairly straightforward rooms. ⑥.

Thriftlodge Los Angeles, 1904 W Olympic Blvd ☎213/380-9393. The name says it all – a real motel bargain with albeit meager rooms and swimming pool. Again, the downside is the somewhat risky location. ②.

Mid-Wilshire

Beverly Laurel Motor Hotel, 8018 Beverly Blvd at Laurel Ave ☎213/651-2441. The hotel coffee shop, *Swingers*, attracts the most attention here, primarily as a hangout for locals and inquisitive tourists (see p.239). The hotel has rather

Accommodation

Accommodation

You can read about the Bullocks Wilshire building on p.74.

A map of Hollywood's hotels can be found on p.95.

mediocre rooms, but its location is good, not far from the Fairfax District and, to the west, Beverly Hills. ④.

Bevonshire Lodge Motel, 7575 Beverly Blvd at Curson Ave ☎213/936-6154. Well situated for both West LA and Hollywood, across from Pan Pacific Park. All of the functionally decorated rooms come with a refrigerator; for a few dollars more you can have a kitchenette. ③.

Chancellor, 3191 W Seventh St ☎213/383-1183. Cheap accommodation near Metrorail stop and Bullocks Wilshire building, with lower-end furnishings and simple, tidy rooms. ⑤–⑥.

Radisson Wilshire Plaza, 3515 Wilshire Blvd ☎213/381-7411 or 1-800/333-3333. Situated in Koreatown, with modern Californian design, adequate rooms, pool, and complimentary breakfast. ⑦.

Wilshire Crest, 6301 Orange St ☎213/936-5131. Small hotel with plain rooms in charming period-revival residential area, just north of Wilshire Boulevard. ⑦.

Wilshire Royale, 2619 Wilshire Blvd ☎213/387-5311 or 1-800/421-8072. MacArthur Park hotel with sleek Art Deco exterior, though rather rudimentary rooms. Sits directly between two Red Line stops. ⑥.

Hollywood

Best Western Hollywood Hills, 6141 Franklin Ave between Gower and Vine ☎213/464-5181. Chain hotel, with cable TV and heated pool, along with standard, though immaculate, rooms. At the foot of the Hollywood Hills. ④.

Holiday Inn Hollywood, 1755 N Highland Ave ☎213/462-7181 or 1-800/465-4329. Massive, but perfectly placed, near the heart of tourist-friendly Hollywood Boulevard and places like the Chinese Theatre. Basic rooms, the price of which lowers with triple occupancy. ⑤.

Hollywood Metropolitan, 5825 Sunset Blvd ☎213/962-5800 or 1-800/962-5800. Sleek high-rise in central

Hollywood, featuring flashy exterior elevator, good views, and somewhat spacious rooms. Good value for the area, though a bit east of major attractions. ④.

Hollywood Roosevelt, 7000 Hollywood Blvd between Highland and La Brea ☎1-800/423-8262. The first hotel built for the movie greats, now in the Clarion chain. The rooms are unremarkable, but the place has been lately revamped and it reeks with Hollywood atmosphere: there's film memorabilia on the mezzanine, and the ever-popular *Cinegrill* restaurant and cabaret (p.280) on the ground level. ⑤.

Hollywood Towne House, 6055 Sunset Blvd at Gower St ☎213/462-3221. Hotel with decayed exterior and 1920s-era phones that connect to the front desk only. Yet the place itself is comfortable enough, with decent rooms, and spare furnishings. ③.

Hollywood Travelodge, 7051 Sunset Blvd ☎213/462-0905. An inexpensive bet just south of Hollywood's major sights, with acceptable rooms (some of which are three-bed suites), sundeck, and pool. Also a location at 1401 N Vermont St (☎213/665-5735), on the opposite side of the area, in East Hollywood. Both ②.

Orchid Suites, 1753 Orchid Ave ☎213/874-9678 or 1-800/537-3052. Offering roomy, if spartan, suites with cable television, kitchens, and heated pool, very close to the most appealing parts of Hollywood. Across the street from the *Holiday Inn*. ⑤–⑥.

Saharan Motor Hotel, 7212 Sunset Blvd at Poinsettia Place ☎213/874-6700. A classic 1950s-style motel with cheesy neon sign, funky pool, brash color scheme, and unexciting rooms. Comparatively good value, especially considering its central location. ③.

Sunset 8 Motel, 6516 Sunset Blvd between Wilcox and Highland ☎213/461-2748. Many of the rooms on this strip rent by the hour, vibrating bed included, but this place, though slightly downtrodden, is a cut above.

Across from the former Hollywood Athletic Club. ②.

Thriftlodge Hollywood, 2010 N Highland Ave ☎213/874-9988. One of the best deals around, with low-end accommodations just a few blocks north of the center of Hollywood. ②.

West Hollywood

The Argyle, 8358 Sunset Blvd ☎213/654-1700 or 1-800/225-2637. An Art Deco landmark, restored as a luxury hotel: metallic ornamentation, sleek 1920s style, but also modern amenities like stereos and VCRs, along with prime views of the Sunset Strip. A memorable experience, if you can afford it. ⑨.

Bel Age, 1020 N San Vicente Blvd ☎310/854-1111. Another of the Strip's top choices, overflowing with quality art and some kitsch, plus lovely rooms and an exquisite lobby. Also with standard pool and health club service. ⑧–⑨.

Chateau Marmont, 8221 Sunset Blvd at Crescent Heights Blvd ☎213/626-1010. Exclusive Norman Revival hotel, which resembles a dark castle or Hollywood fortress – the *Marmont* has seen the likes of Boris Karloff, Greta Garbo, Errol Flynn, Jean Harlow, and John Belushi, who died in one of its elite bungalows. ⑦–⑨.

Le Mondrian, 8440 Sunset Blvd ☎213/650-8999. Like other Strip hotels, this place oozes art and luxury, though with a much heavier dose of pretension. Spacious rooms are well-decorated and fancy, though not quite enough to justify the snooty attitudes. ⑧–⑨.

Le Montrose, 900 Hammond St ☎310/855-1115. West Hollywood hotel with Art Nouveau stylings (including a terrific wood-latticed elevator), featuring upscale restaurant and rooftop tennis courts, pool, and jacuzzi. Most rooms are suites with full amenities such as stereos, sunken living rooms, dual televisions, refrigerators, and expansive views. ⑧.

Le Parc, 733 N West Knoll Drive ☎310/855-8888 or 1-800/578-4837. Very graceful apartment hotel with sim-

ple studios, more spacious one- and two-bedroom suites, stereos, refrigerators, and rooftop pool and jacuzzi with views of the hills. A British rock star hangout. ⑦–⑧.

Le Reve, 8822 Cynthia St ☎310/854-1111 or 1-800/835-7997. Unimposing suite hotel a few blocks north of Santa Monica Boulevard, in residential West Hollywood. Some suites in the style of a French provincial inn, others with stripped-down amenities. ⑥–⑧.

The Park Sunset, 8462 Sunset Blvd ☎213/654-6470 or 1-800/821-3660. One of the Strip's very few affordable hotels, with ordinary rooms and furnishings, pool, and some suites. ④–⑤.

Summerfield Suites, 1000 Westmount Drive ☎310/657-7400 or 1-800/833-4353. Sumptuous hotel in a quiet, residential section of West Hollywood, within easy walking distance to major clubs and attractions, but just far enough away from the Strip's chaos and noise. Impressive, if cozy, rooms with sunken living rooms, refrigerators, and fine views, with pleasant courtyard. ⑧.

Sunset Marquis, 1200 N Alta Loma Rd ☎310/657-1333 or 1-800/858-9758. The *Marquis* is a focus for the local and national rock scene, with pool, jacuzzi, weight room, and outside gardens; most rooms are well-designed suites catering to music figures who can afford them. ⑨.

Beverly Hills

Beverly Hills Hotel, 9641 Sunset Blvd ☎310/276-2251 or 1-800/283-8885. The classic Mission-style Hollywood resort, with a bold pink and green color scheme, and surrounded by its own exotic gardens. Rooms feature marbled bathrooms, VCRs, jacuzzis, and other such luxuries, and famed *Polo Lounge* restaurant is also on the premises. Marilyn Monroe once stayed here, and one of the select bungalows is decorated in her honor. ⑨.

Beverly Hills Inn, 125 S Spalding Drive ☎310/278-0303. A $2 million renova-

Accommodation

A map of West Hollywood hotels appears on p.108.

There's more on the Beverly Hills Hotel on p.115.

Accommodation

A map of hotels in the Beverly Hills area appears on p.113.

tion has improved this old hotel, which now features wood-and-marble features, rooms with refrigerators, pool, sauna, and weight room, along with complimentary breakfast. Located in the middle of the "Golden Triangle" shopping zone. ⑦.

Beverly Hilton, 9876 Wilshire Blvd ☎310/274-7777 or 1-800/922-5432. Prominent hotel at the corner of Wilshire and Santa Monica boulevards, co-owned by Merv Griffin. Fairly nice rooms and decor, though not quite up to the other nearby luxury options. A favorite for actual and would-be movie-stars. ⑨.

Beverly House, 140 S Lasky Drive ☎310/271-2125 or 1-800/432-5444. A steal for this part of town, with sufficiently cozy rooms and complimentary breakfast in an excellent location by the intersection of Wilshire and Santa Monica boulevards. ⑤.

Beverly Pavilion, 9360 Wilshire Blvd ☎310/273-1400 or 1-800/441-5050. Not far from Rodeo Drive, with classic period-revival look, appealing little rooms, and good views of the area. Slightly less pricey than surrounding luxury hotels. ⑧.

Crescent, 403 N Crescent Drive ☎310/247-0505 or 1-800/451-1566. Adjacent to *Hotel del Flores*, with similarly inexpensive prices, commonplace rooms, but a pleasant refurbished Mediterranean atmosphere. Also with complimentary breakfast and afternoon tea. ④.

The Four Seasons Beverly Hills, 300 S Doheny Drive ☎310/273-2222 or 1-800/332-3442. Perhaps the most noted luxury hotel in Beverly Hills, featuring well-furnished rooms with balconies, good amenities, and decent artworks, along with pool and health club facilities. Very high prices, with most rooms at least $350. ⑨.

Hotel del Flores, 409 N Crescent Drive at Little Santa Monica Blvd ☎310/274-5115. Three blocks from Rodeo Drive. Modest, pleasant and surprisingly good value, with faded old period-revival look from 1926 and quaint rooms. ④.

Hotel Nikko, 465 S La Cienega Blvd ☎310/247-0400. Caters mainly to business clients, but offers ample rooms of modern Japanese design, sliding window screens, stereos, pool, and health club. The appealing lobby boasts an Asian rock-and-water garden. ⑨.

The Peninsula Beverly Hills, 9882 Little Santa Monica Blvd ☎310/551-2888 or 1-800/462-7899. Tucked away in a peaceful alcove away from the noise of Wilshire and Santa Monica boulevards, this pricey luxury hotel is a favorite of the stars, and features well-appointed rooms, suites, and villas thick with graceful furnishings and decor, along with pool, sundeck, cabanas, gardens, whirlpool, and weight room. ⑨.

Regent Beverly Wilshire, 9500 Wilshire Blvd ☎310/275-5200. Located near the heart of Rodeo Drive, amid countless boutiques and chic department stores, this 1928 hotel has darkly furnished rooms, three restaurants, palatial design, and views overlooking Beverly Hills. Prices not for the timid. ⑨.

West LA

Century Plaza Hotel and Tower, 2025 Avenue of the Stars ☎310/277-2000 or 1-800/WESTIN-1. In the middle of high-rise Century City, a two-building complex with an older, crescent-shaped main building and newer, uglier modern counterpart to the south. Both offer elegant rooms with outstanding views from Beverly Hills to the ocean, along with countless amenities – pool, health club, business center, rental car outlets, and so on. A popular spot with celebrities, as evidenced by the prominent photos of politicians like Ronald Reagan. ⑦–⑨.

Holiday Inn Brentwood, 170 N Church Lane at Sunset Blvd and 405 freeway ☎310/476-6411. Something of a cylindrical eyesore that pokes out of a hillside below the Getty Center, but with acceptable comfort and furnishings, and pool, whirlpool, and weight room. ⑦.

Hotel Bel Air, 701 Stone Canyon Rd ☎310/472-1211 or 1-800/648-4097.

LA's nicest hotel bar none, and the only hotel in Bel Air, in a thickly overgrown canyon, with lush gardens and waterfall, above Westwood. Go for a beautiful brunch by the Swan Pond if you can't afford the rooms, which will cost you at least $450 for their exquisite decor, spaciousness, and the like. ⑨.

Park Hyatt, 2151 Aveune of the Stars ☎310/277-2777 or 1-800/233-1234. Located just south of the *Century Plaza Hotel* in Century City. Although the area mainly consists of high-speed boulevards and high-rise boxes, this hotel provides good access to sights in West LA and Beverly Hills. Decent rooms with balconies and on-site pool and spa. ⑧–⑨.

Summit Hotel Bel-Air, 11461 Sunset Blvd ☎310/476-6571 or 1-800/HOTEL-411. Not to be confused with the other *Hotel Bel Air*, this establishment is not technically in Bel Air, but almost in Brentwood. Still, impeccable, smartly designed rooms with pool, tennis courts, health club, and in a good location. ⑦.

Westwood and UCLA

Century Wilshire, 10776 Wilshire Blvd ☎310/474-4506 or 1-800/421-7223. Some recent updating has helped this classic old hotel, located along a good section of Wilshire near Westwood Village. Kitchens and complimentary breakfast are standard. ⑥.

Claremont, 1044 Tiverton Ave ☎310/208-5957. An amazingly good deal for the area, this cheerful and inexpensive little hotel sits very close to UCLA and Westwood Village. Rooms are basic, and hotel is located in a peaceful buffer between commercial and residential zones, with the main difficulty being a lack of parking. ③.

Hilgard House, 927 Hilgard Ave ☎310/208-3945 or 1-800/826-3934. Positioned just beyond UCLA's southern boundary, with nicely designed rooms, covered parking, continental breakfast, and some jacuzzis and refrigerators. A reasonable value. ⑦.

Hotel del Capri, 10587 Wilshire Blvd ☎310/474-3511 or 1-800/44-HOTEL. Within a mile of UCLA, this budget hotel provides passable rooms and suites with faded 1980s decor, pool, and complimentary breakfast. A squat building set in one of Wilshire Blvd's high-rise canyons. ⑤.

The Westwood Marquis, 930 Hilgard Ave ☎310/208-8765 or 1-800/421-2317. The height of luxury in Westwood, featuring well-decorated, though not huge, rooms and pool, spa, health club, and ample parking. Popular with rich parents visiting kids at adjacent UCLA. ⑨.

Santa Monica and Venice

Bayside, 2001 Ocean Ave at Bay St ☎310/396-6000. Just a block from Santa Monica beach and the Sixties-style café scene of Main Street. Outside of the colorful, psychedelic bathroom tiles, the rooms are fairly bland, as is the exterior. No phones, but generally comfortable, with ocean views from the more expensive rooms. ③.

Cadillac Hotel, 8 Dudley Ave at Rose Ave, Venice ☎310/399-8876. Stylishly restored Art Deco hotel/hostel on the Venice Boardwalk. Its private rooms are spartan and have few amenities, but given the location and price, there are few better deals in town. With sundeck, pool, gym, and sauna. In the hostel portion of the hotel, a bed in one of the nine dorm rooms costs only a third as much as private rooms. ①–④.

Carmel, 201 Broadway at Second St ☎310/451-2469. The best budget bet for lodging near Santa Monica beach and Third Street Promenade, with the ocean two blocks away. Good, basic accommodation. ⑤.

The Georgian, 1415 Ocean Ave ☎310/395-9945 or 1-800/538-8147. A stunning blue-and-gold Art Deco gem, recently renovated with an airy California interior design. Rooms are acceptable, though pricier suites offer more space and better views, from Malibu to Palos Verdes. The one downside: a single, excruciatingly slow elevator. ⑦–⑧.

Accommodation

A map of Santa Monica's hotels appears on p.132.

Accommodation

Huntley, 1111 Second St ☎310/394-
5454 or 1-800/333-3333. Agreeable, if
pricey, rooms, but the main draw here is
the building's height: twenty stories,
accessible via a flashy, exterior elevator
that takes you to the *Toppers* restaurant
up on top. Food is mediocre, but the
views over the city and ocean are worth
the price of a drink or two. ⑦.

Loew's Santa Monica Beach Hotel,
1700 Ocean Ave at Pico Blvd
☎310/458-6700. One of Santa Monica's
newest and biggest hotels: a deluxe,
salmon-colored edifice overlooking the
ocean and the Santa Monica pier, and
often in demand as a film set. The best
rooms top $400, with lesser rooms being
adequate, though a bit cramped. ⑧–⑨.

Oceana, 849 Ocean Ave ☎310/393-
0486 or 1-800/777-0758. An all-suite
hotel with central courtyard, good oceanside views, pool, spa, fitness room, and
kitchens. Signature pastel design, at the
base of trendy Montana Avenue.
However, even with the luxuries, prices
seem a bit too steep. ⑧–⑨.

Pacific Shore, 1819 Ocean Ave at Pico
Blvd ☎310/451-8711. A popular stop
for package-tour Europeans, with great
bay views, parking spots, and kitchens in

the rooms. However, the overall style is
minimal and its high-rise motel-like
appearance is drab and functional. ⑤.

Santa Monica-Pico Blvd Travelodge,
3102 Pico Blvd at 31st St ☎310/450-
5766 or 1-800/231-7679. At the eastern
edge of Santa Monica, a mile from the
beach. One of the uglier motels you'll
see, the overall look of a stucco jail, but
with fairly good location, unsullied
rooms, and complimentary breakfast. ④.

Santa Monica Travelodge, 1525 Ocean
Ave ☎310/451-0761 or 1-800/255-
3050. Another of the reliable nationwide
chain, a bit more aesthetically appealing
than its counterpart on Pico Boulevard,
with slightly larger rooms and better
location, but also with higher prices. ⑥.

Shangri-La, 1301 Ocean Ave
☎310/394-2791 or 1-800/345-STAY.
Formerly the *Shangri-La Apartments*, a
terrific Art Deco structure with wraparound Streamline Moderne windows
and railings, and alluring white-and-black
design, with some original fixtures.
Rooms are unexceptional but furnished
with Deco motifs and art, and offer
excellent, palm-tree-level views of the
ocean and nearby Third Street
Promenade. ⑧.

Shutters on the Beach, 1 Pico Blvd at Appian Way ☎310/458-0030 or 1-800/334-9000. The seafront home to the stars, a white-shuttered resort south of the Santa Monica Pier. Amenities include jacuzzis (with shuttered screens), pool, spa, sundeck, ground-floor shopping, and ocean views. Easily Santa Monica's best hotel, though you'll pay for the added luxury. No walk-ins – reservations only. ⑨.

The South Bay and LA harbor

Barnabey's, 3501 Sepulveda Blvd, Manhattan Beach ☎310/545-8466. Somewhat of a surprise for the area: a quaint little inn, decorated with belle epoque touches, at the northern edge of Manhattan Beach near the El Segundo oil refineries; it's also adjacent to a lengthy green belt and about a mile from the beach. Tasteful rooms with plush beds and old-time fixtures and detailing, with on-site pool, courtyard, gardens, and jacuzzi. ⑦.

Hotel Hermosa, 2515 PCH, Hermosa Beach ☎310/318-6000. In a busy part of town, between Hermosa and Manhattan beaches, this hotel offers moderate prices, adequate rooms, and a short walk to the beach. ④.

Long Beach Hilton, 2 World Trade Center, Long Beach ☎562/983-3400. One of the better chain hotels in the area, with conventional rooms with wide harborside views overlooking Ocean Boulevard and downtown Long Beach. Within easy walking distance to many sights, with pool, spa, and airport shuttle. ⑧.

Long Beach Travelodge, 80 Atlantic Ave, Long Beach ☎562/435-2471. An obvious bargain in a prime location, with the simple, spare rooms familiar to budget travelers, but also with refrigerators and coffee-makers and good access to major area sights. ③–⑤.

Palos Verdes Inn, 1700 S PCH, Redondo Beach ☎310/316-4200 or 1-800/421-9241. Reasonable luxury on the edge of Redondo Beach, on a busy highway stretch near Torrance and Palos Verdes,

but just a half-mile from the beach. Cheery pastel rooms, pool, spa, and weight room. ⑤.

Rodeway Inn, 50 Atlantic Ave at Ocean Blvd, Long Beach ☎562/435-8369. Safe bet a block from the beach, a serviceable base for exploring Long Beach and its downtown and harbor area. Free in-room movies in rather lackluster rooms. ③.

San Pedro Grand Hotel, 111 S Gaffey St, San Pedro ☎310/514-1414. One of your very few options in San Pedro, and not in a prime spot – several blocks from the end of the 110 freeway. Nonetheless, the quaint decor and antiques, at a decent price, make it worthwhile. ⑦.

Sea Sprite Ocean Front Apartment Motel, 1016 Strand, Hermosa Beach ☎310/376-6933. Acceptable rooms on a busy beachside strip. Ask the manager what's available as there are several options at varying prices, though all are clean and sizable enough. ④–⑤.

Seahorse Inn, 233 N Sepulveda Blvd, Manhattan Beach ☎310/376-7951 or 1-800/233-8050. Typical roadside motel with faded pastel exterior but clean rooms. Further from the beach than others, on another loud stretch of road, but with a pool and good parking. ②.

The San Gabriel and San Fernando valleys

The Artists' Inn, 1038 Magnolia St, South Pasadena ☎626/799-5668 or 1-888/799-5668. Easily the best place to stay in South Pasadena, a themed bed-and-breakfast inn with rooms honoring famous painters and styles. Consider the stylish Fauve and Impressionist rooms – though best of all is the Italian Suite, with dark colors and a sun porch. ⑥.

Best Western Colorado Inn, 2156 E Colorado Blvd, Pasadena ☎626/793-9339. Affordable accommodation and very basic rooms just south of the Foothill freeway and north of San Marino's Huntington Library and Gardens. ④.

Beverly Garland's Holiday Inn, 4222 Vineland Ave, North Hollywood

Accommodation

Accommodation

Disneyland doesn't have a lot of great options for accommodation; the best reason for staying out here is to position yourself for an early-morning jump on the crowds.

☎818/980-8000 or 1-800/BEVERLY. Two-tower complex with pool, sauna, free parking, and screening room, fairly close to Universal City. The proprietor played maternal TV roles on *My Three Sons*, *Remington Steele*, and *The New Adventures of Superman*. ⑦.

Doubletree, Los Robles Ave at Walnut St, Pasadena ☎626/792-2727. Located in the cheesy, postmodern Plaza de las Fuentes complex, this *Doubletree* is an imposing pastel creation with Spanish Revival touches like Mission-style arches and bright, fancy tiling. Luxury rooms have decent amenities, but location is the best feature, near Old Pasadena and grand municipal buildings. ⑧.

Ritz-Carlton Huntington, 1401 S Oak Knoll Ave, Pasadena ☎626/568-3900. Utterly luxurious and refurbished landmark 1906 hotel, located in residential southern Pasadena on an imposing hilltop. Palatial grounds, free parking, ponds and courtyards, three restaurants, expansive rear lawn, and terrific San Gabriel Valley views. Rooms with marble and wood are a bit cozy but quite elegant, and suites start at $350. For even bigger bucks, inquire about the private bungalows. ⑧.

Sheraton Universal, 333 Universal Terrace, Universal City ☎818/980-1212 or 1-800/325-3535. A large and luxurious high-rise hotel on the Universal Studios lot, with health club, spa, and good restaurant, and well-designed rooms with superior valley views. Easily accessible off the 101 freeway. ⑧.

Universal City Hilton, 555 Universal Terrace ☎818/506-2500. A sleek high-rise neighbor to *Sheraton Universal*, with similar appointments and amenities, though a much better-looking steel-and-glass edifice. Rooms are nicely furnished and very close to CityWalk. ⑧.

Vagabond Inn, 1203 E Colorado Blvd at Michigan Ave, Pasadena ☎626/449-3170. Friendly budget chain motel, usefully placed for exploring Pasadena, with clean rooms and limited amenities. Other *Vagabond Inns* at 2863 E Colorado Blvd,

Pasadena (☎626/578-9791 or 1-800/468-2251) and 20157 Ventura Blvd, Woodland Hills (☎818/347-8080), the latter with a large heated pool. All ③.

Malibu and the Santa Monica Mountains

Casa Malibu Inn, 22752 PCH ☎310/456-2219. Located opposite Carbon Beach, a good spot for a stroll, and featuring superb, well-appointed rooms with modern design, and some in-room fireplaces and balconies. A peaceful setting amid bountiful foliage. ⑥.

Channel Road Inn, 219 W Channel Rd at PCH ☎310/459-1920. The house of a turn-of-the-century oil baron, Thomas McCall. Fourteen rooms in a romantic getaway nestled in Pacific Palisades, in lower Santa Monica Canyon, with ocean views, a hot tub, and free bike rental. Eat free grapes and sip champagne in the sumptuous rooms, each priced according to the "view", size and amenities, from the simple Garden Room to a suite with four-poster-bed and capacious living room. ⑥–⑧.

Malibu Beach Inn, 22878 PCH ☎310/456-6445 or 1-800/4-MALIBU. Sunny pink Spanish Colonial resort by the Malibu Pier. With Southwest design, in-room fireplaces, tiled bathtubs, seaward balconies, continental breakfasts, and oceanside hotel deck. Wooden ceilings and quaint period-revival touches add to the charm. ⑧.

Malibu Surfer Motel, 22541 PCH ☎310/456-6169. Frightful interior decor, with eye-straining shag carpets and clashing colors, but just across from the beach and boasting kingsize beds, refrigerators, and TVs. ④.

Around Disneyland

Best Western Stovall's Inn, 1110 W Katella Ave, Anaheim ☎714/778-1880. Elementary, no-frills accommodations in Disneyland area, at fairly cheap prices. ④.

Desert Palm Inn and Suites, 631 W Katella Ave, Anaheim ☎1-800/521-

6420. Very comfortable rooms with refrigerators, microwaves, VCRs, and continental breakfast. Conventions in town make prices jump, but the Inn usually offers good amenities at agreeable rates. ③.

Disneyland Hotel, 1150 W Cerritos Ave at West St, Anaheim ☎714/778-6600. Crude, cookie-cutter rooms in a huge, monolithic establishment, plus several pools, faux beach, and plenty of interior shopping outlets. The Disneyland monorail stops right outside. ⑦.

Motel 6, 100 W Freedman Way, Anaheim ☎714/520-9696. Colorless, almost bare rooms, but with good access to Disneyland. Given the nearby options, it's the best bargain in the area. ②.

Park Place Inn, 1544 S Harbor Blvd (☎714/776-4800). Reliable Anaheim member of a nationwide chain. ④.

Pavilions, 1176 W Katella Ave (☎714/776-0140). Conveniently located and reasonable chain hotel. ④.

Ramada Inn Conestoga, 1240 S Walnut, Anaheim ☎714/535-0300 or 1-800/2-RAMADA. Goofy but fun Wild West decor liven up this otherwise standard hotel, not too far from the Magic Kingdom. ④–⑤.

The Orange County coast

Hotel Laguna, 425 S Coast Hwy, Laguna Beach ☎714/494-1151. In the center of Laguna Beach, near the throngs of tourist crowds. If you have the cash, this is the place to spend it. Nearly every comfortable, luxurious room has an ocean view. ⑥–⑦.

Mission Inn, 26891 Ortega Hwy at I-5, San Juan Capistrano ☎714/493-1151. Rooms at this reasonably priced place come with use of jacuzzi and pool. Located in a distant Orange County city, but close enough to the main draw, the old Spanish Mission. ③–④.

Ocean View Motel, 16196 PCH, Huntington Beach ☎714/592-2700. Family-run roadside establishment with

tidy rooms. As a bonus, get a jacuzzi in your room for an extra $15. ②.

Ritz-Carlton Laguna Niguel, PCH at Ritz Carlton Drive, Dana Point ☎714/240-2000 or 1-800/241-3333. Another of the palatial LA *Ritz-Carlton*s, this one with prime beach access and striking views over the ocean. Also with pool, racquet club, spa, boating, and nicely refined suites with chic design and abundant space. Worth a stay if you have the money and don't mind driving halfway to San Diego. ⑨.

Sail-Inn Motel, 2627 Newport Blvd, Newport Beach ☎714/675-1841. Fairly ordinary rooms on a busy strip, but the motel is the least costly you're likely to find in the pricey Newport area. Close to the trendy Balboa Peninsula. ④.

Seacliff Motel, 1661 S Coast Hwy, Laguna Beach ☎714/494-9717. Unexceptional, rather dull accommodations, but right on the ocean and near an appealing section of Laguna Beach. ④.

Seal Beach Inn and Gardens, 212 Fifth St, Seal Beach ☎310/493-2416. Bed-and-breakfast offering impressive furnishings two blocks from the sands. Rooms on lower level are interesting, with myriad appointments and antiques, but the best room, the exquisite Honeysuckle Suite, is up top overlooking the oceanside. ⑥–⑧.

Surf and Sand, 1555 S Coast Hwy, Laguna Beach ☎714/497-4477 or 1-800/524-8621. One of the best of the Orange County coast hotels, with terrific oceanside views, plentiful beach access, and numerous spacious rooms with many luxurious features. ⑨.

Accommodation

Hostels

As usual, **hostels** are at the bottom of the price scale. Dormitory rooms are sex-segregated, and beds usually go for somewhere around $13–15. Many hostels also offer cut-rate single and double rooms. You can expect little more from your stay than a clean, safe bed and somewhere to lock your valuables. Some do, however, offer tours of surrounding

Accommodation

areas, and some have organized social events – volleyball, pizza parties, and the like. There's often a three-to-five night maximum stay – as hostels are supposed to be preserved for travelers – though this is generally enforced only when demand outstrips supply.

Banana Bungalow-Hollywood Hotel, 2775 Cahuenga Blvd W, in the Cahuenga Pass ☎213/851-1129 or 1-800/446-7835. Popular large hostel near Universal City and US-101, with free airport shuttles, city tours to Venice Beach and Magic Mountain, and a relaxed atmosphere. Outdoor pool, free parking, and as much beer as you can drink every second night for $3. Dorms $12–18 and more expensive private doubles at $45 and up. ①–③.

HI-Anaheim/Fullerton, 1700 N Harbor Blvd at Brea, Fullerton ☎714/738-3721. Convenient and comfortable, five miles north of Disneyland on the site of a former dairy farm, with a rural, isolated feel. The hostel's numerous facilities include a grass volleyball court, golf driving range, and picnic area, along with fireplace, libraries, and laundry facilities. Make reservations first – there are only 22 beds. Summer check-in 5–11pm, rest of year 4–10pm. Mornings open 7.10–10.30am. OCTA bus #43 stops outside. Members $14, others $17. ①.

HI-LA/Santa Monica, 1436 Second St at Broadway, Santa Monica ☎310/393-9913. A few blocks from the beach and pier, the building was LA's Town Hall from 1887 to 1889, and retains its historic charm, with inner courtyard, ivy covered walls, and a skylight. Members $16, others $20 – the price includes laundry machines and huge kitchens. Smoking and drinking are prohibited. Open 24hrs. Reservations essential in summer. ①.

HI-LA/South Bay, 3601 S Gaffey St, building #613, San Pedro ☎310/831-8109. Sixty beds in an old US Army barracks, with a panoramic view of the Pacific. Ideal for seeing San Pedro, Palos Verdes, and the whole Harbor area, and directly adjacent to Angels Gate Park,

Cabrillo Beach, and Point Fermin. Open 7–11am and 4pm–midnight. $11 members, $14 others; private rooms $27 per person. MTA bus #446 passes close by, but it's a 2-hour journey from Downtown. Can also take SuperShuttle from LAX. ①.

Hollywood Hills Hostel, 6772 Hawthorn Ave ☎213/462-3777 or 1-800/LA-HOS-TEL. Not really in the Hollywood Hills, but rather a block south of the center of Hollywood Boulevard, near major attractions and with game room, private baths, main bar, tours of region, and garden patio, as well as airport and train shuttles. Shared rooms $12–17 and private rooms from $30–40. ①.

Hollywood International Hostel, 6820 Hollywood Blvd ☎213/463-0797 or 1-800/750-6561. In the heart of Hollywood, near the Chinese Theatre, with free tea and coffee, game room, gymnasium, patio garden, kitchen, and laundry. Tours of Hollywood offered and also beyond the immediate area to theme parks, Las Vegas, and Tijuana. Shared rooms start at $12 and reach $30 and above for private rooms. ①–②.

Hostel California, 2221 Lincoln Blvd at Venice Blvd, Venice ☎310/305-0250. LA's first hostel, several miles from Venice Beach in a somewhat seedy commercial section of town. Twelve six-bed dorms with kitchens, pool table, big-screen TV, linen, and parking. Cheap shuttle bus to and from LAX. $12 members, $15 others, or $90 a week. ①.

Huntington Beach Colonial Inn Hostel, 421 Eighth St at Pecan, Huntington Beach ☎714/536-3315. Four blocks from the beach and mostly double rooms. Easy access to Disneyland and Knott's Berry Farm. Sleeping bags allowed. Open 8am–11pm. Key rental after 1pm, $1 (plus $20 deposit). Dorms $12, private rooms $16.50 per person. ①.

Share-Tel Apartments, 20 Brooks Ave at Speedway, Venice ☎310/392-0325. Apartments near Venice Boardwalk each hold 6–8 people sharing facilities and bedrooms. $15, including breakfast and dinner Mon–Fri. Private rooms $20. Add $5 to both rates during peak summer periods. ①.

Surf City Hostel, 26 Pier Ave, Hermosa Beach ☎310/798-2323 or 1-800/305-2901. Terrific location near popular beach-side strip, the Strand, and near numerous restaurants, clubs, bars, and famed Either/Or Bookshop. In a nondescript concrete building, with a hard-to-find entrance, and shared rooms from $15 or private double rooms from $35. Also with kitchen, laundry, beer parties, and shuttles to Disneyland and other major theme parks and shopping zones. ①–②.

Venice Beach Hostel, 25 Windward Ave, Venice ☎310/399-7649. Occupying what's left of the old Italian colonnade, with trompe l'oeil Venetian-style windows and painted-on people peering out, this is one of the better-looking hostels in LA. Directly near the heart of the Venice Boardwalk and Muscle Beach, with car rental discounts and shared rooms at $13–17 and private rooms from $32–40. Also with door-to-door trips to major theme parks, homes of the stars, and Getty Center and Museum. Also, complimentary boogie boards for seaside fun. ①–②.

Campgrounds

A company called Destinet (☎1-800/444-7275) processes reservations at many of the **campgrounds** listed below and can look for an alternative if your chosen site is full. It charges a $6.75 fee per reservation per night up to a maximum of eight people per site, including one vehicle.

Bolsa Chica Campground ☎714/846-3460. Facing the ocean in Huntington Beach, near a wildlife sanctuary and bird-watchers' paradise. $14 for campers with a self-contained vehicle. No tent camping.

Chilao Flat, on Hwy-2 twenty miles northeast of Pasadena ☎818/574-1613. The only campground in the San Gabriel Mountains reachable by car, though there are many others accessible on foot. For more details contact the Angeles National Forest Ranger Station at 701 N Santa Anita Ave, Arcadia (☎818/574-1613). $17.

Dockweiler Beach County Park, Playa del Rey ☎310/305-9545 or via Destinet. On a noisy stretch of Vista del Mar, almost at the western end of the LAX runways. Not a pretty beach, but good enough for watching waves and suntanning. Mainly for RVs, tent sites cost $17–25.

Doheny State Beach Campground, Dana Point ☎714/496-6171 or via Destinet, Often packed with families, especially at weekends. Located at southern end of Orange County in picturesque Dana Point. $16–21 per each site.

Leo Carrillo State Beach Park, Malibu ☎818/706-1310 or via Destinet. Near one of LA's best beaches, 25 miles northwest of Santa Monica on Pacific Coast Highway, and served twice an hour in summer by MTA bus #434. Not far from the end of Mulholland Highway. $16.

Malibu Creek State Park 1925 Las Virgenes Rd, fifteen minutes from the center of the San Fernando Valley ☎818/706-8809. A rustic campground in a park which can become crowded at times. Sixty sites in the shade of huge oak trees, almost all with fire pits, solar heated showers and flush toilets. One-time filming location for TV show *M*A*S*H*. $15–21.

San Clemente State Beach Campground, distant campground two miles south of San Clemente ☎714/492-7146 or via Destinet. $20 hook-up sites, $16 others.

Accommodation

Chapter 13

Restaurants and cafés

LA's **restaurants** and **cafés** cover every extreme: whatever you want to eat and however much you want to spend, there are lots of choices, from trendy hybrids of international flavors to good and cheap ethnic food outlets to dingy burger shacks. New cuisines and establishments are constantly appearing, and many of the city's most venerable restaurants still serve their trademark dishes, though some particularly famous names have disappeared in recent years, including *Chasen's* in Beverly Hills and the chic *Brown Derby* branches on the Westside (as well as the downmarket, hat-shaped variant along Wilshire Boulevard). Nonetheless, LA's chefs have invented a number of popular favorites, adding the cheeseburger, hot fudge sundae, french dip sandwich, and Caesar salad to America's, as well as the world's, cuisine.

Eating out is a common event for many Angelenos, and the city's most prominent restaurants rarely lack customers, though knowledgeable locals are more likely to frequent the latest high-end trendsetters or little-known gems than flock to the busier, more touristy spots. Of course, you should try to take at least a few meals in LA's major-name restaurants, which often serve superb food in self-consciously chic surroundings. They tend to drive up their prices on the strength of a good review, and they get away with it because they know the place will be packed with many first-timers, all trying to impress their cohorts by claiming that they've been eating there for years.

Catering appears to be the movie stars' sideline of choice these days, and LA is littered with **celebrity-owned** outfits – like Steven Spielberg's submarine-shaped sandwich store *Dive!* and *Planet Hollywood* in Beverly Hills – but the food is usually so unremarkable there's no reason to list them.

For the majority of restaurants, you won't need to **reserve** ahead, though you should make the effort on weekends and at most expensive or trendy spots. For **dinner**, expect to pay anywhere from $5–10 per person for simple fast food, $15–20 for most ethnic and American restaurants, and $30–50 for the latest hot spots of any cuisine. If you want to sample great food without paying a bundle, you may be better off going for **lunch** at those upscale eateries that offer it, at which prices from $15–25 are common. Consider, too, the all-you-can-eat **buffets** at certain lesser restaurants that usually range around $8–15. The price breaks do not, however, continue downward at those establishments that offer **breakfast**, and unless you're going for a rock-bottom meal at *Denny's* or at *Norm's* diners, you'll end up paying $10–15 for any sort of decent morning meal.

If you simply want to fill up quickly and cheaply, the options are nearly endless, and include free food available for the price of a drink at **happy hours**. No matter where you are, though, don't reach for a cigarette – health-conscious LA banned **smoking** in 1993, and the state of California recently followed that up with a blanket tobacco prohibition in restaurants and most bars.

What to eat

Budget food is as plentiful as in any other US city, ranging from good sit-down meals in street-corner coffee shops and cafés to chain-franchise burgers. Almost as common, and just as cheap, is **Mexican food**. This is the closest thing you'll get to an indigenous LA cuisine – most notably in the burrito, a filled tortilla that's rarely seen in Mexico but here is available everywhere, both from street vendors and comfortable restaurants. These spots are often the city's best deals, serving tasty, healthy, and filling food for as little as $5 per person. They're at their most authentic in East LA, although there's a good selection of more Americanized examples all over the city. You'll have to look harder for authentic food **from other** parts of **Latin America**; much of it is a blend of Peruvian seafood and basic Mexican fare.

LA lacks a wide selection of **African**-style restaurants as well; the ones that do exist are mainly found in Hollywood and Mid-Wilshire. **Moroccan** food is typically quite good, though not particularly concentrated in any one neighborhood; the best **Ethiopian** restaurants are in a small pocket around Olympic Boulevard in Mid-Wilshire, and are fairly inexpensive.

Down-to-earth **American** cuisine, with its steaks, ribs, baked potatoes, and mountainous salads, has a deceptively low profile in faddish LA, although it's available almost everywhere and usually won't cost more than $10 for a comparative blow-out. Much more prominent – and more expensive – is **California cuisine**, based on fresh local ingredients, more likely grilled than fried, and stylishly presented with a nod to French nouvelle cuisine. Spicy **Cajun** food is affordable as well as enjoyable, and there are a number of establishments sprinkled throughout the LA area.

Unlike many ethnic cuisines in LA, those from the **Caribbean** – Jamaican, Cuban, et al – are uncommon in Hollywood and much more visible in West LA and Santa Monica. With only a few exceptions, the affordable food at local Caribbean restaurants leaves subtlety behind in exchange for sweat-inducing flavors and spices. However, California cuisine is increasingly incorporating some Caribbean styles into its complex repertoire.

LA's most fashionable districts offer many delicious **Chinese** and dim sum restaurants, favored by Far East businessmen and fast-lane yuppies alike, in which you can easily eat your way through more than $20. Lower-priced and less pretentious outlets tend to be located Downtown, notably in Chinatown, where you can get a fair-sized meal for around $15. Because **Vietnamese** food has not made much of an official appearance in LA restaurants, your best bet is to venture into the Orange County suburbs of Santa Ana or Westminster, where growing numbers of Vietnamese immigrants can be found.

Predictably, **French** restaurants are among LA's fanciest and most expensive, with most issuing a blend of traditional and nouvelle cuisines, as well as incorporating the elements of California cuisine. On the other hand, LA's **Greek** restaurants provide rich, fairly traditional entrees for acceptably cheap prices. They are, however, fairly thin on the ground, having yet to attract the trendspotting crowd – somewhat of a blessing actually.

Indian and **Sri Lankan** restaurants are increasing in popularity – with restaurant menus often embracing uniquely Californian dishes. Most of the Indian restaurants in Hollywood or West LA fall into a fairly mid-range price bracket – around $15 for a full meal, less for a vegetarian Indian dish.

After years of having nothing more exotic than the established takeout pizza chains, LA has awoken to the delights of regional **Italian** cuisine, with Northern Italian food almost always being the most expensive and trendy. Another

Restaurants and Cafés

Restaurants and Cafés

For more on grocery shopping in LA, see p.306.

recent phenomenon is the **designer pizza**, invented at Hollywood's *Spago* restaurant and made to a traditional formula but topped with duck, shiitake mushrooms, and other non-traditional ingredients. None of this comes cheap, however: even a pasta dish in the average Italian restaurant can cost upwards of $8, and the least elaborate designer pizza will set you back around $15. On the other hand, LA's **pizza** joints are generally tasty and affordable, even if some have incorporated some of the more nouveau stylings into their menus.

Japanese cuisine is available throughout LA, in a wide range of prices, styles, and settings. Not surprisingly, Little Tokyo is the best place for more authentic fare, much of it sushi, with *udon* and *soba* increasing in popularity as you go further west. Along with French cooking, Japanese cuisine is one of the favorites used by California-cuisine chefs for their culinary experiments, making many "Japanese" restaurants more international in style, and good representatives of the city's latest cultural and gastronomic trends.

Korean cuisine has not yet gained much of a widespread cachet in LA. Outside of Koreatown, such restaurants can be found in isolated pockets in the Westside and even in the northern suburbs. Spicy barbequed ribs and *kim chee* (pickled cabbage) are among the more traditional dishes, both worth a try, and you can expect to pay under $20 per person for a decent-sized meal.

Though relatively few exist, **Middle Eastern** restaurants tend to be affordable. Much of the Westside is oblivious to the charms of this cuisine, though that is changing with the advent of citywide pita and falafel chains.

Russian and **Eastern European** restaurants are quite uncommon in LA, and despite the influx of newcomers from former Warsaw Pact countries, no significant pockets of ethnic eateries have emerged in immigrant neighborhoods. The price range, too, is unpredictable, depending on the neighborhood and reputation of the given establishment. **Hungarian** food is rare but appealing (and filling), same with **Polish** cuisine.

Although **seafood** is offered throughout LA in a variety of styles, it should come as no surprise that there are plenty of worthwhile seafood-only restaurants in the city, predominantly along the coast, with a strong concentration near Malibu and Newport Beach. However, often oceanside restaurants are better for their views than their food, and by venturing just a mile or so inland, you can find a better meal than you might at a restaurant located within sight of whales and seagulls.

Although it sometimes figures in California cuisine, **Spanish** cooking, along with **tapas bars**, has not yet made much of a dent in LA's culinary culture. Where they do exist, they're a good spot for a refreshing pitcher of sangria and tasty seafood and pork dishes.

Considering all of LA's options for East Asian cuisines, **Thai** food might be the best deal, both for its succulent, spicy flavors and reasonable prices. The finest restaurants are found in the less trendy sections of town, such as minimalls in Hollywood and run-down storefronts in Mid-Wilshire. If you don't mind sacrificing atmosphere for delicious food, a trip to such ignoble locations is well rewarded.

Finally, it's small wonder that mind- and body-fixated LA has a wide variety of **vegetarian** and **wholefood** restaurants, and even less of a shock that the bulk of them are found on the consciousness-raised Westside. Some vegetarian places can be very good value ($5 or so), but watch out for the ones that flaunt themselves as a New Age experience and include music – these can be three times as costly.

If you'd rather have a picnic than visit a restaurant, try the local Trader Joe's chain – which started as a liquor store with a sideline in unusual food, but now supplies imported cheeses, breads, and canned foods to the locals who crave them most – or the area's frequent **farmers markets**, loaded with organic produce and frequently advertised in the press.

RESTAURANT DIRECTORY

What follows is a list of all restaurants listed in this chapter, sorted by cuisine. To find the review, simply refer back to the relevant neighborhood section listed as a subheading underneath the cuisine.

AFRICAN

Mid-Wilshire
Nyala, 1076 S Fairfax Ave
Rosalind Ethiopian, 1044 S Fairfax Ave

Hollywood and West Hollywood
Dar Maghreb, 7651 Sunset Blvd

Beverly Hills and West LA
Koutoubia, 2116 Westwood Blvd

AMERICAN, CALIFORNIAN AND CAJUN

Downtown
Bernard's, 506 S Grand Ave
Checkers Restaurant, 535 S Grand Ave
Engine Co No. 28, 644 S Figueroa St
New Moon, 102 W Ninth St
Pacific Dining Car, 1310 W Sixth St

Mid-Wilshire
Atlas, 3760 Wilshire Blvd
Ca' Brea, 346 S La Brea Ave
Citrus, 6703 Melrose Ave
Georgia, 7250 Melrose Ave
The Gumbo Pot, 6333 W Third St
Patina, 5955 Melrose Ave
Sabor, 3221 Pico Blvd
Taylor's, 3361 W Eighth St

Hollywood and West Hollywood
Café La Boheme, 8400 Santa Monica Blvd
The Cajun Bistro, 8301 Sunset Blvd
Hollywood Canteen, 1006 N Seward St
Musso and Frank Grill, 6667 Hollywood Blvd
Off Vine, 6263 Leland Way
Pinot Hollywood's Restaurant and Martini Bar, 1448 Gower St
Sabroso, 2538 Hyperion Ave
Spago, 1114 Horn Ave

Beverly Hills and West LA
Arnie Morton's, 435 N La Cienega Blvd
The Cheesecake Factory, 364 N Beverly Drive

The Daily Grill, 11677 San Vicente Blvd
Maple Drive, 345 N Maple Drive
Monty's Steakhouse, 1100 Glendon Ave

Santa Monica, Venice and Malibu
17th Street Café, 1610 Montana Ave, Santa Monica
Crocodile Café, 101 Santa Monica Blvd, Santa Monica
Granita, 23725 W Malibu Rd, Malibu
Hal's, 1349 Abbot Kinney Blvd, Venice
Joe's, 1023 Abbot Kinney Blvd, Venice
LA Farm, 3000 W Olympic Blvd, Santa Monica
Michael's, 1147 Third St, Santa Monica

South and East LA
Harold and Belle's, 2920 Jefferson Blvd, South Central

Orange County
Aubergine, 508 29th St, Newport Beach
Bistro 201, 3333 PCH, Newport Beach
The Cottage, 308 N PCH, Laguna Beach
Five Crowns, 3801 E Coast Hwy, Corona del Mar
Jack Shrimp, 2400 W Coast Hwy, Newport Beach
The Towers, 1555 S Coast Hwy, Laguna Beach

CARIBBEAN

Mid-Wilshire
Prado, 244 N Larchmont Blvd

Beverly Hills and West LA
Bamboo, 10835 Venice Blvd
Versailles, 10319 Venice Blvd

Santa Monica, Venice and Malibu
The Jamaican Café, 424 Wilshire Blvd, Santa Monica
Mobay, 1031 Abbot Kinney Blvd, Venice

South Bay and LA Harbor
Cha Cha Cha, 762 Pacific Ave, Long Beach

Continues over

Restaurants and Cafés

CHINESE AND VIETNAMESE

Downtown
Grand Star Restaurant, 934 Sun Mun Way
Mandarin Deli, 727 N Broadway
Mon Kee, 679 N Spring St
Ocean Seafood, 750 N Hill St
Pho 79, 727 N Broadway
Yang Chow, 819 N Broadway

Mid-Wilshire
Genghis Cohen, 740 N Fairfax Ave
Indochine, 8225 Beverly Blvd

Hollywood and West Hollywood
Chin Chin, 8618 Sunset Blvd
Joss, 9255 Sunset Blvd

Beverly Hills and West LA
Chung King, 11538 W Pico Blvd

Santa Monica, Venice and Malibu
Chinois on Main, 2709 Main St, Santa Monica

San Gabriel and San Fernando valleys
Sea Star, 2000 W Main St, Alhambra

Orange County
Favori, 3502 W First St, Santa Ana
Hue Rendezvous, 15562 Westminster Ave, Westminster

FRENCH

Downtown
Café Pinot, 700 W Fifth St

Mid-Wilshire
Louis XIV, 606 N La Brea Ave

Hollywood and West Hollywood
Fenix, 8358 Sunset Blvd
Le Chardonnay, 8284 Melrose Ave
L'Orangerie, 903 N La Cienega Blvd

Santa Monica, Venice and Malibu
Le Petit Moulin, 714 Montana Ave, Santa Monica

GREEK

Mid-Wilshire
Le Petit Greek, 127 N Larchmont Blvd
Sofi, 8030 W Third St

Santa Monica, Venice and Malibu
Café Athens, 1000 Wilshire Blvd, Santa Monica

South Bay and LA Harbor
Santorini's, 2529 PCH, Torrance

INDIAN AND SRI LANKAN

Mid-Wilshire
The Clay Pit, 3465 W Sixth St
East India Grill, 345 N La Brea Ave
India's Oven, 7231 Beverly Blvd

Hollywood and West Hollywood
Chamika Catering, 1717 N Wilcox Ave
India Inn, 1638 N Cahuenga Blvd

Beverly Hills and West LA
Bombay Café, 12113 Santa Monica Blvd

Santa Monica, Venice and Malibu
Nawab, 1621 Wilshire Blvd, Santa Monica

ITALIAN AND PIZZA

Downtown
California Pizza Kitchen, 330 S Hope St
Cicada, 617 S Olive St
La Bella Cucina, 949 S Figueroa St

Mid-Wilshire
Angeli Caffé, 7274 Melrose Ave
Campanile, 624 S La Brea Ave
Chianti, 7383 Melrose Ave

Hollywood and West Hollywood
Caioti, 2100 Laurel Canyon Blvd
Louise's Trattoria, 4500 Los Feliz Blvd
Palermo, 1858 N Vermont Ave

Beverly Hills and West LA
Barefoot, 8722 W Third St
Jacopo's, 490 N Beverly Drive
Locanda Veneta, 8638 W Third St
Mario's, 1001 Broxton Ave

Santa Monica, Venice and Malibu
Abbot's Pizza Company, 1407 Abbot Kinney Blvd, Venice
Boston Wildflour Pizza, 2807 Main St, Santa Monica
Drago, 2628 Wilshire Blvd, Santa Monica
Giovanni's Salerno Beach Restaurant, 193 Culver Blvd, Playa Del Rey

Valentino, 3115 W Pico Blvd, Santa Monica

Wolfgang Puck Express, 1315 Third Street Promenade, Santa Monica

South Bay and LA Harbor
Mangiamo, 128 Manhattan Beach Blvd, Manhattan Beach

San Fernando and San Gabriel valleys
La Scala Presto, 3821 Riverside Drive, Burbank

Market City Caffé, 33 S Fair Oaks Ave, Pasadena

JAPANESE

Downtown
A Thousand Cranes, 120 S Los Angeles St

Mitsuru Café, 117 Japanese Village Blvd

Restaurant Horikawa, 111 S San Pedro St

Shibucho, 333 S Alameda St

Mid-Wilshire
Mishima, 8474 W Third St

Hollywood and West Hollywood
Katsu, 1972 N Hillhurst Ave

Beverly Hills and West LA
Matsuhisa, 129 N La Cienega Blvd
The Sushi House, 12013 Pico Blvd

Santa Monica, Venice and Malibu
Chaya, 110 Navy St, Venice
Lighthouse Buffet, 201 Arizona Ave, Santa Monica

San Gabriel and San Fernando valleys
Genmai-Sushi, 4454 Van Nuys Blvd, San Fernando Valley

Shiro, 1505 Mission St, South Pasadena

KOREAN

Mid-Wilshire
Buffet Palace, 3014 Olympic Blvd
Dong Il Jang, 3455 W Eighth St
Woo Lae Oak, 623 S Western Ave

Santa Monica, Venice and Malibu
Monsoon Café, 1212 Third St, Santa Monica

MEXICAN AND LATIN AMERICAN

Mid-Wilshire
Casa Carnitas, 4067 Beverly Blvd
El Cholo, 1121 S Western Ave
El Coyote, 7312 Beverly Blvd
Mario's Peruvian Seafood Restaurant, 5786 Melrose Ave

Hollywood and West Hollywood
Burrito King, 2109 W Sunset Blvd
Mexico City, 2121 N Hillhurst Ave
Yuca's Hut, 2056 N Hillhurst Ave

Beverly Hills and West LA
Baja Fresh, 475 N Beverly Drive
El Mexicano Deli & Restaurant, 1601 Sawtelle Blvd
La Salsa, 11075 W Pico Blvd at Sepulveda

Santa Monica, Venice and Malibu
The Gaucho Grill, 1251 Third St, Santa Monica
La Cabana, 738 Rose Ave, Venice
Mariasol, 401 Santa Monica Pier, Santa Monica

South and East LA
Ciro's Mexican Food, 705 N Everery Ave, East LA
King Taco Warehouse, 4504 E Third St, East LA

South Bay and LA Harbor
By Brazil, 1615 Cabrillo Ave, Torrance
El Pollo Inka, 1100 PCH, Hermosa Beach

San Gabriel and San Fernando valleys
Don Cuco's, 3911 Riverside Drive, Burbank
El Tepayac, 800 S Palm, Alhambra
Merida, 20 E Colorado Blvd, Pasadena
Señor Fish, 4803 Eagle Rock Blvd, Eagle Rock

MIDDLE EASTERN

Mid-Wilshire
Al Amir, 5750 Wilshire Blvd

Hollywood and West Hollywood
Noura Cafe, 8479 Melrose Ave, West Hollywood
Shamshiry, 5229 Hollywood Blvd
Zankou Chicken, 5065 Sunset Blvd

Continues over

Restaurants and Cafés

Restaurants and Cafés

Beverly Hills and West LA
Falafel King, 1059 Broxton Ave, Westwood

RUSSIAN AND EASTERN EUROPEAN

Mid-Wilshire
Perestroyka, 5468 Wilshire Blvd

Hollywood and West Hollywood
Diaghilev, 1020 N San Vicente Blvd, West Hollywood
Hungarian Budapest, 7986 Sunset Blvd
Uzbekistan, 7077 Sunset Blvd

Beverly Hills and West LA
The Players, 9513 Little Santa Monica Blvd

Santa Monica, Venice and Malibu
Warszawa, 1414 Lincoln Blvd, Santa Monica

SEAFOOD

Downtown
McCormick and Schmicks, 633 W Fifth St

Santa Monica, Venice and Malibu
Casablanca, 220 Lincoln Blvd, Venice
Geoffrey's, 27400 PCH, Malibu
Gladstone's 4 Fish, 17300 PCH, Pacific Palisades
Killer Shrimp, 523 Washington St, Marina del Rey
Maryland Crab House, 2424 Pico Blvd, Santa Monica
Neptune's Net, 42505 PCH, Santa Monica

Orange County
Claes Seafood, 425 S PCH, Laguna Beach
The Crab Cooker, 2200 Newport Ave, Newport Beach

SPANISH

Hollywood and West Hollywood
La Masia, 9077 Santa Monica Blvd, West Hollywood

Beverly Hills and West LA
Cava, 8384 W Third St, West LA Ω

South Bay and LA Harbor
Alegria Café & Tapas Bar, 115 Pine Ave, Long Beach

THAI

Mid-Wilshire
Tommy Tang's, 7313 Melrose Ave
Vim, 831 S Vermont Ave

Hollywood and West Hollywood
Chan Dara, 1511 N Cahuenga Blvd
Jitlada, 5233 Sunset Blvd

Santa Monica, Venice and Malibu
Flower of Siam, 2553 Lincoln Blvd, Venice
Thai Dishes, 1910 Wilshire Blvd, Santa Monica

San Gabriel and San Fernando valleys
Saladang, 363 S Fair Oaks Ave, Pasadena

VEGETARIAN AND WHOLEFOOD

Mid-Wilshire
Inaka, 131 S La Brea Ave

Hollywood and West Hollywood
The Bodhi Garden Restaurant, 1498 Sunset Blvd

Santa Monica, Venice and Malibu
Figtree's Café, 429 Ocean Front Walk, Venice
Inn of the Seventh Ray, 128 Old Topanga Rd, Topanga Canyon
Shambala Café, 607 Colorado Ave, Santa Monica

South Bay and LA Harbor

Coffee shops, delis, and diners

Budget food is everywhere in LA, at its best in the many small and stylish **coffee shops**, **delis**, and **diners** that serve soups, omeletes, sandwiches, and so forth. It's easy to eat this way and never have to spend much more than $6 for a full meal. There are, of course, the internationally franchised fast-food places on every street; better are the local chains of hamburger stands, most open 24 hours a day. *Fatburger*, originally at San Vicente and La Cienega boulevards on the border of Beverly Hills, has branches everywhere selling deliciously greasy hamburgers; its chief competitor, *In-N-Out Burger*, doesn't rate too far behind.

Sadly, the best of the 1950s **drive-ins** have been torn down, such as *Tiny Naylors* in Hollywood. So, too, have some of the classic "Googie"-style diners: the venerable *Ships* franchise is now just a boarded-up ruin in Culver City and a pair of leftover boomerang signs near a gas station in West LA.

Downtown

Clifton's Cafeteria, 648 S Broadway ☎213/627-1673. Classic 1930s cafeteria, but with bizarre decor: redwood trees, a waterfall, even a mini-chapel. The food is less daring – traditional meat-and-potatoes American, and cheap too.

Grand Central Market, 317 S Broadway ☎213/624-2378. Dozens of market stalls selling tacos, deli sandwiches, and Chinese food – and 24 fresh fruit and vegetable drinks from *Geraldine's* at the Hill Street entrance.

Original Pantry, 877 S Figueroa St ☎213/972-9279. There's always a line for the hearty portions of meaty American cooking – chops and steaks, mostly – in this 24-hr diner owned by Mayor Richard Riordan. Grab one of the charming statistic-filled brochures while you wait.

Philippe's Famous French Dip Sandwiches, 1001 N Alameda St, Chinatown ☎213/628-3781. Sawdust café, a block north of Union Station, with long communal tables, a decor unchanged since 1908, and juicy, artery-clogging french dips – invented at this very spot.

The Yorkshire Grill, 610 W Sixth St ☎213/629-3020. Big sandwiches and friendly service for under $10. Lunchtimes are crowded, so get there early.

Mid-Wilshire

Canter's Deli, 419 N Fairfax Ave ☎213/651-2030. Iconic LA deli with

huge sandwiches for around $7, and excellent kosher soups served by waitresses in pink uniforms and running shoes. Open 24hr.

Cassell's Hamburgers, 3266 W Sixth St ☎213/387-5502. No-frills, lunch-only takeout hamburger stand with plenty of loyal fans, despite its grungy location.

Hard Rock Café, in the Beverly Center, Beverly Blvd at San Vicente Blvd ☎310/276-7605. Rock 'n' roll decor and loud music are the attractions, with greasy food somewhat of an afterthought, except for a few good dishes like the Lime Chicken.

Johnie's, across from May's department store at Fairfax Ave and Wilshire Blvd ☎213/938-3521. Bland food and a drafty atmosphere, but this landmark diner has been home to many a film shoot.

Johnny Rockets, 7507 Melrose Ave ☎213/651-3361. Chrome-and-glass, Fifties-derived hamburger joint, open until 2am on weekends. Many other Westside locations.

Langer's Deli, 704 S Alvarado St ☎213/483-8050. "When in doubt, eat hot pastrami" says the sign, though you still have to choose from over twenty ways of having it. Half a block south of the MacArthur Park Metrorail station.

Maurice's Snack 'n' Chat, 5549 W Pico Blvd ☎213/931-3877. Everything here is cooked to order: spoon bread or baked chicken requires a call two hours ahead, though you can just call in for fried chicken, pork chops, grits, or salmon croquettes. Autographed pictures of celebrity diners – from Sammy Davis Jr to Ted Kennedy – line the walls.

Pink's Hot Dogs, 711 N La Brea Ave ☎213/931-4223. The quintessence of chili dogs. These monsters come with a wide range of messy toppings – and you'll want to lick up every greasy drop.

Swingers, *Beverly Laurel Motor Lodge*, 8018 Beverly Blvd at Laurel Ave ☎213/651-2441. Trendy diner, though the food is basic and low-priced. Late-

Restaurants and Cafés

Restaurants and Cafés

night hours bring out a range of colorful neighborhood characters.

Hollywood

Alex Donut, 6211 Franklin Ave ☎213/464-6148. Good old American donuts served at a 101 freeway-side strip mall. Try the foot-long cinnamon twist if you're up to it.

Barney's Beanery, 8447 Santa Monica Blvd, West Hollywood ☎213/654-2287. A choice of two hundred bottled beers to wash down hot dogs, hamburgers, and bowls of chili, all in a hip, grungy environment.

Duke's, 8909 Sunset Blvd, West Hollywood ☎310/652-9411. A favorite haunt of rock stars, this basic American coffee shop attracts a motley crew of night owls and bleary-eyed locals for its simple American fare.

Hampton's, 1342 N Highland Ave ☎213/469-1090. Gourmet hamburgers with a choice of over fifty toppings, plus an excellent salad bar.

Roscoe's, 1514 N Gower St ☎213/466-7453. Highly caloric guilty pleasures like fried chicken and thick waffles make this a popular hangout. One in a chain of several Westside locations.

Tail o' the Pup, 329 N San Vicente Blvd, West Hollywood ☎310/652-4517. Worth a visit for the roadside pop architecture alone (a thin wiener enclosed by a massive bun; see p.81), though the hot dogs and hamburgers are also good.

Tommy's, 2575 W Beverly Blvd, Silver Lake ☎213/389-9060. Legendary burgers loaded with chili are the main reason to venture to this 24-hr shack.

Village Coffee Shop, 2695 Beachwood Drive ☎213/467-5398. A basic coffee shop in the picturesque hills below the Hollywood sign, and a fine spot for relaxing near the stone gates of a quiet Hollywood neighborhood.

Yukon Mining Co, 7328 Santa Monica Blvd, West Hollywood ☎213/851-8833. Excellent 24-hr coffee shop attracts a diverse clientele of Russian immigrants, elderly pensioners, and glammed-out drag queens.

Beverly Hills and West LA

The Apple Pan, 10801 W Pico Blvd, West LA ☎310/475-3585. Grab a spot at the counter and enjoy freshly baked apple pie and good, juicy hamburgers. Fans of *Beverly Hills 90210* will note that the show's *Peach Pit* was shamelessly copied from this original.

Ed Debevic's, 134 N La Cienega Blvd, Beverly Hills ☎310/659-1952. Fifties-style diner, with acceptable food and pricey beer, as well as a colorful array of singing and dancing waiters.

Jerry's Famous Deli, 8701 Beverly Blvd, Beverly Hills ☎310/289-1811. One of several *Jerry's* locations in LA, this place has a sizable menu of deli food, as well as Mexican offerings, and is open late.

John o' Groats, 10516 W Pico Blvd, West LA ☎310/204-0692. Solid British breakfasts and lunches draw plenty of locals, so come at an off hour: the morning crowd can give you a headache.

Kate Mantilini, 9101 Wilshire Blvd, Beverly Hills ☎310/278-3699. Nicely prepared versions of classic American diner food, served up in one of LA's most stylish interiors. Open late on weekends.

Nate 'n' Al's, 414 N Beverly Drive ☎310/274-0101. The best-known deli in Beverly Hills, popular with movie people and one of the few reasonable places for dining in the vicinity.

Santa Monica and Venice

Bicycle Shop Café, 12217 Wilshire Blvd, Santa Monica ☎310/826-7831. Pseudo-bistro serving light meals and salads; it's also a good place to drink. Don't be deterred by the tired, 1970s-style exterior.

Café 50s, 838 Lincoln Blvd, Venice ☎310/399-1955. No doubts about this place: Ritchie Valens on the jukebox, juicy burgers on the tables. One of several Westside locations.

Café Montana, 1534 Montana Ave, Santa Monica ☎310/829-3990. Good breakfasts, excellent salads, and grilled fish in upmarket Santa Monica.

Gilliland's, 2424 Main St, Santa Monica ☎310/392-3901. Highly eclectic menu of good and hearty foods, from tangy samosas to a thick Irish stew, with plenty of California cuisine, too.

Norm's, 1601 Lincoln Blvd, Santa Monica ☎310/450-0074. One of the last remaining "Googie" diners, this local chain has several other Westside branches and serves $2 breakfasts and similarly cheap lunches.

Rae's Diner, 2901 Pico Blvd, Santa Monica ☎310/828-7937. Smallish 1950s diner behind a turquoise-blue facade. As popular with the late-night crowd as it is with Hollywood filmmakers (the Tarantino-scripted *True Romance*, among numerous others).

The Sidewalk Café, 1401 Ocean Front Walk, Venice ☎310/399-5547. Breakfast on the beach, where you can watch the daily parade of beach people. Live music most evenings.

South and East LA

B 'n' Bar-B-Que, 1958 W Florence Ave, Huntington Park ☎213/671-8190, and 10303 Avalon Blvd, Watts ☎213/757-0221. Slabs of LA's best ribs, smothered in barbecue sauce, served with baked beans and a sweet potato tart.

Johnnie's Broiler, 7447 Firestone Blvd, Downey ☎310/927-3383. Decent American food in a rather bleak corner of LA. On Wed nights, Fifties-car fanatics park outside in their Chevys and Fords and are waited upon by perky, roller-skating teens.

Shabazz Restaurant and Bakery, 3405 W 43rd St, Leimert Park, South Central ☎213/299-8688. Jazz music, photos of luminaries like Malcolm X and Muhammed Ali on the walls, and top-notch chili and bean pie.

The South Bay and LA Harbor

East Coast Bagel Company, 5753 E PCH, Long Beach ☎562/985-0933. In a dreary minimall, but with an excellent,

wide selection of bagels, including California hybrids like the jalapeño-cheddar bagel.

Hof's Hut, 4823 E Second St, Long Beach ☎562/439-4775. One bite of the *Hut's* juicy Hofburger and you know you've found the real deal. One of a chain of several *Hof's* restaurants in the area.

The Local Yolk, 3414 Highland Ave, Manhattan Beach ☎310/546-4407. As the name suggests, everything done with eggs, plus muffins and pancakes.

Ocean View Café, 229 13th St, Manhattan Beach ☎310/545-6770. Enjoyably light breakfasts and soup and baguettes for around $4, all in a pleasant hillside setting on a quiet pedestrian path overlooking the Pacific Ocean, with outside seating for sea-watching.

Pier Bakery, 100-M Fisherman's Wharf, Redondo Beach ☎310/376-9582. A small but satisfying menu featuring the likes of jalapeño cheese bread and cinnamon rolls. Probably the best food around in this colorless tourist zone.

Russell's, 5656 E Second St, Long Beach ☎562/434-0226. Worth a trip to sample the great burgers and fresh pies. Also at 4306 Atlantic Ave in central Long Beach ☎310/427-6869.

Tony's Famous French Dip Sandwiches, 701 Long Beach Blvd, Long Beach ☎562/435-6238. The name says it all, but alongside the delightful and affordable french dips is a beckoning array of soups and salads and other budget foods.

The San Gabriel and San Fernando valleys

Dr Hogly-Wogly's Tyler Texas Bar-B-Q, 8136 Sepulveda Blvd, Van Nuys ☎818/780-6701. Long lines for some of the best chicken, sausages, ribs, and beans anywhere in LA, despite the depressing surroundings in the middle of industrial nowhere.

Fair Oaks Pharmacy and Soda Fountain, 1526 Mission St, South Pasadena ☎626/799-1414. A run-of-the-mill cor-

Restaurants and Cafés

Restaurants and Cafés

ner store transformed into a fabulous old-fashioned soda fountain, complete with authentic and replica antiques and a full assortment of old-fashioned, sugary drinks, from lime rickeys to egg creams.

Goldstein's Bagel Bakery, 86 W Colorado Blvd, Pasadena ☎626/792-2435. If money's tight, feast here on day-old 15¢ bagels; otherwise enjoy fresh pastries, coffees, and teas. Two other area locations in La Cañada Flintridge and Arcadia.

The Hat, 491 N Lake Ave, San Gabriel ☎626/449-1844. Very popular roadside stand selling good burgers and French-dip sandwiches at this and four other nearby locations.

Hidden Springs Café, 23255 Angeles Forest Hwy, Angeles National Forest ☎818/792-9663. The only restaurant on the Angeles Forest Highway serves filling portions of hearty American food in open stone rooms with real fires and rustic decor. Eclectic clientele, too – Hell's Angels, fly-fishers, gold-miners, and a few wide-eyed tourists.

Pie 'n' Burger, 913 E California Blvd, Pasadena ☎626/795-1123. Classic coffee shop near Cal Tech, offering famously good burgers and excellent fresh pies.

Portos Bakery, 315 Brand Blvd, Glendale ☎818/956-5996. Popular and cheap café serving flaky Cuban pastries, cheesecakes soaked in rum, along with more standard muffins, Danishes, croissants, and tortes, as well as tasty cappuccino.

Rose Tree Cottage, 824 E California Blvd, Pasadena ☎626/793-3337. Cream or high tea in a country home setting so thoroughly English that it's the West Coast headquarters of the British Tourist Board. Reservations are essential.

Orange County

Angelo's, 511 S State College Blvd, Anaheim ☎714/533-1401. Straight out of *Happy Days*, a drive-in complete with roller-skating car-hops, neon signs, vintage cars, and, incidentally, good burgers. Open until 2am on weekends.

Belisle's, 12001 Harbor Blvd, Garden Grove ☎714/750-6560. Open late for filling sandwiches, meat pies, and various baked goods.

Café Zinc, 350 Ocean Ave, Laguna Beach ☎714/494-6302. One of Laguna's best and most popular breakfast counters, which also offers simple soup-and-salad lunches and other light fare, good during a day at the beach.

C'est Si Bon, 149 Riverside Ave off PCH, Newport Beach ☎714/645-0447. Small seaside café serving croissants, baguettes, and French cheese, pâté, and coffee, among other inexpensive treats.

The Harbor House, 34157 PCH, Dana Point ☎714/496-9270. Part of a small chain of 24-hr diners on the south end of Orange County, with adequate diner food.

Knott's Berry Farm, 8039 Beach Blvd, Buena Park ☎714/827-1776. People flocked here for the top-notch fried chicken dinners long before Disneyland was around, and they still do. Look out for the steep entry fee to the theme park, though – required for admittance.

Mimi's Café, 18342 Imperial Hwy, Yorba Linda ☎714/996-3650. Huge servings of American food, low prices, and a relaxing atmosphere just down the street from the Nixon Library.

Ruby's, Balboa Pier, Newport Beach ☎714/675-RUBY. The first and one of the finest of the retro-Streamline 1940s diners that have popped up all over LA – and in a great location, at the end of Newport's pier.

Restaurants

The listings below follow (though not slavishly) the chapter divisions of our guide. **Restaurants** are grouped first by neighborhood, then by cuisine. There are also a number of specialty groupings (late night, expense account, etc) that appear in boxes; for a brief overview of those, see opposite.

Downtown

AMERICAN, CALIFORNIAN AND CAJUN

Bernard's, 506 S Grand Ave in the *Biltmore Hotel* ☎ 213/612-1580. Beautifully preserved, lushly decorated dining room in this landmark hotel, serving contemporary versions of classic American meat and fish dishes. *Very expensive.*

Checkers Restaurant, 535 S Grand Ave in the *Wyndham Checkers Hotel* ☎ 213/624-0000. One of the most elegant Downtown restaurants, serving top-rated California cuisine all day; rack of lamb and sashimi are among the finer offerings. *Very expensive.*

Engine Co No. 28, 644 S Figueroa St ☎ 213/624-6996. All-American grilled steaks and seafood, served in a renovated 1912 fire station. Great fries and an excellent wine list. *Expensive.*

New Moon, 102 W Ninth St ☎ 213/624-0186. Straightforward American cooking – salads, soups, steaks, and the like – good mainly for its reasonable prices. *Inexpensive.*

Nicola, 601 S Figueroa St ☎ 213/485-0927. Tasty, experimental culinary hybrids, notably the noodle-and-rice dishes with tuna or duck. On the lower

level of the Sanwa Bank building. *Expensive.*

Pacific Dining Car, 1310 W Sixth St ☎ 213/483-6000. Would-be English supper club housed inside an old railroad carriage. Open 24hr for pricey steaks. Breakfast is better value. *Very expensive.*

CHINESE AND VIETNAMESE

Grand Star Restaurant, 934 Sun Mun Way ☎ 213/626-2285. While the traditional soups and meat dishes here are flavorful and authentic, the real appeal is video karaoke – 8pm–1am on Sun, Tues, and Wed. *Moderate.*

Mandarin Deli, 727 N Broadway ☎ 213/623-6054. Savory and cheap noodles, dumplings, and other hearty staples. *Inexpensive.*

Mon Kee, 679 N Spring St ☎ 213/628-6717. Longstanding favorite for fresh fish and assorted crustaceans, in somewhat grubby surroundings. *Moderate.*

Ocean Seafood, 750 N Hill St ☎ 213/687-3088. Cavernous but often crowded restaurant serving excellent food that's well worth the wait; due to renovation, call first. *Moderate.*

Pho 79, 727 N Broadway ☎ 213/625-7026. Good, cheap Vietnamese fare – all the standard rice dishes and noodle soups are plenty filling. *Inexpensive.*

Yang Chow, 819 N Broadway ☎ 213/625-0811. Delightful Chinese restaurant, where you can't go wrong with the Szechuan beef or any shrimp dish. *Moderate.*

FRENCH

Café Pinot, 700 W Fifth St ☎ 213/239-6500. Next to the LA Public Library, this elegant restaurant offers a mix of California and French cuisines, specializing in grilled chicken and duck dishes, at somewhat less exorbitant prices than you might expect. *Expensive.*

ITALIAN AND PIZZA

California Pizza Kitchen, 330 S Hope St ☎ 213/626-2616. Inventive pizzas; not

Restaurants and Cafés

Restaurants and Cafés

Expense account restaurants

At the following restaurants – good for business dinners or impressing your loved one – you'll definitely need to book ahead and, likely, dress up too. Meals can easily run about $100 per head, including drinks.

Arnie Morton's, 435 N La Cienega Blvd, Beverly Hills ☎310/246-1501; p.251.

Aubergine, 508 29th St, Newport Beach ☎714/723-4150; p.260.

Bernard's, 506 S Grand Ave in the *Biltmore Hotel* ☎213/612-1580; p.243.

Checkers Restaurant, 535 S Grand Ave in the *Wyndham Checkers Hotel* ☎213/624-0000; p.243.

Chinois on Main, 2709 Main St, Santa Monica ☎310/392-9025; p.256.

Citrus, 6703 Melrose Ave ☎213/857-0034; p.245.

Diaghilev, 1020 N San Vicente Blvd, West Hollywood ☎310/854-1111; p.251.

Drago, 2628 Wilshire Blvd, Santa Monica ☎310/828-1585; p.256.

Fenix, 8358 Sunset Blvd, West Hollywood ☎213/848-6677; p.249.

Granita, 23725 W Malibu Rd, Malibu ☎310/456-0488; p.255.

Le Chardonnay, 8284 Melrose Ave, West Hollywood ☎213/655-8880; p.249.

L'Orangerie, 903 N La Cienega Blvd, West Hollywood ☎310/652-9770; p.249.

Maple Drive, 345 N Maple Drive, Beverly Hills ☎310/274-9800; p.251.

Matsuhisa, 129 N La Cienega Blvd, Beverly Hills ☎310/659-9639; p.253.

Michael's, 1147 Third St, Santa Monica ☎310/451-0843; p.256.

Pacific Dining Car, 1310 W Sixth St ☎213/483-6000; p.243.

Patina, 5955 Melrose Ave ☎213/467-1108; p.245.

Spago, 1114 Horn Ave above Sunset Blvd, West Hollywood ☎310/652-4025; p.248.

The Towers, 1555 S Coast Hwy, Laguna Beach ☎714/497-4477; p.260.

Valentino, 3115 W Pico Blvd, Santa Monica ☎310/829-4313; p.257.

---

cheap but worth the extravagance, if you don't mind the crowds. Two branches in West LA and others citywide. *Moderate.*

Cicada, 617 S Olive St ☎213/655-5559. An elegant restaurant in the historic Oviatt Building, that features a range of regional Italian cuisines and light pastas. *Expensive.*

La Bella Cucina, 949 S Figueroa St ☎213/623-0014. Fabulous pizzas and homemade pastas, with the accent on northern and rural Italian cuisine. *Expensive.*

JAPANESE

A Thousand Cranes, 120 S Los Angeles St, Little Tokyo ☎213/253-9255. Located next to the Japanese Garden of the *New Otani Hotel* (see p.221, this is upscale dining at its most refined, with pleasant views of the water and greenery outside and savory, multicourse

servings of Japanese cuisine – notably tempura – in a clean, elegant setting. *Expensive.*

Mitsuru Café, 117 Japanese Village Blvd ☎213/613-1028. On a hot day nothing beats the snow cones at *Mitsuru*, in such exotic flavors as *kintoki* (azuki-bean paste) or *milk kintoki* (sweet custard). On a cold day, try the *imagawayaki* – azuki beans baked in a bun. *Moderate.*

Restaurant Horikawa, 111 S San Pedro St ☎213/680-9355. Upmarket Japanese restaurant, popular with business types, with a sushi bar and open grill. *Expensive.*

Shibucho, 333 S Alameda St, Little Tokyo ☎213/626-1184. Excellent sushi bar in the heart of Little Tokyo. Go with someone who knows what to order, as the waiters don't speak English. Also at 3114 Beverly Blvd ☎213/387-8498. *Moderate.*

SEAFOOD

McCormick and Schmicks, 633 W Fifth St ☎213/629-1929. Upscale seafood joint for business types and known for a great weekend dinner special – call for details. *Expensive.*

Mid-Wilshire

AFRICAN

Nyala, 1076 S Fairfax Ave ☎213/936-5918. One of several Ethiopian favorites along Fairfax, serving staples like *doro wat* and *kitfo* with the delightful *injera* bread. *Moderate.*

Rosalind Ethiopian, 1044 S Fairfax Ave ☎213/936-2486. Spicy goat meat and pepper chicken are among the top exotic treats to enjoy at this modest Ethiopian establishment. *Moderate.*

AMERICAN, CALIFORNIAN AND CAJUN

Atlas, 3760 Wilshire Blvd ☎213/380-8400. One of LA's most stylish interiors, located in the magnificent Wiltern Building. Food is inconsistent, though the chicken and pasta dishes are good, but eclectic musical performances add much to the overall charm. *Moderate.*

Ca' Brea, 346 S La Brea Ave ☎213/938-2863. Hip California cuisine restaurant in newly popular La Brea district. A major draw because of the unbelievable risotto – making the place an increasingly difficult spot to get into. *Expensive.*

Citrus, 6703 Melrose Ave ☎213/857-0034. The trendiest and best of the newer upmarket restaurants, serving California cuisine in an outdoor-style setting indoors, and at garish prices. *Very expensive.*

Georgia, 7250 Melrose Ave ☎213/633-8420. Down-home Southern cooking served in a mahogany dining room for about $25 a plate. Part-owned by a small team of celebrities including Denzel Washington. *Expensive.*

The Gumbo Pot, 6333 W Third St in the Farmer's Market ☎213/933-0358. Delicious and dirt-cheap Cajun cooking

in a busy setting amid a hive of greasy food stalls. Try the *gumbo yaya* of chicken, shrimp, and sausage, along with the fruit-and-potato salad. *Inexpensive.*

Patina, 5955 Melrose Ave ☎213/467-1108. This ultra-chic place delivers exquisite California cuisine, taking duck, chicken, and pheasant, adding exotic spices and herbs, and throwing in the occasional kidney or calf's foot. *Very expensive.*

Sabor, 3221 Pico Blvd ☎310/829-3781. California-cuisine influences on Cajun cooking, with good results, especially the fried chicken, spicy shrimp, and tamales. *Moderate.*

Taylor's, 3361 W Eighth St ☎213/382-8449. Good old-fashioned American steaks and chops in an unlikely setting, with more reasonable prices than similar Westside steakhouses. *Moderate.*

CARIBBEAN

Prado, 244 N Larchmont Blvd ☎213/467-3871. Better than the standard Caribbean offerings in LA, featuring a wealth of tropical fruits and seafood to brighten up the cuisine. A crowded spot in the burgeoning Larchmont Village shopping zone. *Moderate.*

CHINESE AND VIETNAMESE

Genghis Cohen, 740 N Fairfax Ave ☎213/653-0640. Familiar Chinese offerings presented with a touch of Yiddish: food titles are culinary puns, as the restaurant's name might indicate. Standards like Szechuan beef and kung pao chicken are nonetheless quite good, despite the forced humor. *Inexpensive.*

Indochine, 8225 Beverly Blvd ☎213/655-4777. The prototype for pretentious Hollywood dining. The Vietnamese food is tart and colorful, but the chief reason to come here is to watch the sleek clientele strike poses for their movie-industry peers. *Expensive.*

FRENCH

Louis XIV, 606 N La Brea Ave ☎213/934-5102. The prices may be a

Restaurants and Cafés

Restaurants and Cafés

bit lower than at comparable French eateries, but the attitude is just as haughty. Still, the food is tasty and occasionally terrific, especially the steaks and seafood pasta. *Expensive*.

GREEK

Le Petit Greek, 127 N Larchmont Blvd ☎213/464-5160. Sizable servings in quiet Larchmont Village location. Stick to the lamb and fish dishes. *Moderate*.

Sofi, 8030 W Third St ☎213/651-0346. A nice, comfortable place in the vicinity of the Farmers Market, serving classic Greek delights like stuffed grape leaves and moussaka to a loyal crowd. *Moderate*.

INDIAN AND SRI LANKAN

The Clay Pit, 3465 W Sixth St ☎213/382-6300. A great place to eat savory Indian treats like tandoori chicken and naans stuffed with lamb and garlic, with the lunch buffet a popular weekday draw. Additionally, the location – in the Spanish courtyard of the historic Chapman Market – is quietly perfect. Also in Downtown's *Figueroa Hotel*, 939 S Figueroa St ☎213/689-4489. *Moderate*.

East India Grill, 345 N La Brea Ave ☎213/936-8844. Southern Indian cuisine given the California treatment: impressive specialties include spinach curry and curried noodles. *Moderate*.

India's Oven, 7231 Beverly Blvd ☎213/936-1000. Bring your own bottle to this friendly Indian restaurant, with large, delicious portions of old favorites like stuffed naans, vindaloos, and curries. *Moderate*.

ITALIAN AND PIZZA

Angeli Caffé, 7274 Melrose Ave ☎213/936-9086. Old-fashioned ingredients and refreshingly basic pizza styles make this a worthwhile stop. *Moderate*.

Campanile, 624 S La Brea Ave ☎213/938-1447. Rather expensive northern Italian, with good seafood, steak, and rabbit. If you can't afford a full

dinner, just try the dessert or pick up some of the best bread in Los Angeles at the *La Brea Bakery* nearby (see p.309). *Expensive*.

Chianti, 7383 Melrose Ave ☎213/653-8333. Good Italian food, featuring heavy veal and meat entrees and seafood pastas, near the center of the Melrose shopping district. *Expensive*.

JAPANESE

Mishima, 8474 W Third St ☎213/782-0181. *Udon* and *soba* are quickly replacing sushi as the Japanese dish of choice in West LA, and *Mishima* is one of the main reasons. It serves bowls of delicious hot or cold noodles for about what you'd pay at your local burger-chain drive-thru. *Inexpensive*.

KOREAN

Buffet Palace, 3014 Olympic Blvd ☎213/388-9292. Popular restaurant off a busy thoroughfare in the heart of the district. Especially strong on spicy barbecued beef. *Moderate*.

Dong Il Jang, 3455 W Eighth St ☎213/383-5757. Cozy little restaurant where the meat is cooked at your table and the food is consistently good, especially the grilled chicken and beef. *Moderate*.

Woo Lae Oak, 623 S Western Ave, Koreatown ☎213/384-2244. This well-known Korean BBQ is one of the best of its kind in town. Also a more crowded, pricier branch in Beverly Hills, 170 N La Cienega Blvd ☎310/652-4187. *Expensive*.

MEXICAN AND LATIN AMERICAN

Casa Carnitas, 4067 Beverly Blvd ☎213/667-9953. Tasty Mexican food from the Yucatán. The dishes are inspired by Cuban and Caribbean cooking – lots of fine seafood, too. *Inexpensive*.

El Cholo, 1121 S Western Ave ☎213/734-2773. One of LA's first big Mexican restaurants and still one of the best, despite the drunken frat-rats from

USC. Also a branch can be found at 1025 Wilshire Blvd, Santa Monica ☎310/899-1106. *Moderate.*

El Coyote, 7312 Beverly Blvd ☎213/939-2255. Labyrinthine, gloomy restaurant serving heavy, greasy Mexican food, and lots of it; cheap and lethal margaritas are the real draw. *Inexpensive.*

Mario's Peruvian Seafood Restaurant, 5786 Melrose Ave ☎213/466-4181. Authentic Peruvian fare, with the slightest Asian influence. Supremely tender squid, and a hint of soy sauce in some dishes. *Inexpensive.*

MIDDLE EASTERN

Al Amir, 5750 Wilshire Blvd ☎213/931-8740. The Lebanese food is tasty, and you can't help but enjoy the belly dancing at this pricey Miracle Mile restaurant. *Expensive.*

RUSSIAN/EASTERN EUROPEAN

Perestroyka, 5468 Wilshire Blvd ☎213/934-2215. Splendid furnishings and rich, meaty dishes will leave you stuffed and groggy by the evening's end, particularly after a few belts of the restaurant's potent vodka. *Inexpensive.*

THAI

Tommy Tang's, 7313 Melrose Ave ☎213/937-5733. Chic Thai restaurant, home to excellent seafood and noodles, and the incongruous setting for Tuesday night waiters in full drag. *Expensive.*

Vim, 831 S Vermont Ave ☎213/386-2338. With authentic, unadulterated Thai food and low prices, this is one of LA's best options for ethnic food — especially good are the seafood soup and pad thai. *Inexpensive.*

VEGETARIAN AND WHOLEFOOD

Inaka, 131 S La Brea Ave ☎213/936-9353. Located in the newly trendy La Brea district, featuring vegetarian and macrobiotic food with a strong Japanese theme. Live music on weekends. *Moderate.*

Hollywood and West Hollywood

AFRICAN

Dar Maghreb, 7651 Sunset Blvd ☎213/876-7651. The rich, delightful Moroccan cuisine, featuring a range of chicken dishes as well as *b'stilla* — a pastry stuffed with chicken, chickpeas and spices — almost takes second place to the main entertainment at this establishment: belly dancing. *Expensive.*

AMERICAN, CALIFORNIAN AND CAJUN

Café La Boheme, 8400 Santa Monica Blvd, West Hollywood ☎213/848-2360. Yet another quintessentially LA hot spot, this establishment has been variously compared to a film set, theater, and funhouse. Whatever the case, it's pretty good California cuisine, with pan-Asian, continental, and American ingredients dressing up otherwise basic pizza, pasta, chicken, and steak dishes. *Expensive.*

The Cajun Bistro, 8301 Sunset Blvd, West Hollywood ☎213/656-6388. Located in a bleak stretch of the Strip, with satisfying and spicy jambalaya, among other Cajun standards. *Moderate.*

Hollywood Canteen, 1006 N Seward St ☎213/465-0961. No-nonsense fish, steak, and pasta that's tasty enough, though old-fashioned club ambience is the real draw. *Moderate.*

Musso and Frank Grill, 6667 Hollywood Blvd ☎213/467-7788. Since it opened in 1919 anyone who's anyone in Hollywood has been seen in this dark-paneled dining room, though you'll pay plenty for the atmosphere. Standards like chicken pot pie, steak, and seafood are consistently good, but overall, you're better off at the bar (see p.263). *Expensive.*

Off Vine, 6263 Leland Way ☎213/962-1900. A comfortable and spacious bungalow somewhat off the main Hollywood path. Eclectic California cuisine, though the simpler steak and pasta dishes are the best bets. *Expensive.*

Pinot Hollywood's Restaurant and Martini Bar, 1448 Gower St ☎213/461-

Restaurants and Cafés

Restaurants and Cafés

8800. Upmarket American food in a spacious environment, plus 24 types of martinis and Polish potato vodka. *Expensive.*

Sabroso, 2538 Hyperion Ave, Silver Lake ☎213/660-0886. A bit more subtle than most Cajun restaurants, with the highlight being the rich Cajun pasta. *Moderate.*

Spago, 1114 Horn Ave above Sunset Blvd, West Hollywood ☎310/652-4025.

Perhaps LA's most famous restaurant, both for its chef, Wolfgang Puck, the inventor of "designer pizza," and for its star-studded clientele. The trendy pizzas and pastas are tasty enough, though celebrity-watching continues to be the main appeal. The recent expansion to Beverly Hills, 176 N Cañon Drive (☎310/385-0880), has drawn away some of the crowds to more sterile surroundings. Reservations are essential. *Very expensive.*

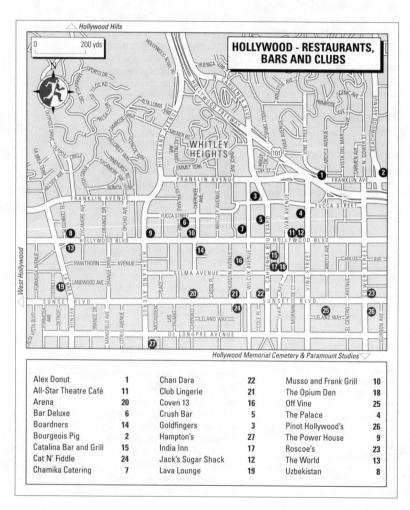

Alex Donut	**1**	Chan Dara	**22**	Musso and Frank Grill	**10**
All-Star Theatre Café	**11**	Club Lingerie	**21**	The Opium Den	**18**
Arena	**20**	Coven 13	**16**	Off Vine	**25**
Bar Deluxe	**6**	Crush Bar	**5**	The Palace	**4**
Boardners	**14**	Goldfingers	**3**	Pinot Hollywood's	**26**
Bourgeois Pig	**2**	Hampton's	**27**	The Power House	**9**
Catalina Bar and Grill	**15**	India Inn	**17**	Roscoe's	**23**
Cat N' Fiddle	**24**	Jack's Sugar Shack	**12**	The World	**13**
Chamika Catering	**7**	Lava Lounge	**19**	Uzbekistan	**8**

CHINESE AND VIETNAMESE

Chin Chin, 8618 Sunset Blvd, West Hollywood ☎310/652-1818. Flashy but not overpriced dim sum café, with lighter fare than comparable restaurants, and open till midnight. One of several Westside branches. *Inexpensive.*

Joss, 9255 Sunset Blvd, West Hollywood ☎310/276-1886. Sitting at the west end of the Sunset Strip, this is the Westside's version of Chinese cuisine: pricey meals with rich, complex flavors and a minimum of excessive color and style – which, of course, makes it all very hip. *Expensive.*

FRENCH

Fenix, 8358 Sunset Blvd, West Hollywood ☎213/848-6677. French cooking on the Sunset Strip, in a rather exclusive establishment popular with culinary trendsetters, in the *Argyle Hotel* (see p.223), *Fenix* offers up a terrific assortment of steaks and seafood prepared with local and exotic ingredients. *Very expensive.*

Le Chardonnay, 8284 Melrose Ave, West Hollywood ☎213/655-8880. The height of French bistro-cooking, an exquisitely decorated homage to turn-of-the-century design, with excellent traditional food – try the foie gras and the roast venison – and a prominent rotisserie as well. *Very expensive.*

L'Orangerie, 903 N La Cienega Blvd, West Hollywood ☎310/652-9770. The closest LA Francophiles can get to Escoffier, though the stylish French food has more than a dash of California cuisine as well. If you haven't got the $150 it takes to sit down, or a fancy enough suit to wear, then enjoy the view from the bar. *Very expensive.*

INDIAN AND SRI LANKAN

Chamika Catering, 1717 N Wilcox Ave ☎213/466-8960. Papadums, *rotis* (garlic and coconut stuffed pancakes), and chicken, beef, or lamb curries, marinated in special Sri Lankan sauces. Wash it all down with a strawberry or mango fruit drink. *Inexpensive.*

India Inn, 1638 N Cahuenga Blvd ☎213/461-3774. Good, basic Indian restaurant in central Hollywood, with a range of deliciously authentic dishes. *Inexpensive.*

ITALIAN AND PIZZA

Caioti, 2100 Laurel Canyon Blvd, Hollywood Hills ☎213/650-2988. Just north of where Hollywood Boulevard fades into the hills, this little pizza place tends toward the experimental topping-wise – duck, curry, cantaloupe, etc. *Moderate.*

Louise's Trattoria, 4500 Los Feliz Blvd ☎213/667-0777. You'll see this restaurant chain all over LA, but this branch is one of the few that isn't swamped by tourists. As with all the *Louise's*, you should stick to the consistently good pizzas and avoid the overcooked noodles. *Moderate.*

Palermo, 1858 N Vermont Ave ☎213/663-1178. As old as Hollywood, and with as many devoted fans, who flock here for the stodgy pizzas and gallons of cheapish red wine. *Moderate.*

JAPANESE

Katsu, 1972 N Hillhurst Ave ☎213/665-1891. Minimalist sushi bar for the cyberpunk brigade. The only splash of color is in the artfully presented bits of fish on your plate. *Expensive.*

MEXICAN AND LATIN AMERICAN

Burrito King, 2109 W Sunset Blvd at Alvarado ☎213/413-9444. Excellent burritos and tasty tostadas from this small stand; open until 2am. *Inexpensive.*

Mexico City, 2121 N Hillhurst Ave ☎213/661-7227. Spinach enchiladas and other Californian versions of Mexican standards served in a quiet corner of Los Feliz. *Moderate.*

Yuca's Hut, 2056 N Hillhurst Ave ☎213/662-1214. Tasty al fresco burritos opposite *Mexico City* and almost as popular with locals *Inexpensive.*

Restaurants and Cafés

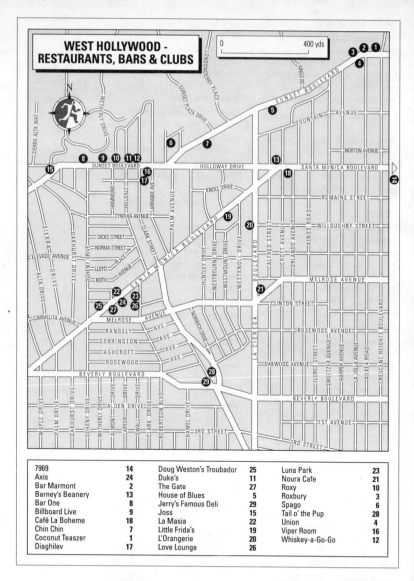

WEST HOLLYWOOD - RESTAURANTS, BARS & CLUBS

7969	14	Doug Weston's Troubador	25	Luna Park	23
Axis	24	Duke's	11	Noura Cafe	21
Bar Marmont	2	The Gate	27	Roxy	10
Barney's Beanery	13	House of Blues	5	Roxbury	3
Bar One	8	Jerry's Famous Deli	29	Spago	6
Billboard Live	9	Joss	15	Tail o' the Pup	28
Café La Boheme	18	La Masia	22	Union	4
Chin Chin	7	Little Frida's	19	Viper Room	16
Coconut Teaszer	1	L'Orangerie	20	Whiskey-a-Go-Go	12
Diaghilev	17	Love Lounge	26		

MIDDLE EASTERN

Noura Cafe, 8479 Melrose Ave, West Hollywood ☎213/651-4581. Moderately priced Middle Eastern specialties. At night the leafy, crowded patio is lit by a central circular sandpit. For beginners, the "taster's delight" plate – hummus, baba ganoush, tabouli, falafel, fried eggplant, zucchini, and stuffed grape leaf – is a good bet. *Moderate*.

Shamshiry, 5229 Hollywood Blvd ☎213/469-8434. The best of

Hollywood's few Iranian restaurants, offering kebabs, pilafs, and exotic sauces. *Moderate*.

Uzbekistan, 7077 Sunset Blvd ☎213/464-3663. Savory, though heavy, servings of mostly lamb-based Uzbekistani food. *Moderate*.

Zankou Chicken, 5065 Sunset Blvd ☎213/665-7845. Easily the top Middle Eastern value in town, with delicious garlicky chicken cooked on a rotisserie, plus all the traditional salads – tabouli, hummus and the like. *Inexpensive*.

RUSSIAN AND EASTERN EUROPEAN

Diaghilev, 1020 N San Vicente Blvd, West Hollywood ☎310/854-1111. Found in the exclusive *Wyndham Bel Age* hotel, an exquisite establishment with classic Russian fare – caviar, Chicken Kiev, borscht, and such – that's quite good, but comes at rather ungodly prices. *Very expensive*.

Hungarian Budapest, 7986 Sunset Blvd ☎213/654-3744. The quite authentic fare here, loaded with meat, cabbage, and paprika, should delight anyone with a taste for Hungarian food. *Inexpensive*.

SPANISH

La Masia, 9077 Santa Monica Blvd, West Hollywood ☎310/273-7066. Dine on a nice selection of tapas, then hit the dance floor and enjoy a spot of salsa and merengue. *Moderate*.

THAI

Chan Dara, 1511 N Cahuenga Blvd ☎213/464-8585. Terrific Thai food, especially the BBQ chicken and Pad Thai, and the locals know it. If you can't get in here, there are other Westside locations at 310 N Larchmont Blvd, Mid-Wilshire ☎213/467-1052, and 11940 W Pico Blvd, West LA ☎310/479-4461. *Moderate*.

Jitlada, 5233 Sunset Blvd ☎213/667-9809. In a dreary minimall, but there's little dreary about the spicy chicken and seafood curries and such. Affordable prices, too. *Moderate*.

VEGETARIAN AND WHOLEFOOD

The Bodhi Garden Restaurant, 1498 Sunset Blvd ☎213/250-9023. Vegetarian Vietnamese food, including fancy dishes like sweet and sour walnuts, bean curd, and black moss. The crowd is eclectic, and the decor features chubby Buddhas resting alongside offerings of fruit. Closed Tues. *Moderate*.

Beverly Hills and West LA

AFRICAN

Koutoubia, 2116 Westwood Blvd, West LA ☎310/475-0729. Good Moroccan food in a comfortable environment, with savory lamb, couscous, and seafood dishes. *Expensive*.

AMERICAN, CALIFORNIAN AND CAJUN

Arnie Morton's, 435 N La Cienega Blvd, Beverly Hills ☎310/246-1501. An unreconstructed 1950s-style homage to the old days of American cuisine, providing hefty steaks (go for the traditional porterhouse) and scrumptious sides of creamed spinach and baked potatoes to the grizzled veterans of Tinseltown. *Very expensive*.

The Cheesecake Factory, 364 N Beverly Drive, Beverly Hills ☎310/278-7270. Beverly Hills' most heavily trafficked restaurant, with adequate salads and entrees but exceptional desserts, notably cheesecakes in a wide variety of styles, including chocolate-chip, peanut butter, and key lime. Come at an off hour if you want a table. *Moderate*.

The Daily Grill, 11677 San Vicente Blvd, Brentwood ☎310/442-0044. Beef, chicken, and fish are the main staples of this Westside chain, which provides pretty good fare for affordable prices. Not glamorous, but one of the few affordable restaurants around this upscale zone. *Moderate*.

Maple Drive, 345 N Maple Drive, Beverly Hills ☎310/274-9800. Fine food from a large culinary palette, from foie gras to meatloaf. If you're lucky, you might spot local celebs sneaking in for an oyster or two. *Very expensive*.

Restaurants
and Cafés

Restaurants and Cafés

Monty's Steakhouse, 1100 Glendon Ave, Westwood ☎310/208-8787. An old-time favorite near UCLA, featuring thick servings of juicy meat and hearty potatoes to a loyal, graying crowd. *Expensive*.

CARIBBEAN

Bamboo, 10835 Venice Blvd, West LA ☎310/287-0668. In a section of West LA full of enticing ethnic restaurants, *Bamboo* stands out for its chicken dishes and spicy Caribbean flavors, as well as its quite reasonable prices. *Moderate*.

Versailles, 10319 Venice Blvd, West LA ☎310/558-3168. Busy and noisy Cuban restaurant with a wealth of hearty fare, including excellent fried plantains, paella, and black beans and rice. Another nearby at 1415 S La Cienega Blvd ☎310/289-0392. *Inexpensive*.

CHINESE AND VIETNAMESE

Chung King, 11538 W Pico Blvd, West LA ☎310/477-4917. The best neighborhood Chinese restaurant in LA, serving spicy Szechuan food: don't miss out on the *bum-bum* chicken and other house specialties. *Moderate*.

INDIAN AND SRI LANKAN

Bombay Café, 12113 Santa Monica Blvd, West LA ☎310/820-2070. Despite its location on the second story of a minimall, this is one of LA's finest

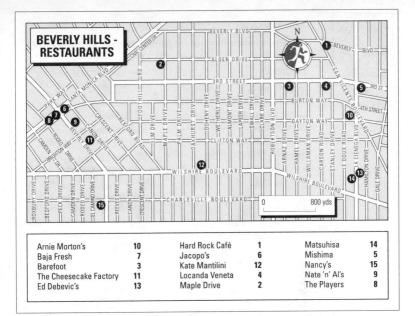

BEVERLY HILLS - RESTAURANTS

Arnie Morton's	10	Hard Rock Café	1	Matsuhisa	14
Baja Fresh	7	Jacopo's	6	Mishima	5
Barefoot	3	Kate Mantilini	12	Nancy's	15
The Cheesecake Factory	11	Locanda Veneta	4	Nate 'n' Al's	9
Ed Debevic's	13	Maple Drive	2	The Players	8

Indian restaurants, with a terrific array of traditional and nouveau offerings and a helpful, friendly staff. *Moderate.*

ITALIAN

Barefoot, 8722 W Third St, Beverly Hills ☎310/276-6223. Good pastas, pizzas, and seafood between Beverly Hills and the Beverly Center. Considering the location, very affordable prices. *Moderate.*

Jacopo's, 490 N Beverly Drive, Beverly Hills ☎310/858-6446. Dumpy little brickhouse surprisingly has some of LA's very best pizzas, served piping hot for fairly cheap prices. *Inexpensive.*

Locanda Veneta, 8638 W Third St, Beverly Hills ☎310/274-1893. This increasingly popular spot near the Beverly Center serves tasty Italian fare, notably the ravioli and risotto. *Expensive.*

Mario's, 1001 Broxton Ave, Westwood ☎310/208-7077. Perhaps the finest pizza in West LA, with a range of scrumptious toppings. Serves a wide range of pasta dishes, too. Also at 1444

Third Street Promenade, Santa Monica ☎310/576-7799. *Moderate.*

JAPANESE

Matsuhisa, 129 N La Cienega Blvd, Beverly Hills ☎310/659-9639. The *nec plus ultra* of Japanese restaurants in Southern California, brought to you by wünderkind chef Nobu Matsuhisa. Along with being a celebrity hangout, it also offers amazingly good, fabulously expensive food with a unique touch of Peruvian style. Most come for the sushi, but everything's worth trying. *Very expensive.*

The Sushi House, 12013 Pico Blvd, West LA ☎310/479-1507. Reggae and sushi coalesce in a hole in the wall bar with only limited seating. Try the "Superman," a rainbow-colored roll of salmon, yellowtail, whitefish, and avocado. *Moderate.*

MEXICAN AND LATIN AMERICAN

Baja Fresh, 475 N Beverly Drive, Beverly Hills ☎310/858-6690. One of the cheapest meals you're likely to have in

Restaurants and Cafés

Late-night eats

The following restaurants serve all or a portion of their menus after 11pm at least twice a week.

DOWNTOWN

Original Pantry, 877 S Figueroa St ☎213/972-9279; p.239.

Pacific Dining Car, 1310 W Sixth St ☎213/483-6000; p.243.

Shibucho, 333 S Alameda St, Little Tokyo ☎213/626-1184; p.244.

MID-WILSHIRE

Atlas, 3760 Wilshire Blvd ☎213/380-8400; p.245.

Canter's Deli, 419 N Fairfax Ave ☎213/651-2030; p.239.

Genghis Cohen, 740 N Fairfax Ave ☎213/653-0640; p.245.

Hard Rock Café, in the *Beverly Center*, Beverly Blvd at San Vicente Blvd ☎310/276-7605; p.239.

Louis XIV, 606 N La Brea Ave ☎213/934-5102; p.245.

Pink's, 711 N La Brea Ave ☎213/931-4223; p.239.

Swingers, *Beverly Laurel Motor Lodge*, 8018 Beverly Blvd at Laurel Ave ☎213/651-2441; p.239.

Tommy Tang's, 7313 Melrose Ave ☎213/937-5733; p.247.

HOLLYWOOD

Barney's Beanery, 8447 Santa Monica Blvd, West Hollywood ☎213/654-2287; p.240.

Burrito King, 2109 W Sunset Blvd at Alvarado ☎213/413-9444; p.249.

Café La Boheme, 8400 Santa Monica Blvd, West Hollywood ☎213/848-2360; p.247.

Caioti, 2100 Laurel Canyon Blvd, Hollywood Hills ☎213/650-2988; p.249.

Chan Dara, 1511 N Cahuenga Blvd ☎213/464-8585; p.251.

Fenix, 8358 Sunset Blvd, West Hollywood ☎213/848-6677; p.249.

Roscoe's, 1514 N Gower St ☎213/466-7453; p.240.

Spago, 1114 Horn Ave above Sunset Blvd, West Hollywood ☎310/652-4025; p.248.

Tommy's, 2575 W Beverly Blvd, Silver Lake ☎213/389-9060; p.240.

Beverly Hills, and a good one at that, with Mexican standards like tacos and burritos. Very popular, however, and your best bet may be to visit any of the chain's other area locations, either 2210 Sawtelle Blvd, West LA ☎310/575-3013; or 10916 Lindbrook Drive, Westwood ☎310/208-3317. *Inexpensive.*

El Mexicano Deli & Restaurant, 1601 Sawtelle Blvd, West LA ☎310/473-8056. Cozy combo deli and restaurant. The deli section is like an old-fashioned general store, selling fruit, vegetables, and canned products from south of the border. *Inexpensive.*

La Salsa, 11075 W Pico Blvd at Sepulveda, West LA ☎310/479-0919. A pilgrimage spot for Spike Jones fans (he immortalized the road junction in his hit, *Pico and Sepulveda*), and for lovers of soft tacos and burritos. *Inexpensive.*

MIDDLE EASTERN

Falafel King, 1059 Broxton Ave, Westwood ☎310/208-4444. Subtlety and authenticity may not be the house specialties, but falafel certainly is, and you can get a lot of it for only a few bucks. *Inexpensive.*

RUSSIAN/EASTERN EUROPEAN

The Players, 9513 Little Santa Monica Blvd, Beverly Hills ☎310/278-6669. Fine salads and hearty goulash top the menu at this traditional, charming Hungarian restaurant. *Expensive.*

BEVERLY HILLS AND WEST LA

The Apple Pan, 10801 W Pico Blvd, West LA ☎310/475-3585; p.240

Barefoot, 8722 W Third St, Beverly Hills ☎310/276-6223; p.253.

Cava, 8384 W Third St, West LA ☎213/658-8898; p.255.

The Daily Grill, 11677 San Vicente Blvd, Brentwood ☎310/442-0044; p.251.

Falafel King, 1059 Broxton Ave, Westwood ☎310/208-4444; p.254.

Jerry's Famous Deli, 8701 Beverly Blvd, Beverly Hills ☎310/289-1811; p.240.

Kate Mantilini, 9101 Wilshire Blvd, Beverly Hills ☎310/278-3699; p.240.

Locanda Veneta 8638 W Third St, Beverly Hills ☎310/274-1893; p.253.

SANTA MONICA, VENICE AND MALIBU

Café Athens, 1000 Wilshire Blvd, Santa Monica ☎310/395-1000; p.256.

Café 50s, 838 Lincoln Blvd, Venice ☎310/399-1955; p.240.

Chaya, 110 Navy St, Venice ☎310/396-1179; p.257.

Crocodile Café, 101 Santa Monica Blvd, Santa Monica ☎310/394-4783; p.255.

Gladstone's 4 Fish, 17300 PCH, Pacific Palisades ☎310/454-3474; p.257.

Granita, 23725 W Malibu Rd, Malibu ☎310/456-0488; p.255.

Hal's, 1349 Abbot Kinney Blvd, Venice ☎310/396-3105; p.256.

SOUTH BAY AND LA HARBOR

Alegria, 115 Pine Ave, Long Beach ☎562/436-3388; p.259.

Cha Cha Cha, 762 Pacific Ave, Long Beach ☎310/436-3900; p.258.

Russell's, 5656 E Second St, Long Beach ☎562/434-0226; p.241.

ORANGE COUNTY

Belisle's, 12001 Harbor Blvd, Garden Grove ☎714/750-6560; p.242.

The Harbor House, 34157 PCH, Dana Point ☎714/496-9270; p.242.

Restaurants and Cafés

SPANISH

Cava, 8384 W Third St, West LA ☎213/658-8898. Latin and Iberian dishes appear on the menu, but the main attraction is tasty tapas accompanied by shots of primo sherry. The sausage *paella* and roasted potatoes are a good start. *Moderate.*

Santa Monica, Venice and Malibu

AMERICAN, CALIFORNIAN AND CAJUN

17th Street Café, 1610 Montana Ave, Santa Monica ☎310/453-2771. Seafood, pasta, and burgers at affordable prices. Not flashy, considering the upscale shopping zone around it, but

consistently good. Also serves breakfast. *Moderate.*

Crocodile Café, 101 Santa Monica Blvd, Santa Monica ☎310/394-4783. Chicken, calzones, and pizzas are all good at this local chain. One of the best budget choices when you're visiting the nearby Third Street Promenade. *Inexpensive.*

Granita, 23725 W Malibu Rd, Malibu ☎310/456-0488. Another of *über*-chef Wolfgang Puck's creations, oceanside *Granita* is a blend of Cal-cuisine, Italian, and various Mediterranean influences. The food is appealing – seafood stew, lobster, salmon, and ravioli all rank high – though most come to spot Hollywood types. *Very expensive.*

Restaurants and Cafés

Hal's, 1349 Abbot Kinney Blvd, Venice ☎310/396-3105. Relaxing restaurant along a hip shopping zone in Venice, with a range of well-done American standards, including marinated steaks and salmon dishes. *Expensive.*

Joe's, 1023 Abbot Kinney Blvd, Venice ☎310/399-5811. One of the less heralded of LA's better eateries, offering appealing American dishes using staples like grilled chicken, pork, and salmon. *Expensive.*

LA Farm, 3000 W Olympic Blvd, Santa Monica ☎310/829-0600. Acceptably tasty California cuisine, with an accent on seafood, though somewhat overpriced. The main draw is not the food, however, but celebrity-watching: here the stars dine in peace, away from the flashier confines of places like *Spago*. *Expensive.*

Michael's, 1147 Third St, Santa Monica ☎310/451-0843. California cuisine served amid modern art. This venerable establishment always attracts the crowds for its rather simple steaks, pastas, and fowl – reservations are essential. *Very expensive.*

CARIBBEAN

The Jamaican Café, 424 Wilshire Blvd, Santa Monica ☎310/587-2626. Spicy ethnic food in an unlikely spot near the Third Street Promenade. Careful not to go overboard in demanding heat – the jerk chicken is spicy enough as it is. *Moderate.*

Mobay, 1031 Abbot Kinney Blvd, Venice ☎310/452-7472. Another establishment with a sharp bite, with jerk chicken and tangy sauces galore. *Moderate.*

CHINESE AND VIETNAMESE

Chinois on Main, 2709 Main St, Santa Monica ☎310/392-9025. Wolfgang Puck, the man who created designer pizza at *Spago* (see p.248) afterward turned his sights across the Pacific to China and opened this enduringly popular restaurant, a mix of nouvelle French and Chinese cuisines designed to go

with the green-and-black decor. Quite pricey, but worth it for a splurge. *Very expensive.*

FRENCH

Le Petit Moulin, 714 Montana Ave, Santa Monica ☎310/395-6619. An old favorite not far from the coastal end of the chic Montana shopping strip, providing surprisingly affordable, provincial French favorites in a comfortable setting. *Moderate.*

GREEK

Café Athens, 1000 Wilshire Blvd, Santa Monica ☎310/395-1000. The spectacle is as important as the food here, as singing and dancing waiters accompany the sizable plates of rich, familiar Greek fare like pitas, tabouli, lamb, and stuffed grape leaves. *Moderate.*

INDIAN AND SRI LANKAN

Nawab, 1621 Wilshire Blvd, Santa Monica ☎310/829-1106. Few surprises on the menu, but pleasing Indian standards like chicken vindaloo do the trick. *Moderate.*

ITALIAN AND PIZZA

Abbot's Pizza Company, 1407 Abbot Kinney Blvd, Venice ☎310/396-7334. Owned by former New Yorkers, this home of bagel crust pizzas tops them with your choice of tangy-sweet citrus sauce or shiitake and wild mushroom sauce. *Inexpensive.*

Boston Wildflour Pizza, 2807 Main St, Santa Monica ☎310/392-3300. Thin, cheesy slices starting at $2, in a yellow shack on the popular Main Street shopping zone. *Inexpensive.*

Drago, 2628 Wilshire Blvd, Santa Monica ☎310/828-1585. The latest of LA's superchic Italian eateries, offering various meats and pastas in an appropriately pretentious setting. *Very expensive.*

Giovanni's Salerno Beach Restaurant, 193 Culver Blvd, Playa Del Rey ☎310/821-0018. The heavy southern Italian food takes second place to the decor: this 30-plus-year-old eatery is a tumult of Christmas decorations, flashy lights, inflatable toys, and various other curiosities – a veritable treasure trove of every sort of kitsch imaginable. *Moderate.*

Wolfgang Puck Express, 1315 Third Street Promenade, Santa Monica ☎310/576-4770. On the second floor of a chain-oriented food mall, but the cheap pizzas, Chinois chicken, and Caesar salads are justly famous. *Moderate.*

Valentino, 3115 W Pico Blvd, Santa Monica ☎310/829-4313. The undisputed heavyweight of Italian restaurants in the region, or anywhere in the US for that matter. Typically, the finest entrees can't be found on the menu and are instead known to a select clique of regular diners. In any case, the listed specials –especially those with veal, duck, and venison – will suit you quite nicely, although your pocketbook won't be quite so lucky. *Very expensive.*

JAPANESE

Chaya, 110 Navy St, Venice ☎310/396-1179. Elegant mix of Japanese and Mediterranean foods, with a suitably snazzy clientele. Also at 8741 Alder Drive, Beverly Hills ☎310/859-8833. *Expensive.*

Lighthouse Buffet, 201 Arizona Ave, Santa Monica ☎310/451-2076. All-you-can-eat sushi. Indulge to your heart's content for under $10 at lunchtime or $18 in the evening. *Inexpensive.*

KOREAN

Monsoon Café, 1212 Third St, Santa Monica ☎310/576-9996. Located on the popular Third Street Promenade. Offers a mix of Pacific Rim cuisines at reasonable prices. Expect anything from sushi to Szechuan to Korean BBQ beef. *Moderate.*

MEXICAN AND LATIN AMERICAN

The Gaucho Grill, 1251 Third St, Santa Monica ☎310/394-4966. Argentine-styled cuisine at affordable prices in this citywide chain, located here along the Third Street Promenade. Known for its garlicky beef and chicken dishes. *Inexpensive.*

La Cabana, 738 Rose Ave, Venice ☎310/392-7973. Corn tortillas as thick as pancakes, and good stuffed quesadillas, at fairly affordable prices. Busy on weekends. *Moderate.*

Mariasol, 401 Santa Monica Pier, Santa Monica ☎310/917-5050. *Cervezas* with a view, hidden away at the end of the pier. On weekend afternoons, the small rooftop deck affords a sweeping panorama from Malibu to Venice. *Moderate.*

RUSSIAN AND EASTERN EUROPEAN

Warszawa, 1414 Lincoln Blvd, Santa Monica ☎310/393-8831. Pleasant establishment with fine Polish cuisine. Don't miss the savory potato pancakes, pierogi, and borscht. *Moderate.*

SEAFOOD

Casablanca, 220 Lincoln Blvd, Venice ☎310/392-5751. *Noir* atmosphere is as important as the food at this combination seafood-and-Mexican restaurant on the edge of Santa Monica. The food is decent, but the margaritas bring in the crowds. *Moderate.*

Geoffrey's, 27400 PCH, Malibu ☎310/457-1519. One of Malibu's most swank locations for seafood-eating and sunset-watching. The predictable menu is secondary to watching the Tinseltown luminaries drop in. *Expensive.*

Gladstone's 4 Fish, 17300 PCH, Pacific Palisades ☎310/454-3474. Near the junction of Sunset Boulevard, this restaurant is known more for its excellent beachfront location than for its seafood, most of which is heavily fried. *Expensive.*

Killer Shrimp, 523 Washington St, Marina del Rey ☎310/578-2293. Big, juicy piles of spicy shrimp are the central, perhaps the only, attraction at this chain of seafood eateries throughout LA. Stuff yourself with mounds of crustaceans for not more than a few bucks. *Inexpensive.*

Restaurants and Cafés

Restaurants and Cafés

Maryland Crab House, 2424 Pico Blvd, Santa Monica ☎310/450-5555. Not surprisingly, crabs of various kinds are the main draw here, and you're encouraged to eat them by the dozen, with your hands. *Moderate.*

Neptune's Net, 42505 PCH, Santa Monica ☎310/457-3095. It's worth a trip to the far reaches of LA County's northwestern border to gorge on clams, shrimp, oysters, and the like, all presented on grimy picnic tables in an otherwise pleasant setting. *Inexpensive.*

THAI

Flower of Siam, 2553 Lincoln Blvd, Venice ☎310/827-0050. Delightful and rich Thai food, chicken satay and noodles especially, often to set your tastebuds on fire. *Moderate.*

Thai Dishes, 1910 Wilshire Blvd, Santa Monica ☎310/828-5634. A citywide chain that provides good, elemental Thai meals for those unfamiliar with the spicier, more extreme versions of the cuisine. *Inexpensive.*

VEGETARIAN AND WHOLEFOOD

Figtree's Café, 429 Ocean Front Walk, Venice ☎310/392-4937. Tasty veggie food and grilled fresh fish on a sunny patio just off the Venice Boardwalk. *Inexpensive.*

Inn of the Seventh Ray, 128 Old Topanga Rd, Topanga Canyon ☎310/455-1311. The ultimate New Age restaurant, serving vegetarian and other wholefood meals in a relatively secluded environment. *Expensive.*

Shambala Café, 607 Colorado Ave, Santa Monica ☎310/395-2160. Apart from organic chicken, the menu is meat-free, with pasta, tofu, eggplant, and some interesting seaweed dishes. *Moderate.*

South and East LA

AMERICAN, CALIFORNIAN AND CAJUN

Harold and Belle's, 2920 Jefferson Blvd, South Central ☎213/735-9023. One of the best and most authentic of the several Cajun-cuisine restaurants in town, with heaping portions of crayfish, catfish, and shrimp, alongside standards like corn-on-the-cob. *Moderate.*

MEXICAN AND LATIN AMERICAN

Ciro's Mexican Food, 705 N Everery Ave, East LA ☎213/269-5104. A split-level cave of a dining room, serving enormous platters of shrimp and mole specials. The flautas are also top-notch, and every meal comes with guacamole. *Moderate.*

King Taco Warehouse, 4504 E Third St, East LA ☎213/264-4067 or 4661. More like a minimall than a restaurant, with every kind of taco imaginable, along with other assorted Mexican treats. *Inexpensive.*

Luminarias, 3500 Ramona Blvd, Monterey Park ☎213/268-4177. Slightly sanitized and with some unappealing views: two freeways and a women's prison. However, the Latin American food is surprisingly good for an area best known for its Chinese cuisine. *Moderate.*

The South Bay and LA Harbor

CARIBBEAN

Cha Cha Cha, 762 Pacific Ave, Long Beach ☎310/436-3900. Paella, black pepper shrimp, and jerk chicken are all highly recommended here, one of Long Beach's better restaurants. Also at 656 N Virgil Ave in Hollywood ☎213/664-7723. *Moderate.*

GREEK

Santorini's, 2529 PCH, Torrance ☎310/534-8898. As good as Greek food gets in the South Bay. Retsina, *tzatziki*, and good fresh bread, in a faceless minimall location. *Moderate.*

ITALIAN AND PIZZA

Mangiamo, 128 Manhattan Beach Blvd, Manhattan Beach ☎310/318-3434. Fairly pricey but worth it for the northern Italian-style seafood, served in a beachside locale. *Expensive.*

MEXICAN AND LATIN AMERICAN

By Brazil, 1615 Cabrillo Ave, Torrance ☎310/787-7520. Hearty Brazilian fare, mostly grilled chicken and beef dishes. *Moderate.*

El Pollo Inka, 1100 PCH, Hermosa Beach ☎310/372-1433. Peruvian-style chicken is the specialty here, and it's quite good, especially considering the low prices. One in a chain of mostly South Bay restaurants, except for a branch at 11701 Wilshire Blvd, West LA ☎310/571-3334. *Inexpensive.*

Pancho's, 3615 Highland Ave, Manhattan Beach ☎310/545-6670. Big portions, comparatively cheap for the area and one of the few decent Mexican establishments down this way. *Moderate.*

SPANISH

Alegria Café & Tapas Bar, 115 Pine Ave, Long Beach ☎562/436-3388. Tapas, gazpacho, and a variety of *platos principales* served with sangria on the patio, and to the beat of live flamenco at weekends. Good location in downtown Long Beach near the harbor. *Expensive.*

VEGETARIAN AND WHOLEFOOD

The Spot, 110 Second St, Hermosa Beach ☎310/376-2355. A staggering array of vegetarian dishes, based on Mexican and other international cuisines and free of refined sugar or any animal products. Purified water, too. *Inexpensive.*

The San Gabriel and San Fernando valleys

CHINESE AND VIETNAMESE

Sea Star, 2000 W Main St, Alhambra ☎818/282-8833. Dim sum at its best: pork *baos*, potstickers and dumplings, and delicious sweets. *Moderate.*

ITALIAN AND PIZZA

La Scala Presto, 3821 Riverside Drive, Burbank ☎818/846-6800. Stylish and tasty antipasti, pizza, and fresh pasta. A more upscale location in Brentwood,

11740 San Vicente Blvd ☎310/826-6100. *Moderate.*

Market City Caffé, 33 S Fair Oaks Ave, Pasadena ☎818/568-0203. Southern Italian cuisine featuring fine pizzas and seafood. Other area locations in the northern valleys. *Moderate.*

JAPANESE

Genmai-Sushi, 4454 Van Nuys Blvd, San Fernando Valley ☎818/986-7060. Genmai is Japanese for brown rice. Alongside the eponymous staple, you can get soft shell crabs in ponzu sauce, regular sushi and seasonal macrobiotic dishes. *Moderate.*

Shiro, 1505 Mission St, South Pasadena ☎626/799-4774. One of LA's few top-notch restaurants in South Pasadena, if not the only one. Seafood – particularly the grilled catfish and smoked salmon – is best here, prepared in an assortment of rich, tangy flavors. Not quite as costly as you might think. *Expensive.*

MEXICAN AND LATIN AMERICAN

Don Cuco's, 3911 Riverside Drive, Burbank ☎818/842-1123. Good local place with familiar Mexican standards and a great Sunday brunch. *Inexpensive.*

El Tepayac, 800 S Palm, Alhambra ☎626/281-3366. Huge, legendary burritos and very hot salsa – be prepared to wait in line. *Inexpensive.*

Merida, 20 E Colorado Blvd, Pasadena ☎626/792-7371. Unusual Mexican restaurant, featuring dishes from the Yucatán. Try the spicy pork wrapped and steamed in banana leaves. *Inexpensive.*

Señor Fish, 4803 Eagle Rock Blvd, Eagle Rock ☎818/257-7167. The best fish tacos this side of Rosarita, and char-broiled halibut for under $10, in a converted house with patio. *Inexpensive*

Wolfe Burger, 46 N Lake St, Pasadena ☎626/792-7292. Rightly praised for its chili, tamales, and burgers. Breakfast, too, with *huevos rancheros*. *Inexpensive.*

Restaurants
and Cafés

Restaurants and Cafés

THAI

Saladang, 363 S Fair Oaks Ave, Pasadena ☎626/793-8123. Pad Thai and Saladang spicy noodles that would pass muster anywhere, but particularly surprising in Pasadena. *Moderate.*

Orange County

AMERICAN, CALIFORNIAN AND CAJUN

Aubergine, 508 29th St, Newport Beach ☎714/723-4150. California cuisine versions of quail, pâté, and other French delights, served with a somewhat surprising lack of attitude. *Very expensive.*

Bistro 201, 3333 PCH, Newport Beach ☎714/631-0111. The salmon and lamb are among the better nouveau American cuisine offerings at this pleasant Orange County coast restaurant. *Expensive.*

The Cottage, 308 N PCH, Laguna Beach ☎714/494-3023. Filling American breakfasts, but other meals offer affordable seafood, pasta, and chicken for hungry beachgoers. *Moderate.*

Five Crowns, 3801 E Coast Hwy, Corona del Mar ☎714/760-0331. Diverse menu, but most locals come to this old favorite for the thick, juicy steaks and clubby English decor. *Expensive.*

Jack Shrimp, 2400 W Coast Hwy, Newport Beach ☎714/650-5577. One in a chain of Cajun dinner establishments in various spots along the Orange County coast, with an appealing assortment of spicy seafoods and fairly authentic Louisiana staples. *Moderate.*

The Towers, 1555 S Coast Hwy, Laguna Beach ☎714/497-4477. Dine on a rich variety of California cuisine, especially the roast duck with a mushroom glaze and grilled salmon with a potato-flaked crust, while the Orange County coast spreads out before you in this sleek hotel restaurant. *Very expensive.*

CHINESE AND VIETNAMESE

Favori, 3502 W First St, Santa Ana ☎714/531-6838. The real thing, way out in distant Orange County between Disneyland and the coast. Worth the drive for what may be LA's best Vietnamese food. In any case, the garlic shrimp, curried chicken with lemon grass, and nicely flavored noodle dishes here are worth the drive. *Moderate.*

Hue Rendezvous, 15562 Westminster Ave, Westminster ☎714/775-7192. In the heart of Little Saigon, more authentic Vietnamese dishes, the best of which are a simple chicken noodle soup (*pho*) and the more adventuresome-sounding rice cakes with beef and pork stuffing. *Moderate.*

SEAFOOD

Claes Seafood, 425 S PCH, Laguna Beach ☎714/494-1151. Stop by this restaurant in the *Hotel Laguna* and sample Cal-cuisine versions of delicious ahi and halibut. *Expensive.*

The Crab Cooker, 2200 Newport Ave, Newport Beach ☎714/673-0100. The hefty plates of crab legs and succulent bowls of chowder make the long lines a bit more bearable. *Inexpensive.*

Chapter 14

Bars, Coffeehouses and clubs

Social **drinking** in LA is far less popular than it is up the coast in San Francisco. Many **bars** are simply places to pose while waiting to meet friends, before heading off to pose again somewhere more exotic. However, it is still possible to have a good time, provided you don't smoke, a practice now banned in most establishments under recent California law (though one which some proprietors and customers are openly flouting). You should be able to get a drink almost anywhere, and for serious, uninterrupted drinking there are bars and cocktail lounges on every other corner – just look for the neon signs. In fickle Los Angeles, bar styles go in and out of fashion quickly, often according to music and showbiz trends, changing from month to month.

If you want something of the bar atmosphere without the alcohol, present yourself at one of the fast-growing band of **coffeehouses**. Lately they've become

the places to be seen, not least because they won't leave a hardened socialite too drunk to drive home – a crime that carries harsh penalties in LA. They can also be a refreshing change of pace from normal bars, especially if you're trying to sate some artistic pretensions rather than just your desire to drink: these spots are usually a hybrid of a café and performance space.

Also quite susceptible to trends and styles – but on the whole, a better option than bars, if you're really interested in checking out LA's drinking scene – are the city's many lively **clubs,** the true focus of social activity. They are usually after-hours oriented, and they feature scenes just as colorful and lively as those at non-musical watering holes. Even if you're not interested in listening to the latest dance or thrasher tunes, there are plenty of secluded spots to hole up with a boilermaker and let the evening slip quietly away.

Bars

The **bar** recommendations below are a mix of spots enjoyable either for an entire evening's socializing or a quick appearance on the way to somewhere else. As you'd expect, they reflect their locality: a clash of beatnik artists and financial whiz kids Downtown, the much greater trendiness of West Hollywood, a batch of jukebox and dartboard-furnished bars in Santa Monica, and the less fashionable spots of the San Gabriel

Bars, Coffeehouses and Clubs

and San Fernando valleys. Ultimately, though, would-be movie stars and leather-clad rock fans make Hollywood the center of the drinking scene, with most of LA's hippest bars around Hollywood and Sunset boulevards.

A few hard-bitten bars are open the legal **maximum hours** (from 6am until 2am daily), though you're likely to be drinking alone if you arrive for an early liquid breakfast: the busiest hours are between 9pm and midnight.

Downtown

Al's Bar, 305 S Hewitt St ☎213/687-3558. In the heart of the trendy loft-district art scene, in a grimy industrial area. Drink cans of cheap beer in post-apocalyptic-looking, smoke-filled rooms, with a pool table and frequent live acts. Homeless people will offer to watch your car for $1.

Bona Vista, at the *Westin Bonaventure*, 404 S Figueroa St ☎213/624-1000. Thirty-five floors up, this constantly rotating cocktail lounge spins faster after a few of the expensive drinks, and offers an unparalleled view of the sun setting over the city.

Casey's Bar, 613 S Grand Ave ☎213/629-2353. White floors, dark wood-paneled walls, and nightly piano music – something of a local institution in entertainment-starved Downtown.

Mr T's Bowl, 5621 N Figueroa Ave, Highland Park ☎213/960-5693. As the name indicates, this was once a bowling alley, though it's now been remodeled into a quirky bar with a regular crowd of slumming Gen-Xers and local characters. On weekends, there's eclectic live music, from rock to surf to punk.

Mid-Wilshire

El Adobe, 5536 Melrose Ave ☎213/462-9421. The Mexican food here is only adequate, so cut to the chase and order the house specialty: lethal and cheap margaritas.

H M S Bounty, 3357 Wilshire Blvd, Mid-Wilshire ☎213/385-7275. Advertising

"Food and Grog," this grungy bar once hosted guests like Jack Webb and Duke Ellington, but has recently been rediscovered by slumming club-hoppers, who come for the dark ambience, lounge music, and kitschy nautical motifs.

Martini Lounge, 5657 Melrose Ave ☎213/467-4068. Dual bars, a dance floor, and live rock music at this hot spot just south of Hollywood.

Molly Malone's Irish Pub, 575 S Fairfax Ave ☎213/935-1577. Self-consciously authentic Irish bar, from the music to the shamrocks to the thick, foaming Guinness.

The Snakepit, 7529 Melrose Ave ☎213/852-9390. One of the better bars along this shopping strip, with a mix of jaded locals and inquisitive tourists.

Tom Bergin's, 840 S Fairfax Ave ☎213/936-7151. Laid-back spot for Irish coffee.

Hollywood

Bar Deluxe, 1710 N Las Palmas St, off Hollywood Blvd ☎213/469-1991. Enjoy sake, beer, and rockabilly music in a bare-bones, crimson-lit bar popular with young club-hoppers. A bizarre giant aquarium adds to the overall atmosphere.

Barragan Café, 1538 W Sunset Blvd ☎213/250-4256. A fairly decent Mexican restaurant, but also allegedly producing the most alcoholic margarita in LA.

Bar Marmont, 8171 Sunset Blvd, West Hollywood ☎213/650-0575. Notable strictly as a place to see Hollywood pretension in all its slick-backed glory; otherwise, it's noisy and unattractive, with mediocre drinks.

Barney's Beanery, 8447 Santa Monica Blvd, West Hollywood ☎310/654-2287. Well-worn pool room bar, stocking more than 200 beers, that attracts jaded youth and graying rebels. It also serves cheap food (see p.240).

Boardners, 1652 N Cherokee Ave ☎213/462-9621. A likably unkempt neighborhood bar in the middle of

Hollywood's prime tourist territory. Attracts an array of salty old-timers and young curiosity-seekers.

Cat N' Fiddle, 6530 Sunset Blvd ☎213/468-3800. A boisterous but comfortable pub with expensive English beers on draft and live jazz on Saturdays (see p.273).

Cheetah's, 4600 Hollywood Blvd ☎213/660-6733. As good a spot for Hollywood slumming as any, with strong drinks, topless entertainment, and an appropriately grubby crowd of regulars.

The Dresden Room, 1760 N Vermont Ave ☎213/665-4298. Wednesday evening is open mike night; otherwise the resident husband-and-wife lounge act takes requests from the crowd of old loyalists and goatee-wearing hipsters.

The Fold, 2906 Sunset Blvd ☎213/666-2407. A spot for serious drinking in Silver Lake, featuring entertainment by rock and thrash groups on weeknights and a bevy of drag queens on the weekend.

Formosa Café, 7156 Santa Monica Blvd ☎213/850-9050. Tiny ex-silent-era film studio decorated in red, pillar-box Chinese style (à la Mann's Chinese Theatre), and known for its potent martinis. Featured in the film *LA Confidential*.

The Garage, 4519 Santa Monica Blvd ☎213/683-3447. With a funky lounge and a pool room, this local Silver Lake bar and club offers live music after 9pm.

Goldfingers, 6423 Yucca St, north of Hollywood Blvd ☎213/962-2913. Fascinating 1960s-kitsch design with striking black-and-gold highlights. Drinks aren't bad, either, and nightly music is a mix of dance and acoustic stylings.

Good Luck Club, 1514 Hillhurst Ave ☎213/666-3524. A hip Los Feliz retro-dive, this Gen-X hangout is popular for its cheesy Chinese decor and drinks straight from the heyday of *Trader Vic's*.

Jack's Sugar Shack, 1707 N Vine St ☎213/466-7005. Eat and drink near the famous intersection of Hollywood and Vine and see various rock and blues bands belt out tunes nightly.

Lava Lounge, 1533 N La Brea Ave ☎213/876-6612. The height of kitschy chic a few years ago, this intentionally seedy strip-mall bar still retains an odd popularity among bored hipsters. Come for a visit and wallow in the lounge music and Brubeck jazz.

Musso and Frank Grill, 6667 Hollywood Blvd ☎213/467-7788. Simply put, if you haven't had a drink in this 1940s landmark bar, you haven't been to Hollywood. It also serves food (see p.247).

Pinot Hollywood's Restaurant and Martini Bar, 1448 Gower St ☎213/461-8800. Twenty-four types of martini and Polish potato vodka, served in airy surroundings. Also a restaurant (p.247).

The Power House, 1714 N Highland Ave ☎213/463-9438. Enjoyable hard-rockers' watering hole just off Hollywood Boulevard. Few people get here much before midnight.

Smog Cutter, 864 N Virgil Ave ☎213/667-9832. A neighborhood joint that attracts a mix of area boozers and youthful poseurs. Don't miss the occasional karaoke, which, like the liquor, can be pleasantly mind-numbing.

Tiki Ti, 4427 W Sunset Blvd ☎213/669-9381. Tiny tiki lounge straight out of *Hawaii-Five-O*, in the middle of East Hollywood.

Santa Monica and Venice

14 Below, 1348 14th St, Santa Monica ☎310/451-5040. At this casual bar, pool tables and a fireplace compete for your attention with rock, folk, and blues performers.

Bob Burns, 202 Wilshire Blvd, Santa Monica ☎310/393-6777. Just around the corner from the Third Street Promenade, this Scottish-themed bar and restaurant offers a nicely gloomy atmosphere, faded tartan decor, and plenty of dour locals drowning their sorrows.

Circle Bar, 2926 Main St, Santa Monica ☎310/392-4898. A rather bleak, claustrophobic space where the main pur-

Bars, Coffeehouses and Clubs

Bars, Coffeehouses and Clubs

pose is getting bombed without spending a wad.

Gotham Hall, 1431 Third St, Santa Monica ☎310/394-8865. The strong drinks and purple pool tables here attract a generally youthful set of drinkers.

The Oarhouse, 2941 Main St, Santa Monica ☎310/396-4725. Occasionally fun, student-oriented bar that gets suitably rowdy on Fridays and sometimes weeknights.

O'Brien's, 2226 Wilshire Blvd, Santa Monica ☎310/829-5303. Irish food and brews served to a vibrant mix of locals and expats from Ireland.

Red Setter Irish Pub, 2615 Wilshire Blvd, Santa Monica ☎310/449-1811. Formerly the popular *McGinty's*, this pub features lots of darts and beer, plus "Lobster Friday," in which you get a pound of the crustacean for under $10.

St Mark's, 23 Windward Ave, Venice ☎310/452-2222. Set among the last of the great colonnades from the old days, this stylish bar and restaurant serves up adequate food, drinks from a full bar, and nicely eclectic live music.

The Tavern on Main, 2907 Main St, Santa Monica ☎310/392-2772. Somewhat boisterous neighborhood bar off the Main Street shopping strip, with sports on TV.

Ye Olde King's Head, 116 Santa Monica Blvd, Santa Monica ☎310/451-1402. Jukebox, dartboards, and signed photos of all your favorite rock dinosaurs. Popular with local British expatriates.

The San Gabriel and San Fernando valleys

Blue Saloon, 4657 Lankershim Blvd, North Hollywood ☎818/766-4644. This San Fernando Valley bar hosts a wide range of live music, but drinking is the main activity here. Pool tables and TVs too.

Clearman's North Woods, 7247 Rosemead Blvd, San Gabriel ☎626/286-8284. A kitsch-lover's delight: fake snow on the exterior and mooseheads on the

walls inside, a great place to dissipate while listening to lounge singers and throwing your peanut shells on the floor.

The Colorado, 2640 E Colorado Blvd, Pasadena ☎626/449-3485. A bright spot along an otherwise bleak Pasadena stretch of asphalt. Salty bartenders, cheap drinks, and a couple of pool tables to boot.

Cozy's Bar & Grill, 14058 Ventura Blvd, Sherman Oaks ☎818/986-6000. Listen to blues on the weekend, or come by any time to throw darts, shoot pool, or knock back a few. A friendly, laid-back San Fernando Valley spot with a devoted clientele.

The John Bull Pub, 958 S Fair Oaks Ave, Pasadena ☎626/441-4353. Colorful drinking joint on the old Route 66. Live music on weekends, mostly journeyman rockers.

JP's Restaurant & Lounge, 1333 Hollywood Way, Burbank ☎818/845-1800. Nightly pop and jazz music, along with karaoke on Sunday and Tuesday nights.

Coffeehouses

You can find **coffeehouses** in LA almost everywhere, from grim hole-in-the-wall dives to brightly elegant hotel lobbies. Well-trafficked tourist strips like Melrose Avenue and Santa Monica's Third Street Promenade are loaded with traditional spots to grab a caffeinated jolt. The listings below, however, tend more toward unique establishments that, while serving coffee – and perhaps tea, food and alcohol – also offer more intellectual amusements like art, music, or poetry.

The places to visit for these nouveau coffee-combos are Hollywood, Santa Monica, and, surprisingly, the San Fernando Valley, which makes up in appealing coffeehouses what it lacks in quality restaurants.

Hollywood

All-Star Theatre Café, 1714 N Ivar Ave ☎213/962-8898. Antique store-cum-café-cum-pool hall with a 1920s feel and comfortably overstuffed armchairs, near Nathanael West's former stomping grounds. Never opens until 7pm.

Bourgeois Pig, 5931 Franklin Ave ☎213/962-6366. Hip environment and outrageously overpriced cappuccinos, though fun for people-watching.

Highland Grounds, 742 N Highland Ave ☎213/466-1507. The poshest and posiest of LA's coffee bars, serving iced latte and pancakes. At night it's a club, with poetry readings and anonymous bands.

King's Road Espresso House, 8361 Beverly Blvd, West Hollywood ☎213/655-9044. Sidewalk café popular day and night with the neo-beatnik crowd and, increasingly, out-of-towners.

Little Frida's, 8730 Santa Monica Blvd, West Hollywood ☎310/854-5421. Healthy food and free-flowing coffee amid poetry readings, eclectic music, and even a bit of comedy now and then.

Lucy Florence Coffeehouse, 6541 Santa Monica Blvd ☎213/463-7585. Drink your java to the sounds of soul, jazz, and R&B several nights a week at this swinging central Hollywood café.

The Onyx, 1804 N Vermont Ave ☎213/662-4187. This Los Feliz coffeehouse hosts musical, poetic, and spoken word entertainment, along with food and coffee.

Tsunami Coffee House, 4019 Sunset Blvd ☎213/661-3476. Music and poetry mid-week at this pleasant Silver Lake space.

Santa Monica and Venice

Anastasia's Asylum, 1028 Wilshire Blvd, Santa Monica ☎310/394-7113. Comfortable place with strong coffee and tea. Also with nightly entertainment, of varying character and quality.

The Novel Café, 212 Pier Ave, Santa Monica ☎310/396-8566. Stacks of used books and high-backed wooden chairs set the tone, but this place also has good coffees, teas, and pastries.

The Rose Café, 220 Rose Ave, Venice ☎310/399-0711. A somewhat trendy, though not pretentious, place for coffee and pastries that also offers occasional blues and jazz music.

Un-Urban Coffee House, 3301 Santa Monica Blvd, Santa Monica ☎310/315-0056. Another combination coffeehouse and performance space, with mostly music and comedy.

Wednesday's House, 2409 Main St, Santa Monica ☎310/452-4486. Step up to the crowd on Wednesday night's open-mike night and bare your soul to jaded young hipsters. A pitch-black shot of espresso helps you get up the nerve.

The World Café, 2820 Main St, Santa Monica ☎310/392-1661; *www. worldcafe.la.com*. Surf the Net with other technophiles on the patio, or drink in the dark café/bar. Often crowded and always touristy.

The South Bay and LA Harbor

Java Man, 157 Pier Ave, Hermosa Beach ☎310/379-7209. Tables lit by halogen lamps, and a rotating display of work from local artists. Not far from the beach.

Sacred Grounds, 399 W 6th St, San Pedro ☎310/514-0800. Combination coffeehouse and club with a sizable stage, close to the LA harbor.

Sponda Music and Espresso Bar, 49 Pier Ave, Hermosa Beach ☎310/370-6735. Open-mike night Thurs at this beachside coffeehouse adjacent to the city pier.

The San Gabriel and San Fernando valleys

Cobalt Café, 22047 Sherman Way, San Fernando Valley ☎818/348-3789. Somewhat grungy, but trendy, with coffee, food, and live music.

Coffee Junction, 19221 Ventura Blvd, San Fernando Valley ☎818/342-3405. If you end up trapped in a remote corner of the Valley, the tasty coffee and earnest folk music here are worth a stop.

Greens 'n' Grounds, 124 N San Fernando Rd, Burbank ☎818/238-9100. Sip your caffeine at this Valley coffee-

Bars, Coffeehouses and Clubs

Bars and Clubs

house while listening to an interesting range of musical and spoken entertainment.

Hot House Café, 12123 Riverside Drive, North Hollywood ☎818/506-7058. High-octane coffee in a Valley joint with art and books, as well as music on the weekend.

i-Browse Coffee and Internet, 11 W Main St, Alhambra ☎626/588-2233. An assortment of the latest cultural rages, from dizzyingly eclectic music to Web browsing to supercharged coffee drinks, at this spot off the main tourist path.

The Kindness of Strangers, 4378 Lankershim Blvd, North Hollywood ☎818/752-9566. Affordable food and coffee in an enjoyable space that provides copious reading material and live performances, namely comedy and music.

Stage Left, 208 N Brand Blvd, Glendale ☎818/551-9791. One of the suburb's best stages, featuring a revolving series of art, poetry, music, and noise performances.

Clubs and discos

Some establishments where alcohol is not served or where the bar is separate from the rest of the club admit patrons ages 18–21.

Like most things in LA, the city's nightlife is very style-conscious, indeed its **clubs and discos** are probably the wildest in the country. Ranging from absurdly faddish hangouts to industrial noise cellars, even the more image-conscious joints are often more like singles bars, with plenty of dressing-up and picking-up (and sometimes not much else) going on, and everybody claiming to be either a rock star or movie big-shot. If you don't fall for the make-believe, the city's nightlife jungle can be great fun to explore, if only to eavesdrop on the vapid chat. Nowadays, many of the more interesting and unusual clubs don't have permanent homes, especially those catering to the house, ambient, and rave scenes. As a result, the trendier side of the club scene is hard to pin down, and you should always check the *LA Weekly* newspaper before setting out.

Not surprisingly, Friday and Saturday are the busiest nights, but during the week things are often cheaper and, though less crowded, rarely any less enjoyable. Regardless, don't bother showing up until at least 11pm or midnight. There's nearly always a **cover charge**, usually from $6 to $10, and a **minimum age** of 21 (it's normal for ID to be checked, so bring your passport or other photo ID), and you should obviously **dress** with some sensitivity to the club's style. That said, prohibitive dress codes are a rarity, and although you may be more welcome if you look completely outrageous, most places will not exclude you solely on your clothing choice.

Most of the top-name clubs are either in Hollywood or along the ten-block stretch of West Hollywood from La Cienega Boulevard to Doheny Drive. Downtown is home to a number of transient clubs operating above- and below-board, and the Santa Monica area has a few worthwhile clubs here and there, while the San Fernando Valley has its own version of a musical scene – usually confined to the weekends.

Downtown

Glam Slam, 333 S Boylston St ☎213/482-6626. Very glam but not too pretentious, a club owned by the Artist Formerly Known as Prince (and named after one of his songs) – hence the purple dance floor. Cover varies.

Mayan, 1038 S Hill St ☎213/746-4287. Convince the doorman that you deserve to be allowed in and your reward is a place among the cool and most fashionable of LA, eager to shake a leg in gorgeous and historic surroundings, a pre-Columbian-style former moviehouse (see p.65). Fri and Sat; $12, no sneakers.

Hollywood

Arena, 6655 Santa Monica Blvd ☎213/462-0714. Work up a sweat to funk, hip-hop, and house sounds on a massive dance floor inside a former ice factory. The fervent crowd is diverse, but leans toward a mix of Hispanics and gays; $8.

Club Lingerie, 6507 Sunset Blvd ☎213/891-2775. Long-established, stylish modern dance club with intimate bar and hip-hop, dance, and R&B music. Tuesday night's "Boogie Lounge" is oriented toward soul and rap; $5–10. (See entry in "Live Music," p.271.)

Coven 13, 1650 Schrader Blvd ☎213/465-7449. Two Sundays a month, this club materializes to offer a grand assortment of eerie attractions, from tarot readings and seances to goth music from the last fifteen years. Just don't forget to bring your fright wig; $10.

Crush Bar, 1743 N Cahuenga Blvd ☎213/461-9017. Soul, reggae, R&B, funk, and assorted dance tracks play at this relaxing, enjoyable club just north of Hollywood Boulevard; $8.

The Derby, 4500 Los Feliz Blvd ☎213/663-8979. Restored East Hollywood supper club with gorgeously high wooden ceilings and a round bar, that has become the new epicenter of LA's burgeoning swing-dancing craze – as seen in the movie *Swingers* (see p.334). Cover varies.

Dragonfly, 6510 Santa Monica Blvd ☎213/466-6111. Despite being on a dismal stretch of Hollywood, this club is continually buzzing, thanks to its two large dance rooms, "eye-contact" bar, and various club nights; $5–15.

Florentine Gardens, 5951 Hollywood Blvd ☎213/464-0706. Stuck between the Salvation Army and a porno theater, but very popular with the faddish LA crowd, many of whom are teenybopper hipsters getting their first taste of club life; $8.

The Opium Den, 16051/2 N Ivar Ave ☎213/466-7800. A good collection of funk and hip-hop create the crowd-pleasing weekend beats at this club just south of Hollywood Boulevard; $6.

The Palace, 1735 N Vine St ☎213/462-3000. A great old blue-and-white historic-revival building triumphantly reincarnated as one of LA's better weekend dance clubs and watering holes, with no less than four bars and two main floors, and a collection of house, funk, hip-hop, and other modern sounds; $10.

Probe, 836 N Highland Ave ☎213/461-8301. Ultra-trendy club with gothic, industrial, and techno beats. If you like the scene, this is one of LA's more enjoyable clubs – if not, Sunday night's "Club 70s" may be more your speed, a tongue-in-cheek tribute to the disco years; $8–10.

The World, 7070 Hollywood Blvd ☎213/467-7070. A wide range of dance styles nightly, from hypnotic ambient to electronica to industrial noise. Added attractions are a wild, diverse crowd and occasional go-go dancers; $10.

West Hollywood

7969, 7969 Santa Monica Blvd ☎213/654-0280. West Hollywood's longest-running gay and lesbian disco, attracting a colorful and eclectic crowd to enjoy the offbeat entertainment: a mind-bending assortment of strip shows, burlesque revues, go-go dancing, frenetic house and dance music, and, of course, drag nights several days of the week; $6–10. Over 18s.

Axis, 652 N La Peer Drive ☎310/659-0472. A predominantly gay crowd, house and dance music, and fervent DJs spinning most nights of the week at one of West Hollywood's more popular clubs; $7.

Bar One, 9229 Sunset Blvd ☎310/271-8355. Bring plenty of attitude to this club frequented by actual and would-be celebrities. For a taste of the peppy dance music, drinks, and food, fancy outfits and reservations are almost always mandatory; $15.

Billboard Live, 9039 Sunset Blvd ☎310/274-5800. The newest kid on the club scene, replacing the classic old rock venue of *Gazzarri's*, this tri-level operation features live and recorded music and leans heavily toward dance, hip-hop, and rock sounds. Exciting enough, though a bit too corporate at times; $10.

Coconut Teaszer, 8117 Sunset Blvd ☎213/654-4773. Poseurs, rockers, and voyeurs mix uneventfully on the two dance floors of this iconic Sunset Strip

Bars, Coffee-houses and Clubs

Bars, Coffeehouses and Clubs

More gay clubs are listed on p.285.

club and concert hall. No cover before 9pm, otherwise $10.

The Gate, 643 N La Cienega Blvd ☎310/289-8808. Retro and contemporary dance and pop sounds shake the walls of this elegant estate setting – a crowded dance floor and two outdoor patios also add to the ambience; $10.

Love Lounge, 657 N Robertson Blvd ☎310/659-0472. One of the better clubs for musical diversity: new wave, dance, rock, house, retro-pop, and house music are but a few of the sounds you'll hear on the weekends; Tues night is given over to drag queens; $10.

Roxbury, 8225 Sunset Blvd ☎213/656-1750. Disco, hip-hop, funk, and dance bring in the crowds to this club, which also features three levels of dance floors and five full bars. Not surprisingly, this sort of entertainment-overload is quite an attraction – waiting in line is almost inevitable; $10–12.

Union, 8210 Sunset Blvd ☎213/654-1001. On a central section of the Sunset Strip, this relaxed supper club provides funk, soul, and R&B grooves. Frequented by an energetic crowd of young actors on Tuesday nights. Cover varies.

Viper Room, 8852 Sunset Blvd ☎310/358-1880. Excellent live acts, a famous owner (Johnny Depp), and a headline-hitting past. The music ranges from house to swing to disco to jazz. Plus, the unpredictable schedule means anyone might show up onstage, perhaps even Depp himself; $10–15. (See also "Live Music" on p.272.)

West LA

The Century Club, 10131 Constellation Blvd, Century City ☎310/553-6000. One of Century City's few forms of reasonably spontaneous entertainment, a dance club with a fine assortment of funk, hip-hop, and pop tunes, an upscale clientele, and high prices to match; $15, or $20 after 10pm.

Orsini's, 9575 W Pico Blvd ☎310/277-6050. Funk, rap, and soul on Friday and

Saturday, and dark, heavy gothic sounds on Sunday; $10, or $5 on Sun.

Santa Monica and Venice

The Pink, 2810 Main St, Santa Monica ☎310/392-1077. Located near the Venice end of the popular Main Street shopping strip, this weekend club typically features both dance and avant-garde music, with the latter offered on Sunday nights; $10.

Scruffy O'Shea's, 822 Washington Blvd, Marina del Rey ☎310/821-SHEA. A pretty good dance and house music club on the edge of Marina del Rey's high-rise commercial blandness. If you're in the area, give it a try – there aren't too many other worthwhile forms of amusement here; $10.

Teasers, 4445 Admiralty Way, Marina del Rey ☎310/641-4494. A somewhat stiff dance and pop club near the marina, albeit in a somewhat bleaker stretch than *Scruffy O'Shea's*. Best for weekend disco or Sunday night salsa lessons; $5.

The West End, 1301 Fifth St, Santa Monica ☎213/656-3905. With a slew of pop favorites and horrors from the 1960s through the 1980s, this is quite an eclectic club, and it also offers reggae, dance, and house music for those without a taste for retro-tackiness; $5–10.

The San Gabriel and San Fernando valleys

Aftershock, 11345 Ventura Blvd, Studio City ☎818/752-9833. Disco and dance music reign supreme at this San Fernando Valley club with four bars and three high-tech rooms. The music also features pop standards and lesser-known curiosities; $6. Wed–Sun.

The Brothel, 4017 Riverside Drive, Burbank ☎213/955-1888. Every Thursday night, the musical low-points of the 1980s are re-created with dazzling effectiveness when AOR and arena rock anthems are dusted off for an enthusiastic crowd; $3.

The Muse, 54 E Colorado Blvd, Pasadena ☎626/793-0608. In the quiet confines of Old Town Pasadena, dance, funk, and hip-hop come together in a three-level club that holds about a dozen pool tables; $5. Thurs–Sun.

Villa Wahnsinn, 8751 Van Nuys Blvd, San Fernando Valley ☎818/894-2876. In the distant Valley burg of Panorama City, weekend DJs spin an upbeat mix of dance, house, and disco music to a mainly suburban crowd; $5–10.

Bars, Coffee-houses and Clubs

Chapter 15

Live Music

LA has many choices if you're looking for **live music**. New bands haven't broken through until they've won over an LA crowd, so there's seldom an evening without something exciting going on.

Besides locals, there are always plenty of big-name American, British and other international acts playing around, and there's an enormous choice of **venues** –the clubs listed below are some of the most established on the circuit. Most open at 8pm or 9pm, and headline bands are usually onstage between 11pm and 1am. Admission ranges from $10 to $20 and you should phone ahead to check set times and whether the gig is likely to sell out. As with clubs, you'll need to be 21 and will almost certainly be asked for ID. As always, the free *LA Weekly* is the best source of **information**.

The music scene

Since the 1960s, LA's **rock music** scene has been second to none, to the extent that it has replaced the film industry as the quick route to riches and fame. The style was first defined by **surf rock**, with the pleasant harmonies of the Beach Boys and Jan and Dean pushing prototypical Southern California beach imagery (bikinis, muscle cars, and the like), though in the late 1960s, the mood darkened somewhat, as **psychedelic rock** took over, with bands like The Doors, Buffalo Springfield, and Love all hanging around these parts. Early-to-

mid 1970s LA witnessed the advent of the laid-back, **country-rock** "California"-sound, defined by the Eagles, Jackson Browne and Linda Ronstadt (even though most of them were from distant places), though that was displaced at the end of the decade by a thriving local **punk** scene, headed by X, the Circle Jerks, and Black Flag. That kind of hardcore thrash is not so much of a staple anymore, but **heavy metal** certainly is, and it has strong forebears in LA in 1970s and 1980s bands like Van Halen, Mötley Crüe, Jane's Addiction and perhaps most importantly (and successfully), Guns'n'Roses, which cut their teeth here.

Today, there's a proto-rock star at every corner, and the guitar case is in some districts (notably Hollywood) an almost de rigueur accessory. The current trends tend toward industrial noise, neo-punk, and the lingering vestiges of the grunge rock of the early 1990s. The influence and popularity of South Central's **hip-hop** and **rap** music is fairly spotty and found mostly in dance clubs – avoid hunting down the local rappers in their home territory.

Other types of music have established somewhat of a foothold, notably **country** and **folk music**; indeed, the northern valleys are hotbeds of bluegrass and swing. There are **blues** and **jazz** venues, too, including a few genuinely authentic downbeat dives, though jazz music is also often found in diluted form to add atmosphere to a

Concert information

Apart from the radio stations listed in "Media Sources" (see p.34), which carry details, previews, and sometimes free tickets for forthcoming events, the best sources of **concert information** are the *LA Weekly* and *LA Reader*, and the "Calendar" section of the Sunday *Los Angeles Times*. You can buy seats for concerts or sports events from Ticketmaster, which has branches in Tower Records stores, and charge-by-phone numbers (☎213/480-3232 or 714/740-2000). A quick way through the maze of LA's theaters is to phone Theatrix (☎213/466-1767 or 888-8023), which handles reservations and provides details on what's playing at several of the smaller venues.

Live Music

restaurant. The lively **Latin** dance music of **salsa**, immensely popular among LA's Hispanic population, was promoted heavily by record companies in the city during the mid-1970s. At the time it failed to cross over into the mainstream, but this is now changing. Even so, it's still found mostly in the bars of East LA, though it's worth pointing out that these are very male-oriented gathering places and some visitors may well feel out of place. Finally, there is a small live **reggae** scene, though nothing too out of the ordinary.

Concert halls and performance spaces

You can find **concert halls** and **performance spaces** spread throughout the LA region, though most of the major rock and alternative clubs are in Hollywood or West Hollywood, with many directly on the Sunset Strip.

Major concert venues

Greek Theatre, 2700 N Vermont Ave, Griffith Park, Hollywood ☎213/665-1927. Outdoor, summer-only venue with a broad spectrum of big-name musical acts.

Hollywood Palladium, 6215 Sunset Blvd, Hollywood ☎213/962-7600. Once a big-band dance hall, with an authentic 1940s interior, and now a showcase for the latest in alternative and grunge.

LA Sports Arena, 3939 S Figueroa St, South Central ☎213/480-3232. Cavernous hall with no atmosphere

whatsoever – perfect for mega-metal bands and dinosaur rockers.

Pantages Theater, 6233 Hollywood Blvd, Hollywood ☎213/468-1770. An exquisite, atmospheric Art Deco theater, with a stunning interior, in the heart of historic Hollywood. Sometimes hosts rock concerts, more often traveling musicals.

Universal Amphitheater, Universal Studios lot, Universal City ☎818/622-4440. A huge but acoustically excellent auditorium with regular rock shows by headline groups.

Wiltern Theater, 3790 Wilshire Blvd, Mid-Wilshire ☎213/380-5005. Art Deco moviehouse that's been converted into one of LA's top concert halls, hosting a range of acts from comedy to rock.

Rock

The Alligator Lounge, 3321 Pico Blvd, Santa Monica ☎310/449-1844. All types of rock, plus cajun and zydeco, are the main attractions, but this energetic club also offers experimental jazz on Monday nights. $8.

anti-club, 4658 Melrose Ave, Hollywood ☎213/661-3913. Occasionally great, but far fewer worthwhile bands play here now than used to. Leans toward punk and thrash music. $7–10.

Café Largo, 432 N Fairfax Ave, Mid-Wilshire ☎213/852-1073. Intimate cabaret venue that features some of LA's more unusual live bands. Free–$10.

Club Lingerie, 6507 Sunset Blvd, Hollywood ☎213/891-2775. Wide-ranging venue that's always at the forefront

For more on the Greek Theatre, see description on p.94.

Live Music

of what's new. $3–8. (See also "Bars and clubs," p.261.)

Doug Weston's Troubadour, 9081 Santa Monica Blvd, West Hollywood ☎310/276-6168. The best-known rock club for the loudest noise, heaviest riffs, and shaggiest manes. Cover varies.

The Lighthouse, 30 Pier Ave, Hermosa Beach ☎310/372-6911. Adjacent to the beach, this club has a broad booking policy which spans rock, jazz, reggae, and more. Cover varies. $5.

LunaPark, 665 N Robertson Blvd, West Hollywood ☎310/652-0611. Eclectic musical mix upstairs at this funky club; downstairs, there's a cabaret. $3–20.

Martini Lounge, 5657 Melrose Ave, Mid-Wilshire ☎213/467-4068. A testing ground for young rockers that also features two bars, a dance floor, and a pool room. $3–5.

The Mint, 6010 Pico Blvd, Mid-Wilshire ☎213/954-9630. A mix of rock, jazz, and blues performers, plus a self-contained studio for recording live concerts. $5–10.

Moguls, 1650 N Schrader Blvd, Hollywood ☎213/465-7449. Catch the city's latest musical trends at this dance and concert hall which hosts rock and punk shows, as well as spoken-word ramblings. Free–$10.

The Opium Den, 1605 N Ivar Ave, Hollywood ☎213/466-7800. Mostly cutting-edge rock at this unglamourous joint in the heart of Hollywood, with some retro 1970s and 1980s thrown in on occasion. Cover varies.

The Palace, 1735 N Vine St, Hollywood ☎213/461-3504. Great looking old building with a performance space hosting mid-level names in rock and grunge. $10–25.

The Roxy, 9009 Sunset Blvd, West Hollywood ☎310/276-2222. The showcase of the music industry's new signings, quite intimate, and with a great sound system. Cover varies.

Spaceland, 1717 Silver Lake Blvd, Hollywood ☎213/413-4442. One of LA's hip music hubs, a concert hall that caters to the punk, noise, and alternative crowd. Cover varies.

The Viper Room, 8852 Sunset Blvd, West Hollywood ☎310/358-1880. Less trendy than many clubs, though it has gained a certain notoriety since River Phoenix overdosed here in late 1993. $3–6. (See listing in "Bars and clubs," p.268).

Whisky-a-Go-Go, 8901 Sunset Blvd, West Hollywood ☎310/535-0579. Legendary spot, thanks mostly to The Doors, and important for LA's rising music stars. Mainly hard rock, though you might catch an alternative act now and then. $10-15.

Country and folk

Blue Saloon, 4657 Lankershim Blvd, North Hollywood ☎818/766-4644. Refreshing lack of attitude at this San Fernando Valley club, where country, rockabilly, and rock are the main offerings. $5.

Cowboy Palace Saloon, 21635 Devonshire St, Chatsworth ☎818/341-0166. Worth a trip to this distant corner of the San Fernando Valley for plenty of down-home concerts and country-fried food. Free.

Crazy Jack's, 4311 W Magnolia Blvd, Burbank ☎818/845-1121. Before the music starts at 9pm, this place offers free dance lessons Tues & Thurs–Sat. Cover varies.

Culver Saloon, 11513 Washington Blvd, Culver City ☎310/391-1519. A country-and-blues venue with an authentic cowboy look and sound. Free.

The Foothill Club, 1922 Cherry Ave, Signal Hill ☎310/494-5196. In a bleak industrial city, this glorious dance hall dates back to the days when hillbilly was cool, complete with mural showing life-on-the-range and pictures of country legends. $4–10.

Jack's Sugar Shack, 1707 Vine St, Hollywood ☎213/466-7005. A fine venue for country, rockabilly, and rock concerts, with decent food and not too much attitude. Free–$15.

McCabe's, 3103 W Pico Blvd, Santa Monica ☎310/828-4403. LA's premier acoustic guitar shop also hosts some excellent and unusual shows. $10–20.

Molly Malone's Irish Pub, 575 S Fairfax Ave, Mid-Wilshire ☎213/935-1577. Traditional Irish music, American folk, rock, and R&B. $5. (See also "Bars and clubs" on p.261.)

Rusty's Surf Ranch, 256 Santa Monica Pier, Santa Monica ☎310/393-7386. With the re-emergence of the pier, a terrific site for folk and rock sounds, along with the inevitable surf music. Cover varies.

Jazz and blues

Babe and Ricky's Inn, 4339 Leimert Blvd, South Central ☎213/295-9112. For many years, one of LA's top spots for blues on Central Avenue, *Babe and Ricky's* has relocated to Leimert Park – and remains a prime music hall. Cover varies.

The Baked Potato, 3787 Cahuenga Blvd, North Hollywood ☎818/980-1615. A small but near-legendary contemporary jazz spot, where many reputations have been forged. $8, or $5 on Thurs.

BB King's Blues Club, 1000 Universal Center Drive, Universal City ☎818/6-BBKING. Has a garish CityWalk exterior, but *Lucilles*, the club room (named after BB's guitar), features decent acoustic blues on weekends. Cover varies.

Blue Cafe, 210 Promenade, Long Beach ☎562/983-7111. Decent nightly blues near the ocean. Also with pool tables and upstairs dance floor. Cover varies.

Café Boogaloo, 1238 Hermosa Ave, Hermosa Beach ☎310/318-2324. A small South Bay club with nightly blues and occasional New Orleans jazz. Cover varies.

Cat n' Fiddle Pub, 6530 Sunset Blvd, Hollywood ☎213/468-3800. This pseudo-English pub has jazz, usually a dual-sax quintet, on Sunday from 7–11pm.

No cover. (See also "Bars and clubs" on p.261.)

Catalina Bar and Grill, 1640 N Cahuenga Blvd, Hollywood ☎213/466-2210. Newly reopened, this central Hollywood jazz institution offers traditional jazz sounds, a good dinner menu, and nice acoustics to an appreciative crowd. $10–20.

Harvelle's, 1432 Fourth St, Santa Monica ☎310/395-1676. A stellar place for blues for over six decades, offering different performers nightly and a popular band showcase on Tuesday nights. Cover varies.

House of Blues, 8430 Sunset Blvd, West Hollywood ☎213/650-1451. Over-commercialized mock sugar-shack, with adequate but pricey live acts. Very popular with tourists and heavily influenced by the life and legend of John Belushi, whose estate has a business interest. Cover varies.

Jazz Bakery, 3233 Helms Ave, Culver City ☎310/271-9039. More performance space than club, and the brainchild of singer Ruth Price. The best local musicians play alongside big-name visitors. $12–22.

World Stage, 4344 Degnan Blvd, South Central LA ☎213/293-2451. Informal, bare-bones rehearsal space that attracts top-name players like drummers Billy Higgins and Max Roach. Thursday jams, Friday and Saturday gigs. Cover varies.

Latin and salsa

El Floridita, 1253 N Vine St, Hollywood ☎213/871-8612. Cuban food and Latin music Thurs–Sun at this popular venue tucked away in a minimall. $8.

Grand Avenue, 1024 S Grand Ave, Downtown ☎213/747-0999. Weekend salsa, Latin, and merengue at this popular club south of Bunker Hill. $10–12.

La Bamba, 61 N Raymond Ave, Pasadena ☎626/584-9771. Terrific Latin performers nightly at this Caribbean/South American restaurant. Weekend cover $5.

Live Music

Live Music

La Cita, 336 S Hill St, Downtown ☎213/972-9785. Traditional Hispanic music played nightly at 9pm in an authentic Downtown bar at the foot of Bunker Hill. Cheap drinks, and free.

Luminarias, 3500 Ramona Blvd, Monterey Park ☎213/268-4177. Hilltop restaurant (see p.258) with live salsa reckoned to be as good as its Mexican food. Free.

Zabumba, 10717 Venice Blvd, West LA ☎310/841-6525. In a colorful building amid drab surroundings, this venue is more bossa nova Brazilian than straight salsa, but it's still great. $3–6.

Reggae

Golden Sails Hotel, 6285 E PCH, Long Beach ☎310/498-0091. Some of the best reggae bands from LA and beyond show up on Friday and Saturday nights. $8.

Kingston 12, 814 Broadway, Santa Monica ☎310/451-4423. Santa Monica's top venue for reggae music on weekends. Small and comfortable. $10–12.

Mobay, 1031 Abbot Kinney Blvd, Venice ☎310/452-7472. Dine on tasty jerk chicken while listening to fine Caribbean and reggae music on weekends. Free.

Chapter 16

Performing Arts and Film

You're rarely at a loss for cultural activities in LA, and there are plenty of **performing arts** and **film** options to keep you busy during a stay here. The city's range of highbrow cultural offerings was for many years quite limited, if not thoroughly inferior to other comparably large American cities. In the last few decades, though, LA has begun to establish itself in the performing arts thanks in part to a renewed push from old-money and corporate interests (many of them Downtown), and the growth of underground, fringe, and alternative venues for the arts.

LA boasts a world-class conductor and orchestra for **classical music**, along with several less familiar entities, and the fields of **opera** and **dance** are represented by several noteworthy companies, though not as many as in eastern US cities. **Theater** is a growth industry here, with more than a thousand shows annually (and more than one hundred running at any one time) and a burgeoning audience for both mainstream and fringe productions. **Cabaret** caters to a select crowd of lounge-music aficionados, but **comedy** is always a big draw, and it comes as no surprise that this is one of the first entertainment options visitors usually seek out. Not surprisingly, however, it's **film** that is still the chief cultural staple of the region, and there is no shortage of excellent theaters in which to catch a flick.

Classical music

LA's **classical music** scene is somewhat unknown to many visitors, despite the prominence of the LA Philharmonic's noted conductor Esa-Pekka Salonen. Also appealing are smaller performing groups, which often tend to float from art centers to universities to church venues, drawing a loyal, though limited, audience. Your best bet for following the cultural trends is to watch the press, especially the *LA Times*, for details. In any case, you can expect to pay from $10 to $40 for most concerts, and much more for really big names.

Classical music companies

LA Baroque Orchestra, rotating local venues 310/458-0425. The local vanguard in the use of period instruments, giving a modern take on seventeenth- and eighteenth-century performance styles and archaic instruments. Old favorites from Bach, Vivaldi, Corelli, Scarlatti, and other notable Baroque names fill the bill when this itinerant company gives concerts throughout town, often in the elegant *Biltmore* hotel Downtown. $24–45.

Los Angeles Chamber Orchestra, rotating local venues 213/622-7001. Appearing sporadically throughout the year, the orchestra presents a range of chamber works from different historical eras. Concerts can vary widely by price and seating choices.

For a review of the Biltmore hotel, see p.220.

Performing Arts and Film

Los Angeles Master Chorale, at the Music Center, 135 N Grand Ave, Downtown ☎213/972-7607. Classic and contemporary works are showcased by this choral institution. Prices vary.

Los Angeles Mozart Orchestra, rotating local venues ☎818/342-3442. Although this group almost always puts on winning programs, Mozart is not necessarily the only composer on the bill. More typically, Amadeus makes an appearance or two, and the rest of the music consists of eclectic selections from the classical canon. $23–34.

Los Angeles Philharmonic, at the Music Center, 135 N Grand Ave, Downtown ☎213/850-2000. The one major name in the city performs regularly during the year, and conductor Esa-Pekka Salonen always provides a diverse, challenging program, from powerful Romantic works – especially those of fellow Finn Jean Sibelius – to craggy modern pieces. Take note when Salonen conducts film music, notably that of Hitchcock composer Bernard Herrmann, as he gives it a depth and richness that you may have missed in the moviehouse. $10–100.

Pacific Symphony Orchestra, Orange County Performing Arts Center, 600 Town Center Drive, Costa Mesa ☎714/755-5799. Although not as groundbreaking or experimental as the LA Philharmonic, this suburban orchestra nonetheless presents enjoyable, engaging programs at much lower prices than its LA equivalent. $17–48.

Classical music venues

The Dorothy Chandler Pavilion, at the Music Center, 135 N Grand Ave, Downtown ☎213/972-7211. From October until May, this center of LA's music establishment is the home of the LA Philharmonic, but is also used by the LA Opera and other top names. Hosts the Oscars on alternate years with the Shrine Auditorium (see below).

The Hollywood Bowl, 2301 N Highland Ave, Hollywood ☎213/850-2000. The LA Philharmonic gives open-air concerts

here Tuesday through Saturday evenings from July to September, though the music can sometimes be drowned out by the noisy atmosphere.

Orange County Performing Arts Center, 600 Town Center Drive, Costa Mesa ☎714/556-ARTS. Home of the Pacific Symphony Orchestra and Opera Pacific, and fairly well suited for the latter.

The Pacific Amphitheater, 100 Fair Drive, Costa Mesa ☎310/410-1062. A big open-air venue capable of drawing sizable crowds. Orange County's answer to the Hollywood Bowl.

Royce Hall, on the UCLA campus in Westwood ☎310/825-9261 or 2101. Classical concerts, often involving big names, occur at this splendid Historic Revival structure throughout the college year (Sept–June, generally speaking).

The Shrine Auditorium, 665 W Jefferson Blvd, South Central ☎213/749-5123; box office at 655 S Hill St ☎213/749-5123. A bizarre white Islamic dome complex that hosts the Oscars and regular performances by choral gospel groups.

Opera and dance

Although far from being dominant cultural presences, **opera** and **dance** in LA are not to be dismissed, either. The few major opera companies in LA and Orange counties are usually worth a look, provided you have the cash for the pricey tickets, though performances are not altogether frequent. By contrast, dance recitals and displays are always taking place. However, dance performances tend to be grouped around major events, so check cultural listings or call the venues listed below for seasonal information. Otherwise, check for performances at universities like UCLA (☎310/825-4401), where some of the most exciting new names in dance have residencies.

Opera companies and venues

The LA Opera, at the Music Center, 135 N Grand Ave, Downtown ☎213/972-7211. Stages productions between

See p.105 for more on the Hollywood Bowl.

September and June, from heavy *opera seria* to lighter operettas. LA Opera also occasionally uses the Dorothy Chandler Pavilion (see opposite). $24–135.

Opera Pacific, Orange County Performing Arts Center, 600 Town Center Drive, Costa Mesa ☎213/480-3232 or 714/740-2000. Performs both grand opera and operettas. $10–120.

Dance companies and venues

Dance Kaleidoscope, John Anson Ford Theater, 2850 Cahuenga Blvd, Hollywood ☎213/343-5120. The year's major dance event is held over two weeks in July and organized by the Los Angeles Area Dance Alliance (LAADA) – a co-operative supported by LA's smaller dance companies that provides a central source of information on events. Prices vary.

Japan America Theater, 244 S San Pedro St, Little Tokyo ☎213/680-3700. This venue presents a range of intriguing dance and performance works drawn from Japan and the Far East.

John Anson Ford Theater, 2850 Cahuenga Blvd, Hollywood ☎213/974-1343. Besides the summer Dance Kaleidoscope, this open-air venue also presents eclectic productions by local groups.

Lankershim Arts Center, 5108 Lankershim Blvd, North Hollywood ☎818/761-8838. Despite being located in a none-too-pretty area, this San Fernando Valley institution puts on graceful dance programs during several periods of the year.

Pasadena Dance Theater, 131 N Marengo Ave, Pasadena ☎626/583-3459. One of the San Gabriel Valley's more prominent dance venues, hosting diverse groups throughout the year.

UCLA Center for the Performing Arts, 10920 Wilshire Blvd, Westwood ☎310/825-4401. Features a broad range of touring companies, and runs an "Art of Dance" series between September and June with an experimental emphasis.

Theater

LA has a very active **theater** scene. You can expect to find anything on any given night in one of the city's large or small venues, including huge Broadway shows, hole-in-the-wall, avant-garde productions, edgy political melodramas, and even modernized revivals of classic works by the likes of Shaw and Ibsen. Aside from the nationally touring megahits (mostly musicals by Andrew Lloyd Webber), some of the productions to attract the most attention in recent years have been multicharacter one-person shows (such as Anne Deavere Smith's *Twilight*, her take on the LA riots) and irreverent stagings of canonical works (notably director Peter Sellars' radical updates of Shakespeare).

Since the region is home to a wealth of **film actors**, many of them unemployed in the movie biz, there is always a good pool of thespians for local productions, and depending on the play, you can expect to find semi-famous TV actors or even big celebrity names like Dustin Hoffman on stage.

While the bigger venues host a predictable array of clapped-out old musicals and classics, there are over a hundred "equity waiver" theaters with fewer than a hundred seats, enabling non-equity-cardholders to perform. This means a lot of fringe perfomances take place, for which prices can be very low and the quality can vary greatly – but you may catch an electrifying surprise now and again.

Tickets

Tickets are less expensive than you might expect: a big show will set you back upwards of $25 (matinees are cheaper), with smaller shows around $10 to $20, and you should always book ahead.

You can get information and book theater tickets through Theatrix (☎213/466-1767) and Theater LA (☎310/659-3678), which also offers half-price tickets for same-day evening admittance, or for next-day matinees. To

Performing Arts and Film

Performing Arts and Film

reserve in person, visit Times Tix on the seventh floor of the Westside's Beverly Center mall (see p.302).

Major theaters

Actors' Gang Theater, 6201 Santa Monica Blvd, Hollywood ☎213/660-TKTS. Something of a cross between a major and alternative theater, with occasionally spectacular productions that feature the odd big-name from film or TV.

Ahmanson Theatre, at the Music Center, 135 N Grand Ave, Downtown ☎213/628-2772. This theater often brings in colossal traveling shows from Broadway. If you've seen a major production advertised on TV and on the sides of buses, it's probably playing here.

Coronet Theater, 366 N La Cienega Blvd, West Hollywood ☎310/657-7377. Home of the LA Public Theater, whose productions include the occasional famous name, and also home to the Youth Academy of Dramatic Arts.

Geffen Playhouse, 10886 Le Conte Ave, Westwood ☎310/208-5454. One of the smaller of the major theaters, in a quaint Spanish Revival building, and often with one-person shows. A decided Hollywood connection – recent playwrights have included comedian Steve Martin.

Mark Taper Forum, at the Music Center, 135 N Grand Ave, Downtown ☎213/628-2772. Theater in the three-quarter round, with familiar classics and frequently innovative new plays. Don't expect fringe-theater radicalism, but if you're interested in more traditional, though not quite orthodox, playwrights like David Hare, this is the spot for you.

Pasadena Playhouse, 39 S El Molino Ave, Pasadena ☎626/356-7529 or 1-800/233-3123. A grand old space that has recently been refurbished to provide enjoyable mainstream entertainment. Actors are often a mix of youthful professionals and aging TV and movie stars.

Shubert Theater, ABC Entertainment Center, Century City ☎1-800/447-7400. Usually Lloyd Webber musicals, among other big-ticket items that draw sizable tourist crowds.

South Coast Repertory, 655 Town Center Drive, Costa Mesa ☎714/957-4033. Orange County's major entry for institutional theater, where you can watch well-executed performances of the standard dramatic repertoire on the order of Shaw and Shakespeare. Adjacent to the Orange County Performing Arts Center.

Small theaters

Actors Forum Theater, 10655 Magnolia Blvd, North Hollywood ☎818/506-0600. Unpredictable venues with a range of topical dramas, one-person shows, and the odd production from non-traditional actors like local weatherman Fritz Coleman.

Cast-at-the-Circle, 804 N El Centro Ave, Hollywood ☎213/462-0265. A small Hollywood theater hosting a variety of unpredictable plays and events. Emphasizes works by local playwrights like Justin Tanner, and typically employs a cast of skilled up-and-comers.

The Complex, 6470 and 6476 Santa Monica Blvd, Hollywood ☎213/466-1767. A number of alternative theaters have sprung up in Hollywood west of Cahuenga Boulevard, revolving around a group of six small theaters here, where you're likely to see any number of small, dynamic productions.

Evidence Room, 3542 Hayden Ave, Culver City ☎310/841-2799. Edgy, startling works by the likes of the Marquis de Sade, alternated with more conventional modern dramas and comedies.

Gascon Center Theater, 8737 Washington Blvd, Culver City ☎213/660-8587. Comedy and satire are frequently on the bill at this venue, along with the occasional drama, which, despite its location outside the Hollywood theater circuit, offers as many interesting plays and skilled actors as most places in LA.

Group Repertory Theater, 10900 Burbank Blvd, North Hollywood ☎818/769-PLAY. The Group Repertory troupe often tends toward plays involving dark, heavy messages and classical themes. Some musicals and comedies are staged, too.

Highways, 1639 18th St, Santa Monica ☎310/453-3711. Located in the 18th St Arts Complex, this adventurous performance space offers a range of topical drama and one-person shows. Not surprisingly, Highways embraces artists like the NEA's "Gang of Four" (Karen Finley et al) and controversial blood-spiller Ron Athey, so any production here is sure to excite at least some measure of controversy.

Hudson Avenue Theater, 6539 Santa Monica Blvd, Hollywood ☎213/566-TIXX. Socially conscious "message" plays alternate with more satiric, comedic works at this theater for young actors.

Knightsbridge Theater, 35 S Raymond Ave, Pasadena ☎818/440-0821. Near the heart of Old Pasadena, this is one of LA's better spots for classical theater works, from Shakespeare to Molière, and while you won't recognize most of the names in the cast, you'll likely enjoy the fresh spins on familiar standards.

Lee Strasberg Theater, 7936 Santa Monica Blvd, West Hollywood ☎818/973-8134. As you might expect, this theater is the home of method acting, and you can expect to see a nice range of straightforward dramas and occasionally comedies here; many of the performances are, of course, impeccable.

Los Angeles Theater Center, 514 S Spring St, Downtown ☎213/225-4044. Despite the institutional name, this former bank is a fringe entity that has gone through numerous ups and downs. Currently, it hosts classical and experimental plays on the weekend, with many performances alternating between Spanish and English.

LunaPark, 665 N Robertson Blvd, West Hollywood ☎310/652-0611. Pushing the envelope of theatrical conventions, this fringe venue puts on outlandish, often bizarre performances, with a bent toward gay-oriented subject matter.

Nudity, profanity, sex jokes, and crude puns are not out of the ordinary.

Matrix Theater, 7656 Melrose Ave ☎213/852-1445. This Melrose theater offers excellent, uncompromising productions that often feature some of LA's better young actors and playwrights.

Odyssey Theater Ensemble, 2055 S Sepulveda Blvd, West LA ☎310/477-2055. Well-respected Westside theater company, relocated in a new home, but still offering quality productions at decent prices. Original plays come from a variety of theater groups, using mostly lesser-known actors.

Powerhouse Theater, 3116 Second St, Santa Monica ☎310/396-3680. On the edge of Venice, this alternative theater presents edgy and risk-taking experimental shows; it's one of the best of its kind in town.

Zephyr Theater, 7456 Melrose Ave ☎213/660-TKTS. Although featuring a range of acting troupes and plays, shows lean toward socially relevant, issue-related content, occasionally with a bit of irreverence.

Comedy

Gags are cracked every night at **comedy clubs** across LA. Although rising stars and hopeless beginners can be spotted on the "underground" open-mike scene, the vast majority of famous and soon-to-be-famous comedians, both stand-up and improvisational, appear at the more established clubs, most of them in Hollywood or Mid-Wilshire. These venues usually have a bar, charge a cover of $10–12, and put on two shows each evening, generally starting at 8pm and 10.30pm – the later one more popular. The better-known places are open every night, but are often solidly booked on Friday and Saturday.

Comedy venues
Acme Comedy Theater, 135 N La Brea Ave, Mid-Wilshire ☎213/525-0202. A fancy new theater with sketch and improvised comedy, as well as variety shows.

Performing Arts and Film

Performing Arts and Film

For more on Canter's Deli, see p.239.

Bang Theater, 457 N Fairfax Ave, Mid-Wilshire ☎213/653-6886. One-person shows and long-form improvisation are the specialties at this recently opened theater/comedy club.

Comedy & Magic Club, 1018 Hermosa Ave, Hermosa Beach ☎310/372-1193. Strange couplings of magic and comedy. Jay Leno sometimes tests material here.

The Comedy Store, 8433 W Sunset Blvd, West Hollywood ☎213/656-6225. LA's comedy showcase and popular enough to be spread over three rooms – which means there's often space available, even on weekends, and usually a good line-up, too, with major names like Jerry Seinfeld and Drew Carey occasionally dropping by.

Groundlings Theater, 7307 Melrose Ave ☎213/934-9700. Another pioneering improvisational venue. Many promising comics make the effort, but only the gifted manage to survive the tough, fickle crowds and competitive atmosphere – among them, the late Phil Hartman, as well as Pee Wee Herman.

HBO Workspace, 733 N Seward St, Hollywood ☎213/993-6099. Free experimental comedy, run by HBO as a proving ground for mostly unknown acts.

The Ice House, 24 N Mentor Ave, Pasadena ☎626/577-1895. The undisputed comedy mainstay of the San Gabriel Valley, where Robin Williams and Steve Martin first came to prominence, but now very established and fairly safe.

The Improvisation, 8162 Melrose Ave, Mid-Wilshire ☎213/651-2583. Known for hosting some of the best acts working in the area, this is one of LA's top comedy spots – so book ahead. Don't be surprised to find Billy Crystal or other celebs lurking in the background, and sometimes stepping on stage.

LA Connection, 13442 Ventura Blvd, Sherman Oaks ☎818/784-1868. An improvisation showcase for highly rated specialists in being obnoxious. Seldom less than memorable.

The Laugh Factory, 8001 Sunset Blvd, West Hollywood ☎213/656-1336.

Stand-up comics of varying worth, with the occasional big name.

Cabaret

LA's **cabaret** scene is where the Cocktail Nation set parades itself most visibly, with the recent rediscovery of lounge music attracting a young, hip crowd. The food at most of the venues leaves much to be desired, but it hardly matters to those who attend. Most of the best and biggest cabarets are in Hollywood.

Cabaret venues

Atlas, 3760 Wilshire Blvd, Mid-Wilshire ☎213/466-4600. On Mondays, fiery chanteuses belt out pop and Broadway standards to a spellbound crowd. Bring a suit and plenty of cash – the show isn't cheap ($15) and the pricey food, mostly California cuisine (see p.245), is some of the best you're likely to get in a cabaret.

Canter's Kibitz Room, 419 N Fairfax Ave, Mid-Wilshire ☎213/651-2030. Located next to *Canter's Deli*, this is one of the more bizarre versions of cabaret in LA, featuring an assortment of pop, rock, and jazz artists – as well as audience members during "Open Mike" nights – performing in a retro 1950s lounge space. Free.

The Cinegrill, 7000 Hollywood Blvd, Hollywood ☎213/466-7000. The biggest name in LA cabaret, housed in the landmark *Roosevelt Hotel* (see p.222) and offering an assortment of acts, from the vocal stylings of Eartha Kitt and Mel Torme to "gender illusionist" Jim Bailey. $10–25; two-drink minimum.

The Dresden Room, 1760 N Vermont Ave, Hollywood ☎213/665-4294. Little-known singers doing your favorite lounge-music covers from Wayne Newton to Tom Jones (see "Bars and clubs," p.261). Free.

The Firehouse, 696 N Robertson Blvd, West Hollywood ☎310/289-1353. Magic, music, and comedy every Saturday; while a bit cheesy, this singing-and-dancing extravaganza can't be beat for value – and you can watch the whole thing without dropping a dime. Free.

The Gardenia Club, 7066 Santa Monica Blvd, Hollywood ☎ 213/467-4444. No self-conscious irony here, only straight-up jazz and adult contemporary tunes presented to a gracious crowd. The odd comedian provides some variation, but music is the real attraction. $10; two-drink minimum.

Masquers Cabaret, 8334 W Third St, Mid-Wilshire ☎ 213/653-4848. Zany comedies, slapdash variety acts, and energetic drag queens at this spirited dinner theater near the Beverly Center mall. Although not always successful, the performers here rarely give up on trying to entertain the crowd. $5–15.

San Gennaro, 9543 Culver Blvd, Culver City ☎ 310/836-0400. On Saturdays, prepare yourself for loving tributes to Ol' Blue Eyes at this swinging "cigar lounge." Along with hearing Sinatra covers, listen to slick crooners belting out favorites from Dean Martin, Tom Jones, and other Vegas acts. $10; two drinks included.

Vitello's, 4349 Tujunga Ave, Studio City ☎ 818/769-0905. If you're a fan of pop standards, Broadway toe-tappers, and operatic showstoppers, this is definitely the place for you: a cozy lounge with decent singers, passable Italian food, and just the right sort of funky, down-market atmosphere. Wed & Fri–Sun; $10 minimum food & drink purchase.

Film

It's no shock to find that many major feature **films** are released in LA months (sometimes years) before they play anywhere else in the world, and a huge number of cinemas show both the new releases and the classic favorites – with fewer screens showing independent and foreign movies. Ticket tend to be around $8. Very few **drive-ins** remain; the ones that do are littered with weeds and offer dilapidated sound systems, and are located in distant burgs miles from anywhere you might want to be.

For **cheap** or **free films**, the places to visit are the Bing Theater at the LA County Art Museum, 5905 Wilshire Blvd, Mid-Wilshire (☎ 213/857-6010), which has afternoon screenings of many neglected Hollywood classics and charges just $2; the USC campus, which often has interesting free screenings aimed at film students (announced on campus notice boards); and UCLA's Melnitz Hall or James Bridges Theater, which show films drawn from the extensive school archive (call ☎ 310/206-FILM for details).

Countless venues for **mainstream cinema** exist, the most notable of which are in Westwood. For **arthouses** and **revival theaters**, there are a few worthwhile choices, some of them surprisingly sited in massive shopping complexes, but mostly scattered across the Westside. Finally, the much-vaunted **movie palaces** described elsewhere in this guide are here listed only as to their value as actual movie theaters; many have been converted into performing arts venues, music halls, churches, or swap meets and flea markets.

Mainstream cinema

AMC Century 14, in the Century City mall, 10250 Santa Monica Blvd, Century City ☎ 310/553-8900. Never mind that it's in a mall – this is the best place to see new films in LA. The theaters are somewhat boxy, but if you're after crisp projection, booming sound, comfy seating, and a rapt crowd – including camera-shy celebs sneaking about – there is no better choice.

Beverly Cineplex, in the Beverly Center mall, Beverly and La Cienega blvds, Mid-Wilshire ☎ 310/652-7760. An enterprisingly programmed venue with fourteen tiny screens that show a mix of artsy, independent film programs and first-run blockbusters.

The Bruin, 925 Broxton Ave, Westwood ☎ 310/208-8998. While smaller than it used to be, this 1930s moviehouse remains a city landmark for its wraparound marquee and sleek Moderne styling.

Performing Arts and Film

For a brief history of the Hollywood studio system, see p.52.

Performing Arts and Film

Cinerama Dome, 6360 Sunset Blvd, Hollywood ☎213/466-3401. Built to cash in on the Cinerama craze, but completed after the fad went bust, this white hemisphere has the biggest screen in California, and perhaps the most distorted, thanks to the internal curvature. In any case, the low balcony, comfortable seats, and spacious interior make this a terrific place to watch Hollywood's latest concoctions.

The Crest, 1262 Westwood Blvd, Westwood ☎310/474-7866. A riot of neon and flashing lights outside, glowing murals of old Hollywood inside. Showing mostly Disney flicks.

Fairfax Theater, 7907 Beverly Blvd, Mid-Wilshire ☎213/653-3117. A relative rarity in town, this is a second-run moviehouse with cheap prices and great old decor that is run by a major exhibitor, the Cineplex Odeon chain, and located in the middle of the Fairfax District.

Fine Arts Theater, 8556 Wilshire Blvd, Beverly Hills ☎310/652-1330. Proof that modern moviehouses don't necessarily have to be ugly concrete boxes. The simple exterior and lobby give way to a grandly opulent theater that shows a mix of mainstream and arthouse films.

The National, 10925 Lindbrook Drive, Westwood ☎310/208-4366. In every way a period piece from the 1960s, this giant, curvaceous theater is another fine Westwood venue in the AMC theater chain.

Universal City 18, end of Universal City Drive ☎818/508-0588. This eighteen-screen complex at Universal CityWalk is one of LA's better multiplexes, featuring a pair of pseudo-Parisian cafés and plenty of greasy snacks. Despite all the screens, though, only six or seven films are typically shown, with multiple theaters reserved for each.

The Village, 961 Broxton Ave, Westwood ☎310/208-5576. Formerly of the Fox chain, this AMC theater is one of the most enjoyable places to watch a movie in LA, with its giant screen, fine seats,

good balcony views, and modern sound system. Come early and take a look at the marvelous 1920s exterior, particularly the white spire on top.

Arthouses and revival theaters

Charlie Chaplin Theater, in the Raleigh Studios complex, 5300 Melrose Ave, Mid-Wilshire ☎213/466-FILM. Thanks to the American Cinematheque film organization, you can watch classic movies in the historic surroundings of an old movie studio site. The fare is typically eclectic and intelligently programmed.

Goldwyn Pavilion, in the Westside Pavilion mall, 10800 Pico Blvd, West LA ☎310/475-0202. Something of a surprise: one of the city's better arthouses located on the third floor of a huge mall. Multiple screens, plus free parking on the roof.

Los Feliz Theater, 1822 N Vermont Ave, Hollywood ☎213/664-2169. Having successfully avoided a descent into the porn movie market in the 1960s, the theater's three small screens show international and low-budget American independent movies.

The New Beverly Cinema, 7165 Beverly Blvd, Mid-Wilshire ☎213/938-4038. Not a particularly attractive theater, with clunky seating and a sound system worthy of a drive-in, this venue nonetheless shows excellent art films and revival screenings, with some imaginative double bills.

Nuart Theater, 11272 Santa Monica Blvd, West LA ☎310/478-6379. Showing rarely seen classics, documentaries, and foreign-language films, this is the main option for independent filmmakers testing their work. Be prepared to wait outside the theater in a lengthy line near the 405 freeway.

Old Town Music Hall, 140 Richmond St, El Segundo ☎310/322-2592. Now that the Westside's Silent Movie theater has sadly closed, the only place to consistently see pre-talkie movies is in this quaint theater, unfortunately sited in a grim industrial location immediately south of LAX.

The Royal, 11523 Santa Monica Blvd, West LA ☎310/477-5581. Although not quite living up to its regal name, this is a prime spot for independent offerings that features a spacious, classically ornamented theater in a rather grubby neighborhood.

The Sunset 5, 8000 Sunset Blvd, West Hollywood ☎213/848-3500. This art-house complex sits on the second floor of the Sunset Plaza outdoor mall and shows a good assortment of edgy independent flicks.

Tales Bookshop and Cinema Café, 667 S La Brea Ave, Mid-Wilshire ☎213/933-2640. Hands-down the finest undiscovered gem among LA's many cinemas. This cozy space is not only a fine place to thumb through used fiction, eat ice cream, or drink a cappuccino, it's also a terrific little place for film screenings four nights of the week. Although the viewing screen isn't large by any means, the cinematic offerings are almost always excellent, with a heavy bent toward the bleak *film noir* flicks of the 1940s.

Movie palaces

Chinese Theatre, 6925 Hollywood Blvd, Hollywood ☎213/468-8111. With its large main screen, six-track stereo sound, and wild chinoiserie design, this Hollywood icon shows relentlessly mainstream films, but the first-night audience's loud participation is entertainment in itself.

Egyptian Theater, 6712 Hollywood Blvd, Hollywood ☎213/466-FILM. Under the aegis of the American Cinematheque film organization, this historic moviehouse has reopened as a center for revival, experimental, and art fare, and promises to remind visitors of the Golden Age of film palaces. Delightfully, the center is a kitschy masterpiece of the Egyptian Revival – all grand columns, winged scarabs, and mythological gods.

El Capitan, 6834 Hollywood Blvd, Hollywood ☎213/467-7674. Whether or not you enjoy the typically Disney-oriented fare offered here, you'll no doubt appreciate the restored splendor of this classic central Hollywood movie palace.

Orpheum, 842 S Broadway, Downtown ☎213/239-0964. The finest of the remaining movie palaces in the historic heart of Broadway, boasting a spellbinding mix French Renaissance and Baroque decor, with leafy, brazen chandeliers, ornamental facial grotesques, a few nude nymphs, and grand arches in gold-leaf.

Palace, 630 S Broadway, Downtown ☎213/239-0959. Mock-Venetian architecture galore, with gilded Corinthian columns, splendid Baroque arches and ornament, and an imitation Tiepolo hanging near the movie screen. Like many Downtown theaters still showing movies, you can expect Spanish subtitles running below the big-budget Hollywood productions.

Rialto, 1023 Fair Oaks Ave, South Pasadena ☎626/799-9567. Despite being on its last legs, the Moorish and pre-Columbian design of this classic moviehouse continues to interest observant viewers who can see past the unfortunate wear-and-tear. The place may look familiar, as this is the spot where Tim Robbins tracked down a pesky screenwriter in the film *The Player*, later killing him in a nearby alley.

State, 703 S Broadway, Downtown ☎213/239-0962. This was once the jewel of movie giant MGM's LA theaters, a staggering display of Spanish Renaissance and Baroque designs with copious mythological ornament, intricate friezes, and two prominent pseudo-opera boxes on the sides. Grime and decay have discolored the old glamour, but when the moody blue-and-orange house lights are on and the eager crowd sits waiting, you can almost envisage the theater's golden age.

Warner Grand, 478 W Sixth St, San Pedro ☎310/548-7672. Definitely worth a trip down to the LA harbor to see the glory of this restored Art Deco masterpiece, with its dark geometry and striking pre-Columbian touches. Thankfully, the theater still shows movies, many of them revival screenings, and also acts as a community center for the performing arts.

Performing Arts and Film

Read more about the Egyptian Theater on p.98.

Chapter 17

Gay and Lesbian LA

For a break-down of hotel price codes, see p.220.

For a definition of our restaurant price-code system, see p.243.

Although not as visible as that of San Francisco, the **gay and lesbian scene** in LA is still quite large, and gay people are out and prominent in workplaces and social environments across the city. Of the specific areas where gay people tend to reside, the best known is the autonomous city of **West Hollywood**, which has become synonymous with the (affluent, white) gay lifestyle, not just in LA but all over California. Santa Monica Boulevard, east of Doheny Drive, in particular has restaurants, shops, and bars primarily aimed at gay men. West Hollywood is also the site of the exuber-ant **Gay Pride Parade** (see p.294, held annually in late June. Another well-estab-lished gay community is **Silver Lake**, home to the gay-oriented bars and restaurants of Hyperion Boulevard, and with more of a Hispanic feel along Sunset Boulevard.

Gay couples will find themselves readily accepted at most LA **hotels**, but there are a few that cater especially to gay travelers and can also be useful sources of information on the LA gay scene in general. Listed below, too, are **restaurants**, **bars**, and **clubs** that cater specifically to gay men and lesbians. Of course, you shouldn't have too much of a problem wherever you go – attitudes in LA are on the whole very broad-minded.

The most prominent local publication, though it's also distributed nationally, is *The Advocate* (www.advocate.com), a bimonthly gay news magazine with fea-tures, general information, and classified ads. Other gay-oriented publications include *Nightlife*, featuring weekly club and event listings, and *Frontiers*, a biweekly with community information and topical articles, as well as listings.

Hotels

Coral Sands Motel, 1730 N Western Ave, Hollywood ☎1-800/367-7263. Exclusively geared towards gay men. All rooms face the inner courtyard pool. ④.

Holloway Motel, 8465 Santa Monica Blvd, West Hollywood ☎213/654-2454. Run-of-the-mill roadside motel, some-what dreary looking – though clean. ③.

Ramada Inn, 8585 Santa Monica Blvd, West Hollywood ☎310/652-6400 or 1-800/845-8585. Very gay-friendly, modern place with brand-new rooms, in the cen-ter of the West Hollywood community. ④.

Restaurants

Figs, 7929 Santa Monica Blvd, West Hollywood ☎213/654-0780. Highly rec-ommended all-American, down-home cooking. *Moderate.*

French Market Place, 7985 Santa Monica Blvd, West Hollywood ☎310/654-0898. Theme restaurant that's a neighborhood staple, and often quite crowded. *Moderate.*

Gloria's Café, 3603 W Sunset Blvd, Hollywood ☎213/664-5732. Popular local hangout near Silver Lake that's a

Gay and Lesbian LA

Gay contacts and resources

AIDS Project Los Angeles, 1313 Vine St, Hollywood ☎213/993-1600. Sponsors fund-raisers throughout the year along with a well-attended annual walkathon in late September.

A Different Light, 8853 Santa Monica Blvd, West Hollywood ☎213/668-0629. The city's best-known gay and lesbian bookstore, with monthly art shows, readings, women's music events, and several comfortable chairs for lounging.

Damron Company, PO Box 422458, San Francisco, CA 94142 ☎1-800/462-6654 or 415/255-0404. Publisher of *Damron Address Book*, a yearbook listing American hotels, bars, clubs, and resources for gay men; *Women's Traveler*, which provides similar listings for lesbians; *Damron Accommodations*, listing lesbian- and gay-friendly places to stay in North America; and *Damron Road Atlas*, pointing out lodging and entertainment in major cities.

Ferrari Publications, PO Box 37887, Phoenix, AZ 85069 ☎1-800/962-2912 or 602/863-2408. Publishes *Ferrari Gay Travel A to Z*, a worldwide gay and lesbian guide; *Inn Places*, a worldwide accommodations guide; the guides *Men's Travel in Your Pocket* and *Women's Travel in Your Pocket*; and the quarterly *Ferrari Travel Report*.

Gay and Lesbian Community Services Center, 1625 N Schrader Blvd, Hollywood ☎213/993-7400. Counseling, health-testing, and information. Also publishes *The Center News*, a useful bimonthly magazine.

Gay Community Yellow Pages, 1604 Vista Del Mar Ave, Hollywood, CA 90028 ☎213/469-4454. Gay businesses, publications, services, and gathering places listed yearly. Available all over LA – write for a copy.

International Gay Travel Association, 4331 N Federal Hwy, Suite 304, Fort Lauderdale, FL 33308 ☎1-800/448-8550. Trade group that can provide a list of gay-owned or gay-friendly travel agents, accommodations, and other travel businesses.

---

great spot for dinner, especially for Cajun food. *Moderate*.

Mark's Restaurant, 861 N La Cienega Blvd, West Hollywood ☎310/652-5252. High-end establishment serving California cuisine. *Expensive*.

Bars and clubs

7969, 7969 Santa Monica Blvd, West Hollywood ☎213/654-0280. Formerly called *Peanuts*, West Hollywood's oldest mixed gay and lesbian disco has drag shows and topless girl dancers, and clubs *Fetish* and *Fuck!* on the weekend. Call for details. $8.

Arena, 6655 Santa Monica Blvd, Hollywood ☎213/462-0714. Many clubs under one huge roof, large dance floors throbbing to funk, Latin, and hi-NRG grooves, and sometimes live bands. *Club*

6655 is another name for the place, used when it becomes a dance, house, and hip-hop club (usually Thurs); on Fri and Sat, it becomes *Circus*, hosting dance, disco, and drag parties. $8.

Detour, 1087 Manzanita St, Hollywood ☎213/664-1189. A friendly and quite cheap denim-and-leather bar along a bleak stretch of Silver Lake. No cover.

Girl Bar, 657 N Robertson Blvd, West Hollywood ☎310/659-0471. Madonna has hung out here and Chastity Bono once worked behind the bar. The cavernous dance floor eventually warms up with the help of go-go dancers. Cover varies.

Jewel's Catch One, 4067 W Pico Blvd, Mid-Wilshire ☎213/734-8849. Sweaty barn catering to a mixed crowd, covering two wild dance floors. Cover varies.

Gay and Lesbian LA

Klub Banshee, 8512 Santa Monica Blvd, West Hollywood ☎310/288-1601. Weekend dance club for women, with international and funk beats. No cover.

Le Bar, 2375 Glendale Blvd, Hollywood ☎213/660-7595. Quiet and welcoming bar in a bland section of Silver Lake. No cover.

The Palms, 8572 Santa Monica Blvd, West Hollywood ☎310/652-6188. Mostly house and dance nights at West Hollywood's most established lesbian bar. $5.

Probe, 836 N Highland Ave, Hollywood ☎213/461-8301. LA's longest-running gay men's disco, playing all the Euro-pop dance hits, with a touch of goth on Weds. $10.

Rage, 8911 Santa Monica Blvd, West Hollywood ☎310/652-7055. Flashy gay men's club playing the latest hi-NRG. Also with drag comedy. Drinks are cheap. $5.

Chapter 18

Sports and Outdoor Activities

In the land of sun and surf, there are always enough **sports** and **outdoor activities** to keep you occupied, wherever your interests may lie. LA may not be the sports town that, say, New York or Chicago is, at least in terms of **spectator sports**, a fact best evidenced by the recent flight of both of the city's football teams to pastures new; but plenty of fans still indulge in viewing a basketball, baseball, or hockey game. If seeing them in person is not your thing – indeed, the most expensive tickets to a hockey game can cost nearly $100 – there are always **sports bars,** where you can catch your favorite team on television.

Regardless of the level of interest in these team sports, it's obvious that **participatory sports** like surfing and hang-gliding are what often define LA to the rest of the country, along with more self-indulgent pursuits like **bodybuilding**. Much of the stereotype of Southern California as a bodily fixated culture can be depressingly accurate at times, but it's a mistake to assume that all sport-related pursuits here are always synonymous with narcissistic tendencies. Rather, if you find the right pastime, you may be able to relax and enjoy yourself without concern for wearing the right clothes, attitude, or musculature.

Water and **beach sports** are still the city's main claims to fame, be they swimming or surfing in the Santa

Monica Bay, snorkeling or scuba diving along the further reaches of the coast, or even kayaking. If you'd rather not get wet, you can always try a bit of in-line skating or bicycling along strips like the Venice Boardwalk, or simply suntanning at a beach.

For less earthbound thrills, you can take part in **airborne activities** such as ballooning above the LA basin, hang-gliding off precarious seaside cliffs, or just traveling safely in a helicopter tour. For more of a physical jumpstart, there are many **fitness sports** to make you gasp and sweat, including jogging, rock climbing, and hiking – not to mention hanging out in any one of the city's many fitness clubs. If all this sounds like too much work, there are plenty of other **leisure activities**, like horseback riding, fishing, and bowling, to keep you amused.

Spectator sports

There are two area **baseball teams**, the **LA Dodgers** (☎213/224-1500), who play at Dodger Stadium not far from Downtown; and the **Anaheim Angels** (☎714/634-2000), who play out at Anaheim Stadium in Orange County. The Dodgers are the more successful and beloved franchise, though they've taken some hits in recent years, both for being purchased by media mogul Rupert Murdoch and for letting go of two of

Sports and Outdoor Activities

their biggest stars, catcher Mike Piazza and pitcher Hideo Nomo, the latter the first Japanese baseball player to find success – and acceptance – in Major League Baseball. Tickets for Dodger games run $6–15; for the Angels, $8–15.

Basketball's flashy **LA Lakers** (☎310/419-3100) have boasted such luminous stars through the years as Kareem Abdul-Jabbar, Magic Johnson and, currently, Shaquille O'Neal. They play at the Inglewood Forum; tickets run $25–70, but can be somewhat hard to come by – though not for many Hollywood stars, who can often be spotted sitting courtside. The lesser light in LA's basketball galaxy, the **Clippers** (☎213/748-8000), have a history of ineptitude; games are held at the ugly LA Sports Arena near Exposition Park; seats run $10–50.

Los Angeles currently has no professional **football** teams – the **Raiders** recently moved back to Oakland, and the **Rams** have shipped out to St Louis – but Pasadena's 102,000-capacity Rose Bowl is used for the annual New Year's Day Rose Bowl football game and is the home field for UCLA's football team (☎310/825-2101).

Hockey in LA didn't mean much until the late 1980s, when the **LA Kings** purchased superstar Wayne Gretzky from the champion Edmonton Oilers. Gretzky's long gone from these parts, but the Kings still play at the Forum in Inglewood (☎310/419-3160); seats are $12–80. They have been joined recently by the **Anaheim Mighty Ducks**, their Orange County equivalent, owned by Disney. The Ducks play out at Arrowhead Pond in Anaheim (☎714/704-2500); tickets $15–90.

One of the newer teams in town, the **LA Galaxy** (☎310/445-1260), play **soccer** in the MLS (Major League Soccer), which formed a few years back. Games take place out at the Rose Bowl in Pasadena, and the season runs much of the year, save winter.

Finally, **horse racing** is a fairly popular spectator sport in the LA area, and there are two main tracks. **Santa Anita**, out in

the San Gabriel Valley, has a winter and spring season (☎626/574-7223); **Hollywood Park**, in Inglewood near the Forum, has a spring-through-autumn season (☎310/419-1500).

Water and beach sports

When it comes to sports in LA, the first place most visitors head for is the ocean. Along the sands from Malibu to Orange County, you can find any number of **water** and **beach sports** to keep you busy. However, for a more passive pleasure at the seaside, **suntanning** with crowds of other locals and visitors is always a popular option.

Swimming, snorkeling and scuba diving

Although you'd never believe it from watching TV, **swimming** in many coastal areas is definitely not recommended. Basically, the further you go from the Santa Monica Pier, the better off you are. Despite being a focus for visitors, the pier is ground zero for water-borne contamination, thanks to the presence of huge crowds, heavy metal and chemical offshore dumping, and nasty drainage ditches that deposit the watery filth of LA into the sea. You may see hordes of people splashing about, but don't follow their lead – the authorities will only inform you of dangerous conditions when heavy rains make the seawater from Santa Monica to the South Bay absolutely off-limits for human activity.

Luckily, the beaches closer to Malibu and those toward Palos Verdes and Orange County are usually less crowded and much safer. **Parking** at major strips of sand will cost you upwards of $7, even for a short time, but there are always sufficient roadside spots to deposit your car should you like to chance a dip along the rockier coves and crags.

Similarly, **snorkeling** and **scuba diving** are better experienced away from the city of LA in places like Long Beach and Santa Catalina island. Prices for excursions taking you to see Catalina's astounding undersea life, kelp forest, and shipwrecks can vary widely, but expect to pay a minimum of $80 for any trip. There are a number of companies to choose from: some of the better ones are Catalina Divers Supply, PO Box 126, Avalon (☎310/510-0330 or 1-800/353-0330), with a range of undersea tours of Santa Catalina; Catalina Island Expeditions, PO Box 386, Avalon (☎310/510-1226), which focuses on snorkeling and kayaking trips, with hourly, half-day, or two-day packages; Scuba Express, 106 E Shoreline Drive, Long Beach (☎562/429-4062), individual or group scuba tours of regional islands, plus whale-watching expeditions; and Sundiver, 106 Marina Drive, Long Beach (☎562/493-0951), with popular package deals including boating trips to area islands for one- or two-day scuba-diving trips.

Surfing, windsurfing and kayaking

Since railroad magnate Henry Huntington began importing Hawaiian talent to publicize his Red Car route to Redondo Beach, **surfing** has been big business in LA. The sport has attracted an excited, and sometimes fanatical, group of participants, while having no small impact on LA's culture and image; indeed, "dudes-peak" is now well known to the outside world. If you want to give the sport a try, it never hurts to pay attention to where these surfer-dudes are catching the waves: mostly along the Malibu section of the Pacific Coast Highway from **Surfrider** to **Leo Carrillo** beaches. Although South Bay and Orange County surfers also have their favorite turf – **Huntington Beach**, to name one – if you want to see local surf culture in its purest form, the Malibu beaches are the obvious places to visit. Don't worry about buying equipment, though: **surfboards** are available for hourly rent (around $25) from dinky rental shacks up and down the coast, such as Ocean Surfboards, 22775 PCH, Malibu (☎310/456-8044).

If you've never been **windsurfing**, a trip to LA might not be the ideal time to start. But if you think you can handle it,

a few outlets along the coast rent windsurfers by the hour or day, for upwards of $20–30. One such place to check out is Long Beach Windsurf Center, 3850 E Ocean Blvd, Long Beach (☎562/433-1014), near the Belmont Pier.

Somewhat easier for novices is **kayaking**, which, unlike windsurfing, allows you to sit down somewhat comfortably. Ocean-going kayaks (at least $10 per hour) are more basic and less forbidding than river kayaks, as you simply sit atop the boat and row with another person. Flipping the boat for kicks is not recommended. Alfredo's Beach Rentals, 5411 Ocean Blvd, Long Beach (☎562/434-6121), provides kayaks for rent, as well as jet skis and small boats. Meanwhile, Adventure Rafting, 103 Pebbly Beach Rd, Avalon (☎310/510-0211 or 1-800/990-RAFT), offers a motorized variation on sea kayaking, where you sit in a small, flat boat with several other people and tour oceanside terrain.

In-line skating and bicycling

The popularity of **in-line skating**, also known as rollerblading, cannot be overestimated at hot spots like the Venice Boardwalk. These dry-surface skates, with a linear row of small wheels, are found on the feet of countless locals and visitors traveling along the **cycling path** from Santa Monica to Palos Verdes. If you're walking, you should avoid this crowded path, as skaters and cyclists race down the narrow asphalt lanes like would-be automobiles, giving little respect to the painted yellow lines.

Typically, this oceanside path is the main choice for **bicycling** in LA, even though there are myriad bike paths throughout the region, from the peaceful, leafy setting of the Arroyo Seco to the post-apocalyptic landscape of the LA River (contact the AAA at ☎213/741-3111 or the LA Department of Transportation at ☎213/485-3051 for maps and information). However, only along the beach can you easily rent equipment from a good number of dealers, many of which may lower their

Sports and Outdoor Activities

Sports and Outdoor Activities

prices to stay competitive in particularly popular spots. Expect to pay from $10–15 for skates or bikes, depending on the dealer's location and equipment.

Some of the better spots to rent either blades or bikes include The Bikestation, 105 Promenade North, Long Beach (☎562/436-BIKE), a nicely located hub that links area bike paths with public transport and rents and repairs bicycles; House of Skates, 4 Rose Ave at Ocean Front Walk, Venice (☎310/399-1728), an in-line skate rental stand, one of many similar dealers along the Venice Boardwalk; Spokes 'n' Stuff, Washington Blvd at Venice Pier, Venice (☎310/306-3332), another of those dealers; and Woody's Bicycle World, 3157 Los Feliz Blvd, Hollywood (☎213/661-6665), good if you're intent on exploring nearby Griffith Park.

Airborne activities

If you'd like to get above the smog, and don't have a private jet at your disposal, LA has several worthwhile **airborne activities** that may interest you. The most affordable, and one of the most enjoyable if you know what you're doing, is **hang gliding**, using a simple glider to drift down from a hill, mountain, or cliff on air currents and slowly coming to a safe landing – preferably, on level ground. Although there are several equipment rental outlets throughout town, one of the more prominent is Windsports International, 16145 Victory Blvd, San Fernando Valley (☎818/988-0111). One-hundred dollars will give you the basic experience, but if you want a greater challenge, more expensive package deals are also available. If you've come to LA as a hang gliding pro, bring your glider to the bluffs overlooking the Pacific near Point Fermin for a strikingly picturesque trip over the seacliffs and toward the beach.

A less precarious option for air enthusiasts is **soaring** in specially designed sail-planes. Using air currents to rise and fall, these simple craft provide a memorable experience, if not quite as awe-inspiring as that of hang gliding. In any case, if you'd like to try it, you'll need plenty of open space for your excursion. North of LA in the Antelope Valley, Crystal Soaring, 32810 165th St E, Llano (☎1-800/801-GLIDE), provides planes and lessons to adventure-seekers. While most of your time will doubtless be spent watching from the back seat of the glider, you'll have a vivid experience that you, and your stomach, will not soon forget.

Finally, if the above ideas frighten you, a **helicopter ride** may provide all the airborne excitement you need. Whether viewing LA's premier sights, like the Hollywood sign, from the air or just escaping the basin's air pollution, there are a number of different packages and tours available, all at fairly steep prices. Outfits offering such trips include Bravo Helicopters, 3401 Airport Drive, Torrance (☎310/325-9565), from which a basic excursion to the South Bay is $90, an overhead tour of LA's top sights is $170, and night tours are available for $140; Group 3 Aviation, 16425 Hart St, Van Nuys Airport, San Fernando Valley (☎818/994-9376), which has movie-oriented trips from central LA to various points along the coast, $90–170; and Helinet, 16425 Hart St, Van Nuys Airport, San Fernando Valley (☎818/902-0229), with Hollywood-related tours of central LA and coastal areas, at $85–140, but also with pricier package journeys that include dinner, limousine trips, and even horseback riding over mountains, from $240.

Fitness sports: working out, jogging and hiking

If you really want a taste of LA's health mania, **working out** at a fitness club or along the beach is an obvious choice. Whether you've come to pump iron yourself or watch the weightlifters go through their paces, there are few better spots than **Muscle Beach** near the Venice Boardwalk – although having the right abs and biceps is essential, unless you don't mind being humiliated. For less conspicuous bodybuilding and fitness training, LA's numerous **health clubs** are found everywhere, with Gold's Gym and Nautilus among the bigger names.

For less social workouts, **jogging** is a popular choice, though you should concentrate your efforts in the safer Westside, rather than anywhere in Hollywood, Mid-Wilshire, or Downtown. The best routes for joggers include San Vicente Boulevard from Brentwood to Santa Monica, Sunset Boulevard through Beverly Hills and West LA (but not Hollywood), the Arroyo Seco in Pasadena, the Lake Hollywood perimeter (see p.88), and most stretches along the beach – except for the busy, chaotic bike path. Also on the beach, you may be able to join a **volleyball** game at any of the sandy courts from Santa Monica to Marina del Rey. Hermosa Beach is another good choice for volleyball, as the city is famous for hosting competitions in the sport throughout the year.

For workouts requiring sports equipment, **tennis** is played at courts across LA, with space available for visitors at city parks and universities. Call the Department of Recreation and Parks for more information (☎213/485-5555). **Rock climbing** has also gained in popularity, and private rock "clubs" or "gyms" allow you to scale vertical surfaces to your heart's content – equipment can also be rented for an additional fee. For further information on the sport, visit the Rock Gym, 600 Long Beach Blvd, Long Beach (☎562/983-5500), one of several LA-area climbing venues.

Hiking

The best workout in town is also one of the cheapest. **Hiking** in LA doesn't have the same reputation as it does in other parts of the country, but under no circumstances is it an inferior, token pursuit. Rather, the Santa Monica Mountains – a huge natural preserve – have many different trails and routes for exploration, most of which feature awe-inspiring scenery, copious wildlife, and interesting rustic sights (see Chapter 11 for specific examples). You can order information and maps for locations throughout LA by calling the National Park Service (☎818/597-1036), the state Department of Parks (☎818/880-0350), the Santa Monica Mountains Conservancy (☎310/589-3200 ext 129 or 310/454-1395 ext 105), or Hiking in LA (☎818/501-1005), a private group that offer tours in several foreign languages, as well as English.

Other leisure activities

If you're interested in less intensive, more casual activities, LA has a sufficient amount of **leisure activities** for your consideration.

Fishing

One of these, **fishing**, is encouraged at some locations, like some of the northern beaches around Malibu. At others, especially Santa Monica and Venice piers, you risk ingesting a lifetime's worth of mercury and cadmium from any fish you're foolish enough to bite into. A better alternative is to take a sport-fishing cruise out to sea and cast your line there, for upwards of $25.

Long Beach Sportfishing, 555 Pico Ave, Long Beach ☎562/432-8993. Overnight and half-day fishing expeditions to deepsea waters, along with seasonal whalewatching trips.

Malibu Sportfishing, 23000 PCH, Malibu ☎310/456-8030. Located on the Malibu Pier, this operator will haul you out to fertile northern waters. Licenses are available for sale and equipment for rent.

Marina del Rey Sportfishing, 13759 Fiji Way, Marina del Rey ☎310/822-3625. Somewhat more commercial, touristy operator, though still featuring the same tour packages as other companies: rental equipment, licenses for sale, day or half-day trips, and so on.

Bowling

Like fishing, **bowling** attracts a die-hard crowd of local enthusiasts, and you can

Sports and
Outdoor
Activities

Sports and Outdoor Activities

find bowling alleys at many spots around town, with some businesses offering "space-age" bowling nights with fancy neon or blacklight decor, glowing balls and lanes, and a goofy Buck Rogers atmosphere. Costs generally run $5 and up per game, with shoe rental a few bucks extra.

Brunswick West Covina, 1060 San Bernardino Rd, West Covina, San Gabriel Valley ☎818/960-3636. Lovers of "Googie" pop architecture will not want to miss this colorful, Polynesian-styled alley – which features its own coffee shop and cocktail lounge – but it's unfortunately located out in the middle of nowhere.

Hollywood Star Lanes, 5227 Santa Monica Blvd, Hollywood ☎213/665-4111. Something of a low-rent cultural institution, with a clientele of sweaty, intense purists and zoned-out rocker types playing in an old-fashioned environment with appropriately kitschy decor. Featured prominently in the Coen Brothers' recent bowling flick, *The Big Lebowski*.

Jewel City, 135 S Glendale Ave, Glendale ☎818/243-1188. Bowling zealots may hate it, but casual fans will enjoy the trek out to this popular Valley spot, where glowing balls, heavy metal music, artificial fog, and headache-inducing lights all serve to distract you from hitting strikes.

Mar Vista Bowl, 12125 Venice Blvd, West LA ☎310/391-5288. Funky old alley east of Venice, which also features Mexican food and weekend karaoke.

Horseback riding

Finally, **horseback riding** is a relaxing pursuit you can experience at several ranches and stables throughout the greater LA region, principally around hills and mountains. Most businesses give you a choice of packages that may include evening journeys, individual or group rides, easy or difficult routes, and various added amenities like dinners or barbeques, which are usually covered in the price. Costs can be anywhere from $20 to $50, depending on the location and package.

K C Malibu Stables, near Mulholland Hwy at 400 N Kanan Rd, Santa Monica Mountains ☎818/879-0444. Provides guided equine tours during the daylight or twilight hours, and occasionally under moonlight, for around $20 per hour.

Los Angeles Equestrian Center, 480 Riverside Drive, Burbank ☎818/840-8401. Offers horse rentals for $15 or evening rides for $33, with a tasty barbeque to boot.

Sunset Ranch, 3400 N Beachwood Drive, Hollywood ☎213/469-5450. A Griffith Park operation that provides evening horse rides through the surrounding area for $35, by reservation only.

Will Rogers Equestrian Center, 1603 Will Rogers State Park Rd, Pacific Palisades ☎310/454-8212. Watch a polo match on the park's front lawn before enjoying a horseback ride around the vicinity for $35.

Chapter 19

Parades and Festivals

With its broad mix of different racial, ethnic, religious, and national groups, LA has a great number of **parades** and **festivals** to celebrate throughout the year. No matter when you come, you'll likely hit some sort of street fair or celebration, especially in summer, when beach culture is in full swing. Still, nice weather year-round means that the outdoor festivities never really stop. The selective list below concentrates on some of the more notable observances, along with smaller, unique events that provide a fun or non-traditional focus. For a list of **public holiday** observances in LA, see "City directory," p.315.

January

Japanese New Year (1st). Art displays, ethnic culinary offerings, and cultural exhibits at this annual Little Tokyo festival. ☎213/628-2725.

Tournament of Roses Parade (1st). Pasadena's famous celebration of floral floats and marching bands along a five-mile stretch of Colorado Boulevard. Coincides with the annual Rose Bowl game. ☎626/419-ROSE.

Martin Luther King Parade and Celebration (9th). The civil rights hero is honored with activities at King Park (☎310/570-6816) and the Baldwin Hills-Crenshaw Mall (☎1-800/945-2589).

February

Los Angeles Bach Festival (throughout month). Revel in the Baroque master's

life and music at the First Congregational Church, just north of Lafayette Park in Westlake, at several times during the month. ☎213/385-1345.

Queen Mary Scottish Festival (14th-15th). All the haggis you can stand at this two-day Long Beach celebration, along with peppy highlands dancing and bagpipes. ☎562/435-3511.

Chinese New Year (first full moon after 21st). Three days of monumental dragon-float street parades and myriad cultural programs, based in Chinatown. ☎213/617-0396.

Bob Marley Reggae Festival (rotating dates). A two-day event that exalts the reggae god with food, music, and plenty of spirit. At the Long Beach Convention and Entertainment Center. ☎562/436-3661.

March

St Patrick's Day (15th). Parade along Colorado Boulevard in Old Town Pasadena. No parade, but freely flowing green beer in the "Irish" bars along Fairfax Avenue in Mid-Wilshire. ☎626/796-5049.

Spring Festival of Flowers (mid-March to mid-April). An explosion of floral color is displayed at Descanso Gardens in the foothill community of La Cañada Flintridge. ☎818/952-4401.

Antelope Valley Poppy Blooms (mid to late March). Although located in the middle of a bleak northern valley, this huge poppy reserve draws big crowds to see

Parades and Festivals

its eye-blinding, fiery orange colors that appear every spring. ☎805/942-0662.

The Academy Awards (end of month). The top movie awards are presented at the Shrine Auditorium or Dorothy Chandler Pavilion. Bleacher seats are available to watch the limousines draw up and the stars emerge for the ceremony. ☎310/247-3000.

April

Blessing of the Animals (Saturday before Easter). A long-established Mexican-originated ceremony. Locals arrive in Olvera Street to have their pets blessed, then watch the attendant parade. ☎213/628-1274.

Long Beach Grand Prix (11th–13th). Zooming around Shoreline Drive south of Downtown are some of auto-racing's best drivers and souped-up vehicles. This city's biggest yearly event. ☎562/436-9953.

San Fernando Valley Jazz Festival (mid-April to mid-May). A good selection of jazz greets your ears at this month-long Valley celebration. ☎818/703-7859.

Renaissance Pleasure Faire (late). Dress up in your best Tudor duds for this olde-fashioned celebration with dancing, theater, food, and the inevitable jousting. Travel to distant Glen Helen park in San Bernardino (☎1-800/52-FAIRE) or to closer California State University in Long Beach (☎562/985-2288).

May

Beach Fest (3rd–4th). Fifty bands and a huge chili cookoff are but a few of the highlights of this annual Long Beach party. ☎562/436-7727.

Cinco de Mayo (5th). A day-long party to commemorate the Mexican victory at the Battle of Puebla. Spirited parade in Olvera Street, and several blocks Downtown are blocked off for Chicano and Hispanic music performances. There are also celebrations in most LA parks. ☎213/624-3660.

Valley Jewish Festival (late). The largest such event west of the Mississippi.

Activities begin at Pierce College, in the San Fernando Valley district of Woodland Hills. ☎818/587-3205.

UCLA Jazz and Reggae Festival (Memorial Day weekend). Plenty of food and music at this two-day celebration on the UCLA campus. ☎310/825-9912.

June

Cajun and Zydeco Festival (first weekend). Long Beach's Rainbow Lagoon is the site of Louisiana-flavored live music, dance lessons, and lots of tasty, spicy cooking. ☎562/427-3713.

Irish Fair and Music Festival (second weekend). Popular music, food, and cultural celebration held at the Santa Anita racetrack in Arcadia. ☎626/503-2511.

Great California Beer Festival (21st–22nd). A wild exaltation of suds, with numerous food stalls, beer vendors, live musical groups, and the requisite rowdy atmosphere, in Long Beach. ☎562/328-8448.

Gay Pride Celebration (late). Parade on Santa Monica Boulevard in West Hollywood. Carnival atmosphere, 250 vendors, and an all-male drag football cheerleading team. ☎213/860-0701.

Aloha Concert Jam (28th–29th). Make colorful leis, race outrigger canoes, indulge in island cuisine, and listen to ethnic music at this celebration of Hawaiian culture. ☎909/606-9494.

July

Independence Day (4th). The *Queen Mary* in Long Beach hosts a particularly large fireworks display, as well as colorful entertainment. Fireworks displays in many places in LA. ☎562/435-3511.

Lotus Festival (first weekend after 4th). An Echo Park celebration with dragon boats, ethnic food, pan-Pacific music, and of course, the resplendent lotus blooms around the lake. ☎213/485-1310.

Garlic Festival (12th–20th). Visit the massive Federal Building complex in

Westwood for a taste of the "stinking rose," courtesy of many different local vendors. Entry fee.

August

Long Beach Jazz Festival (first weekend). At Rainbow Lagoon park downtown, relax and enjoy famous and local performers. ☎562/436-7794.

International Sea Festival (first two weeks). Culmination of the South Bay's sand-and-surf celebration, including cookouts, sports tournaments, and sand-castle contests. ☎562/570-3100.

Nisei Week (10th–14th). Little Tokyo's celebration of Japanese America, with martial arts demonstrations, karaoke, Japanese brush painting, baby shows, and various performances. ☎213/687-7193.

Festa Italia (16th–17th). A rich display of food, music, and culture in the otherwise dreary confines of Santa Monica's Civic Auditorium. ☎310/364-1964.

African Cultural Faire (mid to late). Hundreds of arts and crafts booth and many different entertainers make up this annual celebration at Crenshaw's Rancho Cienega park. ☎213/734-1164.

Long Beach Blues Festival (last weekend). Hear the region's and the country's top blues performers at this annual event at Cal State University. ☎562/985-1686.

September

LA's birthday (5th). A civic ceremony and assorted street entertainment around El Pueblo de Los Angeles to mark the founding of the original pueblo in 1781. Inquiries at City Hall, ☎213/485-2121.

Philippine Arts and Culture Festival (mid). Good food, music, dancing, theater, and film at this annual Cabrillo Beach event near the LA harbor. ☎213/389-3050.

Koreatown Multicultural Festival (18th–21st). Dancing, parading, and Tae Kwan Do exhibitions are the main events at

this colorful Mid-Wilshire celebration. ☎213/730-1495.

Los Angeles County Fair (last two weeks). In Pomona, in the San Gabriel Valley. The biggest county fair in the country, with livestock shows, pie-eating contests, and fairground rides. ☎909/623-3111.

Watts Towers Jazz Festival (late). Two days of community spirit and free music – mostly jazz, R&B, and gospel – with the towers as the striking backdrop. ☎213/847-4646.

Oktoberfest (dates vary). Venture into Alpine Village, in the South Bay suburb of Torrance, to revel in Teutonic culture: hearty German food, music, and dancing abound. ☎310/327-4384.

October

Scandinavian Festival (early). Folk dancing with assorted foods and art, along with vivid displays of ethnic costuming. Held at MGM Plaza in Santa Monica. ☎213/661-4273.

Greek Festival (early). Food and music celebration at St Katherine Greek Orthodox Church in Redondo Beach. Arts and crafts displays and energetic dancing add to the color. ☎310/540-2434.

LA Street Scene (second weekend). Free rock music, community theater, and live comedy on Downtown streets. Held at the same time as West Hollywood's Street Festival, a display of handmade arts and crafts.

Halloween (31st). A wild parade in West Hollywood, where all manner of bizarre and splashy outfits and characters are on display. Or you can opt for the Halloween Shipwreck on the *Queen Mary*, which spends one day as a haunted ocean liner full of favorite ghouls and demons. ☎562/435-3511.

November

Dia de Los Muertos (3rd). The "Day of the Dead," celebrated authentically throughout East LA and more blandly for tourists on Olvera Street. Mexican traditions, such as picnicking on the family

Parades and Festivals

For more on the Watts Towers, see p.153.

Parades and Festivals

burial spot, are grimly upheld.
☎ 213/624-3660.

Intertribal Marketplace (early). At Highland Park's Southwest Museum, many Native American artists and artisans show their vivid, well-crafted works. ☎ 213/221-2164 ext 235.

Doo-dah Parade (Saturday after Thanksgiving). Quintessential LA event that began as a spoof of the Tournament of Roses parade; it's now surprisingly popular, with a cast of absurdly costumed characters marching through Pasadena. ☎ 626/795-9311.

Hollywood Christmas Parade (end). The first and best of the many Yuletide events, with a cavalcade of mind-boggling floats, marching bands, and famous and quasi-famous names from film and TV. ☎ 213/469-2337.

December

Light Festival (throughout month). Hollywood's Griffith Park lights up with this annual showcase that brings a range of bright, ebullient displays to the rustic park setting. ☎ 213/913-4688.

Las Posadas (mid). An Olvera Street event that commemorates the biblical tale of Mary and Joseph looking for a spot to rest on Christmas Eve. Culminates with a piñata-breaking. ☎ 213/968-8492.

Christmas Boat Parade (13th). Marina del Rey is the site for this annual, ocean-going display of brightly lit watercraft. ☎ 310/821-7614.

Kids' LA

LA's attractions are geared mainly for adults, but the city does hold some appeal for **kids**, with a decent enough range of entertaining and educational diversions, from increasingly popular childrens' **museums** to the natural attractions of the city's many **parks and beaches**. If these don't hold the kids' interest, there are always a number of **toy shops** in town where you can undoubtedly pick up something that will. And, of course, there's always **Disneyland** – though you may find this doesn't live up to your expectations.

Numerous cultural institutions, restaurants, and hotels offer **reduced rates** for children, and you'll also see family package-deals sometimes available from tour operators and transport companies (such as VanGo/KidsLimo, which provides 7–14 seat vans with TVs, VCRs, and video games for especially large families; call ☎818/995-3664). However, if bringing kids to the city, you'd be well advised to follow a few general **rules**.

For one, the obvious choices for children's amusement are not always the best. Although many, if not most, kids will doubtless want to experience the thrills and colors of major theme parks like **Disneyland** (p.206), **Knott's Berry Farm** (p.208), and **Magic Mountain** (p.194), it only takes a few days of being jostled by massive crowds, waiting in interminable lines, and eating crummy theme-park food to grow tired of the experience. Children are especially sus-

ceptible to this sort of boredom, particularly if you arrive at the wrong time – like a summer weekend. It always helps to have contingency plans available, which may involve some of the selections below.

Museums

The first and perhaps most obvious choice for children has to be the city's many **museums**, some of which feature kid-friendly exhibits and hands-on, interactive displays. At the **LA Childrens Museum** (p.59), in the Civic Center area Downtown, youngsters can participate in a mock-up of LA's transportation system – without the subway sinkholes – and play with finger paints, discover how an ecosystem works, and press all manner of bright buttons and buzzers. The whole thing isn't terrifically challenging, but for an afternoon's amusement, you could probably do worse by your kid. Pasadena offers a similar experience with its **Kidspace Museum**, 390 S El Molino Ave (☎626/449-9144), where exhibits on natural biology and high technology are the main attractions.

If you prefer your kids' entertainment in smaller packages, visit **Exposition Park** (p.150), south of Downtown, where several different institutions offer more appealing, and less rudimentary, attractions than those found at the kiddie museums. One of these, the **California Museum of Science and Industry** (p.150), has a wealth of displays on

KIDS' LA 297

Kids' LA

ecology, earthquakes, mathematics, general science, and technology, not to mention an exhibit on the artery-clogging dangers of fast food – the kind you might otherwise be eating at the suburban theme parks. Within the complex, an IMAX Theater projects thirty-minute documentaries onto a huge, curved screen and may distract the kids for up to an hour, but not more than the length of two movies, while the nearby Aerospace Hall has a jet stuck to its outside wall and inside shows off a number of aircraft and space vehicles. While not particularly exciting for adults who lack an interest in space travel or aerodynamics, the hall will intrigue most pre-teen visitors. (A similar experience can be found at Santa Monica's **Museum of Flying**, p.137, where mildly interesting, antiquated jets sit in a remodeled airplane hangar.)

Much more appealing to all age groups is the **Natural History Museum of Los Angeles County** (p.150), which, like the **George C Page Museum** in Mid-Wilshire (p.80), is a fine place to view the colossal bones of extinct creatures. The Page Museum mostly features Ice Age-era mammoths, sloths, wolves, and saber-toothed cats dredged up from the adjacent La Brea Tar Pits.

Parks and beaches

Although mainly known for its high-tech spectacles and theme parks, LA also provides plenty of natural outdoor spaces for kids, notably its **parks and beaches**. With many of these bucolic sights being free or minimally priced, these are some of the best choices for kids and can keep them occupied without worrying about high entry fees, long lines, and huge crowds.

The most prominent of LA's natural attractions is undoubtedly **Griffith Park** (p.92), just north of Hollywood. Here you can find an excellent network of hiking, biking, and horse-riding trails amid the rustic charm of a large, mountainous green-space, not to mention prime views of the LA basin and even a glimpse of the Hollywood sign. All kinds of curiosities will pique your children's interest at the park, from a pleasant **bird sanctuary** to the quiet setting of the **Fern Dell**, as well as the imposing profile of the **Griffith Park Observatory**, in which children can experience the projected stars and planets of the observatory, the cloud chamber and other exhibits of the **Hall of Science**, and the always-captivating telescope mounted on the roof.

High Culture for kids

Motivated children with a taste for art and so-called **High Culture** will not be disappointed by LA. Though the **Getty Center** (p.123) and **Los Angeles County Museum of Art** (p.81) are not specifically geared toward children, they both sell headphones and "listening tours" for kids (at least on occasion), and also sell children's guidebooks to fine art in their bookstores.

Children may find **functional art** to be of particular interest in several of the city's galleries as well. Bizarre clocks, chairs, and televisions are but a few of the novelties to look at, and perhaps even touch and tinker with, at places

like the **Gallery of Functional Art** (p.136) in Santa Monica's Bergamot Station, or **Artscape**, 2226 E Fourth St, Long Beach (☎562/434-3224), where educational classes and guest speakers also add to the appeal.

Finally, for a bit of musical edification and symphonic entertainment, the **LA Philharmonic** (p.276) offers seasonal "youth symphonies," playing pieces like Prokofiev's *Peter and the Wolf*, Saint-Saëns' *Carnival of the Animals*, accessible works from Bach, Mozart, and Vivaldi, and occasionally, Britten's *Young Person's Guide to the Orchestra*. Call ☎213/850-2000 for information on this year's offerings.

The observatory, and its attendant displays, will probably appeal to older children more than the **LA Zoo** (p.92) on the other side of the park, where a standard array of animals is shown before the public in mostly outdated displays and cramped environments. Younger kids may enjoy the zoo's central "houses" of reptiles and koalas, though everyone else may be tempted to make for the exits. Similarly, **Travel Town** (p.94) is generally geared to smaller tots, who will appreciate walking on and touching the disused old trains sitting near the LA River.

If you're not planning a stop at Griffith Park but still want a rustic experience for the kids, the **Santa Monica Mountains** are a good place to visit for the many hiking trails and buzzing wildlife. One sight in the mountains, **San Vicente Mountain Park** (p.203), a decommissioned missile base, is a fascinating excursion for older kids, who can learn about the Cold War and get great views of LA at the same time. **Paramount Ranch** (p.203) is equally interesting for kids and adults as the site of many different Hollywood westerns. Not far away, **Malibu Creek State Park** (p.203) is a good choice for a half-day family outing into some of LA's more rugged, unspoiled terrain, while **Tropical Terrace** (p.201) is a modern ruin that kids can gleefully explore.

LA has, of course, a number of popular **beaches**, most of which will be just fine for a supervised day of splashing around. The best can be found around **Malibu** (p.200) and along the **Orange County Coast** (p.210). One beach area that's no good for swimming, but has a better slice of social activity for children (at least during the daytime), is the **Santa Monica Pier** (p.133), a fine place for cotton candy, video games, and carnival rides. Sometimes during the year, the famed Cirque du Soleil circus sets up tent in the parking lot here and amuses young and old alike.

Kids' LA

Toy shops

F A O Schwarz, in the Beverly Center mall, 8500 Beverly Blvd, West Hollywood ☎310/659-4547. The place to go if you're looking for the latest, flashiest, and most expensive toys, from Barbie collector sets to huge stuffed animals to assorted high-tech gizmos.

Hollywood Toys and Costumes, 6600 Hollywood Blvd, Hollywood ☎213/464-4444 or 1-800/554-3444. A one-of-a-kind LA retailer, offering not only a full array of dolls and action-flick figurines for the kids, but also dress-up treats for adults – wigs, Halloween outfits, costume jewelry and the like.

Imperial Toy, 2060 E Seventh St, Downtown ☎213/489-2100. Despite being located in a decrepit strip by the LA River, this toy dealer offers some of the best prices in town on frisbees, dolls, action figures, and especially marbles and "bubble toys."

Pumpkins Toys, 138 N Larchmont Blvd, Mid-Wilshire ☎213/465-4505 or 1-888/400-TOYS. Expect to pay top dollar for the many items at this Larchmont Village designer toyseller, which offers old-fashioned favorites like rocking horses, model train sets, handmade dolls, and colorful puppets.

Chapter 21

Shops and Galleries

Shopping in LA is an art. The level of disposable income in the wealthy parts of the city is astronomical, and touring the more outrageous stores can offer a great insight into LA life – revealing who's got the money and what they're capable of wasting it on. Whether you want to shop for a new light bulb or pair of socks, lay waste to a wad, or simply be a voyeur in the orgy of acquisition, there are, besides the run-of-the-mill retailers you'll find anywhere, big **department stores** and mega-sized **malls** where most of the serious shopping goes on. Not to be missed are LA's countless **clothing** stores, which sell everything from ritzy designer apparel to moth-eaten thriftwear, and its **hair** and **makeup salons**, which give the fanciest dos and looks to the city's fashion elite, as well as anyone else who can afford them.

LA also has a good assortment of **bookstores** and **record stores**, both of which are in abundance throughout the city. Whether you're in search of a cozy secondhand shop or a megastore with all the latest releases, plus a café to boot, you won't have a hard time finding it. There's an equally diverse array of **food stores**, from corner delis and supermarkets to fancy cake stores and gourmet markets. You'll also find several **specialty stores** selling perfectly weird LA souvenirs, from colorful wind-up toys to macabre beach towels.

If you have bags of money to spend, LA provides plenty of cultural shopping as well, in the form of both trendy and ultratrendy **galleries**, where you can spot the latest works from the city's hottest young artists offered for sale at jaw-dropping prices. For a cheaper indulgence, try the beachside artists found along the Venice Boardwalk, where you can pick up a kitschy sunset or unicorn or, if you're lucky, perhaps a masterwork by an undiscovered genius – but don't count on it.

Shopping districts

While you can find souvenirs and touristy merchandise in most consumer zones, there are a few **shopping districts** that are especially worth noting. Downtown's buying focus is undoubtedly the **Garment District**, just east of Old Downtown, where you can get a variety of fabrics and clothes, as well as designer knock-offs and markdowns, for some of the cheapest prices anywhere in LA. Mid-Wilshire has no less than four main shopping areas: **La Brea Avenue**, just north of Wilshire, a collection of clothing, furniture, and antique stores arrayed along each side of a busy thoroughfare; **Third Street**, a short strip of boutiques and restaurants near the Beverly Center mall; **Larchmont Village**, a mix of small retailers and chain stores; and the irrepressible **Melrose Avenue**, between Mid-Wilshire and Hollywood, LA's most conspicuously hip area, a place where you can get anything from used clothing to cut-rate antiques to designer dog collars – for humans.

To the north, **Hollywood Boulevard** is one big shopping zone, especially for movie memorabilia and discount T-shirts, with particular concentrations of merchandisers from La Brea Avenue to Gower Street. West Hollywood is more self-consciously chic, and you can expect to find small boutiques along **Santa Monica Boulevard** and numerous music and book stores along the **Sunset Strip**. Beverly Hills is, of course, the hub of upscale shopping, especially in the downtown core known as the **Golden Triangle**, highlighted by **Rodeo Drive**. West LA is, for the most part, lacking in popular retail areas, except perhaps for Brentwood's **San Vicente Boulevard**, another ritzy zone, and **Westwood Village**, full of inexpensive bookstores, clothing outlets, and record stores. Out in Santa Monica, the **Third Street Promenade** is one of LA's most trafficked strips, with a good mix of small retailers

and chain stores; linked from the Promenade by a free bus (in summer), Santa Monica's **Main Street** is popular for its collection of book dealers, clothing stores, and trinket shops.

In the outlying areas, there are countless malls, minimalls, and chain-store outlets, but only a few truly interesting places to shop or browse. **Downtown Long Beach** is appealing for its used book stores and scattered clothing shops, as well as its architecture and restaurants; **Old Pasadena** – notably Colorado Boulevard – offers music stores, apparel merchandisers, and used book sellers; **Ventura Boulevard**, running north of the Santa Monica Mountains in the San Fernando Valley, just east of the 405 freeway, is a good place to buy new and used music, assorted souvenirs, and cheap clothing; and Newport Beach's **Balboa Peninsula**, along the Orange County Coast, sells expensive designer duds and similarly pricey outfits at smaller boutiques..

Department stores and shopping malls

Each of LA's neighborhoods has a collection of ordinary stores and minimalls. You'll find many of the best sources of cheap toiletries and staples at places such as K-Mart and Target. A step up from these in price and quality, though still good for general shopping, are **department stores**, which more often than not are included within massive **shopping malls**, sometimes resembling self-contained city suburbs, around which Angelenos do the bulk of their buying.

Department stores

Barneys, 9570 Wilshire Blvd, Beverly Hills ☎310/276-4400. At the base of the Golden Triangle, this New York retailer offers five levels of dapper clothing for exorbitant prices; if you don't have the right look, expect the sales clerks to ignore you.

Bloomingdale's, 10250 Santa Monica Blvd, in the Century City Mall, Century City

Shops and Galleries

Shops and Galleries

310/772-2100. A recent arrival to LA, this East Coast chain features all the standard men's and women's apparel, kitchen items, and assorted jewelry and trinkets.

Macy's, 8500 Beverly Blvd, in the Beverly Center mall ☎310/854-6655. Another newcomer to the LA department store scene, offering a broad selection of clothing and personal effects. Other branches at 10250 Santa Monica Blvd, in the Century City Mall, Century City (☎310/556-1611); 315 Colorado Ave, in the Santa Monica Place mall, Santa Monica (☎310/393-1441); and 10861 Weyburn Ave, Westwood (☎310/208-4211).

Neiman-Marcus, 9700 Wilshire Blvd, Beverly Hills ☎310/550-5900. With three fancy restaurants, opulent displays of jewelry, and a plethora of fur coats, this store is quintessential Beverly Hills. Don't forget to ask about the his 'n' her leopard skins.

Nordstrom, 10830 Pico Blvd, in the Westside Pavilion mall, West LA ☎310/470-6155. Mostly clothing and accessories at this Westside department store. If you can't decide on the right party dress or power tie, ask for a "personal shopper" to do your bidding – for a steep price.

Robinsons-May, 103 Santa Monica Place, in the Santa Monica Place mall, ☎310/451-2411. Two old LA retailing warhorses forged into a single corporate entity; the resulting department store has better prices than some of its competitors to go along with a wide selection of clothing and housewares.

Saks Fifth Avenue, 9600 Wilshire Blvd, Beverly Hills ☎310/275-4211. Expensive perfume, eye-popping jewelry, and high fashion – everything you need for a day strolling around Rodeo Drive and looking like you belong there.

Shopping malls

Beverly Center, 8500 Beverly Blvd, between Mid-Wilshire and West Hollywood. Chic shopping for the masses:

seven acres of boutiques, Macy's and Bloomingdale's department stores, a multiplex cinema, and a *Hard Rock Café*, all in one complex that resembles a giant brown concrete bunker, trimmed in hideous green and purple.

Century City Marketplace, 10250 Santa Monica Blvd, Century City. An outdoor mall with one hundred upscale shops, including a branch of New York's Metropolitan Museum gift shop and a Rand McNally map outlet. The place to come to see stars do their shopping, and a spot to catch a first-run movie in excellent surroundings (see p.281).

Del Amo Fashion Center, Hawthorne Blvd at Carson St, Torrance. A huge mall in the South Bay, with five major anchor stores – Macy's, Montgomery Ward, J C Penney, Robinsons-May, and Sears – and a convenient location just south of the 405 freeway.

Media City Center, E Magnolia Blvd at N San Fernando Rd, Burbank. Branches of Sears, Macy's, and the low-cost furniture retailer IKEA at this complex of buildings just outside the heart of old Burbank, immediately adjacent to the I-5 freeway.

The Plaza Pasadena, E Colorado Blvd at S Los Robles Ave, Pasadena. Near the center of Old Pasadena, this giant, bunker-like mall features the usual suspects – Macy's, J C Penney, Sears – but completely lacks the historic charm of the resurrected neighborhood around it.

Santa Monica Place, Broadway at Second St, Santa Monica. Sunny, skylit mall with three tiers of shops and an outdated postmodern-pastel decor. The third floor is almost empty of consumer traffic much of the time, and the chain-link-walled parking garage is of minor note as a Frank Gehry design experiment.

Seventh Street Marketplace, Seventh and Figueroa sts, Downtown. Anchored by Macy's department store, at the foot of the Citicorp office towers, this subterranean three-level mall primarily caters to office workers in the surrounding towers. Nothing here you haven't seen elsewhere.

Sherman Oaks Galleria, Ventura and Sepulveda blvds, San Fernando Valley. The original home to the notorious "Valley girls" of popular lore, this aging behemoth sits near the 405 freeway and has limited commercial appeal, with only Robinsons May department stores at both ends to provide interest.

South Coast Plaza, 3333 Bristol St, north of 405 freeway, Costa Mesa. Orange County's main supermall, with nearly three hundred shops and huge crowds of locals and tourists. Seven anchor stores – among them Macy's, Saks Fifth Avenue, and Nordstrom – plus a good mix of low- and high-end retailers. At the least, you're sure to get a good workout from navigating the place.

Third Street Promenade, Third St between Broadway and Wilshire Blvd, Santa Monica. A rare successful attempt to lure back consumers to the heart of the city. Despite its prime location, this commercial stretch was an eyesore until redevelopment money turned things around, to the point where the place is now absolutely packed on weekend evenings: mobs scurry about in a fervor to get to the many bookstores, fashion outlets, restaurants, cinemas and such, amid the throngs of itinerant musicians, homeless folks, street lunatics, and ivy-covered dinosaur fountains. Easily the most worthwhile mall in the region.

Westside Pavilion, Pico and Westwood blvds, West LA. Postmodern shopping complex centered on the Nordstrom department store – a clothes, shoes, jewelry, and cosmetics retailer that provides regular customers with a personal "shopper" (ie an employee who does all the legwork around the store and comes back with a cache of goods). Overall, though, no real surprises here.

Clothes and fashion

LA's **clothing** stores are some of its most prominent, and most heavily visited, retail outlets. Of course, there is always a slew of **chain stores** to choose from, where you can pick up a jacket, gloves,

or pantyhose for standard, and occasionally discounted, prices, but it's in the city's own unique retailers that you can really get a sense of how LA dresses and what its stylistic attitudes are. **Designer boutiques** are conspicuous along Rodeo Drive, but there are branches throughout the rest of town as well, and they are always interesting in revealing what the upper class is wearing – though you can expect a few haughty sneers if you're not considered to be the right kind of customer. Much more relaxed are the **funky shops**, many along Melrose Avenue, where you can get black club outfits, garishly sequined dresses, or tight, Day-Glo vinyl pants for a night on the town, as well as a broad array of sexy, skintight lingerie and fetish attire. On the other hand, if you're just looking for cheap duds, LA has a good selection of **secondhand** clothiers, with **vintage clothing** dealers charging somewhat more for nicely preserved artifacts from previous decades.

Chain stores

Giorgio Armani, 436 N Rodeo Drive, Beverly Hills ☎310/271-5555. One of the elite fashion dealers in LA, with sleek, well-cut suits that are standard issue to movie biz agents, lawyers, and other self-anointed big shots. For cheaper, though still expensive, clothing, try the Emporio Armani just down the road at 9533 Brighton Way ☎310/271-7790.

Ralph Lauren, 444 N Rodeo Drive, Beverly Hills ☎310/281-7200. An incomparable place to get yourself outfitted as English gentry. Pick up a gilded walking cane, finely tailored suit, and a smart tweed cap, all for a small fortune.

Designer boutiques

Betsey Johnson, 7311 Melrose Ave ☎213/931-4490. An upscale boutique well suited for Melrose, where stiletto heels, micro-miniskirts, and fashionably dingy attire are all part of a funky look for which you'll pay plenty.

Chanel, 400 N Rodeo Drive, Beverly Hills ☎310/278-5500. As you'd expect, a

Shops and Galleries

Shops and Galleries

pricey selection of perfumes and clothes from Paris. You'll get a healthy dose of attitude, too, if you've only come to browse.

Fred Segal, 8100 Melrose Ave ☎213/651-4129. For those poseurs and party-hoppers who wouldn't be spotted dead in Beverly Hills, this Melrose store provides just the right mix of designer gloss and funky edge with its stylish shoes and clothing.

Frederick's of Hollywood, 6606 Hollywood Blvd, Hollywood ☎213/466-8506. The pink-and-purple tower of Frederick's houses a panoply of frilly, lacy, and leathery lingerie, of varying prices, as well as a Hall of Fame devoted to famous celebrity undergarments (see p.98).

Gucci, 347 N Rodeo Drive, Beverly Hills ☎310/278-3451. Aside from the outlandishly priced shoes, wallets, and accessories you can find here, there's also a fair assortment of men's and women's clothing, though most tourists head straight for the leather purses.

Kenneth Cole, 8752 Sunset Blvd, West Hollywood ☎310/289-5085. Leather jackets, tapered boots, sleek earrings, and hip-hugging pants – all in black – to help you get in to the chic nightclubs in town.

Louis Vuitton, 307 N Rodeo Drive, Beverly Hills ☎310/859-0457. Designer wallets and luggage, with plenty of expensive styles from which to choose. Soon to expand into 273 N Rodeo, formerly occupied by the now-closed Fred Hayman.

Spike's Joint West, 7263 Melrose Ave ☎213/932-7064. Colorful hats, shirts, and jackets at this boutique operated by director Spike Lee, who can sometimes be spotted between the aisles when he's in town to make a movie.

Todd Oldham, 7386 Beverly Blvd, Mid-Wilshire ☎213/936-6045. Smart, quirky clothing designed to fit size-2 runway models. Still, a bit less pretentious than the snooty fashion outlets crowding the Golden Triangle to the west.

Funky Clothing

Don't Panic!, 802 N San Vicente Blvd, West Hollywood ☎310/652-9689. The racy counterpart to the many bland T-shirt shops in LA, a place that offers more than a hundred shirts with shocking, crude, or off-color slogans.

Dream Dresser, 8444 Santa Monica Blvd, West Hollywood ☎213/848-3480. Corsets, dresses, and lingerie made from rubber, leather, vinyl, and such, with custom-designed outfits for either women or men.

Ipso Facto, 517 N Harbor Blvd, Fullerton ☎714/525-7865. Piercing supplies, goth clothing, and a full range of skull-emblazoned belts, rings, and boots at this retailer out in, of all places, Orange County.

Na Na, 1228 Third St, Santa Monica ☎310/451-5998. Near the end of the Promenade, Na Na sells funky shoes and high-heeled boots, as well as a good number of goofy T-shirts, incense candles, and off-kilter greeting cards.

Necromance, 7220 Melrose Ave ☎213/934-8684. A window skeleton invites you in to sample all the latest ghoulish clothing at this morbidly themed apparel shop, which sells outfits suitable for TV's Elvira, Mistress of the Dark.

Retail Slut, 7308 Melrose Ave ☎213/934-1339. An essential Melrose stop, where you can pick up all the vinyl fetishwear, club outfits, leather dog collars, and spiked wristbands you'll ever need.

Syrens, 7225 Beverly Blvd, Mid-Wilshire ☎213/936-6693. A wide selection of poured-on latex outfits for sexual adventures or simple club-hopping. Ring the bell for entry.

Trashy Lingerie, 402 N La Cienega Blvd, West Hollywood ☎310/652-4543. Not only can you find the sort of risqué undergarments suggested by this store's name, you can also browse through a wide variety of more traditional satin and silk bras, teddies, and bustiers. All of the revealing items are handmade, and you'll have to pay $2 for an annual "membership fee" to get in.

Urban Outfitters, 1440 Third St, Santa Monica ☎310/394-1404. An odd clothing store that offers ragged retro-1970s jackets, wrought-iron candlesticks, abstract chunks of jewelry, dirty-joke books, and off-the-wall T-shirts.

Secondhand and vintage clothing

Aardvark's, 7579 Melrose Ave ☎213/655-6769. This is one of LA's best spots for buying used garments, whether wild psychedelic shirts, nasty old leisure suits, goofy ball caps, frumpy pants, or more recent – and more fashionable – shirts, skirts, dresses, and suits.

American Rag, 150 S La Brea Ave, Mid-Wilshire ☎213/935-3154. Though supposedly a secondhand clothing store, the beaten-up denim jackets, floral-print dresses, and retro shoes for sale here are strictly upper-end material, often restyled enough to be brand-new items.

Cheap, 705 S Pacific Ave, San Pedro ☎310/547-1000. Worth a trip down to the harbor area to pick up bargain-basement coats, dresses, shoes, and skirts from $2–10. The secondhand garments vary in quality, though some are in surprisingly good condition.

Golyester, 136 S La Brea Ave, Mid-Wilshire ☎213/931-1339. Very vintage stuff, with clothes dating as far back as the nineteenth century, in every sort of fabric imaginable.

Julian's, 8366 W Third St, Mid-Wilshire ☎213/655-3011. No retro-kitsch here, only ultrachic vintage clothing from the 1950s and before, including hats, furs, dinner jackets, dresses, and scarves.

Muskrat, 1248 Third St, Santa Monica ☎310/394-1713. The best place to look if you want an old, postwar Hawaiian shirt. Also a good collection of jackets, dresses, and outfits from around the 1940s.

Polkadots and Moonbeams, 8367 Third St, Mid-Wilshire ☎213/651-1746.

Dresses, swimsuits, and sweaters from the pre-1970s era, most in fine condition and some quite affordable. If it's more modern clothing you crave, drift down to the pricier contemporary outlet at 8381 Third St (☎213/655-3880).

Reel Clothes, 12132 Ventura Blvd, Studio City ☎818/508-7762. Sells all types of used clothing and props from movie and TV show sets that have wrapped production. Buy the scarf, hat, or dress or complete outfit of a lead character in a recent movie of your fancy.

Star Wares, 2817 Main St, Santa Monica ☎310/399-0224. If you desperately want something previously owned by a movie or TV celebrity, here you can buy old junk from the closets of the stars, including freakish black dresses from Cher, tough-guy duds from Mel Gibson, and worn-out jackets from Don Johnson.

Finishing touches: hair, makeup and nails

As the capital of self-centered indulgence and personal transformation, LA has a large array of **hair** and **makeup salons** where you can be teased, sprayed, made up, and slicked down. While cheap spots for a haircut are everywhere (Supercuts is one of the more widespread names), if you're really looking to get a fancy makeover, or a **manicure**, to fit in with the trendsetting crowd, there are a few top-notch salons that will work quite nicely for you, as well as some that offer more quietly affordable prices.

Christophe, 348 N Beverly Drive, Beverly Hills. No listed number. Although you may have a tough time getting into this salon if you're not at least a low-level celebrity, the place is worth a look for its showman/hair stylist – the man who famously cut President Clinton's hair on the tarmac of LAX a few years ago.

Colleciones de Raquel, 9873 Little Santa Monica Blvd, Beverly Hills ☎310/203-9240. While this store also sells lingerie and skin care products, its upscale, handmade cosmetics are the main attraction to the local fashion elite.

Shops and Galleries

Delux Beauty Parlor, 727 N Fairfax, West Hollywood ☎213/658-8585. Whether you're going clubbing or to a power lunch, the hair styling, makeovers, skin care, and manicures at this parlor will do the trick for around $50–85.

Jessica Nail Clinic, 8627 Sunset Blvd, West Hollywood ☎310/659-9292. The place where the stars get their manicures, and you can too, often for around $25 – a bargain for clients like Julia Roberts and Nancy Reagan.

Larchmont Beauty Center, 208 N Larchmont Blvd, Mid-Wilshire ☎213/461-0162. Features a comprehensive, and pricey, assortment of beauty care treatments, from hair styling, manicures and pedicures, makeovers, and skin care to Swedish massage and aromatherapy.

Raphaël, 9020 Burton Way, Beverly Hills ☎310/275-5810. Watch this haircare wizard do masterful things to your tangles and split ends; in the process, you might even glimpse a celebrity or two.

Robinson's Beautilities, 12320 Venice Blvd, West LA ☎310/398-5757. Along with a good selection of hair care products and makeup, this supply house stocks a fascinating assortment of designer and fright wigs, facial glitter, and special-effects makeup for the movie biz.

Drugstores and pharmacies

LA Medical Center pharmacy, in the Kaiser Permanente building, 4867 Sunset Blvd, Hollywood ☎213/667-8301. 24 hr.

Horton & Converse Pharmacy, 11600 Wilshire Blvd, West LA ☎310/478-0801. 24 hrs.

Rite-Aid, 226 N Larchmont Blvd, Mid-Wilshire ☎213/467-1397; 463 N Bedford Drive, Beverly Hills ☎310/247-0838.

Sav-On, 201 N Los Angeles St, Downtown ☎213/620-1491; 2505 Wilshire Blvd, Santa Monica ☎310/828-6056.

Thrifty, 501 S Broadway, Downtown ☎213/626-0947; 3420 Wilshire Blvd, Mid-Wilshire ☎213/380-9797; 300 N Cañon Drive, Beverly Hills ☎310/273-7293; 1808 Wilshire Blvd, Santa Monica ☎310/829-7651.

West LA Medical Center Pharmacy, 6041 Cadillac Ave, West LA ☎323/857-2151. 24 hrs.

Food and drink

Since eating out in LA is so common, you may never have to shop for **food** and **drink** at all. But if you're preparing a picnic, or want to indulge in a bit of home cooking, there are plenty of places to stock up. **Delis** and **groceries**, many open around the clock, are found on more or less every corner in LA, and supermarkets are almost as common, with some open 24 hours or at least until 10pm – Lucky, Alpha-Beta, Gelson's, Pavilions, Ralph's, and Trader Joe's are the names to look out for. There are also a number of interesting **ethnic groceries** and **health food stores**, the latter of which are decidedly expensive, as well as a disparate collection of outlets for **baked** and **dairy goods**, among other items, mainly clustered in West LA. To buy alcohol, you need go no further than the nearest supermarket – Trader Joe's is the cheapest and best.

Delis and groceries

Bristol Farms, 606 Fair Oaks Ave, South Pasadena ☎626/441-5450. One of the best grocers in the region, with branches throughout the LA suburbs. It's worth a trip to South Pasadena to sample their delicious meats, cheeses, and caviar and pick up a bottle of wine as well. Prices can be rather high. Another location in Long Beach, 2080 Bellflower Blvd (☎562/430-4134).

Greenblatt's, 8017 Sunset Blvd, West Hollywood ☎213/656-0606. A Sunset Strip deli that is a neighborhood favorite, offering thick, meaty sandwiches, good chicken soup, and a nice array of wines – plus it stays open until 2am.

Jerry's Famous Deli, 13181 Mindanao Way, Marina del Rey ☎310/821-6626. One of several LA locations for this local culinary icon, where you can nosh on traditional favorites while keeping an eye out for wandering celebrities, especially in the middle of the night – the deli chain is open around the clock.

Langer's, 704 S Alvarado St, Mid-Wilshire ☎213/483-8050. In the middle of the high-crime Westlake district, this is nevertheless one of LA's finest delis, with an excellent selection of meats and baked goods, as well as succulent pastrami sandwiches. Open daylight hours only.

Nate 'n' Al's, 414 N Beverly Drive, Beverly Hills ☎310/274-0101. Perhaps LA's best deli, in the middle of Beverly Hills' Golden Triangle. Tinseltown old-timers and modern high-rollers swear by its delicious meats, breads, and sandwiches – all at surprisingly affordable prices.

Smart and Final, 7220 Melrose Ave, Mid-Wilshire ☎213/655-2211. A bulk retail chain, which packs its stores with big, industrial-sized boxes of cereal, paper towels, fruit juice, and just about anything else you might need in massive quantities.

Stan's Produce, 9307 W Pico Blvd, West LA ☎310/274-1865. A favorite neighborhood grocer with a fine seasonal display of fruits, vegetables, and exotic produce. Just south of Beverly Hills.

Vicente Foods, 12027 San Vicente Blvd, Brentwood ☎310/472-5215. If you're in this neighborhood, hunting down O J Simpson-scandal sights, this is a good place to stop and commune with the locals, who come here for the terrific selection of quality foods and aren't deterred by the high prices.

Wally's, 2107 Westwood Blvd, West LA ☎310/475-0606. A gourmet grocery that caters to the local wine-and-cheese crowd and also features a fine assortment of caviar and other assorted foodstuffs.

Ethnic groceries

Alpine Village, 833 W Torrance Blvd, Torrance ☎310/327-2483. Quite a hike, and in a rather drab area, but this place has all the bratwurst and schnitzel you'll ever need.

Bangluck Supermarket, 5170 Hollywood Blvd, Hollywood ☎213/660-8000. Thai grocer in Los Feliz, one of several branches in a local chain, with meat, fish, sauces, and noodles to help you cook a Southeast Asian feast, or to provide a simple snack.

Bay Cities Importing, 1517 Lincoln Blvd, Santa Monica ☎310/395-8279. This Westside retailer offers piles of fresh pasta, along with spices, meats, sauces, and many French and Middle Eastern imports.

Bharat Bazaar, 11510 Washington Blvd, Culver City ☎310/398-6766. One of several excellent Indian grocers around this stretch of Culver City.

Cañon Deli, 338 N Cañon Drive, Beverly Hills ☎310/246-9463. Pick up a bottle of wine or a pound of Italian meat, but don't miss the cheap turkey sandwiches during lunchtime.

Claro's Italian Market, 1003 E Valley Blvd, San Gabriel ☎626/288-2026. A compact but well-stocked haven of Italian wines, chocolate, crackers, and store-brand frozen meals. A second room houses a deli and bakery with at least forty varieties of cookies.

Domingo's, 17548 Ventura Blvd, San Fernando Valley ☎818/981-4466. A good reason for traveling to Encino: authentic Italian meats, pastas, and cheeses.

Elat, 8730 Pico Blvd, West LA ☎310/659-7070. Mainly Middle Eastern staples at this colorful market, located near other ethnic grocers on Pico Boulevard just southeast of Beverly Hills.

Gastronom, 7859 Santa Monica Blvd, West Hollywood ☎213/654-9456. Catering to the burgeoning Russian community, but popular with just about everyone; the smoked fish and caviar are the highlights.

La Canasta in El Mercado, 3425 E First St, East LA ☎213/269-2953. Three floors

Shops and Galleries

Shops and Galleries

of authentic Mexican and Central American food: chiles, chayotes, and tasty desserts.

Market World, 2740 Olympic Blvd, Koreatown ☎213/382-2922. A good range of Korean meat, vegetable, and noodle dishes here – one of the better and larger groceries in Koreatown.

Nijiya Market, 2130 Sawtelle Blvd, West LA ☎310/575-3300. Bentos – elemental rice-and-meat combinations – are some of the succulent takeout items you can get from this Japanese grocer.

Olson's Deli, 5560 Pico Blvd, Mid-Wilshire ☎213/938-0742. Herring, meat-balls, and assorted sausages at this Swedish grocer, one of the few Scandinavian food retailers in LA and definitely worth a look.

Portos Cuban Bakery, 315 N Brand Blvd, Glendale ☎818/956-5996. Tasty pastries and desserts, along with spicy sandwiches.

Standard Sweets and Snacks, 18600 Pioneer Blvd, Artesia ☎562/860-6364. A good Indian finger-food joint selling vegetarian *dosas* (pancakes) and delicious desserts, along with other traditional fare. North of Long Beach.

United Foods, 736 N Broadway, Chinatown ☎213/624-3788. A colorful display of traditional and exotic meats, from pork to boar, at this Chinese food retailer, which also has a nearby branch at 419 Alpine St ☎213/620-0368.

Health food stores

Co-Opportunity, 1525 Broadway, Santa Monica ☎310/451-8902. A very popular seller of organic and vegetarian foods, which are unfortunately arranged in too-cramped spaces, making shopping here a nerve-wracking experience during peak hours.

Erewhon, 7660 Beverly Blvd, Mid-Wilshire ☎213/937-0777. Next door to the CBS studios, selling pricey health food and all the wheat grass you can swallow. The epitome of health-obsessed LA.

Full o' Life, 2525 W Magnolia Blvd, Burbank ☎818/845-8343. This mother of all health food stores dates back to 1959 and offers an organic market, deli, dairy, restaurant, and book department, and there are two nutritionists and a naturopath on the premises daily.

Mother's Market, 225 E 17th St, Costa Mesa ☎714/631-4741. A large health food retailer in Orange County. If you're traveling along the coast, this is the perfect place to stock up on bulk supplies of juice, vitamins, and veggie cuisine.

Nowhere Natural Foods, 8001 Beverly Blvd, Mid-Wilshire ☎213/658-6506. This shabby-looking old building has a loyal following of hard-core acolytes and veg-ans willing to pay a bit more for clean, sanctified food.

Quinn's, 1864 N Vermont Ave, Hollywood ☎213/663-8307. One of the oldest organic food stores around, with an adequate selection and decent prices, but without the hip cultural cachet currently attached to Westside health-food-ers. Also at 8466 Melrose Ave, West Hollywood (☎213/651-5950).

Whole Foods Market, 11666 National Blvd, West LA ☎310/996-8840. Similar to many other Westside wholefood operations, with a fine assortment of health food, a nice environment, high prices, and a sometimes haughty clientele. This citywide chain's nearest other branch is at 239 N Crescent Drive, Beverly Hills (☎310/274-3360).

Wild Oats Community Market, 603 S Lake Ave, Pasadena ☎626/792-1778. The best selection of organic wine in LA in a pleasantly European market atmosphere. Produce is also quite good for selection and taste, and the prices reflect this fact.

Baked and dairy goods

Al Gelato, 806 S Robertson Blvd, West LA ☎310/659-8069. That old Italian version of ice cream – gelato – is here served with Southern California panache: delicious flavors doled out in sizable helpings. The espresso gelato is mouth-watering.

Beverlywood Bakery, 9128 Pico Blvd, West LA ☎310/550-9842. Old World desserts and baked goods, from heavy strudels to chewy, thick-crusted breads. The premium prices reflect the store's proximity to Beverly Hills.

The Cheese Store, 419 N Beverly Drive, Beverly Hills ☎310/278-2855 or 1-800/547-1515. More than four hundred types of cheese from all over the world, including every kind produced in the US, with many of them suspended invitingly over your head.

Cobbler Factory, 33 N Catalina Ave, Pasadena ☎626/449-2152. With a range of fruity desserts and a faithful local following, this place sits in a prime spot near Old Pasadena, where you can snack on these tempting sweets – especially anything with berries – as you wander about the grand architecture of this shopping precinct.

Diamond Bakery, 335 N Fairfax Ave, Mid-Wilshire ☎213/655-0534. In the heart of the Fairfax District, this Jewish bakery provides a good number of traditional favorites, including cheesecakes, breads, and rugalach, and sells mostly to devoted local customers.

Eiger, 124 S Barrington Place, Brentwood ☎310/471-6955. Whether in cones, dishes, or pies, the ice cream at this Westside favorite is always good and rich.

Hansen Cakes, 1072 S Fairfax Ave, Mid-Wilshire ☎213/936-4332. A local institution that features a collection of resplendently decorated, and rather tasty, cakes. Also at 193 S Beverly Drive, Beverly Hills ☎213/272-0474.

La Brea Bakery, 624 S La Brea Ave, Mid-Wilshire ☎213/939-6813. This bakery (adjacent to the upscale *Campanile* restaurant; see p.246) is a serious treat for anyone with an interest in fine breads, from traditional sourdough offerings to fancier olive- and cherry-laden loaves.

LA Desserts, 113 N Robertson Blvd, Beverly Hills ☎310/273-5537. If you don't mind a few snide looks from the

Hollywood swells, step into this terrific bakery inside the swank *Ivy* restaurant and try the delicious cakes and tarts, all available for absurdly high prices.

Mousse Fantasy, 2130 Sawtelle Blvd, West LA ☎310/479-6665. A Japanese version of a French patisserie, featuring a range of tasty tarts and pastries, all found in a crowded strip mall. Particularly notable is the Green Tea Mousse cake – a taste of heaven.

Robin Rose, 215 Rose Ave, Venice ☎310/399-1774. With chocolate and fruit flavors among its best desserts, this ice cream boutique is known for its high calories, rich flavors, and actual and pseudo-bohemian customers. In any case, the dairy treats are a perfect complement with a trip to the nearby beach.

Röckenwagner, 2435 Main St, Santa Monica ☎310/399-6504. Chocolate desserts, rich pastries and scones, and hearty breads are some of the items featured at this Westside culinary delight, which also serves as a restaurant, in the sleek Edgemar shopping complex.

Say Cheese, 2800 Hyperion Ave, Silver Lake ☎213/665-0545. A fine array of French and international cheeses nicely priced below the comparable goods at other Westside stores.

Viktor Benes Continental Pastries, 8718 W Third St, West LA ☎310/276-0488. The place to go for freshly baked bread, coffee cakes, Danish pastries, and various chocolate-oriented treats, and appreciative local fans know it. Three other area locations as well.

Bookstores

There are almost as many **bookstores** in LA as there are people. All the ubiquitous **chains** and **superstores** that have spread across the US in the last few years have made it out here, and they have the enormous stock that you would expect. Aside from the national chains, there are also some good **general interest** booksellers locally, with Dutton's being the biggest. The city is also exceptionally well served by a wide

Shops and Galleries

range of **specialist** and **secondhand bookstores**, which reward several hours' browsing along the miles of dusty shelves. Also, while not too common, there are a few good **travel bookshops** worth noting, where you can usually find a decent number of titles, including many *Rough Guides*.

Chains and superstores

Barnes and Noble, 1201 Third St, Santa Monica ☎310/260-9110. There are many of these high-volume bookstores citywide; this branch is the best: three floors of general and specialty books overlooking the end of the Third Street Promenade. Highlights include the many racks of bargain books and a sleek, glass-walled central elevator.

Bookstar, 12136 Ventura Blvd, Studio City ☎818/505-9528. One of the bigger branches of this chiefly suburban discount chain, with plenty of space for browsing, a nice selection of books, and an always-crowded magazine rack.

Borders, 1360 Westwood Blvd, West LA ☎310/475-3444. Easily the top LA branch of this omnipresent retailer, and supposedly the biggest Borders in the US, with two sprawling floors, an upper-story café with outside seating, expansive music section with listening stations, and as many new books on general topics as you're likely to find on the Westside.

Crown Books, 2800 Wilshire Blvd, Santa Monica ☎310/829-3388. Big discounts on recent books – some up to 40 percent off – are the chief reasons to visit this chain store. The selection here isn't as wide as other major chains, but the prices are unmatched.

General interest and new books

Book Soup, 8818 W Sunset Blvd, West Hollywood ☎310/659-3110. Great selection, right on the Sunset Strip, and open daily until midnight. Narrow, winding aisles packed with books on a variety of subjects. Especially strong in entertainment, travel, and photography.

Dutton's, 11975 San Vicente Blvd, Brentwood ☎310/476-6263. The best of the stores in this LA chain, an ungainly complex built around a central courtyard. Its aisles tend to be cluttered, and the category sections scattered across the unlinked rooms, but it's a good store; just try to visit during the less-crowded weekdays.

Either/Or, 124 Pier Ave, Hermosa Beach ☎310/374-2060. An excellent fiction selection and a wide variety of New Age tomes, with free publications littering the floor. Supposedly once a haunt of Thomas Pynchon. Open until 11pm.

Midnight Special, 1318 Third St, Santa Monica ☎310/393-2923. A large general bookstore on the Promenade, with hardwood flooring, high bookcases, eccentrically filled shelves, and a broad focus on lefty politics and social sciences.

Vroman's, 695 E Colorado Blvd, Pasadena ☎1-800/769-2665. A large retailer for new books that offers a café and fairly good selection. Don't expect any bargains, though.

Secondhand books

Acres of Books, 240 Long Beach Blvd, Long Beach ☎526/437-6980. Worth a trip down the Blue Line Metrorail just to wallow in LA's largest, though most chaotic, secondhand collection. You may not be able to find the exact title you're looking for, but chances are you'll stumble across something good.

Aladdin Books, 122 W Commonwealth Ave, Fullerton ☎714/738-6115. With what may be the region's finest assortment of film titles, both new and used, this shop is a rather unknown commodity to most Angelenos, but shouldn't be missed by visitors. Due to its irregular hours, you should call before driving all the way out here.

Atlantis Book Shop, 144 S San Fernando Rd, Burbank ☎818/845-6467. Just down the street from the huge Media City Center mall, and adjacent to the 5 freeway, *Atlantis* specializes in history, fiction, politics, and – as the name might indicate – the speculative and the paranormal.

Berkelouw, 830 N Highland Ave, Hollywood ☎213/466-3321. An easy-to-miss dealer with large and voluminous stacks of titles, with notable sections in fiction, biography, entertainment, and history – and a knowledgeable owner who'll be glad to help you sift through his collection.

Book City, 6627 Hollywood Blvd, Hollywood ☎213/466-2525. This central Hollywood institution is tightly packed from floor to ceiling with eclectic titles, many of which are physically well out of reach on the looming bookcases.

Brand Bookshop, 231 N Brand Blvd, Glendale ☎818/507-5943. A San Fernando Valley used-book seller with a broad range of liberal art titles and particular strengths in entertainment, history, and politics.

The House of Fiction, 663 E Colorado Blvd, Pasadena ☎626/449-9861. Not only fiction, but also an assortment of scholarly titles at this bookseller – one of many in this particular stretch of Pasadena.

Wilshire Books, 3018 Wilshire Blvd, Santa Monica ☎310/828-3115. An excellent used bookstore for its smallish size, with a nice collection of tomes on art, politics, religion, music; all of them coherently organized in a cozy, crowded space.

Specialist bookstores

A Different Light, 8853 Santa Monica Blvd, West Hollywood ☎310/854-6601. The city's best-known gay and lesbian bookstore, in the heart of the city's gay community, with monthly art shows, readings, and women's music events.

Amok Books, 1764 N Vermont Ave, Hollywood ☎213/655-0956. Mayhem, true crimes, fanzines, and paranoid conspiracy rants: the extremes of information in print. A small shop with a large mail order clientele favored by tabloid TV researchers. Now publishing its own authors.

Bodhi Tree, 8585 Melrose Ave, West Hollywood ☎310/659-1733. At this ultra-trendy Westside book retailer, you can find a range of New Age, occult, and psychobabble titles, along with all things spiritually chic, including plenty of information on the healing power of crystals, pyramids, and the like.

Hennessey and Ingalls, 1254 Third St, Santa Monica ☎310/458-9074. An impressive range of art and architecture books makes this Promenade bookstore the best in LA in its field, and it also sells rare posters, catalogs, and hard-to-find books.

Larry Edmunds Book Shop, 6644 Hollywood Blvd, Hollywood ☎213/463-3273. Stacks of books, many of them out of print, on every aspect of film and theater, with movie stills and posters. Located at the center of tourist-oriented Hollywood.

Mysterious Books, 8763 Beverly Blvd, West Hollywood ☎310/659-2959. Pick up a rare edition of Raymond Chandler, or any other crime-genre writers, at this terrific seller of old and new mysteries and thrillers.

Norton Simon Museum Bookstore, 411 W Colorado Blvd, Pasadena ☎626/449-6840. Prices in this museum-attached store are lower than in any other art bookstore in LA, and the stock is superb, including numerous titles on museum specialties like Impressionism and early modern art.

Samuel French, 7623 Sunset Blvd, Hollywood ☎213/876-0570. LA's broadest selection of theater books are found in this local institution, along with a good collection of movie and media-related titles. In the back room, you can sometimes find discounted or used titles.

Travel bookstores

California Map and Travel Center, 3211 Pico Blvd, Santa Monica ☎310/829-6277. Atlases, maps, and books of outdoor activities and local adventures at this bookshop near the 10 freeway.

Shops and Galleries

Distant Lands, 56 S Raymond Ave, Pasadena ☎626/449 3220, *distant-lands.com*. Well-stocked travel bookstore, with some fairly hard-to-find titles, which also carries maps, travel gear, and has the occasional speaker.

Rand McNally, in the *Century City Mall*, 10250 Santa Monica Blvd, Century City ☎1-800/333-0136. A narrow little store loaded with travel books, maps, and even a good selection of globes. One of several regional branches.

Thomas Brothers Maps, 521 W Sixth St, Downtown ☎213/627-4018 or 1-888/277-6277. The well-known map-makers who produce good local and national maps, plus vend a decent assortment of travel publications.

Traveler's Bookcase, 8375 W Third St, Mid-Wilshire ☎213/655-0575, *www.travelbooks.com*. Located along the trendy Third Street shopping strip, this bookseller offers a voluminous amount of travel guides, maps, and publications, along with a fine assortment of literary travel stories and essays.

Music stores

If anything, **record stores** are even more plentiful than bookstores in LA. However, with the rise of the CD, the number of stores selling vinyl has dropped dramatically – a plunge that has stopped for the moment, if only because of the demand of die-hard vinyl fans. We've confined our selection to LA's more one-off record stores, many of which carry used LPs, although they often also sell new CDs and cassettes.

Aron's Records, 1150 N Highland Ave, Hollywood ☎213/469-4700. Secondhand discs – all styles, all prices, and a sizable stock, though nothing too out of the ordinary from what else you'll find in Hollywood to the north and along Melrose to the west.

Compact Disc/Count, 10741 Pico Blvd, West LA ☎310/475-4122. Located across from the giant Westside Pavilion, this beats any of the mall's CD sellers for price and selection. New, used, and rare discs, with several listening stations to assist you in finding the right records to buy.

Moby Disc, 28 W Colorado Blvd, Pasadena ☎626/449-9975; also at 3731 E Colorado Blvd, Arcadia ☎626/793-3475. Secondhand and deletion stocklist; the outlet in Old Pasadena is preferable to the Arcadia location, which is quite bleak.

Music and Memories, 5057 Lankershim Blvd, North Hollywood ☎818/761-9827. Three hundred Sinatra LPs, and plenty of others that sound like he should be on them, but in a somewhat seedy location.

Penny Lane, 12 W Colorado Blvd, Pasadena ☎626/564-0161. New and used records at reasonable prices. Always crowded, this local chain features listening stations from which you can sample up to a hundred eclectic discs. Also at 1349 Third Street Promenade, Santa Monica (☎310/319-5333).

Poo-Bah Records, 1101 E Walnut Ave, Pasadena ☎626/449-3359. Plenty of American and imported New Wave sounds, along with 1980s technopop.

Pyramid Music, 1340 Third St, Santa Monica ☎310/393-5877. Now that the Santa Monica branch of Rhino Records has closed, this is the Third Street Promenade's best source of music, providing a range of new and used CDs, cassettes, and vinyl.

Record Surplus, 11609 W Pico Blvd, West LA ☎310/478-4217. A massive LP collection of surf music, ancient rock 'n' roll, 1960s soundtracks, and unintentionally hilarious spoken-word recordings. Prices are excellent, with many CDs offered for ridiculously low prices.

Rhino Records, 1720 Westwood Blvd, West LA ☎310/474-8685. A great selection of international independent releases at this terrific retailer that features a fine assortment of new and used CDs, as well as the entire stock of recordings produced on its own label.

Rockaway Records, 2390 Glendale Blvd, Silver Lake ☎213/664-3232. Great place to come for both used CDs and LPs, as well as laserdiscs. Also offers old magazines, posters, and memorabilia.

Top Shelf, 1768 N Vermont Ave, Hollywood ☎213/660-5877. Wide-ranging selection includes punk, blues, jazz, and rock, on both vinyl and CDs. The adjacent clothing store is filled with clubwear.

Vinyl Fetish, 7305 Melrose Ave, Mid-Wilshire ☎213/935-1300. Besides the punk and post-punk merchandise, a good place to discover what's new on the ever-changing LA music scene and even to buy a cheesy Gen-X T-shirt or two.

Specialty stores

With a huge range of strange and exotic goods, LA's **specialty stores** almost resist description, but generally include shops that sell unorthodox fashion accessories, inventive toys, refurbished antiques, morbid gift items, and sex paraphernalia. While any list can only hint at the great range of such shops in LA, the stores below are some of the more colorful you'll find.

Condomania, 7306 Melrose Ave ☎213/933-7865. A huge assortment of prophylactics in a variety of colors, textures, and sizes, all inflated on a central rack – so you can see what they look like when in use.

Forbidden Fruit, 9960 Glenoaks Blvd, San Fernando Valley ☎818/504-1871 or 1-800/258-1999. Take a trip back in time when you visit this novelty store in the Sun Valley district, which sells incense, clove cigarettes, lava lamps, water pipes, and even blacklight lamps.

Jurassic, 1340 Third St, Santa Monica ☎310/393-9622. One of the few places to purchase memorabilia from eighty`million years ago, with such curiosities as fossilized dinosaur eggs and trilobite casts, as well as a more affordable range of reptilian trinkets.

LA County Coroner Gift Shop, 1104 N Mission Rd, Downtown ☎213/343-0760. Selling everything from skeleton-decorated beach towels and T-shirts to toe-tag key chains, this peculiar gift shop is a great place to buy unique LA merchandise.

Le Sex Shoppe, 6315 Hollywood Blvd, Hollywood ☎213/464-9435. Hollywood's prime sex-paraphernalia dealer, with magazines and videos, as well as handcuffs and the like, catering to a mix of curious Westsiders and seedy regulars.

Name That Toon, 8483 Melrose Ave ☎213/653-5633. An impressive gallery for animation art – cels, drawings, and the like – that includes a broad assortment of cartoon characters including Gumby, Homer Simpson, and, of course, Mickey Mouse.

Off the Wall, 7325 Melrose Ave ☎213/930-1185. Amazing roadside junk cleaned up and sold as antiques, from neon-lit gas-station signs to cigar-store Indians, as well as faded consumer items like outdated board games and old telephones.

Panoptikum, 5050 Vineland Ave, North Hollywood ☎818/985-2837. A spot to revel in the macabre, where you can find creepy, gnarled candelabras, coffin-like furniture, ghoulish ornaments, and a collection of demonic figurines.

Raven's Flight, 5042 Vineland Ave, North Hollywood ☎818/985-2944. Tools of the trade for local witches and pagans, including books on casting spells, magical herbs, ceremonial masks, and druidic jewelry.

Wound & Wound Toy Company, 7374 Melrose Ave ☎213/653-6703. Wind-up toys of every size and variety, from the crude tin toys of the 1940s to collectible Star Wars figurines to contemporary dinosaurs, rockets, and killer apes – all animated at the turn of your wrist.

Galleries

More so than any other area, the Westside is the province of LA's best **galleries** for painting, mixed-media, sculp-

Shops and Galleries

For more toy shop listings, see "Kids' LA," p.299.

Shops and Galleries

ture, and, especially, photography. Indeed, snapping pictures is what a city based on the movie industry does best, and you're likely to find terrific retrospectives of long-departed artists like Weston and Stieglitz among the breakout shows of up-and-coming local photographers. Although Santa Monica, Hollywood, the La Brea district, Beverly Hills, and parts of the Wilshire Corridor are not the only places to find good art in town, they're usually the most consistent, and a visit to any one of the galleries below will be rewarded by general proximity to other, similarly interesting establishments.

Beyond Baroque, 681 Venice Blvd, Venice ☎310/301-8035. This gallery and art center prides itself on community outreach, making it a bit less pretentious than LA's other top galleries. Yet, the offerings here are as interesting and unpredictable as anything else in town, with a wide spectrum of performance art, fiction and poetry readings, assemblage and mixed-media works, painting, drawing, photography, and so on.

Fahey-Klein, 148 N La Brea Ave, Mid-Wilshire ☎213/934-2250. Contemporary work, particularly local photography, much of it in black-and-white. Don't be deterred by the forbidding, windowless exterior – the gallery is open and accessible most days of the week.

Gallery of Functional Art, 2525 Michigan Ave, Santa Monica ☎310/829-6990. Noise-emitting clocks, ornamental wooden furniture, and funky, Space Age wall sconces are for sale at this Bergamot Station gallery, where function and form mix with intriguing results.

Jan Kesner Gallery, 164 N La Brea Ave, Mid-Wilshire ☎213/938-6834 Featuring retrospectives of noted artists, many of them photographers, and openings by up-and-comers, this gallery sits among numerous other art shops on La Brea.

Koplin Gallery, 464 N Robertson Blvd, West Hollywood ☎310/657-9843.

Etchings, paintings, and drawings offered at this elite dealer, which tends toward contemporary art from both inside and outside the city.

Los Angeles Contemporary Exhibitions, 6522 Hollywood Blvd, Hollywood ☎213/957-1777. Also known as LACE, this regional institution hosts a wide-ranging selection of mixed-media, painting, drawing, and video work, while its various community outreach programs bring art to the masses. Additionally, an autumn competition, the "Annuale," draws visitors eager for a look at the latest hotshots on the LA art scene.

Margo Leavin Gallery, 812 N Robertson Blvd, West Hollywood ☎310/273-0603. The eclectic collection almost pales in comparison to the outside facade designed by Claes Oldenburg, which features the blade of a knife slicing into the curving stucco exterior.

Pace Wildenstein, 9540 Wilshire Blvd, Beverly Hills ☎310/205-5522. Don't come here expecting any bargains: this gallery sits at the base of Beverly Hill's elite Golden Triangle shopping zone. You're also unlikely to find too many risky, cutting-edge exhibitions, as most of the works are tasteful, mainstream photography.

Rosamund Felsen Gallery, 8525 Santa Monica Blvd, West Hollywood ☎310/652-9172. One of LA's more noteworthy galleries, featuring established Southern California artists and more recent arrivals. The mostly eclectic collection is often striking, but you can forget about buying anything: the prices here are almost always stratospheric.

Track 16, 2525 Michigan Ave, Santa Monica ☎310/264-4678. The politically oriented artworks here tend toward mixed-media and assemblage, though you can also find more traditional painted and sculpted works, with most of them having one blatant message or another boldly attached.

Chapter 22

City Directory

AIRLINES Air Canada ☎1-800/776-3000; Air France ☎1-800/321-4538; Alaska Airlines ☎1-800/426-0333; America West ☎1-800/235-9292; American Airlines ☎1-800/433-7300; British Airways ☎1-800/247-9297; Continental Airlines ☎1-800/525-0280; Delta Airlines ☎1-800/221-1212; Finnair ☎1-800/950-5000; Icelandair ☎1-800/223-5500; Japan Airlines ☎1-800/525-3663; KLM ☎1-800/284-6210; Korean Air ☎1-800/438-5000; Lufthansa ☎1-800/645-3880; Northwest Airlines ☎1-800/225-2525; SAS ☎1-800/221-2350; Southwest Airlines ☎1-800/435-9792; Swissair ☎1-800/221-4750; TWA ☎1-800/221-2000; United Airlines ☎1-800/241-6522; USAir ☎1-800/428-4322; ValuJet ☎1-800/825-8538; Virgin Atlantic ☎1-800/862-8621.

AIRPORTS Hollywood/Burbank ☎213/840-8847; John Wayne/Orange County ☎714/834-2400; LAX ☎310/646-5252; Long Beach ☎310/421-8293; Ontario ☎714/785-8838. Left luggage at LAX for $1 a day ($2 for larger lockers).

BEACH INFORMATION Weather conditions ☎310/457-9701; surfers' weather ☎213/379-8471; Coast Guard search-and-rescue ☎562/980-4444.

BUS STATIONS Main Greyhound bus station at 1716 E Seventh St – open round-the-clock, but access restricted to ticket holders. Other terminals: Hollywood, 1409 Vine St; Pasadena, 645 E Walnut St; North Hollywood, 11239 Magnolia Blvd; Santa Monica, 1433 Fifth St; Anaheim, 1711 S Manchester Blvd. All have toilets and left luggage lockers. Green Tortoise: stops in Hollywood at *McDonald's* on Vine Street, a block south of Sunset Blvd; in Santa Monica at *HI-LA/Santa Monica* hostel, 1434 Second St at Santa Monica Blvd.

CAR INFORMATION The Automobile Club of Southern California, 2601 S Figueroa St, south of Downtown (☎213/741-3686), provides maps, guides, and other motoring information for members.

CONSULATES Australia, 611 N Larchmont Blvd, Mid-Wilshire (☎310/469-4300); Canada, 300 S Grand Ave, Suite 1000, Downtown (☎213/346-2700); Mexico (tourist office), 10100 Santa Monica Blvd, Suite 224, Century City (☎310/203-8151); New Zealand, 12400 Wilshire Blvd, West LA (☎310/207-1605); United Kingdom, 11766 Wilshire Blvd, Suite 400, West LA (☎310/477-3322) – call for general information or pick up a tourist card, which is necessary if you're crossing the border (Mon–Fri 9am–5pm).

CURRENCY EXCHANGE Offices are scattered inconveniently throughout town. Most reliable is at LAX, outside of banking hours open daily until 11.30pm.

DENTAL REFERRAL SERVICE ☎1-800/422-8338.

DIRECTORY INQUIRIES Local ☎411 (a free call at pay phones); long distance ☎1 + area code + 555-1212.

City Directory

DRUGS Absolutely illegal (excepting the use of medical marijuana) and worth avoiding, especially with the US near the apex of its "War on Drugs" and mandatory minimum sentences crowding American prisons with pot-smokers and crack-users alike.

ELECTRICITY 110V AC. European appliances typically require two-pin plug adaptors for lower US voltages.

EMERGENCIES Dial ☎911. For less urgent needs: ambulance ☎213/483-6721; fire ☎213/384-3131 or 262-2111; paramedics ☎213/262-2111; police ☎213/625-3311; poison control center ☎1-800/777-6476; earthquake tips ☎818/787-3737.

HOLIDAYS New Years Day (Jan 1); Martin Luther King Jr birthday (third Mon in Jan); Presidents Day (third Mon in Feb); Memorial Day (end of May); Independence Day (July 4); Labor Day (first Mon in Sept); Veterans Day (Nov 11); Thanksgiving (last Thurs in Nov); Christmas (Dec 25). Most federal holidays are observed by private businesses, except the King birthday and Presidents Day, which vary by company. On all holidays, grocers and pharmacies and some retailers stay open, though often at reduced hours.

LAUNDRY Most hotels do it, but they charge quite a bit for the service. You're better off going to a laundromat or a dry cleaner (see *Yellow Pages* under "Laundries").

LIBRARIES Downtown's Central Library is the city's best (see p.68), with branches throughout LA. Other cities also have good main libraries, notably Beverly Hills (see p.115) and Santa Monica, Main St at Ocean Park Blvd. County libraries are notoriously deficient, having been wiped out by budget cuts in recent years.

MEASUREMENTS AND SIZES If you're used to the metric system, you're out of luck here: measurements of length are in inches, feet, yards and miles; weight in ounces, pounds and tons. American pints and gallons are about four-fifths of imperial ones. Clothing sizes are two fig-

ures less than they would be in Britain (a British size 12 is an American size 10). To calculate your American shoe size, simply add one to your British size.

MEDICAL CARE The following have 24hr emergency departments: Cedars-Sinai Medical Center, 8700 Beverly Blvd, Beverly Hills (☎310/855-6517); Good Samaritan Hospital, 616 Witmer St, Downtown (☎213/397-2121); UCLA Medical Center, Tiverton Drive at Le Conte Place, Westwood (☎310/825-8611 or 2111). Dental treatment: cheapest fees at the USC School of Dentistry (☎213/743-2800), on the USC Campus, costing $20–200. Show up and be prepared to wait all day.

NEWSPAPERS Newsstands are scattered throughout the region, and both the USC and UCLA campuses have libraries with recent overseas newspapers. Day-old English and European papers are on sale in Hollywood at Universal News Agency, 1655 N Las Palmas Ave (daily 7am–midnight), and World Book and News, 1652 N Cahuenga Blvd (24hr). See "Media," p.33, for a rundown of LA's papers.

POST OFFICE Main Downtown post office at 900 N Alameda St (☎213/617-4543), next to Union Station; zip code is 90086; pick up letters Mon–Fri 8am–3pm.

PROSTITUTION Police lay traps for johns throughout Hollywood, where prostitution is frequent in some areas. Hollywood and Sunset boulevards are rife with both male and female prostitutes, while Santa Monica Boulevard is a center for transgender activity. Illicit sex is also available on the Westside through "escort services" and "private modeling" companies, though the threat of venereal disease and police sting operations is always present. Don't forget, too, that this is the place where Hugh Grant gave Divine Brown her fifteen minutes of fame, and, more recently, Eddie Murphy had to explain the presence of a transsexual hooker in his car at 4am.

PUBLIC TOILETS Uncommon outside of hotels and restaurants, though sometimes found at retailers. Street toilets are a rarity – and rarely clean.

SMOG LA's smog is more hype than reality, yet its air quality *is* often very poor, and, especially in the valleys in late summer, can sometimes be quite dangerous. An air-quality index is published daily, and if the air is really bad, warnings are issued on TV, radio, and in the *Los Angeles Times*.

SMOKING Frowned upon, perhaps more than in any other major US city (only San Francisco comes close). Considered antithetical to a healthy lifestyle by the majority of Angelenos, though a requisite badge of rebellion in counterculture clubs and cafés. Forbidden in restaurants and, more recently, bars – though the latter prohibition is scantily enforced and often openly skirted.

TAX LA sales tax is 8.25 percent; hotel tax variable, generally 12–14 percent.

TELEVISION STATIONS KCBS, CBS affiliate on channel 2; KNBC, NBC on 4; KTLA, WB network on 5; KABC, ABC on 7; KCAL, unaffiliated on 9; KTTV, Fox on 11; KCOP, UPN network on 13; KCET, PBS on 28 UHF.

TIME Pacific Standard Time (PST), 3 hrs behind US Eastern Standard Time and 8 or 9 hrs behind GMT, depending on seasonal observance of Daylight Savings Time.

TIPPING Generally 15 percent for restaurants, though upscale eateries may expect closer to 20 percent (still, it's up to you). $1 per carried bag at hotels and $1 per day for maid service (with a minimum $2 tip).

TRAFFIC Check AM radio news channels for frequent updates on which freeways are suffering from gridlock or congestion; if a highway section is particularly immobile, a "Sig-Alert" will be issued, meaning "avoid at all costs."

TRAIN STATION Union Station, located Downtown at 800 N Alameda St, connects to Gateway Transit Center, an access point for local bus lines. Amtrak trains stop at the station and at outlying stations in the LA area; for all listings call Amtrak (☎1-800/USA-RAIL).

City
Directory

Contexts

A brief history of Los Angeles

To most, Los Angeles seems a place with little sense of history, a modern urban sprawl that lives up to a lot of vapid stereotypes: the land of sunny skies, carefree surfers, and Hollywood movie stars. However, since the founding of modern-day LA some two hundred years ago, there have been enough violent outbreaks and sordid episodes to give some credence to myth beneath the myth – that of a city with a dark and dangerous underbelly. The following account is meant to give a sense of LA's overall development, with special attention to episodes of particular importance. For a list of figures who helped – or help – shape the city, see p.341.

Native peoples

For thousands of years prior to the arrival of Europeans, **native peoples** lived rather peacefully in the area we now know as Los Angeles. The dominant groups in these parts were **Tataviam**, **Chumash**, and **Tongva** (whom the Spanish called Gabrieleño) peoples. These tribes, however, had little in common, and were an easy target for the **Spanish** – although it's true to say that they were wiped out by epidemics as much as Spanish aggression.

Surprisingly, LA County today is home to the greatest number of native peoples of any county in the US – up to two-hundred thousand by some estimates. Most Native Americans in these parts are now Navajo, though, and little remains to mark the existence of the early tribes.

■ NATIVE PEOPLES

Discovery and exploration

The first explorer to use the name California, and to reach what's now the US state, was **Juan Cabrillo**, who sighted San Diego harbor in 1542, and continued north along the coast to the Channel Islands off Santa Barbara. He bestowed a number of other place names that survive, including, in the LA area, San Pedro Bay.

Other European explorers followed, charting the California coast and naming more of the islands, bays and coastal towns, but it was the Spanish, moving up from their base in Mexico, who were to colonize Southern California and map out the future city of Los Angeles.

Colonization and mission life

The **Spanish** occupation of California began in earnest in 1769 as a combination of military expediency (to prevent other powers from gaining a foothold) and Catholic missionary zeal (to convert the heathen Native Americans). Father **Junipero Serra** began the missions, setting off from Mexico and going all the way up to Monterey; assisting him was soldier **Gaspar de Portola**, who led the expedition into LA.

The first mission sited in Los Angeles was **Mission San Gabriel** (northeast of today's Downtown), in 1771; from that beginning, Spanish military garrisons served to hold the natives subject to the demands of Franciscan friars, who ordered them to abandon their religious beliefs, cultural rituals, and languages. The penalties for disobedience were stiff: flogging with twenty to forty lashes was standard practice. Needless to say, while the Spanish were trying to "convert the savages," they were also decimating the native population, reducing their ranks by 95 percent over the course of 150 years. By World War I, fewer than 17,000 natives remained.

The Spanish era

Aside from abusing the natives, the Spanish who colonized Southern California effected the first crude designs for LA, which they established in 1781 at a site northwest of the current Plaza. The city's original **pobladores**, or settlers, of which there were less than 50, set a multicultural precedent for the region, as they were made up of a majority of black, mestizo, mixed-race, and native peoples, with the white Spanish being a distinct, though powerful, minority. The early **pueblo** (town), designed by California's governor **Felipe de Neve**, grew in short spurts, aided by the creation of the *zanja madre*, or "mother ditch," that brought water into town. Despite the Spaniard's half-hearted efforts to make the settlement grow, it took a devastating 1815 flood for large-scale development to begin, namely with the construction of the current Plaza and its Plaza Church and Avila Adobe buildings.

As the town grew from remote outpost to regional centerpiece, the power of the Spanish crown began to fade. While the military and missions exercised official power, the functional operation of the little burg was increasingly the province of a small group of mestizo families whose names are still reflected in LA's street monikers – Sepulveda, Pico, and so on – along with a few white American expatriates who for various reasons found the region to their liking. By the early 1800s, the Spanish were playing only a de jure role in city administration; soon after, they would be forcibly removed from power.

Mexican rule

Mexico gained Independence in 1821, calling itself the United States of Mexico, and over the next four years, the Mexican residents of Southern California evicted the Spanish and made the region into a territory of Mexico itself.

The 22 subsequent years of Mexican rule were marked by some dramatic changes in governance and the social architecture – and the destruction of many missions – but no end to the oppression of native peoples. The Tongva and others now found themselves at the bottom level of a new hierarchy, where rich land barons controlled huge parcels of land known as **ranchos** and reduced the natives to a state of near-serfdom.

This period was largely a lawless and wantonly wasteful one, well-described by Richard Henry Dana in his book *Two Years Before the Mast*. Internal political squabbles and outright clashes

were common, and by the time Governor **Pio Pico** successfully established his Alta California capital in Los Angeles (long his preferred spot for governance), the period of Mexican rule was almost at an end, its demise assured by the factional struggles and laggardly ways of the ranch owners.

The Mexican-American War

From the 1830s onward, inspired by the concept of **Manifest Destiny**, a belief that Americans should occupy the country from coast to coast, the US government policy regarding California was to buy all of Mexico's land north of the Rio Grande, the river that now divides the US and Mexico. The offers failed, and when President James Polk went ahead and annexed Texas – still claimed by Mexico – war broke out. Most of the fighting in the **Mexican-American War** took place in Texas, though one battle was fought near San Diego.

By the summer of 1846, after the American capture of Monterey and San Diego, Pico and his colleagues had difficulty even finding significant numbers of loyal Mexicans to defend LA against the Yanks. A truce was signed to avoid bloodshed and American troops walked into the city virtually unopposed. However, despite this relatively pacific start, the military chieftains left local government in the hands of the incompetent **Archibald Gillespie**, who promptly instituted martial law and just as quickly turned the populace against the American presence. The situation further degenerated, with outbreaks of local hostilities, and by the time Mexican general Andreas Pico and American "pathfinder" John C Fremont signed the final **peace treaty** in January 1847, after several battles and much bloodshed, the chasm between the Mexican residents and their new American conquerors had grown considerably.

Early American Rule

California was admitted to the US as the 31st state in 1850, a move quickly followed by the **1851 Land Act**, in which the new white settlers targeted the rancho owners, forcing them to legally prove their right to the land they had been granted. The countless legal battles that ensued left many of the owners destitute, and while the rancho boundaries and some of their elemental chunks continued to linger for up to a century or more, the central goal of the new settlers had been accomplished: the old-line Mexicans were driven out and replaced by a Yankee elite. However, even as this process was taking place, and the latest real estate magnates were consolidating their power, the city's social structure was sliding into chaos.

For many good reasons, LA was called "**Hell Town**" in the middle of the nineteenth-century. The lives of the native peoples got even worse, as they were subject to all manner of mob aggression and legal disenfranchisement. Because the city had no effective municipal authority, and because it was crowded with hordes of aggressive fortune-hunters who failed in the northern gold rush, it became a magnet for violent criminals and other ne'er-do-wells, and was peppered with gambling halls, saloons, and brothels – a Wild West town decades before the idea officially came into being. The bellicose citizenry usually focused their rage against the groups at the bottom of the social hierarchy, tactics that eventually backfired when roving groups of Mexican bandidos emerged to counter the threats.

The local situation got so bloody that "**vigilance committees**" were created to deal with the crime, which had reached the same levels as San Francisco even though LA only had a tenth as many people. The committees had some measure of success, but LA remained a city beholden to mob rule until after the Civil War.

During the height of its social strife, the area managed to sketch out the outlines of what would later become the metropolitan area. Post offices, banks, newspapers, and churches were a few of the emblems of encroaching civilization, and the activity of such pioneering entrepreneurs as **Phineas Banning** – the developer of the Wilmington harbor plan – also brought early growth to the city.

In 1860, LA's citizens chose the wrong side in the **Civil War**, casting only a meager 18 percent of their ballots for Abraham Lincoln and soon becoming possessed by secessionist anger and racial hatred. Adding to the rancor, many in the city and region were clamoring to split from northern California and create their own autonomous enclave, where they wouldn't be subject to state or federal power. Thirteen-thousand soldiers were stationed in Wilmington's Drum Barracks to insure domestic order (also acting against Southwest rebel activity and, later,

native uprisings). Just as tellingly, a merry crowd of revelers gathered in LA after hearing news of Lincoln's assassination. Their celebration was broken up – but only with the aid of the federal soldiers.

Late nineteenth century growth

The last three decades of the nineteenth-century were an era of **rapid growth** and **technological change** in LA, principally because of three key factors: periodic real-estate booms that often involved the subdivision of the old ranchos into smaller, more profitable chunks; the building of railroad lines externally, to spots like San Francisco, and internally, from Downtown to the port at San Pedro; and the most important factor, the mass arrival of Midwesterners.

From the 1870s, LA gained a reputation as a paradise for healthy living. While eastern American cities were notorious for sooty air and water pollution, LA was touted as a sunny, clean-air paradise where the infirm could recover from their illnesses and everyone could enjoy the fruits of the invigorating desert lifestyle. The **orange** was the perfect symbol of this new arcadia, and groves were planted by the thousands. Huge numbers of Iowans and Kansans moved to the city in the Victorian era, spurred on as well by cheap one-way railroad tickets: thanks to a price war between the Santa Fe and Southern Pacific railroads, fares from Kansas City to LA dropped to a mere dollar; before long, the passenger cars were full of church-going Protestants seeking desert salvation.

The Midwesterners of the 1880s did much to displace lingering Hispanic influences, meanwhile exacerbating racial tensions, which flared up in such instances as the **anti-Chinese riot of 1871**. After a disagreement left a white man dead at the hands of a Chinese shopkeeper, a mob assembled and quickly set about attacking, maiming, and murdering what Chinese residents it could get its hands on. While there were only about two hundred Chinese in LA at the time, the mob managed to strangle, shoot, stab, and hang 22 of them. Naturally, few of the perpetrators faced jail time, and those that did only served a year or so.

Beyond its racial animus and Midwestern migrations, LA was becoming an odd sort of attraction for a few of the nation's more colorful characters. **Charles Fletcher Lummis** was the first of these, a fervent supporter of the rights of native peoples, yet also an isolationist who saw an ominous threat from foreign immigration to the eastern seaboard. Aside from that, Lummis was a bit of a crank who was so committed to his own notion of healthy living that he created a boulder house, "El Alisal," which still stands in Highland Park, and he took the unusual step of coming to LA from Cincinnati **on foot** – a distance of nearly three-thousand miles. Lummis would be just one of many individualists to inhabit the LA region, others including the Pasadena artisans who created **"Arroyo Seco culture"** just after the turn of the century (an arts-and-crafts philosophy that owed much to Lummis), and political activists like **Job Harriman**, whose commune in the northern desert town of Llano was intended to be the blueprint for a socialist utopia.

While the dreamers and artists experimented with alternative living, the politicians and businessmen were busy expanding the city by every means possible: **railway lines** were added throughout the region, in the form of Henry Huntington's electric Red Car transit system; the **harbor** was developed at San Pedro, and entrepeneurs such as Edward Doheny grew rich drilling for **oil** throughout the region.

The early twentieth century

Around the turn of the century, LA's population reached 100,000; perhaps more important to the city's development, **William Mulholland** was put in charge of the city's water department. Mulholland was the engineering catalyst for a water-stealing scheme that even now remains legendary: various bankers, publishers, and railway bosses purchased large land holdings in the San Fernando Valley, and shortly thereafter, a small cadre of city bankers secretly began buying up land in California's distant Owens Valley 250 miles away. By the time the northern farmers realized what had happened, the bankers had consolidated control over the valley watershed and were making plans to bring the bulk of the region's water to the seemingly drought-stricken citizens of LA. Seemingly is the key word, for modern evidence suggests that massive amounts of water were being deposited into the city sewers so area dams and reservoirs could drop precipitously, thus making it looking like the region was on the verge of drought.

Following the land grabs, Mulholland built a

giant canal system – one of the country's biggest public works projects – that carried the stolen water to Southern California, but not LA proper. Instead, the aqueduct ended in the San Fernando Valley and city politicians had little choice but to **annex** the valley, thus making the real-estate interests there wealthy beyond imagination. The entire enterprise surely ranks as one of the country's biggest municipal swindles, and one which the Owens Valley farmers did not soon forget. In the 1920s, when Mulholland and company set about acquiring more land for the canal system, the farmers responded by destroying sections of the system with carefully placed dynamite charges. This violence, coupled with the unrelated bursting of the St Francis dam north of LA – a catastrophe that killed more than four hundred people – destroyed Mulholland's reputation. However, by that time, his main work had already been accomplished: the aqueduct had helped turn LA into a metropolis.

Accompanying the development of the modernizing city was the growth of **organized labor**. In 1910, a series of strikes at breweries and foundries crippled the city, and local labor was also responsible for nearly bringing socialist Job Harriman to power. However, when the main building of the *Los Angeles Times* – the right-wing organ of labor's arch-enemy **Harrison Gray Otis** – was bombed, a slow erosion of leftist support took place and ultimately led to defeat for Harriman, who then retreated to his northern desert commune.

World War I to the Great Depression

LA still displayed its regressive character in many ways, especially in its **treatment of minorities**. Chinese residents were still subject to all manner of exclusionary laws, as were the Japanese, who were profoundly affected by the passage of the **1913 Alien Land Bill** that kept them from purchasing further land tracts and limited their lease tenures. Finally, even though industrial production during World War I doubled the black population of the city, the total number of **African-Americans** was still fairly small (less than three percent of the population).

Despite its lack of progressiveness, rapid growth continued, and after World War I, LA became quite a **tourist magnet** – decades before the arrival of Disneyland. Sights like Abbot

Kinney's pseudo-European Venice, Ocean Park in Santa Monica, Long Beach's carnival midway, Santa Catalina island, and the Mount Lowe Railroad in the San Gabriel Mountains all drew good numbers of seasonal visitors.

Soon, another great **wave of newcomers** began arriving, from all across America. By the 1920s, LA was gaining residents by one hundred thousand per year, most coming by car and flocking to spots that were then and still are **suburbs**: Glendale, Long Beach, Pasadena, and so on. **Petroleum** was adding to the boom, from places like Signal Hill to Venice, with oil wells popping up all over the region, usually without regard to aesthetics or environmental pollution. The quintessential symbol of the dynamic, forward-looking atmosphere of the time was **City Hall**, built as a mix of classical and contemporary elements, and topped by none other than a small replica of one of the long-lost ancient wonders of the world – the Mausoleum at Halicarnassus. This was civic ego on a grand scale, a fitting reflection of the haughty attitudes of the time, but also a symbolic portent of the 1930s.

Into this highly charged environment also came the first **movie pioneers**, whose typically Jewish backgrounds were sneered at by the Downtown elite. Because of exclusionary housing laws, film titans like Adolph Zukor and Samuel Goldwyn developed the Westside as their base of operations, an action which had long-lasting effects. Even today, West Hollywood, Beverly Hills, and West LA remain the cultural focus of the city, with Downtown far behind, despite the continued financial efforts of the remaining Downtown elite to remedy the situation.

The boom years ended with the onset of the **Great Depression**. Banks collapsed, businesses went bankrupt, and Midwestern drought brought a new round of immigrants to Southern California, much poorer and significantly more desperate than their forebears. These hard times spawned a number of movements. Religious **cults** gained adherents by the thousands (this, long before the advent of 1960s flower-power), communist and fascist organizations trawled for members among the city's more frustrated or simple-minded ranks, and the muckraker **Upton Sinclair** emerged as the greatest threat to LA's ruling hierarchy since Job Harriman.

With his **End Poverty in California** (EPIC) campaign, Sinclair frightened the upper crust across the region, and was countered not only by the usual Downtown suspects, but also by their Westside adversaries, the Hollywood movie bosses, who rightly perceived a danger in Sinclair's message to their control over the film industry. Fraudulent newsreel propaganda (showing hordes of homeless men and various halfwits testifying their allegiance to Sinclair) helped speed Sinclair's demise in the gubernatorial contest, but no one could stop the tide of reform, which brought down LA's corrupt mayor **Frank Shaw** and his attendant cronies. The entire political and social mess was reflected in the most famous literary works of the time: Nathanael West's *Day of the Locust* and Raymond Chandler's entire body of detective fiction, all of which portrayed a morally decayed society on the verge of collapse.

World War II and after

By the time of World War II, West and Chandler looked to be quite right about LA. The misery of the continuing Depression and the ugliness of the war exacerbated the underlying social tensions and unleashed new rounds of violence and oppression against the perceived enemies of white Protestants. Although Chinese citizens had suffered after Union Station was plunked on top of the destroyed site of Chinatown, it was the city's Japanese population who now received the full brunt of the region's, as well as the nation's, racial animus. One of Franklin Roosevelt's executive orders gave the green light to mass deportations of Japanese-American citizens, who were forcibly relocated to bleak desert internment camps for the duration of the war. Minorities who hadn't been shipped away made for fat targets as well, especially Mexican-Americans.

The **Sleepy Lagoon Murder case** – in which seventeen Hispanics were rounded up and sent to jail for a single murder, only to be later released by a disgusted appellate court – was but a prelude to the turmoil that would become known as the **Zoot Suit Riots**, named for the popular apparel Hispanic youth wore at the time. Over the course of several days in early June 1943, two-hundred sailors on leave attacked and beat up a large number of Mexican-Americans – with the assistance of local police, who made sure that the black-and-blue victims were promptly arrested on trumped-up charges. The violence continued until it became a federal issue causing a rift in international relations between the US and Mexico. After the chaos had concluded, the LA City Council responded aggressively to the ugly events – by banning the wearing of zoot suits.

Although anti-Asian and -Hispanic feelings still remained, the end of the war brought a shift in hostilities. A growing contingent of **black migrants**, drawn by the climate and defense-related jobs, became the focus of white wrath, and the reason was clear: from 1940 to 1965, the number of blacks in LA increased from 75,000 to 600,000. The white elite did what it could to marginalize the new residents – keeping blacks confined to eastern sections of town and "redlining" them out of personal loans and business financing – but these tactics only served to heighten the hostility that would later erupt in mass violence.

In the meantime, LA was becoming one of the USA's largest cities almost overnight, with the almost nonstop arrival of newcomers from across the country, the rebirth of the local economy, and the construction of a **vast freeway network** to replace the old Red Cars – due principally to a decline in public transit users and active subversion by oil, gas, and automotive interests. Defense industries, notably in aerospace, began a decades-long dominion over the local economy, replacing, most notably, the movie industry, which experienced a sharp decline in the 1950s because of television's impact and governmental antitrust actions.

Concurrently, suburbs like Orange County drew old-time residents from the heart of the city into expanding towns like Garden Grove, Huntington Beach, and Anaheim – where **Walt Disney's theme park** also acted as a pop-culture beacon. The northern valleys traded orange groves for subdivisions and asphalt, and before long, the entire LA basin was swelling with people in every conceivable direction. Much of the wealth from the Hollywood and Mid-Wilshire sections of town had been drained by the loss of upper- and middle-class business interests and residents, and these areas were increasingly becoming the home of many working-poor minorities.

Modern LA: 1960s to the present

The type of conservative leadership evident in LA's postwar politicians, such as race-baiter Sam Yorty,

and the city's so-called **Committee of 25**, a business cabal that acted as a sort of shadow government for many years, got its comeuppance with 1965's **Watts Riots**. The riots – which started with the arrest of one Marquette Frye for speeding, lasted a week, and ended with the arrival of 36,000 police and National Guard troops – caused $40 million worth of property damage and permanently dismantled white LA's beliefs about the perceived laziness of minorities and willingness to accept overt subjugation. While many blacks did not see, and still have not seen, a diminution in poverty levels, the old municipal overlords couldn't help but take notice at the potent brew of anger and frustration they had helped create.

Along with this, the late 1960s **protests** by student radicals, mostly against the involvement in Vietnam, and the emergence of flower power and hippie counterculture caused a dramatic break between generations: the staid Orange County parents versus their rebellious, pot-smoking kids.

Eight years after the riots, LA's first black mayor, **Tom Bradley**, was elected by a coalition of blacks, Hispanics, and Westside Jewish communities. The political success of these historically disenfranchised groups galvanized others into action on the LA political scene, notably women and gays. Accordingly, the LA Times, long a paragon of reactionary yellow journalism, underwent a historic change through the efforts of **Otis Chandler**, son of archconservative former publisher Harry Chandler, who turned the paper into a neoliberal icon with a range of world-class writers and critics.

Bradley's twenty-year tenure was also marked, less fortuitously, by the disappearance of LA's manufacturing base. South Central and Southeast LA ceased to be centers for oil, rubber, and automotive production, the San Fernando Valley saw its car plants closing, and heavy industries like Kaiser's mammoth steel-making operation in Fontana shut down. Though this was somewhat tempered in the Eighties by the infusion of foreign money, heavily invested in Downtown real estate, the decade ended hard with the **demise of aerospace jobs**, which had provided the region with its military-industrial meal ticket since early Cold War-era.

The early Nineties continued the hard times, which only got bleaker when black motorist **Rodney King** was videotaped being beaten by uniformed officers of the LA Police Department. The officers' subsequent acquittal by jurors in

(soon to be Goldwyn) and vaudeville producer Jesse Lasky, established the basis for the big studios that would follow. The film made in the barn, *The Squaw Man*, was a huge commercial triumph; DeMille became one of the early industry's most bankable directors of historical and biblical epics, and Lasky and Goldwyn later teamed with Adolph Zukor to create the colossus known as **Paramount Studios**.

Paramount used a number of tactics to push its product, including "block booking" (in which film packages, rather than individual films, were sold to exhibitors, thus maximizing studio revenue) and buying up theater chains across the country (to ensure exhibition spaces for its films). These practices, which were adopted by other film companies, served to consolidate the industry. By the end of World War I, three major studios had risen to dominance: Paramount, **Loew's**, and **First National** – though only Paramount would survive in name during the height of the studio system.

The 1919 creation of **United Artists** (UA) looked promising for actors and directors. This studio, formed by Douglas Fairbanks Jr, Mary Pickford, D W Griffith, and Charlie Chaplin, seemed to suggest a greater role might be in store for the creative individuals who actually made the films, instead of just the studio bosses and executive producers. Things didn't quite work out that way, and the next decade saw UA in the role of bit player, along with Columbia and Universal, principally because it didn't own its own theaters and had to rely on one of the major studios for booking its films.

The golden age

The five largest studios from the 1920s to the 1940s comprised **Paramount**, the **Fox Film Corporation** (later 20th Century-Fox), **Warner Brothers**, **Radio-Keith-Orpheum** (a major conglomeration known as RKO), and the biggest of them all, **Metro-Goldwyn-Mayer**, or MGM, which was controlled by the still-powerful Loew's corporation in New York. The majors used every method they could to rigidly control their operations, and they did much to industrialize the business, breaking down the stages of production and using specialists (editors, cinematographers, and so on) to create the product. The arrival of **sound** in the late 1920s further specialized the industry, and the possibility of a lone professional with a camera shooting a nationally released film vanished.

Ince's original system had been perfected into rigorous, clinical efficiency. Even the content of the movies was controlled, in this case by Hollywood's censor-in-chief **Will Hays**, who was hired away from the corrupt Harding administration. He wielded such power that, in the late 1930s, no suggestion or implication that involved taboos like sex, miscegenation, blasphemy, and such would be allowed. With the Catholic organization the Legion of Decency also looking over its shoulder, Hollywood produced a brand of entertainment that was safe, fun, and mostly non-controversial. That filmmakers like John Ford, Orson Welles, Howard Hawks, and Preston Sturges were able to make classic films out of such a stifling environment says much about the degree of talent the studios were employing during this time.

The demise of the studios

The emergence of the **film noir** style at the end of World War II should have sounded a warning to the old studio system. With bleak storylines, chiaroscuro photography, dubious heroes, and dark endings, film noir was a sudden break from many of Hollywood's previous aesthetic conventions. This stylistic change, and the postwar disillusion it reflected, preceded several major transformations that permanently altered the way the studios did business.

The greatest threat to the system, the **federal government**, in its anti-trust prosecution of Paramount, was beginning to dismantle the practices of block booking and theatrical ownership that had kept the majors in firm control over the exhibition of their films. The increasing power of independent producers, helped by this and other structural changes, also removed some of the majors' control over the industry, as did the increasing ability of actors to use the **star system** (in which film product was driven by celebrity) to their advantage, not allowing the studios to lock up their careers for interminable lengths of time. Along with these changes, television reduced film viewership by great numbers and the studio bosses had to resort to desperate devices like 3-D, widescreen, and Cinerama to try to lure back its audience.

Furthermore, the institution that Will Hays had censored, and promoted to his allies in Congress, began to come under direct attack from McCarthyite politicians. The House Un-American

Activities Committee (HUAC) dredged up information on the alleged presence of communist and left-leaning groups in Hollywood, and many screenwriters, actors, and directors were either humiliated into testifying or found themselves on an internal **blacklist** that kept them from working.

After the HUAC proceedings, Hollywood was creatively damaged, but the government's activities didn't keep directors like Otto Preminger from challenging the Hays Production Code. Through a series of legendary battles, on films like *The Moon Is Blue* and others, Preminger and other filmmakers succeeded in throwing off the yoke of the code, which had been in place for over thirty years. This change, combined with the diminishment of pressure groups like the Legion of Decency, further loosened the control of the studio bosses over movie content and later led to the establishment of the **ratings system** in place today.

The aftermath

By the end of the 1950s, the studio system, at least as it had been known, was finished, and it took many years for the majors to regain much of the ground they had lost. However, while the industry eventually rebounded, and moviemaking has become profitable once more to the studios (if not necessarily for their investors), it's unlikely that we'll see a return to Depression-era days, when each studio churned out hundreds of films per year.

Currently, Hollywood only manages to pump out a few big-budget spectacles and a declining number of medium-budget flicks – often cumulatively less than twenty annual films per studio. Modern American filmmaking, driven by exorbitant talent costs, is quite different to the old mechanized industry between the wars. Television-film studio mergers, videotape sales, and multimedia production have only served to highlight the differences from the old way of doing business. In one way, though, the studios have reasserted their dominance: by bringing innovative independent companies like Miramax under their wing, they have ensured that risky, lower-budget productions come under their direct control, to their direct benefit – just like the old days.

LA on film

Since its birth in the 1910s, Hollywood has always searched its own backyard for compelling scenes and interesting stories. While not always successful in conveying the truth of LA to a film audience, Hollywood filmmakers have nevertheless created a version of the city that has slowly shaped the country's, and the world's, attitudes about what kind of a place LA seems to be. Below are the films that best use their LA backdrop or are most significant to LA's status as film capital.

Hollywood does Hollywood

The Bad and the Beautiful (Vincente Minnelli 1952). A cynical, satiric melodrama from one of the best directors of the form. Kirk Douglas is a ruthless movie producer manipulating and ruining those around him.

Barton Fink (Joel Coen 1991). Tinseltown in the 1940s is depicted by the Coen brothers as a dark world of greedy movie bosses, belligerent screenwriters, and murderers disguised as traveling salesmen.

The Big Knife (Robert Aldrich 1955). An incisive portrayal of Hollywood politics, in which a weak-willed actor can't get free from the tentacles of a hack director, despite the pleas of his wife. Based on a play by Clifford Odets and filmed like one as well.

Day of the Locust (John Schlesinger 1975). Somewhat maladroit realization of the classic satire by Nathanael West. The author's vivid colors are rendered here as bland pastels.

Ed Wood (Tim Burton 1994). The ragged low-budget fringes of Fifties Hollywood are beautifully re-created in this loving tribute to the much-derided auteur of *Plan Nine from Outer Space* and *Glen or Glenda*. Gorgeously shot in black and white, with a magnificent performance by Martin Landau as an ailing Bela Lugosi.

Hollywood Canteen (Delmer Daves 1944). In a celebrity club based on an actual Hollywood establishment, your favorite movie stars from the World War II era sing and dance to a bevy of toe-tapping tunes. Most of Warner Brothers' stars were featured in the picture – those that wouldn't appear were labeled "unpatriotic."

Hollywood on Trial (David Helpern Jr 1976). Interesting documentary offering insight about the early 1950s witch hunts in Hollywood and the blacklisted screenwriters, actors, and directors.

Hollywood Shuffle (Robert Townsend 1987). Ultra-low-budget, scattershot satire on movie hiring practices and racial bias. When it's on target, though, it's scathingly funny.

LA Story (Mick Jackson 1991). Plenty of local in-jokes and movie allusions in this low-key comedy that verges on the sentimental.

The Last Action Hero (John McTiernan 1993). Somewhat unfairly lambasted, this rare Schwarzenegger flop makes great use of LA locations and has lots of Hollywood jokes, some of which hit the mark.

Last Tycoon (Elia Kazan 1976). F Scott Fitzgerald's unfinished, would-be masterpiece is here rendered as an interesting failure: a rich, opulent world of Hollywood gloss that translates into slow, clumsy storytelling.

The Loved One (Tony Richardson 1965). A version of Evelyn Waugh's pointed satire about the dubious practices of the funeral industry, inspired by a trip to Forest Lawn. An effective adaptation.

The Player (Robert Altman 1992). Tim Robbins is a studio shark who thinks a disgruntled screenwriter is out to get him; he kills the writer, steals his girlfriend, and worries about it later. A wickedly sharp satire about contemporary Hollywood, with some great celebrity cameos.

Postcards from the Edge (Mike Nichols 1990). Written by Carrie Fisher, an insider's look at behind-the-scenes Hollywood, with Meryl Streep as the drug-addicted daughter of pushy glamor-queen Shirley MacLaine.

Singin' in the Rain (Stanley Donen/Gene Kelly 1952). A merry trip through Hollywood set during the birth of the sound era. Gene Kelly, Donald O'Connor, and Debbie Reynolds sing and dance to many classic tunes, including "Good Morning," "Moses," "Broadway Melody," and countless others.

A Star Is Born (William Wellman 1937; George Cukor 1954). Based on the film *What Price Hollywood?* (see below), these adaptations tell the story of the rise of a starlet mirroring the demise of her Svengali. Janet Gaynor and Fredric March star in the early version, Judy Garland and James Mason in the later. Both are worthwhile, while a 1977 remake with Barbara Streisand and Kris Kristofferson runs a distant third.

The State of Things (Wim Wenders 1982). A European filmmaker sees his financing disappear while stranded in LA and is beset by boredom in his mobile home. Essential if you're a fan of Wenders or of music by the band X.

Sullivan's Travels (Preston Sturges 1941). A high-spirited comedy about a director who wants to stop making schlock pictures and instead create gritty portrayals of what he thinks real life to be. The first two-thirds are great, though the film ends in mawkish fashion.

Sunset Boulevard (Billy Wilder 1950). Long before the musical came this award-winning film about a screenwriter falling into the clutches of a long-faded silent movie star. William Holden was near the beginning of his career, Gloria Swanson well past the end of hers. Erich von Stroheim nicely fills in as Swanson's butler.

The Way We Were (Sydney Pollack 1973). Aside from the Barbara Streisand-Robert Redford pairing and cloyingly memorable songs, a worthwhile portrait of the dark days of the Red Scare and Hollywood blacklist of the 1950s.

Whatever Happened to Baby Jane (Robert Aldrich 1962). Bette Davis and Joan Crawford are former child stars who plot and scheme against one another in a rotting Malibu house. A fine slice of modern horror.

What Price Hollywood? (George Cukor 1932). The template for the *A Star Is Born* movies that followed: Constance Bennett is the starlet, an ambitious waitress, and Lowell Sherman is the drunken director.

Who Framed Roger Rabbit? (Robert Zemeckis 1988). Despite being a live-action/cartoon hybrid, a revealing film about 1940s LA, where cartoon characters suffer abuse like everyone else and the big corporations seek to destroy the Red Car transit system. An enjoyable ride.

LA crime stories

Beverly Hills Cop (Martin Brest 1984). Still-amusing Eddie Murphy flick, in which the actor plays an unorthodox, fast-talking Detroit detective who takes LA by storm while trying to solve a murder case.

The Big Sleep (Howard Hawks 1946). One of the key films noirs of the 1940s, with Humphrey Bogart playing Philip Marlowe, and featuring a wildly confused plot – even screenwriter Raymond Chandler admitted he didn't know who killed a particular character.

Chinatown (Roman Polanski 1974). One of the essential films about the city. Jack Nicholson hunts down corruption in this dark criticism of the forces that animate the town: venal politicians, black-hearted land barons, crooked cops, and a morally neutered populace.

Dead Again (Kenneth Branagh 1991). The director's take on LA is a creative adaptation of film noir, and features plenty of plot twists, humor, and a gallery of notable American and British actors.

Devil in a Blue Dress (Carl Franklin 1995). Terrific modern noir, in which South Central detective Easy Rawlins (Denzel Washington) navigates the ethical squalor of elite 1940s white LA and discovers a few ugly truths about city leaders – most of which he already suspected.

D O A (Rudolph Maté 1949). The ultimate high-concept storyline: a victim of poisoning must discover who killed him before the toxin in his veins finishes him off.

conservative Simi Valley sparked the April 1992 **riots**, which highlighted the economic disparities between rich and poor, along with the more obvious abuses of police power and privilege. The aftermath of the riots (which involved all races in mass chaos and were not simply black vs. white) has not yet been fully realized or understood, and new initiatives promised by local and federal authorities to combat LA's endemic violence and poverty have yet to materialize. Meanwhile, episodes like the **O J Simpson** trial have only served to further confuse matters. In 1995, Simpson, a black former football star, was acquitted of killing his wife and her friend, in what was termed the "Trial of the Century," an ugly and protracted affair in which public opinion was split right along racial lines.

For now the public seems fine without grand solutions. The current mayor is **Richard Riordan**, a multimillionaire technocrat with little real power. Effective control over the region lies in the hands of five county commissioners, who, with about two million people per district, each represent more people than the mayors of every US city except New York and Chicago.

The recent resurgence of the regional economy, spurred on mainly by economic growth at the federal level, has defused many of the animosities and enabled many hard-hit economic sectors to recover. Yet, being far too diverse to experience economic or social trends in a singular fashion, the city remains as unpredictable as ever – the one thing about LA that will probably never change.

The rise of Hollywood

To this day, the word "Hollywood" remains synonymous with the motion picture industry, even if the reality of that association has not always held true. What follows is a brief history of how the movie business came to Los Angeles and how the studio system took root in Hollywood.

Westward migration

While we now think of Hollywood's emergence as a simple matter of abundant sun, low taxes, and cheap labor – all important factors, to be sure – the original reason the first filmmakers established themselves here was due to something much simpler: fear. But for the strong-arm tactics of Thomas Edison and company, the movie business might never have come to Southern California.

Edison and his competitors (companies like Biograph, Vitagraph, and Pathé, among many others) had by 1909 consolidated their various patents on film technology and processing to form what was known as the **"Trust"**: the Motion Picture Patents Company (the MPPC). Although it didn't even last a decade, thanks to bad business practices and a federal anti-trust suit, the MPPC did manage to scare off many directors and producers in the first years of its existence, including producer William Selig and director Francis Boggs, both of whom wanted to get as far away from the MPPC's seat of power, New York City, as they possibly could. Southern California was their choice, and more prominent film industry figures soon followed, finding the taxes, labor, and abundant shooting locations much to their liking.

Early Hollywood

Thomas Ince, **Mack Sennett**, and **D W Griffith** were the early film legends who helped to establish Hollywood as the focus of the American movie business. Ince, with his studios in Culver City and Edendale and his coastal "Inceville" north of Santa Monica, founded the elemental model of the studio system which was to hold sway for many decades: writers would prepare detailed scripts in collaboration with directors

and Ince himself, after which a tightly budgeted production would be filmed at pre-arranged locations, and a final cut of the movie would be carefully edited. This sort of precise planning minimized the possibility of surprises during shooting and contributed to the factory-like character of Ince's operation.

By comparison, Sennett's **Keystone Film Company** in Edendale, in East Hollywood, produced Keystone Kops comedies in less rigorous fashion. However, with production needs mounting, Sennett adopted his former colleague's model (both had worked for Triangle Films) and went on to a two-decades-long career making his signature brand of wacky entertainment.

The largest creative presence in early Hollywood was, however, **D W Griffith**, who began as a theatrical actor and director of one-reel shorts. Something of a Victorian romantic, Griffith was entranced by Helen Hunt Jackson's Mission legend and jumped at the chance to direct an adaptation of her novel *Ramona*, a bowdlerized and revisionist bit of history. He was to reach the apex of his fame with *Birth of a Nation*, a runaway hit in 1914 – despite its glamorization of the Ku Klux Klan, its epic length (2hr 40min), and its unprecedented $2 admission fee. Woodrow Wilson praised the film for "writing history with lightning," overlooking that its source was not actual history, but the bigoted ramblings of Southern preacher Thomas Dixon, on whose book, *The Clansman*, the movie had been based.

Generating a firestorm of controversy the film, Griffith fired back at his critics with his next film *Intolerance* – a bloated historical epic – but only succeeded at shooting himself in the foot. Griffith would make a slow slide into obscurity in coming decades, but not before he perfected the essential aesthetic components of later Hollywood filmmaking: close-ups, flashbacks, cross-cutting, and the like.

The birth of the big studios

In 1913, **Cecil B DeMille**, an itinerant theatrical actor and director, came west to rent a horse barn for a movie. From this simple act, DeMille and his partners, glove-maker Sam Goldfish

Double Indemnity (Billy Wilder 1944). The proto-typical film noir. Greedy insurance salesman Fred MacMurray collaborates with harpy wife Barbara Stanwyck to murder her husband and cash in on the settlement. Edward G Robinson lurks on the sidelines as MacMurray's boss.

Heat (Michael Mann 1995). Big names like De Niro and Pacino, but this crime drama, which does include some stunning set-pieces (eg a Downtown LA shootout), is ultimately less than the sum of its parts.

In a Lonely Place (Nicholas Ray 1950). One of the all-time great noirs, and an unconventional one at that. Humphrey Bogart is a disturbed, violent screenwriter who causes trouble for those around him, particularly girlfriend Gloria Grahame – the director's real-life ex-wife.

LA Confidential (Curtis Hanson 1997). Easily the best of all the contemporary noir films, a perfectly realized adaptation of James Ellroy's novel about brutal cops, victimized prostitutes, and scheming politicians in 1950s LA. Even the good guys, Russell Crowe and Guy Pearce, are morally questionable.

The Long Goodbye (Robert Altman 1973). Altman intentionally mangles noir conventions in this Chandler adaptation, which has Elliott Gould play Marlowe as a droning schlep who wanders across a desaturated landscape of casual corruption, encounting bizarre characters like nerdy mobster Marty Augustine, played with relish by movie director Mark Rydell. Old-time screenwriter Leigh Brackett freely changes Chandler's original ending.

Murder My Sweet (Edward Dmytryk 1944). One-time Busby Berkeley crooner Dick Powell changed his tune and became a grim tough-guy detective in the best work from this director, who was briefly blacklisted for his former communist ties.

Point Blank (John Boorman 1967). Engaging, somewhat pretentious art-house flick with Lee Marvin as a hit man out for revenge. Begins and ends in Alcatraz, but in between successfully imagines LA as an impenetrable fortress of concrete and glass. Recently reissued.

The Postman Always Rings Twice (Tay Garnett 1946). Lana Turner and John Garfield star in this seamy – and excellent – adaptation of the James M Cain novel. Awkwardly remade by Bob Rafelson in 1981 with Jessica Lange and Jack Nicholson.

Touch of Evil (Orson Welles 1958). Supposedly set at a Mexican border town, this noir classic was actually shot in a seedy, decrepit Venice. A bizarre, baroque masterpiece with Charlton Heston playing a Mexican official, Janet Leigh as his beleaguered wife, and Welles himself as a bloated, corrupt cop addicted to candy bars.

Apocalyptic LA

Blade Runner (Ridley Scott 1982). While the first theatrical version flopped, the recut director's version establishes the film as a sci-fi classic, involving a dystopic future LA where dangerous "replicants" roam the streets and soulless corporations rule from pyramidal towers.

Earthquake (Mark Robson 1974). Watch the Lake Hollywood dam collapse, people run for their lives, and chaos hold sway in the City of Angels. Originally presented in "Sensurround!"

Falling Down (Joel Schumacher 1993). Fired defense-worker Michael Douglas tires of the traffic jams on the freeways and goes nuts in some of the city's poorer minority neighborhoods.

Kiss Me Deadly (Robert Aldrich 1955). Perhaps the bleakest of all noirs, starring Ralph Meeker as brutal detective Mike Hammer, who tramples on friends and enemies alike in his search for the great "whatsit" – a mysterious and deadly suitcase.

Lost Highway (David Lynch 1997). A lurid, frightening take on the city by director Lynch. Non-linear storytelling and actors playing dual roles had critics screaming for the exits, but if you like Lynch, this is unquestionably his glorious return to form.

The Terminator (James Cameron 1984). Modern sci-fi classic, with Arnold Schwarzenegger as a robot from the future sent to kill the mother of an unborn rebel leader. Bravura special effects and amazing set-pieces here were successfully followed up with the director's 1989 sequel, in which Arnold becomes a good robot.

LA in the Nineties

Boys N the Hood (John Singleton 1991). An excellent period piece that cemented the LA stereotype as a land of gangs and guns.

Clueless (Amy Heckerling 1995). Jane Austen's *Emma* transplanted to a rich Southern California high school, with a fine performance by Alicia Silverstone as a frustrated matchmaker.

Grand Canyon (Paul Mazursky 1992). Made at the nadir of LA's early 1990s self-loathing, involving folks from various races and classes trying to rediscover their humanity.

Mi Familia (Gregory Nava 1994). The saga of the Sanchez family, featuring fine performances by a range of Hollywood's best Hispanic actors, including Jimmy Smits, Edward James Olmos, and Esai Morales. Overly earnest and sentimental in places, though.

Pulp Fiction (Quentin Tarantino 1994). A successful collection of underworld stories presented in non-linear fashion, by then-hot director Tarantino. Set against a down-at-the-heels backdrop of LA streets, bars, diners, and would-be torture chambers.

Short Cuts (Robert Altman 1993). Vaguely linked vignettes tracing the lives of LA suburbanites, from a trailer-park couple in Downey to an elite doctor in the Santa Monica Mountains. Strong ensemble cast bolsters the intentionally fractured narrative.

Speed (Jan de Bont 1994). Ultimate LA action flick, in which a bus careers through the freeways and boulevards of the city – and will blow up if it slows below 50mph.

Swingers (Doug Liman 1996). Cocktail culture gets skewered in this flick about a couple of dudes who flit from club to club to eye "beautiful babies" and kibbitz like Rat-Pack-era Sinatras.

"Way-out" West

Barfly (Barbet Schroeder 1987). Mickey Rourke channeling writer Charles Bukowski, a liquor-soaked romp through a seedy world of low-lifes, fistfights, and general depravity.

Beach Blanket Bingo (William Asher 1965). A cult favorite – the epitome of sun-and-surf movies, with Frankie Avalon and Annette Funicello singing and cavorting amid hordes of wild-eyed teenagers.

The Big Lebowski (Joel Coen 1998). The latest Coen foray into LA, exploring the lower-class underbelly of the city. Not their best, but engaging nonetheless – with a lot of bowling scenes.

Bob and Carol and Ted and Alice (Paul Mazursky 1969). Two married couples and their sexual pro-

clivities amid a washed-out Southern California atmosphere.

Boogie Nights (Paul Thomas Anderson 1997). A suburban kid from Torrance hits the big time in LA – as a porn star. Mark Wahlberg, Julianne Moore, and Burt Reynolds tread through a sex-drenched landscape of LA in the disco years.

Car Wash (Michael Schultz 1976). Laid-back party flick about laboring in LA during the de-romanticized 1970s. Fun disco soundtrack.

Down and Out in Beverly Hills (Paul Mazursky 1986). A West Coast adaptation of Jean Renoir's classic *Boudu Saved from Drowning*, with homeless Nick Nolte salving the nerves of upscale nouveau riche neurotics.

Rebel Without a Cause (Nicholas Ray 1955). Brash colors and widescreen composition in this troubled-youth film, starring, of course, James Dean. A Hollywood classic with many memorable images, notably the use of the Griffith Park Observatory as a shooting location.

Repo Man (Alex Cox 1984). Emilio Estevez is a surly young punk who repossesses cars for Harry Dean Stanton. Very imaginative and fun, and darkly comic.

Seconds (John Frankenheimer 1966). One of Rock Hudson's better performances, as a bored suburbanite who's transplanted into the body of a younger, bulkier man. Creepy and bleak.

Shampoo (Hal Ashby 1975). Using LA as his private playground, priapic hairdresser Warren Beatty freely acts on his formidable, though nonchalant, sex drive. A period piece memorable for its 1970s look.

Valley Girl (Martha Coolidge 1983). Early Nic Cage flick, in which he winningly plays a sort of new wave freak trying to woo the title character (Debra Foreman), in a clash of LA cultures. Good soundtrack, too.

Drama and history

Colors (Dennis Hopper 1988). An early chronicle of gang warfare in LA, directed with flash and vigor by Hopper.

Fat City (John Huston 1972). Great late-Huston film starring Stacy Keach as a washed-up pugilist and Jeff Bridges as his young, incompetent charge. Quietly and effectively depressing.

La Bamba (Luis Valdez 1987). The fictionalized story of Ritchie Valens, the LA rocker who died in an untimely plane crash with Buddy Holly. Lou Diamond Phillips gives an effective performance, despite looking nothing like Valens.

Less Than Zero (Marek Kanievska 1987). More valuable as a period piece than as inspired cinema, a depiction of the drug habits of fatuous LA youth. The book wasn't much better.

Nixon (Oliver Stone 1996). A long, dark look at the first president from Southern California, starring Anthony Hopkins.

Stand and Deliver (Ramon Menendez 1988). Inspired by the story of East LA's miracle-working teacher Jaime Escalante, played effectively by Edward James Olmos. Better suited for TV than the big screen.

They Shoot Horses, Don't They? (Sydney Pollack 1969). Gloomy story set during the Depression, in which contestants desperately try to win money in a relentless dance contest. Reflects the fatalistic attitudes of the late 1960s.

To Sleep With Anger (Charles Burnett 1990). An interesting view of LA's overlooked black middle-class, directed with verve and polish by a very underrated African-American filmmaker.

True Confessions (Ulu Grosbard 1981). Priest Robert De Niro and cop Robert Duvall play brothers who cross paths in the atmosphere of 1940s LA. An uneven film with a few appealing scenes, based on the John Gregory Dunne novel.

Zabriskie Point (Michelangelo Antonioni 1970). Muddled, fairly pretentious misfire from the director that nonetheless features some promising early work by Jack Nicholson and visually interesting shots of the LA basin.

Zoot Suit (Luis Valdez 1981). A simplified overview of the Sleepy Lagoon Murder case and resultant anti-Hispanic violence, told as a musical.

Books

In the following listing, wherever a book is in print, the publisher's name is given in the format US;UK. Where books are only published in one country, we have specified which one; when the same company publishes the book in both, it appears just once. O/p signifies an out of print title.

Travel and general

Jan Morris *Destinations* (OUP UK). Collection of essays that appeared in *Rolling Stone*, only one of which is about LA, but as Joan Didion said in response to the piece, "She got it."

Leonard Pitt and **Dale Pitt** *Los Angeles A to Z* (UC Press US). If you're truly enthralled by the city, this is the tome for you: six-hundred pages of encyclopedic references covering everything from conquistadors to movie stars.

Cecilia Rasmussen *Curbside LA* (LA Times Syndicate US). A newspaper writer lists her favorite picks in an array of familiar and quirky categories: ancient burial grounds, adobes, stairways, and so on.

Peter Theroux *Translating LA* (Norton). The author seems to know more about the Middle East than LA, but manages to record a few interesting tidbits about life in the region, especially Long Beach. Not to be confused with travel writer/novelist Paul Theroux – a relative.

John Waters *Crackpot* (Random House; Fourth Estate). The irreverent director of cult classics like *Pink Flamingos* and *Hairspray* takes you on a personalized tour of the city's seamy underside.

History and politics

Jean Baudrillard *America* (Verso). A sacred text for some academics (mere ramblings to others), posing such profundities as Disneyland being the real America and everything else being fake.

David Brodsly *LA Freeway* (UC Press US). An essay concerning the supposed glories of the Southern California highway system. Not always convincing, but often interesting.

Mike Davis *City of Quartz: Excavating the Future in Los Angeles* (Vintage; Pimlico). Something of a leftist counter-perspective to Kevin Starr's mainstream history (see below). Written in the early 1990s, Davis' descriptions of racial hatred, security-system architecture, shifty politicians, and industrial decay have dated slightly, but there's still plenty here worth paying attention to.

Gordon DeMarco *A Short History of Los Angeles* (Lexicos US). Just that, a brief 180-page summary of the major events and phenomena that have shaped the city, with particular regard to class and racial struggles. Excellent reading.

Umberto Eco *Travels in Hyperreality* (Harcourt Brace US). A pointed examination of "simulacra," discussing such things as a now-closed museum in Orange County that re-created the great works of art as wax figurines.

Robert Fogelson *The Fragmented Metropolis: Los Angeles 1850–1930* (UC Press US). A hefty chunk of local history covered deftly and with significant insight. A sweeping story from the early "Hell Town" to the go-go days of the 1920s.

William Fulton *The Reluctant Metropolis: The Politics of Urban Growth in Los Angeles* (Solano Press US). A highly readable account of political and economic conflicts in contemporary LA, with notable sections on modern Chinatown and the aftermath of the 1992 riots.

Lynell George *No Crystal Stair* (Anchor; Verso). A depressing reminder of the struggles of LA's African-American community, rendered in precise, painful detail.

Robert Gottlieb and **Irene Wolt** *Thinking Big: The Story of the Los Angeles Times* (Putnam US). An insightful look at the way the city's biggest and most important newspaper has reported and manipulated the news through the years.

Paul Greenstein, et al. *Bread and Hyacinths: The Rise and Fall of Utopian Los Angeles* (Classic Books US). A chronicle of the attempt to create communal living by some city activists, particularly the socialist Job Harriman.

Abraham Hoffman *Vision or Villainy: Origins of the Owens Valley–Los Angeles Water Controversy* (Chronicle US). An introduction to the messy business of water politics around the turn of the century, a topic which still engenders debate and anger after ninety years.

Carey McWilliams *Southern California: An Island on the Land* (Gibbs-Smith US). One of the most important books about the city yet written, detailing the social clashes and intrigues that rocked LA in the first half of the twentieth century. McWilliams adds special insight to his story through his background as the lead defense attorney in LA's shameful prosecution of the Sleepy Lagoon Murder case. Enjoyable, essential reading.

Harris Newmark *Sixty Years in Southern California: 1853–1913* (Houghton Mifflin US). One of the great nineteenth-century leaders of the Jewish community, and an insider to LA's politics and secrets of the time.

Merry Ovnick *Los Angeles: The End of the Rainbow* (Balcony Press). A riveting story of the city's political and social struggles, as seen through its institutions and architecture. Hard to find outside LA, but well worth seeking out.

WW Robinson *Ranchos Become Cities* (San Pasqual Press US). A chronicle of the changes that turned the old Mexican rancho system into subdivided plots of land fit for real estate speculation, urban growth, and massive profit-taking.

Jack Smith *Jack Smith's LA* (McGraw-Hill US). A collection of the author's wry, incisive columns for the *Los Angeles Times*, which detail the daily mechanics of the city and its many assorted urban characters.

Kevin Starr *Material Dreams: Southern California through the 1920s* (OUP). The third of the author's five volumes on the history of LA from the late-rancho period to the years after World War II. This book is perhaps the most interesting, covering the city's boom years and its attendant

scandals, and colorful celebrities. More volumes are on the way.

Danny Sugarman *Wonderland Avenue* (Sphere; Abacus). Former Doors' publicist gives a mind-bending tour of the local rock scene from the late 1960s on, with many lurid accounts of the actions of famous and infamous figures.

Architecture

Reyner Banham *Los Angeles: The Architecture of Four Ecologies* (Penguin). The book that allowed architectural historians to take LA seriously, and still enjoyable reading. Valuable insights on the city's freeways, vernacular buildings, and cultural attitudes.

Federal Writers Project *The WPA Guide to California* (Pantheon US). Recently republished, this 1939 guide is a remarkable handbook to the architecture and neighborhoods of the time.

David Gebhard and **Robert Winter** *Los Angeles: An Architectural Guide* (Gibbs-Smith US). The latest, and final, edition of the most comprehensive guide to the city's architecture, which covers a full range of structures from programmatic to Art Deco to modern.

Philip Jodidio *Contemporary California Architects* (Taschen). An overview of the city's most vibrant and influential architects, including Frank Israel, Eric Owen Moss, and Frank Gehry. Somewhat lacking in analysis, but plenty of splendid color pictures.

Sam Hall Kaplan *LA Lost and Found* (Crown US o/p). Adequate commentary and great pictures in this former newspaper critic's lament for the good old days of local architecture.

Robert McGrew and **Robert Julian** *Landmarks of Los Angeles* (Abrams). A list of the sights and structures that have been worthy of historic preservation in LA. A large-format guide with numerous large, glossy photos.

Charles Moore *The City Observed: Los Angeles* (Random House US). Maps, pictures, anecdotes, and recommendations to set you on your way to exploring the nooks and crannies of LA.

Robert Winter *The Hollywood Bungalow* (Hennessey and Ingalls US). A discussion of the vernacular housing style that can be found throughout the city, and a good companion to an informal tour of such homes.

Hollywood and the movies

Kenneth Anger *Hollywood Babylon* (Bantam; Arrow). Deliciously dark and lurid stories of sex scandals, bad behavior, and murder in Tinseltown. Not great writing, but it holds your attention throughout.

Peter Bogdanovich *Who the Devil Made It* (Random House US). Acclaimed new book of conversations with great Hollywood filmmakers.

David Bordwell, Janet Staiger and **Kristin Thompson** *The Classical Hollywood Cinema* (Columbia UP; Routledge). Learn all about the techniques used by filmmakers and studios up to the 1960s: cross-cutting, eyeline-matches, the shooting line, and other devices that you may not know by name, but have seen in countless old movies.

Kevin Brownlow and **John Kobal** *Hollywood: The Pioneers* (Knopf US). An intriguing look at the founders of American cinema in the silent era, told from the points of view of an esteemed film historian and preservationist, and a prolific writer on movie topics.

Bruce Crowther *Film Noir: Reflections in a Dark Mirror* (Columbus US o/p). An overview of the loner flicks, detective movies, and chiaroscuro filmwork of the late 1940s and 1950s.

Carrie Fisher *Postcards from the Edge* (Pan/Picador UK currently o/p in US). Fisher starred as Princess Leia, the goody-two-shoes heroine of the Star Wars trilogy, and later – faced with the mother from hell, the pressures of teenage stardom and the unstoppable force of the Hollywood Movie Machine – caved in to chemical comfort, before cleaning up her act, rebuilding her relationship with Mom and writing the book. Filled with the raw stupidity of the drugs world (swapping the Porsche for an evening's-worth of coke, for example) and illuminated by some very funny, embarrassingly honest scenes, this is a *Heart of Darkness* for 1980s Hollywood.

Otto Friedrich *City of Nets: A Portrait of Hollywood in the 1940s* (UC Press/Headline). Descriptions of the major actors, directors, and studio bosses of the last good years of the studio system.

Charles Higham *Hollywood Cameramen* (Thames and Hudson US o/p). A discussion of seven of the great masters of cinematography, whose work in lighting movie classics has been all too frequently overlooked. A classic read, with copies still available in some used bookstores.

Colin McArthur *Underworld USA* (Viking US o/p). One of the best analyses of the Hollywood gangster film, as realized by directors from Fritz Lang to Don Siegel.

Michael Munn *The Hollywood Murder Casebook* (St Martin's Press US o/p). If you really want to dive into the ugly side of Tinseltown, this is your opportunity: an examination of the gory details of Hollywood murders, presented with clinical efficiency.

Julia Phillips *You'll Never Eat Lunch in This Town Again* (Signet; Mandarin). Amusing, if somewhat self-serving portrayal of the drugs and violence behind the Hollywood gloss.

Alain Silver and **Julia Ward** *Film Noir: An Encyclopedic Reference to the American Style* (Overlook). A large-format guide to the bleak films of the 1940s to the present, and a popular title that has gone through many editions.

Jerry Stahl *Permanent Midnight* (Warner). When his employers heard star scriptwriter Stahl ("Moonlighting", "thirtysomething") was spending more than his already-huge paycheck to support his heroin and other habits, they gave him a raise to cover the difference and keep him on the job. The result is another gritty descent into (and miraculous recovery from) well-heeled drug hell, in which LA and the entertainment business provide the brutal but at times hilariously funny backdrop.

Fiction

TC Boyle *Tortilla Curtain* (Penguin; Bloomsbury). Set in LA, this book boldly borrows its premise – a privileged white man running down a member of the city's ethnic underclass – from Tom Wolfe's *Bonfire of the Vanities*, but carries it off to great satiric effect.

Ray Bradbury *The Martian Chronicles* (Bantam; Flamingo). A collection of short stories that features a memorable tale of a trip to Mars, which ends up looking a lot like LA – which the author refers to as the "Beast."

Charles Bukowski *Post Office* (Black Sparrow). An alcohol- and sex-soaked romp through some of LA's more festering back alleys, with a mailman surrogate for Bukowski as your guide. One of several books the author wrote exploring his encounters with the city's dark side.

James M Cain *Double Indemnity, The Postman Always Rings Twice, Mildred Pierce* (Vintage; Picador). With Raymond Chandler, the ultimate writer of dark, tough-guy novels. His entire oeuvre is excellent reading, but these three are the best explorations of LA.

Raymond Chandler *Farewell, My Lovely, The Long Goodbye, The Lady in the Lake* (Random House; Penguin). All of these books, and several more, have been adapted into movies, but Chandler's prose is inimitable: terse, pointed, and vivid. More than just detective stories (centered on gumshoe detective Philip Marlowe), these are masterpieces of popular fiction.

Susan Compo *Life After Death and Other Stories* (Faber). The club life of the black-clad inhabitants of the local Goth-rock scene is the subject here, and the author's prose animates it in sordid detail.

Joan Didion *Play It As It Lays* (Vintage US). Hollywood rendered in booze-guzzling, pill-popping, sex-craving detail. Oddly, the author went on to write the uninspired script for a third adaptation of *A Star Is Born*.

John Gregory Dunne *True Confessions* (Dutton o/p; No Exit Press). The noted author, and husband of Joan Didion, here pens a tale of an LA cop and his priestly brother, who interact amid allusions to the city's notorious Black Dahlia murder case. A first-rate book, made into a second-rate movie.

Bret Easton Ellis *Less Than Zero* (Vintage; Picador). Whining, drug-addicted LA youth are criticized and glorified in this prototypical 1980s novel.

James Ellroy *The Black Dahlia, The Big Nowhere, LA Confidential, White Jazz* (Warner; Arrow). The LA Quartet: an excellent saga of city cops from the postwar era to the 1960s, with each novel becoming progressively more complex and elliptical in style.

John Fante *Ask the Dust* (Black Sparrow). The first and still the best of the author's stories of itinerant poet Arturo Bandini, whose wanderings during the Depression highlight the city's faded glory and struggling residents.

Robert Ferrigno *The Horse Latitudes* (Avon; Pocket Books o/p). A drug-dealer-turned-academic begins a descent into a bizarre LA world

when he encounters a corpse at his home, possibly left by his departed wife.

F Scott Fitzgerald *The Last Tycoon* (Macmillan; Penguin). The legendary author's unfinished final work, a major novel on the power and glory of Hollywood. Intriguing reading that gives a view of the studio system at its height.

David Freeman *A Hollywood Education* (Carroll & Graf; Michael Joseph o/p). Another hatchet piece on Tinseltown, this time from a writer's perspective and employing all manner of subtle and overt criticism.

Joseph Hansen *Gravedigger* (Holt; No Exit Press). Entertaining tale revolving around a gay insurance claims adjuster; one in a series.

Chester Himes *If He Hollers Let Him Go* (Thunder's Mouth Press; Serpent's Tail). A fine literary introduction to mid-century race relations in LA, narrated by the jaded character of Bob Jones, whose struggles mirrored those of author Himes, who eventually ended up living in Spain.

Aldous Huxley *Ape and Essence* (I R Dee; Flamingo). Imaginative depiction of postnuclear LA, in which books are burned in Pershing Square for warmth and the *Biltmore* hotel is the site of an annual orgy.

Christopher Isherwood *Down There on a Visit* (Noonday Press; Minerva). Incisive, involving read by a British expatriate, who penned much of his later fiction in and on Southern California.

Helen Hunt Jackson *Ramona* (New American Library; Fisher Press). Ultra-romanticized depiction of mission life that rightfully criticizes the American government's treatment of Indians while showing the natives to be noble savages. Not particularly good reading, but a valuable period piece – and perhaps the most influential piece of fiction ever written about LA.

Elmore Leonard *Get Shorty* (Bantam; Penguin). Ice-cool mobster Chili Palmer is a Miami debt collector who follows a client to Hollywood, and finds that the increasing intricacies of his own situation are translating themselves into a movie script.

Ross MacDonald *Black Money* (Vintage; Allison & Busby). Private detective Lew Archer pilots himself through the nasty underworld of LA society, high and low. A captivating read.

Walter Mosley *Devil in a Blue Dress, A Red Death, White Butterfly, Black Betty, A Little Yellow Dog* (Pocket Books; Pan). Five excellent modern noir novels that involve black private detective Easy Rawlins, who "does favors" from his South Central base. Mosley compellingly brings to life pre-riots Watts.

Thomas Pynchon *The Crying of Lot 49* (HarperPerennial; Vintage). The hilarious adventures of techno-freaks and potheads in Sixties California, among other things revealing the sexy side of stamp collecting.

Danny Santiago *Famous All over Town* (NAL US). Set in the barrio of East LA, and featuring a cast of street gangs, this is a good slice of life in a struggling Hispanic community.

Budd Schulberg *What Makes Sammy Run?* (Vintage). A classic criticism of Hollywood by one of its insiders, a long-time novelist and screenwriter, whose vitriolic portrait of the movie business is unmatched.

Mona Simpson *Anywhere but Here* (Vintage; Faber). Engaging story of a mother's desire to put her daughter on the fast track to Hollywood stardom. A strangely involving read.

Upton Sinclair *The Brass Check* (Ayer Press o/p). The activist author's vigorous criticism of LA's yellow journalism and the underhanded practices of its main figures. Sinclair also wrote *Oil!*, about the city's 1920s oil rush, and *The Goose Step*, concerning collegiate life at USC.

Michael Tolkin *The Player* (Grove Atlantic; Faber). A convincing look at the depravity and moral twilight of the filmmaking community, with special scorn for venal movie execs.

Joseph Wambaugh *The Onion Field* (Dell US). One in a group of crime novels by a former LAPD cop. The most worthwhile in the author's series of LA tales, all of them gripping, popular reading, even if none is up to the rarefied levels of Cain and Chandler.

Nathanael West *The Day of the Locust* (Signet; Picador UK o/p). The best book about LA not involving detectives, an apocalyptic story of the fringe characters at the edge of the film industry, which culminates in a glorious riot and utter chaos.

Glossaries

LA people

AUTRY Gene The "singing cowboy" who starred in a string of successful Westerns, reaching the height of his popularity in the years before World War II. Wrote "Here Comes Santa Claus"; also owned baseball's Anaheim Angels.

BALDWIN Lucky Wealthy mining investor who developed the Santa Anita racetrack in 1873, also founding and becoming the mayor of Arcadia, where the track is located. In 1909, he acquired the future site of the 1932 summer Olympics, now known as "Baldwin Hills."

BANNING Phineas The "Father of the LA Harbor," Banning founded the town of Wilmington, though it never actually became the harbor site. He also built the first rail line in Southern California (connecting Downtown LA with the ocean).

BRADLEY Tom A former police officer who became LA's first black mayor in 1973, Bradley was instrumental in building up Downtown and in staging the 1984 Olympics.

CABRILLO Juan Portuguese explorer who claimed the coast of Southern California for his employer, Spain. More associated with San Diego than LA, though he did name several local geographic points such as San Pedro Bay.

CALL Asa Insurance executive who exercised inordinate control over city politics and affairs of the 1950s and 1960s, including electing mayors and spurring Downtown investment. As a prime mover in the elite, secretive "Committee of 25," Call was nicknamed "Mr Big."

CHANDLER Harry Publisher of the *Los Angeles Times* from 1917 to 1941 and son-in-law of Harrison Gray Otis. The classic right-wing conservative, Chandler and his paper fought against unions, socialism and the like.

CHAPLIN Charlie Seminal comedy actor/director whose character is known to audiences worldwide. He was also the co-founder of United Artists and a prime force behind the emergence of the star system.

DEMILLE Cecil B Larger-than-life director of biblical epics like *The Ten Commandments*, but also one of the creators of the silent movie success *The Squaw Man*, which helped lead to the creation of Paramount Studios.

DISNEY Walt Legendary creator of Mickey Mouse, Disney Studios, and a bevy of theme parks, of which Disneyland was only the first, in 1955. Guarded, sometimes paranoid, personality who was not nearly as animated as his films.

DOHENY Edward Wildly successful oil entrepreneur who was implicated as the man who bribed Interior Secretary Albert Fall in the 1923 Teapot Dome scandal.

DOMINGUEZ Juan Jose Spanish soldier and cattle rancher who owned the 76,000 acres of Rancho Palos Verdes and Rancho San Pedro.

EISNER Michael Disney CEO and one of the most powerful executives in Hollywood today, running a multimedia empire of music, movies, theme parks, and television that aims to inhabit most corners of the globe.

FAIRBANKS Douglas Popular Hollywood swashbuckler and husband to Mary Pickford, both of whom helped found the United Artists studios. One of the few stars to successfully make the transition from silent to sound films.

GATES Daryl Controversial LA police chief from 1978 to 1992, Gates was popular with politicians and fellow cops, though many residents blame him for helping create the hostile climate that led to the riots of 1992, which cost him his job. Appropriately, he has recently resurfaced as a radio talk show host.

GEHRY Frank Perhaps LA's most famous architect – creator of the Geffen Contemporary museum and his own bizarre Santa Monica house. His finest work, however, can be found overseas, such as the Vitra Design Museum in Germany and Guggenheim Museum in Spain.

GETTY J Paul LA oil baron turned art collector. His holdings, originally contained in his small oceanside residence, now reside in the hilltop colossus of the Getty Center, which has a $3 billion endowment to buy art.

GOLDWYN Samuel One-time glove manufacturer who helped create the film *The Squaw Man* in a horse barn with Cecil B DeMille and Jesse Lasky. Despite his prominence in the industry, Goldwyn left his various partnerships before they became the legendary studios (Paramount and MGM) of Hollywood.

GREENE Charles and Henry Architects and brothers whose firm built many local examples of Craftsman houses, notably Pasadena's Gamble House – which, like other of their works, also includes a number of Japanese influences.

GRIFFITH David Wark Known by his initials "D W," one of Hollywood's most prominent early directors and a co-founder of United Artists. Made his name with *Birth of a Nation*; undid much of his success with the bomb *Intolerance*.

GRIFFITH Griffith J Mining millionaire who gave LA the land for a large, centrally located park on the crest of the Hollywood Hills. Also known for shooting his Catholic wife in the eye, in a drunken rage against a supposed papal conspiracy, and spending two years in San Quentin Prison for attempted murder.

HAMMER Armand Oil-industry executive who founded Occidental Petroleum and greatly helped business relations between the US and Soviet Union. Also an intrepid art collector who relocated his stash of paintings from the LACMA to his own eponymous museum in Westwood.

HARRIMAN Job Utopian socialist who ran for LA mayor in 1911, though his candidacy was undone by his association with confessed bombers of the LA Times building. Defeated again in the next election, Harriman withdrew to his social colony of Llano del Rio in the Antelope Valley, the ruins of which still stand.

HUGHES Howard Tool-dynasty heir behind Hughes Aircraft who later controlled TWA as well. As a movie producer, he scored big with *The Outlaw*, a Jane Russell vehicle that dared to show cleavage.

HUNTINGTON Henry Nephew of railroad magnate Collis Huntington and developer of the Pacific Electric Railway. As the largest landowner in California, Huntington was able to bring his "Red Cars" to cities across the basin; after selling out to the Southern Pacific Railroad in 1910, he developed philanthropic enterprises like the Huntington Library and Gardens in San Marino.

INCE Thomas Early movie producer whose studios, in Culver City and the San Ynez Canyon (nicknamed "Inceville"), helped standardize and streamline the filmmaking process. Died near the height of his success in 1924 – rumored to have been accidentally shot by William Randolph Hearst while aboard Hearst's yacht.

KING Rodney Black motorist whose beating at the hands of LA cops was captured on videotape and replayed for the nation to see; the 1992 riots ensued after the cops were acquitted. Amid the violence, he famously remarked "Can't we all just get along?"

KINNEY Abbot Wide-ranging entrepreneur who devised Venice of America, a city of quasi-quattrocento buildings and canals near the sea that was meant as a beacon for cultural activity.

LUMMIS Charles City editor of the *Los Angeles Times*, early historic preservationist, city librarian, and founder of the Southwest Museum. Lummis created El Alisal, a boulder house in Highland Park that served as the model for many other local wood-and-stone structures.

MORRISON Jim Lead singer of legendary 1960s rock group The Doors, which often performed on the Sunset Strip. Artistic pretensions, occassionally obscene stage antics, and, perhaps inevitably, an unseemly death in a Paris hotel.

MULHOLLAND William Engineer who constructed the LA Aqueduct from Northern California, commenting on the public arrival of the water, "There it is! Take it!" Later defamed for shoddy building methods in the St Francis dam collapse that killed 450 people, though exonerated after his death.

MURRAY Cecil Leader of the First AME Church in South Central LA and one of the city's more visible and respected ministers, whose calls for calm in the days after the 1992 riots were somewhat heeded.

NIXON Richard The 37th president's checkered political career includes starting the Cambodian bombing campaign, opening ties with China and the Soviet Union, and engaging in a variety of "high crimes and misdemeanors" that led to his 1974 resignation. His birthplace and library are out at Yorba Linda in Orange County.

O'MALLEY Walter Owner and president of the Dodgers baseball team, who moved the club to LA from Brooklyn in 1958 – an action still held in contempt by old-time New Yorkers. O'Malley quickly stirred up local controversy by siting the new Dodger stadium (finished in 1962) on land slated for low-income housing.

OTIS Harrison Gray Brigadier general and real-estate magnate who owned and edited the *Los Angeles Times*, a newspaper he shaped into a paragon of right-wing, anti-labor ideology.

OVITZ Mike The head of the Creative Artists Agency in the 1980s and early 1990s, the most powerful group of Hollywood agents in Tinseltown history, which drove up actor salaries and made the film business less profitable for the major studios. More recently, he had a less than successful stint under Michael Eisner at Disney.

PARKER William LA supercop from 1950 to 1966, who fought corruption in the force, which had reached epidemic levels under some of his predecessors. Unfortunately, he also allowed minorities to be brutally treated, which led in no small part to the Watts Riots in 1965.

PICKFORD Mary Queen of the silent screen, known as "America's Sweetheart," and best remembered for starring in films like *Rebecca of Sunnybrook Farm*. Also co-founded United Artists studios with husband Douglas Fairbanks in 1919, and built the lavish – now demolished – Pickfair mansion in the Hollywood Hills.

PICO Pio The last Mexican governor of California, who fled after the Mexican-American War but later returned to LA to own several sizable ranchos and properties. Unfortunately, bad luck and poor judgment led to the collapse of his finances, and he died in poverty in 1894.

PORTOLA Gaspar de Leader of the first Spanish exploratory mission into the current area of LA, in 1769, which trekked around the basin near the current Plaza and Sepulveda Pass. A soldier and governor of Baja California, Portola later became Alta California's first governor.

PUCK Wolfgang Masterchef and culinary celebrity, the man who made the restaurant *Spago* synonymous with chic California eating.

RIORDAN Richard Multimillionaire powerbroker and current mayor of Los Angeles. A staunchly Catholic Republican, Riordan is actually a fairly moderate figure, promoting business investment in LA and trying to streamline city bureaucracy.

ROGERS Will Cowboy philosopher and entertainer, mayor of Beverly Hills, political commentator, and Depression-era movie star, Rogers met a tragic end in a 1935 plane crash.

SENNETT Mack Actor, director, and producer whose Keystone Studios launched the careers of entertainers like Fatty Arbuckle, Charlie Chaplin, and the bumbling Keystone Kops.

SEPULVEDA Francisco Mexican leader and landowner whose claim to Rancho San Vicente y Santa Monica gave him title to over 30,000 acres in what is today LA's Westside.

SERRA Junipero Franciscan missionary who somewhat coercively established a chain of 21 missions in Alta California, including Mission San Gabriel and San Fernando.

SIMON Norton Business titan, controlling major food and publishing companies, and failed politician, but most familiar as an art collector, especially of seventeenth-century Dutch art and Impressionism, shown at his self-named Pasadena art museum.

SIMPSON Orenthal James Star running back for the NFL's Bulls and 49ers franchises, as well as a fixture in a series of Hollywood B-movies, who was accused – and acquitted – of murdering his ex-wife Nicole and her friend in 1994.

SMITH Jack Columnist for the *Los Angeles Times* whose insightful, piquant observations did much to define the city as a colorful, chaotic metropolis. His attempt to nickname LA the "Big Orange," however, never really caught on.

STERLING Christine Amateur historic preservationist who helped engineer the rebirth and re-creation of Olvera Street in the Plaza. Sterling also attempted – less successfully – to create pseudo-cultural zones, like "China City," complete with rickshaws and chinoiserie kitsch.

STREISAND Barbra Singer, actress, director, and producer. A primal force in Hollywood, Streisand has also donated her Malibu estate to create a nature preserve and a walk-in movie-star habitat.

UEBBEROTH Peter Travel-company executive and organizer of the 1984 LA Olympics, an economic success that helped him become baseball commissioner in the late 1980s. He also headed "Rebuild LA," a committee that, less successfully, set out to solve South Central's economic woes after the 1992 riots.

WARNER Jack Movie executive who, with his three siblings, founded the Warner Brothers film studio in 1918 – which made its name with the release of the first sound pic *The Jazz Singer.*

WILSHIRE Gaylord Oil entrepreneur who founded the Orange County town of Fullerton and widely promoted his own brand of utopian socialism. Named, modernized, and developed Wilshire Boulevard.

WRIGHT Lloyd Son of Frank and a long-term LA architect who designed scores of memorable buildings, best of all the Wayfarer's Chapel in Palos Verdes.

ZUKOR Adolph New Yorker who established Hollywood film production company, Zukor's Famous Players, that merged with Jesse Lasky's company in 1916 to become Paramount. Zukor was active head of the new company for twenty years and remained Chairman Emeritus until his death – at age 103.

LA architectural terms

Art Deco Catch-all term for Zigzag Moderne, Streamline Moderne, governmental WPA, and some other styles, often identified by geometric motifs, sharp lines, and sleek ornamentation.

Craftsman Early twentieth-century style, using exposed wood beams, overhanging rooflines, large shingles, cobblestones, and prominent fireplaces to create a rustic, rough-hewn look.

Googie Free-spirited coffee-shop architecture, with bright colors, sharp curves and boomerang shapes, pitched roofs, and neon trim.

Historic Revival The early twentieth-century use of various older architectural styles.

Minimall Collection of small, independent businesses arrayed in a strip (also known as a "strip mall").

Modern Severe 1920s and 1930s design aesthetic, seen locally in houses built by R M Schindler and Richard Neutra for one Dr Lovell.

Moderne A popular architectural style that used Art Deco ornamentation and sleek lines to convey quiet elegance.

Period Revival See "Historic Revival".

Postmodern Contemporary rehash of neoclassical architecture, often in pastel colors.

Pre-Columbian Quirky 1920s architecture, employing blocky sunbursts, abstract floral motifs, and stylized faces to create an ancient look for the modern city.

Streamline Moderne Buildings resembling ocean liners and sometimes airplanes, borne of a 1930s worship of all things mechanical.

Victorian General term for late 1800s housing styles – Eastlake, Queen Anne, Stick – few of which remain in the city.

Zigzag Moderne A late-1920s version of Art Deco that had particular popularity in LA, with strong verticality, narrow windows, geometric ornament, and occasional use of pre-Columbian or Egyptian motifs.

LA movie industry terms

Above the line Budgeted costs for actors, writers, directors, and producers.

Below the line Budgeted costs for camera, lighting, and all other technical and behind the scenes costs.

Blockbuster Now a well-known word, its original meaning meant a film that appealed to all audiences and thus "busted" the "blocks" of disparate segments of viewers.

Bomb A financial disaster, or a movie that does not meet minimal levels of capital return. Confusingly, "the bomb" is also street slang for something (not necessarily a movie) that is considered very good.

Box office The weekly money generated by a particular film. Also called the "take."

Green light A verb meaning to approve the actual production of a given film.

High concept A movie plot that can be summarized on a cocktail napkin, or more specifically, by a single, basic sentence, eg "A chimpanzee detective solves crimes in Hollywood."

Open Verb meaning "to begin playing" and, more importantly, "to draw an audience."

Player An extant 1980s term for an important studio executive, film producer, or rising director able to command financial respect throughout town and get a movie project "green lighted."

Points A percentage of profits taken from the gross earnings of a film, often as payment by actors and directors in lieu of salary.

Sleeper A familiar term for an unheralded flick that manages to be a surprise hit.

Other LA terms

Angeleno A resident of LA.

Blood Gang member wearing red apparel, though the blue vs. red conception of gang warfare has lately become somewhat inaccurate.

Catch basin A dry reservoir used to contain mud-slides during periods of heavy flooding. Often visible throughout the foothills of the San Gabriel Mountains.

Community policing A new method of law enforcement used in the aftermath of the 1992 riots, in which cops regularly patrol given neighborhoods and try to ingratiate themselves with the residents.

Crip Gang member wearing blue apparel; see "Blood" above.

Drive-by A fatal shooting that takes place from the window of a passing car. Traditionally associated with South Central gang activity, but not exclusive to that district.

Exurb An extreme version of a suburb, a growing community of urbanophobes located in distant places at the fringes of the metropolis.

Gridlock A state of absolute automotive immobility, typically found on major highways. Increasingly the status quo for many LA freeways, especially during rush hours.

Sig alert A warning for motorists regarding particular freeways that are experiencing gridlock due to traffic congestion, accidents, or whatnot.

Smog Smoke plus fog, or more precisely, a noxious mixture of ozone, nitrous oxide, carbon monoxide, and hundreds of assorted chemicals. Worst during summer months in eastern suburbs like Azusa and Glendora.

Swap meet Similar to a flea market, where cheap goods are bought and sold on tables and floors, typically in poorer sections of LA.

White flight The hurried emigration from urban areas by the white middle class.

Index

the perfect getaway vehicle

low-price holiday car rental.

rent a car from holiday autos and you'll give yourself real freedom to explore your holiday destination. with great-value, fully-inclusive rates in over 4,000 locations worldwide, wherever you're escaping to, we're there to make sure you get excellent prices and superb service.

what's more, you can book now with complete confidence. our £5 undercut* ensures that you are guaranteed the best value for money in holiday destinations right around the globe.

drive away with a great deal, call holiday autos now on **0990 300 400** and quote ref RG.

holiday autos miles ahead

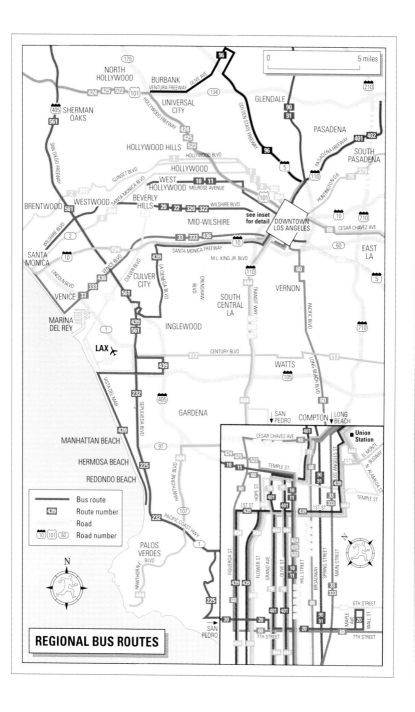

REGIONAL BUS ROUTES

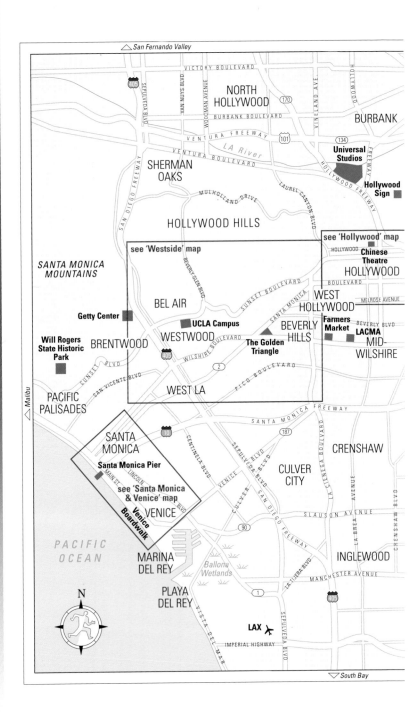

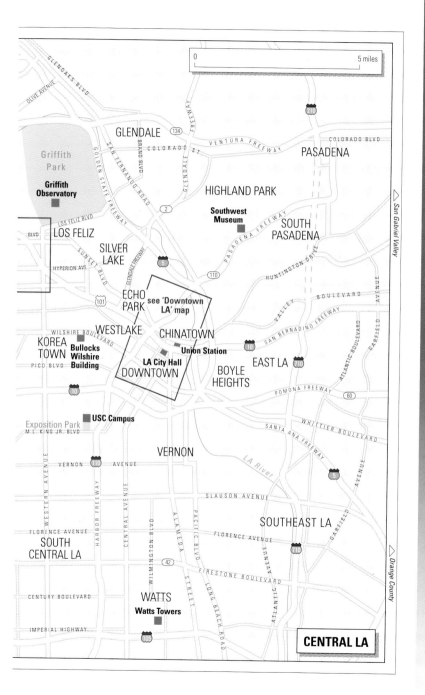

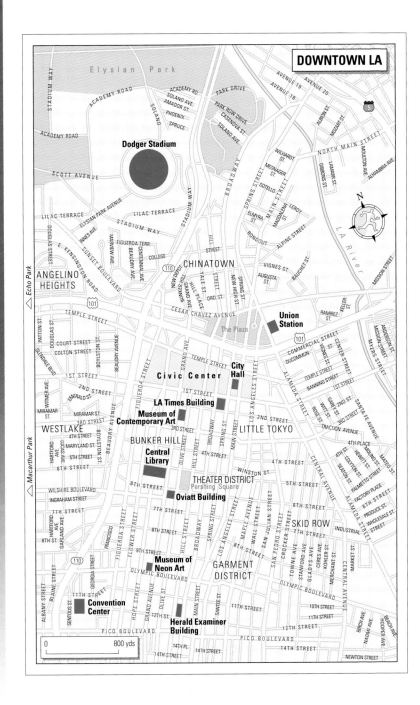

DOWNTOWN LA

Elysian Park

STADIUM WAY

ACADEMY ROAD

AVENUE 19
AVENUE 20
AVENUE 18

ACADEMY RD.
SOLANO AVE.
AMADOR ST.
PHOENIX
SPRUCE

PARK DRIVE
PARK ROW DRIVE
CASENOVA ST.
SOLANO AVE.

AURORA ST.
MOZART ST.
MOULTON AVE.
ALHAMBRA AVE.
LAMAR ST.
GIBBONS ST.

NORTH MAIN STREET

Dodger Stadium

SCOTT AVENUE

WILHARDT ST.
MESNAGER ST.
SOTELLO ST.

BROADWAY

SPRING STREET
MAIN STREET
MAGDAMAR ST.

LA RIVER

LILAC TERRACE
ELYSIAN PARK AVENUE
INNES AVE.
LILAC TERRACE
STADIUM WAY

STADIUM WAY

ELMYRA ST.
LEROY
ALPINE STREET
RONDOUT

E. KENSINGTON ROAD
SUNSET BOULEVARD
MARVIEW AVE.
BEAUDRY AVE.
CENTENNIAL AVE.
COLLEGE

FIGUEROA TERR.

HILL STREET

VIGNES ST.
BAUCHET ST.

MISSION STREET

ANGELINO
HEIGHTS

△ Echo Park

DOUGLAS ST.
GLENDALE BLVD.

BUNKER HILL
HILL PLACE
GRAND AVE.
YALE ST.
NEW HIGH ST.
SPRING ST.

AUGUSTA ST.

KELLER ST.

CESAR CHAVEZ AVENUE

CHINATOWN

**Union
Station**

RAMIREZ ST.

PATTON ST.

TEMPLE STREET

COURT STREET
COLTON STREET

1ST STREET

COMMERCIAL STREET
DUCOMMUN
VIGNES ST.
CENTER STREET

The Plaza

TEMPLE STREET
BANNING STREET

ANDERSON STREET
MYERS STREET

2ND STREET
EMERALD ST.

GRAND AVE.

TEMPLE STREET
City
Hall

Civic Center

TEMPLE STREET
1ST STREET

MIRAMAR
ST.
MIRAMAR ST.
3RD STREET

WESTLAKE

WITMER AVE.

BEAUDRY AVENUE

FIGUEROA STREET

LA Times Building

**Museum of
Contemporary Art**

LOS ANGELES STREET
BROADWAY
SPRING ST.
MAIN ST.

1ST STREET
2ND STREET
3RD STREET

GARY ST.
ROSE ST.
WITT ST.

2ND ST.
3RD ST.
SANTA FE AVENUE
TRACTION AVENUE

LITTLE TOKYO

4TH PLACE
HEWITT ST.
MOLINO ST.
MATEO ST.

△ Macarthur Park

HARTFORD
AVE.
3W SCOTT
MARYLAND ST.

4TH STREET
5TH STREET
6TH STREET

BUNKER HILL

**Central
Library**

HILL STREET
OLIVE ST.
4TH STREET

BROADWAY

WINSTON ST.

4TH STREET

COLTON ST.
SEATON ST.
PALMETTO STREET
4TH PLACE
STANFORD AVE.

CENTRAL AVENUE

5TH STREET
6TH STREET

ALAMEDA STREET

WILSHIRE BOULEVARD
INGRAHAM STREET

6TH STREET

THEATER DISTRICT
Pershing Square

Oviatt Building

FACTORY PLACE
PRODUCE ST.
WHOLESALE ST.

HARTFORD
AVE.
GARLAND AVE.
7TH STREET
8TH STREET

FRANCISCO ST.
FIGUEROA STREET

7TH STREET

FLOWER STREET

8TH STREET

HILL STREET
BROADWAY
SPRING STREET

LOS ANGELES STREET
MAPLE AVENUE
WALL STREET
SAN JULIAN STREET

7TH STREET

SAN PEDRO STREET
CROCKER STREET

SKID ROW

7TH STREET

INDUSTRIAL STREET

ALBANY STREET
BLAINE STREET

GEORGIA STREET

9TH STREET

OLYMPIC BOULEVARD

**Museum of
Neon Art**

HOPE STREET
GRAND AVENUE
OLIVE ST.

HILL ST.
MAIN STREET
SANTEE ST.

8TH STREET

GARMENT
DISTRICT

TOWNE AVE.
STANFORD AVE.
GLADYS AVE.
CERES AVE.
KOHLER ST.
MERCHANT ST.

MARKET ST.

OLYMPIC BOULEVARD

11TH STREET

**Convention
Center**

SENTOUS ST.

12TH STREET
PICO BOULEVARD

**Herald Examiner
Building**

11TH STREET

12TH STREET
PICO BOULEVARD

10TH STREET
11TH STREET

12TH STREET

14TH STREET

BIRCH AVE.
NAOMI AVE.
HOOPER AVE.
BEACH AVE.

0 _____ 800 yds

14TH PL.
14TH STREET
14TH STREET

14TH STREET

NEWTON STREET

N

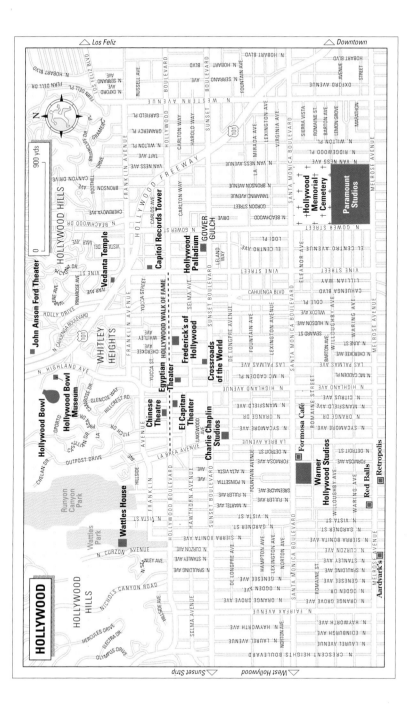

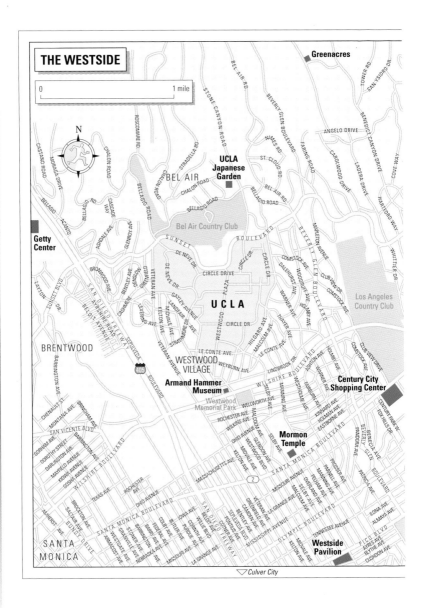

THE WESTSIDE

0   1 mile

N

Greenacres

TOWER RD.
SAN YSIDRO DR.

BEL AIR RD.

BEVERLY GLEN BOULEVARD

ANGELO DRIVE

BENEDICT CANYON DRIVE

CARGWOOD DRIVE

LADERA DRIVE

COVE WAY

HARTFORD WAY

WHITTIER DR.

STONE CANYON ROAD

ROSCOMARE RD.

CASTANO ROAD

MORAGA DRIVE

CHALON ROAD

STRADELLA RD.

NIMES RD.

ST. CLOUD RD.

FARING ROAD

UCLA Japanese Garden

BEL AIR

CHALON ROAD

BEL AIR RD.

BELLAGIO ROAD

BELLAGIO ROAD

BELLAGIO RD.

CASCADE WAY

ACANDO

BELLAGIO

ASHDALE AVE.

GLENROY AVE.

Getty Center

LAYTON

SUNSET DR.

BROXWOOD AVE.

BENTLEY AVE.

BENSON AVE.

GREEN AVE.

CASHMERE

Bel Air Country Club

SUNSET BOULEVARD

DE NEVE DR.

DE NEVE DR.

CIRCLE DRIVE

CIRCLE DR.

CIRCLE DR.

PLAZA

COMSTOCK AVE.

DALEHURST AVE.

WOODRUFF AVE.

BEVERLY GLEN BOULEVARD

MARKETON AVENUE

CLUBVIEW DR.

COMSTOCK AVE.

Los Angeles Country Club

SAN DIEGO ROAD

BEVERLY FREEWAY

BEVERLY AVENUE

GAYLEY AVENUE

LEVERING AVE.

MIDVALE AVE.

KELTON AVE.

LANDFAIR AVE.

GLENROCK AVE.

UCLA

WESTWOOD

CIRCLE DR.

HILGARD AVE.

MALCOLM AVE.

HOVER AVE.

WARNER AVE.

HOLMBY AVE.

CLUB VIEW DRIVE

COMSTOCK DR.

BRENTWOOD

BARRINGTON AVENUE

405

VETERAN AVENUE

STRATHMORE DR.

LE CONTE AVE.

WESTWOOD VILLAGE

WEYBURN AVE.

LE CONTE AVE.

LINDBROOK DR.

ASHTON AVE.

WARNER AVE.

HOLMBY AVE.

Armand Hammer Museum

WILSHIRE BOULEVARD

WESTHOLME AVE.

MANNING AVE.

FAIRBURN AVE.

Century City Shopping Center

CHENAULT ST.

BRINGHAM AVE.

MONTANA AVE.

SAN VICENTE BLVD.

Westwood Memorial Park

WELLWORTH AVE.

ROCHESTER AVE.

WILKINS AVE.

OHIO AVENUE

WESTWOOD BLVD.

MIDVALE AVE.

KINNARD AVE.

HOLMAN AVE.

EASTBORNE AVE.

CENTURY PARK W.

FOX HILLS DR.

BENICIA AVE.

PANDORA AVE.

BEVERLY GLEN BOULEVARD

PATRICIA AVE.

GORHAM AVE.

DOROTHY STREET

DARLINGTON AVE.

MAYFIELD AVENUE

IOWA AVENUE

GOSHEN AVENUE

BARRINGTON AVENUE

Mormon Temple

MASSACHUSETTS AVE.

KIOWA AVE.

SANTA MONICA BOULEVARD

MISSOURI AVENUE

OVERLAND AVE.

SELBY AVE.

PROSSER AVE.

PARNELL AVE.

MANNING AVE.

MALCOLM AVE.

PROSPECT AVE.

WILSHIRE BOULEVARD

ROCHESTER AVE.

OHIO AVENUE

SAN DIEGO FREEWAY

VETERAN AVE.

LA GRANGE AVE.

MALCOLM AVE.

2

TEXAS AVE.

BROCKTON AVE.

SALTAIR AVE.

AMHERST AVE.

BUNDY DRIVE

SANTA MONICA BOULEVARD

GRANVILLE AVE.

STONER AVE.

BARRY AVE.

BUTLER AVE.

FEDERAL AVE.

IOWA AVE.

PURDUE AVE.

CORINTH AVE.

SAWTELLE BLVD.

SEPULVEDA BLVD.

ARMACOST AVE.

COTNER AVE.

PONTIUS AVE.

GRANVILLE AVE.

MISSISSIPPI AVENUE

OLYMPIC BOULEVARD

TENNESSEE AVENUE

Westside Pavilion

PICO BLVD.

AYRES AVE.

ALMAYO AVE.

BYTHE AVE.

CUSHDON AVE.

KEITH AVE.

NEBRASKA AVE.

MISSOURI AVE.

LA GRANGE AVE.

SANTA MONICA

▽ *Culver City*

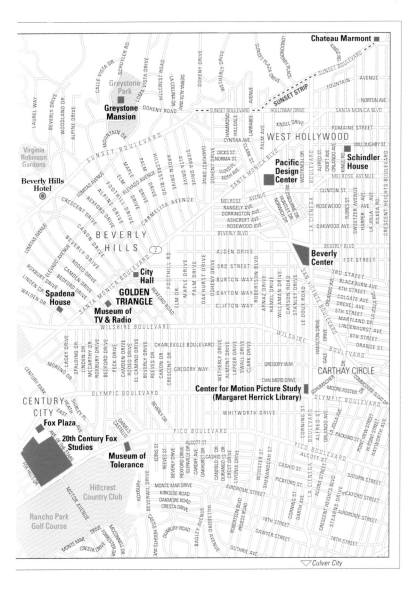

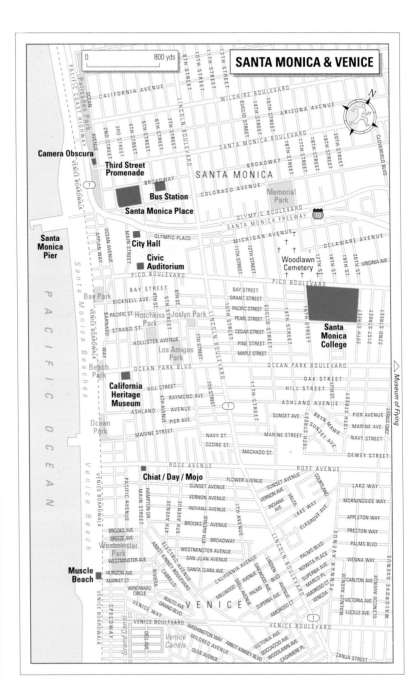

SANTA MONICA & VENICE

0 — 800 yds

Camera Obscura

Third Street Promenade

Bus Station

Santa Monica Place

SANTA MONICA

CALIFORNIA AVENUE

WILSHIRE BOULEVARD

ARIZONA AVENUE

SANTA MONICA BOULEVARD

BROADWAY

BROADWAY

COLORADO AVENUE

Memorial Park

OLYMPIC BOULEVARD

SANTA MONICA FREEWAY

Santa Monica Pier

City Hall

OLYMPIC PLACE

MICHIGAN AVENUE

DELAWARE AVENUE

Civic Auditorium

Woodlawn Cemetery

PICO BOULEVARD

PICO BOULEVARD

BAY STREET

BAY STREET

GRANT STREET

Bay Park

BICKNELL AVE.

PACIFIC STREET

Hotchkiss Joslyn Park

PEARL STREET

Park

CEDAR STREET

Santa Monica College

STRAND ST.

HOLLISTER AVENUE

PINE STREET

Los Amigos Park

MAPLE STREET

Beach Park

OCEAN PARK BLVD.

OCEAN PARK BOULEVARD

Park

OAK STREET

California Heritage Museum

HILL STREET

HILL STREET

ASHLAND AVENUE

Ocean Park

RAYMOND AVE.

ASHLAND AVENUE

PIER AVENUE

SUNSET AVE.

MARINE AVE.

PIER AVE.

MARINE STREET

MARINE STREET

NAVY STREET

NAVY ST.

OZONE ST.

MACHADO ST.

DEWEY STREET

ROSE AVENUE

ROSE AVENUE

Chiat / Day / Mojo

FLOWER AVENUE

SUNSET AVENUE

LAKE WAY

VERNON AVENUE

VERNON AVE.

MORNINGSIDE WAY

INDIANA AVENUE

INDIANA AVE.

APPLETON WAY

BROOKS AVENUE

PRESTON WAY

BROOKS AVE.

BROADWAY

PALMS BLVD.

BREEZE AVE.

WESTMINSTER AVENUE

PALMS BLVD.

Westminster Park

SAN JUAN AVENUE

VIENNA WAY

WESTMINSTER AVE.

SANTA CLARA AVENUE

Muscle Beach

HORIZON AVE.

MARKET ST.

WINDWARD CIRCLE

VENICE

VICTORIA AVE.

LUCILLE AVE.

VENICE WAY

GRAND BLVD.

VENICE BOULEVARD

VENICE BOULEVARD

Venice Canals

DEL AVE.

WASHINGTON WAY

MILDRED AVENUE

OLIVE AVENUE

ZANJA STREET

PACIFIC OCEAN

Santa Monica Beaches

Venice Beach

Venice Boardwalk

Museum of Flying